SEASON
of INFAMY

SEASON
of INFAMY

*A Diary of War
and Occupation,
1939–1945*

Charles Rist

Compilation, Notes, and Introduction
to the 1983 French Edition
by Jean-Noël Jeanneney

Translated from the French
with Additional Text and Annotation
by Michele McKay Aynesworth

Foreword by Robert O. Paxton

INDIANA UNIVERSITY PRESS
Bloomington & Indianapolis

This book is a publication of

INDIANA UNIVERSITY PRESS
Office of Scholarly Publishing
Herman B Wells Library 350
1320 East 10th Street
Bloomington, Indiana 47405 USA

iupress.indiana.edu

Originally published as *Une saison gâtée: Journal
de la guerre et de l'occupation (1939–1945) Établi,
présenté et annoté par Jean-Noël Jeanneney*
© 1983, Librairie Arthème Fayard
English translation © 2016 Michele
McKay Aynesworth

This English translation was made possible by
generous grants from the Kittredge Foundation
and the National Endowment for the Arts.

NATIONAL
ENDOWMENT
FOR THE ARTS

The paper used in this publication meets the
minimum requirements of the American
National Standard for Information
Sciences – Permanence of Paper for Printed
Library Materials, ANSI Z39.48–1992.

Manufactured in the United States of America

Library of Congress Cataloging-in-Publication Data

Rist, Charles, 1874–1955.
[Saison gâtée. English]
Season of infamy : a diary of war and occupation,
1939-1945 / Charles Rist ;
translated from the French with additional
text and annotation by Michele McKay
Aynesworth ; foreword by Robert O. Paxton ;
compilation, notes, and introduction to the
1983 French edition by Jean-Noël Jeanneney.
   pages cm
   Includes index.
   ISBN 978-0-253-01944-8 (cl : alk. paper) – ISBN
978-0-253-01951-6 (eb) 1. Rist, Charles, 1874-
1955 – Diaries. 2. World War, 1939-1945 – Personal
narratives, French. 3. World War, 1939-1945 – France.
4. France – History – German occupation,
1940-1945. 5. Diplomats – France – Diaries. 6.
Economists – France – Diaries. I. Aynesworth,
Michele McKay, 1947– translator. II. Jeanneney,
Jean Noël, 1942– compiler. III. Title. IV. Title:
Diary of war and occupation, 1939–1945.
   D811.R56513 2016
   940.53´44092 – dc23
   [B]
                                          2015035243

1 2 3 4 5   21 20 19 18 17 16

frontis: Charles Rist, c. 1935.
Courtesy of the Rist Family.

*This translation is dedicated to Michelle Rist (1932–2010),
Colas Rist (1940–2014), and the other members of the Rist family for
whom Charles Rist wrote his wartime diary and whose enthusiasm
and support for the publication in English have been unflagging.*

But how, in this season of infamy, can we believe anyone talking about himself?

MONTAIGNE, "OF GIVING THE LIE," IN *ESSAYS*
QUOTED BY CHARLES RIST, 17 JUNE 1941

Later people will say of those in the Vichy regime: some acted
shamefully, others treacherously, and all of them, abjectly.

CHARLES RIST, 17 APRIL 1942

Contents

Foreword

ROBERT O. PAXTON

BAD TIMES MAKE FOR GOOD DIARIES. FRANCE EXPERIENCED ITS worst time since the Black Death of 1381 with defeat by the German army in May–June 1940, followed by a military occupation until August 1944. Humiliation was followed by cold, hunger, and internal division. On one side was the collaborationist government of the World War I hero Marshal Philippe Pétain, located at Vichy, a spa town in the southern hills of the Auvergne, while Paris was occupied by the Germans. On the other side was a growing opposition. The opposition itself was divided between underground Resistance movements within occupied France and the Free French government-in-exile in London (in Algiers after summer 1943). The two oppositions were gradually pulled together by the imperious personality of General Charles de Gaulle. Marshal Pétain had personally brought France into an armistice with Germany in June 1940, and he was determined to maintain French neutrality under the armistice even when the Germans exceeded their allotted powers. De Gaulle thundered on the BBC that the armistice was illegal and that the true France, which he embodied, was still at war with Germany. An increasing number of French people listened to him, and the Vichy and German police increasingly tracked them.

The wartime diary of Charles Rist, first published in France in 1983, appears here in English to join other classic diaries of this period such as Jean Guéhenno's *Diary of the Dark Years,* Marc Bloch's *Strange Defeat,* and Hélène Berr's *Journal.* These four diaries are very different, each one the product of a strong mind and particular circumstances. But they are similar in their acute powers of observation, their moral exigency, and their eloquence. Guéhenno, a writer and literature professor in preparatory classes for university applicants, employed formidable powers of intellectual and ethical judgment as he examined the occupation and Vichy's responses to it from an outsider's perspective. He was a true recalcitrant, refusing, exceptionally, to publish anything at all during the occupation except in the underground press, but, then, he had his professor's salary. Marc Bloch's *Strange Defeat* is not, properly speaking, a diary at all, but a commentary written down in white heat during the weeks following the military campaign of 1940 in which Bloch, an internationally celebrated medieval historian, had served as a reserve staff officer. He was shot by the Germans in June 1944 for Resistance activity. Hélène Berr, a university student, chronicled the ever tightening noose around Jews in occupied Paris. Her diary stops abruptly on 15 February 1944, shortly before she was taken off to her death in Auschwitz.

Former participants in the Vichy government also wrote a host of self-exculpatory memoirs after the Liberation of 1944, usually amending their accounts with the advantages of hindsight. Charles Rist's diary differs even more sharply from that genre. It seems to be a fully authentic record of what he was thinking and doing each day. Dr. Aynesworth, who had access to the original handwritten pages, has verified the authenticity of the text and explained clearly what she has restored to the French edition of 1983 (see "A Note from the Translator Regarding the English Text").

Charles Rist observed the travails of occupied France from a perspective that was unique for being simultaneously inside and outside the French power elite. Rist's life and professional accomplishments are expertly presented below by Jean-Noël Jeanneney, a prominent French historian and sometime government official whose father was a close colleague of Charles Rist. I need point out only that Rist was a highly respected economist who began in academia and moved into government service and then onto the boards of important French and foreign banks and businesses. He knew Marshal Pétain and many ministers and high Vichy officials personally. He belonged to an inner circle of experts who were taught to believe that serving the State is a high calling, and he was prepared on two occasions to serve the Vichy State. The first occasion, a report on prewar economic policy for the Vichy government's trial of the French prewar leadership of 1940 (a proceeding that Rist disdained) was minor (see diary entry for 11 May 1942). The second occasion, Rist's proposed economic mission to Washington and eventual appointment as Vichy French ambassador to the United States, did not work out, as Rist discovered the preference of Admiral François Darlan, Pétain's prime minister, for a German victory rather than a British one, and his scorn for American military potential, views repugnant to Rist. At the same time, Rist had considerable doubts about the Resistance and de Gaulle's Free French, although his eldest son, Jean, was active in the Resistance, as will be seen below.

As a board member of several important banks, Rist met in the course of his duties with German officials, particularly with M. von Falkenhausen, the German aristocrat, nephew of the military governor of Belgium, who had been appointed to monitor French banks. These meetings were marked by the courtesy traditional in such circles but altered in no way Rist's fervent desire for an Allied victory. Rist was secretly delighted when von Falkenhausen told of having to spend nights in a basement air-raid shelter during visits to Berlin. Rist resigned from the board of the Banque des Pays de l'Europe Centrale when he concluded that it was serving primarily German interests.

Rist's contacts within the regime and with some German occupation officials made him extremely well informed about the attitudes of the Vichy and German authorities and about the course of the war. His record of conversations with Pétain, Darlan, and other Vichy leaders in the fall of 1941 are particularly precious historical evidence. Soon after, in December 1941, with German armies stalled in the east and the United States engaged in the war, Rist concluded that German defeat was a certainty.

Yet Charles Rist was also an outsider. He descended from and married into a network of Protestant families who were socially and professionally prominent without ever feeling fully at home in Catholic France. The Protestant upper class (HSP, or *haute société protestante*), to which Rist belonged, included some people who served the new regime actively. There was the banker Baron Jacques de Neuflize, who worked closely with the Germans in 1940, and there was General Charles Théodore Brécard, the actively pro-Vichy grand chancellor of the national honor society, the Legion of Honor. Rist felt scorn for their conformism. He reacted more like other members of the HSP who had not forgotten the Saint Bartholomew's Day massacre of 1572 and who feared that if the French government singled out Jews as enemies of the State, the Protestants would be next. The French extreme right had always amalgamated Jews and Protestants in their invectives. Charles Rist's second son, Claude, was married to a Jewish woman, and Rist worked hard to protect that family from Vichy's harsh measures of discrimination against Jews, and from the even more dangerous German deportations. He was related by marriage to pastor André Trocmé, the celebrated protector of Jews in his village of Le Chambon-sur-Lignon.[1] Rist's youngest son, Mario,

---

1. André Trocmé was the first cousin of Henri Trocmé, husband of Charles Rist's sister Ève. Charles Rist's nephews Daniel and Charles, the sons of Henri and Ève, were also active in protecting Jews. Daniel Trocmé, who headed two shelters for young refugees in Le Chambon, was arrested by the Gestapo in 1943 and ended up in a Nazi death camp (see diary entry for 30 June 1943). Charles Trocmé worked alongside Rist's son

who had just been admitted to the position of judge, was almost alone among government officials who resigned their positions in protest against the Vichy government's measures of exclusion against Jews. His cousin Gustave Monod, an official in the education ministry, resigned similarly with a brilliant letter of denunciation of Vichy policies. Another son, Jean, was killed on a Resistance assignment in 1944. Charles Rist and his wife, Germaine, sheltered a Jewish family in their country house.

Charles Rist poured out in his diary the scorn and contempt he felt for the Vichy government, both for the reactionary authoritarianism of its internal policies and for its external policy of collaboration with Nazi Germany. One day in April 1941 while reading Chateaubriand (Rist was a highly cultivated man), he fell upon a phrase that matched his mood perfectly: "There are times when we must ration our alms of contempt, for there are so many needy ones." At the same time, he rejected the visitor (who remains unknown) who tried in January 1943 to recruit him for a resistance movement. He thought that the Liberation of France was a military matter, and that afterward France should align itself with the Protestant "Anglo-Saxon" nations, as the French persist in calling them. Fluent in English and German, Rist drew his information from Swiss radio and the BBC rather than from the Gaullist broadcasts from London and Algiers. Rist was not the only highly trained professional person in France who struggled to balance a commitment to upholding the State with opposition to the government temporarily in charge of it. The complexities of his position, greater than those of Jean Guéhenno, make Rist's diary an eloquent example of a virtuous man trying to reconcile his professional duties with his moral obligations.

Rist believed, with a touch of snobbery, that a frightened middle class lay behind the timidity of the armistice and collaboration, and that the dictators of the modern world – Hitler, Stalin, Mussolini, Pierre Laval – were lower middle-class arrivistes maddened by ambition and resentment. "No pure peasants or pure workers, no aristocrats or 'grands bourgeois' among them" (8 November 1940). He believed that "the people" were more capable than the elite of healthy judgments about the world. Here the older Rist returned to his origins as a young economist concerned with social inequities and political injustice (he had been a defender of Captain Alfred Dreyfus, a Jewish officer wrongly accused of treason in 1894 and finally exonerated after years

---

Jean to shelter refugees in the town of Saint-Étienne (see diary entry for 10 November 1942). Information provided by Françoise Nicolas, daughter of Charles Trocmé, and André Rist, email of 13 September 2010. [TF]

of controversy in 1906). He had been in his early years a leading advocate of cooperatives as the best way to alleviate poverty.

Charles Rist's diary is full of memorable moments. There are the meetings in which Pétain asks him to go to Washington as French ambassador; on Rist's return visit to Vichy, the old marshal gets sidetracked and proudly shows Rist a volume of colored illustrations of his own life. He wants to send a copy to General John J. Pershing, the American commander in chief in 1917–1918. Like all Parisians, even the relatively affluent Rist struggles with extraordinary difficulties in everyday existence. There is a plague of fleas. There are endless struggles with the search for food and heating. Paris is bombed by the Allies, killing or wounding thousands. A son and two nephews are killed in combat before the Liberation comes. Rist's life was accompanied daily by anxiety and the immediacy of death. His diary opens an authentic window onto that harsh time.

A Note from the Translator Regarding the English Text

THIS TRANSLATION WAS GREATLY ENRICHED BY MY RESEARCH IN France during the fall of 2010. Charles Rist's grandson Jean-Pierre Rist allowed me to photograph Rist's original manuscript, which was written in longhand, entirely on stationery – some on Rist's Versailles letterhead, some showing his summer home address near Lake Geneva, and some on hotel stationery obtained during trips to London or Washington.

Having a copy of the manuscript, I can attest to the integrity of the published diary. I have also been able to restore a few lines or passages that were omitted in the French publication of 1983, which was based on the typescript prepared by Germaine Rist after her husband's death. An example of such a restoration is this telling passage from 8 September 1940: "Mario has been busy cutting up the great chestnut tree that collapsed the other day – like the French government – under the weight of too heavy a burden."

Rist's efforts to protect his son Claude's Jewish wife and their three daughters caused him intense anguish ("I believe nothing has aged me more over the past two years, especially this last one, than the anxiety I have suffered for these three children" [23 October 1942]), but the threads of this drama are only cautiously woven through the diary, and some of those threads disappeared entirely in the 1983 publication. I have therefore restored this passage from the manuscript:

> On Tuesday Françoise was summoned by the Gestapo in Maisons-Laffite for an interrogation regarding two denunciations that had been received against her: one accused her of not wearing her yellow star, the other, of traveling between Le Vésinet and Paris. I went with her so that she would not have to face these worrisome characters alone. But I was not allowed to be present at the interrogation. I had to wait in the hall. After she came out, she told me she had been able to clear herself on all points. She had signed a record of the interview and was told that she would be summoned again once her statements had been checked. (31 October 1943)

Two whole pages left out of the typescripts prepared by Germaine Rist have been translated directly from the manuscript and included here. These are the entries for 29 and 30 August 1944, relating to the wounding of Charles Rist's sister Ève "during the Allies' arrival in Verneuil." The fact that she was wounded by friendly fire may have been the reason for the omission.

At the urging of grandson André Rist, I have also reinserted the entries (between 16 February and 16 May) relating to Charles Rist's early 1940 blockade mission to North America, during which he met with Franklin Roosevelt. This section, though included in the typescripts prepared by Germaine Rist, was omitted from the French edition on the grounds that the entries were too dry and telegraphic.

Rist's "Report on My Mission to the United States" and "Notes for Conversation with Prime Minister Paul Reynaud," included in the original manuscript after the 25 April 1940 entry, have been reinserted here. Going beyond the telegraphic notation of meetings, in the "Report" Rist focuses on the intricate politics involved in achieving any sort of blockade. In order to bring the United States on board, it was first necessary to placate Southern Democrats:

> Agricultural purchases immediately became the priority issue. As France had not stopped buying tobacco or cotton, it was not really involved. . . . In contrast, England abruptly declared that it was going to stop buying tobacco. The biggest outlet for this important American product was thus cut off from one day to the next, and prices fell, leading to loud complaints from entire regions in the South. Since these regions belong to the Democratic Party and since Secretary of State Hull was then engaged in the difficult task of persuading the Senate to renew the law that authorizes him to make trade agreements, the problem had become acute when we arrived.

The "Notes" for Prime Minister Reynaud are telegraphic but trenchant:

1. Good intentions on the part of the Roosevelt administration.
   Official Report. Obliged to hedge with Congress.
2. Bad state of public opinion.
   Republicans: hatred of Roosevelt
   Democrats and the left: fear of war; focus
   on the struggle of empires
   Intellectuals: skepticism born of brainwashing during the last war
   Certain industrialists: arrangements with Germany

One entry that is *not* in the original manuscript is that of 19 June 1940: "Last night I heard on the radio the courageous and moving appeal of General de Gaulle, who is giving us back hope and trust." This entry does not appear in Rist's original manuscript or in the Box 45 typescript of 1940 diary entries housed in the *Papiers Charles Rist*, but grandson André Rist confirms that it *is* included in the typescript distributed by Rist's wife after her husband's death in 1955. Few Frenchmen are said to have heard de Gaulle's famous 18 June appeal to resist broadcast by the BBC,[1] and indeed the language of the diary entry does not accord very well with Rist's style or attitude toward de Gaulle. On the other hand, it is probable that the Rists did hear the speech and that Germaine later deemed it necessary to correct the unfortunate lacuna in the diary.

The Rists did listen regularly to the BBC while they were at Le Très-Clos, their summer home near Lake Geneva: "We clung to the hopes conveyed by radio as we listened to broadcasts from Switzerland and London. But by evening, the BBC's program was heavily scrambled; we will have a hard time hearing it from now on. However, this evening we heard de Gaulle's appeal to the navy not to surrender the fleet" (27 June 1940). In fact, Rist apparently refers to de Gaulle's 18 June appeal in a letter to U.S. Army Colonel Sosthènes Behn dated 12 September 1944: "General de Gaulle, in an unforgettable radio speech, affirmed his faith in France and in the future.... Among so many people who remained silent for fear of spies or informers, there existed a common thought, a deep unity, that was rekindled every night by listening to the BBC." (See appendix 4.)

In an email (6 March 2011) to me, granddaughter Isabelle Rist Pinard recalled de Gaulle's radio speeches being excitedly talked about at Le Très-Clos. Grandson Colas Rist, in an email of 4 March 2011, recalled Germaine later talking about de Gaulle's initial appeal: "I remember very well my grandmother telling me about the unforgettable surprise of hearing the speech on the evening of 18 June 1940. She had tears in her eyes as she recollected the moment, sitting before the very same radio by which the speech had reached them. This was in August, 1958, at Le Très-Clos."

The Rists' situation on the eighteenth of June was incredibly tense, which may explain why there was no diary entry the next day, and subsequently only a brief summary dated 18–22 June. Rist and his family, including his Jewish daughter-in-law, her children, and an expectant German daughter-in-law, were essentially refugees who had raced to Le Très-Clos for shelter

---

1. Yet Jean Guéhenno begins his diary *Journal des années noires (1940–1944)* with this recollection: "Last night the voice of General de Gaulle on London radio. What joy finally to hear, in this shameful debacle, one who can speak with pride" (19 June 1940). [TF]

as the Germans marched on Paris: "Chaos and uncertainty everywhere. No discipline anywhere. We arrived around five o'clock. They were anxiously awaiting us. Still no word from our sons" (18 June 1940).

The Rists had the special radio required to pick up broadcasts from abroad. They arrived at Le Très-Clos in plenty of time to have heard de Gaulle's speech, which was broadcast at 7:00 PM London time, and given their anxiety at the time and their habit of tuning in at every opportunity (see, for example, 18–22 June, "hanging on every word of radio news"), it would have been strange if they had not turned on the radio after their ten-hour trek to find out what was happening.

Would Charles Rist have had mixed feelings as he listened to the speech? In it de Gaulle appealed directly to engineers like Rist's son Jean, chief engineer in one of the Holtzer steel mills, who indeed later joined the Resistance: "I call upon French engineers and skilled armaments workers who are on British soil, or have the means of getting here, to come and join me."[2]

: : : : :

At the Banque de France I was able to photograph the following documents, which tell their own story of the passionate doer and thinker who wrote this diary:

· Notes on Rist's visit to the slums of London when he was eighteen
· His letters as a Dreyfusard
· His lectures to workers at the "Open University" of Montpellier
· His notes for speeches representing the League of the Rights of Man
· Letters to him from Romain Rolland and Jean Jaurès
· Numerous letters from Jews and other refugees seeking his help
· His great speech "Resist" (delivered in September 1945 at l'Assemblée du musée du désert in Mialet, Cévennes), in which he urged the nation to resist seeking vengeance on collaborators and to return instead to the rule of law

During my stay in France the Rists' numerous family members not only made me welcome, but they also provided invaluable interviews, some of which I videotaped. The most memorable of these is the one of Isabelle

---

2. "Charles de Gaulle Speech," BBC News UK, 17 June 2010, http://www.bbc.com /news/10339678.

showing me the yellow star that her mother, Françoise, had left to her and her sisters.

In the United States I also interviewed Isabelle's sister Antoinette Rist Constable, as well as Antoinette's daughter Marianne, who had taped interviews with her grandmother Françoise before the latter died. Their memories and insightful comments on the situation of Françoise and her daughters during the war became incorporated in various ways into this translation. Antoinette's poem "As Many Stars . . . Under Nazi Rule, 1943" has been included in appendix 3.

: : : : :

The French title given to Rist's diary by Jean-Noël Jeanneney is "Une Saison Gâtée," a phrase taken from an essay by Montaigne (see the epigraph), translated by Charles Cotton in 1894 as "so corrupt an age," and cited by Rist on 17 June 1941. I owe thanks to Raymond H. McKay for suggesting the more resonant English translation "Season of Infamy." The words echo Franklin D. Roosevelt's own assessment of the war a bare six months later in the aftermath of the 7 December 1941 attack on Pearl Harbor, a date, he said, "which will live in infamy."

As Dan Aynesworth has pointed out to me, "Season of Infamy" also echoes Voltaire's catchphrase *"Écrasez l' infâme"* – "crush the infamous." In his diary, Charles Rist does his share of crushing the infamous, the likes of Jacques Doroit, Pierre Laval, Marcel Déat, Admiral Darlan, and others in Pétain's inner circle. Voltaire's primary target was irrationality and superstition, and Rist picks up where Voltarie left off, repeatedly denouncing the bourgeois fear of communism, which he saw as the driving force behind France's capitulation and collaboration with Hitler.

: : : : :

I have prepared this English version with the general reader in mind, not just World War II buffs and historians. To give the daily entries more context, the diary has been divided into chapters with brief introductions. I have also added a timeline of Rist's movements, a brief Who's Who of the Rist family, and a list of Rist family members who were imprisoned or killed during the war.

I am indebted to Jean-Noël Jeanneney and his research assistant Renaud Fessaguet for much of the annotation found here. The footnotes from the

1983 French edition have been either retained, incorporated into the text, or used in the glossary created for the English translation. All footnotes here are translated from the French edition except where indicated otherwise in brackets: [TF] means Translator's Footnote; [JNJ/TF] means I have added information to the original French footnote. In addition, all translations of text quoted in the diary are mine unless otherwise noted.

Acknowledgments

I AM DEEPLY GRATEFUL TO ROBERT J. SLOAN, WHO, AS EDITOR IN chief at Indiana University Press, undertook on behalf of IUP to publish this translation of Charles Rist's diary, and to incoming director Gary Dunham and the team at the press whose work has been so conscientious.

This English version of Charles Rist's diary would not have been possible without a great deal of help. Generous grants from the National Endowment for the Arts and the Kittredge Foundation allowed me to spend three years working on the translation and three months doing background research in France. If it were not for Jean-Noël Jeanneney, the eminent French historian, the diary would never have been published in the first place. With the help of Noël Rist and researcher Renaud Fessaguet, M. Jeanneney compiled the original annotated French edition, wrote an incisive introduction for it, and saw it through publication by Fayard. His continued advice and support have been invaluable.

Rist's descendants likewise contributed enormously to this effort. My heartfelt thanks go to Rist's grandson André Rist in particular for his encouragement and active involvement in this project. André served from the beginning as a liaison, connecting me with other sources of information as well as providing me with his own extensive knowledge of events and people discussed in the diary. André was a teenager during the war and thus privy to much that was happening, including his parents' efforts to hide refugees and his father Jean Rist's participation in the Resistance. André and his wife, Michelle, provided many helpful documents, including family photographs, Jean Rist's brief 1941–1942 diary, and a copy of *Charles Rist et les siens*, with helpful essays on Charles and Jean Rist by André and cousin Colas Rist.

I am grateful to André's sister Simone Rist for a helpful interview in which she shared her memories of the family and their wartime experiences. Other grandchildren were equally forthcoming. Jean-Pierre Rist allowed me to view and photograph the entire handwritten manuscript, which remains in his possession. Franklin and Colas Rist hosted a family get-together in March 2010 so that their family could meet my husband, Dan, and me on our initial visit, and Colas arranged for us to tour the house in Versailles where their parents were raised by Charles and Germaine Rist. Franklin, a lawyer, provided important information regarding the history of the diary's publication and was able on several occasions to locate expert help with translating the diary's more difficult economic terms. Colas Rist and his wife, Denise, spent a memorable evening with us at André's house during which we discussed ways to structure the English-language version of the diary. Colas shared his own writings about Charles Rist and helped me to see his grandfather as a *moraliste* in the tradition of Montaigne. He also provided the section in appendix 2 titled "The Anti-Jewish Laws of Vichy."

Granddaughters Isabelle Rist Pinard and Antoinette Rist Constable, daughters of Claude Rist and his Jewish wife, Françoise, provided photographs, documents, and personal accounts that helped to round out Charles Rist's circumspect references to their perilous situation and to his efforts to protect them. Françoise Nicolas Trocmé, the granddaughter of Rist's sister Ève, was a fount of information about people and events in the diary. Aside from interviews and emails, she provided me with a copy of her extensive genealogy of the Rist family, and she and her husband, Robert, helped me decipher Rist's handwriting in the two pages I translated directly from the manuscript (29 August and 30 August 1944).

Several of Charles Rist's great-grandchildren deserve mention as well: Jean-Daniel Rist, for facilitating my access to the Charles Rist papers donated by Jean-Daniel's father, Marcel, to the Banque de France; Marianne Rist Ravenscroft and Line Rist Billaud (along with her spouse, Jean-Pierre) for their interest, support, and informative reading of the translation; and Marianne Constable, who possesses taped interviews with her grandmother, for helping me to understand Françoise's situation better.

I am extremely grateful to Frédérik Grélard and all the staff at the Banque de France archives for their help and support during my frequent visits to the reading room to study the Charles Rist papers; to Benoît Klein for sharing his research on the trial of Pétain; and to Sylvia Simpson, a longtime friend of the Rist family, for her support and encouragement.

I am indebted to Robert Paxton for his encouragement and for showing me *la diritta via* in regard to Rist's belief that a right-wing conspiracy led to the German occupation of France. Thanks, too, to translators David Ball, Marian Schwartz, and Patrick A. Saari for their enthusiastic support and advice.

Evenings of discussion with journalist and educator Raymond H. McKay resulted in the English title "Season of Infamy" (see "A Note from the Translator") and fresh perspectives from one who lives in Argentina on the fine line walked by those who wish to serve in infamous times.

My deepest gratitude goes to advisory reader Norman Thomas di Giovanni and to my husband, Dan (Donald D. Aynesworth), who introduced me to Rist's diary. I could count on master translator di Giovanni and French scholar Dan Aynesworth to spot those infelicities that, like Charles Rist's floor fleas, seem so hard to eradicate.

Introduction to the 1983 French Edition

JEAN-NOËL JEANNENEY

HERE IS THE DIARY OF CHARLES RIST, JUST AS HE RECORDED IT from 1939 to 1945, during the whole of our national drama. It is a *livre de raison* – an account for his heirs by a member of France's bourgeoisie – free of later embellishments or regrets.

Forty years have gone by, yet the upheaval of those years still haunts our collective memory. Shaped by successive generations, legacies of defensive pride, and newly colored views imposed by the march of history, the story continues to be rewritten. The time has not yet come – will it ever? – when interpretations of occupied France could be set in stone.

Any new testimony, if well developed and written by a qualified observer, merits consideration. It seemed to me that the unpublished diary of Charles Rist, a rich and truthful account, was worth bringing before a public eager to know more. His family have agreed with complete generosity of spirit, convinced that not only would it serve his memory, it would also add to our knowledge of a collective past that we continue to pore over, searching for answers.

: : : : :

Charles Rist, who lived from 1874 to 1955, came from a Protestant family of the Alsatian bourgeoisie.[1] After the defeat of 1871, the family relocated from Strasbourg to Lausanne, settling finally in Versailles in 1890. Rist's

---

1. This summary of Rist's life is based largely on the special issue of the *Revue d'économie politique* (November–December 1955) dedicated to Charles Rist. In addition to homages written by his friends and students, it includes a biography (977–1045) written by Rist himself for his successor at the Académie des sciences morales et politiques, as well as a bibliography of his works.

father was a doctor. But Charles, after *lycée* studies in Versailles, chose to study law and specialize in political economy, a calling to which he was drawn by concern for "the social question." A trip to England at the age of eighteen, during which he saw for himself the abject misery of working-class neighborhoods in London, resulted in his two doctoral theses: "Journée de travail de l'ouvrier adulte en France" [The Work Day of an Adult Worker in France] and "Législation anglaise sur la responsabilité en matière d'accidents" [Accident Liability Law in England]. Not at all influenced by Marx, whose work he found deeply repugnant from the beginning, Rist was a strong proponent of Saint-Simonianism. He considered the *Doctrine de Saint-Simon* [The Doctrine of Saint-Simon], written by [Amand] Bazard and [Barthélemy Prosper] Enfantin, to be a "great book, a classic of French language and thought" (*Revue* 979).

In 1899 Rist qualified to become a professor. "When I arrived as a young professor at the University of Montpellier," he wrote at the end of his life, "I hardly knew anything about political economy; in particular, monetary matters were completely foreign to me, banking seemed mysterious, and only social issues struck me as worthy of study and observation. My union sympathies and my penchant for taking up social causes had been nurtured and rekindled by the Dreyfus affair, during which we had the constant support of labor organizations" (*Revue* 978–79).

While in Montpellier Rist devoted considerable energy to the Dreyfus cause, and because of his recent marriage to Germaine Monod, the affair took on even more importance in his formation. Germaine's father was Gabriel Monod – famous Protestant historian, founder of the *Revue historique*, and one of the leaders of that young group of intellectuals who at last brought about a reversal of Dreyfus's conviction. Her mother was the daughter of Alexander Herzen and the loquacious, enthusiastic heir to the cosmopolitan traditions of Russian socialism in exile.

In the diary one encounters several allusions to "the affair," a critical experience for a whole generation of young members of the bourgeoisie eager to escape the selfishness and hypocrisy of social conformity. In a note dated 13 September 1899, Rist wrote the following:

> The most important . . . consequence of this horrible drama, the one that strikes me today more than ever, is the need to introduce into our whole way of judging and thinking the greatest objectivity possible. Listen to testimony, examine the facts, and if possible, stay calm until the truth emerges, then pursue it with vigor and passion – that is the rule to obey in all matters. In France, we flee from anything that goes beyond a simple impression. As soon as the facts cohere and lead to a conviction that is contrary to a conviction backed up by other facts, we

try to slip away. We would rather entertain simple opinions that are easy to talk about, but we quickly turn away once those opinions become certainties requiring action. I recognize the usefulness of skepticism grounded in a natural sense of reserve, but I detest the cowardice that can no longer hide behind doubt, that exaggerates the uncertainties of our judgment in order to escape the need to judge.[2]

Faithful to his early enthusiasms, Charles Rist undertook to create at Montpellier one of those "Popular Universities" with a mission to "go to the people" and raise the consciousness and intellectual abilities of the working class. At the same time, he wrote a regular column dedicated to the development of unionism for the *Revue d'économie politique*.

Such was the point of departure. The next stage brought Rist nearer to economics proper. He spent a number of years in collaboration with Charles Gide, his senior, writing the monumental *Histoire des doctrines économiques* [History of Economic Doctrines]. This work, his most famous, was published in 1909. Since then it has been reprinted many times and translated into nine languages.

In 1913 Rist was elected to the Law Faculty in Paris. His scientific curiosity began to gravitate strongly toward monetary problems as he witnessed the disruptive impact of the Great War on currencies, exchanges, and budgets. By the end of that war he had become one of France's top experts on financial matters. At the urging of André Lichtenberger, Rist spent the war working with a team of specialists on German matters; their aim was to supply the government with more expert and better-monitored data regarding Germany's economic and financial resources. His 1920 book on the subject, *Les Finances de guerre de l'Allemagne* [Germany's War Finances], raised him to immediate prominence in the field. His reputation grew still further with the appearance in 1924 of *La Déflation en pratique* [Deflation in Practice], a critique of postwar financial policy. That same year Rist wrote the chapter on economics for *La Politique républicaine* [Republican Policy], a collective work constituting the left-wing coalition's radical political platform.

Thus, two years later, at the time of the coalition's decline, Finance Minister Raoul Péret appointed him to the famous committee of experts who for the first time, in the spring of 1926, proposed that the de facto devaluation of the franc be officially acknowledged as irreversible. The purpose of this "stabilization" – a euphemism – was to sweep away the illusion of a pure and simple return to the way things were before the war. Péret's successor Joseph Caillaux adopted the experts' plan as his own. Because the governor

2. Family archives.

(Georges Robineau) and board of the Banque de France insisted on the franc's rise, Caillaux made a spectacular move. He dismissed Robineau and his second in command, naming in their place his protégé Émile Moreau, director of the Banque d'Algérie, and Professor Charles Rist with the explicit mission to implement the policy of stabilization. Rist's hesitations were swept aside by Caillaux's admonition, likely to wound any academic comfortably settled on the sidelines as teacher and commentator: "Surely you don't want to spend the rest of your life teaching grammar!"

Thus was Charles Rist suddenly launched into action. Theory gave way to practice. He was fifty-two. At a time when the world of university economists remained rather distant from political, business, and government circles, this new role meant that Rist's experience and social network would rapidly expand.

At Moreau's side, Rist played an important role in the difficult two-year process culminating in the introduction of the Poincaré franc on 25 June 1928.[3] The bank's governor, who did not speak English, named Rist as his representative to the first organized meeting among the central bank heads of Great Britain, the United States, Germany, and France. The meeting took place in New York City in 1927. Numerous meetings followed, most notably in Paris and Rome. Then once the stabilization was successful, Rist asked [Raymond] Poincaré to be relieved of his duties and once again donned his professor's robes at the Law Faculty. But as he now enjoyed an international reputation, he continued to represent France at various meetings of experts. At a time when the great crash was about to multiply the war's upheavals, he was called in as a consultant for endangered foreign currencies in Romania, Austria, Spain, and Turkey. He was equally in demand with large private corporations, which were just as unprepared as the nation-states to confront, after a century of monetary stability, the era's unprecedented jolts. Clearly valued as a consultant, he was soon asked to become even more involved and to serve on numerous boards.

This was the third phase of his career. The expert took on additional roles as banker and board member. In 1933 Rist once again requested leave from the Law Faculty (this time for good) in order to serve on the boards of the Suez Canal Company and the Banque de Paris et des Pays-Bas, two of

3. Moreau himself, eager as he was to proclaim his own influence, acknowledged Rist's role throughout his posthumous memoir, *Souvenirs d'un gouverneur de la Banque de France, Histoire de la stabilisation du franc (1926–28)* [Recollections of a Governor of the Bank of France: History of the Stabilization of the Franc, 1926–28] (Paris: Marie-Thérèse Génin, 1954).

the most desirable, prestigious – and lucrative – posts in the worlds of French and international business. He served also on the boards of the Banque de Syrie, the Banque du Maroc, and Matériel Téléphonique, a Franco-American industrial corporation. Finally in 1937, in the course of his travels to Turkey, he became chairman of the Ottoman Bank's Parisian board.

A change of direction – a material change, as well. The professor, now head of a large family, knew for the first time the prosperity required to ease his five sons' entry into professional life. But he was far from renouncing the advantages and interest of his "multipositionality," as current sociologists' jargon would label it. Each year he gave several lectures at the École Libre des Sciences Politiques[4] and, above all, devoted most of his time to research. In 1938 he published an important *Histoire des doctrines relatives au crédit et à la monnaie depuis John Law jusqu'à nos jours* [History of Monetary and Credit Theory from John Law to the Present Day], and in 1933, with help from the Rockefeller Foundation, set about creating ISRES. This Scientific Institute for Economic and Social Research was established the following year at 4 rue Michelet in Paris near the Observatory Gardens. Rist's goal was clear: with no theoretical agenda, he aimed to provide researchers, particularly those with political and economic responsibilities, the best concrete data on the development of French economics, from a contemporary, international perspective. The Institute published a quarterly review, *L'Acitivité économique* [Economic Activity]; some *Tableaux de l'économie française* [Graphic Representations of France's Economy] issued in 1935; an important survey of unemployment in France (three volumes, 1935, 1942, and 1949); and a collection of graphs relating to the French economy from 1914 to 1936. At a time when availability of concrete economic facts was still quite poor – as French economist Alfred Sauvy often sadly observed – this was a new and useful contribution. Moreover, Rist made an effort to create strong links with researchers in neighboring countries by holding regular meetings. Though we remained far behind compared to Anglo-Saxon countries, the impetus had been given for a new way of doing things.

Meanwhile, those in high public office continued to regard Rist as an expert (the word enjoyed an almost magical prestige in those years). Repeatedly, his name was pronounced when a technical expert was needed at the finance ministry. From 1935 until the war, Rist presided over a committee charged by the Ministry of Commerce with adapting customs regulations to prevailing economic conditions. In particular, he had the difficult

---

4. An institution of higher education in Paris specializing in the social sciences and political affairs (aka Sciences Po). [TF]

mission of doing away with some of the quotas that had multiplied after 1932 and had erected, in Rist's words, "a veritable Wall of China around principal French industries, and even more so, around agriculture." When in March 1937 the Popular Front government proclaimed a "pause" and sought to restore "confidence" in the business world, Rist, along with Paul Baudouin and Jacques Rueff, became part of a committee set up to manage the exchange stabilization fund, in collaboration with the Banque de France. On the fourteenth of June, Baudouin, Rist, and Rueff resigned. Given existing economic circumstances and unable to answer for financial measures of which they disapproved, they felt powerless. Their resignation delivered one of the final blows to Léon Blum's government, resulting in its precipitate collapse in the Senate a few days later.

This episode in the trajectory of Charles Rist's career is significant. Without a doubt, his image in informed circles had shifted toward the right. The explanation is not just his entry into the world of business, nor the possible psychological changes that might have affected him as a result. One must also consider intellectual reasons. At the beginning of the 1920s, he had been one of the first to advocate publicly a bold stabilization policy; he had approved Keynes's political and technical diatribes against those who supported a policy of merciless reparations imposed on Germany; and he had sided against the nationalist right wing, favoring Aristide Briand's advocacy of collective security pacts and Franco-German reconciliation: all attitudes that, in the eyes of the public, identified him with the left. From then on, to his enduring theoretical and practical anti-Marxism was added an unshakable hostility toward the man on his way to becoming, for Anglo-Saxons at least, the prophet of choice for capitalism's new age – namely, John Maynard Keynes. Rist severed all links with him, believing his *General Theory* (which appeared in 1936) was just the skillful packaging of a purely economic approach to the problem of unemployment, and was effective (if that!) only in Anglo-Saxon countries. His view henceforth was that Keynes had introduced "in all subjects that he touched, confusion, ambiguity, and obscurity."[5] At the same time, his repugnance toward all systems with global claims was thus reinforced: "Political economy," he would write after the war, "does not deserve to be called a science as long as it relies on systems."[6]

5. "La Pensée économique de Proudhon" [Economic Ideas of Proudhon], *Revue d'histoire économique et sociale*, no. 2 (1955): 129–65. The essay was written as an introduction for a reprint by Marcel Rivière of Proudhon's *Manuel de spéculation en Bourse* [Stock Exchange Speculator's Manual].

6. Ibid.

We should add that in the great debate of the years 1934–1936 – a debate sprung from the fact that French prices were too high in relation to those in other countries – when it came time to choose between deflation and devaluation, Rist delayed taking sides for a long time, preferring to play the Sphinx in public.[7] As late as 1935 he appeared to lean toward the deflationist policy of Laval's government, and it was only in the spring of 1936, at the very moment of the Popular Front election, that he finally opted for devaluation in an explosive article contributed to the *Petit Parisien*. The least one can say is that this time he did not play the guiding role, either in the realm of ideas or the realm of action, that he had during the 1920s.

Thus had Charles Rist evolved as an individual when World War II and this diary began. He was sixty-five years old. His health, which had once raised alarms (he had been declared unfit for military service in 1910 following an attack of tuberculosis), was now sound thanks to a very strict regimen, leaving him free for his pursuits. The Phoney War brought him new tasks, on top of his usual activities. Blockade Minister Georges Pernot asked him to create and preside over a consultative committee charged with providing Pernot with a program and some guiding principles. The policy Rist inspired, consonant with that of the English, rejected as illusory the idea of a general, universal blockade, concentrating rather on a limited number of products. A trip to the United States in March and April 1940 was the occasion for an encouraging meeting with Roosevelt on matters of general policy, and he obtained some concrete results, putting a stop to shipments of Canadian nickel and American molybdenum to the enemy. He returned to Paris in early May. A few days later saw the German offensive of 10 May and the brutal beginning of the long, four-year tunnel of occupation.

After suffering through the exodus, along with millions of French people, Rist returned to Versailles, to the Villa Amiel, which belonged to his mother-in-law, Olga Monod-Herzen, and which his family had occupied since 1913. His activities necessarily slowed. A certain lightening of his industrial, financial, and scientific responsibilities allowed him to consecrate his leisure to writing "for postwar youth" a *Précis des mécanismes économiques* [A Handbook of Economic Mechanisms], in which he summarized in the simplest way possible the reflections and observations of his whole life as an economist. His concern for the welfare of those close to him took up much of his time and labor. Could he do more? Try to influence the course of political

---

7. Alfred Sauvy criticized him sharply for this in *Histoire économique de la France entre les deux guerres* [Economic History of France between the Two Wars] (Paris: Fayard, 1965), 2: 104.

events? He saw only a momentary possibility of doing that. At the end of 1941, Pétain wanted to send him to Washington as France's ambassador – with the explicit intention of reassuring Americans regarding the foreign policy of the new regime. But the project quickly foundered. Rist also rejected a call from members of the Resistance to go to Algeria in June 1943. He said he felt too burdened with family responsibilities and that "some men must stay in France," though his real motive, noted by himself, was different: "The truth is that I don't know what I would be doing over there, what purpose I would serve; I know in advance I would be disgusted by all the political hot air" (4 June 1943).

It therefore remained for Rist to stay in Versailles and Paris as a passionate observer of the war's developments, questioning himself on the causes of the disaster, placing the behavior of the "common people" and the "elite" in historical perspective, and reflecting on the country's destiny, its past, its present, and its future. To this do we owe the book.

: : : : :

To appreciate the scope of this document, we must first clarify the author's motivation, the psychological and intellectual reasons why Charles Rist wrote so continuously in his diary, and, finally, the public for which he intended it.

At other moments in his life he had been accustomed to making journal notes – but in a sporadic fashion. Some of them have been preserved by his family. They are often so laconic as to lack interest. But this time he chose to write with detachment and regularity. He clearly needed to offset the depressing effects of his curtailed activities and decreased influence, even as an expert, on the course of events. To comment, classify, prioritize – this is a kind of mental hygiene that helps one to dominate emotion and to nurture clarity of mind by focusing on the essential. Beyond compensating for the uncertainties of memory, Rist wanted to keep a record so that his children might at a later time better understand the evolution of his feelings and the reasons for his actions. After news arrived in September 1944 that his eldest son, Jean, had been killed by Germans that August, Rist put down his pen. "For a month now I have written nothing," he observed on the fifteenth of October. "The shock was too great. And I asked myself if I would ever again have the heart to take up these notes, written in large part for his eyes. It seemed so useless to continue."

Three years earlier, on another of the rare occasions on which he explained the persistence of his diary entries, Rist had written: "Sometimes I tell myself that this diary is useless and will perhaps serve someday to show me my own errors of judgment. Even if that were the case, I should not regret having written it and having kept the memory of my impressions day by day, during such an infamous time, a time people will be eager to forget when peace has come. It will perhaps be the measure of my illusions, perhaps also the measure of what I managed to preserve of good sense in the storm" (17 June 1941).

Such were his motivations, and such was the small audience he had in mind: himself, later, plus his family circle and a few close friends. That he did not imagine future publication of his diary is precisely what gives it a rare interest. Certainly, he did not tell all regarding his emotions or the information that he gathered, modesty and prudence combining their effects. But in the end sincerity shone through, restoring to the passing days their truth – or truths. There is no posing before posterity and very little egotistical introspection; what we get instead is a sustained effort to record his worries, his hopes, and his indignation regarding others, a constant effort (one welcome to the historian) to situate the shock of the moment in the continuity of time, to connect it to precedents, and thus to weigh the essential and the absurd. This is the chronicle of a head of family constantly concerned, in the middle of the storm, not just for the fate of his loved ones, but for his own moral and civic responsibility.

: : : : :

To which France? At the heart of the collective drama every Frenchman, depending upon his situation, had his own image of France.

The trajectory of Charles Rist's life described so far helps to convey the various circles of his universe, which gradually evolved and helped shape his personal outlook during the war.

His five sons, first of all, opened several windows for him on occupied France. Jean, the oldest, born in 1900, was a graduate of the École Centrale engineering school. Assigned to an artillery unit at the beginning of the war, he returned two months later to his previous job as chief engineer in one of the Holtzer steel mills near Firminy. After the Nazi invasion of France's southern zone, however, seeing that the mill had resigned itself to work for Germany, he quit and made numerous trips to the Paris region, where he was asked to found a national research laboratory for the French steel industry. At the same time he became increasingly involved in the active Resistance. Of this Charles Rist speaks sparingly – restrained by his own prudence and by that of his son. In June 1944 the Secret Army entrusted him with the job of liaisons and communications for the entire Loire department. And on 21 August, during a skirmish with retreating Germans who had unexpectedly halted, he was killed.[8]

Claude, born in 1902, was the second son. Also an engineer, he headed the lab at Lyonnaise des Eaux, a public utility located near Le Vésinet. He and his family, as one will see, are very present in the diary. Since Claude's wife, Françoise, was of Jewish origin, Charles Rist had to make great legal efforts and engage in much maneuvering in order to protect her and her three little girls from danger.

Léonard, born in 1905, was the only one to enter the world of economics and finance – but on the practical side. Since 1928 he had worked for the Morgan Bank in Paris. Taken prisoner in 1940 and freed in September 1941, he returned to his job at the bank, a fact to which we owe several original insights into the life of American financiers in Paris. When the capital was liberated, Léonard found himself momentarily acting as interpreter for General de Gaulle and reported his impressions of the atmosphere during these great moments.

Noël Rist, thirty-four years old in 1940, was a medical researcher at the Pasteur Institute.

Lastly, Mario, the youngest, who had qualified as a judge in 1939, resigned when the Vichy government promulgated its anti-Jewish "laws of exception" and went to work for the Société d'Ugine's legal department.

Still others complete the family circle. Charles Rist's brother, Édouard, was a prestigious pulmonologist and hospital physician. His sister Ève was married to Henri Trocmé, assistant principal of the École des Roches, an elite secondary school, and Gabrielle, his other sister, was the wife of General Constant Schaller. The extent of this circle's suffering during the war will become clear during the course of the diary.

The Trocmés, the Monods, and others close to Rist – the Boegners, the Ullerns – this universe was largely of Protestant persuasion. In the "social space" of Charles Rist, the Protestant bourgeoisie into which he was born held an important place, though Rist himself had long been agnostic. It was not that he had a special love of this group; he could be quite acerbic about the wealthiest. "Well-off Protestants," he wrote on 6 August 1941, "generally consider themselves to be the salt of the earth; most often they are just the vinegar." But in the end, he was visibly influenced, on many occasions, and

---

8. *Jean Rist, 1900–1944,* biographical brochure (with a fine piece by Charles Rist in memory of his eldest son), 64 pages, no place or date.

not just from the Chambon side,[9] by the residual effects of this minority's historical solidarity – a solidarity that the Dreyfus affair had reinforced and extended to the Jews, and sometimes to the Freemasons, two other "confederate states" singled out by Charles Maurras[10] for the hatred of "good Frenchmen."

Though Charles Rist had left the university in 1933, he retained some friends and many acquaintances there. These included former students or researchers at his institute on rue Michelet, people such as Robert Marjolin, Jean-Marcel Jeanneney, René Brouillet, and René Courtin, who consulted Rist about the economic program Courtin was secretly drafting for the General Studies Committee of the Resistance.

Some distance away was the Académie des Sciences Morales et Politiques, where other generations held sway. In 1928 Charles Rist had been elected a member in the economics division, nominated by Clément Colson. He was rather assiduous about attending the weekly Saturday meetings (the diary of fellow member Jacques Bardoux, published after the war, gives more detail in this regard than his own notes). The Academy was for him one of those rather rare places where one could find, with a center-right coloration, and with perhaps more social and political influence than in our own time, personalities from academia, high government office, politics, banking, and industry.

In the world of business, the boards of Paribas[11] and the Suez Company provided Rist with privileged observation posts, and he could further inform himself at Matériel Téléphonique, the Banque du Maroc, the Ottoman Bank, and the Banque de Syrie: each contact offered original insights into the relations maintained with various foreign countries. The historian as a rule is less informed about the ethos of those in business than about the worlds of politics, journalism, or literature, whether for lack of access or available records. Thus Charles Rist's observations are invaluable. Though for years he had invested much of his energy in these new activities, he kept more distance from the beginning than others would have, and so he was able to tell us more, and with a greater sense of perspective. What is more, despite the harsh measures of the Nazi occupation, which lessened international

9. Le Chambon-sur-Lignon, a Protestant enclave in south-central France, became a haven for Jews during the war under the leadership of André Trocmé, a Protestant minister, and his wife, Magda. [TF]

10. Charles Maurras was an influential leader of L'Action Française, advocating monarchism and a return to the ideas of pre-Revolutionary France. [TF]

11. Paribas: Banque de Paris et des Pays-Bas. [TF]

exchanges and strained his Anglo-Saxon friendships, he continued to meet with foreign businessmen: his American friends from the Morgan Bank, in particular, up to the end of 1941; [Marcus] Wallenberg, a great Swedish financier; and also, until 1942, a few Germans.

As for Vichy, Rist's diary is rich in firsthand information about the actors, the atmosphere, the decision-making process. Even aside from the 1941 episode of the proposed ambassadorship, he strove constantly to find out as much as he could through his personal relations with [Lucien] Romier and [Henri] Moysset, both longtime acquaintances of Rist's who served in Pétain's cabinet, one very close to the marshal, the other to Darlan. The American diplomats posted to Vichy – [Harrison Freeman] Matthews, [Maynard B.] Barnes, and [Pinckney] Tuck – also spoke freely with him.

Let us not overlook, finally, how often daily life was the focus of Rist's reflections. His direct observations proliferate over the course of the diary: the simple atmosphere of a street; the conduct of his neighbors on the rue Mansart in Versailles; the comings and goings of Germans in requisitioned houses; the comments of merchants, the conversations snatched on the fly in public places, and anecdotes gleaned on trains and trolleys that provided a member of the bourgeoisie with glimpses of what the "people" thought and felt.

: : : : :

If one attempts to sum up the contributions of Rist's diary, it is this simple flavor of the time that must be mentioned first. Let us cite at random the difficulties of securing food and heating (a persistent topic of conversation); the parcels arriving from the country; the bicycle taxis and the "floor fleas"; the new epidemics; the gaunt, starving children and the patience of poor people in the snow; the man on the Versailles train tearing apart his cigarette butts; the humble laborers; the carters and the woodcutters who cynically took advantage of their new status; the uncertainties of the mail and surprise that the telephone continued to function during the entire time that Paris was under siege ... The Diary of a Parisian Bourgeois: this is a noble genre, of which past centuries have given us remarkable examples. Rist's daily notes easily take their place in that tradition.

The day-by-day character of Rist's diary entries, moreover, charts for us what might be called the chronology of a hope: the highs and lows of a French patriot's morale could almost be tracked on a sine curve.

The frequent accuracy of his predictions is to be commended. If he wrongly believed in September 1939 that Germany would not attack France on its eastern front, and in January 1943 that a second front would open in the Balkans, on the other hand he predicted early on the entry of the United States into the war, the efficacy of Soviet resistance, and also (wishful thinking?) the final crushing of Germany. His impatience often led him into error regarding the future calendar of operations, but rarely in regard to the general movement of the war. He mistook the rhythm, but not the overall direction. And this lucidity does much to heighten the credit one may accord the document as a whole.

The direct experience that Rist had long since acquired of Anglo-Saxon countries did not blind him to their weaknesses. Several times he had personally taken the measure of the "sacrosanct individualism" of America. He was bitter toward the English for their conduct between the wars, "their perpetual collusion with the Germans after the peace of 1918" (2 November 1940), their minimal financial sacrifices in the military sphere, their tenacious illusions about the nature of Hitler's regime. But with all that, he never ceased to admire these two nations (not without some Huguenot influence) for the efficiency of their democracy, their prodigious energy, and their implacable determination once it became clear there was but one path to follow – all strong indicators that many disheartened French people were incapable of noticing, believing until the end in the possibility of a compromise peace: "Their faint hearts make it impossible to understand more passionate ones," he wrote on 12 May 1943.

That Rist's hopes were partly based on faith is clear, but one also finds here a level of information on the general unfolding of the conflict that appears in retrospect to have been rather good. The reader will note, with the help of footnotes, that credence given to false rumors is on the whole rather rare.

An interesting reminder in this regard: radio, for the first time in history, played an essential role in this war. The cultural privilege Rist enjoyed of having an excellent command of German and English took on considerable importance, giving him access to German-Swiss radio and to British and American networks. But vitally significant also, in all the social circles that Rist frequented, were transatlantic and trans-Channel broadcasts in French. We read of the worker on the Versailles train who was quietly enlightened by Germaine Rist when he complained that he could no longer hear the broadcasts very well because of scrambling. We note in passing that Charles Rist heard and applauded General de Gaulle's 18 June appeal, of which certain authors have said once too often that only a handful of random listeners knew about it.[12]

However attentive Rist was to distinguishing truth from falsehood, the diary nonetheless provides, presented with varying degrees of mistrust, a remarkable array of rumors and tall tales, the false news that any system of censorship causes to spring up and quickly spread under the radar of official, controlled information.

These abundant, often picturesque, and sometimes frankly mad rumors were peddled by the most levelheaded people, whose credulity grew as time passed. There were two types. On the one hand, the "rose-colored" rumors – from the point of view of the Resistance – reflecting an unconscious desire (or, in some cases, a concerted will) to reassure the public and encourage hatred of the occupier. The death of Jacques Doriot, invented in November 1942, or the imagined presence of General [Alphonse-Joseph] Georges in the U.S.S.R. in January 1943, was apt to lend a patriotic French coloring to the unexpected successes of Stalin. In contrast, the "black" rumors, the depressing ones: the alleged failure of the meeting of the Allies in Teheran in December 1943, or the frightening plan attributed to the Germans, 15 August 1944, to round up all male children over ten years old... Sometimes the psychological import of a rumor was more uncertain, as in the case of the one spread in July 1944, according to which Hitler was to be taught a "doctrine of sacrifice" by a Japanese teacher belonging to a mysterious sect.

It was rare, in truth, for Charles Rist to fall for these rumors or for him to present such information as true. This was owing to his sangfroid in the face of such stories, as well as to the critical spirit with which he weighed his sources.

:   :   :   :   :

The episode of the aborted American mission constitutes, at the heart of the diary, one of its strongest moments – casting a bright light on the suffocating inner circle where the new masters' intrigues were being hatched.

At the end of August 1941, passing through Vichy, Charles Rist learned from an American diplomat that his name had come up for the ambassadorship to Washington, as a replacement for Senator Gaston Henry-Haye, who

---

12. See "A Note from the Translator." It appears that this entry was in fact added to the diary after Charles Rist's death. [TF]

had occupied the position since 1940 and who had little authority. In spite of Rist's lively antipathy toward the Vichy regime, he surprisingly did not rule out the possibility of accepting. It is less surprising if one knows that during the course of the 1930s his name had already been advanced on occasion for the Washington post. He had even noted one day that it would be one of the few public positions he could find attractive. This may explain a weaker psychological resistance than one might have expected after reading the diary up to this point.

In mid-September matters began to crystallize. Yves Bouthillier, minister of finances, called him in to say that the mission would begin as a politico-economic one parallel to the ambassadorship, and only afterward might there be the possibility of his becoming ambassador. Leaving the ministry, where he also consulted two ministry directors, Paul Leroy-Beaulieu and Maurice Couve de Murville, Rist succinctly summarized the ambiguity of the project from the outset: "In short, Pétain wants me to persuade Washington to follow the Vichy agenda (in which concern for domestic politics predominates), whereas my goal is on the contrary to bring Vichy over to America's way of thinking" (21 September 1941).

It took several weeks and two visits to Vichy for Rist to be struck by the impossibility of founding his mission on such ambiguous grounds. The sticking point was North Africa. Rist made it a sine qua non of acceptance that, armed with an explicit message from Pétain, he could assure President Roosevelt that Vichy would never allow the Germans to set foot in North Africa. He drafted a letter to that effect, and Pétain signed it on 26 October 1941 – in spite of the accord that had already been signed the preceding May allowing the Germans to do so, an accord whose discovery made Rist uneasy. He returned to the occupied zone the following day, persuaded that "the die is cast" and the thing would go forward.

But when he returned to Vichy two weeks later, 9 and 10 November 1941, all bets were off. Pétain had given up trying to restrain his number two man, Admiral Darlan, out of spite for his mortal enemy General [Maxime] Weygand, commander in chief in North Africa, and the admiral left no doubt about the policy of frank collaboration he intended to follow. He gave Rist to understand that under these conditions his mission would only serve to take advantage of Roosevelt's presumed naïveté. It was clear that Darlan was going to have Weygand dismissed and thus dispose of the last guarantor of a will to hold firm in the Maghreb in the face of possible German pressure. As for Pétain, he sheepishly confessed one evening to Charles Rist: "We forgot about you." And the latter concluded in plain language: "End of my mission to the United States" (11 November 1941).

He had yet to discover the profound abyss that had opened up between the northern zone, which he described as very anti-German, and the ideas of Vichy, "all directed toward . . . new capitulations" (11 November 1941). We owe to this episode some strong comments on the small closed world of the new regime. Pétain himself remained somewhat dignified, but he was wavering and childishly vain. "He is the only one who has not completely folded. Unfortunately, he no longer has the will or the memory. He forgets recent events. He no longer puts facts together in order to draw conclusions" (15 November 1941). We get a life-size portrait as well of Admiral Darlan: vindictive and obsessive, with a habitual scorn for Americans and hatred of the English, driven by the "absurd" idea that the Germans were moved only by economic motives and that France must consequently "become part of the new Europe" (11 November 1941).

And the entourage! The description of Pétain's Vichy court is etched in acid. Rist has several meals at the marshal's table, where he hears remarks that he finds "enlightening": "That little clique of idolatrous reactionaries who surround Marshal Pétain have reached the height of folly with their allusions to Freemasonry, their aversion to the word 'republic,' and their general lack of culture. This suggestion of holy secrecy, this hatred of anyone who does not rally round the new cult, it is all grotesque" (15 November 1941).

Hence his conclusion: "How is it that this little court, in which the stale ideas of French conservatism have found refuge with an old soldier, cannot see that it will perish at the first shock? The impression of unreality that emerges is incredible" (15 November 1941).

:   :   :   :   :

Is this tone harsh? It is the tone of the entire diary. One must not expect to find here the prudence of academia or the civilities of the *juste milieu*. As he was writing for himself, Rist was not moved by considerations of courtesy and thus gave free rein to his readily caustic temperament and the force of his spontaneous outrage.

I imagine that among all the features of the testimony here published, it will be the harsh nature of his judgments that will cause the most surprise – judgments made not just against the Vichy regime but against the French bourgeoisie as a whole, particularly in the realm of business. Rist's constant concern to remain faithful to his social role as a reasonable intellectual and to his Protestant temperament formed in the spirit of free inquiry, as well as his will to restrain the transports of passion with sangfroid, made the vengeful force of this long philippic against the country's social elites all the stronger. If the man seemed, on the eve of the war, to have drifted toward the comforts of a gilded conservatism, the celebrated critical comments aimed at the bourgeoisie at the same time by Marc Bloch in *L'Étrange défaite* [Strange Defeat], or by Léon Blum in *A l'Échelle humaine* [For All Mankind], seem pale by comparison.

It is true that Rist himself, describing his personal reactions and the reactions of several of those close to him, contributed considerable ammunition against the temptations of Manicheism; he writes of numerous members of the bourgeoisie who, endowed with simple patriotism and quick insight as to the outcome of the global conflict, engaged in courageous actions whose wisdom would be validated in the end. Sometimes, moreover, he made a conscious effort not to generalize too quickly; for example, when he observed on 23 August 1942, that "[at board meetings] minds clash – envisaging that [unknown] future with hopes, fears, and desires that differ from one person to another and are only indirectly expressed. The majority, however, wait and hope for the Allies' victory. The rest consider themselves better informed and more intelligent." In the end, however, the moments of intense suffering, of exasperated anxiety, quickly lead to other simplifications. After describing his conversation with a reactionary engineer on 8 May 1944, Rist exclaims, "Poor country! Poor bourgeoisie!" Often he concludes with the global condemnation of an entire class. At such times his interpretation of the French drama ends up as an oversimplification in black and white: on the one hand the masses who think clearly; on the other the bourgeoisie obsessed by social fears.

Let us compare a few significant excerpts in hopes that the reader will be inspired to examine them more closely, though their effect may be a bit exaggerated by their juxtaposition here:

23 November 1940: "A young man from a 'good family' . . . [confessed] that he preferred defeat without Freemasons to English victory with them! This is the spirit of the Holy League and of the émigrés . . . a mixture of reactionary panic (hatred of anything new) and anarchistic rebellion against any national discipline."

15 April 1942: "The 'nobility' have too often acted *against* France. They are still doing this, even after having absorbed part of the bourgeoisie. 'Common people' have always *felt* French."

28 December 1942: "It is the peasants and the workers in this country who have a proper sense of their national obligations and duties, of the honor and true glory of the nation; in momentous circumstances, they are the ones who truly represent the 'national spirit' in contrast to the spirit of caste and party."

On the patriotic virtues of the people . . . We are here quite far from the pessimistic and "revisionist" view that for a while, at the beginning of the

1970s, was incarnated by the hit film *The Sorrow and the Pity* yet quite near at times to the Manicheism of a Guillemin. And our author, this great bourgeois intellectual, this banker by adoption, reassures himself with the pride one sees in the following passage:

> Decidedly, in this war I am seeing once again that my reactions are always those of the people. In the Dreyfus affair, I felt "people." During the previous war, I felt "people." After the war, confronted with the stupid nationalism of the *Chambre bleu horizon*[13] and Poincaré's boastful bluster, I felt "people." During the Stavisky affair and again on 6 February, 1934, I felt "people." . . . And now, during this new war, I again feel "people," and like the people, I believe the military and the reactionaries have committed treason. (28 December 1942)

In contrast to the people, there was the moneyed class. Returning to Versailles after board meetings, Rist assuaged his rancor by adding to his store of comments from the "panic-stricken Bolshiephobes" among the bourgeoisie, those who for years had "preferred Hitler to Stalin." "They are obsessed," he noted on 23 October 1943, "by this fear of the Russian. . . . I collect the echoes of these fears at each meeting of the Ottoman Bank and of the Banque de Paris, but this week I felt it growing in everyone. People no longer bother to conceal it."

This social fear obsesses such men, and their understanding of a world at war is all the more compromised because they are – yet another painful grievance – ignorant of global realities: above all, of foreign languages. To their "imbecility" is added "laziness."

> What I read disgusts me. What I hear sickens me. . . . Hardly any of them have traveled. Some know a little German or English. But the vast majority of those who express an opinion would be incapable of understanding one column of a German or English newspaper. They know nothing of the literature or history of these countries. Thus they judge everything according to their petty political ambitions. . . . They dream of a world in which all foreign countries would remain calm and unchanging in order that the French bourgeoisie, which has a horror of all movement and of all change, could continue to lead their petty lives in peace; they would like to immobilize the world around this sleeping, frightened, and uncomprehending axis – the French bourgeois. (22 January 1942)

Hence their inability to understand the greatness of the United States: "Some criticize Americans for their jazz, others for their 'naïveté,' still others for their 'materialism.' All to avoid having to admire the tremendous enthusiasm, the zest for life . . . of this people." This systematic anti-Americanism

---

13. The *Chambre bleu horizon* ("sky-blue" chamber) was elected in 1919 and named for the color of French uniforms, the color of the political right. [TF]

is "one of the countless forms of backward, cantankerous stupidity on the part of the French bourgeoisie" (6 January 1943).

Such is the tone of these pages. Who among left-wing polemicists, for whom Charles Rist came to represent cautious conservatism, would have dared such brutal severity before the war?

Consider this expression of rage:

> Their hatred of the majority of French people (for they are, in spite of all, a minority) has reached such an extreme that the externally induced catastrophe has been welcomed. Moreover, German despotism . . . relieves them of the dreadful fear that has gripped them for the last ten years – fear of communism and fear of economic crises, fears they do not dare to admit but that explain in truth all their actions, all their hatreds, all their uncritical acceptance of the worst calumnies and the worst crime fiction aimed at the previous regime, calumnies that help them justify themselves on the grounds of "morality," their so-called love of "right-thinking" people, their inexpiable hatred, and their hidden fear. And in the end, their love of "right-thinking" people leads them to acclaim Laval – precisely because they sense he can handle all the dirty work. (28 May 1941)

This infamous complacency in regard to [Pierre] Laval, stupidly taken on by Pétain as instrument and shield, is itself a glaring sign of failure. Toward Laval, Rist showed none of the consideration he had shown toward Pétain over a long period. Laval represented corruption itself, abject ignominy, and he fit right in with the other repugnant dictators.

> Mussolini a teacher; Stalin a seminarian; Hitler a mediocre artist, son of a low-grade customs employee; Laval a lycée proctor, son of a butcher. All petty bourgeois with elementary educations, phony intellectuals; all without scruples, full of resentments and repressed desires for wealth, and endowed with a strong will backed by cunning . . . An extreme passion for power and hatred of those more fortunate or more cultivated, with scorn for the all too real weaknesses of their "betters," even more so for the "scruples" born of upbringing or tradition. (8 November 1940)

Also complicit in "reactionary" circles, in Charles Rist's eyes, was the military. It is as if the fiery emotions evoked by the Dreyfus affair still smoldered. Before the war the high command seemed to him both "infested with politics" and "knowing nothing about their profession, thanks to vanity and laziness" (13 May 1941).

As for the leaders of the conquered army – the very ones who shamelessly divided up so many good jobs among themselves – he begins by reproaching them for being blind to the economic dimension of modern conflicts (between the wars, Rist was never consulted by the high command). He quotes with a sad gourmandise, on 12 August 1941, these lines of Henri de Man: "In no profession (as in that of the military) have I seen such an abundance of bad judgment based on unfounded dogmatic assurance, routine conservatism, indifference to new experiments, scorn for imagination, and intolerance of opposing views." The glory of General [Henri Honoré] Giraud? "It is clear today that his prewar halo owed to his status as a militant reactionary. This is the origin of all military reputations in France so long as the officers have not been tested in time of war" (25 January 1944). Only de Gaulle escapes this mistrust for long – until the disappointments of the provisional government remind Rist that decidedly a general is running the show. "Here we are, in full military rule," he wrote on 22 August 1944. "Only madmen are not worried about our future. For all of these people come more or less from the Action Française and hate the Republic."

Rist's intellectual proclivities and the cruelty of the national situation led him to harden his construction of things and to embrace with surprising ease the hypothesis of a very cunning and efficacious conspiracy, supposedly cooked up long before against the Third Republic. It is notable that Marc Bloch and Léon Blum, the other two good men whom I earlier associated with Rist, were better able to resist this temptation.

Rather greedily and somewhat naïvely, Charles Rist collected versions of the plot that, since 1934 (or 1937?), Pétain, [Raphaël] Alibert, and Laval had supposedly hatched – namely, to rise to power thanks to the defeat and with Hitler's support. The House of Worms, naturally, was suspected of playing a prominent role: this was the famous Synarchy.[14] We know almost certainly today (failing some improbable, shocking revelation) that the "plot" just amounted to the momentary influence of a network of ambitious friends who were well positioned and ready and willing to seize the occasion, sinister though it be, of a political role that would allow them to put into practice their reactionary and pre-technocratic ideas. It was not a conspiracy based on prodigious clear-sightedness, perversity, and efficiency. How can one not be struck by the ease with which a man such as Charles Rist, so concerned to treat the facts with levelheadedness, could have believed these conspiracy theories? It is a measure of his desperation to explain the appalling collective misfortune – and, as Rist himself admitted, a kind of mental hygiene: better for one's morale to accept the corruption of a few traitors than to risk admitting the horrifying corruption of France as a whole.

---

14. According to a conspiracy theory that gained popularity during the war, the Synarchy was a right-wing coalition including La Cagoule and the Banque Worms that plotted to bring about France's defeat in order to avoid a communist takeover (or to profit the presumed bankers and industrialist conspirators). [TF]

: : : : :

Another resource for Rist's discerning judgment was his unceasing quest for precedents. From his youth, history had held a strong attraction for him, an attraction that grew as he aged. On 21 November 1943, he explained it this way:

> Old men know that the end – their end – is coming. They face a wall beyond which they know they cannot go. What happens beyond the wall no longer interests them. . . . As we age and approach the final wall, we are seized by a growing desire to know all that is still within our reach of the beautiful, noble, and grand that our short life has not allowed us to see, admire, and touch. . . . That is why the old man gives others the impression he is living in the past. He is only trying, before he disappears, to take once again, and in his own way, "possession of the world."

But above all, he found in the past the means to give some order to his present emotions, to distinguish the essential from the nonessential and profound changes from trivial events: not a philosophy of history – "the most inane occupation of mental defectives" (10 December 1943) – but a reservoir of references useful for sifting the lasting from the momentary. Chateaubriand, Tocqueville, Sainte-Beuve, Balzac, Michelet, Victor Hugo, Edgar Quinet, Renan, Albert Sorel, Lavisse's great *Histoire de France*: such were the writers and works he would reread.

One thing of permanence that impressed him more each day: the conduct of the "reactionary party," those who never accepted the French Revolution, of which Rist made a kind of stubborn cult – presenting himself here again as the heir to Protestant culture. The Revolution was for France "revenge for the failed Reformation, a French version of the revolution of ideas that made Prussia, England, and the United States the great nations of the nineteenth century" (17 October 1943). Those countries – where Rist, in his later years, would surely have been quite at home – had a conservative party open to the spirit of the age. But, in France, there was nothing of the sort: in opposition to the offspring of the Revolution was "a single great party successively known as nationalist, Boulangist,[15] or national, and united under the sign of anticommunism by that schemer and lackey called Laval" (2 May 1943). He repeated on several occasions that a history of the reaction, spread over two centuries, remained to be written. The genius of the Third

---

15. Georges Boulanger (1837–1891) was an anti-republican general whose Boulangist movement advocated revenge on Germany, revision of the constitution, and restoration of the monarchy. [TF]

Republic was "to give the bourgeoisie sufficient social security and a strong enough guarantee of property to prevent them from interfering violently or by military means in the life of the democratic republic and, little by little, to educate the working classes in the ways of freedom" (2 May 1943). For they alone could provide the new blood necessary for a country's progress and even survival. But alas! At the slightest opportunity, "reaction" would raise its head, ready to build on the wreckage of defeat a restoration for which it had never given up hope – as Vichy proved.

Historical comparisons offered other subjects for reflection, such as the fate of great conquerors – Alexander, Belisarius, Philip II, Wallenstein, Bismarck, and especially Napoleon, toward whom the thoughts of Charles Rist went spontaneously from the moment Hitler attacked Russia in June 1941. He saw Napoleon as head and shoulders above Hitler for his "sense of the universal" and also for his "fund of bourgeois good sense." But it was naturally the collapse of conquering dictators that he avidly scrutinized. On the fourth of January 1942, to raise his morale, he recalled Metternich's telling comment about Napoleon, dating from 1807. There was, Metternich said, nothing to do but wait for "the great day when Europe would put an end to this essentially precarious state of things, because it is against nature and against civilization."

:   :   :   :   :

I shall leave to the reader the pleasure, and often the surprise, of discovering in more detail what our witness's intelligence drew from these historical comparisons, but there is one last remarkable aspect of his thinking that merits being noted in closing: his efforts to divine the future.

Let us note first of all the relevance of his visions for the postwar period. His August 1941 portrayal of what General de Gaulle's provisional government would be like in 1944–1945 was shrewd. Also of interest is this political program that he outlined as early as December 1940 for postwar France: strengthening of the executive power, restructuring of the administration, a reform of the venal press, an increase in the number of school years required for lycée and university students, creation of a more technically proficient army resembling a corps of engineers. . . . Many of Rist's ideas would be encountered again during the following decades. Living for ten years after the victory, he was able to see several of his wishes suitably fulfilled. With one great exception, however: his hope that the economic role of the State would be reduced.

He maintained his faith that the family would continue to provide a counterbalance, in spite of the prophets who proclaimed its decline. Far from idealizing the family, however, he mocked those homes that "tyrannically confined their members in suffocatingly close quarters" (21 November 1943) but in the end rejected outright any prediction of its demise.

Is it possible that one's hopes might prove valid beyond the near future, beyond the generation that follows one's exit from the tunnel? Can one sketch a few lines of a future fit to live in? Rist's intelligence was enriched by his constant efforts to alter the lighting, to take his distance, to change the zoom, as a cinematographer would say.

The idea Charles Rist formed about human destiny was ambiguous: skeptical that intelligence could be a guide, so unpredictable is the virulence of passion, yet convinced at the same time that it was a worthy endeavor to strengthen democracy against all dictatorial temptations. Even if only because dictatorships necessarily lead to war. "Experience shows," he wrote, "that this system inevitably leads to war, for only war offers free rein to passion, fear, enthusiasm, and hatred" (9 January 1943). Thus, if reason could speak loudly enough, it would not leave any opening for democracy's enemies. But can it? He who mistrusts collective passions will always be comforted by the conviction that popular common sense gives reason to hope. Readers will see how strongly concerned and irritated he was to note that true "republicans" were thinking of limiting, after the Liberation, by diverse juridical procedures, the right of voters to choose the members of the Constituent Assembly.

It remained only to know in which direction the enduring influence of spirituality and religion would lead humankind. Doubtless people grow less attached to dogmas, and that is not a bad thing. But always "the masses demand to *believe* in something" (23 August 1942). And so? "Could we not imagine a religion that is purified, but made simple and concrete for the masses, one that would be different from the political passion-religions left us by the nineteenth century as a consequence of the universal criticism of Christianity?" (23 August 1942). Could not the religion of France be an idea of the perfectibility of humans and their institutions? A false idea, perhaps – but so what? It is also a salutary idea. The antithesis of Christianity? Only if one confuses "Christianity with Catholicism – or even with clericalism" (14 July 1942). Without dogma, without repression, this religion (was it not for Charles Rist an extreme version of Protestantism's spirit of free inquiry?) could not be easily defended in calmer times. But in great crises, for noble souls, what a spiritual renewal!

The reader will have understood: the economist who speaks in these pages believes in the predominant role of politics, religion, and culture in the human adventure, counting for much more than the development of production and commerce. "Today as always," he wrote, "it is the passions – the same passions as long ago – that govern the course of history, only with different weapons" (10 April 1943).

In a study dedicated in 1955, the last year of his life, to the ideas of [Pierre-Joseph] Proudhon,[16] an article that he presented as a kind of intellectual testament, he recalled that if he had always rejected Marxism, it was primarily as a "construct combining Jewish prophesying and German nationalism." And he added in more general terms: "The truth is that political economy is a perfectly down-to-earth discipline. . . . Looking closely, one sees that it is an almost sordid science that, in its elementary acts, is associated with the least elevated decisions of human nature." Here is an author who resists every temptation to impose his discipline as supreme. Can one deny that this uniquely enriched his observations over the course of five tragic years of our national history?

16. "La pensée économique de Proudhon," 130 and 141.

Regarding the History and Annotation of the French Text

JEAN-NOËL JEANNENEY

CHARLES RIST'S DIARY WAS WRITTEN IN A SINGLE DRAFT, MOSTLY on both sides of loose-leaf paper. Later additions appear to be quite rare; I have indicated them from time to time. After Rist's death, his widow had a few copies of the journal typed for members of the family and a few intimate friends. The title *Une Saison gâtée* is mine.

From the beginning of the war in September 1939 until the May 1940 invasion, the entries are brief, sometimes almost telegraphic. The text is thus rather dry. But it seemed best to include these early entries, even if readers prefer to pass rapidly over them, for they help to set the social scene.

I did, however, omit the pages having to do with Rist's trip to America in March–April 1940, as they are unfortunately nothing more than an annotated date book, with the tedious listing of people's names.

From May 1940 on, the entries become much more interesting, more fully developed and "literary." For this period covering the occupation, a period all too often subject to subsequent revisionism, it is vital that readers know they are getting the original text, complete and unedited. I have restored some passages that Germaine Rist, for charitable reasons, had felt best to leave out of the first typed copies. Though these passages were rather hard on certain contemporaries, each reader must conscientiously bear in mind the date at which they were written. In a few rare cases, for legitimate family reasons, Rist's descendants wished to leave out some words or phrases, in all some fifteen lines. With these minor exceptions, this publication constitutes Rist's complete journal. Revisions have been limited to a few slips of the pen, a few skipped words, a few first names needing clarification.

I have tried to keep the annotations to a minimum in order not to distract attention from the text and make the book too dense. They serve to give context to people who are not widely known; to cite sources for works mentioned; to clarify obscure allusions; to indicate a few factual mistakes on the part of the author; and to provide the testimony of others who have written about meetings mentioned in Rist's journal.

An index of people's names has been provided in order to facilitate the reading of this journal and to allow for varying approaches to the entries.

To Renaud Fessaguet, I express my gratitude for his efficient help in documenting the critical apparatus, and to Noël Rist, my thanks for the invaluable aid of his memory, friendship, and trust.

A Brief Who's Who of the Rist Family

Note: Rist habitually shortens references to his sons' families by pluralizing the sons' names: the Claudes, the Marios, etc.

Charles Rist (1874–1955), French economist
Brother of:
- Édouard (1871–1956), a physician at Hôpital Laennec in Paris, specializing in the treatment of tuberculosis
    + Lilian von Glehn (1872–1951)
    + Madeleine Roy (1887–1988)
- Ève (1875–1944), philosophy teacher; co-founder and assistant head of the École des Roches
    + Henri Trocmé (1873–1944)
- Gabrielle (1882–1980)
    + Constant Schaller (1871–1951)

Married to:
- Germaine Monod Rist (1875–1960)

Father of:
- Jean (1900–1944), chief engineer for the Jacob Holtzer Steelworks (resigned in the spring of 1943 in order not to make parts for Nazi Germany); member of the Resistance
    + Jeannette Cestre (1902–1975), BA, Mills College, California; daughter of Charles Cestre, who held the first chair in American Literature and Civilization at the Sorbonne
        Children: Marcel (1925–2004), André (b. 1927), Simone (b. 1931)
- Claude (1902–1950), agronomist and lab director at Société Lyonnaise des Eaux, a public utility

    + Françoise Gorodiche (1909–2006), of Jewish
    descent; called Françoise because her father loved
    France so much, according to daughter Isabelle
    Children: Isabelle (b. 1930), Antoinette (b.
    1932), Marie-Claire (b. 1935)
· Léonard (1905–1982), banker at the Morgan
Bank in Paris during the war
    + Eva Cornier (1902–1989), Jeannette Rist's
    classmate at the École du Service Social, a school
    for training health and social workers
· Noël (1906–1990), department head at the Pasteur Institute
    + Marie de Lacroix (1912–1996)
    Children: Jean-Pierre (b. 1948), Arianne
    (b. 1948), Patrick (b. 1949)
· Mario (1915–1979), resigned as a judge when Vichy promulgated
the anti-Jewish "laws of exception," then worked in Paris as
head of the legal department of Ugine's steelworks plant
    + Éléonore (Lolli) Gaede (1919–2009)
    Children: Colas (1940–2014), Jean-Franklin
    (b. 1942), Dominique (b. 1945)

SEASON
of INFAMY

One

War Begins

2 SEPTEMBER 1939–23 JANUARY 1940
On 2 September 1939 France and England issued an ultimatum to Germany that resulted in a declaration of war the next day.

Charles Rist, sixty-five years old at the time, was working in Paris and commuting some 15 kilometers to Versailles, where he lived at 18 bis rue du Parc de Clagny with his wife, Germaine, and her mother, Olga Monod-Herzen. His home office was on the top floor of their three-story house, the Villa Amiel. The Rists also owned a country house, Le Très-Clos, near Lake Geneva.

Their five adult sons, three of whom would soon be enlisted, were scattered in several directions. Jean was employed as chief engineer at the Jacob Holtzer Steelworks in Fraisses, about 100 kilometers southeast of Vichy and another 300 southeast of Paris. Claude directed a water safety lab near Le Vésinet, 15 kilometers west of Paris. Léonard, Noël, and Mario worked in Paris: Léonard as a banker, Noël as a researcher at the Pasteur Institute, and Mario as a judge.

In Paris Charles Rist oversaw his economic research institute, ISRES, and served as an expert on various government committees as well as on the boards of several banks and corporations. These included the Banque de Syrie, Banque du Maroc, Paribas, the Ottoman Bank (of which he was board president), the Suez Canal Company, and Le Matériel Téléphonique.

The chaos of war was soon to disrupt this busy middle-class life. Three of Charles Rist's sons would be mobilized, Rist would be asked to head a blockade mission to North America, and many members of his extended family would find themselves in peril.

SATURDAY, 2 SEPTEMBER 1939 We set off early to visit Jean in Moulins.[1] Cars full of children and suitcases, with mattresses on the roof. Crowds

---

1. Jean was Charles and Germaine Rist's oldest son. See "A Brief Who's Who of the Rist Family" and Jean-Noël Jeanneney's "Introduction." [TF]

1

at Nevers. Crowds at Moulins, but we found a room at Jean's hotel, across from the railroad station. He showed up at 7:30. Happy to see us: "What a great surprise!" Dinner in the dining room, with officers everywhere. Jean plainspoken and unassuming, talking quite openly about everything. His job is to shoe the horses for four regiments, and he is amazed by the detailed instructions given to him in a little notebook. He says if there were no blacksmiths with cars of their own, not to mention ironmongers, in the town, nothing would get done. The military command foresaw all except the fact that horses from the Bourbonnais region have hooves that do not fit any of the three regulation sizes. He is amused by communism, an insoluble problem.

The next day we were shown the cathedral and his gardener friend's flowers. At 11:30 Jean came in from work, angry at the lack of news and the stupidity of censorship. He fears – as do his comrades – that the French government will cave in at the last moment. We left him at 1:30. What serenity, overlying a deep melancholy. When he talks about his children one feels they are his whole life. His wife spent two hours with him a couple of days ago. She is taking the children to Le Chambon.[2]

Return in a line of cars. At 4:00, getting out of my car at a railroad crossing, I learned from another driver that, according to the radio, war had been declared at 2:00. We got back to Versailles at 7:00. A boy called out to us, "War has been declared," as we passed some houses just before Longjumeau. Everywhere, requisitioned horses led by peasants. Groups of people talking in every street. Everyone is serious.

MONDAY, 4 SEPTEMBER 1939 Trade Minister Gentin has asked me to serve on a consultative committee with Julien Durand and Bonnefon-Craponne.

Suez Company board meeting at 11:30. Not a single one of our English colleagues present. Lord Hankey has been appointed to serve as minister without portfolio in Chamberlain's War Cabinet. Company head Georges-Edgar Bonnet brought us up to date on measures taken to safeguard the canal. We are in complete agreement with the English army and admiralty. Income will be negligible in the face of enormous expenses. A probable deficit of two to three million.

---

2. Le Chambon-sur-Lignon: a Protestant enclave in south-central France where Jean Rist had close connections. [TF]

At the Banque de Syrie, de Cerjat[3] informed me of an urgent request for 200 million to be sent to Syria. We discussed how to transport the 75 million we have on hand, as well as how to make up the rest. Shipping services have been partially resumed.

The English financial and commercial attachés came to see me. They believe it is too soon to negotiate with Italy. Why? Do they want to close the Mediterranean first? The general embargo on imports to France was undertaken in agreement with England. I told them I find the measure a bit abrupt. They asked me some questions regarding French finances, but I know no more than they do. They assured me that the oil supplied by Russia to Germany cannot amount to much, as the Russian surplus is scarcely a million tons.

TUESDAY, 5 SEPTEMBER 1939 This evening Noël drove us to Le Vésinet to visit the Claudes.[4] Total darkness; forbidden to use headlights, drivers run the risk of running down pedestrians, both soldiers and civilians, who have to walk in the middle of the road. We were stopped by two traffic guards, who scolded us for using lights. What can one do?

The Claudes doing rather well. Claude, back from Chantilly, worries about what his wife will do if he is called up.

During the night, alarms. We would be up for half an hour then go back to bed. I thought it was a bad joke. Luckily, little Isabelle did not wake up.

Board meeting of the Banque de Paris et des Pays-Bas. Nothing new.

WEDNESDAY, 6–THURSDAY, 7 SEPTEMBER 1939 Suez Company committee. Nalèche confirmed that the alarms are deliberately exaggerated. Ten million people have been put on alert as far away as Rouen and Le Havre.

At 2:30, visited Mme Le Verrier.[5] Present were Robert de Billy, the Duke of Harcourt, and the French vice-consul at Dusseldorf, who had just returned from Germany. He crossed the border on Sunday and told us the most amazing things about the state of German spirits. Eighty-five percent of their

---

3. Charles de Cerjat, like Rist, was a trustee for the Banque de Syrie et du Liban. Syria and Lebanon became French mandates after World War I. [JNJ/TF]

4. The Claudes: Claude Rist, his Jewish wife, Françoise, and their three daughters – Isabelle, Antoinette, and Marie-Claire. Rist habitually abbreviates references to his sons' families by this use of the plural. [TF]

5. Mme Le Verrier: head of the weekly *L'Europe nouvelle*. Rist was a contributor to this anti-Munich publication.

generals are against the war. Heads of industry in the Rhineland are hoping
for defeat. On the sly, workers gave him maps of airports, fortifications, etc.
The German communists consider the Russo-German pact to be a trick by
Stalin to force Hitler to go to war, etc., etc.

Visit from Lorch and Ostersetzer, forced to report to an internment
camp as citizens of an enemy country. Poor devils.[6]

Evening visit from the Claudes. Claude will be commuting between
Chantilly and Le Vésinet.

FRIDAY, 8 SEPTEMBER 1939 Noël in bed with a bad sore throat. Burial
of poor Jean-Jacques Bizot, deputy governor of the Banque de France, dead
at forty.

Am informed that the *Washington,* the American liner carrying Mario
and Lolli, will arrive tomorrow evening at Le Havre.

At *L'Europe nouvelle,* Mme Le Verrier tells me what a hard time they are
having to replace Georges Bonnet with Herriot at Foreign Affairs. Bonnet
is keeping a tight grip. Along with de Monzie he is impatiently awaiting
Hitler's peace offensive after the fall of Poland. Indeed, it was necessary for
Chamberlain to threaten to resign if Bonnet, on Saturday, did not follow
Sir Nevile Henderson's example in dealing with Hitler. A bitter conversation
took place between Lord Halifax and Bonnet. The upshot was to refer the
matter to Prime Minister Daladier, and that is when Chamberlain delivered
his ultimatum.

Piatier came to say good-bye.[7] News from the front, as well as the form of
the communiqués, has exasperated the officers. The current offensive seems
ridiculous. He considers Bonnet a traitor.

Rueff asked what I think about a possible control on exchange rates.[8] I
said it seems inevitable.

Strange war, in which there will doubtless be no encounters on France's
eastern front. The essential thing is to control the Mediterranean and to
persuade America to declare an embargo on goods to Germany. The same
goes for the other neutral countries. The legal proceeding would be for those

---

6. A. Lorch and Wilhelm Ostersetzer: anti-Nazi Austrian refugees who were sent to
French prison camps after war was declared.

7. André Piatier: economist, secretary of the Institut International de Finances
Publiques, and colleague at ISRES, Rist's research institute.

8. Jacques Rueff, former director of money transfers at the finance ministry, had just
been appointed as second vice president of the Banque de France.

countries at war to come up with lists of things that they would have the neutral countries agree to.

The war will no doubt be shorter than expected – if a real blockade is put in force. Gasoline will be vital, and the same goes for oils and cotton.

What the future will probably overlook, and what must be remembered, is the formidable role that social conservatism – the fear of communism and Bolshevism – has played in the foreign policy of France and England these last few years. Obsessive fear on the part of hundreds of people has made them incapable of comprehending events other than through this distorting lens. Hence their hidden but certain sympathies extend even to Hitler, his methods, and his aggressions. People no longer believe that a democratic government in France will be strong enough to protect them. They are not reassured by seeing order maintained and social conflict avoided here at home. They need the public show of police force, just as they need the image of a violent communism; and for that reason, they don't hesitate to commit attacks themselves for which they blame the communists (C.S.A.R.)![9] The war frightens them because they foresee at its end concessions to the workers, which for them is the same as concessions to communism.

The reality is that we are all under a state of siege today, and the military are our masters. Will they be able to contain themselves?

SATURDAY, 9 SEPTEMBER 1939 With Ambassador Bullitt this morning at the U.S. embassy. I gave him the document received from Goerdeler, via Simon, regarding the momentous days in Berlin leading up to 31 August.[10] An extremely interesting document, as it indicates the uneasiness of German generals and their final submission to Hitler's will. Bullitt told me that in order for the United States to act, Americans must suffer a direct attack. He is considering a trip to Washington in the hope of influencing Congress to

---

9. This is a reference to attacks committed in September 1937 by the secret extreme right organization Comité Secret d'Action Révolutionnaire (known as "La Cagoule") at the Parisian headquarters of two employers' organizations, provocations meant to be taken as communist actions. [JNJ/TF]

10. Carl Friedrich Goerdeler and Manfred Simon were German informants who provided Charles Rist with information on Nazis and anti-Nazis. Goerdeler, a ringleader of the generals' revolt (20 July 1944) against Hitler, was hanged in February 1945. He played an important role as an informer for the western democracies, notably Great Britain, for which he represented the idea of a "national opposition" to Hitler. Simon was a journalist and attaché at the French embassy in Switzerland. The date 31 August was when Hitler signed the order to invade Poland. [JNJ/TF]

change the Neutrality Act. He said he will pass on any suggestions I might bring him.

Next saw Cochran's replacement as first secretary. His name is Matthews. He wants the same relationship of trust that I had with his predecessor. I told him how important it is for the war to be short and for Germany to understand at once that America's full economic strength will be brought to bear against it. He agreed and asked what legal and practical form such a message could take.

Tonight it was announced that England and America have agreed to control all imports entering the Mediterranean. This would be vital.

Later I saw Philippe Vernes. His sons and nephews have been called up. He advised me to keep my dollars and to wait before converting them to francs.

Lunched with [Charles S.] Dewey, former American financial adviser to Poland, and his wife. He is returning to the United States full of admiration for the way children were evacuated from Paris and received in the provinces. They witnessed their reception in Normandy and promise to show photographs and spread the word about this in America.

Osusky at a nearby table with Élie-Joseph Bois.[11] We had an amiable conversation.

Back in Versailles at 4:00.

SUNDAY, 10 SEPTEMBER 1939   Took a walk with Isabelle, rather impressed by the gas mask she had to try on. She was fascinated by the soldiers and the cars clogging the streets of Parc de Clagny. All the villas have been requisitioned. She let me know, incidentally, that Poland is too far away for France to be obliged to wage war on its behalf. Fortunately, she has not heard the nightly sirens and alarms.

During the evening we went to meet Mario and Lolli, who had been in the United States visiting Lolli's parents. The Saint-Lazare train station in total darkness. The streets of Paris, black. Luckily, a bit of moonlight allows one to more or less find one's way. Our driver, Gustave Monod's chauffeur, was horrified. The train was forty minutes late; it took nine hours to arrive from Le Havre. The trip over on the *Washington* was good. They picked up some torpedo survivors. We drove Mario and Lolli to Versailles, both in good spirits.

During the night, sirens. One hour of alarms.

11. Stefan Osusky: Czechoslovakian representative in Paris during the Munich crisis; Élie-Joseph Bois: editor in chief of *Petit Parisien* and a "power" in the world of journalism.

MONDAY, 11 SEPTEMBER 1939 Phone call this morning from Raymond Philippe. He assured me that Daladier is going to replace Georges Bonnet. I felt relieved, as if we had carried off a great victory. Bonnet's weakness, cowardice, and pathological ambition have made him a traitor.

Philippe wants me to put my name on *L'Europe nouvelle* alongside his. I have decided to do nothing of the sort. This man is extraordinarily vacuous, and I foresee risks.

Lunch with Simon, back from Switzerland. He continues his information gathering, receiving direct communications from the "Ribbentrop Bureau."[12] He considers Italy's current attitude to be most dangerous. Once the Polish affair has been taken care of, Mussolini is contemplating a joint venture with Germany to sue for peace, then once the peace has failed, to make a surprise submarine attack on the English and French fleets. Thus all depends on the Poles' ability to resist.

This afternoon phone calls to the naval ministry about the Banque de Syrie banknotes, to Billecart about the Ostersetzers, to Rueff about the Ottoman Bank. Dropped in on Gentin and, finally, on Osusky. The latter tells me that our military know nothing of Polish military plans thanks to the mistrust sewn between the two military high commands by Josef Beck, Poland's foreign minister. He attributes Russia's nonaggression pact with Germany to the Russians' discouragement following the invasion of Czechoslovakia. Needing to protect themselves on the western front in the event of problems in the Far East, they believed Germany's guarantee was more valuable than that of the Allies, which they considered worthless. Not to mention the "resentment" of an Oriental like Stalin against the disdainful democracies. We agreed that the role played by resentment in current politics is appalling: Hitler, Mussolini . . .

TUESDAY, 12–WEDNESDAY, 13 SEPTEMBER 1939 First meeting yesterday of the Foreign Exchange Committee, which will convene every day at 3:00. Our task is to draft rules for controlling exchange rates.

Saw Léger[13] to talk about the Simon affair and about his information.

Conversation with former ambassador de Marcilly, completely in agreement.

THURSDAY, 14 SEPTEMBER 1939 Georges Bonnet was finally removed from Foreign Affairs and sent to Justice!

12. Joachim von Ribbentrop: Nazi Germany's foreign minister. [TF]

13. Alexis Léger (Saint-John Perse): general secretary at the French foreign ministry until 1940.

Mario has been assigned to Le Mans.

Foreign Exchange Committee meeting. Visited by General Tilho. Lunch, Georges-Edgar Bonnet. We shared our joy at the departure of his namesake from Foreign Affairs. The story goes that Daladier, out of desperation, had asked Roosevelt to approve Bonnet as ambassador. Roosevelt's reply: "That is the greatest sacrifice France could ask of me."

FRIDAY, 15 SEPTEMBER 1939 Double meetings, the Commerce Committee (Charmeil, Durand, Michaud, Bonnefon-Craponne, and myself, with Fougère as presiding secretary) and the Foreign Exchange Committee, till 6:00 PM.

The news from Russia (mobilization of four million men, press campaign against Poland) is becoming worrisome.

SATURDAY, 16 SEPTEMBER 1939 Mario left at 8:00 AM for Le Mans, where he was inducted into the army. His wife went with him to the station. Poor thing, she will be stateless for another month, a situation that is creating problems for her.[14] At noon we headed to Moulins to see Jean before he leaves for an unknown destination.

WEDNESDAY, 20 SEPTEMBER 1939 We had a better visit with Jean this time. At first very bitter about the stupidity of the newspapers and the reluctance of the government to stress the struggle against Hitler – the only thing that matters, he says, for the draftees. Still not sure where he will be sent, impatient to see his children in Le Chambon. He has had no news of them.

On our return, we noticed that the wheat that was still in bundles two weeks ago has been brought in, and haystacks are being built everywhere. Many cars coming back to Paris from Fontainebleau. Some still traveling in the other direction, carrying children and beds.

On Monday I take Lolli to my office in an effort to keep her busy.

Almost all the Paris shops are closed.

Everyone is shocked by the Russian invasion of Poland. All kinds of hypotheses are being floated.

---

14. Lolli Gaede, wife of Mario Rist, was of German origin. She became stateless because her parents had immigrated to the United States and had not yet obtained citizenship.

Monday evening my brother Édouard called to announce the death of Jean Sueur, killed in a plane crash.[15] He had suffered greatly because of Munich. He came this summer to Le Très-Clos with his father-in-law and agreed with me that war was inevitable. As brave as his father was.

Yesterday Blockade Minister Pernot asked if I would work with him on the blockade. That is the only thing that seems useful to me.

Cards and letters from Mario, transferred from Le Mans to Laval. He has injured his foot.

This war looks more and more like a great coalition against England of all those with grudges – Russians, Germans, and even neutral states. Lindbergh has given a radio address appealing to Americans to remain neutral! What would his father-in-law, Dwight Morrow, have said? This is the difference in sensibility between a primitive technician like Lindbergh and a man of high culture! It is the technicians and traveling salesmen who shape opinion today. They are all for Germany. Naturally, the French newspapers are saying nothing of this speech.

England is disappointed because the Norwegian fleet on which they were counting was not made available. Barnaud[16] managed to acquire two Norwegian ships for the Worms line: the crew refused to sail! Why? Fear? Communist ideas? Hatred of England? Pro-Germanism? One wonders.

THURSDAY, 21 SEPTEMBER 1939 Ottoman Bank and Suez Company committee meetings. The first incidents have occurred in the Suez Canal. A Russian ship loaded with cement traveled down the canal, then again from south to north. It was accompanied and occupied by our government officials. But we were uneasy. A nephew of Vogüé,[17] having returned from Egypt via Lisbon and Madrid, gave us a report. Both of our embassies are convinced that Spain is supplying the German submarines.

Afternoon, Foreign Exchange Committee. Afterward, my committee approached Gentin to insist that the Banque de France accept commercial instruments drawn on draftees who are eligible for the moratorium. In England, according to the financial attaché, there is no moratorium for draftees.

I am still waiting to hear from Pernot.

---

15. Jean Sueur, a cousin of the Rists, had been killed in an air raid.

16. Jacques Barnaud: inspector of public finances and managing partner of Worms et Cie, a shipping company that began by importing English coal to France and maintained close ties with England during the war. [JNJ/TF]

17. Marquis Louis de Vogüé: board chairman of the Suez Company (1927–1948).

FRIDAY, 22 SEPTEMBER 1939 Saw Paul Reynaud at the finance ministry this evening. Impassioned as ever; worried about Russian purchases of oil from the United States on behalf of the Germans. He would like to have a general policy on purchases of raw materials.

Paperwork for Lolli at the justice ministry. She will become French on 17 October.

SATURDAY, 23 SEPTEMBER 1939 Stormy session at Foreign Exchange. Pierre Fournier showed up to oppose certain committee decisions. He wants to be able to monitor foreign branches of French companies and has no intention of permitting the freedom of action that the foreign exchange decree confers on them. Rather heated discussion with Laurent and me.[18] The committee kept the text as is.

Jean has received orders to return to his factory for two months.

SUNDAY, 24 SEPTEMBER 1939 Visit from Charles Bedaux, author of the system of scientific management named after him. He wants to make his management consulting firm available to us. And give himself importance. He owns the Château de Candé, where he housed the Duke of Windsor, and will house the American embassy in case of trouble in Paris. He had lunched in Berlin with Schacht and von Stauss. He says Schacht was arrested at that same lunch by the prefect of police, then let go. According to him, von Stauss continued the conversation as though nothing had happened and told Bedaux, "As long as Hitler is in power, there will be no peace in Europe." I accepted Bedaux's offer of help.[19]

This evening Simon brought me the reports of his latest intelligence: Italy will evidently soon throw its support to Germany with a surprise attack on Suez and the Anglo-French fleets. All signs to the contrary will be mere camouflage. Simon believes this intelligence is confirmed by Mussolini's speech. There is also evidence of a formal military pact between Russia and Germany to put pressure on Romania. Rumors of a possible falling out

18. Pierre Fournier: governor of the Banque de France, France's central bank, from 1937 to 1940; Jacques Laurent: industrialist who, as a member of the Banque de France board of trustees, served on the Foreign Exchange Committee. [JNJ/TF]

19. Hjalmar Schacht: former minister of economics for the Reich, 1934–1937, and president of the Reichsbank, 1923–1930 and 1933–1939; Emil-Georg von Stauss: director of Deutsche Bank. [JNJ/TF]

between the bear and the jackal, it seems, are just illusions of the "democracies." Spain is also apparently in on it. All this comes from the "Ribbentrop Bureau" and from Hess's doctor!

MONDAY, 25 SEPTEMBER 1939 Pernot has asked me to put together a consultative committee.

TUESDAY, 26 SEPTEMBER 1939 Took steps on behalf of the Banque de Syrie, to which Fournier is refusing the necessary funds. Foreign Exchange Committee at three o'clock; it was decided to have Syria included in the controls. Visited Dayras, Pernot's chief of staff, and gave him the names of the committee Pernot asked me to set up: Mercier, Barnaud, de la Baume, Charguéraud, Auboin, and myself.

This evening we learned of the dissolution of the Communist Party. It was dead from the moment the Russo-German pact was signed.

WEDNESDAY, 27 SEPTEMBER 1939 Went to the finance ministry with Georges-Edgar Bonnet to declare the Suez Company's foreign assets. Lunch with Bolgert. Saw Auboin – agrees with my suggestions for the committee. Conversation with Hargrove, of the *Wall Street Journal*. He tells me the newspaper has become isolationist; they are so convinced American entry into the war is unstoppable that they want to put on the brakes starting now. He believes that if Italy enters the war, England has powerful ways of making her pay dearly for it.

THURSDAY, 28 SEPTEMBER 1939 Along with Gentin, met with Finance Minister Reynaud regarding the extension of Banque de France credit facilities to draftees. Fournier reluctant. Decision on a finance ministry communiqué. After the meeting, I insisted to Reynaud that Syria be satisfied with regard to exchange rates. I told Fournier that I will not attend future meetings of the Foreign Exchange Committee until I get satisfaction for the Ottoman Bank.

All is arranged with Pernot for the Blockade Committee. I asked Gentin to release me from the Commerce Committee. He insisted that I stay on. Arrangement with Auboin.

SATURDAY, 30 SEPTEMBER–SUNDAY, 1 OCTOBER 1939 Traveled to Le Havre and returned with Léonard.

MONDAY, 2 OCTOBER 1939 Stopped by the premises reserved for me at the blockade ministry. Saw Barnaud, who accepted. Herberts has been inducted into the army.[20] Meeting at Commerce – useless.

TUESDAY, 3 OCTOBER 1939 Saw Pernot. Problems with the quarters where my committee was to meet. Foreign Affairs considers it an intrusion and is making trouble. Laboulaye[21] has taken over the offices destined for my use – in order to install his "Reconnaissance Française," an association of distinguished ladies and Americans. What idiocy.

Pernot asked me to add Ferrasson, president of Paris's Chamber of Commerce. After that the list will be closed.

At Commerce, Fougère asked me to reassure Julien Durand, who is afraid I will leave and feels depressed.

Fournier making problems for the Banque de Syrie – in spite of a telegram from Weygand and Puaux.

Pernot knows as little as I do regarding Italy. Some are for flooding Italy with orders for war materiel in order to give it a stake in our success. Is this the right approach?

THURSDAY, 5 OCTOBER 1939 Ottoman Bank and Suez Company in the morning. Talk is about the great German "peace offensive." An editor with Havas [news agency] thinks he knows that Hitler will offer to reconstitute Poland and the Czech Republic and then withdraw, having Goering replace him. Stupidities! In Paris some people, especially some legislators, could not ask for better.

Visited by Commandant Perruche of military intelligence to discuss telegram communications and information for the blockade. Very good impression. A perceptive, unaffected officer. But I have acquired the habit of not trusting first impressions.

Went to see Ferrasson, president of the Chamber of Commerce. I asked him on behalf of Pernot to join the Blockade Committee. Ecstatic. He insists that the members of the committee be made public. "When the Germans see your name and mine, they will say: This is getting serious." (!!!) He is magnificent in his colonel's uniform and rejoices loudly at the communists' arrest.

Saw Marx at the Hotel Continental. What a great music box of writers, professors, and journalists! Much ado about nothing. Marx is distraught

---

20. Jean Herberts: anti-Nazi German refugee and colleague at Rist's research institute, inducted into the French army. [JNJ/TF]

21. André Laboulaye: former French ambassador to Washington.

over the concentration camps for Jews and Austrians. Men like von Unruh, the anti-Nazi dramatist, have been arrested. But up to now Marx has got nowhere and does not see how he can help those I am trying to protect. He suggested I talk to Pernot about them; Pernot could then talk to Daladier. The effect of these camps on American journalists is disastrous – he fears there will soon be a reaction. The military and the civilian police are passing the ball back and forth. It seems someone has come across two Germans said to have "advanced" opinions who are Gestapo agents. This will serve as a pretext to do nothing.

What would death be at this moment? A great comfort. At my age you keep living only out of duty. How little of lasting value has been accomplished! You cannot help judging yourself at your true, minuscule size next to so many men you have admired and loved. And yet life was worth living for those moments of joy that are so perfect, all the meaning of life is contained within them. I am not speaking merely of the great joys of youth that illuminated everything and upon which I still draw. But the affection and tenderness of grandchildren! This exquisite trust from Isabelle or Antoinette. I still remember when Jean was born. It seemed I could *physically* feel my heart suddenly expand. Today, worries about him and his children!

The current struggle is strange – inspiring and obscure. We are present at a mingling of peoples, from which a world unlike the one we loved will emerge. We are caught up in a maelstrom, with no light on the horizon. And yet, even if we should succumb, it is crystal clear that our absolute duty, without reserve, is to fight. This is somewhat like the Arab invasion or, later, that of the Turks. Europe in the end managed to free herself. How long will she take to free herself from the dreadful German advance? How despicable this people and the systematic training it has undergone for a century to worship brute force! What a miserable thing is undiluted politics. We must once more look to the Mediterranean for salvation. Even strategically, it is only there, it seems today, that the way out may be found.

FRIDAY, 6–SATURDAY, 7 OCTOBER 1939 Lunch with [Tracy Barrett] Kittredge, the Rockefeller Foundation's representative. The Rockefellers believe preparation for peaceful conditions should begin now, and they intend to provide money for this work.

Kittredge gave me his impression of Stalin based on stories told about him by the Patriarch of Sofia, a university dean. Stalin was a thief who ended up being expelled from the seminary in which he and the patriarch were classmates. Kittredge believes Stalin's grand idea is to take advantage of the general impoverishment resulting from this war to create a unified communist Europe. I told him that these ambitions are remarkably similar to the old ambitions of Pan-Slavism.

Hitler's proposals are only communicated to us in incomprehensible, truncated form. The censors seem to fear that the French public is incapable of resisting them. What imbeciles!

MONDAY, 9–MONDAY, 16 OCTOBER 1939 A busy week. Futile attempt on Monday to fly to London. The weather is too bad. On Tuesday we succeeded, Pernot, Dayras, and I. Afternoon session with British Blockade Minister Cross and the staff of Economic Warfare. The minister in charge of that department, Leith-Ross, proposed some strange ideas over dinner. He thinks it is difficult to justify the war "now that the economic goals have been met thanks to the Russian influence in the Balkans and along the Danube." I pointed out that the current war has greater scope than that. Next morning saw Jean Monnet, who is trying to organize Franco-British cooperation. Saw Gwatkin,[22] Hugh Smith, Truptil, etc. Returned to the air terminal with Paul Morand,[23] who apologized for being the head of his department. Ran into François Trocmé at the airport. Spent Thursday and Friday organizing our information for the blockade. Mény, president of the French Petroleum Company, came by to say he cannot be part of my committee. Saw Barnaud regarding de Vitry. Preposterous meeting at Commerce to talk about Fougère's request to be general secretary of the ministry. On Saturday met morning and evening with Pernot, first regarding negotiations with Italy, later those with Romania. Sunday, rest, visits from Mario and Léonard.

MONDAY, 16 OCTOBER 1939 Deliberations with the minister regarding the Belgian agreement. Went to see Raoul de Vitry. He will agree to be on the committee if Dautry okays it.

Loss of the *Royal Oak* and the attack on the Forth Bridge seem to indicate that the war is being fought more and more at sea and in the air. England is the primary target. Let us hope she understands that.

TUESDAY, 17 OCTOBER 1939 Got nowhere today. Conversation with Moreau at the Banque de Paris – he declared, as if it were a monumental occurrence, that he has broken with the Comte de Paris's adviser, Monsieur

---

22. Frank Ashton-Gwatkin: economic counselor in the British foreign office and Rist's British counterpart on the blockade mission to the United States undertaken in 1940. [JNJ/TF]

23. Paul Morand: novelist-diplomat, head of the French mission for economic warfare in Great Britain.

de la Rocque, and that everything is badly organized in the entourage of the future king of France.[24] How odd to worry about such things in the midst of the current turmoil!

SATURDAY, 21 OCTOBER 1939 At midday saw the new Turkish ambassador at the Ottoman Bank. Behiç Erkin is quite different from his predecessor. He is an old general, head shaved like the Boches' – slow, awkward gait, speaks French with difficulty. He has just spent twelve years in Budapest. Full of Hungarian affairs. Claims the Hungarians are brimming over with hostility toward the Germans. In the wake of the new Anglo-Franco-Turkish treaty, he is convinced that a rapprochement between Yugoslavia, Hungary, and Romania is in the works. He thinks the Transylvanian question could be resolved by separating the Hungarian and Romanian populations and returning a strip of territory to Hungary for the relocation of Hungarians remaining in Transylvania. He also believes the Bulgarian attitude is undergoing a change. He complained about the darkness in Paris. He was clearly nostalgic for his former post.

TUESDAY, 24 OCTOBER 1939 The Turkish ambassador returned my visit. He told me he has never believed in Hungary's joining the "Axis." "Besides," he said, "this steel axis seems to me more like a wooden axis." He thinks the Germans might very well send some small submarines via the Danube to the Black Sea.

SUNDAY, 29 OCTOBER 1939 Busy week finishing up the organization of my Blockade Committee. First meeting on Wednesday: de Vitry, Barnaud, Ferrasson, de la Baume. Unanimous agreement on how to proceed: begin right away consulting engineers and working on the list of staples that must be purchased to keep the Germans from having them. Good rapport with the minister. We decided to choose a small number of goods on which to focus the whole effort. As for food, it will be limited to fats and livestock feed. Frequent meetings with the minister regarding the agreement with the Belgians and Yugoslavs. All this is moving very slowly. The minister of agriculture understands nothing.[25] He refuses to buy any pigs for fear of lowering the price of pigs in France!

24. Henri d'Orléans, Comte de Paris: pretender to the throne of France from 1940 until his death in 1999; Pierre de la Rocque: brother of Colonel François de La Rocque, head of the far-right Croix-de-Feu. [JNJ/TF]

25. Henri Queuille: radical senator from Corrèze and minister of agriculture, 1938–1940.

Paid a visit on Wednesday to "General" Julius Deutsch, the Austrian who led the armed resistance of Viennese socialists against Dollfuss in 1934. This good man's task is to identify the "loyal" Austrians in the concentration camps. I spoke to him about Ostersetzer. He said it would take at least four weeks to resolve the matter. He is also charged with organizing the "Austrian Legion." He meets with Starhemberg![26] We talked about Dollfuss and the events of February 1934. He assured me he had done everything possible to avoid the conflict but knew in advance that resistance was futile!

On Friday I went to the war ministry to see General Ménard, whose job is to choose the Germans to be liberated. I left him some notes regarding Lorch, Adler, and Neisser. He told me that all these refugees are forming hostile groups – Jews, Nazis, anti-Nazis, etc. – and do not want to be grouped together. No real nationality. He confirms they are being offered the chance to sign up "for five years" with the Foreign Legion (a fact that has been denied in the newspapers in the face of all evidence).

Lunch on Thursday with Grünfelder.[27] He would like to see Belgium invaded.

Frightful weather. Endless rain. The Seine very high.

The American Senate has at last modified the law of neutrality! This will light a fire under the Germans.

THURSDAY, 2 NOVEMBER 1939 Yesterday another meeting of my committee. A report was presented on the goods that should be the target of blockade purchases. Absurd observations on the part of Ferrasson. Ill-disguised opposition by Delenda, who is replacing de la Baume as managing director for the blockade ministry. The three other members support me. There is increasing disorder at the ministry. The staff complain that there are not enough of them yet resist any external help, especially any assistance from engineers or businessmen. In spite of this, I have arranged a system for getting information from industrialists and merchants. Everything is slow.

MONDAY, 6 NOVEMBER 1939 A busy, tiring week. Dreadful weather, nonstop rain, nightly returns to Versailles in almost total darkness. At Block-

---

26. Prince Ernst Rüdiger von Starhemberg: Austrian politician who took part in Hitler's 1922 putsch in Munich, then organized the *Heimwehren* (a militarist organization) in 1927 before becoming minister, then vice-chancellor, in 1934–1936. However, he did not support the Anschluss and left for Argentina during the war.

27. Jean-Georges-Henri Grünfelder: retired French general and former student of Charles Rist.

ade, Delenda complained that my committee might commit some indiscretions! We met in the minister's office, where we agreed to finish the list of goods that must be bought up in order to deprive the Germans of them. The minister asked me to determine the total amount this might cost. After a quick calculation, I told him three to four billion, of which we would be responsible for half. Negotiations with Belgium have resumed in Paris. In fact the English have already fixed our positions. Alphand, from the commerce ministry, complained forcefully that the English are trying to dislodge us from our commercial positions on almost all fronts.

On Friday lunched with English financial attaché Young, Georges-Edgar Bonnet, and Engineer Solente. We all agreed that France should immediately come to an understanding with the English regarding war goals. We tried to persuade Young that Germany must be diminished politically and militarily. He endlessly repeated, "You cannot kill eighty million Germans." Bonnet proposed that we make the Rhine our frontier. This solution clearly annoyed Young. "Unless," he said, "you are going to displace the populations." (After all, why not?) It is now clear that the English and French war aims are quite different.

Boissonnas said the captain of a French freighter recently told him he had been boarded and inspected four times by German submarines during the course of his voyage. They let him go with the words, "We are not at war with you"!

We agreed that the Germans will not attack on the western front – and wondered how the morale of four million inactive men can be maintained.

WEDNESDAY, 15 NOVEMBER 1939 Had the U.S. embassy's Matthews to dinner on Saturday. He assured me that the question of molybdenum interests him and that they are ready to help us by, for example, prohibiting exportation of the ore. He and Pernot agreed that I should see the ambassador.

On Friday evening I had a long conversation with Stucki, the Swiss ambassador. He said he has had *direct* confirmation of the assassination of General von Fritsch on the Polish front.[28] "If that were not from an absolutely certain source, I would not tell you." He expounded upon the Swiss position in the upcoming negotiations, the restrictions that they have already brought to bear upon trade with Germany, the fact that all their exports are finished products, the total absence of raw materials. For us, I told him, the

---

28. General Werner von Fritsch, commander in chief of German ground forces from 1934 to 1938, when he was sacked by Hitler, was killed on 22 September 1939 during the siege of Warsaw. The rumor of his assassination was false.

essential thing is that they not send war materiel to Germany. (Afterward I learned that their trade agreement with the Germans does in fact exclude direct war materiel but still includes machines destined for the manufacture of war goods.)

Bellet telephoned with information on the Moscow talks between Stalin and Saradjoglou, the Turkish foreign affairs minister – very curious.

The attack on Hitler in Munich is the momentous event being talked about by everyone.[29]

For ten minutes on Monday we heard antiaircraft fire. On Tuesday, at the Banque de Paris, I learned that it was a mistake and the planes were French!

THURSDAY, 16 NOVEMBER 1939 On Wednesday, advisory committee and session with industrialists Leverve and de Metz regarding companies particularly affected by the war. I noticed that de la Baume is being more cooperative. Discussed the Trans-Siberian and Spanish railways.

Saw Matthews regarding the molybdenum question. He has already telegraphed Washington. Bullitt is very interested, but he is not yet back in Paris. Meeting of my committee. De Vitry tells us that a means has been found for extracting the magnesium we lack from sea water!

Meeting with the minister about the potassium question. We are going to declare we can provide the whole world with potassium! Curious efforts by the Germans to maintain (with English support) their foreign sales of potassium, the production of which is intended to pay off the interest on a loan previously made by London to the German potassium syndicate. The English say it is better that they should be paid this money than that the Germans be allowed to bank it! And the latter want to take advantage of the situation to maintain their global exports! Curious coincidence of interests resulting from these international syndicates.

Auboyneau, arriving from London, told us that the British minister of economic warfare is concerned about the worthless reports sent him by our intelligence service. He is sure that the English would like to see me at the head of this service.

During the evening Jeanne Amphoux came to our house to say good-bye to my nephew René, who is suddenly being sent to the front.

WEDNESDAY, 22 NOVEMBER 1939 The lack of coordination and the compartmentalization among the services is becoming more and more an-

---

29. On 8 November a bomb exploded in a room that Hitler had just left.

noying. From Bellet's letters on Yugoslavia I have learned that the different attachés are working independently and do not share their information – not even with their ambassador. Thus National Defense knows things that only pertain to the blockade, but does not communicate them.

Last night I took Tyler, the American banker, to dinner. He told me some interesting things about Hungary. He would like to see a federation established: Austria-Hungary-Czechoslovakia.

Saw Rodenbach, back from Bern, complaining about the total lack of coordination among the blockade offices – jealousy on the part of the commercial attaché.

Disasters at sea (six boats in two days) caused by German mines along the English coast, finally bring about the blockade of exports.

MONDAY, 27 NOVEMBER 1939 Saw Bullitt last Thursday. In his opinion, only air power will allow victory over Germany. As for the Russians, he believes their sole objective is to make the war last as long as possible. He declared himself ready to do everything in his power to facilitate the blockade.

Took various steps to help those in the camps. On Saturday saw Combes, director of the territorial police. Spent a long time discussing Ostersetzer's case with him.

TUESDAY, 28 NOVEMBER 1939 Stucki came to complain about the difficulties he is having in negotiations with France. He asked me to intervene with Pernot and set up a meeting for him.

MONDAY, 4 DECEMBER 1939 Reception for Cross, the English blockade minister, lunch at the Quai d'Orsay. After lunch, meeting of the two delegations – and (finally!) resolution of certain problems with purchasing (Turkish chrome and cotton) and with the application of the new blockade of German exports. We decided to facilitate imports of coal from Italy. We must take the Germans' place.

Gwatkin told me that Goerdeler is in Stockholm. Gwatkin thinks Goerdeler will be the intermediary for the German generals when they decide to overthrow Hitler and sue for peace in Hitler's place! Goerdeler is counting on General Halder and one other who, it is said, has his troops massed behind the Siegfried Line.

MONDAY, 11–TUESDAY, 12 DECEMBER 1939 Matthews phoned to tell me that Washington has decided to stop molybdenum exports to Russia. He is quite happy about it. When I told Pernot about this on Tuesday, he was delighted.

FRIDAY, 15 DECEMBER 1939 Lunch at the Cercle de l'Union with Prince Starhemberg, Clauzel, and Dunan. I had requested a meeting with Starhemberg in order to ask him some questions about the role of Chancellor Dollfuss during the socialist uprising in Austria on 12 February 1934.[30] Starhemberg, Austria's vice-chancellor at the time, said Major Fey was behind the search for weapons that set off the uprising in Linz, but added that the socialists were ready to fight and accepted the idea willingly. The hatred between the officers and the socialists goes back, he says, to the time when the former, returning from the Great War and arriving in Vienna, had their insignia torn off by the Viennese crowd as they left the station. According to him, Dollfuss was completely flustered by the insurrection in Vienna, and in a meeting that took place that Monday afternoon with Starhemberg and Fey, he lost his head. Prince Starhemberg regrets above all the hangings that occurred afterward and declares that he had advised against them. It seems Dollfuss also had regrets but said he could no longer hold back the mechanism of military justice that had been set in motion. Starhemberg expressed admiration for the courage with which some of the condemned socialists died, then talked about his relations with Hitler, whom he knew in the early days and whose influence upon him was unquestionable. He said Hitler would talk to them as if they belonged to a religious order.

SATURDAY, 16 DECEMBER 1939 Saw Campinchi to obtain the support of his "Deuxième Bureau" military intelligence officers for our own intelligence gathering.[31] Campinchi spoke to me at length about the difficulties of the situation, the military's ignorance of economic necessities, Daladier's slowness to make up his mind, etc. On Thursday Clauzel had told me about the rumors that were circulating in the Chamber halls: replacement of Daladier by Paul Reynaud – Foreign Affairs to de Monzie (!), the departure of Dautry, etc.

---

30. Rist was on a mission to Vienna at the time of the armed struggle begun in Linz and continuing in the capital itself between social democracy and the "moderate" government of Chancellor Dollfuss. The result was the bloody suppression of Austrian socialism.

31. César Campinchi: Radical Deputy from Corsica (1932–1940); minister of the Navy under Léon Blum, Édouard Daladier, and Paul Reynaud. [JNJ/TF]

MONDAY, 18 DECEMBER 1939 Lunched with Moysset in Versailles (our car was almost overturned).[32] He said morale in parliamentary circles is appalling. As for Germany, he is sure the generals are hostile to Hitler and are seeking to replace him with Goering – but naturally they do not want Germany to be in any way diminished! A peace offensive on the part of the generals would find us very badly prepared. He is full of admiration for the job the French navy is doing. I told Moysset what I know about Goerdeler and his connection with General Halder, whom Moysset knows and about whom he is sure we will hear more in a few weeks . . . or a few months.

FRIDAY, 29 DECEMBER 1939 Conversation with Admiral Darlan in his office on the rue Royale. He complained that the blockade is not effective enough. He told me that at the last meeting of the Supreme Council the English displayed no interest until they were handed the Thyssen report (actually just a small part of the report) showing the importance of Swedish iron. Currently this iron goes through Narvik in the North Sea but cannot be seized, because the boats stay in Norwegian territorial waters. That, he says, is where they should be attacked. A few days later I learned that efforts in this direction were thwarted by a personal telegram from King Haakon to George VI!

I had stopped by Moysset's before going to see Darlan and reported my conversation with Schairer, who had come to see me a few days earlier. Schairer, a German refugee in England and friend of Goerdeler, had told me about Thyssen's[33] having fled to Switzerland; announced a projected offensive that would take place between the second and fifteenth of January; and said that the planned invasion of Holland in November had failed because of the opposition of some generals, of whom one, General Reichenau, had been convinced by a three-hour conversation with Goerdeler. Moysset, very interested, said to me, "If the new offensive fails, one may be certain that the generals are opposed to Hitler."

During all this time there has been talk of sending me to the United States along with Gwatkin in order to expound to the president and to U.S. Secretary of the Treasury Morgenthau what we at Blockade are doing – and to seek American support for stopping shipments of ferro-alloys. Personally,

32. Henri Moysset: minister of information, then minister of State, under Pétain. Moysset and Charles Rochat were Rist's usual contacts in the Vichy government. [TF]

33. Fritz Thyssen: German industrialist who backed Hitler in the beginning but became disillusioned. It seems it was he who suggested that the Allies make an expedition to Norway in order to cut off the Swedish "iron route." [JNJ/TF]

I am not enthusiastic, convinced that these conversations should remain on the level of technical conversations among experts.

FRIDAY, 12 JANUARY 1940 Phoned Bullitt to talk about my possible trip to the United States. He invited me to lunch. We were alone. He had just come back from Algeria, Daladier having asked him not to leave yet for the United States. Thus he had not set off for Lisbon to take the Clipper.[34] I outlined the situation and told him that in my opinion an expert would do a better job than I would, given the conditions surrounding the problem of ferro-alloys. He agreed. He said, "I must have men who are completely trustworthy around the president. Pleven[35] is there for now and that is perfect." He lamented that he did not have all the contact with the president he would like; the English hold back his mail. A letter of great importance dated 12 November had reached him at the beginning of January. The Germans intercept wire communications. Besides, official telegrams sooner or later will appear before the Senate. Now Roosevelt has decided to stretch the limits of neutrality. As an example, Bullitt said he has decided to give France two hundred planes of a certain kind taken from the U.S. Army, since an order for the same number would not be ready until August. Ever anxious about the Russians, he would like to see Baku bombed. He does not seem enthusiastic about the idea of invading Sweden to seize the iron.

Bullitt said he has information regarding an impending German offensive. An American having come from Berlin apparently told him that one of his friends, a German officer, had begged him not to pass through Holland again but to travel via Switzerland. Bullitt does not believe there will be an offensive just yet. I told him I shared his opinion.

Maurice Bérard, back from London, said that the English still do not understand the situation and are doing everything halfheartedly. In his eyes, only two things count: oil and iron.

On Thursday the eleventh I went to see Marlio, who had been to see Thyssen.[36] He gave me the main points of his meeting. The Germans believe that in two years they can organize Russia and live off her. Reasonable Germans know that even a victorious war will end in general ruin. But Thyssen would like to be assured that the French will not take part in "dismembering"

---

34. Clipper: long-range flying boat produced by the Boeing Airplane Company between 1938 and 1941. [TF]

35. René Pleven, general director for Europe of the Automatic Telephone Company, was well connected in Washington.

36. Louis Marlio: aluminum and hydroelectricity mogul.

Germany. He and his friends are apparently ready to give back Czechoslovakia, Poland, and Austria. But not the left bank of the Rhine. It is true (as Schairer had told me) that he drafted an economic report; Hitler supposedly asked for it, promising that in exchange Thyssen would get all of his property back.[37] Thyssen sees two things to focus on: Swedish iron and Baku oil.

SATURDAY, 13 JANUARY 1940 Lunch with Blockade Minister Pernot and his brother Maurice, also his chief of staff, Dayras, and Paribas trustee Maurice Bérard. The latter talked about England and the role that special interests are playing to put a brake on aggressive measures. In his opinion Hore Belisha has been the victim of anti-Semitism.[38]

FRIDAY, 19 JANUARY 1940 Incident with François-Poncet resolved by an extremely friendly letter from him. I told Norman Young about it.

Lunch yesterday with Georges-Edgar Bonnet. He recounted his impressions of Egypt. He is quite worried by the anti-English vehemence of King Farouk. The English ambassador has assured him that if the king keeps it up, he will be pushed out. His uncle is all set to replace him.

Early in the week a visit from Matériel Téléphonique manager Raymond Jaoul, back from Lisbon, very anxious to have all the tungsten in Portugal and China bought up. The Germans are making great efforts to get it from Portugal.

Lunch on Wednesday at Matthews's, rue Vaneau, with Couve de Murville and Dayras. They were discussing possible bombings of London and Paris. I expressed the wish that the neutral nations not remain indifferent. And I added: "I say that in the presence of Mister Matthews, who is almost a member of the blockade ministry, but I would not say it in front of others." The possibility of my trip to Washington is becoming remote. Neither Bullitt nor Matthews seems to favor the idea. Maurice Bérard thinks domestic politics has much to do with this.

---

37. After Thyssen fled to Switzerland, his property in the Ruhr was confiscated. [TF]

38. Baron Isaac Hore Belisha was a controversial war minister in Neville Chamberlain's cabinet from 1937 to January 1940. In the spring of 1939 he instituted the draft, favored the promotion of men from the ranks to officer status, and undertook to inject new blood into the British army's general staff. Faced with a hue and cry on the part of high-ranking officers provoked by these reforms, Chamberlain was obliged to break with Hore Belisha in January 1940. The claim was then made that Chamberlain was prevented from conferring another portfolio on Hore Belisha owing to an anti-Semitic smear campaign.

SATURDAY, 20 JANUARY 1940 Meeting yesterday at the blockade ministry concerning tungsten. Present: Painvin, Jaoul, Delenda, representatives of Armament and of Foreign Affairs, Labbé, and myself. Dayras chaired the meeting, as the minister is ill. The industrialists demanded that France be allowed the lead in this matter. The English have all the tungsten they need. France can monitor production in Portugal and receive it in Indochina (where 4,500 tons were just intercepted) by way of China. It is clear that everyone is in it for himself! It was decided that instructions will be sent to Bérard and that I will then go to London, with Jaoul and Painvin if possible.

Icy cold, minus 14 degrees this morning!

MONDAY, 22 JANUARY 1940 Visit from Léonard yesterday, a bit dismayed by the absurd military milieu in which he lives in Le Havre. His commander, a career soldier, is furious that fate has handed him a second war. Visit from Herberts, extremely discouraged and weary. Visit from Papi, an Italian who, from his first words, took pains to make clear that there is a difference between his government and the Italian people. He is secretary-general of the International Institute of Agriculture. Augé-Laribé sent him. Papi asserted that the sole cause of Mussolini's anti-Comintern declarations is his resentment of certain statements by Stalin. He seems to have no faith at all in the less Francophobic sentiments expressed by Ciano.[39] I pointed out to him that Italy has no real oil reserves. And with the embargo on German exports, the Allies control the coal that was reaching Italy by sea from Antwerp. The Allies are now Italy's coal suppliers.

On Friday we had lunch at Langeron's with the Campinchis, Élie Bois, and General Héring. Élie Bois told me that Georges Bonnet is continuing his intrigues; he is convinced that if we attacked the Russians, the Italians would take advantage of the situation to strike a nasty blow.

TUESDAY, 23 JANUARY 1940 Yesterday Garr came to have lunch at our house.[40] Happy to be back in Paris, but rather bitter about his forced stay in Évian. Nothing important at the ministry. At five o'clock I introduced Auboin's lecture on Franco-British coordination, rue de Varenne. I am preparing for my departure to London.

---

39. Galeazzo Ciano: Italian minister of foreign affairs and Mussolini's son-in-law. [TF]

40. Max Garr: Viennese journalist who kept Charles Rist informed about Austrian problems at the time of his missions to Vienna.

Two

Blockade Mission,
Visit to Roosevelt

24 JANUARY–25 APRIL 1940

Rist's record of the blockade mission he undertook with his British counterpart, Frank Ashton-Gwatkin, is fascinating for the political wrangling it reveals. The aim of the mission was to persuade the United States and Canada to stop exporting to Germany the metals used in manufacturing armaments. An agreement was achieved quickly in Canada, but was more difficult to reach in the United States. This was because of strong isolationism in the U.S. Congress. Charles Lindbergh, spokesman for the powerful isolationist "America First Committee," influenced public opinion through rallies and radio speeches. Although President Roosevelt recognized the danger posed by fascist Germany, he hesitated to support the Allies openly.

Negotiations with the United States had to reconcile America's interest in maintaining exports to European countries with the Allies' focus on stopping shipments of essential metals to Germany.

In Washington Rist was cordially received by Secretary of State Cordell Hull and by Roosevelt himself. According to letters contained in the Rist Papers at the Banque de France, Roosevelt and Rist discussed an idea that had been suggested to Rist by economist M. J. Bonn: that downgraded South American securities held by Europeans could be sold back to the respective South American countries as a way to settle the inter-Allied debt. This may have been linked to an issue that Rist discussed with others: the question of possible credit that the United States could extend to the Allies (see 10 and 24–25 April 1940).

A timeline of the trip is provided in appendix 1.

WEDNESDAY, 24 JANUARY 1940 Left Le Bourget Airport at ten o'clock. A sea of clouds for a quarter of an hour, then good weather for the rest of the trip to London, where it is not nearly so cold as in Paris. Lunch at the

Savoy – Painvin, Jaoul, and I – then Picard of the Foundries Committee. At three o'clock the first meeting, presided over by Leith-Ross, with Monnet, Bérard, and Gwatkin present. Monnet told us that Secretary of State Hull was furious over Morgenthau's secret negotiations regarding ferro-alloys. That is the reason for the delay in Gwatkin's and my trip to Washington. I let Monnet know that in my opinion this trip should be postponed.

The meeting focused exclusively on the possibility of the trip and on British instructions to prevent the experts who were sent from taking any action that might lead to trouble with Japan. The English are not favorably disposed toward the Japanese, but neither do they wish to run the risk of seeing them enter the war. On the other hand, Leith-Ross says the United States is steadfast in its refusal to renew the trade agreement.

Later, a long meeting on the question of tungsten. It was agreed that we will be allowed to deal with China regarding the 4,500 tons requisitioned in Indochina. The question of price, which is much on the minds of the English for "imperial" reasons, was similarly resolved in our favor. Afterward, we discussed future blockade purchases, as well as the projected American loan to China. In order to give ourselves time to reflect on these issues, we postponed making decisions. This morning we decided that we must first have certain vital information (Chinese production, Japanese and American needs, etc.) and that we would take up the problem again on the basis of China's monopoly and weapons payments via the United States. On Thursday, lunch with Leith-Ross at the Atheneum. He is leaning more and more toward placing quotas on the neutral nations. He wants to respect the rules of international law. Four o'clock visit to Corbin, France's ambassador in London.

On Wednesday evening, dinner with Bérard. The future worries him. After the war he would like some kind of military and economic dictatorship.

FRIDAY, 26 JANUARY 1940 The morning taken up with conversation regarding the French mission on tungsten, then lunch at the Atheneum with Gwatkin and Bérard. The latter gave us his take on things: we can only satisfy the demands of neutral nations by producing weapons for export, but production is lagging. We must thus approach General Headquarters to ask if they can slow down provision of the front and use the surplus to buy products from the neutral nations so they will not fall into German hands. Gwatkin showed me a telegram received from the British ambassador to China, mentioning the difficulty of negotiations on tungsten going on in Chungking between the French ambassador and the Chinese, who demand arms in exchange for tungsten. We agreed to call off the trip to the United States.

In the afternoon, conversation at Auboyneau's with Dudley Ward[1] regarding the Committee on Financial Oversight. Bérard was there.

Dinner at Hugh Smith's in the evening, with Master of the Rolls (appeals court presiding officer) Wilfred Greene. We talked about Loisy, about Tereschenko,[2] and about Schairer's ideas regarding German generals. Gwatkin arrived at the end. We returned together. He told me it was Goerdeler who warned the Belgian king in November and convinced him to proclaim resistance, putting a stop to the projected German invasion. Gwatkin believes that the intelligence received by Schairer from Germany contains a great deal of truth.

Pitch black in the streets. Awful, snowy rain. We managed nevertheless to find a taxi to take us back to the hotel.

SATURDAY, 27 JANUARY 1940 Rain and snow. The plane could not take off. Phoned Dayras to explain our position in regard to tungsten. I stopped by to see Leith-Ross, who showed me the telegram he plans to send Purvis to let him know we are calling off the trip to the United States. I concurred.

Lunch at the embassy.

SUNDAY, 28 JANUARY 1940 Spent the whole afternoon with the Contraband Committee.

MONDAY 29–WEDNESDAY, 31 JANUARY 1940 This morning visited Bruce, Australia's high commissioner to the U.K. We discussed the 12 February meeting in Amsterdam and the Ostersetzer affair.[3]

---

1. Dudley Ward: London economist and banker (British Overseas Bank) who served as the British representative to the Dawes Commission on German reparations.

2. Mikhail Ivanovitch Tereschenko: revolutionary Ukrainian economist and financier; Russian foreign minister for a brief period in 1917. [TF]

3. Ostersetzer was liberated from his camp and given shelter at the Rists' house while Charles Rist tried to obtain an Australian visa for him. Claude Rist's daughter Antoinette Rist has this recollection: "It was at Claude Rist's home that Ostersetzer, his wife and daughter took refuge: this is how we learnt German, since the little girl didn't speak French, and we were fond of repeating what she said. They stayed with us for several months and then managed to immigrate to the U.S." Antoinette's sister Isabelle also remembers the Ostersetzers: "I remember the mother and the little girl going every day to the 'commissariat de police' to register on the list of Jews living in the sector; the mother had to go a good two kilometers each way, pushing the little girl's stroller." [JNJ/TF]

The dreadful weather kept us from returning yesterday, as it did the day before. I spent Sunday afternoon attending the Contraband Committee meeting chaired by Lord Finlay. Three and a half hours deciding on the navicerts and the cargoes to release or retain.[4] Dinner at the Savoy with bankers Bérard and Denis. Bérard's ideas: quick nomination of the commission for making purchases in the Balkans; need to furnish arms to the Balkan countries, China, etc., as the sole demand of these countries is for weapons; planning of industrial accords and unloading sites with the English.

During the evening Gwatkin called to tell me they are sending Colonel Griffith to talk to Thyssen. I said he should have Griffith see Léger and Marlio before any such conversation.

This morning a huge snowfall. We decided with Jaoul to take the boat to Le Havre via Southampton this evening. Arrived in Le Havre Tuesday evening at five only to learn there is a five-hour delay on trains to Paris owing to downed telephone poles all along the line. The poles were upended by ice forming on the wires.

I spent the night at the Fascati and on Wednesday took the 7:00 AM train, which did not reach Paris until three in the afternoon!

THURSDAY, 1 FEBRUARY 1940 Went to the blockade ministry, phone call from Gwatkin wanting to talk more about the trip to the United States. Meeting concerning the intelligence service.

WEDNESDAY, 7 FEBRUARY 1940 Yesterday dined at Mercier's to meet with Prince Otto von Habsburg – as well as Lachenal from Geneva, the Coudenhoves with their daughter, and the d'Audiffret-Pasquiers. The prince was accompanied by his mentor, whom I sat next to at the table.[5] We talked about Dollfuss and Schuschnigg, who became chancellor of Austria following Dollfuss's assassination. He criticized Schuschnigg for his lack of decision. The prince spoke to me primarily about the Belgian situation, about Degrelle, who, he said, was paid by Rome, and about the Flemish, who seem even more anti-German than the Walloons. He said that at Aix-la-Chapelle there is apparently a German propaganda center targeting both the communists and the extreme right. He said Austrian workers have formed an

4. Navicerts: permits for neutral ships to pass through the blockade. [TF]
5. Prince Otto co-founded the Pan-European Union in 1922 with his mentor, Count Richard Coudenhove-Kalergi, in 1922. The prince, both anti-Nazi and anticommunist, promoted the restoration of the Habsburg monarchy. [TF]

organization that is first and foremost anti-German; by contrast, "General" Deutsch, though Jewish, has remained Pan-Germanic (as was Bauer). As for Germany, he does not expect to see any movement, not even on the part of the generals. General Halder is supposedly anti-Hitler, but *for* the war! The prince speaks perfect French. We said nothing about the possibility of restoration. He foresees Austria, Hungary, and Czechoslovakia forming a union, or at least a common military command. Poland might participate. He finds Beneš to be very indecisive, Osusky much more open and understanding.

Received Michel Mange (former assistant to Leverve) in the afternoon. He explained railway surveillance operations in Italy. He said Italy is "feverishly" preparing for war, but which war is not clear, probably against the Yugoslavs, who are becoming quite concerned. The evening before, at the Suez Company, Sir Malcolm Graham (former English ambassador to Italy)[6] had told me that 80 percent of the Italian population favor the Allies, as does the king, who seems to be on good terms with Mussolini and much more influential than people think. Mange assured me (1) that Mussolini is extremely hostile toward the English and will demand an air base near Suez, though he appears to be friendlier toward the French, and (2) that the Romans, fearing inflation, are purchasing land in order to protect themselves.

MONDAY, 12 FEBRUARY 1940 Lunch on Saturday at Coudenhove's with Cambó, former Spanish finance minister under Alphonse XIII, and Heinemann, president of SOFINA. Cambó praised the gold standard, as did Heinemann. The conversation, which Coudenhove tried to steer toward Pan-Europe, kept getting sidetracked. The two great financiers were clearly interested solely in the war's repercussions on business.

On Saturday morning saw Serruys[7] to ask him to help with the publication of statistical data. Lengthy exposition of his economic policy and attacks on Reynaud, his bête noir. His fervent hope is that the secret committee that is still meeting will bring about a cabinet reshuffle.

I received Monnet in the afternoon. We talked about my trip to the United States, which is now on.

TUESDAY, 13 FEBRUARY 1940 Saw Bérard at the Banque de Syrie and at the blockade ministry. He and Gwatkin have agreed that we will take the

---

6. Actually he meant Sir Ronald Graham, ambassador to Rome, 1921–1933. [TF]

7. Daniel Serruys: high commissioner at the Ministry of National Economy in Daladier's cabinet. [TF]

Clipper on the twenty-fifth. Telegram from Lord Lothian saying we will be asked about all the financial and monetary problems, not just about the blockade.

WEDNESDAY, 14 FEBRUARY 1940 Consultative committee. Discussed the report on goods shipments in the Balkans. Barnaud very worried about the size of our foreign purchases. Dinner at Istel's in the evening. Spoke at length with Maurice Rueff, the banker. According to him the war will cause vast impoverishment and the splitting up of companies that have become ridiculously large. Late return to Versailles. Cold and snow once again.

THURSDAY, 15 FEBRUARY 1940 Spent the morning in Versailles. During the afternoon, discussed the organization of the committee on financial oversight with Drouin and Auboyneau. We are told that the Clipper will not resume passenger flights until March 15! Our mission to Washington may be considerably delayed.

FRIDAY, 16 FEBRUARY 1940 Matthews phoned to tell me of a wire from Ambassador Bullitt saying our arrival in the United States would be well received. He came to lunch.

SATURDAY, 2 MARCH 1940 Our trip to the United States having been decided upon, on 24 February Gwatkin and I left for New York from Genoa aboard the *Washington*. The crossing, which was quite calm and beautiful at first, ended with several days of terrible squalls. Gwatkin was a charming traveling companion; extremely intelligent and interested in everything, he did much to make this long and disagreeable voyage more bearable.

MONDAY, 4 MARCH 1940 Having landed at 11:00, on the dock I found Garreau-Dombasle, the French commercial attaché; Tcherichowsky, sent by Public Works Minister de Monzie; and Morgan Bank's Carter and Leffing-well, with whom I shook hands.

Right away Arthur Purvis, head of the British Purchasing Commission, invited us to lunch and laid out the Morgenthau–Cordell Hull position. It seems Morgenthau is the one who needs to be reassured. I telephoned him and was told that I must be presented to him by the ambassador. Thus everything will become official.

Trip to Washington with Garreau-Dombasle and Gwatkin. Had dinner on the train.

TUESDAY, 5 MARCH 1940 Visited Saint-Quentin, the French ambassador. I explained the new situation to him. This would be discussed during the afternoon. Lunch at the embassy. Returned to the hotel, then at 4:00 went to the British embassy to chat with Gwatkin. Lord Lothian, the British ambassador, is most charming and highly intelligent. At 5:00 tea and discussion. In the interim Purvis came back from a conversation with Morgenthau. All had changed. Morgenthau wants us to go through Cordell Hull. For his part, he will do all he can to support us. This has taken the wind out of our sails. We decided to see Cordell Hull tomorrow.

Dined at the Mayflower with Purvis, Gwatkin, and Bloch-Lainé.[8] Gwatkin depressed. We will have to fight hard.

News of the seizure of Italian ships loaded with coal. Which is it? War or bluff!

WEDNESDAY, 6 MARCH 1940 At a quarter past noon visited Bullitt, the U.S. ambassador to France. Very impassioned, he told me that the attitude toward the English is rather bad. He advised me to trust Feis, telling me there was a "row" between Feis[9] and Morgenthau, and that the latter has decided to leave issues relating to metals to the State Department. The president, he said, is in good health but deeply discouraged; he does not want to have a third term and will leave the presidency to Hull.

Lunch with Gwatkin, who, on behalf of Lord Lothian, insisted that I speak to Hull this afternoon. After lunch I polished the little speech prepared this morning. Gwatkin and Garreau-Dombasle helped me put it in suitable English.

At 4:15 introduced to Cordell Hull by the two ambassadors. Some words of welcome from Hull, who kindly remembered having seen me. I made my little speech, and Hull replied that we had come in a "very fine spirit."

Afterward, a preliminary conversation in Assistant Secretary of State Berle's office – in which Berle reacted testily to an apparently (but unwittingly) ironic remark. A schedule of meetings was worked out, and Gwatkin and I took a drive along the Potomac and back to the Capitol.

We shall deal with serious matters tomorrow.

THURSDAY, 7 MARCH 1940 Two meetings presided over by Grady, another assistant secretary of state. A discussion of navicerts in the morning.

8. François Bloch-Lainé: inspector of public finances, later finance minister. [TF]
9. Herbert Feis: economic adviser for international affairs at the State Department. [TF]

The Americans want two things. First, they want us to promise that navicerts will not be rejected because of the sender, but only for reasons of the nature of the cargo and of the intended receiver (who is not an American); actually, they want to be given a way to say the United States has not been "black-listed." Second, they want us to give reasons for our rejections.

Second meeting in the afternoon regarding agricultural purchases. They are afraid we will suddenly stop purchasing a series of products, including tobacco, the most important one, as well as fruit, cotton, wheat, and peas. This threat has irritated some senators whose vote is needed to pass a law giving Hull the right to make trade treaties. The Americans let us know they are not asking that *all* purchases be resumed, but only some. Grady explained that this is just a matter of psychology. Garreau-Dombasle said we have resumed our purchases of tobacco and that we are prepared to make a declaration. Agreements can also be arranged regarding the other articles. The English want to think about it.

FRIDAY, 8 MARCH 1940 Dinner with Purvis last night. Afterward Gwat-kin and Purvis came to my room. Purvis said everything has been arranged with Morgenthau and that he is expecting us.

Another meeting with Grady during the afternoon regarding the trade agreements. Actually this was the same matter dealt with the day before, just in another form. It was pointed out to us that we are no longer comply-ing with the clauses of Franco-American and Anglo-American agreements relating to agricultural purchases. We countered by indicating our increased purchases of other goods, inadequate tonnage, and the absence of credit. Gwatkin said the Dominions have given them long-term credits.[10] Grady insisted on the political aspect of the problem.

SATURDAY, 9 MARCH 1940 No meeting today. This morning I saw the naval attaché. Discussed with Ambassador Saint-Quentin the composition of a long dispatch to the Blockade Committee. Lunched at de Lamure's with Pleven, the European head of Automatic Telephone Company.

10. "Dominions were semi-independent polities that were nominally under the Crown, constituting the British Empire and British Commonwealth, beginning in the later part of the 19th century. They included Canada, Australia, Pakistan, India, Malta, Ceylon (Sri Lanka), New Zealand, Newfoundland, South Africa, and the Irish Free State. The Balfour Declaration of 1926 recognised the Dominions as 'autonomous Com-munities within the British Empire' and, in the decades afterward, the dominions each became fully sovereign from the United Kingdom." Wikipedia. [TF]

During the afternoon saw the *Washington Post*'s Eugene Meyer, who took me to his bungalow on the Potomac. General discussion. Dined at the British embassy, seated next to Berle. Conversation with Lord Lothian about our attitude and that of the United States in regard to Japan.

SUNDAY, 10 MARCH 1940 Long conversation with Pleven, then Gwatkin came to take me to lunch with Chinese ambassador Hu Shih, one of today's greatest Chinese philosophers. He is a friend of Gwatkin. The news from Finland was causing us considerable uneasiness.

I had the most charming lunch imaginable at the Chinese ambassador's. He is short, with a powerful mind and extraordinarily intelligent eyes. In attendance were an attaché and his Chinese-robed wife, as well as another Chinaman who was my student at the Law Faculty around 1918. He remembered my course very precisely. Lunch Chinese style: at first I was alarmed to see two elegant ivory chopsticks beside my plate, next to which a knife and fork were soon placed, but the others, including Gwatkin, applied these instruments with remarkable skill. In the middle of the table was a large wooden turntable that brought the various dishes around to the guests. After the soup, which was served in little cups, there was just one dish, a chicken so well cooked that it was easy to take apart with the chopsticks. Then the turntable was covered with an infinity of varied dishes including soy (in the form of beans, cheese, and sauce), while next to each of us a bowl of very white, unseasoned rice appeared. All served on the same plate.

The ambassador had been a professor for twenty years and had a huge influence on his students.

MONDAY, 11 MARCH 1940 Strange reception by Morgenthau. During the afternoon a discussion with Berle on some points regarding the retention of certain American goods bought and paid for before 1 January this year. Saw journalists at 12:45.

Lunch with Mrs. Kittredge.

Dinner at Dumaine's with Feis and E. Meyer.

TUESDAY, 12 MARCH 1940 Talks this morning at the British embassy. Visited the Freer Gallery.

WEDNESDAY, 13 MARCH 1940 Lunch at the French embassy, then a conversation with Berle regarding the postal service and the establishment of a port of control in the United States. The Canadian minister was there.

Not much headway. At 5:00 tea with Grady. In the evening, big dinner with journalists at Eugene Meyer's.

THURSDAY, 14 MARCH 1940 In the morning we had a review meeting in Grady's office. Agriculture gave us a report. Then Garreau-Dombasle, Gwatkin, and I talked about "moral embargoes." Grady seemed encouraging, but again brought up the question of agricultural purchases. He said, "The English treat us like a colony."

All smiles are for the French, and I am a beneficiary of this attitude. Despite the injustice, I am delighted by this general friendliness. It is clear there is a great desire here to help us.

At 5:00 a meeting at Lord Lothian's regarding Halifax and Saint-John Perse.

FRIDAY, 15 MARCH 1940 Saw Berle to offer my excuses for not being able to attend the afternoon meeting. He spoke to me about agricultural products. Next I went to the embassy to submit my long letter to Blockade Minister Pernot. There, received a phone call from Cochran asking me to receive Pubston on behalf of Morgenthau. He came to talk about agricultural purchases.

Left by plane for New York. I sent a letter to the ambassador saying he should speed up the English decision on the agricultural question.

Dinner with Lolli's parents at the Waldorf.[11]

SATURDAY, 16 MARCH 1940 Conversation with Purvis, later with Leroy-Beaulieu, during the morning; lunch with Purvis. At 2:15 I went to the Waldorf to look over the draft of my interview with Mrs. Kittredge;[12] then another conversation with Purvis and Pleven. The ambassador telephoned in response to my letter regarding agricultural products and to let me know about some telegrams that had come in. Dinner at the Ritz-Carlton with the Jays[13] and an evening of theater: *Life with Father.*

11. Lolli Rist's German parents, the Gaedes, had immigrated to the United States. [TF]

12. Mrs. Eleanor Kittredge, wife of the Rockefeller Foundation representative in Paris, published her interview with Charles Rist in the *New York Times*, 31 March 1940. [TF]

13. Nelson D. Jay: president of the Morgan Bank in Paris. [TF]

SUNDAY, 17 MARCH 1940 Conversation with Dumont, secretary of the Comité France-Amérique [France-America Committee], about Wednesday's lunch. Lunch at the home of Roussy de Sales, a French journalist; went on to the Metropolitan with Mrs. Kittredge to see the old American dwellings; dinner at the Garreau-Dombasles'; then briefly returned to the Roussy de Saleses', where I met Valrun. It was raining when I got back. At 6:30 Gwatkin came to fill me in on some conversations he had had in Washington on Saturday.

MONDAY, 18 MARCH 1940 Conversation at the embassy yesterday with Purvis, the British purchasing commissioner; decided to wire Monnet to give Purvis more freedom of action. Long telegram to the Blockade Committee summing up the status of our conversations; lunch at the Morgan Bank; conversation with Leffingwell regarding agricultural purchases and the possibility of a government loan. Dinner at the Purvis's with Pleven and Douglas. At 6:30 visited by the naval attaché and by Altschuhl of the Lazard Bank.

TUESDAY, 19 MARCH 1940 At the embassy, drafted a telegram and an explanatory letter to Monnet; lunch at the Rockefellers'; conversation with Miss Walker. Returned to the embassy; conversation at Purvis's with the molybdenum people, very important; visited Mrs. Leffingwell from 6:00 to 7:00. Returned to the hotel and dined with Dumont.

WEDNESDAY, 20 MARCH 1940 Lunch at France-Amérique, then flew to Washington. Dinner at Berle's with the governor of Alaska.

THURSDAY, 21 MARCH 1940 Lunch at the Press Club. As Gwatkin had not come back yet, I was on my own to answer their questions. Dinner at the Swiss ambassador's along with Secretary of Agriculture Wallace and his wife. There was talk of the new French cabinet. Everyone is happy to see Bonnet go. Gwatkin present.

22 MARCH 1940, GOOD FRIDAY Gwatkin returned last night. He stayed until one in the morning telling me the results of his Canadian conversations. The Americans want nothing more to do with Lord Halifax, after having proposed him themselves. During the morning a meeting with Grady to sum up our conversations.

Lunch at the ambassador's. With Dumaine[14] and Garreau-Dombasle we prepared a communiqué. At 4:00 we went to the British embassy, where Gwatkin translated my draft and coordinated it with that of Sir Owen Chalkley, the British commercial attaché; 5:30 at the State Department with Hickerson.[15] Their idea is to make a simple official statement noting our desire to resume complete compliance with the trade agreement after the war.

Dined with Dumaine at the hotel. Talked about anything and everything.

SATURDAY, 23 MARCH 1940   Asked the ambassador to request an interview with Roosevelt on my behalf. Sent telegrams and letters to New York. Lunched at the British embassy with Gwatkin and Feis. The latter spoke to us about issues relating to Mexico; then Gwatkin asked him questions about metals and agricultural purchases. The other evening Wallace had suggested to him that corn could be purchased at a reduced price. Feis is uneasy about our sales of nickel and Indochina's sales of tin to Japan.

I accompanied Feis to the gym where he played badminton. A nice game, Cathedral School style.

Dinner in the evening with Cochran at the Mayflower. He explained what had happened with Morgenthau. Matthews's telegrams informing the State Department of our negotiations on molybdenum raised fears that these official letters might reveal the president's personal position. Hence the dispute with Morgenthau, who decided not to see us. Cochran recommended that Purvis be the only channel for dealing with Morgenthau – and that we speak with Grady about blockade issues.

24 MARCH 1940, EASTER   Icy cold outside. Stayed indoors all day, except for a short walk after lunch. Read Carl Snyder's book.[16] My secretary brought me an important telegram from Monnet to Purvis this morning.

Our conversations here have been quite different from what we had been led to expect. We must start from scratch and persuade London. Extremely difficult from such a distance. The personal reception everyone has given me is excellent.

14. Possibly Rist was referring to Cyrille Dumaine, Canadian legislator. [TF]

15. John D. Hickerson: member of the Permanent Joint Board on Defense (U.S. and Canada), 1940–1946. [TF]

16. Carl Snyder: American statistician and author of several books, including *Capitalism, the Creator* (Macmillan, 1940), which blamed the Depression on the Federal Reserve. [TF]

25 MARCH 1940, EASTER MONDAY Conversation this morning with Feis. I talked about tungsten as a good example of parallel efforts by the Allies and the United States, pointing out that a successful embargo depended upon an intelligent exchange of information. I spoke about nickel. He said that obviously they are not pleased by the exports to Japan, nor by the sales of wool on credit that Australia is preparing to make, whereas the whole effort by the United States has been to stop their own sales on credit to the Japanese.

Conversation with Grady on the same subject this afternoon. He told me that we can do as we like regarding nickel – that it will be hard to establish new moral embargoes – but that we will be able to obtain some things via the Munitions Board. Then saw Dumaine, with the draft of the State Department's communiqué and various telegrams.

TUESDAY, 26 MARCH 1940 Lunch with the French embassy's Baeyens,[17] met an American journalist – very chatty, especially on financial matters. At 7:00 Purvis and Bloch-Lainé came for dinner and talked about the absurd telegrams of London's Coordination Committee. Purvis was furious. Gwatkin returned from New York around ten. We stayed at it until eleven, when I sent them away.

WEDNESDAY, 27 MARCH 1940 This morning discussed the statement to be published with Hickerson. Then met with Purvis at the British embassy to talk about the telegram to send regarding nickel. Back at the hotel, having packed and sent the telegram on nickel to the Blockade Committee, took the plane, got to Lamont's at 6:00. Dinner at 8:00 with Stanley of the *Nickel*, Merz of the *New York Times*, and Cooper of Associated Press. Plane trip with Offrey, Bullitt's secretary.

THURSDAY, 28 MARCH 1940 I spent the morning with Purvis talking about several metals and the policy to apply to each; reviewed and discussed the final text of the long telegram to send to the Coordination Committee regarding the general policy on nickel and molybdenum. Lunch with Aldrich, who spoke to me exclusively of his charitable works.[18] He would like to play a big role, though he is not capable. The next day I asked Roussy de Sales to take him in hand. At 6:00, visit from my niece Élisabeth Aubin and her

17. Jacques Baeyens: consul general of France. [TF]
18. Richard Steere Aldrich (1884–1941): U.S. Representative from Rhode Island. [TF]

husband. Later saw a journalist from the *New York Times* wanting to interview me. Dined with John Foster Dulles. They say he is pro-Dewey, Dewey's future secretary of state. I spoke to him about Montagu Norman[19] and the Germans. Norman is openly friendly toward them and said it is up to Europeans to determine the necessary balance of power. Went back to Lamont's.

FRIDAY, 29 MARCH 1940 Received many letters from Europe all at once. Finally! Garreau-Dombasle kept me in his office showing me the blockade arrangements. Later I was led by Dumont to Coudert, who spoke to me of the French embassy's plan to have Dumont head up the blockade office. Lunched with Dumont. Magnificent murals by Sert[20] in the Waldorf's dining room. Stopped by Purvis's; back to Lamont's, had tea with Mme Lamont, packed my bags; stopped in to see Roussy de Sales; dinner with Butler, president of Columbia University (ridiculous invitation); a telephone call from the ambassador telling me that London has thrown everything back into question. Took the train to Washington at midnight.

SATURDAY, 30 MARCH 1940 Meeting at the State Department; discussion of ports, navicerts, and German exports. We have made no progress. As for the navicerts, Hickerson told us, "We give you our blessing," but he rejected any formal declaration regarding the issue of ports; then a quite intelligent statement by one of the Englishmen. But he was told it is up to the ambassador to come discuss the matter with Mr. Sumner Welles.[21]

Lunch at Dumaine's. At 3:00 PM I found Maurice Boure, who spoke to me of various possible financial projects – exchange of securities, etc. He believes the matter of inter-Allied debts should be taken up again. We decided to dine together at Harvey's. At 6:00 visited Mrs. Wood. Went to bed early for once.

SUNDAY, 31 MARCH 1940 Eugene Meyer invited me to lunch at his bungalow on the Potomac. This morning I wrote to Vogüe. Conversation with Eugene Meyer regarding inter-Allied debts. I suggested that some strategic points in the Caribbean be ceded. It was understood that he would put out

19. Montagu Norman: governor of the Bank of England, 1920–1944, and member of the Anglo-German Fellowship. On his watch in 1931 the United Kingdom abandoned the gold standard, a standard that Rist spent much of his life defending. [TF]

20. Josep Maria Sert i Badia (1874–1945): Spanish muralist and friend of Salvador Dali. [TF]

21. Sumner Welles: U.S. undersecretary of state from 1937 to 1943. [TF]

feelers regarding the possibility. Dinner at Feis's; had a long chat with the head of the Far East bureau. Bullitt arrived at the end of dinner. He asked me if we were getting anywhere with our discussions. I said that as far as France was concerned, all was well.

MONDAY, 1 APRIL 1940 Lunched at the French embassy with Paswolski[22] and packed my suitcase to catch the 3:00 PM plane to Canada; arrived in Ottawa at ten in the evening and was received by the high commissioner, Sir Gerald Campbell.

In Montreal I was astonished to see soldiers wearing British uniforms but speaking French. Joy, seeing at last some soldiers in a country that is, at least theoretically, at war, and to be, for a few days at least, out of the awful atmosphere of haggling and recrimination in America.

Flying over Montreal, a vast, luminous city, one sees on the heights an enormous lighted cross towering above it. From the outset this symbol lets you know where French Canada stands.

TUESDAY, 2 APRIL 1940 Morning talks with Purvis, Gwatkin, the Canadian Robertson, and Assistant Secretary of State Skilton. The subject was nickel. Lunch at Campbell's with Mackenzie King, the administrator replacing the viceroy, the finance minister, etc.[23]

Afternoon discussion of the Canadian naval base with members of the navy; paid a visit to Graham Towers, governor of the Bank of Canada.

Dinner this evening at Gerald Campbell's.

WEDNESDAY, 3 APRIL 1940 Talks resumed this morning in regard to metals: cobalt, asbestos, radium. Meanwhile, an important telegram arrived giving the English carte blanche in regard to nickel – evidently as a follow-up to my telegram of 27 March. The Canadians quite constructive and cooperative.

Lunch at La Geneste's – visit from the new legation – then left for dinner at the country club, Skilton's treat.

THURSDAY, 4 APRIL 1940 Took the train to Montreal. Gwatkin had agreed to speak at the Canadian Club, and I was thus obliged to make a

22. Leo Paswolski: special aide to U.S. Secretary of State Cordell Hull. [TF]

23. Sir Gerald Campbell: British high commissioner to Canada from 1938 to 1941; Mackenzie King, Canadian prime minister. [TF]

speech, which was broadcast via radio, before an audience of five hundred people. Afternoon reception at the École des Hautes Études Commerciales Françaises with some French teachers and with the head of the Catholic University. A charming reception at which I must admit I was rather moved. Finding myself suddenly in a completely French environment at such a distance from Europe left quite an impression, especially at a time like this when everything French is so close to one's heart.

FRIDAY, 5 APRIL 1940 Arrived in Washington after a one-hour plane ride. In Jimmy Dunn's office[24] we resumed talks on the naval base; it was decided to refer the naval memo to Sumner Welles through the offices of Lord Lothian. Afterward at the British embassy we discussed among ourselves the terms of the communiqué, which had been juggled about by Sir Owen Chalkley during our absence!!

Dined with Garreau-Dombasle at the hotel.

SATURDAY, 6 APRIL 1940 A 10:00 AM meeting with Grady, quite unhappy with the English. He was ready to accept the older version agreed upon last Friday. I urged a decision that this text be submitted to the respective governments. Chalkley was furious. Lunched at the Federal Police Association, then drafted a long telegram asking the government to adhere to the communiqué.

SUNDAY, 7 APRIL 1940 Got up late, letter to Versailles; lunched with Benech, the French naval attaché, and dined alone at the hotel – early to bed.

WEDNESDAY, 10 APRIL 1940 Received by Roosevelt.[25] Telegraphed my conversation with him.

---

24. Jimmy Dunn: political adviser to the U.S. secretary of state. [TF]

25. The White House Stenographer's Diary, located in the Roosevelt Presidential Library, confirms that Rist met with Roosevelt at noon that day. There is a hint of what this conversation touched on in a letter to Rist dated 9 May 1940 from Yves Bouthillier, French minister of finances: "Our attaché, M. Leroy-Beaulieu, tells me that President Roosevelt spoke with you about a plan to sell South American securities belonging to the Allies. Could you give me the broad outlines of this plan?" Another letter in the *Papiers Charles Rist*, dated 5 April 1940, just five days before Rist's meeting with Roosevelt, touches on the same topic. In this letter Dr. M. J. Bonn, a German professor of political economy teaching at Bowdoin College in Maine, suggests an intricate plan to sell downgraded South American securities held by Europeans back to the respective South

THURSDAY, 11 APRIL 1940 Dinner at Morgenthau's. Unimportant. At 3:30 I was received by Cordell Hull. He kept me there for an hour. As I was leaving he said, "I wish you to live a hundred years."

FRIDAY, 12 APRIL 1940 Lunch at the Canadian Legation with Minister Christie. Conversation with Frankfurter, member of the U.S. Supreme Court. Dinner with W. Stewart, Viner, Riefler.[26]

FROM 12 TO 19 APRIL 1940 Completed conversations regarding the communiqué.

WEDNESDAY, 24–THURSDAY, 25 APRIL 1940 My departure has once again been postponed, the foul weather preventing Clippers from taking off. Thus my stay in New York has been prolonged from the nineteenth to the twenty-ninth of April.

I am assured by everyone here, especially the French, that my mission has been a great success, that I have been a "persona grata" . . . and that I must come back.

Yesterday Morgan Jr. gave me a tour of his library, with the magnificent works of art still housed there.[27] The rest had been donated to the Metropolitan Museum. He insisted that I spend Thursday and Thursday night at his house in the country.

I had a long conversation with George Harrison[28] Thursday afternoon. He introduced me to his wife and we spoke of old memories and of Montagu Norman, much more Nazi-loving than I could have imagined. I saw Burgess, president of the National City Bank. With all of them I brought up the question of possible credit that the United States could extend to the Allies. In their opinion it is not yet opportune to discuss the matter. They have been alarmed by the Nazis' invasion of Norway and by the methods used.

American countries as a way to settle the inter-Allied debt. However, says Dr. Bonn, "It is quite possible that the isolationists would see in the offer to settle the debt an endeavor to drag [the United States] into the war." (See also the diary entry for 11 November 1941: "I reminded [Darlan] of the ideas Roosevelt had discussed with me, his fear for South America and for Greenland.") [TF]

26. Rist is probably referring to economists Jacob Viner, Walter W. Stewart, and Winfield W. Riefler, the first a Canadian, the latter two Americans. [TF]

27. Morgan had founded the Pierpont Morgan Library in 1924 to honor his father. [TF]

28. George Harrison: president of the Federal Reserve Bank of New York. [TF]

Visited Hartman, editor of *Harper's* magazine.[29]

Tuesday, a visit to Roussy de Sales, who has an American wife. He is the best French journalist here, and he and I discussed what could be done regarding American public opinion. He has at last found an invaluable support in the person of the good, intelligent Lewis Douglas.[30] Douglas, who comes every year to see me in Paris and is a great friend of Purvis, decided to publish a "letter" of the kind popular here to make clear to Americans that it is in their interest not to let the Allies fall. It was a great success. Douglas is influential and has influential friends. Then, too, the Norwegian affair has resulted in a flow of goodwill and readiness to act.

Lunch with Shotwell at Columbia.[31]

REPORT ON MY MISSION TO THE UNITED STATES

Originally intended as talks regarding metals, our official mission was in the end devoted to general blockade matters and to agricultural purchases – matters much more relevant to the British government than to ours – and which Germany's occupation of Norway simplified in an unexpected way.

If the British government had been more attentive to American sensibility to the way, not in which things were resolved, but in which things were announced to the American government, most issues relating to the blockade would not have taken on the urgency they had when we arrived in Washington.

Agricultural purchases immediately became the priority issue. As we had not stopped buying tobacco or cotton, France was not really involved. This will only come later with regard to fruits. In contrast, England abruptly declared that it was going to stop buying tobacco. The biggest outlet for this important American product was thus cut off from one day to the next, and prices fell, leading to loud complaints from entire regions in the South. Since

29. The visit to Lee Foster Hartman concerned an article by Frank Henighen, an American journalist, that had appeared in the March issue of *Harper's*. The article begins: "While French and German armies have been fighting, French and German industrialists have been . . . selling each other the materials [coke and iron ore] out of which shells and cannon are made." In a letter dated 29 April 1940, Mr. Hartman concludes: "Dr. Rist . . . called upon me last week and I have invited him to set forth his protest in *Harper's* magazine." According to a letter dated 2 April 1940, Mr. Hartman had acknowledged that these claims of underground trafficking with Germany were false. [TF]

30. Lewis Williams Douglas: American diplomat, academic, and politician who lobbied Roosevelt to aid the Allies. [TF]

31. James T. Shotwell: professor of international relations at Columbia University. [TF]

these regions belong to the Democratic Party, and since Secretary of State Hull was then engaged in the difficult task of persuading the Senate to renew the law that authorizes him to make trade agreements, the problem had become acute when we arrived. Everyone, including the president himself, considered it his duty to back the secretary of state. We were simply being asked to provide a formula that would avert the looming storm, which, if it should hit, could even lead to Mr. Hull's resignation.

The formula that was finally adopted does not commit us to anything at all. The goodwill with which we proceeded to discuss the matter allowed them to tell the senators that England and France had understood their error and would do everything possible to continuing buying goods from the United States.

A little diplomacy on the part of England would have avoided the incident. It would have been a simple matter of not stopping their purchases from one day to the next, but of informing the U.S. government ahead of time that after a certain period England would be obliged to end them. One got the impression, however, that Great Britain was once again treating the United States like a colony. "They always treat us like colonials," Assistant Secretary of State Grady told me. Sir Owen Chalkley, the English commercial attaché, contributed in no small part to this impression. Chalkley continuously hobbled our mission, just as he did Purvis's; his surly, provocative manner got the Americans' dander up.

The result, however, was positive. My colleague Gwatkin made it clear to his ministry that a more continuous contact with the Department of State would avoid such incidents in the future. Since the active goodwill of this department – not just on the part of the head, but of all the staff – in regard to the Allies is not in doubt, it can be expected that such things will not happen again.

The issue of German exports was handled in like fashion. We were simply asked to allow the shipment of a certain number of goods that had been bought before the blockade became effective.

NOTES FOR CONVERSATION WITH PRIME MINISTER REYNAUD

1. Good intentions on the part of the Roosevelt administration.
    Official Report. Obliged to hedge with Congress.
2. Bad state of public opinion.
    Republicans: hatred of Roosevelt.
    Democrats and the left: fear of war; focus on the struggle of empires.

Intellectuals: skepticism born of brainwashing during the last war.

Certain industrialists: arrangements with Germany.

3. Unfortunate view of England.

England is the only one they are paying attention to.

Role of Lothian. He is reproached for his ineffectiveness. Taxi drivers and intellectuals are of one mind.

Hatred of three men: Neville Chamberlain, Horace Wilson, Montagu Norman.

4. Propaganda. Nothing needed from France. To get help from the Americans:

L. Douglas and Roussy de Sales. Let the administration do it.

5. Embassy: Nothing to change. It is doing its job correctly.

6. Role of France: to moderate the English and take their place if possible.

7. High opinion of the French army.

Issue of debts (Colonel Knox, Eugene Meyer)

8. The Americans will mobilize if we have some victories.

Recent shifts of opinion subsequent to events in Scandinavia.

Three

Occupation and Exodus

16 MAY–12 JULY 1940

As the French government, banks, and corporations vacated Paris, Rist's attention turned to protecting the vulnerable members of his family, especially his Jewish daughter-in-law and three granddaughters.

The armistice with Nazi Germany, signed on 22 June 1940 and dividing France into an occupied zone and a "free" zone, found Charles Rist and his wife, Germaine, taking refuge at their country house near Lake Geneva, along with most of their sons' wives and children.

THURSDAY, 16 MAY 1940 Lunch at Édouard's, arrived at the ministry to find all the green boxes thrown out into the courtyard.[1] Labbé was as outraged as I was. I got back to work and called Charguéraud, who came down to tell me they had been ordered to leave at 5:30. I went to see the minister, who told me about the motorized division that had completely disappeared. "Under these circumstances," I told him, "I am going to see to the safety of my granddaughters." Passed by Eva's; she decided to come to Versailles with me. Stopped by my ISRES office, where I found Mme Sterne. I paid everyone for the month of May and returned to Versailles. The de Lacroix were there for dinner.[2] Claude and I decided to take his little ones[3] to La Bouffource, Noël's farmhouse in Mayenne.

---

1. After the Sedan breakthrough (see note 4 below), the Germans' arrival in Paris had been declared probable in the next few hours, and an order was given to burn a large number of diplomatic files on the grounds of the Quai d'Orsay in case there was not time to remove them.

2. Victor de Lacroix: French ambassador to Prague until 1939 and future father-in-law of Noël Rist. [TF]

3. Rist was referring to the daughters of Claude and his Jewish wife, Françoise. [TF]

FRIDAY, 17 MAY 1940 Left with Germaine and the children around 10:00 AM, had lunch in Nogent – lines of refugees along the roads. Arrived in the afternoon. The children were delighted. Bad news on the radio tonight. Reynaud's speech to the Senate – on Corap's army.[4]

SATURDAY, 18 MAY 1940 Stayed at La Bouffource, took the children to the lake for a stroll.

SUNDAY, 19 MAY 1940 Returned alone to Versailles, spent some time at the blockade ministry during the afternoon. Paid a visit to Léger, who has just been sacked – Baudouin's doing.[5]

MONDAY, 20–TUESDAY, 21 MAY 1940 Claude and Françoise at the house, telling me they are going to consult Baume[6] tomorrow. In that case, I said, I will have Mother and the children return from La Bouffource. I phoned Germaine accordingly.

WEDNESDAY, 22 MAY 1940 Claude called to tell me Baume thinks his wife and children should come back. I told him to get everything ready for our departure to Le Très-Clos.[7]

THURSDAY TO SATURDAY, 23–25 MAY 1940 Telegram from Jeanne saying she is sending Magna back from Le Havre because of the bombings.[8]

---

4. "The Nazi Army on the Western Front broke through at Sedan, crossed the Meuse River, and started the drive that ended in the defeat of France. In command of the Ninth French army protecting the Meuse was General André Georges Corap. Six days after the break-through Premier Paul Reynaud took to the air [and] told the French Senate of the Meuse disaster, which he blamed on 'the total disorganization of the Corap Army.'" *Time,* 21 April 1941. [TF]

5. Alexis Léger (aka Saint-John Perse), an anti-Nazi, was general secretary of the French Foreign Office until he was dismissed by Paul Baudouin, undersecretary of state for the council presidency as of 30 March 1940. [TF]

6. Baume: Swiss manager at Lyonnaise des Eaux, where Claude Rist directed the lab. According to Antoinette, the daughter of Claude and Françoise, the primary place where her mother would hide out was at the Baumes', "some distance from us, in Chatou." Françoise would go there "sometimes at night, without a light on her bike, in black streets." Email to translator, 8 December 2010. [JNJ/TF]

7. Le Très-Clos: property of the Rist family in Haute-Savoie near Évian. The house was built in 1932 using Charles Rist's own design.

8. Olga Monod-Herzen, known as "Magna": mother of Charles Rist's wife, Germaine. [TF]

We decided to let her come and then to send her on immediately to Évian by train. She will be accompanied by Eva. On Friday Noël left, taking Isabelle and Mario's wife, Lolli, as well as the Polish cook and her little girl. The Claudes called to tell us they will start for Le Très-Clos on Sunday.

MONDAY 27 MAY–MONDAY 3 JUNE 1940 The week of Dunkirk. The Blockade Committee once again took up the question of oil. I wrote the report for the minister. Saw Charles-Roux, Léger's successor at the Quai d'Orsay – convinced that Italy will enter the war.

Mario leaves his camp nearly every day to see us.

TUESDAY, 4 JUNE 1940 Meeting about oil presided over by Herriot, president of the Chamber of Deputies!

WEDNESDAY, 5 JUNE 1940 Saw Bullitt and asked him to stop oil shipments to Italy. He told me that the new offensive against Paris had begun. Impossible to see Mario, who has to stay in camp.

THURSDAY, 6 JUNE 1940 Called and cabled Lolli not to return to Versailles. This evening went to the Béléba camp to see Mario briefly. He has not slept for three nights.

SATURDAY, 8 JUNE 1940 The minister had someone phone me; when I saw him, he said the Blockade Committee would be discontinued. I told him I would leave the next day to rejoin him in Langeais. In the evening we went to see Mario in his camp. He is in the process of relocating his men to Jouy-en-Josas. How long before we see him again?

SUNDAY, 9 JUNE 1940 Packed this morning. Waited to leave until Noël got back from Paris. No orders have been given at the Pasteur Institute, where he works. Left at 1:30. Arrived in Langeais at the Family Hotel, where we had a room reserved. Ran into Philippe Monod[9] in the evening. The other members of the Blockade Committee are arriving this evening or tonight. General chaos.

MONDAY, 10 JUNE 1940 Returned from the foreign affairs ministry. In the evening we learned by radio that Italy has entered the war. There is

9. Philippe Monod: minister plenipotentiary of France.

nothing more to be done for the blockade. The German advance on Paris is intensifying from the right and from the left.

TUESDAY, 11 JUNE 1940 I went to see the minister after lunch. I explained that there is nothing more to be done for the blockade and told him I wanted to go to Le Très-Clos for a few days to see if there is anything that needs doing there. He agreed. We left at four o'clock, taking along Jullien,[10] whom we dropped off in Tours. Spent the night in Bourges. Air alert. Ran into Mme Zuckerkandl.[11]

WEDNESDAY, 12 JUNE 1940 Arrived at Le Très-Clos around five o'clock after a flat tire and constant stops to show our papers. Astonishment of everyone at Le Très-Clos.

THURSDAY, 13 JUNE 1940 Saw Widmann,[12] who tells me a German division may land in Haute-Savoie using hydroplanes. Twenty sailors have been summoned! Just in case, I went to the sub-prefect to obtain safe-conduct passes for everyone. He proposes to put an inspector at my disposal who will take care of everything.

FRIDAY, 14 JUNE 1940 The matter of the safe-conduct passes was easily arranged. We have discussed what each of us must do now. Stay? Leave? This evening we learned that the Germans have occupied Paris. We know nothing of Léonard, surely cut off from everyone. Nothing from Noël, Claude, or Mario. We suppose the first two are evacuees, the last, in retreat south of Paris.

SUNDAY, 16 JUNE 1940 Set off again for Firminy – saw Jean this evening – we had dinner with him at the Pertuiset. Crowds of workers from Givors, Rive-de-Gier, and Saint-Étienne. Jean is very worried. No orders in case the enemy arrives. Uncertainty and incompetence all around. His children are in Le Chambon with Jeannette. As for Jean, he is clear-sighted and straightforward. After dinner we listened to the radio. There has been a change of ministers. Pétain is replacing Reynaud. Noël sent a telegram saying he is in Cholet.

---

10. Armand Jullien: assistant manager of the Banque de Paris et des Pays-Bas.

11. Mme Zuckerkandl: widow of a Viennese jurist and a friend of Charles Rist.

12. Marcel Widmann: forestry inspector in Thonon, Haute-Savoie, and friend of Noël Rist.

MONDAY, 17 JUNE 1940 We left for Vichy via Thiers. Roads packed with refugees. In Vichy saw bankers Bellet and Planque, as well as Bouthillier.[13] The military's general staff, having arrived two days earlier, are already preparing to set off again. Telegram from Claude saying he is in Châteauroux. Vichy is a gridlock of cars, a cacophony of horns. It is already hard to find gasoline. On the radio the speech of a disheartened Pétain announcing the request for an armistice. No explanation of the change in ministers. The papers have announced the resignation of Jeanneney and Herriot – the last vestiges of the parliamentary system.[14] After consulting with Bellet, seeing that I have nothing to do and no service to render the Ottoman Bank, I decided to leave with Germaine and return to Le Très-Clos. I had intended to go from Vichy to Bordeaux.[15] But I do not know anyone in the new ministry. This would be a useless trip, and meanwhile the roads to Le Très-Clos would doubtless be cut off. What would our sons, from whom we have been separated, say if I were to leave their wives to fend for themselves? We went back using side roads in order to avoid the lines of refugees. We were not sure we would find gasoline and had only thirty liters. Durand[16] made a wrong turn, so we ended up going through Roanne. Luckily, at the big bridge over the Loire, we found all the gasoline we needed. We flew through the night and arrived at Jean's at ten o'clock. Good conversation with him – we are all overwhelmed by the catastrophe.

TUESDAY, 18 JUNE 1940 We left at 8:30, happily with gasoline. After Rive-de-Gier, lines of cars filled with refugees. They say that Lyon has been taken – people are abandoning the city en masse. In Vienne, huge traffic jam before the bridge, on the bridge, and after the bridge. Lines of army trucks. Finally, on our way out of Vienne we took the road that leads to Saint-Genis, and from there on to Seyssel, leaving the congestion behind. Some soldiers with nice manners, evidently part of the Alps army. Very few officers. The soldiers say they have no orders. Stopped for lunch at La Tour-du-Pin. Many soldiers. We were held up so long in Vienne that I feared the roads would be cut off beyond Seyssel. The bridges have been mined, but there are so few soldiers they could hardly have been defended. Everywhere, entering and

13. Yves Bouthillier had just been appointed as Pétain's finance minister. [TF]

14. Jules Jeanneney: president of the Senate; Édouard Herriot: president of the Chamber of Deputies. The news of their resignation was false. [JNJ/TF]

15. The French government was in Bordeaux until 1 July 1940, when it moved to Vichy. [TF]

16. Durand: Charles Rist's chauffeur.

leaving the towns, there are tie-ups. At last Bellegarde. The Fort-l'Écluse road is being mined, so it was blocked. We detoured to Frangy and Saint-Julien. In spite of our fears, we got through with no problems. From Annemasse on, things smoothed out once again. The people are calm. We no longer see the cars or the cyclists with suitcases on their backs rushing headlong to reach the Rhône valley. They say the Germans have reached the Jura. Many automobiles are coming from Ain. Chaos and uncertainty everywhere. No discipline anywhere. We arrived at Le Très-Clos around five o'clock. They were anxiously awaiting us.

Still no word from our sons.

WEDNESDAY, 19 JUNE 1940 Last night I heard on the radio the courageous and moving appeal of General de Gaulle, who is giving us back hope and trust.[17]

TUESDAY, 18–SATURDAY, 22 JUNE 1940[18] Hanging on every word of radio news concerning the request for an armistice. The only news of interest comes from Switzerland and London. We are kept in the dark about Bordeaux. One gets lost in conjectures about the character of the new government. Is it just a government for negotiating – or are we also being steered in a new direction? The latter case is becoming increasingly evident. Everything favorable to England is being jettisoned. Pitiful speech by Pétain in which he cast blame on the weak birth rate and the desire for leisure. Reynaud, more to the point, had denounced the military errors. Our sole hope now is English energy and the growing shift in American opinion toward war. But, meanwhile, what suffering, privation, and humiliation!

How will I manage to get work somewhere? One must wait and see what comes after the armistice.

SUNDAY, 23 JUNE 1940 The radio brought news during lunch that the armistice has been concluded with Italy. Thus the armistice with Germany will now enter into effect. And therefore very probably this region will be occupied, whether by Germans or Italians, with many dangers for Lolli and Françoise[19] and the impossibility for me to do anything. I decided at least to

---

17. For a discussion of the apparent insertion of this entry after Rist's death, see "A Note from the Translator." [TF]

18. The date has been corrected from "Wednesday, 19–Saturday, 22 June," in accordance with the original manuscript. [TF]

19. Lolli was stateless; Françoise, Jewish. [TF]

spend a few days in Switzerland, if only to see Ambassador Coulondre and make up my mind. We packed our things and took everyone with us. I do not want my sons to reproach me later for having left their wives alone.

Passage to Saint-Gingolph, facilitated by the police inspector. The Swiss on the other side, especially the soldiers, greeted us with concern (I must say even with compassion). They are as shattered as we and feel, as we do, the moral calamity for all concerned. The conditions of the armistice are as infuriating to them as they are to us. We left Saint-Gingolph around seven in the evening. Everything went fine as far as Montreux. Françoise drove ahead of us with Lolli and two of the children in her car. At La Tour-de-Peilz we heard some cries. I looked out of the window and noticed Françoise's car moving slowly, and in front of her wheels, a young woman on the ground. I got out of the car. People were already gathering around. Luckily, Françoise's car stopped. It was pushed back. The young woman was bleeding but had not lost consciousness. She had been riding a bicycle. Her fiancé was next to her. Names were taken. Gendarmes were called to make a report; also an ambulance. La Tour's justice of the peace arrived and took preliminary statements. A Swiss major peremptorily declared that Françoise was going too fast. But a good man who was following behind us declared that on the contrary we were going too slowly. The truth is that the woman's bicycle got caught in the rail of the tramway, she raised her arms, let go of the handlebars, and fell. Françoise, frightened, did not stop immediately, and that is how her car hit the young woman, a nurse at the canton's hospital.[20]

At last we moved on. We decided to spend the night at Vevey. The justice of the peace accompanied us to the Hôtel d'Angleterre and asked the owner to give us reasonable accommodations. He took fifty Swiss francs for everyone – which, at the exchange rate, represented more than one thousand French francs.

MONDAY, 24 JUNE 1940 We went with Françoise to Lausanne. While Germaine and Françoise stopped by the hospital for the latest news (luckily, the young woman is doing well; no fever, and simple dislocation of her hip, quickly put back in place), I called Coulondre, who told me to "come as soon as possible." I departed for the French embassy in Bern. Ambassador Coulondre had just lunched with Rodenbach, de Menthon,[21] and a professor

20. According to Françoise's daughter Isabelle, Françoise had taken driving lessons while the family was at Le Très-Clos, and this incident was the first and last time she would ever drive a car. [TF]

21. This must be François de Menthon, law professor and French minister of justice after the Liberation.

from the Catholic University of Fribourg. Coulondre quickly took me aside. He was extremely worried. The naval clauses of the armistice (of which he does not yet know the text) seem monstrous to him. He is thinking of resigning if they are in fact what he believes them to be. He regrets that the dissident French government has settled in London. He would like to see it set up in Algeria, a French territory. He suspects, as I do, that Pétain's entourage has taken him over and is contemplating a total change of policy. He said he wants to stay in touch with me. To be able to act, he thinks, one is best outside France. He observed that the Swiss government is leaning more and more toward acceding to German pressure on all its borders. The Fribourg professor shared his information on the German campaign and German plans regarding England. He cited examples of the Germans' meticulous preparation – a dress rehearsal for the taking of Liège, heat-producing bombs creating such temperatures inside the forts that the guns could no longer fire. Plans regarding England are apparently just as precise and complete: simultaneous air attacks on Scotland from Norway, on the east coast from Holland, on the south coast from France, and on the west coast from Ireland; troop landings from planes capable of transporting fifty to a hundred men and light-tank carriers; reliance on England's not knowing where to deploy her troops when confronted with these attacks on all sides at once. At that point the attack on Gibraltar will begin, and once Gibraltar is taken, the Italian fleet will enter the Atlantic. Such are the plans.

I returned to Vevey. Everyone wanted to go back to Le Très-Clos. This stay at the hotel has been extremely painful. It is awful to feel we are "refugees."

WEDNESDAY, 26 JUNE 1940 I left for Aigle to ask for a pass to enter the military zone of Saint-Gingolph. Lieutenant Delachaux, who gave me the pass, asked if I were related to the economist! He was kinder than I can say and asked if the Swiss had received us well. I told him we would never forget the friendship they have shown us. Returned to Vevey. I stopped by Gerhardt's to ask that he mediate the situation with the injured woman and gave him full power to arrange everything. The newspapers have published the complete text of the two armistices (still not available in France!). Dreadful. We learned that Haute-Savoie is not occupied. Le Très-Clos remains one of the only safe places.

We left at 1:30 in three cars, one of which is rented. No problems. In Saint-Gingolph the Swiss soldiers told us that an attacking Italian division had been wiped out by French troops. At 3:00 we arrived at Le Très-Clos!

We were "home." For how long? And how shall we organize our lives? Above all, when will we receive news of our sons? At least, knowing we are here, they will not worry about their wives. Where is Eva, no doubt trapped in the occupied zone? How will she get news of Léonard? Where is he now? Prisoner? Or wounded? Where is Mario, whom Lolli thinks must have retreated to Brittany? Did he fight? Or has he been taken prisoner? The Red Cross in Geneva writes to us that the lists of prisoners received from Berlin do not contain the names of our sons. The *Tribune de Lausanne* has published a map of the occupied zone. Firminy does not seem to be included. Thus it seems Jean will not be forced to work for the enemy.

On the radio this evening we were given a summary of the declarations of Baudouin, who, by the most brazen of intrigues, has become minister of foreign affairs. Sickening language. He spoke of our "disagreements" with Italy. Not a word of courage or of protest. The radio also announced an attempt by the Japanese to claim Indochina from us. We heard according to an article in the *Times* of London, the two old generals Pétain and Weygand have been manipulated by the most unbelievable intrigues of a clique whose "influence will continue to increase, however improbable this may seem." We already knew that Laval is vice president of the Council!

THURSDAY, 27 JUNE 1940 A visit this afternoon from the Widmanns. Like us, they cannot understand the attitude in Bordeaux. We exchanged news, saying that the generals commanding the colonies, especially Mittelhauser in Syria, are about to disobey the orders from Bordeaux. We clung to the hopes conveyed by radio as we listened to broadcasts from Switzerland and London. But by evening the BBC's program was heavily scrambled; we will have a hard time hearing it from now on. However, this evening we heard de Gaulle's appeal to the navy not to surrender the fleet.

During the day, I talked to a peasant from Verlagny whose three sons are on the front lines. He said to me, "We've been badly governed. How do you expect things to go well when government 'employees' have been given the moon? Isn't it disgusting? Teachers earning ten thousand francs for doing nothing? In the old days, a nun would teach school for four hundred francs a year."[22]

I replied, "Well, now, that's not what lost us the war."

"True," he said.

22. The institution of public schools and the training of teachers were viewed as propaganda tools of the Third Republic. [TF]

FRIDAY, 28 JUNE 1940 We have learned that Spain is claiming Oran from us and that the Japanese are going to send their navy and troops to back up their claims in Indochina. The whole empire is collapsing. It has been reported that Mittelhauser will disarm our Syrian troops! And so the last hopes of resistance are collapsing.

Visit from the Bernards in the afternoon. They want to believe in a feint on the part of the Bordeaux government. I set them straight. From here on out we are going to witness an attempt to cut France in two: those who are for England, and the partisans of Germany. That will be the great conflict – and France once again torn apart! In the United States Willkie has been nominated as the Republican candidate. He is an ardent supporter of the Allies. How sorry I am not to have seen him when I was in New York as Mrs. Page had arranged for me to do. Now we see the United States rejecting the awful isolationism of the Lindberghs and Hoovers. Is it not too late? We are about to witness a magnificent effort by England, the struggle of the Anglo-Saxon world with that of the Germans. Prodigious spectacle – of which we shall be momentary victims, but beneficiaries if the Anglo-Saxons triumph! One must cling resolutely and steadfastly to this hope.

After dinner we spent the evening reading together in order to escape for a moment from this nightmare. Dard's book on Talleyrand.

Telegram from Noël telling us he is in Sainte-Foy-la-Grande! The telegram took two days to arrive. Where are the others? What are they doing? How are they being treated? What they are thinking, we can easily guess. But what they are suffering?

We hear of the occupation of Bukovina and Bessarabia by the Russians – prelude to what?

Balbo killed in a plane crash. Suicide? Assassination? On the radio the English say there were no English planes engaged in battle when his went down.[23]

TUESDAY, 2 JULY 1940 The day before yesterday, a telegram from Mario in Garlix (Basses-Pyrénées) saying he will soon be demobilized. The previous evening, a letter from him had arrived from Limoges. Great relief to us all! Still no word from Léonard. Yesterday I sent a letter to Jay via Coulondre and one to the president of the Bank for International Settlements via Rodenbach.

---

23. Italo Balbo was heir apparent to Mussolini. [TF]

Demoralized letter from poor Herberts in Pamiers, to which his unit has retreated. This morning I got a letter saying he is in Dun (Ariège)!

Postal communication seems to be picking up. Correspondence with Switzerland is once again possible. Still no word from Jean. It seems the Germans are still in the Loire region, from which, however, they will presumably withdraw. We can still clearly hear radio broadcasts from England and Switzerland. Speech by Chamberlain saying that the English are united, contrary to what the Germans are reporting. What the French fleet will do is still a mystery. Paris radio puts all blame on the English. How easy it will be, as restrictions become more onerous (ration stamps for everything already, and no more gasoline), to make people in this country believe that their suffering is a result of the continuing war with the English!

The great air attack on England is clearly under way. Jersey and Guernsey have been occupied by the German air force. Will the Americans supply planes in time? To think that no one had suspected the extent of German preparations. Enormous responsibility on the part of those charged with monitoring them, in England as well as in France.

There is nothing to do but wait, and while waiting, work.

Word has it that the government will relocate to Vichy. But what is the government? What does it want? What does it believe? People are even talking about a reconvening of the legislative chambers. What freedom will they have? Is this a military government? Or a right-wing Croix-de-Feu government? A government of retaliation? Or a government of national union? We have stored up so much hatred over the past ten years, urged on by an irresponsible press. . . .

Russian enigma! They have announced a general arms buildup. Against whom?

We must expect universal ruin after this war.

THURSDAY, 4 JULY 1940 We stopped briefly at the Widmanns' yesterday and talked about Noël. Like us, they are waiting for news of their loved ones, scattered here and there. We discussed the reconvening of the chambers. Under whose control will they be? We suspect there was a sort of coup d'état in Bordeaux before the fall of Reynaud. By whom? And how?

What is appalling about this situation is the incredible swiftness with which it came about. From one day to the next, we have had to pass from the utmost faith in an invincible resistance to the deepest abyss of defeat. It is still hard to accept the reality. This could only have resulted from an incredible failure of leadership.

Last night the radio informed us that the new constitution must duly authorize the government and that the focus will be on protecting family, work, and fatherland. These are lovely words that we have often heard – and we know too well what they conceal. There is no end to internal politics!

An article in the *Petit Dauphinois* explains that in reality no one has ever understood why the war broke out. That is the drama of this war. Ordinary people knew why they were fighting. Others claim ignorance.

Mme Widmann read us a letter from her mother, who writes that fifth-column espionage and trickery have been marvelously successful in the Nord.[24] Her witness is a perfectly calm, balanced man. Fake telephone calls, German officers disguised as French officers, etc., etc. It is said that General D. was taken prisoner at the Valenciennes station, already in German hands, as he arrived by train with his staff. No one had warned him! Who had so demoralized France?

One must find one's way amid all the false news that reaches us by radio and the newspapers. In the end, the success or failure of England and the United States will decide the "truth."

Began reading aloud Chateaubriand's *Napoléon* yesterday. Parallels with today.

FRIDAY, 5 JULY 1940 Radio announcement yesterday of the destruction of French ships at Mers el-Kébir by Admiral Somerville's English fleet.[25] The operation must have taken place on Thursday, and Churchill has given the reasons for it in the House of Commons. Nothing so clearly demonstrates England's tragic situation and her decision to use every means possible to keep her dominance of the seas while waiting to have air superiority. The consequences will be grave for Anglo-French relations, as well as, perhaps, for relations with Germany and Italy – if the latter wish to retaliate. Here we can only wait . . . and hope. Still no news of Claude, nor of Jean, nor of Léonard. Nothing from Noël, who must have received neither our letters nor our telegrams.

England's action recalls the shelling of Copenhagen in 1807.[26] Similar circumstances, similar means. But the men? Are they the same?

24. The Nord is a northern French department bordering Belgium. [TF]

25. The port of Mers el-Kébir is just 7 kilometers to the west of Oran in northwestern Algeria. [TF]

26. During the summer of 1807, Britain's foreign secretary, George Canning, may have feared that neutral Denmark would go over to the French side and put its fleet at Napoleon's disposal. As the Danish government refused to ally itself with England,

TUESDAY, 9 JULY 1940 England's action at Oran has shocked everyone. France has decided to break off diplomatic relations. Are we heading toward the horror that war with our allies would be? In the end, will our fate depend upon this colossal struggle between Berlin and London, for which London is so badly prepared? How much more excusable the English would be for their brutality against France if they had encountered and beaten some German and Italian battleships! On the radio yesterday de Gaulle was quite frank. But up to now they have only been successful against merchant ships. Their unwillingness to take the offensive is almost pathological. Their ignorance and miscalculation of their enemy's spirit are tragic. The only excuse for the Oran affair is that they feel caught by the throat and want to keep "ruling the seas." Yet they continue limiting themselves to a statistical superiority, instead of demonstrating it by fighting. Every day they announce successes of the Royal Air Force. But no extension of the action to Italy has occurred. Do they have no idea of the resources that Germany can bring to bear against them? Or what a dangerous base Ireland may prove to be? Is America providing them with substantive backup? One can only answer these questions with hope and a kind of mystic faith.

Letter from Noël, who received our telegram – and says he will try to come here if he can find transportation. Nothing from the others. Via the Bovets, who came here on Sunday, I have written Leffingwell of the Morgan Bank in New York asking him to intervene on behalf of Léonard. Also wrote the American president of the Bank for International Settlements.

The first task of the government should be the reestablishment of postal and wire services. They are worse than ever. Except for Switzerland, from which letters arrive in two days, it takes six days and more to get a reply. Jean told us *a week ago* to expect some letters from Mario. We have yet to receive any. The administrative incompetence of this country is past all imagining. The cause of our failures is right there.

According to the papers, the Germans left Lyon and Aix-les-Bains the day before yesterday.

Wrote to Thuillier[27] in Toulouse yesterday asking for news of Claude. Maurice Bernard came by and told me he had received a letter from his accountant in Ruffec, which is in the *occupied* zone!

Copenhagen was bombarded on 2 September and capitulated on the fifth. Some of the Danish ships were destroyed; the rest were seized. [JNJ/TF]

27. Joseph Thuillier: manager with the Société Lyonnaise des Eaux.

TUESDAY, 9–FRIDAY, 12 JULY 1940 We now have letters or telegrams from all our children – except Léonard. Claude in an old château in Dordogne, near Les Eyzies. Mario in the Basses-Pyrénées. Noël on his way here. (Got here Thursday by car after having stayed overnight in Cahors with Father Sol, in Firminy at Jean's, and at Aix-les Bains at the de Lacroix's.)

On Thursday M. Hillaert, a Belgian sugar producer from the Oise, partner in the Béguins' paper manufacturing firm – encountered by chance at Bouchet's garage – called to say he is leaving for Vichy and proposed I take advantage of his gasoline and go too. At the same time, I received a telegram from Bellet saying there is talk of relocating the banks to Paris and suggesting in reply to my letter that I go to Vichy.

Four

Vichy and the "French State": Beginnings

12 JULY–29 SEPTEMBER 1940

After briefly relocating to Tours and then Bordeaux, the French capital moved to Vichy on 1 July 1940. Nine days later the National Assembly granted full powers to Marshal Pétain, under whose command the French Republic was renamed the French State.

Rist made three trips to Vichy for consultations with representatives of the companies and banks on whose boards he served: one in July, one in August, and another in September. While there he also conferred with U.S. embassy officials; the Turkish ambassador; Jules Jeanneney (president of the French Senate under the Republic); and François Charles-Roux, general secretary of foreign affairs.

On these trips Rist also paid visits to son Jean and his children, who lived about 100 kilometers southeast of Vichy in Fraisses, near Saint-Étienne.

FRIDAY, 12 JULY 1940 Left for Vichy. We took Noël with us and dropped him off in Annecy, where he will request orders to return to Paris.

We traveled from Annecy to Lyon by way of La Chambotte, where we saw a small German cemetery, freshly made, very neat. There had been a battle there recently. Sign on a cross: "Gefallen für Deutschland."

Quick lunch in Lyon. Fabre-Luce, having come from Vichy, approached me. He said he had thought of me during the vote by the National Assembly[1] and thought to himself that I would no doubt have been among the eighty who voted no. He told me that Marcel Déat has been given the task of forming a "single state party." Already! – the abject imitation of totalitarian methods. The same people who seized power in the night and in defeat are preparing to bind up the country so tightly it will be helpless when it awakens.

---

1. Rist is referring to the vote of 10 July giving full powers to Marshal Pétain and putting an end to the Third Republic. [TF]

We arrived in Vichy around five in the afternoon. Discussed with Bellet and Bouthillier the possible move of the Ottoman Bank to Paris. I am against any transfers before having all guarantees and assurances that connections with London and Istanbul will be possible (and no one will touch our stocks and shares). Besides, the atmosphere has changed. The Germans have created all sorts of problems, and the Ministry of the Interior has announced that departures for the occupied zone have been suspended. The return of the government to Versailles and Paris – proclaimed by Pétain immediately after the vote by the National Assembly naming him head of state – has been postponed *sine die*. A grave turn of events!

During the evening the new cabinet was announced. More or less the same names as before. Rivaud, after a short stint at National Education, has been replaced by Mireaux of *Le Temps*. I have been told that Rivaud showed too much concern over the Nazis' increasingly active propaganda in the north of France (regarding a scheme to unite France's northern departments with Flanders). No one at the helm of Ministry of Industry and Labor. Both Peyrecave and Daum, well-regarded industrialists, declined the post. They are falling back on Belin, an extreme pacifist, of the C.G.T. [Confédération Générale des Travailleurs]. What does this former post office worker know about the country's industry and economy? Piétri at communications. Thus a cabinet of partisans, not competencies.

Vichy is full to overflowing with gendarmes and police. The hub is the Hôtel du Parc, serving as the Ministry of Foreign Affairs. All the usual anteroom crowd are there – the beggars, the pro-Munich contingent, those who would have liked to play a role but did not and who now cry loudly that it was they who were right! As if peace could have been safeguarded. An atmosphere heavy with suspicion, bitterness, and suppressed ambition, also fear and worry. Time wasting and laziness in the ministries. Ran into Tirard, Barnaud, Detoeuf, Max Hermant, Mireaux, and Jahan (turned back from the occupied zone when he tried to enter it).

Visited Jeanneney. His wife told me that Noël Monod[2] is gravely ill with typhoid fever, contracted while taking some of the Peugeot personnel to Bordeaux under the most difficult conditions. Jeanneney was calm, serene, perfectly clear-sighted. The old fellow's sense of dignity, along with his beautifully lucid intelligence, is quite moving. This country, he told me, is headed for an acute crisis of antimilitarism. I gave him some examples of incompetence. "There are hundreds like that," he said. He told me how the

---

2. Noël Monod: executive with Peugeot and a distant cousin of Germaine Rist; his sister married Jean-Marcel Jeanneney, Jules Jeanneney's only son.

passage from Reynaud to Pétain came about. A simple majority vote. Then the business of the *Massilia*.[3] He asked me to visit him again.[4]

Back at the hotel, luckily ran into Michel Carsow, who promised to provide me with gasoline. Our return is assured!

Came across Captain Samson. "It's not easy," he said, "for our sailors to accept defeat when they've always been victorious." He gave me Moysset's address and added, "Our poor army, it's even worse than we thought."

SUNDAY, 14 JULY 1940 Long conversation with Moysset. He does not defend the members of Parliament. He criticizes England for having put us in the hands of the Polish. The business in Oran – "a shot of whiskey for Churchill." He thinks Schacht will return when it comes time to discuss the economic terms of the peace treaty.

In the evening, visit to Charles-Roux. Morand has assured continuing communications with England. Certain members of the cabinet were pushing for a break in diplomatic relations, but the rupture almost went beyond that. He is struck by the menacing tone of German and Italian radio toward the new French regime. I told him that a definitive rupture with England would force the United States to side against us. There are some who want us to believe that the Americans are distancing themselves from England in order to draw closer to us! Marlio has been sent on a mission to the United States. He told the government, "I'm not asking you for anything, just the right to export my money." (!!!) The finance ministry refused. The aim of the mission is supposedly to explain our situation and to obtain American aid for the reconstruction of France. I told those who spoke to me about it that this is all pie in the sky. The position of the United States is unshakable. (Yesterday Roosevelt was selected by acclamation as the Democratic candidate, with a platform of aid to England.)

Returned Monday in dreadful weather. My traveling companion was as impressed as I by the chaos, the inefficiency, the lack of men. Relieved to leave Vichy for Évian.

---

3. On 21 June the *Massilia* sailed for North Africa with some thirty members of Parliament – Daladier, Mendès France, Yvon Delbos, Jean Zay, etc. They left with the approval of Pétain, Laval, Darlan, and the presidents of the Senate and the Chamber, with the initial intention of continuing the struggle from Algeria. As events in France took a different turn, the new rulers unleashed a campaign against the supposed "runaways" on board the *Massilia*.

4. Jules Jeanneney, in his *Journal politique, septembre 1939–juillet 1942* (ed. Jean-Noël Jeanneney and Armand Colin, 1972, 107) has only this to say about the visit: "Charles Rist, resolute."

In Vichy everyone is skeptical about the possibility of England's defending herself against a well-managed attack. This is the logical position for people who throw themselves at the feet of their conquerors. As Auboin says (having arrived at Le Très-Clos on Sunday in my absence), "The defeat of England would be the only justification for these people." That they should hope for it is not surprising.

FRIDAY, 19 JULY 1940 Yesterday I went to Thollon with Noël to order 6 cubic meters of firewood for this winter. Current price eight hundred francs, delivered. Stopped to pay the Bernards a visit on the way back.

At last heard news of Léonard from Eva! He is in Saint-Lô, having disembarked at Cherbourg after some tough combat. Taken prisoner *after* the armistice. We hope he can be liberated.

SUNDAY, 21 JULY 1940 The de Lacroix paid us a visit today. Like me, de Lacroix is dumbfounded by the ignorance and negligence that have characterized the conduct of the war. Anecdotes and facts of all kinds point up the indifference and lack of foresight. Deep humiliation to think of the judgment the world will pass on this event. The very same people who demonstrated their incompetence as military professionals are now at the helm of our civil administration, about which they know nothing! The worst is that the old disputes persist. Everyone feels betrayed, some by the communists, others by those on the right. Many today certainly take comfort in knowing that "their ideas (!?) are in power." But what ideas did the party in power have? And how did it defend them?

FRIDAY, 26 JULY 1940 Claude arrived on Wednesday! He had to leave his car along the way for lack of gasoline. He has moved into the cabin[5] with his wife. But they must prepare for a return to Le Vésinet right away. Noël must leave, too. What we know about the occupied zone (especially according to English radio, which dramatizes the situation) does not reassure us. Édouard wrote from Paris, giving us Léonard's address.

Three days ago Marquet, minister of the interior, gave a speech on the radio. We must not, he said, blame either soldiers or civilians. "The cause is the worm-eaten state of a liberal and parliamentary capitalist system." (!) Judgments and sanctions were announced against those who pushed for war. Such stupidities will gradually poison the public. This former dentist was treating us to his social and political philosophy. Two days later German

---

5. This was a one-room cabin near Le Très-Clos overlooking Lake Geneva. [TF]

radio insulted him – because in his speech he made a timid appeal for German authorities to cooperate in returning refugees to France.

In a letter from his sister Jacqueline we learned that Alexandre Parodi[6] is very worried about a presumed German plan to set up a new government in the occupied zone with people even more submissive to German authority than those in Vichy.

London radio broadcast General Alexander's speech to the House of Commons announcing that the *Meknès,* bringing twelve hundred French sailors home to France, was hit by a German torpedo boat. They say a thousand men were saved by the English. This morning not a word on the subject in the *Petit Dauphinois.* Horrible drama, a prelude to others; the French people will know nothing about it. Two days later, French radio simply stated that the government had not been warned of the departure (a lie).

The Americans are sending arms to England at an accelerated pace. Hearst[7] announced that the United States will be at war "somewhere, against someone" within six months.

I have written to Jay, Meynial, and Deroy[8] asking them to do what they can to free Léonard, as necessary for the economic well-being of the country.

SUNDAY, 28 JULY 1940   Noël left this morning. We went with him to the bus stop at 7:00. We have burdened him with many questions that he will have to answer. Above all, what is the state of our villa Amiel?[9] We learned only three days ago that it had been searched, the wine drunk, and the drawers turned inside out. And the other villa, the one destined for Mario and Lolli?

At ten we learn that the train that was to transport refugees to Annecy tomorrow has been canceled, along with all other refugee departures! Noël phoned to say he will leave tomorrow for Lyon, just in case. These openings and closings of the occupied zone, what is behind them? Harassment? A means of putting pressure on the Wiesbaden Commission? Who knows? What will people say later when we tell them it took eight days to go from Évian to Paris?

---

6. Alexandre Parodi: Council of State attorney, former managing director for Labor, and future chief representative of the provisional government of occupied France in 1944.

7. Presumably, Rist is referring to William Randolph Hearst. [TF]

8. Jay and Meynial of the Morgan Bank in Paris; Henri Deroy, general secretary for public finance. [JNJ/TF]

9. Amiel: the house where Charles Rist and his family lived in Versailles; it belonged to his mother-in-law, Olga Monod, née Herzen, who lived with them.

The English have announced that the Germans are organizing Brittany as an autonomous country whose political relations with France and Germany will be worked out later (?). A response no doubt to Maurras's campaign demanding the dismemberment of Germany. Why is it that we have so often provided the political model *not* to follow? The Germans want to give us an ad hominem lesson.

De Lacroix was saying to me just the other day, "The only attitude worthy of a government in our situation is silence." Why is ours talking so much?

The newspaper campaign against the English is gradually having an effect. We are all deeply sickened by the Battle of Oran. Around us, all the peasants are repeating what they read in the *Petit Dauphinois*. A few months from now, common sense will prevail once again, because people will prefer anything to the invader. But in the meantime! Yet everyone knows that salvation can come only with an English victory. Contradictions and confusions! That is exactly what the enemy wants.

Daily anxiety as we await the expected German attack on England. The fate of Europe depends on the outcome! And we wait like spectators who have no role in the drama unfolding on the stage.

Who knows, after all, if the end result will not be a solid Anglo-German entente – at the expense of France? On that day it will be Italy, no longer France, that will rank number one among the second-rate powers. This country is its own undoing.

TUESDAY, 30 JULY 1940 The trials of Paul Reynaud and Daladier have been announced (on English radio, as French radio is silent on the subject). This kind of vengeance is appalling. Paul Reynaud will apparently be jailed in Vichy.

When the history of the last twenty years is written, I think England will be severely judged. We can scarcely be proud of ourselves. But that the English, by their blindness and incredible arrogance, have allowed things to come to this life-and-death struggle between them and the Germans, that is one of those mistakes the future will not forgive, whatever the outcome of the struggle.

I have learned by means of a letter from Lemaître that ISRES[10] has been saved. We can thus return to work. That will hasten my return to Paris.

---

10. ISRES: Scientific Institute of Economic and Social Research, founded by Charles Rist in Paris; Henri Lemaître, graduate of the École des Chartes, was the assistant manager.

SATURDAY, 3 AUGUST 1940 No sooner had Claude phoned from Annecy on Tuesday to say they were leaving than we read in the *Petit Dauphinois* that as of 31 July postal communications between the occupied zone and ours have been "temporarily" interrupted; thus we will have no news of our children's arrival. Nor shall we hear anything of Léonard, from whom we have as yet received no replies to our cards and letters! Why these interruptions? Impossible to understand or to learn more. A postal communiqué warns employees who must be repatriated that the Germans will not allow Jews to reenter the occupied zone.

On French radio the day before yesterday a list was read of Jews who had left France between 25 May and 30 June (Jonas, André Meyer, Maurice de Rothschild, etc.). They added that these runaways prefer their Jewish identity to their French one.

A letter from Jay informs me of what he has done on behalf of Léonard. He says he hopes to see me again soon, but adds in English: "*I feel you would be well advised to remain at Lake Geneva and try to store up health for the winter, when we shall have many hardships.*" Warning? Advice? That is what I think.

Yesterday the radio announced that de Gaulle has been given a death sentence in absentia. At the same time, a list of those on the court of justice. I noted that Ripert, dean of the law faculty, was among those named.

If one is to believe the German and Italian communiqués, the attack on England is being postponed. Would it be more difficult than had been supposed? In any case, that means the war will be a long one. Speech in the United States by Secretary of Defense Stimson stating that obligatory military service is the only way to face the danger.

The mayor of Maxilly[11] told me the other day, when I asked where Senator Jacquier and Deputy Bernex were, "One no longer dares to speak."

Changes in the diplomatic postings. Henry-Haye sent to Washington in place of Saint-Quentin, who has been assigned to non-active status. Henry-Haye is going to have problems, given the current state of mind in America! Massigli likewise relieved of duty in Ankara. Personal vendettas and obedience to enemy orders.

SUNDAY, 4 AUGUST 1940 Our grandchildren will find it hard to imagine the atrocious humiliation we are suffering. Comparable only to that expressed by Chateaubriand in his *Napoléon*, when the Allies controlled Paris in 1815. Greater still. Compounded by the shameful degradation of the men

---

11. The Rists' country home, Le Très-Clos, lies within the precincts of Maxilly-sur-Léman, a small village near Lake Geneva. [TF]

responsible (and who took the responsibility upon themselves) for leading France in these tragic circumstances. To convince this country that everything it has believed for the last 150 years, everything upon which its glory is founded, is a colossal error! Humiliation, finally, for those who know the true cause of this dreadful defeat: laziness, complaisance, and arrogance on the part of those who were charged with the country's defense; their criminal ignorance of preparations going on in their own backyard; the same laziness, the same complaisance on all fronts, civilian or military, industrial or agricultural. Complete failure to recognize the new conditions of modern life. Is this a sign of irreversible decadence? Must we truly despair?

WEDNESDAY, 7 AUGUST 1940 Telegram from Mario the day before yesterday telling us that he has been demobilized and will arrive in a few days. First good news in the midst of all this darkness.

Yesterday had a chat with Jacquier – the son of the boat rental owner – back from the front. A frank, intelligent boy. He stayed in the Alps all winter and only suffered from the cold. "Why didn't they send us to the northern front to build fortifications, since nothing could have happened where we were? What a mess! They'd send buses 40 kilometers to pick up four of us! As if we'd have minded walking! Our lieutenant alone smashed up four cars. And these officers – simple postmen in civilian life made lieutenants! For them, it was like living in a castle. That's all they wanted!"

I said, "There are still the English."

The father replied, "And if they're defeated?"

SATURDAY, 10 AUGUST 1940 Mario arrived this morning. In good shape and happy to be here. But it pains him to tell his stories of the retreat. Chaos, negligence. There were trucks, rifles, etc., available. They were just not given to them. The soldiers were using Gras rifles. In Orléans they were given only four hundred trucks of the eight hundred available. The others, left behind, were taken by the enemy. The soldiers were refused gasoline, which was in plentiful supply. The officers were the first to leave.

What is the source of this shamelessness? This general disorganization? Since when? Who tolerated it? Who noticed nothing? Who carried out, or rather did not carry out, the training of reserve officers? And the leadership?

In his *Mémoires d'outre-tombe* Chateaubriand speaks of the shame and humiliation experienced between 1814 and 1815 when the Allies were in Paris. But that was after the extraordinary French campaign. How can that be compared to the shameful debacle our military has made us endure? Even after

1814 the Allies feared France. Today she is bound hand and foot, completely powerless. No one fears her now. Does anyone still respect her?

MONDAY, 26 AUGUST 1940 Last week I spent two days in Vichy. I left here on Monday at 8:30 A M, had to wait five hours in Annecy (which I took advantage of to see the prefect and reserve a room in Lyon), arrived in Lyon at nine in the evening, slept at the Hôtel Terminus, and set off again around 6:00 A M on Tuesday in order to be in Vichy at 11:30. Thirty hours for a trip that normally takes six. Packed trains, passengers standing in the corridors, no light when night fell. On the station platforms (at Aix, one stands around for an hour to change trains) the crowds wait anxiously to rush at arriving trains in order to get a seat. Yet transport is said to be improving! There are few cars and locomotives in the rail yards. In spite of myself, I think of Austria in 1922. Station buffets with no food and salons full of passengers spending the night on chairs and sofas for lack of accommodations.

In Vichy, long conversations with Boissière[12] regarding the chances of having the Ottoman Bank return to Paris. The idea strikes us as absurd. The Germans in Paris are demanding to see all the accounts.

I went to see the Turkish ambassador, Behiç Erkin. Smiling and Oriental. He no longer believes that Greece will defend itself or that Turkey is obliged to come to its aid. He questioned me regarding the United States; I expressed strong optimism.

Lunch with Matthews on Wednesday, as well as the next day, when we were joined by Tyler, the American banker. He shared his impressions of the grim days in Bordeaux. "That's the most horrible two weeks I've ever spent." "We did our best to push for resistance." "Baudouin was among those pushing the hardest for surrender." He was concerned to resupply the free zone and asked me what the essential needs are. I told him gasoline, coal, sugar, and fats. He considered Henry-Haye the best of the three ambassador candidates under consideration. The other two were Georges Bonnet and Chautemps! During the course of Thursday's lunch, Tyler offered us an excellent old Burgundy. I told them, "Leave a little for the American soldiers in 1942!" Matthews retorted, "Why 1942? Much sooner, I hope." Tyler, who accompanied me as far as Lyon that evening, said, "All the American diplomats I've met with these last few weeks are convinced the United States can't stay out of the war."

12. Gustave Boissière: head of the Ottoman Bank in Paris.

On Wednesday morning in nearby Châtelguyon I paid a visit to Gravière at the Banque de France, to Morgan Bank trustees Pesson-Didion and Arragon (spoke of Léonard), and to Chase Bank, where I complained of their attitude and their silence.

Pétain has given an interview to some American journalists in which he declared that France must once again become "agricultural and Christian." The stupidity of these remarks is truly breathtaking. In France Christianity = Catholicism. Does he believe he will please the Germans? And does he believe he will please the French clergy who detest National Socialism?

I saw Homolle,[13] whom Georges-Edgar Bonnet has ordered to stay in the non-occupied zone, the only way to stay in contact with Egypt. He is thinner, deeply sickened by what he has just gone through. "The general staff has lost its head," he told me.

Returned to Évian on Friday evening. From Lyon to here, it took me fifteen hours! Part of the trip standing up. I spoke with a lady, the wife of an officer currently in Syria; she is bringing her five children here from Niort (occupied zone). She said that in Niort everyone is pinning their hopes on the English. A fine woman, energetic and courageous.

SATURDAY, 31 AUGUST 1940 In the current catastrophe the worst thing is that the political beneficiaries of the disaster have a stake in its continuance. In these circumstances the people in power (and those who rejoice to see them there) must hope for the defeat of England and soon that of the United States! For an English victory will spell their downfall. Though this situation is not of their making, and though they do not wish to admit it, they are hoping for the continuation of the German triumph and the subjugation of France. Thus in France there is a faction that favors humiliation and defeat, preferring this shame to a France that is free, but one in which they fear a group of their fellow citizens – the ones they call communists. It is this fear that is at the heart of all the perversion of recent years.

The new French slogan is clear for those who know the history of France: "family" means obedience to the church, "work" means obedience to the boss, "fatherland" means obedience to the military. These fine words, "family," "work," and "fatherland," are smoke screens, and every person in France knows what lies behind their use as a political slogan.

French radio in England up to now would begin its broadcasts with the words "Liberty, Equality, Fraternity." As of two days ago, they have been replaced by "Honor and Fatherland." The Republic has fallen, even in England.

---

13. Michel Homolle: general secretary of the Suez Company at the time; he would be its general director after the war.

That the colonies of Chad and Equatorial Africa have rallied to General de Gaulle is simply owing to the fact of their being surrounded by English territories; they cannot survive without the support of the English. The same for New Caledonia. But the immediate motivations matter little. That is the fact of the matter.

Mme Parodi, who arrived yesterday, tells me that in certain military units there was talk of a *sixth* column!

I have been told that in certain regions of the occupied zone, the invader has reestablished the communist municipalities. The great crime of our country's governments during these last few years is to have encouraged moral confusion by their own lack of conviction. Germany is continuing their work. We must recreate a common ideal that will have to be worked at.

SUNDAY, 8 SEPTEMBER 1940 I have not written for several days because of too many distractions – departure of the chauffeur and the maid; getting back to my book; errands in Évian and Lugrin to fetch mail, butter, or sugar. That's how we spend part of our days. Mario has been busy cutting up the great chestnut tree that collapsed the other day – like the French government – under the weight of too heavy a burden. Likewise the apple tree, thanks to an incredible bounty this year.

Received a visit from the good Widmann and the Auboins, who arrived from Château-d'Oex, but without bringing important news.

I talked to Widmann about military responsibilities. A serious historian of the Third Republic will one day have to focus primarily upon relations between the Republic and the army. Between 1870 and 1894 it was necessary to live with the old Bonapartist, clericalist army. Its hostility erupted with the abscess of the Dreyfus affair. After 1900 an effort was made to republicanize it. Then came 1914, with the triumph of an army that was more and more democratized by the reserve officers and enlisted men. After 1918 nothing more was done except that the corps of career officers once again had the upper hand – covered with its triumphs of 1918. The army was less and less accountable to Parliament; it rested on its laurels, on the general conviction that there would be no war, and on the Maginot Line. How was its spirit altered during this period? Who was giving military orders? What were the political attitudes? No doubt they were strongly tinged with the spirit of Six February![14]

But above all they counted on the reduction of the German army. And then, in 1935, obligatory military service was reinstituted in Germany! This

14. An anti-Parliament riot in Paris, 6 February 1934, was thought to have been inspired by fascism. [TF]

was the great turning point. A first-rate leader would have understood that everything in the army's organization should have been subordinated to this new fact, and that an immense effort was required. There was no one to awaken the dreamers. De Gaulle, who tried to do it, found himself alone. The old routines continued – they were still preparing for the war of 1914. Meanwhile, Germany was innovating; once again, it put its trust in technology, as well as in the unexpected and in new methods. The servility of our press, the cowardice of the Republic's leaders, their lack of interest in military matters, allowed everything to continue as before.

But all that went on in the shadows. We were all still overwhelmed by the memory of 1914–1918. It seemed impossible that one would be forced to contemplate a new and similar slaughter. And in fact the present war is not a slaughter of masses, but a multitude of separate battles in which civilians are the main victims.

Last night we got news of the greatest attack on London so far. This morning the English announced sixty German planes shot down. This is what we have been waiting for.

Here people are rallying more and more to this hope. They are a bit hesitant to speak. But then one notices they are listening to London radio.

There has been an attack on the bridge that joins Annecy to La Roche-sur-Foron and Évian. Total silence in the papers. Naturally, hypotheses are circulating. First hypothesis: the English. But they would have announced the thing on the radio! Since no one but us listens to the radio in English, in any case, everyone believes it. Another hypothesis: some French officers, indignant at the sight of convoys passing through Switzerland on their way to Germany, blew up the bridge. Imbecilic argument, since trains can now again go through Bellegarde, Collonges, Annemasse. But as everyone repeats that their butter is going to Switzerland (where, with the exchange rate, the price is double the official price here), the argument appears patriotic and responds to public sentiment. In my opinion the officers would have done better to blow up the bridges useful to the Germans during the war! A personal hypothesis: thugs looking to create trouble, and possibly paid by the occupying forces! Last suggestion: the Germans may have demanded the right to inspect trains arriving via Bellegarde to Geneva; Switzerland may have refused, preferring to go through Annecy-Évian. Thereupon the Germans may have blown up the bridge over the Fier near Annecy. Of course there is still the Bellegarde-Collonges-Annemasse line. But it is controlled by the Germans, and no merchandise entering this zone can pass on to Chablais, a free zone. This hypothesis is by far the most probable. The Germans did not hesitate to make it impossible for the whole French side of the lake to receive goods from the south. Above all, they act the same in the free zone as in the occupied territory. Of no small significance are the papers' systematic silence and indications that the French railway company has interrupted service and will replace it by buses.

Fournier has been replaced at the Banque de France by Bréart de Boisanger, Bonnet's protégé.

Cabinet reshuffle three days ago. Disappearance of Mireaux, Ybarnégaray, etc. Weygand is also leaving. No doubt he did not want to be responsible for the arrest of Gamelin, who, it was announced this morning, is going to appear along with Reynaud and Daladier before the Riom court! I pity the accusers when the wheel of fortune has turned.

Abdication of King Carol in Romania. I had always predicted he would end badly.

At two o'clock London radio announced eighty-eight German planes shot down over London, four hundred civilians killed, fourteen hundred seriously injured. What will London's response be? What will America do? My American friends always told me that American opinion "would not tolerate a bombardment of London or Paris." We shall see if that is true.

The drama is reaching its climax.

MONDAY, 16 SEPTEMBER 1940 One of my young neighbors tells me that every evening they listen to London radio.

The Banque de Paris has written to express the desire to see me return, and we expect to leave on Friday after all sorts of complicated preparations. We shall travel via Vichy.

Visit on Tuesday from Tyler and Charron. I entrusted Tyler with a spoken message for Morgan and Rockefeller.

SUNDAY, 29 SEPTEMBER 1940 Returned to Versailles with Isabelle, Antoinette, and Marie-Claire on Wednesday morning after a complicated trip during which, having left Le Très-Clos by car on Friday the twentieth and arrived in Vichy that evening, we had to spend four days in Vichy, from which we set off again on Tuesday the twenty-fourth at 10:00 PM.

In Vichy I saw Behiç Erkin, the Turkish ambassador, very confident about the outcome of events in Egypt – then Matthews of the U.S. embassy, more and more convinced of an American intervention and annoyed by Baudouin. The Dakar affair exploded on Monday.[15]

15. This concerns the failed Anglo-Gaullist landing intended to rally French West Africa to the Resistance.

Also saw Jeanneney, who spoke of the growing pro-English sentiment in the country and of the deep divisions between the marshal and his "designated successor." Jeanneney is very alarmed by the prospect of food shortages and cold temperatures in the occupied zone. The new food rationing was introduced as of the nineteenth under direct pressure from the occupiers, who calculate that the conquered country must have rations that are 30 percent less than those of the conquering country.[16]

Saw François Charles-Roux, general secretary of foreign affairs, to whom I spoke energetically about the danger of alienating the United States by a policy of provocation with regard to England. In his office former ambassador Georges-Picot, today mayor of an arrondissement in Paris, told us of the Germans' ruthless plans regarding France – which they themselves had revealed to him – and described as delusional those who think a "reversal of alliances" will result in favorable conditions from the enemy. On Sunday saw Jean, who brought his children to us and told me about his mission to Turin and to Rome.

In Chambéry the pastry cook at the Fidèle Berger, very pro-English, told me people are saying "the triumph of England will mean the return of Freemasonry." Not unlike the Swiss man who said that the victory of France would mean the "victory of communism." To what degree of ignominy have the so-called nationalists and patriots fallen!

Meeting at the Ottoman Bank on Thursday morning. It was decided that I would go to see M. von Falkenhausen, the German civilian commissioner overseeing French banks, in order to point out that, as this is a Turkish bank, it should be placed under the regulations of American, not English, banks. Neuflize[17] seemed quite perturbed that I was insisting on this point. We went there together on Friday at four o'clock. Bellet accompanied us. Falkenhausen appeared to be rather intimidated, very red, and very likeable. He gave us to understand that the situation of the Ottoman Bank could be changed gradually; he said they began with the idea that it is entirely under English influence. I told him that the capital is in French hands, that the branch in

16. Jules Jeanneney, president of the Senate when war broke out, recorded the following in his journal: "Of a much higher quality [than that of Jacques Bardoux] is the language of Charles Rist, with whom I was able to converse at length. . . . One of his sons is a prisoner. The bankruptcy of our military command, the poverty of government ideas, their falsity in economic matters, have naturally not escaped him." *Journal politique*, 24 September 1940, 137–38.

17. Baron Jacques de Neuflize: director of the Protestant bank of the same name and trustee of the Ottoman Bank.

Turkey is dependent on Paris. When we arose to go, Neuflize stayed behind to chat, very *Kamaradschaftlich*. When I brought this to Bellet's attention, he informed me that Neuflize gets along very well with the Germans, who are considering the formation of a big Protestant bank with Neuflize as the president! Decidedly, the H.S.P. [High Protestant Society] is not through discrediting itself. All these partisans of Doriot or of Colonel de la Rocque are ready to grovel at the feet of the conqueror!

I have decided not to read any newspapers. We shall be content with English radio. Last night it announced 150 enemy planes destroyed over England.

All the houses in the neighborhood are occupied. One sees only *Feldgrau*[18] in the streets. No cars except for the Germans'. Twenty-two years ago we were victorious!

Horrible failure of General de Gaulle in Dakar!

Our three granddaughters have been taken back to Le Vésinet by their parents.

It is hard to obtain things one wants and one must stand in line for food. But up to now, no real deprivation; the thing we fear most is the cold.

How long must we wait to see a ray of light?

Constant Schaller[19] came to say he has learned that his son Marco is in a camp at Arès near Bordeaux (after a failed escape attempt).

18. *Feldgrau*: German soldiers. [TF]
19. General Constant Schaller: husband of Charles Rist's sister Gabrielle.

Five

Promulgation of
Anti-Jewish Laws

4 OCTOBER–15 DECEMBER 1940

As Vichy compounded Nazi persecution of the Jews by promulgating its own anti-Jewish laws, the Rist family grew increasingly worried about the fate of Claude Rist's Jewish wife, Françoise, and their three little girls, Isabelle, Antoinette, and Marie-Claire.

In his diary Rist writes on numerous occasions of measures taken by Vichy to persecute the Jews: the first anti-Jewish law (4 and 6 October 1940), roundups of Jews (13, 15, and 20 December 1941 and 24 July 1942), the second anti-Jewish law (2 January and 23 October 1942), the requirement to wear a yellow Star of David (2 June 1942), and deportations (6 July 1942).

Because Claude was in a sanatorium with tuberculosis, Charles Rist took on the responsibility of protecting his son's family. His efforts to save his Jewish granddaughters led Rist to say in October 1942, "I believe nothing has aged me more over the past two years, especially this last one, than the anxiety I have suffered for these three children."

Other diary entries concern individual Jews – or other refugees – whom the Rist family protected or tried to protect. The Schneiders, for example, spent the war at the Rists' country home in Haute-Savoie.

FRIDAY, 4 OCTOBER 1940 Yesterday on the train to Paris, a young woman offered her neighbor one of her newspapers. "Ah! No," replied the latter, laughing, "I don't read the papers, I intend to keep my sanity." A moment later she added, "In forty years they'll have become curiosities for historians; that's how long it will take for us to leave this time behind." She had a fine-featured, intelligent face.

The newspapers yesterday were vile, announcing measures for the registration of Jews and the preparation of special legislation in the free zone.

I had lunch yesterday with O'Brien and Strode, the Rockefeller Foundation doctors. We discussed the possibilities for keeping my institute going.[1] According to them, people in the United States do not realize that the Vichy government is not free and that the measures taken reflect pressure from the occupier. They are amazed that, given the floods of evacuees, epidemics have not broken out. They are worried about the flu epidemic that is apparently raging in the Antilles and the danger that it may cross the Atlantic.

Many here imagine that by returning to Catholicism and suppressing secular schools they can restructure the nation. The Vichy government is reinstituting the teaching of Latin and abolishing teachers' colleges! As if the German government had become victorious by reestablishing religious education and the teaching of Latin! The reverse is true: it is by making a sharp break with the past and trusting in technology alone that Germany has triumphed! The same goes for royalism. Cruel utopian thought to believe the Germans would allow it in France. And when the Germans have left, what stupidity to believe that the French nation will seek salvation in a "legitimate" king!

Laurent-Atthalin[2] does not believe that the English, if they are triumphant, will bother about France. In any case he thinks that, economically speaking, we must go along with Germany. He is following a bit too closely the notions of the Spanish ambassador, Lequerica.

SUNDAY, 6 OCTOBER 1940   Yesterday the Anti-Jewish laws were made public![3] A shameless newspaper, *Le Pilori,* has a great red headline: "The Hunt Is On." Nothing so appallingly ignominious since the time of the Saint Bartholomew's Day Massacre.

At a request from the woman who cares for the Winters' house, yesterday Germaine managed to arrange for the coal in their cellar to be left for her and for us to be given ours. To achieve this she had to deal with a certain army captain, and the NCO who took her to him asked along the way, "Why have all the villas in the neighborhood been abandoned? *Sind wir alle* 'brutes'?" (He said the word in French.) After a moment's thought, Germaine answered, "*Nein, nicht alle.*"[4] Curious, this feeling of inferiority,

1. ISRES owed its existence principally to the Rockefeller Foundation.
2. Baron André Laurent-Atthalin had recently been made president of the Banque de Paris et des Pays-Bas.
3. See appendix 2. [TF]
4. "Are we all brutes?" "No, not all." [TF]

and this uneasiness with regard to the feelings these conquerors inspire! They want to be liked as individuals. They are much friendlier to the French who speak German.

People who pass German soldiers in the street pretend not to see them and consider them "nonexistent."

Baudouin, in a speech to the press, has declared that the policy of the French government is perfect loyalty with regard to the occupier! It is in the name of this loyalty that it is abandoning Indochina to the Japanese and Dakar to the Germans.

The only result of the new tripartite Germano-Italo-Japanese pact, designed to scare off or forestall the United States, will be for the latter to enter the war sooner than expected. The great question mark remains the U.S.S.R. In Vichy the Turkish ambassador told me that, as far as he knew, Japan had decided to wage war on the United States.

SUNDAY, 13 OCTOBER 1940 Very busy week. Visits from anxious Jews. On Monday I had lunch with Édouard after the Suez Company meeting, at which only a few of us were present in the committee's small room. Georges-Edgar Bonnet announced his intention to leave, and on Thursday we learned he has acquired an Italian visa. Lucky him, to go to Egypt, where men are fighting! At the Ottoman Bank, Bellet, who had recently returned from Vichy, told us of the Turkish ambassador's persistent optimism despite the Germans' entry into Romania. On Saturday Noël returned with the authorization to go to Évian. He leaves this evening and will at last rejoin Marie after a year of tension – a letter from her this morning shows her full of joy.

A manifesto from the marshal yesterday morning. What sorry ideas! What cowardice in his foreign policy. He speaks of the war being "lost from the beginning." Was he not part of the High Council of National Defense? Was it not his duty to speak up? "Franco-German relations conducted with such frivolity!" Indeed, but who always refused to come to an understanding with them? Was he not among the front ranks?

Mme Le Verrier, editor of the old *Europe nouvelle,* came for dinner last night and said that Laval, having come to Paris with the intention of declaring war on England, sensed such strong Anglophilia everywhere that he has changed his mind! Up to now I have not met anyone, humble or rich, who does not listen to English radio. Flouret tells me that all of his colleagues at the Cour des Comptes hang on every word. In the shops everybody openly says the same. Are these just empty words? Is this country still capable of making an effort? The return of the flame we are all awaiting, will it come?

The U.S. government has refused permission for the Rockefeller Foundation to send us money. I must try to keep the Institute going without that.[5]

THURSDAY, 17 OCTOBER 1940 Yesterday a visit to Dr. Schaefer, *grand maître* of the Banque de France,[6] accompanied by Bellet, Neuflize, and von Falkenhausen. I renewed my mild protest against a German commissioner's having been given oversight of the Ottoman Bank, which is Turkish, not English, and thus neutral.

Schaefer is a heavy-set man with a shaved head. He took careful note of what I told him. The heart of what he said was in the asides. He announced that we were going to have a system of exchange similar to Germany's. "It is," he said, "a historic occasion for France!"

"I call a currency thus regulated a currency under siege," I replied.

"What will you do," he said, "if Germany occupies Turkey? Of course, this is a purely theoretical supposition!" That is in fact what worries us all. We shall cross that bridge when we come to it, we answered, and I said to him, *"Morgen ist auch ein Tag"* – that is to say, "sufficient unto the day is the evil thereof." His only answer: "Ah, so you know German." He expressed his regret regarding the total separation of the two zones. A new regulation now allows a monthly remittance of two thousand francs to an individual in the free zone.

On the way back, Falkenhausen offered to drive me to the Saint-Lazare railway station. I asked if he was pleased with his stay in Germany, from which he had just returned. "Yes," he said, "but in Berlin and in Essen I had to spend almost every night in the cellar. In one's own house one can get by, but in apartment buildings it is terrible." (He did not suspect the pleasure he had given me!) I pointed out to him that Schaefer is occupying my former office at the Banque de France, and I asked him for news of Schacht. He seemed to hesitate, but replied, "He is one of the most intelligent men I know."

5. See Robert Marjolin, "Le directeur de l'Institut scientifique de recherches économiques et sociales," *Revue d'Économie politique*, November–December 1955, 918: "Resources were lacking. Charles Rist made prodigious efforts to maintain ISRES, moved by the conviction that better days would come again and also by the determination to keep those personnel who stayed in Paris employed."

6. Dr. Carl Schaefer was the German commissioner appointed to oversee the Banque de France and chief surveillance officer over all French banks in the occupied zone (July 1940–July 1941). [TF]

SATURDAY, 19 OCTOBER 1940 The first letters from Léonard have arrived. We are trying to figure out where he is. He says the hills of the Sudetes are to the north and east. Perhaps this is near Prague? He fears the cold and is eating little. He is giving German lessons! My heart contracts each time I think of him.

Yesterday I talked to Barnaud about Schneider,[7] obliged as a Jew to quit his job. Afterward, we discussed more general topics. I expressed my uneasiness at seeing the government carrying on a campaign against England, the effect of which is to completely alienate America. The United States will without a doubt be the one to rule the end game and, above all, the only one able to take our side at the treaty table. This aggressive policy toward England would only make sense if one could count on German or Italian promises. In that respect, however, the expectation of any sort of accommodation is pure illusion. Barnaud acknowledged this. I added that Laval's foreign policy has always been wrong, as he completely ignores the feelings of those with whom he is dealing, whether German, Italian, American, or English. Barnaud twice said to me, "Laval is an abominable man." He defended the armistice. He talked about the resentment of those in Vichy against the English, given the efforts the former had made to save the navy. He said the price of that rescue operation had been abandoning ten to twenty more French departments to the enemy. I told him he must realize the degree to which the campaign against England flies in the face of general feeling in both the occupied and free zones. They could not even make French people admit that their hunger resulted from the English blockade. He readily acknowledged this, saying they should renounce all foreign policy and concentrate on domestic policy instead. And there the man showed his true colors!

SUNDAY, 20 OCTOBER 1940 Yesterday we went to pick up the little ones in Le Vésinet. Very impressed by the multitude of German soldiers. Isabelle said to me, "At night I'm scared when I hear the planes; in the daytime I tell myself I shouldn't be afraid, but when I wake up at night, I'm afraid anyway!"

Decree regarding the Jews came out yesterday. Shameful. Clearly, the government is getting embroiled in a policy it believes will please the Germans and bring about the adhesion of extremists among the French. The foolish illusion that the enemy will be grateful is unfathomable. The government has become prisoner of a policy whose clearest effect is to divide the French at an hour when unity should be the first priority. What personal aims

---

7. Georges Schneider: chief engineer at Mines; he and his family took shelter at the Rists' house in Haute-Savoie during the war.

is Laval pursuing? What obscure revenge, for what, and upon whom? What concept does he have of the future destiny of France? The coming to power of this adventurer is an appalling twist of fate. After 1870 we had Thiers and Gambetta. After Jena, Prussia had Stein and Scharnhorst.

People say to me, "The English may well be able to defend themselves, but how could they be victorious?" My reply: by air and naval superiority. It was thanks to the superiority of our armed forces that we were victorious in 1918. It will be the same this time. Of course, one must take into account German tenacity. In 1918 they stuck to ground fighting. What will happen this time?

But what role can France still play in this war? She is bound hand and foot. Impossible to see a way out for the time being. Keep silent, wait, feed one's hope. But what can one *really* depend on?

MONDAY, 21 OCTOBER 1940 Read de Gaulle's 1938 book, *La France et son armée*. Dedicated to Marshal Pétain! The problem is always the same. To have a high command that understands the technical changes required and puts them into action. The preparation of 1914 was almost as lamentable as that of 1939. The great mistake after the war of 1914 was to have once again separated the middle and lower classes in the army. The bourgeoisie, mixed with the peasants and workers in the barracks, as they were in my time by the law of 1889, found there the only national, popular contact of their whole lives. But after 1918, young bourgeois were put in special schools and courses. Who did that? Who is *responsible*? The consequences have been disastrous. The bourgeoisie turned in upon itself. It took only twenty years to make of them, militarily and socially, a class apart. They believed themselves to be an "elite." They were, on the contrary, totally decadent. In my day the officers had a certain respect for and a bit of fear of the educated youth mixed in with the troops. It was stimulating. All that disappeared. In the time of danger, cohesion was lacking.

The role of the "leader" has never been so much discussed as in these last twenty years. All the young bourgeois egotistically prepared themselves for the role of "leader," for which they believed themselves to be predestined. And they began by not knowing how to obey. Mothers reveled in the word. After twenty years of these hollow phrases, there were no more leaders! What imbeciles!

Received Noël's letter from Annemasse this morning. He is engaged to be married. His long wait has finally been rewarded. A bit of happiness in these sad days.

SATURDAY, 26 OCTOBER 1940 We have received a letter from a member of Mario's regiment, Roger Raffard, in which he writes, "I was just a simple soldier under the orders of officer cadet Rist, who was able to share the troubles and the great weariness of his men with a simplicity that has won him the hearts of us all!"

Three days ago, an edict regarding Jewish organizations, declaring Jewish all those in which a third of the directors are Jewish or whose president is Jewish. Will my institute be considered Jewish? Yesterday at the board meeting of the Banque des Pays de l'Europe Centrale we realized that, in spite of the Aryans sitting around the table, the bank might be considered Jewish!

The newspapers have announced the Laval-Pétain-Hitler talks.[8] Everyone is silent and filled with dismay. A new humiliation? A deeper descent into the abyss? English radio and echoes from the United States indicate that those countries are increasingly annoyed with the Vichy government.

According to Ambassador Clauzel, Finance Minister Bouthillier thought about prohibiting all retired state employees from sitting on any board of directors! Nearly all the French members of the Suez Company would thus have to resign. What a windfall for placing one's friends. And a source of anxiety for many.

News from Léonard is scarce. He must be suffering from the cold. We suppose he is now in Silesia or Bohemia.

On Monday I saw Dayras at the Ministry of Justice to talk about my trip to Switzerland scheduled for 26–27 June. I gave him a letter addressed to the minister to be used as needed.

In judging Laval it must not be forgotten that this man has been the hope of the bourgeoisie since 1934. This fact reflects on their patriotic and psychological state of mind. They could not choose between Coty, Bailby, and Laval when it came to handing out awards for respectability and political wisdom. Without the terror of communism, such aberrations would not have been possible. It is thanks to this terror that even today Laval has his partisans. I fear they will very soon be disillusioned. Projects like those of Bouthillier, the recent decree regarding organizations, etc., are far more effective anticapitalist propaganda than all the communism in the world. Everyone is reduced to the role of a state employee, and as these are granted neither liberty nor a future – that is the ideal.

---

8. These talks took place on 24 October in Montoire.

THURSDAY, 30 OCTOBER 1940 Conversation with Moreau, who kept repeating his friends' set phrases. This is a continuing conspiracy to minimize the military's responsibility and accuse the "regime." "All these teachers with their internationalist ideas didn't want to fight." But he added the following fact, which, without his suspecting, sheds light on the situation: "I know that two reserve officers, *belonging to old aristocratic families*, told their colonel, we don't want to die for Dantzig!" Thus, it is among the aristocratic families that the spirit of defeat prevailed, not among the teachers. The latter knew perfectly well that they were fighting for freedom. And today joy in the fall of the "regime" is the old aristocrats' reward for the humiliating amputation of France. How shameful!

Spent the afternoon at the Banque de Syrie. Thomasson and Bérard think "the end of all this will be Bolshevism." I told them I saw no signs of this, and that the worst Bolshevism is "Bochevism."[9]

Saw Achille Villey, the new prefect of the Seine. When I told him of my faith in the English, he shook my hand.

SUNDAY, 2 NOVEMBER 1940 This week I visited Chase Bank in an attempt to obtain credit for my institute. Bailey, the director, told me that he has formal orders not to grant any more credit and to have outstanding loans reimbursed. Many Americans with substantial sums of money in the United States are having difficulty getting any here. Certain American banks are reimbursing their clients, returning their acceptances, and simultaneously reducing their assets and liabilities in order to have the fewest possible commitments when America enters the war. He himself is taking precautions so he can leave in a timely fashion when the moment comes, thus avoiding the concentration camp whose victims today are the English remaining in France. Meanwhile, Laval and Chambrun[10] are spreading the word everywhere that the United States will not enter the war.

The substance of the Laval-Pétain-Hitler negotiations is still unknown. Georges-Picot assured us that upon his return to Vichy, Laval said nothing to the Council of Ministers, who were anxiously awaiting him. The truth is that nothing has been done. Laval has his friends saying behind the scenes that the conditions will be very favorable! French radio from London carries warnings against an agreement that will no doubt cause Anglo-French incidents and lead us directly into war with England.

9. "Boche": French slang for German, like "Jerry" or "Kraut." [TF]
10. René de Chambrun: son-in-law of Pierre Laval; like all the Chambruns, he inherited dual American and French citizenship.

German and Italian radio broadcasts continue threatening France. Charles-Roux has resigned. Likewise Baudouin, offended that he was not invited to the talks, but he remains in a secondary post at the ministry. He hangs on to any portfolio whatsoever! Laval has been named minister of foreign affairs. His picture appears in the newspapers next to that of Brinon, who engineered the whole thing.

Certainly, one could reproach England for many things, most especially her way of using France as a bastion against Germany. In the preceding war, she waited until 1917 to take over an important sector of the front. During that period France lost a million men. When Baldwin proclaimed that the English frontier was on the Rhine (that was in 1935), the English did nothing to prepare themselves. That is because they were still counting on France to hold out until England was ready. The draft came only much later; three months ago, English men over twenty-seven years of age had still not been mobilized! On each of his trips to France, Churchill wanted to be reassured that the Germans would not attack before 1941, because he needed more time to prepare. And what can one say regarding their perpetual collusion with the Germans after the peace of 1918? All of this might indeed make one think that France should reach an understanding with Germany. But today it is too late. Entente means submission, amputation, reduction to nothing. Perhaps now they are under attack, the English will understand that they are the ones directly targeted by German hegemony. Vanity prevented their understanding that in 1918.

Italy has declared war on Greece. Who knows? Can this be the beginning of an Italian disaster? But one has hoped too often – the Germans in Romania are too near. Naples bombarded by the English! At last!

THURSDAY, 6 NOVEMBER 1940 Logan[11] tells me of a conversation he had with a German officer, wearing the Iron Cross, to whom he said, "You have been decorated!"

"Yes, in the first war."

"But won't you be for this one as well?"

"Oh, this one, this is not a victory. We are not proud of it."

"Why not?"

"It is not a victory, it is the collapse of a rotting nation."

This is what the shameless press, busy slandering France during the last eight years, has made people think of us!

11. Logan: the Rists' dentist.

Yesterday Bérard said to me, "There has been treason, and by people in very high places." I replied, "I'd rather believe that than think the whole of France is corrupt." The more I reflect, the more I believe, in fact, that treason has been committed. How can one otherwise explain the non-distribution of arms, even though they existed? Besides, the haste with which everyone was forced to lie, the tales that are being spread everywhere – the order to blame the communists or the teachers, to say that the soldiers were the first to flee, the recruitment of members of the C.S.A.R. and the Croix-de-Feu into a secret police – all of that smells of conspiracy. The first duty of historians will be to track down this conspiracy begun some ten years ago. The leader? Always the same man, the one found everywhere – Laval.

Triumphant election of Roosevelt. The Vichy government has let it be known that this is a "purely internal matter of the United States" and that it "has no right to offer an opinion!" In truth, this is a terrible blow to its political insight. If Willkie had been elected, what a noise would have been made to persuade France that Roosevelt's policies had been condemned! This and the Greek resistance are surprising and encouraging. French radio from London was so scrambled last night that for the first time we understood nothing. But we could hear Boston and New York quite clearly.

SATURDAY, 8 NOVEMBER 1940 Last night, alert! The first time since the "end" of the war. Germaine came rushing into the living room, where I was reading, and exclaimed, "It is the English!" No antiaircraft guns or bombs. Great turmoil in the street among the "occupiers." Cars roaring, men running, etc. But nothing happened. Anglo-French radio totally jammed.

Doctors Strode and O'Brien of the Rockefeller Foundation came to lunch today. We drank to Roosevelt's health.

Not enough attention has been paid to the origins of dictators: Mussolini a teacher; Stalin a seminarian; Hitler a mediocre artist, son of a low-grade customs employee; Laval a lycée proctor, son of a butcher. All petty bourgeois with elementary educations, phony intellectuals; all without scruples, full of resentments and repressed desires for wealth, and endowed with a strong will backed by cunning. No pure peasants or pure workers, no aristocrats or *grands bourgeois* among them. An extreme passion for power and hatred of those more fortunate or more cultivated, with scorn for the all too real weaknesses of their "betters," even more so for the "scruples" born of upbringing or tradition. All without religion and disdaining religious beliefs.

The German soldiers often sing when they are marching. They sing well and on key. But the songs themselves are hardly musical. Short, jerky phrases pounding out the beat – all so dull, without color, without grace, without harmony, without life.

THURSDAY, 13 NOVEMBER 1940   The eleventh of November passed without ceremony. But today we learned that some two hundred college and lycée students met at the Arc de Triomphe and sang the *Marseillaise* – and the Germans fired shots and made arrests. Yesterday the Gestapo visited certain lycée heads to tell them that if their students participated in demonstrations, they would be held responsible. Today all students, girls and boys, have been ordered to register with the police! I shall know tomorrow what really happened. Someone laid flowers before the statue of Clemenceau. News from Greece: the Italians have been pushed back. And a number of Albanian troops are passing over to the Greeks.

Molotov is in Berlin. They say the Germans are offering Constantinople to the Russians.

This morning, at last, a card from Léonard!

FRIDAY, 14 NOVEMBER 1940   Yesterday the radio announced that on Monday night the English sank four Italian ships (including two of the biggest kind) in the port of Taranto. Meanwhile, Greek successes against Italian troops continue. Today's papers, which of course say nothing of these events, have given full coverage to Molotov's arrival in Berlin.

Since the election of Roosevelt and the attack on Greece, it is crystal clear that the war is taking a turn for the better. German diplomatic ardor and the haste with which Laval is trying to take advantage of it would be enough to demonstrate this.

When will someone write the history of Laval? He will be found behind everything that has been poisonous to France for the last ten years, but always hidden, always invisible. He is at the heart of the Stavisky affair (through his protection of Hudelo), at the heart of the Prince affair (having forced the councilor to postpone prosecution), at the heart of propaganda for Franco and Mussolini.[12] I shall never forget the improbable entourage of corrupt or ultra-reactionary journalists who went with him to Washington in 1931 – and as for Laval, he was self-absorbed, without a single idea, testing the waters to see which side he should support.[13]

---

12. Hudelo and Prince were both connected with the Stavisky affair. See the glossary. [TF]

13. This is an allusion to Pierre Laval's trip to the United States as president of the Council in October 1931. The purpose of the trip was to negotiate the consequences of

SATURDAY, 15 NOVEMBER 1940 Tonight, around 9:30, two waves of bombardment by the English. Yesterday a brief one around 10:00. People here say that in Villacoublay some people were killed, some wounded.

Mlle S.[14] tells us that a few days ago, at the Comédie-Française, when an actor came out on the stage to announce that the play was being interrupted because of an air-raid alert, the hall erupted in applause.

Everyone is talking about the students' demonstration. It seems they marched carrying little poles and yelling "Vive de" – the pole representing a *"gaule."*[15] They say the Germans fired at and wounded several students. All students whose families are in the provinces have to go home – the rest must register every day at their local police station. The universities and other schools of advanced study are closed. Roussy, rector of the University of Paris, has been ousted and replaced, they say, by Carcopino.

Speculation is rife regarding the results of the Molotov talks. Molotov spent his second night in Berlin in an air-raid shelter. Many parents in Versailles have no news of their children, who were arrested following the demonstration.

SUNDAY, 17 NOVEMBER 1940 The newspapers are carrying the list of prison camps. Léonard's is in Ober Langendorf, in the Sternberg district. This seems to be near Olmütz.

Yesterday Barnes, U.S. chargé d'affaires in Paris, came to lunch. He told me of his two-hour conversation with Laval three days ago. Barnes asked him, "Has it never occurred to you that the United States might break off diplomatic relations?" Laval appeared to be quite astonished and asked that a dispatch be sent as soon as possible explaining the situation. "France must choose between destruction and collaboration," he explained. "Besides, the Germans are sure to win. The advantage of France's having reached an understanding with them is that France will be 'the principal Latin nation in Europe.'" (How can a statesman believe in such clichés as "the Latin nations"?) "Above all, we must prevent France from being wrecked and impov-

---

the "Hoover moratorium," which suspended payments of all debts and reparations resulting from the war. In his "Notice biographique," Charles Rist comments on the mission: "This mission was fruitless. Our conversations with the Treasury secretary, who was intent on maintaining the gold standard, held no attraction for M. Laval, who said to me very simply, 'You know, I do not give a damn about the gold standard. You can say what you like in the communiqué'" (1026–1027).

14. Unidentified.

15. *Gaule*: a fishing pole. [TF]

erished." Barnes asked him if he realized that the United States was firm in its decision not to deal with a Europe led by Hitler – and what the consequences could be for France if America refused to enter into commercial relations with the new Europe. Laval had not thought about this possibility, which really astounded him. "If Germany is victorious, why would the United States not renew relations? That's what France would do in a similar case." Barnes observed that Laval has no notion of the great wave of feeling that is rising in the United States; besides, he does not believe in emotional movements, he is purely a "realist." Barnes asked him if he was aware that French opinion is in large part against him. Laval said he was but declared that public opinion is of no importance. He explained that in 1936 he was overthrown by "occult forces" (read Freemasons and the English). "Today there are only two opposing belief systems: Bolshevism and fascism." As for him, he has opted for fascism. Besides, he is convinced that, with its mastery of the continent, Germany has access to all the resources necessary for its industry and for the organization of Europe (!!!).[16]

I was appalled by the mediocrity and the triteness of these ideas, by the alarming ignorance that they reveal of moral forces and economic realities.

Later in the afternoon, a visit from Alexandre Millerand.[17] He told me about General Buat's remark that Pétain, during the Great War, "did nothing but plan for retreat." Millerand also reported Laval's words to Knickerbocker, the journalist, toward the end of June: "You greatly exaggerate the importance of what is happening *here* (here, meaning conquered France). The only battle of importance is the one that will take place against Bolshevism, and we've sided with Germany."

SATURDAY, 23 NOVEMBER 1940   It is curious to observe the face of Paris. People pass by the Germans without seeing them. The latter are surrounded by silence. You can sense the hidden hostility of every Frenchman. Silence in the trains, in the subway, in the street. All keep their thoughts to

---

16. The summary of this Barnes-Laval conversation cannot be found in the *Foreign Relations of the United States Diplomatic Papers*. On the other hand, a memo from Matthews, the State Department's chargé d'affaires in Vichy, making note of a meeting with Laval, exists under the following reference: 740.00119 – European War 1939/606 telegram dated 14 November 1940 (*Foreign Relations*, 1940, vol. 10). Another telegram gives an account of a conversation between U.S. consul Murphy and Laval (9 December 1940).

17. Millerand: former president of the Republic, senator from the Oise; a neighbor of the Rists in Versailles who became friends with them there.

themselves. And yet one *feels* the enmity. Everyone is awaiting something. No one despairs. People talk about food, heating. In every conversation, one feels the mounting bitterness. The Italian defeat at Taranto and the failure in Greece, we all think about them, and hope is building. The actions of the Vichy government have something unreal about them. The truth is elsewhere. These puppets have no control over opinion and feelings. One looks to the future – that is where reality lies. The impression that our lives have been suspended (horrible, certainly, but just an interregnum). You hear, "Yes, the English, that's all well and good, but can they really win?" That is the only worry. Everyone feels ashamed, as well, that we are purely *passive* in this drama.

Over lunch, Marjolin said that Darlan has placed his admirals everywhere in order to reserve a personal role for himself later. All these people spend their time concocting schemes to advance their petty ambitions.

This morning I saw Lequerica, the Spanish ambassador, on behalf of my nephew Marco Schaller.[18] The ambassador says there is little he can do. The Germans observe set rules without ever breaking them. There is an admirable folding screen done by Sert that held my attention while I waited to see him.

Lunch with General Grünfelder, my former student. He told me of his visit to General Georges this past January. Georges was complaining bitterly about the organization of powers between him and the general in command. Why did he not resign? Today he brags to civilians about his sound judgment. And what about his courage?[19]

Vichy has apparently shut down fifteen newspapers in the free zone for having spoken too liberally of the Italian defeat at Taranto. This is emblematic of the situation. A government that takes desperate measures to prevent France from rejoicing at events that are favorable to her! An infamy unequaled until now! For what purpose? To protect itself! Moreover, the gap between public opinion and the government becomes more noticeable each day. Its salvation is fear of a Doriot-Déat-Flandin government. But one sees no results from the Laval-Führer negotiation – except for the mass expulsion of peasants in the Lorraine region. The lot of prisoners remains deplorable.

---

18. Marc ("Marco") Schaller, son of General and Mrs. Schaller, Charles Rist's sister Gabrielle, was killed at Neufchâteau, but a con man who pretended to have news of him kept his parents in a state of anxiety.

19. The two "houses" of Gamelin (general in command) and Georges (commander of the North/East forces) had been in a notorious state of constant rivalry, to the detriment of strategic success.

André Amphoux, prisoner in Koblenz, writes that his "fate is cruel." Elsewhere it seems the officers at least are better off. But the soldiers!

Marjolin too told me of a conversation, this one with a young man from a "good family," confessing that he preferred defeat without Freemasons to English victory with them! This is the spirit of the Holy League and of the "émigrés." Replace "Huguenots" with Jews, Freemasons, and communists, and you have the same state of mind. The spirit of the League is a French tradition. We have seen it reborn with Boulangism, with anti-Dreyfusard nationalism, with Larocquism,[20] and today, with Lavalist defeatism. Replace the Spain of Philip II with the Italo-Germany of Mussolini-Hitler, and you have the same situation as in the time of Charles IX. This spirit is a mixture of reactionary panic (hatred of anything new) and anarchistic rebellion against any national discipline, particularly the payment of taxes; of creative imagination, using novels to justify disobedience to an odious government (Michelet has noted the Jesuits' use of romance and the novel to at once *move and rouse to fanaticism* – as with the Prince affair in our own time) and belief in violence, on the naïve assumption that violence will always work in your favor; and of the passionate search for material comfort and the satisfaction of desire along with a blind certainty that some of your countrymen are capable of every conceivable crime and thus deserve no mercy. The intellectual ingredients of this mix, in frightful confusion, are memories of the Revolution; a passion for "Liberty" (for oneself exclusively); a great need for "Equality" (by bringing others down to one's own level); a romanticized contemporary history composed of behind-the-scenes machinations; a patriotism that is quick to react to any criticism of military authorities and extraordinarily tolerant vis-à-vis foreign insolence and encroachments; a deep skepticism regarding all moral values; an artist's taste for highly colored, melodramatic spectacle – and underlying all this, a palpable fear for one's wallet and a complete ignorance of *real* political and social problems.

Last Monday, a long conversation with Admiral Durand-Viel.[21] This old sailor spoke harshly of his army colleagues. Above all, he reproached them for their indifference to materiel. He told me that when the air ministry was created, engineers were blithely left out. Weygand was afraid they would leave for jobs in private industry. Result: panic whenever a technical question came up. A similar situation with the Maginot Line: it was Durand-Viel who, after noticing that the soldiers' barracks were *outside* the line, pointed

20. Colonel François de la Rocque led the Croix-de-Feu, a far-right league of World War I veterans. [TF]

21. Admiral Georges Durand-Viel was navy chief of staff and president of the navy's high command from 1931 to 1937.

out that they might as well house sailors outside their battleships! After three months he was asked to send some sailors to show army officers how one learned to use military machinery I pointed out to him that civilians who had experienced the last war concluded that modern wars were wars of materiel. He observed that the military had not arrived at this conclusion!

If Vichy were a serious government, it would focus on improving technical instruction in all areas. But it is doing the contrary: reestablishing the teaching of Latin!

Everyone rejoices to see the Italian army following its ancient tradition – namely, "to run like hell" when face-to-face with the enemy. The famous Mussolini reforms have clearly not destroyed the essential character of this people, which is to disdain getting oneself killed. Already, in one of his essays, Montaigne recalled the words of an Italian who said that evidence of the livelier intelligence of his countrymen was that they could spot danger from farther away than the French or the Germans and would flee the sooner.[22]

MONDAY, 25 NOVEMBER 1940 Yesterday Germaine was at the Winters' house to retrieve part of their furniture. German soldiers very accommodating. Seeing that she speaks German, they started a conversation. (Nothing is so painful for them as their enforced isolation.) One of them said to her, "The owner of this house is Jewish; do you not think, *Gnädige Frau*, that the Jews are to blame for all of this? If I have not returned home for two years, it is the Jews' fault." Another said, "Do you know that *Negroes* were sent to Germany after the last war? My family was reduced to living in one room – there were five of us children – and there were Negroes next to us. I will never forget it."[23]

Germaine responded, "Yes, I know, and we disapproved."

The soldier appeared quite astonished. He said, "Yes, we were told that in France there were some who disapproved."

Another said, "But this Jewish woman, where is she?"

"In Marseille."

"But Marseille is occupied not by us, but by the Italians."

"Oh," said Germaine, "the Italians are much too busy in Greece to be able to occupy Marseille" – and one of them laughed. Another asked if she had children and if they had suffered from the war.

22. Montaigne, *Essais*, Livre II, Chapitre XI, "De la cruauté" [On Cruelty]. [TF]

23. During the Franco-Belgian occupation of the Ruhr in 1922–1924, Senegalese soldiers, against whom German nationalist propaganda had been particularly excessive, were sent to Germany.

"Yes," said Germaine, "I have a son in prison."

"Then," replied the soldier, "if he is with peasants (we are all peasants), he is no doubt doing O.K. Our relatives all have prisoners staying with them, and the prisoners get along fine and are well fed."

WEDNESDAY, 27 NOVEMBER 1940 A lot is said these days about the prisoners, and Scapini[24] emphasizes the advantages he supposedly has obtained for them. All those who have prisoners know that these vaunted advantages are just jokes, that their prisoners are not receiving packages or letters, and that they are at the mercy of more or less benevolent camp commandants. Léonard seems to be doing rather well, but André Amphoux in Mainz complains bitterly and demands that he be sent "anything at all to eat." Who will ever pardon the Vichy government for its negligence and its impudent lies? I hold it personally responsible for the fate of my son, who should never have been imprisoned, having been taken after the armistice. I hold Laval and Baudouin personally responsible for what he is suffering and will suffer. I hold them personally responsible for the cold and hunger that they cause my children and my grandchildren to suffer. Personally responsible for adding to these ills the cynical lies published in their newspapers. Personally responsible for prolonging these sufferings by providing Germany with the help of our industry. Personally responsible for the intellectual degradation imposed on our newspapers and for keeping us in total ignorance of what is going on, were it not for American and English radio. It is impossible to think that the day of vengeance will not come, and that these cynical *provocateurs* and profiteers of France's defeat will not be punished.

Burthe, our notary, tells me some French corporation trustees are saying that even if the Germans take 51 percent of the shares, the intelligence of the French is so superior they can "hoodwink" the Germans. What better proof could these gentlemen give of their imbecility and their ignorance than these boastful words?

SATURDAY, 30 NOVEMBER 1940 Removal of Gustave-Adolphe Monod[25] by Minister Ripert following Gustave-Adolphe's declaration that he did not share the government's ideas regarding the Jewish question. Ripert received him, saying, "We're purging, we're purging!" They would like

24. Georges Scapini, deputy from Paris, had just been named head of diplomatic services for prisoners.

25. Gustave-Adolphe Monod: Germaine Rist's cousin, inspector general of education, and a former adviser to Jean Zay, French legislator.

to say publicly that Monod himself asked for the change for "personal reasons." This great disabled veteran of Douaumont, dismissed by that wretched professor of commercial law with the mind of a Marseillais store clerk, and who during the war of 1914 was in who knows what bureaucratic post, is a symbol unto himself.

There is much talk that the marshal may be moving to Versailles. But in reality no one knows – and the Germans appear to be keeping the matter in suspense.

Bellet, back from Vichy, where he saw the Turkish ambassador, told me that the ambassador was very optimistic and twice said to him, "Trust me, the Axis powers have lost the war." That proves, in any case, that the Turks are not afraid of a Russian military operation at their back door.

This morning a great hustle and bustle by the troops moving out. Will they be replaced? And will we see others in two days?

News from Romania: Iorga and poor Madgearu,[26] cut down by revolvers. The latter was the only energetic and courageous financier that I met in Bucharest. The former was a phrase maker, but eloquent, and a kind of bard of the Romanian renaissance.[27]

Soriant and two others assassinated with them! Everywhere, savagery unleashed. To tell the truth, the infamous King Carol, by having Codreanu assassinated in prison, had sown the seeds of this harvest. How many of those I met and with whom I worked in Austria and Romania have died violent deaths – or almost died, as in the case of poor Schuschnigg! Dollfuss, Buresch, Künwald in Austria – and now the Romanians. That is National Socialism. When will this universal frenzy, born in the soul of a degenerate Austrian, come to an end?

FRIDAY, 6 DECEMBER 1940 When a German officer, a patient of our dentist, had a gold tooth replaced, Dr. Logan asked him for fourteen hundred francs instead of the twelve hundred agreed upon at the beginning, invoking various pretexts. "No problem," said the German, "I will pay what you want," and took out some bills. Then, showing his tooth and the bills: "For me, gold, and for you, toilet paper." There is one, at least, who does not share the Nazi doctrine that gold is useless!

The Germans are leaving Versailles – at least those who are near us. They say they are going to Saint-Cloud or Chaville. Perhaps that is to allow for the

---

26. Both were assassinated by Codreanu's Iron Guard. [JNJ/TF]

27. The fascist National Renaissance Front was created by King Carol as a rival to the Iron Guard. [TF]

installation of Pétain here. Dr. Logan, wishing to thank the German dentist lodging with him for his courtesy, asked Germaine to serve as interpreter. The conversation got under way. The German, very happy to find someone who could speak his language, took advantage to ask some questions. "Soon we will be collaborating, accept the hand that is offered to you," etc. Germaine replied that no Frenchman would do so and that no German would either under the same circumstances. The German responded, "But, *Gnädige Frau*, do you know what we suffered?" And he resumed, "The Ruhr, the Negroes, and the French officers in the Rhineland who pushed civilians off the sidewalks with their riding crops. And then, of course, the Jews, the cause of all this suffering." That is evidently the lesson they have been taught – to our shame! While moving out, they have looted everything from uninhabited houses – beds, linens, etc., all ransacked, ruined.

Georges-Edgar Bonnet has returned from Egypt and conveyed his impressions of the deep mistrust the English feel toward us – and their double fear that we will aid the Germans with our fleet and that Syria will allow the Italians or the Germans to pass through.

He tells me that Chiappe's plane was machine-gunned not by the English, but by the Italians. Naturally, the press say nothing of this and let the public believe that those awful English have killed this "great citizen" who had been boldly asked to serve the nation![28]

MONDAY, 9 DECEMBER 1940 Kept at home recently by swollen feet, I have written the preface to Marjolin's thesis.[29]

Two attacks by English planes, one yesterday and another two days before. They came to Villacoublay. The English tactic now consists of preventing German attacks on England by bombing German airbases just as their planes are taking off. The method apparently works, for German flights seem to have stopped three days ago.

The Greek advance, the taking of Santi Quaranta, and yesterday Argyrokastron, has thrilled everyone. The resignations (forced, or voluntary?) of Badoglio, of the governor of the Dodecanese, and of the navy chief of staff are evidence of Italian disarray. But what will the German reaction be?

---

28. The former prefect of police, whose replacement by Daladier had unleashed the events of 6 February 1934, was appointed by the Vichy government to be governor general of the Levant (the French Mandates of Syria and Lebanon), but the plane that was carrying him there was shot down near Cyprus.

29. Robert Marjolin, *Prix, monnaie et production. Essai sur les mouvements économiques de longue durée* [Prices, Money, and Production. Essay on Long-term Economic Movements] (Paris: Presses Universitaires de France, 1941).

Lieutenant Renard,[30] back from Syria, came to see us yesterday, bringing me a letter from Ambassador Puaux. What he says about the Syrian army's lack of preparation is sickening. Everywhere the same chaos, the same incompetence of the officers, the same absurd swelling of the staffs, the same rivalry among the leaders resulting in impotence. Arrived in Marseille with three thousand men, nothing had been done to prepare for them! Not even food. Their two boats were caught in the Anglo-Italian naval battle west of Sardinia. He admires the guts of the English. A small destroyer advanced fearlessly to attack the Italian ships. The latter made a U-turn as soon as the English (much less numerous) came into view and took shelter behind the two French ships to keep the English from firing.

WEDNESDAY, 11 DECEMBER 1940 The day before yesterday the English launched a major attack on the Italian troops at Sidi-Barani (Graziani's army in Egypt). This time we are full of hope. Some of General de Gaulle's French soldiers are taking part in the attack. The Greek successes have given us confidence. We can already glimpse, from our prison, the Italian collapse.

The former French partisans of Mussolini are very upset. They had been saying that we needed a Mussolini. Alas! We did not need him to teach us how to be defeated.

It seems Pétain has decided not to come to Versailles for the time being. What is going on? Is it possible that he is showing more resistance to the German demands conveyed by Laval? Does he hope to make France participate in the defeat of Italy? If that were the case, would we ever emerge from this appalling impasse?

What will the French government be like after the war? Laval's idiotic idea that fascism will triumph and that France will be the beneficiary seems now and forever impossible. But what measures will this ignominious specimen take to remain in power? If de Gaulle triumphs, it is he who will be the master. But he will need to have popular representation with an executive power stronger than the previous one. A more independent administration, one that is more forceful; otherwise, we will go back to the eternal complacency that got us where we are. Technical progress is a priority. Systematic libel in the press must be kept in check by the courts. Keep a tight rein on the purely reactionary faction, which is in any case small. Shore up the industrial and agricultural middle class – do not let it perish for fear of the workers. Avoid any involvement with religious affairs, leaving the churches

---

30. Pierre Renard, a friend of Mario Rist, volunteered in Syria but was brought back to France at the end of 1940 for having tried to go over to the Resistance.

free. Have legislative chambers that are much smaller in number. Do not let them take the initiative regarding expenditures. Have ministers who are responsible to the chambers. Reduce the economic functions of the state. Restore its independence vis-à-vis customs; leave the initiative to heads of industry; deny them the hope of enriching themselves via customs duties. Commercial and industrial education. Create a technical army resembling a corps of engineers. Rely on England and the United States. Secondary and higher education simplified and reformed. Make the independence of judges and the integrity of the legal system the primary ideological principle. Make education available to the working class up to the age of fourteen or fifteen.

THURSDAY, 12 DECEMBER 1940 In Lavisse's *l'Histoire de France,* I read this passage from Mariejol's book on Richelieu, p. 328:

> The art of war had been transformed. Wallenstein raised and supplied armies that were 50,000 strong. Gustav Adolf had inaugurated those races across Germany at which his lieutenants would excel. He had abandoned deep linear formations, and when outnumbered, simply organized a line of musketeers, covered by a line of pikemen, to present a more extensive front to the enemy. His regiments, consisting of battalions and units of equal strength, maneuvered in an orderly fashion and moved speedily. *But the tactical and strategic lessons were lost on the French generals; they did not know how to lead either a campaign or a battle. They dragged along from siege to siege....* But in the school of experience, a second generation was formed, much superior to the first.

It was generals Turenne and Condé who emerged from that school.

The tradition that led us to disaster in 1940 is thus quite old. In times of peace, the French army sleeps.

Great English victory at Sidi-Barani. More than twenty thousand Italian prisoners in three days. Egypt has been liberated. It will be impossible to attack the Suez for a long time unless the Germans try to go through Turkey (!?). The Italians have been obliged to send reinforcements simultaneously to Albania and Libya. Their three armies (Abyssinia, Libya, Albania) are all dependent on communication by sea, which the English control. And we were absent!

Here the politics of reaction continues. From now on it is the government that will appoint all the mayors, who in turn will appoint the city councilors. A municipality will have less to say about the appointment of its administrators than an assembly of shareholders about that of its board. Happily, all this will be swept away at the end of the war.

> When news was heard that at Sidi-Barani
> The English were pounding Signor Mussolini,

More than one Frenchman said, "How proud I'd be
If France had been there, and as before, free
To cudgel this wretch, this treasonous ghoul
Who'd be nothing at all if we hadn't been fools."[31]

SATURDAY, 14 DECEMBER 1940 Certain newspapers, having lost all sense of shame, are now openly recommending the beauties of Nazi doctrine for France. That deceitful dupe M. Flandin sings the praises of currency "based on national wealth"! Others praise the racial doctrine. What treason, when we know that National Socialism prides itself on being a purely German doctrine, exclusively interested in the grandeur of Germany alone!

If it is inevitable to have religious doctrines, since men live by their passions and their feelings, let them at least be doctrines that lead toward greater humanity. Christianity and the French Revolution were religions of this kind. But the exaltation of violent instincts in order to set in motion foreign and civil war, how despicable! Understandable when it fires up the conquered against the conqueror to take revenge. But when it glorifies the voluntary submission of the conquered to the conqueror! What cowardice!

At heart, these partisans of Hitlerism in France are idolaters of force triumphant. As Michelet put it in his entry on Catherine de Médicis, they believe only in fact.[32] They overlook the deep feelings that justly rouse men against fact and give them the heroism to move mountains and transform fact. The preaching of servility in France for the past ten years by people who are frightened or bribed is the dreadful cancer that has contaminated our blood and ruined our patriotism. Helped by the stupidity of the military, it has put us in the last rank of peoples, by a defeat not only suffered but accepted.

The terrible question remains: what will be done with Germany after the war? How to deal with the horrifying presence, in the heart of Europe, of eighty million people who love war? The English will no doubt do away with the German fleet and perhaps its air force. But the army? It is we who are threatened by the army, and we alone.

---

31. Quand la nouvelle vint qu'à Sidi-Barani / Ces bons Anglais rossaient signor Mussolini, / Plus d'un Français s'est dit: "Que je serais plus fier / Si la France était là, comme elle y fut hier, / Pour bâtonner ce fol, faquin, maître en traîtrise, / Qui jamais ne fut rien sauf par *notre* sottise." Several words of the poem are crossed out in Rist's original manuscript, thus indicating that he was its creator. [TF]

32. Jules Michelet, "Catherine de Médicis," *Histoire de France,* Tome X [History of France, Volume 10].

Lord Lothian[33] has just died, predicting English victory in 1942! A brilliant, energetic, restless man, who had flirted with the English Germanophiles! Deep down, without convictions. How I would have liked to see him again after the war. Through him, one could have known England's true intentions. This great politician was a Christian Scientist. Example of the super-intelligent naïveté of certain Englishmen.

SUNDAY, 15 DECEMBER 1940 Yesterday, Saturday evening, Pétain announced on the radio that Pierre Laval has been replaced by Flandin and that the constitutional decree naming Laval as successor to the marshal has been revoked. "The change does nothing to alter our relations with Germany, it concerns only domestic policy." All other ministers remain in place. The marshal added, "The National Revolution continues!"

This is a shell game. Even with Parliament, ministerial shufflings were not so frequent. France today no longer has the right to know why her ministers have been changed. Most probably one must assume the opposite of what Pétain says. The change is a matter of foreign policy (otherwise, the other ministers, Alibert and company, would not still be in place). But what change? Flandin belongs to the Germans even more than Laval. Now is the moment when Italy is collapsing and the chances of the English are increasing. Is Flandin charged with striking a blow for the Germans in order to keep all the French from becoming Anglophiles? Do people think he will succeed in attenuating the reactionary policies of Laval? But what chance of that as long as Alibert and Peyrouton are there? Confusion and uncertainty. Only one thing is certain: the dirty stain that the very presence of Laval constituted for France has been removed. This infamous French chief of state, illegitimate son of a gypsy and a butcher from Auvergne, is with us no more. This conglomerate of all personal corruptions – parliamentary, journalistic, and financial – is disappearing from the scene. At no time has France ever fallen so low as during the six months during which she has had to tolerate this shame.

The Germans are bringing back the ashes of the Duke of Reichstadt, which will be interred next to Napoleon. The newspapers say that the gift was made by Hitler to Pétain in a letter "of rare elevation." Who do the Germans take us for? For imbeciles, that is certain!

---

33. Lord Lothian was British ambassador to Washington when Rist traveled to the United States in the spring of 1940.

Six

"National Renewal":
Harem Hijinks

17 DECEMBER 1940–14 MARCH 1941
Pétain's sacking of Pierre Laval on 13 December 1940, along with other ministerial maneuvering, smacked of harem hijinks in Rist's opinion. Vichy's National Renewal, also referred to as National Revolution, instead of bringing stability, had brought the reverse. Rist blamed the reactionary "bonne bourgeoisie," who had embraced defeat with open arms, fearing a return to the French Republic.

TUESDAY, 17 DECEMBER 1940 Yesterday at the Banque du Maroc conjectures were rife regarding recent events. Complete silence in all the papers. The Germans are evidently not pleased about Laval's removal, and tension seems to be building between them and the marshal. But that is all. They say Déat was arrested in Paris on Sunday then released at German insistence.[1]

Leaving the board meeting, Moreau took me aside to tell me about the little intrigue that obliged him to resign from the Banque de Paris. He quoted Laval's words to him in Vichy: "You know, the Germans are all-powerful; if they decide to arrest you, I will be unable to prevent them." He told me in passing that he was wrong to allow himself to be seduced by the one and a half million francs stipulated in his contract when he returned to the Banque de Paris. But he hopes nevertheless to be compensated.

This morning, finally, London radio gave some explanations regarding the Laval-Pétain mystery. Already yesterday Boston – based on news from Bern – announced that after Laval let loose against Pétain at a meeting of the Council of Ministers, Pétain had Laval arrested. Today word is that, in cahoots with Abetz,[2] Laval was preparing a coup d'état against the marshal.

1. The rumor was correct.
2. Otto Abetz was the German ambassador to Paris (November 1940–July 1944). [TF]

The latter, summoned to Versailles, would have had to defend his policy of collaboration. France was supposed to replace Italy to form a new Axis. It seems Laval was going to take control in case of resistance on the part of Pétain. The ceremony for the Duke of Reichstadt's reburial would have served as a pretext for the arrival of Hitler (?). Word leaked to Peyrouton, who apparently warned Pétain, and Saturday's decision was taken.[3]

Moreau told me that on Saturday his housekeeper came to him and said, "Ah, monsieur, at last some good news – there's not much these days! – they say Laval has been assassinated." Everyone here (except for the Laval crowd) is of a mind with this good woman.

"National Renewal" was supposed to give us, along with other benefits, stability. Yet ministers and ministries are constantly changing. Even the constitution (!), six months after its promulgation, has been changed by the suppression of the act naming Laval as the successor. These changes are no better than harem hijinks. The public is given no information. The silence is complete. Evidently one must keep quiet in the presence of the Germans. But what a lack of dignity! As for Laval, he ends up where he started: committing treason. The man was born a servant to the Germans. For this money-hungry individual, war is a nuisance. He was twenty-nine years old when he went to Stockholm in 1917.[4] Today he is fifty-five, but he is doing the same as always: reaching an understanding with Germany, for his personal profit, to keep France from fighting. When there was still time, under Brüning, he was adamantly opposed to any gesture of reconciliation! And forbade me the least concession at the Basel conference.[5]

This man is so base that one can hardly imagine the ambition that drives him. His association with Guimier at the Havas news agency – the most brazenly corrupt kind of journalism – plus his social rise via the Chambruns help to explain this lycée proctor's disgusting character. His use of La Rocque to

---

3. On 27 November Pétain let it be known that he would be moving to Versailles; Laval opposed the move, however, and on 3 December the move was vetoed by Ribbentrop. Then "it was learned suddenly on December 12 that Pétain was supposed to go to Paris on German conditions to participate in the reburial of Napoleon's son [the Duke of Reichstadt] at the Invalides." (See Paxton, *Vichy France*, 99–100). [TF]

4. Pierre Laval was in fact among the French socialists who hoped to attend a Russian-inspired international convocation of socialists in Stockholm, but the French government denied them passports.

5. This was a meeting of experts deliberating on war debts remaining from World War I. [JNJ/TF]

secure the services of thugs,[6] his ties with Franco in Spain and Mussolini in Italy, even as France was reinforcing her ties with England against Hitler – these things reveal a concerted betrayal and systematic blindness with regard to French interests (or to the strength of opposing countries), with the single goal of obtaining personal profit. We know Laval long admired Stalin, whose age is the same as Laval's and who shares the same lowly origins and the same sordid resentments against those who are wealthier and better educated. An old story goes that he would mention at the drop of a hat, "We were born in the same year; what a harvest."

WEDNESDAY, 18 DECEMBER 1940 Everywhere people confirm the interpretation that has been given to Laval's departure. American radio announced last night that he was freed at the demand of Abetz, who went to Vichy and talked with Pétain for three hours. In fact, the marshal was expected to come to Paris, where he would have met Hitler himself, and where they would have communed under the aegis of the Duke of Reichstadt. But Laval was preparing, as soon as the marshal arrived, to change the cabinet and team up with Déat, Doriot, etc. He reportedly responded to Pétain by asking what guarantees of his personal liberty he would have once in Versailles: "The word of Chancellor Hitler!"

Meanwhile, the newspapers here are completely silent. If it were not for the marshal's radio appeal, no one here would know anything about the change in the government. That is because the Germans consider this unfinished business.

These are political games, with the royalist team on one side (Alibert, Weygand) and the demagogic-authoritarian on the other (Déat, Laval) playing tug of war around the marshal. The second team is closer to the Germans than the first and clearly has their sympathies, as they are vehemently anti-English. We are going to see increasing pressure on the part of the Germans, which will translate as material sacrifices and persecutions. But if that could induce the marshal to exercise a policy of true neutrality (the only one possible in this moment) rather than one of aiding the Germans against England, it would be an enormous improvement.

THURSDAY, 19 DECEMBER 1940 Conversation yesterday with Admiral Durand-Viel. He said Darlan evidently told Pétain that he must take into

6. This is an allusion to the secret funds that Laval and Tardieu, according to the latter's testimony, gave Colonel de La Rocque in 1930–1931. The colonel denied this consistently during the course of the 1937 trial linked to the episode.

account three new facts: (1) the defeat of the Italians by the Greeks, (2) the defeat of the Italians by the English, (3) the refusal by the French people to accept the policy of collaboration. The change in Darlan, if that is true, would be a matter of the greatest importance. Durand-Viel thinks that Weygand has a big role to play in Africa at this juncture. Bellet, back from Marseille, tells me that the order has been given to repair the *Dunkerque* and the *Jean Bart* with all speed. To what end?

Laval, brought back to Paris by Abetz (in an armored car, they say, a curious reminder of Lenin's return to Russia in 1917), has been definitively unmasked as an agent of Germany. In the future he may continue to do evil, but no longer will it be evil consented to by the mob of imbeciles who have let themselves be led by the nose up to now (all the morons hitched to the wagon of the moron La Rocque).

The problems of food and heat are becoming more acute with each passing day. On the trains it is the only thing you hear people talk about. Everyone has a suitcase or bag carrying provisions found in Paris or elsewhere. This week we had meat only once. In Marseille the oil mills are overflowing with oleaginous grains that the English allow through from West Africa. But the Germans take 90 percent. Two supply specialists have told me that the Germans requisition 25 percent of the oil produced. In the buildings where the Germans are staying, they heat their own apartments but close the radiators of apartments inhabited by the French, sealing them with lead. Before leaving Versailles (to make room for Pétain), they grabbed everything in the stores. One could see all the soldiers loaded down with packages and boxes. Vogüé, back yesterday for Suez business, told me that at the Verrerie (his property in the Cher, which has been occupied for a long time) the Germans invoked all the suffering that had been imposed upon them in the Ruhr to justify their methods of impoverishing France. Many prisoners receive no packages (André is of their number). Hellot[7] assures me that packages are redirected to the Germans. I find it hard to believe, but faced with the scientific organization of plunder that operates here, one ends up believing that anything is possible.

SATURDAY, 21 DECEMBER 1940 Yesterday Eva told us that Léonard has received *all* the packages sent to him. Just one excuse for the packages that do not arrive: the difficulty of organizing the distribution to two million

---

7. Frédéric Hellot was a retired general and board president of Matériel Téléphonique.

prisoners! What would be the result if it were we, with our administration, who had such a task?

Something is going on in Vichy. But what? What German demands? What maneuvering among these ministers divided among themselves, pre-occupied with domestic politics and preparing the accession of their respective candidates? They have already ceded so much to the enemy, there is no reason not to continue.

FRIDAY, 27 DECEMBER 1940 My sister Gabrielle has lost hope for her Marco. He was surely killed at Neufchâteau, the last place his captain saw him, and where it is known that a great air attack took place. The letter from the captain is pathetic. His only concern was to hide, and afterward he thought no further of his men. What had given Gabrielle some hope was a visit three months ago (after they advertised in *Le Matin*) from a young man who claimed to have been with Marco in the Arès camp (near Arcachon), from which he himself supposedly escaped. He proposed setting off for Bordeaux to learn what he could, and the Schallers gave him money for the trip. Now it just so happened that a police inspector came to see them and told them that this young man (who called himself Comte de Wulf) was a crook, an air force cadet who had stolen the papers of one of his comrades (the real de Wulf) at the hospital in Montpellier and had already swindled several soldiers. The Schallers are devastated. This scam of preying on the hopes of parents who are waiting in vain for news of their loved ones is apparently widespread. Naturally, the military command know nothing of it. Not one of the families we know who have lost someone has been informed by the army. What they learn they have always got from comrades. The wholesale assassination of our country by the high command is reflected at the retail level as well: the families of our dead are being destroyed by their indifference and neglect. I do not believe that in the entire history of France there has ever been such a demoralization of the instrument to which the nation's defense has been entrusted. Yet it is of this that the nationalists, having declared the government and Parliament to be corrupt, said, "At least, we still have the army." For them the army was more than anything a gendarmerie charged with defending them against "communists."

SATURDAY, 28 DECEMBER 1940 Working-class people jokingly say, regarding the return of the Duke of Reichstadt's ashes, "We would rather have coal than ashes." The coal ration is 100 kilos (or 50?) per month per person.

On Thursday afternoon I ran into one of the board members, a graduate of the École Polytechnique, at the Société Commerciale Franco-Turque. The conversation turned to the prisoners. His sole concern is to know whether they will come back as Bolsheviks. He is confident that the Germans are bombarding them with propaganda to get them fired up against their bosses. Nothing is more sickening than this exclusive preoccupation on the part of the "*bonne bourgeoisie*," in the middle of the country's most horrific mourning, to know if there will be a popular uprising against it. These same people who for years have tossed around the most vicious slander against the government and pushed for civil war, etc., today dream only of a government that will suppress popular discontent and defend their property. They really have no other concerns. Compared to that, the humiliation of France seems to them relatively minor. In answer, I told him that in my opinion there would be neither revolution nor Bolshevism – the prisoners would be only too eager to return to their jobs and their families – but that it would be important to demand an accounting from the military command, which in two weeks caused France to lose the war, and for my part I hoped very much to see this happen.

SUNDAY, 29 DECEMBER 1940   Yesterday Roosevelt delivered the great speech announced several days ago. The essential part is this: "I do not believe that the Axis powers will win this war. The most recent and certain information I have received has persuaded me that they will not win." Another important sentence, responding to threats against the United States appearing in recent German articles: "Others' interpretations of our attitude will not change it and will not alter our policies one whit." (The threats consisted of warning the United States of a possible attack by Japan.) He then announced a significant increase in aid from American industry. He declared that no expeditionary force would be sent to Europe. That is no doubt the only bit the censors here will allow through.

MONDAY, 30 DECEMBER 1940   The two most noticeable material deprivations we have to suffer are the absence of vehicles and the morning darkness that has resulted from the application of central European time in the occupied zone. The first of these problems is the more serious, as it makes any undertaking slower and more complicated. Nothing serves better to make us feel conquered: the "masters" use cars; the "vanquished" use their legs, or at best bicycles, which are more and more difficult to obtain. There are certainly some Frenchmen with driving permits who go around in cars. I notice that the brutality and lack of consideration they show with regard to pedestrians far outstrips that of the Germans, who are nevertheless soldiers. What can have caused the French, when left alone and believing themselves immune from punishment, to become in all areas so lacking in scruples – and consequently, courtesy and consideration? Or has it always been like this? As for the women, the great torment is having to wait in line at shops, even at administrative offices, in the cold, at night. The day before yesterday the maid stood in line *four hours* at city hall for ration cards. Some women fainted, others got into fights. Bureaucratic negligence is worse than ever. The indifference of the pencil pushers, not to mention their stupidity, has never attained such heights. I learned today that the person charged with organizing distribution is a colonel! That explains everything. There is nothing to be done with these wretched imbeciles who have no imagination whatever. Imagination for the French consists of constructing images, never of empathizing with what others might be feeling or thinking. Napoleon was the only one who knew how to manipulate such people, using the twin motivations of fear and vanity.

THE FOLLOWING IS AN UNDATED TEXT FROM RIST THAT MUST HAVE BEEN WRITTEN DURING THE LATTER HALF OF 1940. THE TITLE OF THIS FRAGMENT IS "CAUSES" (OF THE DEFEAT).

1. Lack of technical know-how on the part of the military. This is just one aspect of the general technical deficiency of French administrative units.

The first characteristic is the absence of information. This applies to all branches: witness my experiences at the Ministries of Commerce, Foreign Affairs, and National Education, as well as at the Banque de France. Everywhere the lack of curiosity about new things being achieved abroad and the lack of information regarding what was going on in France itself. The principle is to "stick with the status quo." The principle *should be* to envisage new problems that require solution and to arrive at relevant decisions by applying modern methods of information. "*Think*" war and "*think*" peace. Examples in all fields. The reform of the "State" should consist above all of a reform of "administrative methods": simplification and concentration of bureaucratic machinery; in each administrative office, a small staff in charge of solving "new" problems, with enough authority to implement the new solutions. It is for this reason that "technical" ministries such as Public Works, where the corps of bureaucrats consists of people accustomed to "problem solving," have more success than others. The worst is the Ministry of Commerce. Somewhere in between, the Ministry of Finance.

The conservative political parties in France make the same mistake as in Germany. They see National Socialism as a means for returning to the old political and economic structure in which they held sway. In France is added the hope of seeing the Church's influence reborn. They fail to recognize the democratic and egalitarian nature of the National Socialist movement. Its primary strength (aside from methods of physical constraint) is to have pursued technical efficiency in all areas and to have rejected all ideological conflicts in order to subordinate the entire activity of the country to one single goal: military triumph over neighboring states. From this point of view, the National Socialist government has *modernized* all industrial, agricultural, and military activities. It is not by talking (as B.[8] did in his speeches) about the conservation of "spiritual forces" that one will achieve an organization capable of standing up to it. It is by exciting the nation's ability to invent, imagine, and conceive with vigor and originality. Any political action seen as taking revenge on popular parties in order to boost the influence of conservative parties will only create new conflicts. England and the United States look to the intensification of industry and the union of political parties for salvation.

What has weakened this country over the last ten years is the politicization of the entire bourgeoisie. In bourgeois circles one no longer talked of anything but politics. Real problems and real solutions were studiously ignored. Difficulties, even those that resulted directly from the new forces unleashed outside our borders, were interpreted as consequences of the "regime." And as difficulties had been on the rise since 1930, bourgeois discontent has not ceased to grow, along with bourgeois incomprehension.

2. Psychological causes. Impossible to believe that the systematic campaigns of defamation over the past several years, having become increasingly intense, did not gradually undermine, among the ruling classes (by now completely hostile to the "regime"), confidence and, above all, their enthusiasm for defense.

Probability that these campaigns have been run from "outside." In the face of this movement, no serious reaction from the leaders and parties in power. A sort of skepticism on their part regarding their own doctrine and a stupefaction in the face of monetary and economic problems that could not possibly be solved using the old purely political formulas that make up the substance of party platforms. Socialist rehash of old economic credos even more retrograde than conservative credos in these fields. Paralysis of activity on the part of industry as well as of the army during the eight-month war of position.

A "management school" must be created. Not with a political agenda, as the Blum government would have liked, but simply to form the administra-

8. Perhaps Rist is referring to Léon Blum.

tive staffs of the various ministries. They will be charged with studying the "new" problems in accordance with methodical procedures of information and solution. L'École [Libre] des Sciences Politiques did not err by being "liberal," but by not being modern, not having a program adapted to modern conditions; refusing to confront the need for administrative concentration and unification; and assuming that the methods of the period 1870 to 1910, methods based on free trade among nations and on spontaneous adaptation by industry to new situations, were widely accepted, whereas industrialists no longer relied on anything but customs duties.

1 JANUARY 1941 Terrible air raid on the city of London. The Guildhall and part of St. Paul's were on fire two days ago. The English declare three thousand enemy planes shot down since the start of the war. What is that? A month's production! If America does not hurry up, it will be too late. The Germans are preparing to strike a decisive blow. Today we received a circular letter signed by Léonard himself. Sent to all the relatives and friends of prisoners, it announces that cards and letters must be restricted to the polite formulas expressed by the prisoner himself! What a horrid New Year's gift! The appalling idiots who made us lose the war and who now govern could not even protect the prisoners' lives and morale from enemy abuse. But they strut around like that miserable Scapini, with ambassadorial titles to cover up their nothingness, their laziness, and their foolishness. Do they have any idea of the savage, indestructible rancor they are building up in French souls?

3 JANUARY 1941 Conversation at the Ottoman Bank yesterday with Banque Mirabaud's J. B., who has kept up with developments in the Bor affair from the beginning.[9] The company only agreed to negotiate with the German governor on express orders from the government. (It is known that the order was given by Laval following a private conversation with the Germans; he revealed this after the fact to the Vichy government while French representatives were still negotiating in Wiesbaden.) Terms were agreed upon. The company set the price for its shares at thirty-five hundred francs, an amount that the Germans were to offer the bearers – and that capitalized

9. From the beginning of the occupation, Nazi Germany sought to take the place of France, often with the consent of Vichy, in the major business concerns in which France had an interest, notably in Central Europe. This was the case with the Bor copper mines in Yugoslavia, where Vichy ceded French interests under extremely disadvantageous conditions. "J.B." is probably Jean Boissonnas.

twenty-five years of excellent management. Insiders who bought enough shares at the current rate – namely, between nineteen hundred and twenty-five hundred francs – assured themselves of a tidy profit. This is what Laval did. As for the Germans, nothing was demanded in return for this great loss.

I have been told that the military has been put in charge of all provisioning. The president of the Seine, Seine-et-Oise, and Seine-et-Marne Federation of Bakers tells me that the essentials of flour, salt, and firewood had been very well organized by Villey, the Seine's former prefect, but now supplies have been completely disrupted. Decisions are made by the prefects of the three departments meeting together at the military supply office.

Everyone is asking whether the silent protest suggested by de Gaulle for the first of January (all French people staying home at the same time in the two zones) was successful. At four we heard the *Marseillaise* played in London to end the protest. Not without emotion. Strange, this unity realized via the airwaves.

SUNDAY, 5 JANUARY 1941 On the subway a worker saw me standing and, before sitting down himself, gestured for me to take the seat that had become available. Which proves two things: (1) that I look much older than I imagine; (2) that the general boorishness that has taken hold with the bourgeoisie over the last twenty years has not yet completely overtaken the working class.

Conversation yesterday with Barnes, the U.S. chargé d'affaires. He told me that the Germans have given Vichy an ultimatum: by the eighth of this month, Vichy must turn over to Germany the warships remaining to us – if not, complete occupation of France. I expressed doubts about whether the Germans actually intend to go to that extreme, with the risk of North Africa's resuming the war. Barnes thinks the intent is to replace Pétain with Laval. In his opinion the German leaders are convinced of the *total* support that the United States has decided to give England, in spite of a conversation he had recently with a German dignitary who expressed his skepticism. I said the important thing is to persuade the Vichy government. He assured me that Admiral Leahy, the new U.S. ambassador, would not leave any doubt on that score. He is due to arrive in two days. For Barnes there would be a psychological advantage if the United States did not declare war but had war declared against it. He does not fear an attack by Japan. Even if Japan took the Philippines, he said, it would not reduce the chances of defeating Germany in Europe, which is the only important thing.

TUESDAY, 7 JANUARY 1941 Bardia has been taken with thirty thousand men.[10] The Italians say this is just one episode. The Vichy and Swiss radio broadcasts say the same thing. In truth, it is of capital importance because the Egyptian route is closed to the Italians. The danger now is that the Germans will attack via Turkey. But then it will be the war on two fronts that they dread so much.

When, with hindsight, people realize the blindness of the English and American governments and the unbelievable stupidity of the French military command, they will wonder how what is happening today was possible. The answer must be: (1) because of the conviction that after the war of 1914 the horror of all war would persist with *everyone*; (2) because of the profound and persistent misunderstanding of all things German, of the mechanical genius and the breathtaking willpower of this people; (3) because of the incredible foolishness and pettiness of French politics since 1918, which simultaneously sowed the seeds of discord with the Anglo-Saxons and the seeds of resentment in Germany. How wise the policies of Briand appear in retrospect! From the moment England refused to crush Germany, our only option was to seek an entente with the latter. I am proud today of having said, written, and thought this at the time. But I did not have enough authority to be listened to. I have a complete right, on the other hand, to look with irony on those who, having rejected any reconciliation at that time, preach entente to us now with an enemy that no longer needs our consent in order to do what it wants with us.

I really think the true characteristic of the French bourgeoisie is stupidity. A list of their objects of admiration over the last fifty years: Esterhazy, Syveton, Coty, Bailby, Pierre Laval. The very smell of corruption and ignominy emanating from all these men should have alerted them. But they have lost all sense of smell. They erect patriotic statues in honor of men who are no less than traitors . . . because they imagine they will save us from communism.

SUNDAY, 12 JANUARY 1941 Nothing makes us take the measure of our humiliation better than what has happened since Pétain's sacking of Laval. A violent newspaper campaign was unleashed here against the Vichy government. Not a word about what is really at stake: the surrender of our ports and

---

10. The Italians had a major fortification in Bardia, a Libyan seaport close to the Egyptian border. In early January 1941 Commonwealth forces gained control of the town. [TF]

our fleet to the Germans in order to combat England in the Mediterranean, comfort a distressed Italy, and allow Germany to prepare its invasion of Great Britain in total tranquility. The attacks target only domestic issues: insufficient provisions reaching Paris, the reactionary nature of the Vichy government. The hope obviously is to win over whatever pacifist radicals and socialists remain. Vichy radio talks only about trifles such as the discovery of sarcophagi in a church in Poitiers! But nothing about the crisis. The public struggles in this darkness and the most extravagant rumors circulate. The day before yesterday it was the entry of the Germans into the free zone. Noël left that very day without difficulty for Aix-les-Bains, from which he expects to rejoin his fiancée in Annemasse.

Laval's policy is revealed more and more cynically in the pro-German papers: wage war against England in order to save whatever is left of the empire! And rediscover our continental power! This insane program is flaunted today in the *Nouveaux Temps*. And Pichon[11] told me the day before yesterday that Laval, incapable of any passion, is now making a show of his fierce hatred of the English, declaring he wants to "see their bones broken" (verbatim) and accusing them of having brought about his fall from power in 1936 – an unforgivable crime, it seems! Thus it must be shown that, no matter what, England will lose. According to the same newspaper, Lord Halifax's trip to America is proof that Churchill believes he will be defeated! Indeed, according to this hypothesis everyone knows England and the United States "will unite as a single nation," and Halifax has been charged with preparing their union; his mission is thus the first symptom of English demoralization. These insane fantasies have only one redeeming feature: they demonstrate the Germans' uneasiness. But Laval clearly believes them, and in his mad admiration for himself, thinks he can show France the way to salvation, not realizing that he is being used and will be thrown out with the garbage when his treason is accomplished. What is encouraging is the public's complete indifference to these campaigns. It does not believe a word. And it knows who is behind the food and coal shortages and why people must endure the increasingly harsh cold. The public is counting on Pétain to be firm and calmly contemplates the total invasion of France if, as is hoped, North Africa and the colonies respond by resuming the fight at England's side.

But what is Pétain doing? What is this phony triumvirate, which seems to have been constituted by Darlan, Huntziger, and Flandin, thinking? Is it using cunning with regard to the Germans? Is it playing for time? Does it

11. Adolphe Pichon, with the Union of Metallurgic and Mining Industries, was an old friend of the Rists.

really imagine it can save what is left of the fleet? Is it beginning to believe that the English can win? And Admiral Leahy, Roosevelt's personal delegate, will his influence make itself felt? About all this no one has a clue. Vichy's hatred of Laval is still the best trump card. Because none of the men of the triumvirate inspire confidence. Their past is too problematic. They are driven by personal ambition alone.

Thus we are led by night, while the imbeciles go on talking about "national renewal." No doubt by lies, stupidity, and impotence. Great assets to "form the soul of a people," as the journalists who are paid, indoctrinated, and bound by censorship like to say. We must hope that this people, so full of good sense and patriotism, does not allow anyone to "form" – or deform – its soul, but keeps the soul that was formed by 150 years of struggles and of liberty and that the everlasting internal exiles, who have not changed since Valmy, and whose ranks have been swelled by bourgeois fearing for their valuables, would so much like to turn to their own profit.

SUNDAY, 19 JANUARY 1941 I read in Paul Cambon's *Correspondance* this passage, written 20 May 1873, speaking of the attitude of the center right: "These men no longer know themselves and are capable of anything, even of devoting themselves to a Bonaparte. This is the point on which they must be confronted, forcing them to *admit that they would rather see France perish than see it become a republic.*"[12]

What the reactionaries of that age were thinking but dared not avow, today they think *and* avow. They welcomed the defeat – and what they fear in an English victory is the return of the Republic (which they characterize for the know-nothings in the language of Freemasonry). They sustain themselves with what Cambon calls "Bonapartism," that horde of unscrupulous social climbers and wheeler-dealers who for the last ten years have been hawking the beauties of Mussolini's government and have always sided with France's enemies (Italy, Franco's Spain, Hitlerian Germany). The press controlled by them has gradually poisoned French opinion. The mediocrity of the republican party and its leaders' total lack of conviction prepared the way for them. The war of 1914–1918 was a huge disappointment to them. France's victory consolidated the Republic. They swore that would not happen a second time. Toward that end they found this magnificent distraction: the fear of Bolshevism. They accused the republicans of setting the scene for communism, just as they accused Thiers and Gambetta of being *communards* (or as we say to-

12. Paul Cambon, *Correspondance, 1870–1924* (Paris: Grasset, 1940–1946), 39–40; Rist's emphasis.

day, "fellow travelers"). What do they offer us in the way of government? That which we see and which already disgusts all of France. But when the English, with the help of the United States, have won, Thiers's words will once again hold true: "What divides us least is the Republic." In order to understand this, the French will have had to suffer the dreadful experience of German occupation. Stimson has declared to the House Foreign Affairs Committee that Roosevelt's policy allows American warships to accompany convoys of food and munitions to England, and that this was essential – a clear affirmation that the United States is ready for naval warfare. The Germans surely have no illusions as to the proximity of this war.

At last a letter from Léonard, passed on to us by his wife. It ends thus: "Courage, confidence, dignity." He and his friends were preparing a melancholy Christmas party. It is not the prisoners who will give in by "collaborating."

A little while ago I paid a visit to Millerand. Given Pétain's last interview, Millerand thinks "collaboration" is dead.

A letter from Theodore Simson's wife tells us he was arrested in Bouron as an Englishman and put in a barracks in Besançon along with others of his countrymen. He is seventy-two! She, as an American, was allowed to go free, and begs us to intervene.

A letter from Noël, who hopes to get married on Wednesday.

TUESDAY, 21 JANUARY 1941   Weather much milder for the last two days. Great thaw after three very difficult weeks.

Yesterday the newspapers announced the Pétain-Laval meeting. One wracks one's brains to guess what the outcome will be. I went to see von Falkenhausen yesterday morning to dissuade him from attending our bank's board meetings. (He gets eight thousand francs a month from the Ottoman Bank.) I told him that up to now the Turkish government, upon which we depend, was not worried, as we had explained that the commissioner's only aim was to verify that no money trafficking had been going on. But the commissioner's presence at our meetings would give the impression that we are no longer free. The reaction we fear is that we would be blacklisted in Constantinople and that the head office, in order to continue functioning effectively, would feel obliged to break off relations with us and deal only with London. I added that down the road I foresee equally serious difficulties, because the Turkish government, remembering this situation, would draw conclusions unfavorable to the bank. Von Falkenhausen replied that an "interimistic" solution could be worked out; we would convey to him the meeting dates and afterward a summary of what had occurred, but he would not attend. I told him: "Yes, that's a solution, but why not take this opportunity to review the whole situation that is causing our bank's present difficulties?" I also told him that, while willingly accepting this "interim" solution, I did not see why our whole situation could not be reviewed in order for us to be placed on a footing more in line with international law; we would return to our position as a neutral bank, and if Doctor Schaefer had something to communicate to us, he, von Falkenhausen, would be the designated intermediary. He then suggested that I present him with a written explanation of our difficulties. This suits me very well and will allow me to make a written record for the Turks of the position we have taken.

Von Falkenhausen was clearly in a hurry to end this part of our interview and take advantage of the fact that we were alone in order to ask how I felt with regard to France's collaboration. He told me how necessary it was, whatever the name given to it. I said the name had little importance, it is the substance that concerns us, and we do not know what that is – and besides, we only know what we read in the press, over which we have no control. "But," he said, "it is the government that must choose. You people in France are not familiar with totalitarian methods; the important thing is that the government choose a path that leads to success." I answered: "What an immense responsibility for one man to divine the direction in which success lies!" He went on: "This is above all a political issue; as I always tell my friends, problems must be prioritized. Politics first, and the economy will follow on its own." Reply: completely in agreement with you on condition that the ladder have three steps: the military first, then politics, then the economy. I do not know if he understood.

SATURDAY, 25 JANUARY 1941 Last Tuesday at the Suez Company, Jacques Georges-Picot, back from Algeria, told us about his conversation with Weygand. The latter agrees with the Resistance but said he is too old to take the initiative. He will await orders. The English and the Americans are exerting strong pressure on him to make up his mind. Yet another bit of bad luck for us that we have had to turn to soldiers who are all over seventy years old. And they talk about "National Renewal!" It is enough to make you weep.

According to Georges-Edgar Bonnet, Hitler supposedly told Darlan during their conversation at the end of December, "You have only two men in France: Laval and General de Gaulle."

Gustave-Adolphe Monod, back from Marseille, where he buried his father-in-law, tells me that "respectable people" are all saying, "If the English win, we will once again have a government of Jews and Freemasons." Understand the Republic, which, however, was founded and sustained by men such as Thiers, Gambetta, Waldeck-Rousseau, Léon Say, Poincaré, Briand, the Cambons – all of whom were republican and none of whom was a Jew or Freemason. Cambon's characterization of reactionaries' thinking is still true: "Better to see France perish than to have the Republic." Too bad for them: they shall have it anyway.

The other evening, 21 January, we were able to hear a direct radio broadcast of President Roosevelt's third inaugural ceremony at the Capitol building, including his speech. From six to six-thirty, London rebroadcast the American announcer, then the prayer, then the reading of the oath by Chief Justice Hughes of the Supreme Court – then Wallace's oath of office, then Roosevelt's, followed by his fifteen-minute speech saying that the United States would not remain passive in defending the democracies, but would take the lead. This direct contact across the ocean was moving. I know all of these men and they know me. I used to think that one day, because of this, I could serve my country. But today the dream has vanished!

Tobruk was taken two days ago. The English claim to have taken fourteen to twenty thousand prisoners. In all, counting the dead, wounded, and prisoners, they took half to two-thirds of Graziani's army. This is the predictable end for dictators: war and defeat! They say here that the Germans would like to take Bizerte, which could save the Italians from disaster. Will we give them a hand? Or will we escape this last dishonor?

Bellet, back from Geneva, learned from a telephone call that Noël's marriage was apparently going to take place on the twenty-fourth. We had believed it was on the twenty-second. So yesterday we began again to follow the ceremonies at Blonay in our thoughts.

FRIDAY, 31 JANUARY 1941 I ran into Lammers,[13] in Paris for three days on an industrial mission! I welcomed him, and we had lunch together Wednesday at the Café de Paris. He said he no longer has an automobile and his house in Berlin has been requisitioned, as has his office. So they are in the same boat we are. Always a good Catholic, he talked about the "Nazi Party" with the same antipathy as before. He is impressed by the coming together in these times of Catholics and Protestants in Germany in order to defend simple "Christianity." Priests and pastors have been meeting together with the blessing of the pope. Lammers has been corresponding with the latter.

---

13. Clemens Lammers: German economist and international expert.

We spoke very little of the war. However, he declared that in his opinion the Germans would not be able to land in England, nor the English in Germany. "How, then, will it end?" Naturally, I did not reply. As he left, he asked if he could get in touch if he made another trip to Paris. I replied, "Gladly."

Yesterday morning all the newspapers let loose at once against Vichy. "It seems France is at a turning point: collaboration or hostility. She must choose." But the threats are vague. One gets the impression that the enemy is not sure of itself and does not know exactly what to do. The imprecations against Flandin are truly amusing. The dithyrambic praise for Laval shows him definitively for the traitor he is. All of this is excellent.

An afternoon visit to Villard, deputy governor of the Banque de France, to get his permission for the Ottoman Bank to transfer part of its loan accounts from Paris to Châtelguyon. He agreed without hesitation. We spoke of general matters: the sum of 400 million francs being sent every day to Germany is his big worry. And rightly so! Who agreed to that amount of money?

The list of the two hundred "National Councilors" being paid one hundred thousand francs each to form a consultative committee for the marshal is viewed with scorn by everyone here: Cortot, Germain-Martin, La Rocque, Joseph Barthélemy – all the small-time *arrivistes* and unprincipled mediocrities.

Likewise the constitutional decree requiring that State officials take an oath of allegiance before the marshal and establishing his right to punish in their person and in their estate those who fail to take the oath, according to a procedure to be chosen by him in every case. The people who decide these things are grotesque, odious puppets. This is what they call the National Revolution! And we are condemned to prefer them to their possible replacements because of their relative independence vis-à-vis the enemy. The decree, moreover, seems to be aimed at Laval.

SUNDAY, 2 FEBRUARY 1941 For three days the rumor has spread that Langeron has been arrested.[14] In the 28 January issue of *l'Oeuvre*, Déat (servant of the Germans) cites Maurras's article in *Candide* in which he says the "most improbable turn of events" had brought him "what a poet calls a *divine surprise*." The surprise is that on the evening of 10 June "the stars were favorable on only one point: amid the undeniable disaster and collapse, our ideas

14. The rumor was correct: Roger Langeron, prefect of police since 1934, was arrested by the Gestapo on 24 January 1941 and removed from office by Vichy on 23 February 1941. See his journal, *Paris, juin 1940* [Paris, June 1940] (Paris: Flammarion, 1946); the narrative was interrupted on 20 January 1941.

happened to be extremely close to acceding to power." Déat was indignant! One could be indignant for much less. That a Frenchman could write such things! And think them! Déat for once was right: these people's disgraceful behavior must never be forgotten . . . nor should his.

Yesterday and the day before, I saw Jaoul and Painvin to talk about Mario. They make me very hopeful that a position can be found for him.

WEDNESDAY, 5 FEBRUARY 1941 On Tuesday I went to see Doctor Courteauld, who had been to the Ober Langendorf camp and seen Léonard. Precise information about heating, which is inadequate, and food, which is meager. But they are with one another and not in direct contact with the German officers.

Afterward visited Charles Jacob, who has been put in charge of Vichy's Scientific Research Center.[15] I was trying to obtain a grant to print the second volume of my work on unemployment. Like all academics thrown abruptly into administration, he talks a lot and decides nothing. He expounded upon his plans, his views, etc. But he said he needs a week to think about the thirty thousand francs I am asking for and in fact requested a month ago.

FRIDAY, 7 FEBRUARY 1941 The newspapers are full of Darlan's comings and goings between Vichy and Paris. Laval is demanding a sort of blank check; the Germans speak of him bluntly as their man. English and American radios are still reluctant to believe that Vichy will give in to him. We also. It all seems to be a matter of threats. Clearly, the Germans do not yet dare to back up their threats with force. Why not? There must be something that is not going well for them! One still fears for Bizerte. But the English are scoring victories on all fronts, and the Italians are caving in.

Yesterday I had lunch with Georges-Edgar Bonnet after the Suez meeting. We spoke about the future and about what kind of government France would have. I told him I would not be displeased with de Gaulle as leader. He replied that he no longer has the slightest confidence in any generals. We searched in vain for a name the French could agree on. This country has been so deeply divided by the Action Française, ten years of Lavalist intrigues, and the scarcity of republicans, that there is no longer any common ground. We are at odds over "regimes!" When what we need is men to do some simple

---

15. Charles Jacob: geology professor and member of the French Academy; as a Vichy appointee, he headed the CNRS (National Scientific Research Center) from 1940 until the Liberation. [TF]

tasks that constitute the permanent activity of a state. The problem is that each of these tasks requires intelligence and conscience, two things that have been terribly lacking since the last war.

The difficulty in getting supplies has created a whole system of private shipments from the countryside to the city. Here packages of two, three, and five kilos containing butter, beans, and canned goods are piling up at the station. The cold of the last few days and the heavy snow have slowed down distribution. There are still some rural areas (Brittany, Haute-Savoie) where one can find everything. The farmer's wife who supplies Marie and Noël sent a rabbit a week ago. But it did not arrive! Mario sent us three or four packages; so did a fine Breton lady, Mme Plusquelec, whose husband is in prison with Léonard. She says her region is a "paradise." She offers to send a package every week. How long can this go on? The Germans confiscate the cattle feed, the meal, etc. The dairy woman declares she does not know how she can continue to feed her cows. People want to set up chicken coops, but it is hard to find grain to feed the chickens, etc., etc. On top of that, the scarcity of transportation. Our small supply of coal is running low. Each new freeze means we must light the stove again. Then as soon as the temperature rises above freezing, we hurriedly turn it off. The trains have been cut back, and a shortage of lubricants is expected in a few weeks. Doctor Veslot tell us that for every fifty thousand bottles of Gallia milk produced, the Germans take forty-five thousand. The rest is for French babies. Germaine has just told me that the butchers will have no meat this week.... We will do without. The old can be vegetarians. But the young! And the poor! We are fortunate.

MONDAY, 10 FEBRUARY 1941 Three important events on the radio: the English fleet has bombarded Genoa, the English troops are already 200 kilometers west of Benghazi and are heading by forced march toward Tripoli, and, finally, Pétain and Laval were not able to come to an agreement. The post as minister of state offered by Pétain was not enough for the traitor, who wants the presidency. In that regard we have learned that Darlan will be vice president of the council and will also take charge of the navy and Foreign Affairs (Flandin is resigning). What will Laval do? Set up a separatist government? Keep quiet? Will the Germans dare to attack North Africa? It would mean a resumption of the war with many advantages for us.

At ten last night we heard Churchill's powerful and moving speech broadcast to the whole empire, full of pride for what has been accomplished, full of trust in the future, and ending with the most skillful and eloquent appeal to the United States: "Give us the tools and we shall finish the job."

WEDNESDAY, 12 FEBRUARY 1941 Monday at 12:30, Marie and Noël burst unexpectedly into the dining room! Eventful trip crossing the Demarcation Line. But they are so happy, as are we, to see them at last and to hear their stories.

Yesterday I visited Barnes, the U.S. chargé d'affaires. We discussed the meaning of the latest events, which I think constitute an out-and-out failure for Laval. Barnes thinks so, too. According to him, this is what happened: Abetz left for Berlin last week. It seems the Führer told him, in effect:

> You, Goering, and Hess advised me to follow a policy of collaboration. I never believed in it, but I let you have your way. Today it is clear that I was right. I am too busy right now to follow French internal affairs. Their significance will only be clear later. At this time Laval is going to be invaluable to us. The French people will be treated harshly. If Laval appears to be the only person capable of improving the situation, he will have everyone behind him and will play a great role.

This language explains why after Laval's plans fell through and Darlan was chosen as vice president (and heir apparent), the press remained calm instead of flying into fits of rage as one would have expected. Rather, it has presented Laval's failure as a success – the marshal having offered him a post that he refused, according to the press, believing the time was not ripe.

Barnes had told me about a conversation with Laval two months ago that of course had been relayed to Washington. Barnes read the text of that transmission to Laval some twelve days ago. The latter expressed his approval except for one point, where Barnes had Laval say he was convinced that a compromise peace would be arranged. Laval stopped him, saying, "No, that is not what I think – or, in any case, it is no longer what I think. England will be defeated, and it *must* be defeated." Thus, rather than softening, Laval's initial position has become even stronger in spite of events. Laval added that the next time he takes power, he will be careful to arrange in *advance* certain "details"... "which you understand without further explanation" – meaning he will arrest his enemies. I asked Barnes if it is true that Roosevelt is considering a compromise peace (as Georges-Edgar Bonnet had told me a few days ago). Barnes protested vehemently against this idea. His only concern is that Darlan might actually agree with Laval on the policy to follow in regard to England.

Laval's stubborn illusion, which in reality ignores everything connected with Germany, not to mention England and the United States, is that Germany, psychologically, would really like to "spare" France (and not reduce it to impotence) and that, economically, Germany can take the place of England and the United States. *On these two points illusion is fatal.* The evidence as to the first is glaring. As for the second, illusion is just as dangerous. Monetarily, Germany will only recover thanks to French gold, and it must therefore begin to confiscate it – making us dependent upon Germany and bringing about the loss of our foreign assets, the sole means by which we will be able to resume essential purchases for rebuilding after the war, and without which our depreciated currency will be able to buy neither oil nor iron (if the Germans take the east and the north of France), nor coal, nor cotton, nor copper, nor wool. In the absence of foreign exchange, we will need to export massively. But export what, if not manufactured goods (lacking the iron that will be commandeered)? And these goods, how can we manufacture them without importing raw materials? We shall be obliged to borrow. But who will make us a loan? In the case of an Allied victory, it will be easy to obtain one, but if the Germans should win, who believes Germany will lend us money? We will have to beg or else turn over part of our industry to Germany. The only other recourse is the "re-agriculturization" of France, impossible without painful relocations of the population and a prodigious decline in activities of all kinds.

All of this presupposes, moreover, the destruction not just of France but of England and its dominions, as well as of the United States. Germany needs these great markets, and the more it industrializes, the more it will need them. Does Germany believe it can *impose* its exports? Do without some of their raw materials – cotton, wool, copper? The idea is absurd. From this point forward, destruction of the Anglo-Saxons is out of the question. It will thus be a compromise, and only by relying on them will France be able to retain some of her assets.

On Tuesday I went to see Madame Langeron, wife of the prefect, and Langeron's niece Laurence.[16] Langeron was taken away this morning – they gave him time to eat breakfast first. The excuse for taking him: an inquiry. Since then no news except that his health is good. It has been three weeks now. He was taken by soldiers – the military authority at work. Both are very courageous but worn down by waiting.

SATURDAY, 15 FEBRUARY 1941 Rueff came to see me the day before yesterday to express his appreciation for my intercession on his behalf. Thanks to the marshal, he has been exempted from the restrictions imposed

16. Laurence Ballande, future countess of Bourbon-Busset, worked on economic chronology at ISRES.

on Jews – and he is still an inspector at the finance ministry. He is profoundly sickened, however. Bouthillier had tampered with Pétain's decree just to get at Rueff. The decree maintaining restrictions on Jews outlined in Article 2 was dated 22 December but was not published until the twenty-sixth in *l'Officiel*. Rueff went to the marshal to protest.[17] Bouthillier was asked to show the original text. He replied that the text was in Paris and that he could not provide it. Bad impression. Thereupon a friend of Rueff's photographed the original text in Paris and sent it to Rueff. Bouthillier was summoned before Du Moulin de la Barthète, Pétain's chief of staff. He swore by all the gods, rejecting the accusation with scorn. Du Moulin pulled out the photograph. Bouthillier collapsed and asked what he should do. He was required to publish a correction. This minister had thus tampered with a public document in order to harm a Jew.

Rueff used the word "abjection" in speaking of Vichy. That was the word used by Marcilly back in August. This same Bouthillier dismissed Marcel Borduge, president of the Banque d'Indochine, to replace him with Baudouin, who is as repugnant as Bouthillier but not as stupid. Bouthillier, in order to remove Borduge, accused him of being a Freemason; Borduge demonstrated that he was not. He was removed anyway to make way for the man who declared he wanted to "rescue the spiritual values" of France and handed over Indochina.

Marcel Déat, in *l'Oeuvre* of 13 February, names all those who in his eyes are opposed to the "true Revolution": the capitalists who emigrated as well as those who did not emigrate, "with all sorts of nuances, ranging from reluctant collaboration to the glorification of the rebels and the extremes of Anglophilia"; the "roving Jesuits"; the "international Freemasons in the service of the English" – "all those destined by ambition, greed for profit, fear of European revolution, religious fanaticism, or passionate conservatism to be

17. Jacques Rueff had left his post as deputy governor of the Banque de France on 22 January and taken up that of inspector with the finance ministry. Pétain had told him his name would be on the list of Jews who were exempt from the law that required their resignation from professional offices, yet his name did not appear on the document published in *l'Officiel* on 26 December. Yves Bouthillier, who had been finance minister since 16 June 1940, had deleted Rueff's name on Pétain's document, a crime that goes by the name of a "faux en écriture publique." Rueff's daughter Passerose Rueff-Pigeat and her husband, who explained the back story to this passage in a telephone interview with the translator (20 March 2011), said Pétain's decree actually dated from 17 December. In his memoirs, *De l'aube au crépuscule* [From Dawn to Dusk] (Paris: Plon, 1977), Rueff is quite brief regarding this period and does not mention his quarrels with Bouthillier. [JNJ/TF]

the unconscious but zealous agents of Yankee gun merchants." At work in the United States is "Jewish solidarity, Masonic ideology, Puritan hypocrisy." In brief, M. Marcel Déat is out to conquer Catholics, Protestants, republicans, and free thinkers, in France as well as in England and the United States – in a word, all of France, England, and the United States. Q.E.D. But, then, for whom does M. Marcel Déat work? Obviously, for the adversary of those three countries.

Our neighbors' son – a young nineteen-year-old preparing for admission to the Polytechnique – was arrested on Thursday for belonging to the Scouts of France, a forbidden association, and taken to Paris; his parents have no way of knowing where he is.

FROM WEDNESDAY, 26 FEBRUARY, TO THURSDAY, 6 MARCH 1941 Trip to Vichy, Saint-Étienne, Évian. Left on Wednesday in the dead of night. Monday, Mme Langeron had asked me to see Moysset upon my arrival in Vichy in order to prevent Marchand's being named as her husband's replacement at the police prefecture.[18] As soon as I arrived I asked to see Moysset. He told me, "Nothing more can be done. Marchand has been appointed. We had to avoid having the Germans name a new prefect themselves. The delegation in Paris insisted that it be done right away. Langeron will be given whatever satisfaction he may desire. Besides, the only way to rescue him from their clutches was to make him an ordinary private individual. The case is much more serious than Mme Langeron believes. In any event, we know nothing more." I told him that the dismissal of Langeron will make it appear that the French government has lost interest. But its decision has been made. My impression that Vichy feared above all displeasing Paris-Berlin was to be confirmed two days later. I had asked to see Moysset to talk about some general matters. I was able to talk at greater length. First he asked me to tell him what I thought. I told him, with as much force as I could, of reactions here during the Laval crisis, the abrupt increase in the marshal's prestige, the decision of the United States, the decisive role that the United States would play when peace arrives, etc. "And you?" I asked. "As for the broad outline of the future," he replied, "I agree with you. *But they are there.* That is a fact." "At least Laval won't be back?" I asked. He answered with a gesture of uncertainty, which did not inspire great hopes for the future. In short, a very bad impression.

18. The political context for Rist's trip to Vichy was marked by two recent events: Pétain's dismissal of Laval on 13 December 1940, which offered a ray of hope, and the arrest of police prefect Roger Langeron on 24 January 1941, a source of anguish. [TF]

I saw Rochat[19] on Wednesday afternoon to lay out Mme Le Verrier's case for him. He asked my opinion on general matters, and I spoke of the essential role of the United States. Then he asked, "But will they continue their support even if England should be defeated?" One gets the strong feeling that what Vichy fears most is to bet on the wrong horse. However, Rochat appears to be firmer than Moysset. But what influence does he have? Not much. He doubts that the Germans will persist in their invasion plans.

On Saturday morning, spent a good deal of time with Matthews at the U.S. embassy. I shared my impressions, the uncertainties of the Vichy government. He told me forcefully, "We will never allow England to be beaten." At ten he presented me to the ambassador, Admiral Leahy. Imposing figure of a man, sure of himself and speaking with authority. He was especially concerned about supplies to the free zone (the bread ration has just been reduced by 20 percent). He asked questions about the situation in the occupied zone. Very good impression of the role he can play, given his firmness.[20] Matthews told me that America is now sending nine hundred planes a month to England. As for supplies here, he said, "The Vichy government needs to get its information from someone other than Henry-Haye."[21] And again, "The marshal has one weapon: the threat of his resignation."

Marjolin arrived on Thursday evening. He was in Vichy to report on negotiations in which he had participated regarding supplies for the free zone. He had dealt with the problem in Morocco and Algiers. He said the English have asked him, "Why don't you send us men we can trust? For example, M. Rist." As for Weygand's attitude, he confirmed what Georges-Picot had told us: Weygand will take no initiative. Noguès and Weygand are in a situation of rivalry and conflict. Marjolin and I dined together and chatted at length. The same the following evening. He has made up his mind. He will leave for the United States or England. Pathetic stories about the role Mme de Portes[22] has played with Paul Reynaud and about her influence on recent events. Marjolin says that in Africa it is the navy that dominates everything (secret agents, etc.).

19. Charles Rochat was general secretary at the Ministry of Foreign Affairs, Charles-Roux's replacement. Moysset and Rochat were Rist's usual contacts in the Vichy government. [JNJ/TF]

20. For Admiral William D. Leahy's impressions upon his arrival in Vichy, see his book of reminiscences, *I Was There* (New York: Whittlesey House, McGraw-Hill, 1950), chapter 2 and following. [JNJ/TF]

21. Gaston Henry-Haye: French ambassador to Washington since July 1940. [TF]

22. Mme de Portes: Reynaud's mistress. [TF]

Paid a visit to the Turkish ambassador. Much less talkative than usual. "Thrace is a difficult terrain in which to maneuver. The last war was much longer for us than for you. We had scarcely begun to emerge from our economic difficulties when here came a new threat. Kemal Pasha made quicker decisions. Ismet takes more time to think about things." All of that was evidently meant to explain the indecisiveness of his government. On Friday he invited me to tea. I saw him right after my visit to Moysset. He was quiet, with a troubled air. During this time the radio was broadcasting news of Anthony Eden's trip to Ankara and Athens. The news is rather vague. All of this, added up, makes me uneasy as to the Turkish decision. The ambassador also told me that Sir Stafford Cripps is not a good ambassador to Moscow, that it would have been better to send a conservative lord; that way at least the Russian government would have known with whom it was dealing. It seems as always that the equivocal attitude of the U.S.S.R. is keeping Turkey on tenterhooks. Behiç told me that eight hundred thousand French workers were apparently employed in Germany. I exclaimed that, to my knowledge, this was a very exaggerated figure, that even one hundred thousand would be enormous. The next day at tea, Behiç barely spoke, passing his hand over his brow as if half asleep.

Spent half an hour with Jeanneney. In truth, he has been left out of things. The government had asked him to send in a list of Jewish senators. He went with Herriot to see Pétain and explain that he himself had been elected president of the Senate but was not their leader and could not require them to do anything. The marshal understood.[23]

Left on Saturday for Saint-Étienne, where I arrived at 4:30, just in time to see the streets still decked out after the marshal's reception. Jean joined me on the train to Firminy, along with his two sons[24] in their boy scout uniforms. They had been standing for six hours. Jean's cheeks are hollow and he does not look well. Arrived in Fraisses around 6:30. Simone had left to see the marshal at the Firminy station, where he was to speak.[25] Upon her return she

---

23. Regarding this episode, see the note written by Jules Jeanneney himself and published in the appendix to his *Journal politique*, 274–87.

24. Jean's two sons were Marcel and André Rist.

25. Jean Rist lived in Fraisses, a small village located some 2 kilometers from Firminy and near the Jacob Holtzer Steelworks, where he was head engineer. He surprised his father by showing up to meet him in Saint-Étienne, where he and the boys had come to hear Marshal Pétain address the people of this mineral basin. The children had evidently been drafted to help swell the crowd, and Jean had come along, perhaps, to see what kind of propaganda his children were being exposed to. After the Rists arrived in Fraisses, Charles Rist learned that Simone, Jean's nine-year-old daughter, had also been

reported the marshal's words: "France has been looted, and if you do not have enough to eat in the coming months, you know whom to blame." A stroll with Jean and the children on Sunday morning, then lovely music as the children performed a Schubert sonatina and some sonatas by Bach, Corelli, etc. They are their father's only joy. Jean tells me that all the workers are "Gaullists."

I left them on Sunday at 2:30 to take the train to Saint-Étienne, arrived in Annecy at 10:00 PM and left again the next day at 10:00 AM, arriving in Évian at 1:30. Found the Marios in good health. Mario had returned from the Ugine steelworks, where he had met with de Maublanc and Lebreton to discuss his prospective employment. Very anxious for matters to come to a head so he can end his inactivity.

The local village is in a state of (national!) revolution. Maxilly's city council has been dismissed "for bias," according to the letter addressed to the old mayor Viollaz, who showed it to me. They have been replaced by a "delegation" of three members (Ducret, Blanc, Christin). The first two came to see me at Le Très-Clos and spoke to me about some municipal irregularities. To spend their time looking for irregularities – that is just the way to bring peace to the village again! If things like this go on throughout the free zone, what a pretty prospect for national unity! Reprisals, vengeance, legal proceedings, etc. "Now it is friends of the priest who govern," Lugrin said to me. Indeed, it is the most well-to-do who are in charge. Meanwhile, everyone listens to English radio.

FRIDAY, 14 MARCH 1941 Back in Paris, I went to the Société d'Ugine on Monday about Mario's affair. Jaoul told me it has been arranged. All it takes now is Painvin's approval.

On Tuesday the Lend-Lease Act was signed in the United States.[26] A great event that is troubling to the Germans. This is evident in the newspapers here, which – contrary to the truth – announce that American warships will not be able to escort merchant ships.

At almost the same time, Darlan has declared that French merchant ships may be escorted by warships. Just a threat for now.

No news on what is going on in the Balkans. Negotiations must be difficult. Just a simple military display by the Germans? Or a real intention to take the war there? Who knows?

---

recruited along with others from her school to hear Pétain give a speech at the Firminy train station. André Rist, interview, Gif-sur-Yvette, Fall 2010. [TF]

26. This law authorized Roosevelt to "lend" war materiel to any country whose defense he deemed vital to the interests of the United States.

Yesterday I was paid a visit by François Legueu. He is preparing to resume publication of an economic weekly with the remaining editorial staff of the *Bulletin quotidien*, formerly the voice of the Foundries Committee.[27] He said it would be dull but intended to keep people, especially in the provinces, from getting lost "in daydreams." Naturally I said that was excellent, though I could not yet see clearly where he was headed. He continued: "I have a committee of three generals, Anthoine, Maindras, and Bineau, whom I ask for military advice. Well, then, the German army is something so powerful it can carry out any operation it wants, including the invasion of England, and that will be the end of the war."

"I have little tactical expertise," I said, "but the invasion of a country like England is something completely without precedent for which the military itself has no special competence. Moreover, people in France misunderstand or systematically ignore two things: the moral character and tenacity of Anglo-Saxons on the one hand, and, on the other, the will and power of the United States. I know the Americans in charge, Stimson, Hull, and above all, Roosevelt. In France people have no idea of the will that inspires them, nor of the impossibility that they might ever accept, as long as their country exists, a German victory. So that even with a defeated England, there would not be a lasting peace, and, consequently, no possible European reconstruction. The Germans have four months to deal London a great blow, and such a blow, even if it should succeed, would still not be decisive."

He replied, "I admit that if in four months they have not succeeded, it will be too late."

"Well, then! We shall see each other again in four months."

This fellow is the perfect example of today's middle-class Parisian. He is well-off, has no need to earn a living. He was a Croix-de-Feu, even fought well during the last war and was wounded. Yet he is already coming to terms with defeat. What he is actually going to do is make propaganda for Laval. He cannot even wait to see whether the attack on England will succeed. He must begin right away in order to take credit in case the Germans are successful so that he can claim his place in the new order, of which, moreover, he knows nothing and understands nothing from the little he has said to me about it. The only thing he knows is that he will be saved by the Germans from the fear of communism, the great fear that has suffocated them all for the past fifteen years and has taken the place of their great fear of the Germans dur-

---

27. The *Bulletin quotidien*, founded in 1920 on the initiative of Robert Pinot, general secretary of the Foundries Committee, was an influential and highly intellectual mimeographed newsletter.

ing the four years of the last war. Of these two fears, it is still the first that
is the worse. The defeat delivers them from both at once. These people no
longer have any courage, whether faced with external or internal threats. The
future frightens them. They would like to live in peace. And like Gribouille,
they jump in the water to keep out of the rain. . . . What is really dead is the
French bourgeoisie!

Today one could rewrite Marx's book on the class struggle from 1848
to 1851. All events were interpreted as a function of bourgeois fear of the
proletariat. Today this is still the great motivator. One sees it as the origin of
almost all political attitudes, and it continues in the face of the enemy. The
successful union of parties and classes that has occurred in England and the
United States has not been possible in France.

Last Tuesday, the eleventh, Pesson-Didion asked me to drop by Morgan's for a meeting. Bonny Carter, Arragon, and Pesson-Didion were there.
They had received a message from New York saying that, all things considered, the New York partners thought the bank should either hand itself
over to another Parisian bank or become a limited liability company. They
asked my opinion. I replied that it would be a great misfortune to see them
disappear, that appearances could be deceiving, that everyone in France was
counting on an Allied victory, that the day after this victory there would be
considerable room for an American bank with Morgan's choice clientele to
serve as a link between America and a France that would not want to have
exclusive financial ties either with Germany or with England. In any case,
there could be no question of offering itself to other banks. I could see that
what I said reassured and pleased them. At lunch Arragon told me, "You
have lifted a great weight off my shoulders." And Carter asked me to write a
letter summarizing what I had said so that he could send it to his associates
in New York.

*This note has not been found, but we have the text of a letter written by Rist
and addressed to Jay on 10 January 1941 regarding the same matter. It reads:*

My dear friend,

There are, in my opinion, some extremely strong reasons for your bank to remain
in Paris.

From afar one may have the impression that France has definitively lost its
independence and that it is destined in all future engagements to follow in
Germany's wake. But this view seems to me completely wrong. It is true that
France is reduced to silence. In the terrible confusion of the defeat and the
exodus, our nation watched stupefied as a government it had neither chosen

nor desired was imposed upon it. Aside from the marshal, none of the men who compose it had either authority or reputation. France had to accept it, however, because all resistance was physically impossible: all communications among the French were temporarily suppressed, along with the freedom to speak and write, in both the free and occupied zones. Moreover, the best of its citizens had been transported to Germany.

But behind this misleading appearance, there is in all of France, with the workers, the peasants, and the great majority of bourgeois, an absolute resistance of opinion, a refusal to recognize the defeat as definitive, and a passionate expectation that there will be an English or an Anglo-American victory that will bring a return of freedom, both internal and external, to our country. The only exceptions are those impressed by the rapidity of the German victory and ignorant of the moral and material resources of the Anglo-Saxon democracies. Some of them belong to the little anti-English clique that has always existed in our country. But the vast majority of the public believe the war is not over. Peasants and workers get together to hear the news broadcast in French by London radio; this happens in Normandy or in Brittany, in Burgundy or in Gascony, in the occupied zone or in the free zone. Everywhere you go in the free zone you see travelers with Swiss newspapers in their hands, even in third class, because people no longer have any faith in the French papers. Daily conversations show that there is not any difference on this point among the workers, the retail merchants, or the managers and administrators of big business. To say that 90 percent of the French await the victorious end to the war in order to reorganize the country on a foundation of freedom is, if anything, a conservative estimate.

Under these conditions, and admitting, of course, the hypothesis of an Anglo-American victory, the presence of an American bank such as yours in Paris will be a great advantage for both countries. It will very quickly regain its American clientele and an even more extensive French clientele. It will be able to serve as a link between America and a France that will not wish to associate itself too closely with Berlin or London. It will be the ready-made intermediary and, thanks to its unequaled reputation, the most sought-after intermediary for all operations of interest to the two countries. It seems clear to me that in the aftermath of such a war foreign loans will be necessary for private industry as well as for the State. Management of the gold and securities held by French people in the United States will become a matter of urgency. Of course it would not be a concern if a victorious Germany seized French assets in the United States, but if we leave aside this possibility, it is essential that the best use of these assets be made, both for individuals and for the general economy. This cannot happen, however, without the collaboration of the American financial market.

In a word, far from despairing over the future of your bank, I believe on the contrary that its role will only grow larger if the war ends as we, of course, hope (and even if it ends with a compromise peace). Its absence on the day of the peace treaty would mean a gap impossible to fill at a moment when the United States will be called upon, and rightly so, to play a very big role, as France and the French financial market will need the advice and support of the New York market.

It is not easy for me to give an opinion as to the best legal form to give the bank in order for it to remain in Paris and keep its name. The form of a corporation with the same name and with capital in line with that of other French banks could be an acceptable solution in lieu of the bank's current legal status, which would be difficult to maintain. The essential thing in my opinion is that, after the decades during which the bank has played, vis-à-vis the French government and the Paris market, a historic role that no other bank could have fulfilled in its place, it should not put an end, at the very moment when our future prospects appear to be brightening, to a relationship that in the past has been so efficacious and that can be even more so after the war.

Very truly yours, my dear friend.

Seven

The Spreading
Conflagration

16 MARCH–17 AUGUST 1941

As 1941 wore on, the contagion of war quickly spread. The Allied and Axis powers struggled for control over the Atlantic, Scandinavia, the Baltic States, Central Europe, and strategic Mediterranean lands, including Greece, North Africa, and the Middle East. Uprisings and civil wars paralleled the Axis expansionist wars as European colonies and Soviet satellites took advantage of the chaos to fight for independence.

With France occupied by Germany, French colonies made easy targets. Axis ally Japan, long at war with China in the east, had occupied northern Indochina in September 1940 for strategic reasons and in March 1941 pressured Vichy to cede Laotian and Cambodian territory to Thailand, which had been fighting to regain lost territories. In May, the same month the French-Thai War ended, the Viet Minh revolted against French rule in Vietnam.

In April 1941 Rashid Ali al-Gaylani led a pro-Nazi coup in Iraq, fanning Arab nationalist sentiment. By June, Free French and Vichy French troops were fighting each other in France's Middle East mandates Syria and Lebanon.

Which side would the Soviet Union join? This was the great unknown. Germany provided the answer on 22 June when it began Operation Barbarossa, targeting Leningrad, Moscow, and the Caucasus oil fields. In July the U.S.S.R. signed a mutual defense pact with Britain.

Later that month Hermann Goering ordered S.S. General Heydrich to submit a plan for "carrying out the desired final solution of the Jewish question," meaning a more systematic extermination of Jews in the Nazi death camps.

The United States was moving ever closer to entering the war. On 11 March President Roosevelt's signing of the Lend-Lease Act signaled increased American support of the Allies, and on 10 April the United States occupied Greenland to facilitate the creation of military bases and patrols in the Atlantic. An oil embargo against aggressor nations began on 1 August. Five days later Roosevelt warned

Japan not to invade Thailand and on 9 August met with Churchill to sign the Atlantic Charter.

SUNDAY, 16 MARCH 1941 In the history of this war the present moment will mark a turning point. This will be the time of greatest anxiety about the war. In the Balkans the Germans are preparing who knows what, massing troops in Bulgaria, threatening Yugoslavia and perhaps Turkey. The attitude of these two countries remains even more uncertain than that of Russia. Mussolini has made a great effort, so far in vain, to penetrate the Greek front. Will the invasion of England be attempted or not? The Americans are sending ships and weapons. Will they arrive in time? It is a race with Germany. Where will the German force be unleashed? Will they want to, and can they, pull Japan into the fight against the United States? Will Matsuoka's[1] trip to Berlin mark the arrival of a new enemy in the Pacific? Or, on the contrary, an abstention that would indicate a doubt as to German victory? In France partisans and adversaries of Germany put forward their contrasting predictions. In four months we will know who is right. For the losers, it will be a catastrophe. Faced with all of these question marks, French anxiety is growing. The passionate hopes of some and the self-interested skepticism of others are in direct opposition. Who later could imagine this tension of our minds and our hearts, which has never been greater, and from which the fate of France will issue? We will always remember, and later we will look on this as our time of greatest illusion or truest intuition.

SATURDAY, 22 MARCH 1941 On Thursday I went to see Marcus Wallenberg[2] (seventy-six years old!), who is in Paris representing Norwegian Nitrogen Products. Full of sympathy and very friendly. He gave me half a pound of Swedish butter for Germaine. A valuable gift! He filled me in on events in Sweden. Everyone (including the crown prince and, of course, the military) was in favor of going to war to support Finland. The king alone held out (energetically advised by Wallenberg himself). There was not, he told me, any armaments preparation: very few planes, nonexistent tanks, etc. He is proud that he succeeded and that Sweden has remained neutral. "Besides, we have sent the Finns some seven billion francs worth of materiel, provisions, etc. Today," he said, "even Ryti (Finland's current president) agrees that we did the right thing." This is questionable, for at that time Germany had not attacked Norway, and, as Wallenberg himself admitted, the Soviet army was

1. Yōsuke Matsuoka: Japanese foreign minister, 1940–1941. [JNJ/TF]
2. Marcus Wallenberg headed a dynasty of Swedish bankers and businessmen.

worthless, with no power. But he spoke scornfully of all the "idealists" who were pushing for war.

He believes Germany is quite reluctant to invade England; he is sure the military are against the idea. For the moment, they are depending on their submarine units for success. He made no forecasts as to the outcome of the war. But it is easy to see he is very impressed by German strength. He will be spending a couple of days in Berlin and made a very friendly offer to see what he could do there to hasten Léonard's release. He assured me that the Soviet army has four hundred thousand well-trained and well-equipped men who enthusiastically support the government and that all the rest are worthless.

The Germans are transforming the country house of poor Mme C., whose son was killed in the war, into an airmen's bordello. Her protests have been in vain. The renovations were already under way.

SATURDAY, 29 MARCH 1941 Saw Langeron, finally freed, on Thursday. Ran into Serruys[3] at the door! We went in together, he left shortly afterward. Langeron in perfect physical condition. Some boxes in his living room. On Monday he is returning to his private residence. He spoke with satisfaction of his meeting with Abetz, which, he said, lasted for two hours. The Germans want him to stay in his post. He is eager to let the world know how well he gets along with them. Obviously Lavalist. (His niece attributes his arrest to the fact that on the morning of 14 December, noticing that Laval had not returned, the prefect put out an alert, in Lyon, Vichy, etc., and in Paris. She claims that is what saved Laval, who was severely threatened.) Langeron is very upset with the French government, which had arranged his compulsory retirement while he was in prison. He is thinking of going into business. He is confident that he will be welcomed with open arms as a liaison with Germany. He seems to have no inkling of the way most people feel about Laval. I talked to him at length about the United States' position and of their certain entry into the game. He listened without saying anything, clearly not convinced. He attributes his imprisonment to the declaration of a secretary who had been part of Chiappe's staff and who had been arrested for imprudent remarks. She is said to have responded that the prefect agreed with her. But he believes it was personal French enemies who used this pretext to undermine him.

Dramatic weekend. The Tripartite Pact was signed by the Yugoslav ministers in Vienna, followed the next day by General Simović's coup d'état and

---

3. Daniel Serruys: former high commissioner at the Ministry of National Economy (September 1939–March 1940). [TF]

young King Alexander's accession to power.[4] Also Cheren and Harrar were taken, opening up Eritrea and Abyssinia. Everyone is exultant.

Saw this written inside a street toilet: "To clean verdigris, use de Gaulle polish."[5] Everywhere now one sees the *V* on doors, on street surfaces, on railroad cars, etc. Often accompanied by a Cross of Lorraine. This proves how closely the English radio broadcasts are followed.

SUNDAY, 30 MARCH 1941 Laveleye once wrote a book about the decadence of Catholic peoples.[6] He targeted in particular the France of 1870. France has made an enormous effort since 1871 to redress that decadence. Primary education, higher education, and technical education have been improved. (Secondary education has remained humdrum and uninspiring.) But even with all of this, France has not caught up with the enormous advances made since the Reformation by countries that saw education as the means of renewal par excellence and created schools everywhere, thanks to which in Switzerland, in Germany, in Holland, in England, the illiteracy of the masses has practically been wiped out for two centuries; even their peasants are cultivated.

When during the last fifty years it became necessary to inculcate the masses with new methods required by the modern technological revolution, the Germans, Swiss, English, and Dutch were well prepared. Whereas in France a great effort went into teaching the masses just to read and write, in all of these other countries, because the effort had already been made, new techniques – agricultural, industrial, and commercial – could be introduced through education. From twelve to fifteen or sixteen years old, children were able to acquire the elementary knowledge that would help them, once they got out in the world, to adapt to the new way of working, to take an interest in new advances, and to read and understand informative periodicals with practical articles about what was new and changing, thus preparing them to accept certain economic disciplines that were essential in a complex and changing world.

---

4. Actually, King Alexander was assassinated in 1934, and this was followed by a regency. After the regent signed the Tripartite Pact, which had established the Axis powers in September 1940, Yugoslavia's antifascist military staged a coup on 27 March 1941 and Alexander's son, seventeen-year-old Peter, became king. [TF]

5. "*Les vert-de-gris*" was pejorative usage for "German soldiers" during World War II. [TF]

6. Émile de Laveleye, *De l'avenir des peuples catholiques* [The Future of Catholic Peoples] (Paris: G. Baillière et Cie, 1876).

In France the Third Republic will be deserving of history for its enormous efforts to make up for lost time. But advances in other countries were too great to catch up with in so little time, and we are still behind. This is especially true in agriculture; French peasants cannot compete in terms of information and knowledge with those in the Protestant countries. The imbecility of the clerical and authoritarian reaction of the "National Revolution" ignores all of that. Rather than looking at what has been done in progressive countries, it is trying to lead France back to the past, which has, precisely, assured its inferiority. Once again it is pushing the press – whose baseness and stupidity over the last twenty years have surpassed the bounds of the most shameful imaginations – to focus on lies, futility, and foolishness.

As for secondary education, it has always aimed at teaching our children *knowledge* and *doctrines.* Yet its only purpose should be to supply young people with *working tools* (mathematics, modern languages, the gift of observation, and inductive methods of the physical and natural sciences) as well as *tastes* and *curiosity* through literary and historical education. We must prepare adults capable of acquiring *later, on their own,* in the changing and variable circumstances of their profession, the knowledge and doctrines they will need.

Yesterday I went to the supply ministry at Hannotin's request. They want to create a statistical bureau capable of capturing the movements of goods among the French departments, letting them know the existing quantities of each product, etc., etc. I discouraged them from attempting this wacky, superhuman enterprise and suggested instead that they free up communications among departments and rely on merchants to practice their trade in response to market prices. They replied that the Ministry of Finance reserves the right to control prices. The Germans are behind this mountain of red tape and general interference in production and distribution. These poor wretches are completely overwhelmed by a task that is beyond them and that the individualism of the French peasant condemns to failure. When I spoke of the merchants, they replied: "But then they will make money!" That is the great fear of these interventionist bureaucrats.

MONDAY, 31 MARCH 1941[7] Snow today!

As Marjolin left me in Vichy, he spoke these words: "It is now clear that the only names to stand out in accounts of this war by French historians will

---

7. This entry is dated 30 March 1941 in the French publication; I have used the date given in the manuscript, 31 March 1941, and combined it with the second entry for that same day. [TF]

be those of de Gaulle, Larminat, and Catroux. This is overwhelmingly obvious to those who wish to see. In Prussia after Jena, Clausewitz abandoned the soil of his country to head for Russia, declaring that the true patriot must scorn accusations of treachery or mutiny that would unfailingly be aimed at him. Who today does not smile at the name of traitor given to a man who wished to keep fighting? Those are the examples to follow." I did not think I could argue with him.

Naval battle in the Mediterranean, leaving Italy minus three cruisers and two destroyers. Our Algerian coastal batteries chose this moment to fire on an English ship inspecting one of our merchant ships transporting rubber!

Impatience at being powerless and inactive at such moments.

The economic collaboration, the European union that is being advocated today, who wanted this more than I after the last war? In any case, it is going to be imposed upon us after this one, whether by the Germans or by the Anglo-Saxons. A protectionist France will stand out as reactionary in either system and, being a second-rate power from now on, must go along with the one or the other. Great commercial and industrial alliances, approved by the states or imposed by them, will achieve a certain unity. But the momentum and drive will come as always from perfected technology and a trained work force. New competitions will arise, from which new conflicts will be born. The struggle is in reality between completely different forces. The Anglo-Saxons have conceived a civilization based on economic well-being and the growth of individuals. Germany is holding on to the idea of a military power to which all else is subordinate. It is the struggle between naval and land-based dominance – air dominance capable of tipping the scales in one direction or the other. Thus, in reality as always, the power of arms. And we can no longer make any claims in that regard. The sphere of real action is tilting more and more toward the west. It is only there that one will breathe freely.

Stopped by the Morgan Bank. They have just received the answer from their branch in New York. Their associates "regretfully" reject their disappearance as a solution. They approve of a corporation bearing the name "Banque Morgan & Co." But they do not want to figure as administrators (which bothers Pesson-Didion, who sees this as a desertion by the Americans). This entity would limit itself for the moment to an inactive existence. I tell them this is the most acceptable solution. From what Carter tells me, in New York the European situation is considered, to use their English word, *hopeless*. People do not realize the power of opposition in the occupied countries. Or else they suppose that real peace will not be possible and that after this one, another war awaits. Or even that German ascendancy has been definitively attained over the continent and that a great Anglo-Saxon community will be established that France will be unable to join. They forget that France, if she is intelligent, can become a great power, both in the Atlantic and in the Mediterranean, if she knows how to make use of her African empire after Italy's African collapse. A close relationship with England on this side, and with America on the Atlantic side, may still herald fine days ahead for France. But for that to happen, Germany must not be part of the picture – contrary to Darlan's policy.

The important thing is that after the war young Frenchmen find confidence in a mission for their country – a mission that is appropriate for France, not one belonging to the framework outlined by a hostile and barbarous Germany.

FRIDAY, 4 APRIL 1941 Since Monday a German accounting officer (*Wirtschaftsprüfer*) has been installed at the Suez Company to examine its financial situation. The aim is clearly to look for English influence at the Paris branch.

All attention is focused on events in Yugoslavia and Abyssinia, where the surrender of Italy's troops in Addis Ababa is expected any time now. Meanwhile, the English are withdrawing from Benghazi in the face of a new Italo-German push.

Current efforts of the Lavalists are all meant to persuade us that a German victory is inescapable and that French adhesion to the new order must proceed with all haste. Complete silence in the newspapers of this zone regarding English successes in Africa. (However, in all the bookstores African maps are on display.) False news regarding Croatia. It is said to be seceding from old Serbia, contrary to news on English radio that Maček has been retained in the new Yugoslav government and that the union of the country is complete.

Corroborating eyewitness reports indicate that German preparations for aggression in the north of France have given way to defensive preparations and that the troops are leaving to go elsewhere, probably to the Balkans, where the Russian and Turkish tilt in favor of Yugoslavia is becoming clear. Rumor of an Italian proposal to mediate between Yugoslavia and Germany (Boston radio)!

Where is this German push to the east headed? Is it toward the sea, to fight the English fleet with submarines? Is it toward Turkey, to reach Syria, Mosul, and perhaps Egypt? No one knows. Yet one has the impression that the enemy is hesitating. It appears to me, from numerous accounts, that German airfields in this zone are beginning to experience a gasoline shortage. Will petroleum play a decisive role in the end? I remain skeptical. With their Romanian wells and their own refineries, the Germans have what they need to supply planes and submarines. Perhaps not, however, *both at once.* . . . In that case, English chances of victory would be even greater!

SUNDAY, 6 APRIL 1941 Suicide of Count Teleki three days ago.[8] Proof that it is impossible for a man of honor to collaborate with the Germany of today. He had signed a nonaggression pact with Yugoslavia. Now they wanted him to violate it. Besides, Teleki knew better than anyone the dangers of alliance with Germany. His death is a symbol.

This morning the German declaration of war on Yugoslavia and Greece was announced. At the same time, the Russo-Yugoslav friendship pact. Now we are faced with new worries and uneasiness. The taking of Addis Ababa by the English consummates the fall of Italy's colonial empire. But it is not there that France's fate will be decided.

The most appalling thing in the face of these events that inspire at once hope and anxiety is uncertainty as to Vichy's attitude. Are we going to aid Germany? The shame would be complete, and the lunacy as well. Here, in the powerless state in which we find ourselves, there is a strong sense that we are no more than phantoms. One comes, one goes, one attends to business, but in a world that no longer seems real. From all that really lives, all that thinks, hopes, vibrates with normal human feelings, we are cut off. Our world is covered by a lid underneath which the only air we have to breathe is contaminated by the falsification of all news, of all ideas, where good is called evil; honor, shame; where what we do no longer has a clear goal – where the future, like the past, is cut off from us. Only the most elementary human acts, and solidarity in the hope of one day getting out of this prison, have meaning anymore.

A new order declares that property owners will from now on be responsible for any writing on their walls or doors! These inscriptions have become so common: the only outlet for opinion.

Nothing better characterizes the true feelings of Vichy than this constant assertion that France has been on the wrong path for the last seventy years! The Republic alone is targeted, whereas the empire that brought us the

---

8. Pál Teleki had been head of the Hungarian government since February 1939.

capitulation of Sedan has been left out of the picture! Reactionary passion is so idiotic that it does not even know how to hedge.

THURSDAY, 10 APRIL 1941 Yesterday Belgrade and Niš taken. The English have withdrawn to Darnah in Cyrenaica, but are occupying Massawa.

EASTER SUNDAY, 13 APRIL, AND MONDAY, 14 APRIL 1941 Noël and Marie came to spend Easter Sunday with us. Dark news from Africa. This morning the Germans are at Bardia, thanks to an astonishingly bold maneuver. During the naval battle against the Italian fleet, triumphantly celebrated by London as a great victory, the Germans were having their heavy tanks moved from Sicily to Tripoli! A crafty stratagem that will be remembered as an astonishing example of their military genius and audacity.

TUESDAY, 15 APRIL 1941 Pesson-Didion called to tell me his associates have left. This indicates the increasingly rapid evacuation by Americans. The United States will soon be at war with Germany. The Morgan Bank has refused to change its status for the time being. This is wise.

SUNDAY, 20 APRIL 1941 The Serbs have been crushed. Horrible raids on London. Lord Stamp[9] killed along with his wife and son, according to the radio. One of the most brilliant English brains I have known. With a certain tendency to sympathize with the Nazis! A mixture of Christian, businessman, and economic dialectician.

Uncertainty for the future. The public on the whole are easily impressed by German victories. They become discouraged. The Nazi-run French papers try to turn this situation to Laval's advantage. For Darlan is no longer enough for them. They must have Laval again.

If history confined itself to the struggle of nations among themselves, there would be plenty to cause despair. The growth of the Nazi state, destroying and subjugating everything around it, deprives others of any raison d'être, any purpose in life! Happily, the history of the world consists of something else: scientific advances, the desire to live with more humanity and solidarity; the representation of life by art – all of that counts more than the states' falling upon one another, and that is exactly what constitutes the meaning and the grandeur of this war. The fate of nations, that is to say, is not

---

9. Lord Charles Stamp (1880–1941): statistical economist and former British representative to the Dawes and Young committees on German reparations.

the only thing at stake – but also that of "civilization," as that old reactionary Metternich remarked on the subject of Napoleon. How many analogies between the history of Napoleon and that of Hitler! The situation today resembles that of Napoleon after Tilsitt. The whole continent at his feet, and only England against him. Prussia hostage like France today. The differences are air power and the United States; these will constitute the end for Hitler. Napoleon encountered Spain and then Russia. It seems neither will play a role this time, whereas Russia . . . ? But the air and naval might of the two great Anglo-Saxon powers?

TUESDAY, 22 APRIL 1941 Visit from Guy Merle d'Aubigné, a comrade of Léonard's in the internment camp, sent back, as the father of four children. Léonard always full of spirit and courage, the least "collaborating" of all. He is brave.

Disaster for Yugoslavia and Greece. The intrigues are worse than ever, as are insinuations in the papers affirming Germany's definitive victory.

FRIDAY, 25 APRIL 1941 Freezing cold since yesterday, and this morning, snowstorms. Yesterday another Suez Company lunch. There were at most ten of us. Emmanuel Rousseau announced that Laval's return to the ministry would be made public today.[10] Every day the calls for his return in French-language German papers get stronger. Bellet tells me of his conversations in Vichy, where he spent two days with Behiç and the Yugoslav minister. Behiç declared that German pressure to cross the free zone and enter Spain in order to attack Gibraltar is increasing daily. In Spain Franco is putting up a weak resistance. The Germans would like to occupy the whole coast, from Dakar to Portugal, to stop the Americans from landing there. They would simultaneously press on toward Suez and trap the English in the Mediterranean. Their plans are beginning to smack of fantasy. What could help them is the astonishing aptitude of the Anglo-Saxons to let themselves be preempted. The infinity of German ideas always surprises them after the fact. Their imagination cannot admit that this is a reality. Roosevelt, they say, wants to wait until he has finished with the Japanese. That may take some time. Meanwhile, the Germans are targeting Dakar as a response to the occupation of Greenland by the American air force. Dakar and Greenland! This is what war has become in a world transformed by aviation and the occupa-

10. The rumor turned out to be false. Emmanuel Rousseau, honorary member of the Council of State, was on the board of trustees for the Suez Canal Company.

tion of Africa. The Americans must decide to make a surprise attack, with no declaration of war, on the Japanese fleet. Will they dare? Their speeches are preparing American opinion for war.

The famous passage in Chateaubriand's *Mémoires d'outretombe* – "There are times when we must ration our alms of contempt, for there are so many needy ones" – has never found a more astonishing occasion for its application than in the France of today. The impossibility of imagining that Germany really is what it is must perhaps be recognized as having played a role in this prodigious accumulation of despicable acts. Many find the enormity of Germany's faith in force alone and its unheard-of contempt for other peoples beyond belief. They are sure that, in spite of everything, Germany is like others, that it can be "had" or cajoled by those who are more astute. Such people are in fact being "had" by Germany. When one thinks that *no one*, not in France, not in England, not in the United States, suspected the weapons revolution that Germany was silently preparing with a view to taking revenge for the war of 1914! The few men who knew of it did not manage to convince their governments that Germany was resolved to take advantage of its monopoly. For it is the governments' *incredulity* more than their ignorance that is staggering. One must reread in Rivière's book the profound chapter on German belief in the "possible": "Whatever is possible is permitted."[11]

The Yugoslav minister told Bellet that victory was not in doubt, and in his country, moreover, notwithstanding the capitulation of two armies, the remaining troops would continue to resist in the mountains.

SATURDAY, 26 APRIL 1941 The two speeches by Cordell Hull and Colonel Knox lead one to believe that the United States will very shortly enter the war for good. These are two responses to those who thought a resounding English defeat would make America hesitate. On the contrary, America has declared that her choice is made and that she has gone too far now to turn back. England's war is *America's* war, she declares. After that there will still be three great unknowns: Japan? Russia? Turkey? At the end of this war everyone will be courting Russia!

Tsouderos was appointed prime minister of Greece five days ago. This charming man, so simple and conscientious, was exiled a year ago by Metaxas (for having criticized the government in a *private* letter later stolen

---

11. Jacques Rivière wrote a memoir of his time as a German prisoner: *L'Allemand: Souvenirs et réflexions d'un prisonnier de guerre* [The German: Memories and Reflections of a Prisoner of War] (Éditions de la Nouvelle Revue Française, 1918). See the chapter titled "La morale du possible," 53ff.

from the recipient by a spy). He did not like totalitarian governments. As I was comparing such governments to that of the Soviets, he said to me in a melancholy tone, "At least that one has an ideal!" Nothing is further from his way of thinking, however, than Bolshevism. Now he is charged with the heaviest responsibilities. The Greek government has announced that it is abandoning Athens for Crete. Soon Europe will have only governments in exile. Happy those that are on islands!

Exasperating difficulties for Mario's return. He has a pass. But they will not give his wife one!

Growing problems with food. Practically no more meat. Some vegetables are once more appearing in the marketplace. Prices double or more. Forbidden to ship potatoes.

TUESDAY, 29 APRIL 1941 Amusing story of de l'Hôpital's arrest. Young Ratier,[12] finally freed after two and a half months' detention in the Cherche-Midi prison, tells us of an encounter he had there with de l'Hôpital's commanding officer, Marshal Foch's former aide-de-camp – the very one who had asked me at the burial of German ambassador Roland Köster to help establish a new Franco-German organization inspired by the Croix-de-Feu! What happened to this fellow is truly comical. He was amusing himself by setting up a group to prevent the return to power of "Jews and Freemasons" in the event of an English victory! Now, there is a farsighted man who continues, like other Frenchmen of his ilk, to put partisan concerns above all else! But the Germans arrested him because he did not ask for their authorization! He responded (and here is where the thing becomes magnificent) that if people knew he was operating with their authorization, no one would follow him! If anything depicts the unfathomable abyss of stupidity on the part of French reactionaries, not to mention their narrow-minded confusion of ideas, it is this little anecdote.

THURSDAY, 1 MAY 1941 "Labor Day." The workers will collect all of their wages for this day off, in spite of an attempt to confiscate half for the "Secours National." This idea was scuttled in the face of unanimous disapproval. Almost no one here knows that 1 May was introduced in Germany as a national holiday by the Nazis, a new effort at *Gleichshaltung.*[13] Posters

---

12. Rist was referring to the son of one of the Rists' neighbors in Versailles.

13. *Gleichshaltung* is German for "assimilation" or "bringing into line."

everywhere show the marshal extending his hand to a worker and saying, "I keep all promises, even those of others." Mystification and ignominy.

Talking yesterday with Laurent-Atthalin at the Banque de Paris, I was told that those English "swine" are on the point of throwing in the towel, that those American "swine" will never enter the war, and that if Greece and Yugoslavia have done so, it is the fault of the English and the Americans! I explained to him why I was sure that the Americans would enter the war. This blindness on the part of the "Lavalists" is quite encouraging for others. They will not forgive the English for not allowing themselves to be beaten in September 1940, thus upsetting Lavalist predictions.

FRIDAY, 2 MAY 1941 A visit from Bolgert and his wife. Bolgert states with certainty that the penetration into Morocco is much greater than people think.

Nazi propaganda makes a very effective point, which is that we must above all develop virile traits such as courage, endurance, and loyalty in our men, especially our young people. These moral virtues are essential; all else is secondary. This idea appeals to many with a certain nobility of spirit. But the same mistake is always made. Courage, stamina, and loyalty are admirable and necessary virtues in all political systems. The mistake consists in claiming that these virtues are sufficient and that democratic or liberal regimes hinder their development. The political problem is transposed onto a purely moral plane, disguising the fact that political organization is one thing, moral education, another. It is thus possible to avoid examining the question of political organization and to take for granted that these virtues develop better in a totalitarian regime – under the pretext that in democratic regimes many men are inclined to subordinate these virtues to financial and political advantages or to party interests. The problem posed by the current crisis is altogether different.

It is a matter of knowing *what ends will be served* by these avowedly indispensable virtues. The subordination of weak countries to the strong? The suppression of national ideals? Internal political repression? Or the preservation of independent nations and the free development of individuals within them? It is a matter of knowing if these virtues, necessary for all regimes, will not finally be suppressed, cynically used for personal political ends by the heads of totalitarian governments, and, consequently, finally condemned to a withering away, while universal warfare, without term and without limits, is unleashed. But the discussion of such problems is "political." It thus ceases to be truly accessible to the masses, who judge everything on the "moral" plane of their feelings, their passions, and their grudges. Hence the power of Nazi propaganda.

SATURDAY, 3 MAY 1941 A senator who was minister of agriculture ten years ago has solemnly explained in *Les Nouveaux Temps* that the gold standard is the worst of monetary systems.[14] He thinks this will show he is "in the know" so that he can pass as an economist in the eyes of the Germans. He does not realize that their aim is simply to accumulate gold in Berlin and persuade *everyone else* to do without a commodity they confidently expect to have the monopoly on. Otherwise they would not be prowling around Martinique and would not have demanded Belgium's gold. How they must laugh to read such wild flights of fancy!

The more it develops, the more foolish the German enterprise appears. Already the diversion of its push toward the Balkans on the heels of the Italians and the abandonment of an invasion of Great Britain (at least for the moment) mark a change in plans that postpones the *real* decision. The complications that could arise in Turkey, Russia, Iraq, and Palestine are infinite. Even the taking of the Suez Canal would not resolve the problem. More than anything else, the goal must be to stop the United States from arriving in time. But the latter appear to have understood and are feverishly speeding up production. Precise airplane production figures for the two adversaries remain unknown. It seems certain, however, that German production will be surpassed in six months by that of the Anglo-Saxons. When that happens, life in Germany could become intolerable. The Allies' two weak points: (1) current powerlessness to repulse German attacks on Great Britain; (2) insufficient mastery of the seas, especially in the Mediterranean. Enemy transports are still in circulation, whereas they should be stopped. If these two weaknesses are overcome, the odds will change.

MONDAY, 5 MAY 1941 Magnificent weather for three days now. All night planes were passing overhead. Toward London? No doubt. Strange impression, the passing of those machines on their way to deliver death in a few hours – without our being able to do anything.

According to English radio, American ships have arrived in Suez. If the news is true, this is a crucial juncture.

---

14. Victor Boret: senator from La Vienne beginning in 1927 and twice minister of agriculture (1917–1919 and 1930–1931). His article appeared in the 11 April 1941 issue of *Les Nouveaux Temps* with the title "L'Illusion de l'or" [The Gold Illusion].

Yesterday a visit from Pesson-Didion. He said, "The same men I had known as brilliant officers at the end of the last war I have found to be leading our country in this one, but asleep, sclerotic, intellectually stagnant. At the beginning of the war we suggested that they have their staff officers do exercises to get the foot soldiers used to planes flying overhead. They responded, 'It's not worth the trouble.'" He talked about the crossing of the Meuse, which was accomplished by all means possible: "Even if the bridges had been destroyed, the result would have been the same; we were beaten as of that moment."

Encounter on Saturday at the Academy with Dean Ripert, during whose short spell at the education ministry he sent Gustave-Adolphe Monod packing. I told him what I thought of this measure taken against a grand *mutilé* whose conduct during the Great War was heroic. And I turned my back on him.

WEDNESDAY, 7 MAY 1941 Party for Germaine with Marie, Noël, and the Claudes. Played the 13th Quartet. At times the noise of planes passing above us headed for London on their mission of death drowned out the sound of the music.

THURSDAY, 8 MAY 1941 Little Antoinette, wishing to tell me something about May the first, began thus: "You know, May the first, called Saint Pétain's Day . . . !" (May the first is Saint Philip's Day).

Read Proudhon's book *La Révolution sociale démontrée par le coup d'État*.[15] How many similarities with what has been happening for the last five years! Fear of the "Popular Front"[16] corresponding to that provoked by the days of June 1848. Afterward, conservatives doing everything in their power to overthrow the republic and limit voting rights. They formed an alliance with the Bonapartist rabble just as they have today with the Lavalist crowd – in both cases, calling themselves republicans in order to get the popular vote. Fear of the 1852 elections and the new electoral law denying Louis-Napoléon the right to be named president again led to the coup d'état of 1851. It is here that the analogy breaks down or, rather, becomes tragic. Defeat by Germany has suddenly put power in the hands of Laval, who made

15. Pierre-Joseph Proudhon, *La Révolution sociale démontrée par le coup d'état du 2 décembre 1851* [The Social Revolution Made Manifest by the Coup d'État of 2 December 1851] (1936; Paris: Garnier, 1852). [TF]

16. The Popular Front: left-wing coalition that governed France from 1936 to 1938 (Blum, Chautemps, and Daladier revolved in office as head of state). [TF]

haste to stage his anti-Parliament coup d'état in June with the applause of everyone on the right. To the internal coup d'état is now added external treason! That is what the people of 1852, at least, did not have to witness. That is what will be the eternal shame of today's France. As for the republicans, their leaders abruptly disappeared from the scene, then as now.

TUESDAY, 13 MAY 1941 I always come back to the same idea: until we can unmask the reactionary conspiracy begun ten years ago to destroy the Republic by preparing defeat, we will be unable to understand what happened in 1940. The main character is always the same: Laval. The groups vary: the upper middle class, licking its wounds from the Great Depression; former conservatives, disillusioned by the results of the 1918 victory that consolidated a detested regime; pacifist, internationalizing socialists refusing to see in Germany anything other than a victim; speculators, determined not to relive the problems arising from deflation nor the personal sacrifices made necessary by war; all those frightened by Russian communism and affecting to believe that French communism is dangerous – and relying upon the French taste for scandal to spread their ideas. On the other side of the coin, republicans who are overwhelmed by economic problems and willfully blind to external danger, coupled with a vain and slothful military command infested with politics and knowing nothing about their profession, thanks to vanity and laziness.

The Germans take only 25 percent of the oil that arrives in Marseille, true. But they require the government to stockpile enough oil *for one year.* This explains why Bordeaux and Marseille are swimming in oil and we have none.

WEDNESDAY, 14 MAY 1941 Lunch with Dard, de Tarde, and Sommier.[17] Sommier spoke of Marlio's letter from the United States describing the unimaginable speed and power of America's industrial war effort. I shared my absolute conviction that America's leaders have the will to carry through to the end. These Americans whom I know well – it seems no one here has any idea who they are and what they can do.

THURSDAY, 15 MAY 1941 A radio announcement of Vichy's decision to make Syrian airports available to the Reich. Humiliation and disgust. Never in its entire history has this country fallen so low! Are we going to be

---

17. Émile Dard: diplomat and historian; Guillaume de Tarde: state councilor and railway vice president; Edme Sommier and Louis Marlio: industrialists. [JNJ/TF]

drawn into the war with Germany *against* the United States and England? Infamous prospect!

Rudolf Hess's flight and his landing in Scotland! He is the subject of all conversations. What a revelation of the Reich's internal machinations!

SATURDAY, 17 MAY 1941 Yesterday Pastor Pannier told me what happened on 11 May at the Joan of Arc statue. He was there with his wife. Several thousand people (five thousand he said) were gathered in groups on the sidewalks (controlled by amenable French police officers). Some girls started singing the *Marseillaise*, which the crowd took up in chorus. After that the pastor went away, but he found out how the incident ended from a very reliable source. Suddenly a German officer appeared in front of the statue and, at his side, a Frenchman. People did not realize what was happening, but the officer took out his revolver. Immediately, a dozen men (veterans?) surrounded him to keep him from firing. Worried that he was about to be set upon, the officer withdrew, and some moments later it was learned that the *Kommandantur* having been alerted was sending vans with machine guns. The policemen begged the crowd to disperse, which apparently it did. During the first part of the ceremony, a German officer in a car had passed by the statue (as the rue de Rivoli was open to traffic) and given Joan of Arc the Nazi salute. He was jeered by the crowd (and he himself, no doubt, imagined he was making a courteous gesture of sympathetic understanding!).

That same eleventh of May, Admiral Darlan was in Berchtesgaden.[18]

We have learned that two days ago the English bombed the Syrian airfields where German pilots had landed.

That evening the marshal, speaking on the radio, gave his approval to the Darlan accords, asking the French to have confidence in him, but without bothering to reveal the content of the accords.

This war has demonstrated that the British Empire is incapable of defending itself *alone*. The British had to rely on France to resist and allow them to ready their armaments. Now that France has fallen, they would be powerless without the United States. What a sorry commentary on their policies of the last twenty years!

SATURDAY, 24 MAY 1941 Last Wednesday, after the Suez Company meeting, Mathieu de Lesseps[19] let loose with a sadistic outburst regarding

18. Berchtesgaden: site of an extensive Nazi retreat in the Bavarian Alps. [TF]

19. Mathieu de Lesseps: grandson of Ferdinand de Lesseps, a Suez Canal Company administrator.

France's degradation: "She has sunk even lower than the French think." He said this with undisguised joy, a kind of satisfaction in revenge. He is regurgitating all the bitterness of Panama at a distance of fifty years. At last he has his vengeance on that filthy regime. Let France perish, provided that the republic dies with it. This state of mind on the part of reactionaries is unbelievable, yet all too real. It is at once their condemnation and their curse. What a buildup of stale hatreds among these wretches! What retaliations from *others* are they driving us toward! When a country has reached such an extreme of internal hatreds, can it recover? Rohan[20] took me aside to say that in 1936 it was the English who brought down Laval, and never had they spent so much money to overthrow a French minister! Such are the fairy tales that those imbeciles on the right, crowding around the man from Stockholm, have swallowed.

WEDNESDAY, 28 MAY 1941 Grave events these past few days. In Crete, whose conquest is not yet complete, one sees once again the inadequacy of English air power. Yesterday, a better piece of news – after the blowing up of the battle cruiser *Hood,* widely touted by the Germans – the *Bismarck* was pursued and sunk off the coast of Greenland by the English. Last night a major speech by Roosevelt. Germaine got up at 4:00 AM to hear it. This is the saber-rattling before their entry into the war. The night before, the Germans had Laval address a speech to the Americans! Sheer stupidity – when we know that the very name of this man nauseates even the most ignorant farmers of the American Far West.

Yesterday at lunch (with Farnier and Auboin), Mme Auboin told me that soon after the armistice she received a letter from a reactionary friend, containing these words: "At last we are victorious!" She said she was speechless.

This past Sunday lectured on Sully at the Musée Social.[21] This spurred me to reread the history of finances during the ancien régime – that period of ready violence and scandalous exploitation for the sake of sustaining fantastic wars! And this is the model they offer us today. Besides, it is the only financial system that our Radical Socialists understand.

Negotiations to reduce our tribute to the Germans would appear to aim at lowering by a hundred million the four hundred million a day we are paying, but part of the balance would have to be *paid in gold*!

Future generations will find it hard to believe that so many are *indifferent* to this tragedy – a drama in which the moral fate and entire historical destiny

---

20. Jean H. de Rohan, Vicomte de Rohan-Chabot, was on the Suez board.
21. Musée Social: research institute focusing on social economics. [TF]

of France is being played out. Among the indifferent one finds almost all of those who followed Laval and the Action Française over the course of the last few years. Their hatred of the majority of French people (for they are, in spite of all, a minority) has reached such an extreme that the externally induced catastrophe has been welcomed. Moreover, German despotism will free them from thinking about all the internal problems that would require a little courage and sacrifice. It relieves them of the dreadful fear that has gripped them for the last ten years – fear of communism and fear of economic crises, fears they do not dare to admit but that explain in truth all their actions, all their hatreds, all their uncritical acceptance of the worst calumnies and the worst crime fiction aimed at the previous regime, calumnies that help them justify themselves on the grounds of "morality," their so-called love of "right-thinking" people, their inexpiable hatred, and their hidden fear. And in the end, their love of "right-thinking" people leads them to acclaim Laval – precisely because they sense he can handle all the dirty work.

At ten o'clock this morning, following Roosevelt's speech, English radio broadcast the proclamation of a state of "emergency" in the United States, placing all powers of civil and military requisitioning in the hands of the president. This is the last step before war.

Yesterday, after his return from a trip to Algeria and Morocco, Wibratte[22] described for us the rapid economic changes that the war has triggered there. The embargo has spurred the development of industries such as coal mining, and wine is being used to make alcohol, replacing gasoline in automobiles. However, the mining of minerals is declining for lack of export potential. But railways, electric grids, dams, and irrigation are expanding rapidly. The prices of agricultural products are rising. Money is pouring in, and lodging can no longer be found – because of so many immigrants. This is "war prosperity." Beware the aftereffects once peace has arrived. But who is thinking about peace?

SUNDAY, 8 JUNE 1941 On Thursday I waited for Lolli and Mario at the Gare de Lyon, hoping they would return on the train with those being repatriated. But no luck! In a letter yesterday Mario said he is obliged to consider coming back alone! Decidedly, the Darlan negotiations, far from easing communications between the two zones, have made them less frequent. Ten days ago I was refused the pass I had asked for.

---

22. Louis Wibratte, vice president and future president of Paribas, was also during this period head of the board for Chemins de Fer Marocains [Moroccan Railway].

The day before, Jaoul had asked for me, so I went to see him at the Ugine office. He insisted that I see the marshal and explain to him how insane it would be to fall out with the United States. I accepted but made it clear that the marshal would have to ask me to come himself. That is what he meant, he said. He had recently returned from the free zone, where he had seen Perrin.[23]

Great anxiety this week because of the negotiations under way. I have not seen anyone up to now who does not feel it. For many people Pétain is losing his charm. They say that in Dijon his portraits have disappeared from the shops. Meanwhile the disciples of Vichy are spreading the rumor that peace is at hand. Their stupidity has no bounds: one of them assured me that Rudolf Hess's flight is proof that negotiations are under way – and that Hess had seen Sir Samuel Hoare in Madrid.[24] I replied that Germany can easily negotiate in Bern, Stockholm, or Madrid. But nothing is going to change the minds of those who believe England is floundering, do not believe in the arrival of the Americans, and ardently hope for a peace that, in their eyes, would maintain the current regime in France and assure that other nations remain in the grip of dictators.

Today we are told that the English and General Catroux[25] have entered Syria. Will this be a success? Or the beginning of Frenchmen fighting one another in the colonies? This war will have inflicted upon us the most frightful of conflicts, the kind that can divide a country, tear it apart, and rip it to shreds while the enemy looks on.

Today visited our potato fields, or, rather, patches, to see if the beetles have invaded. This is the great occupation of all French people. Food is more and more difficult to come by. Another fine result of the collaboration.

MONDAY, 9 JUNE 1941 Ship captain Bion (with Matériel Téléphonique), who headed maritime communications during the previous war, told me that upon arriving in Vichy after the armistice he ran into an army friend, a colonel or general, who said: "At least this time you won't be able to say it was for lack of technology that we were defeated!" So it was not enough for this imbecile that the Germans were superior in tanks and planes and rolling stock! Nor was it enough that at *no* time did French soldiers even glimpse any French airplanes! At all costs, he had to discover some "moral causes." In the face of such total obliviousness, one wonders how this wretched, routine-

23. René Perrin: head of Aciéries d'Ugine [Ugine steelworks] and of the Compagnie Française de Raffinage [French Refining Company].

24. Sir Samuel Hoare was at the time Great Britain's ambassador to Madrid.

25. General Georges Catroux was in command of Free French forces. [TF]

bound army can be saved. And this is the moment they have chosen to fill all civilian posts with army officers.

At times we feel gripped by a terrible anguish. What if England, after all, even in spite of help from America, were unable to resist for lack of competent military and naval leaders? The other day a newspaper article carried this headline: "Where is our Nelson?" Since the loss of Syria, whose conquest had aroused so much hope, each of us is secretly asking this question. Here we are in the month of June, and there is not an impressive naval power in sight. The Italian bases have not been touched. Rhodes, which could have been taken long ago, is only blockaded – whereas French Syria has been invaded. English daring is exercised more readily against vanquished France than against Italy. This is an astounding thing. Is it incompetence or ignorance, or are there second thoughts? Do the leaders still lack the imagination required to understand their enemy? And if so, can one not fear the worst – especially if America persists in not declaring war, in not taking the final step that alone would make the enemy lose confidence in its ability to stop her, a confidence it clearly has and is fully exploiting with its propaganda?

In rereading the histories of Alexander and Napoleon, one is struck by the futility of those great victories and triumphs of romantic conquest. It is all we can do to interest ourselves in those battles, those triumphs, those acts of vengeance on peoples or individuals. What remains of all that today, if not astonishment that one man could have shaken up whole populations only to see the borders and nations return in the end to their starting point! Meanwhile the masses lived on and had reasons to live. In the past they lived for religious reasons, focusing on the value of individual lives; today they live for reasons of civilization, the desire to contribute to improving the common good through scientific discovery and a more complete understanding of the universe. This is what endures in spite of such immense cataclysms. Otherwise, human life at such times would have no more meaning than that of a herd of cattle.

What can one divine of the future? Nothing, if not that nations will need to focus on their defensive forces, recreate professional armies, and, consequently, reduce political freedom and put an end to party squabbling. But how will they cope with *social* struggles exacerbated by poverty? By despotism from above? Or from below?

THURSDAY, 12 JUNE 1941 Here is an example of the rumors spread by Germany's defenders, intended to make the public believe peace is at hand. The following explanation of Rudolf Hess's flight was reported to me as making the rounds in so-called informed circles. Hess had met privately with Sir Samuel Hoare in Madrid and they had exchanged views on a compromise Anglo-German peace. This peace would supposedly be made at the expense of France, which would divide its colonial empire between the two . . . thieves. Having returned to Berlin, Hess is said to have brought the Führer up to date. The latter was supposedly vastly irritated, wishing, he said, to crush England. Hess, alarmed by this anger, is then said to have taken the same airplane that brought him back from Madrid and fled. Everything in this story is clearly biased: the readiness of England to deal, English perfidy vis-à-vis France, and Germany's resolve. At the same time, the rumor is being put about that in Berchtesgaden Darlan obtained substantial promises from the Führer himself concerning Alsace-Lorraine, which would be granted some form of autonomy. I asked my interlocutor if France would get her army back.

The only way such insinuations can succeed is if there are Frenchmen who willingly lend themselves to these inventions, pretend to believe them, or, in their total ignorance of Germany and hatred of England, really do believe them.

SUNDAY, 15 JUNE 1941 The other day, in Guerbois's small coffee shop across from the Bon Marché, where only calm, discreet people come, I saw a man at a neighboring table rise, walk over to two seated women, converse with them a moment, then suddenly raise his voice, as though to give everyone present, ten people at most, the benefit of his lecture: "We must tolerate everything happening to us as a punishment for having put up with Léon Blum. We deserve all this for not having stood up to him sooner – even those who did not vote for him. We can only bow our heads in the face of justice." This imbecile was obviously proud of giving his civics lesson to everyone in the small café. I watched him. He was a well-dressed bourgeois with a rather stern face, convinced of his superiority. His demeanor was that of the classic Croix-de-Feu – stubborn and sure of himself. For him, the great European and global drama could be summed up by the case of Léon Blum, and its causes could all be found in the error his compatriots made in accepting this man. Of the Anglo-German conflict, of the reconstitution of Germany by Hitler and the army, of its sixty-year struggle for hegemony, of Poincaré and Roosevelt, he was hardly even aware. As far as he was concerned, the Popular Front and Léon Blum summed up the causes of the drama. There are many such cretins in this poor country.

TUESDAY, 17 JUNE 1941 In Isabelle's little notebook, where she jots down the things that are important to her and which she has left with us, we found the following page written during her stay with us last week: "Non-collaborators of France, listen, you French non-collaborators, it's to you I am speaking. You do well not to collaborate. I am your young eleven-year-old friend. Pray to God that he will make the English, our brothers, our fellows, win, and make the Germans, who are neither our brothers nor our fellows, but the brothers of demons, lose!" Such is the reflection of this horrible war in the good, sensitive soul of this child. Her need to share in the feelings of those who surround her and are loved by her.

The current rumor here concerns the imminent invasion of the Ukraine and the German divisions massed from Lithuania to Romania. It is difficult to reconcile the intentions attributed to the Germans with those revealed by other simultaneous rumors, according to which they are massing more and more soldiers on the French coasts and have warned the inhabitants that they could be evacuated within twenty-four hours! There are many Frenchmen who believe both rumors at once – the impending invasion of England and that of the Ukraine.

The Syrian affair has finally undermined the little remaining good sense of our poor people.[26] All those in Paris who did not dare openly voice opposition to England – all the while cursing them silently for continuing a war whose end they themselves desire *at any price* – now find themselves free to declare that the actions of the English vis-à-vis France are infamous. They have at last found an apparently honorable pretext for coming out in favor of the approaching German peace. At heart, all of these people were counting on domestic reaction to this event, but their plans are postponed as long as the war continues. As for France, its history, its future, they don't give a toss.

Meanwhile, the English and Free French advance in Syria appears to be moving a bit slowly, but no one here seems to doubt their success.

Sometimes I tell myself that this diary is useless and will perhaps serve someday to show me my own errors of judgment. Even if that were the case, I should not regret having written it and having kept the memory of my impressions day by day, during such an infamous time, a time people will be eager to forget when peace has come. It will perhaps be the measure of my illusions, perhaps also the measure of what I managed to preserve of good sense in the storm.

I am copying this passage from Montaigne (book 2, chapter 18, "Of Giving the Lie"):

---

26. This concerns the attack by the English and the Free French on Syria, which had remained loyal to Vichy (Darlan having previously agreed to allow German planes to fly over Syria). The hostilities lasted five weeks.

But how, in this season of infamy, can we believe anyone talking about himself? – given that there are few, or none at all, whom we can believe speaking of others, when there is less temptation to lie. The first stage in the corruption of morals is the banishment of truth: for, as Pindar said, to be truthful is the beginning of great virtue and the first thing Plato requires of the Republic's ruler.

And these words, which are so magnificently applicable to our own time:

Our truth today is not what is but what others can be convinced of: as we call "money" not only that which is genuine but also that which is false – if it will pass. Our nation has long been criticized for this vice.... One might even say that for the French it has become a virtue. They form and fashion themselves accordingly as if this were an honorable exercise; for dissimulation is among the century's most remarkable traits....

Does this reproach not seem also to include cowardice and faintheartedness? Can they be more expressly indicated than by failing to honor one's word? Even worse, failing to honor one's own knowledge!

WEDNESDAY, 18 JUNE 1941 Still impossible to predict the arrival of Mario's family. Yesterday we received three letters from him. He complains about not receiving any news and says there is no way to know when the refugee trains will leave. Perhaps Noël will manage to obtain a pass by way of the "French delegation from Paris." (!) It is three months now that we have been waiting for him.

They say the Boche threaten to cut off our supplies (to deprive Paris of bread, etc.) if the Vichy troops do not fight well enough for them in Syria! The same if we do not send reinforcements! Abominable, atrocious situation. The enemy would like to make the conflicts between the English and the French, between the Free French and others, inexpiable. They laugh at this appalling imbroglio. Had they ever hoped for such a success in their most sadistic dreams about France? Robert de Caix,[27] whom I ran into as I left the Banque de Syrie yesterday, said, "Never in all its history has the French government stooped so low."

Yesterday Bérard, back from Châtelguyon, explained to us all the measures he has taken so that the Banque de Syrie will not suffer as a result of the change in sovereignty that is about to take place. The most intelligent thing is to have a special bureau set up, separate from the bank, in case the English want to issue new currency based on the pound. He calculates, moreover, that as the English are getting near to Syria's two wheat repositories in the north, the struggle cannot last much longer in that country. First General

27. Robert de Caix: journalist and Middle East specialist.

Huntziger, then Weygand, assured him in Vichy that, according to their information, the English would not enter Syria! Two days later the entry was announced. It is hard to imagine by what mental mechanism the French military always foresee the opposite of what actually comes to pass. In the end the grotesque grandeur of such consistent error is almost Shakespearean!

SUNDAY, 22 JUNE 1941 The Marios returned on Saturday. Lolli had to cross the Demarcation Line on her own. Eighteen kilometers on foot. Some fifteen people with her. The price: 250 francs. They met up again in Dijon, Mario with his pass and the baby. We picked them up at the Gare de Lyon and at last got them settled in their villa.

This morning the radio announced the entry of German troops into Russia. Now we are facing a new unknown. And what an unknown! Does Germany want to hold back Russia so that Japan will be encouraged to attack the United States? Or is it a question of their taking over the Baku oil fields to counterbalance the oil being sent to England by the United States? Or both at once? What is certain is that the move is aimed at the United States, a riposte to their intervention that suffices to demonstrate the degree of German concern.

This evening at 9:00, a speech on the radio by Churchill announcing that the British Empire stands firmly with all the enemies of Germany, and, therefore, with Russia. Vichy is going to accuse him of Bolshevism!

MONDAY, 23 JUNE 1941 Mario has told us of Jean's refusal to make airplane parts for the Boche! Mario begins work in Ugine today.

Now we will have to combat the new sophism by which it will be shown that the English are defending communism while the Germans are protecting us from it. The number of simpletons among us is so high we can rest assured of this new slogan's success.

What is strikingly obvious is the increasingly insane character of the German enterprise. Its dimensions are becoming inhuman, its consequences unpredictable. The very effort imposed on this hitherto invincible army seems bound to wear it down. Evidence of the risk run by the whole world makes a desire for German failure universal. Are they going to replace Stalin with the White Russians? Are they going to put a *Gauleiter*[28] in Moscow? Starve the Russian peasantry by depriving it of the oil necessary for its tractors? Once they reach the Caspian Sea, are they going to turn toward Suez or India? All of this smacks of Dionysian frenzy.

---

28. The *Gauleiters* ruled Nazi political regions. [TF]

Turkey's attitude shows once again the Germans' art of isolating their adversaries. But how long will this friendship pact last?

WEDNESDAY, 25 JUNE 1941 Everyone is rejoicing at the outbreak of war in Russia. I very much fear that ideas of the Russians' ability to resist are vastly exaggerated. And the Germans generally advance only with certainty of success. At most one can say that this new "incident" gives more breathing space to England and the United States and allows them to reinforce their air power for attacks on Germany. In any case, it means the prolonging of the war for an indefinite period. Once again everything depends upon military operations. It is a great Anglo-Saxon illusion to have believed they could use economic weapons against an enemy that was determined to wage "real" war, by all means. And perhaps it will reach Egypt via the Caspian Sea and Armenia!

THURSDAY, 26 JUNE 1941 Someone remarked to me, "Marshal Pétain truly stands tall." . . . Yes, but he's losing stature by the day.

It is entertaining to watch all the people who have no opinion, and are incapable of having one, take refuge behind the marshal. And that is his great usefulness. Not for what he does or does not do, because he does nothing and, deep down, knows nothing. But he represents a rallying symbol rather than a point of view. He shelters all those who for so many years have suffered from understanding nothing and from being obliged in spite of that to have an opinion on everything. Obviously, it was not possible to hide like that behind M. Lebrun,[29] the man chosen by Poincaré.

FRIDAY, 27 JUNE 1941 Certain remarks overheard at the Suez Company lunch have given me an idea of the state of mind in certain milieux.

"Well, then," de Lesseps said to me, "do you want the Russians to win or the Germans?"

"The Russians, without a doubt."

"So you are a Bolshevik?"

"No, but I think we have only one enemy."

"Oh, I beg your pardon, but first we must defeat communism, then we can worry about the Germans!"

---

29. Pétain replaced Lebrun as head of state on 10 July 1940 by vote of the Parliament. [TF]

As for the marquis (de Vogüé), he assured me in all seriousness that the English were wrong to occupy Syria because the Germans can do nothing with it. Moreover, he is convinced that in the event of an English victory, we will be thrown out of Suez. He also told me, "A victory by the Russians would lead immediately to Bolshevism in Germany and France." All those people are sick.

At the Ottoman Bank people are more reasonable. No one really believes in a Russian victory. But they are delighted by the delay granted the English.

It would be quite interesting to know what psychological reactions this new war will trigger in Germany. But we know nothing at all about that. We go on living in our prison, where nothing our guardians think or say filters through.

SATURDAY, 28 JUNE 1941 Whatever the outcome of this Russo-German war, it is in any case a huge event. Let us suppose the Germans win in a short time. Most probably that would mean the collapse of the government in Moscow, its replacement by a German *Gauleiter*, and an attempt to impose on this vast country an economic administration run by the military. A result fraught with consequences for the future of Russia and Asia. Its immediate repercussion on England would present a sudden danger. If this same result takes a long time, the effects on Russia's future would doubtless remain the same, but the repercussion on England would be considerably lessened. It might even be very favorable. On the other hand, if Russia resists, if the German penetration is insufficient, then the German position will be strongly undermined – whereas the Anglo-Saxon influence in Russia might provoke unexpected internal changes, and the whole psychological situation of Europe, having been freed from the communist phantom, would be transformed. Once again, we are entirely dependent upon the fortunes of war. Germany is playing a wild game of chance. After Ludendorff, the "dicey" army officer, it has handed itself over to Hitler, the "dicey" civilian.

WEDNESDAY, 9 JULY 1941 We spent the last week at La Bouffource with Noël. Beautiful weather. Not a single German. A long green and blue horizon of grasslands cut by hedges and faraway hills. We have everything in abundance here: bread, eggs, cream, butter. Only meat is missing. We brought back some supplies of butter and eggs. It was touching to see the Noëls spending some of the time making packages of eggs for their friends. Read some Shakespeare and Balzac with them. Their welcome, so warm and simple, was delicious. They are loved by everyone in the area. All of these people are for the English. They were passionately following the Russian resistance.

Received a letter from Léonard. Vichy is now sending food to the prisoners! A sudden demagogic measure after having done nothing for them during the past year! No doubt they had caught on that the returned prisoners did not have a "good attitude" – that is to say, were still patriotic. The impending release of prisoners still in France has been announced. These are Moroccans and Negroes. The goal is only too clear: to have troops available to retake the colonies from the hands of the Gaullists. There is increasingly less effort to hide the alliance with Germany. But results will depend exclusively on military operations. A surprise in Russia could change many things. Since the military brass have assured us that the Russian army is worthless, there is every chance that it is rather good. American and English radio point out that the stunning successes proclaimed by the Germans from the beginning are slow to manifest themselves. Already we can be sure that things will not happen as they did in Poland. And then? People are beginning to hope and to believe again.

On the trains, no one reads the papers. In normal times, people would be eagerly devouring them! This abstention says much about public opinion. People no longer believe any of the news they are given and rely instead on the radio.

Formation of a French legion to fight side by side with the Germans against Bolshevism!

The Americans have occupied Iceland. One step closer to war.

SUNDAY, 13 JULY 1941 Alfred Zuber[30] has recounted to me this declaration by General Gamelin, who, early in the war, had come to visit the officers of the Thann garrison. "Gentlemen, understand once and for all that this war is 50 percent economic, 30 percent diplomatic, and only 20 percent military!" Proof that one should never have spoken to the military of economics. But Gamelin did not come up with these ideas all by himself. Who filled his head with them? Where among the high command could one find the super-cultivated and simultaneously super-cretinous who could have encouraged our leaders' laziness by talking such nonsense? No one has ever paid me the honor of even asking for my advice or a simple opinion on these matters.

Resumption of the German attacks on Russia. They claim to have made a great advance. Today France's fate depends on the greater or lesser degree of energy with which a Russian peasant will stand behind his machine gun.

---

30. Alfred Zuber: paper mill industrialist in Thann and a distant cousin of Germaine Rist.

The Syrian affair has finally come to an end with more slapstick comedy from Vichy: it has rejected the terms of the English armistice but allowed General Dentz[31] complete latitude to negotiate! The terms made public yesterday in Paris have outraged certain Frenchmen! On the subway ran into Paul Valéry, who told me, "They are unacceptable." Thus we have gone along with everything the Germans wanted, but when it comes to the English, we feel dishonored by conditions whose moderation is evident. It is scandalous that Vichy had Frenchmen fired upon, and even more so that it did so knowing the situation was untenable. General de Gaulle's position has thus been strengthened. Now we must see whether Catroux will know how to maneuver with the necessary skill. If the English had been in this campaign alone, people would have said, "See, they're taking Syria from us." Since some Gaullists are with them, people are saying, "See, the 'traitors' are taking Syria from us."[32]

At two o'clock English radio announced the conclusion of the Anglo-Russian treaty, which dictates that neither party will make a separate peace. A good precaution to take against Stalin.

WEDNESDAY, 23 JULY 1941 The Russo-German War still has the world in suspense. It has been four weeks now. Nothing points toward a rapid advance on Moscow, Leningrad, or Kiev. Everyone thinks that such an advance may happen. But how long will it take? That is the question.

The Germans apparently have nothing better to do than to appropriate the *V* campaign for their own. An enormous *V* rises above the Bourbon palace. Below, an immense banner with the inscription "*Deutschland siegt auf allen Fronten.*"[33] These childish measures are looking more and more like newspaper accounts when the favorite wins a bicycle race. What a degradation of victory itself! Is it not enough to have it? Must one convince others that one does? In any case, this is clear proof that the *V* campaign has stung the Germans where it hurts.

31. General Dentz: French army officer in charge of defending the French mandates in Syria and Lebanon under the Vichy regime. [TF]

32. Free French forces under Catroux fought alongside the Allies in Syria. Catroux initialed the Armistice of Saint Jean d'Acre (14 July 1941), an action that was seen as a betrayal for having ceded control of the French mandate to the British. The terms of the armistice were subsequently protested by de Gaulle for having made no mention of the Free French and for having treated the French mandate as conquered rather than liberated territory. For Rist the incident with Valéry was cause once again to deplore the fact that so many Frenchmen were mistaking their enemy, ignoring the fact that England had been their ally in opposing Germany. [TF]

33. "Germany is victorious on all fronts." [JNJ/TF]

We know less and less of what is happening in France. In Vichy, Darlan has given the interior ministry portfolio to Pucheu, who is, Buisson tells me, a follower of Doriot. Things continue to develop in the same direction. There is no longer any connection with public opinion, which has become more and more divided along the lines of the split that followed the riot of 6 February 1934. Except that many who were then lukewarm or neutral, or inclining toward indulgence for the rioters, today are patriots. It is this unity of the "patriots" that must be achieved: bourgeois, workers, and peasants.

SATURDAY, 26 JULY 1941 The week has concluded with the Germans more or less in the same positions as two weeks ago when they announced that great advances and encirclements would shortly be achieved. This is already Eylau, where for the first time after a victory Napoleon did not advance, and his troops, worn down by enormous losses, were content to stay put. Emmanuel Rousseau, returning on Thursday from Vichy, told me, "People are beginning to ask whether we bet on the wrong horse." At the same time, English bombardment of Germany and northern France is intensifying. American armaments and planes are finally beginning to arrive in substantial numbers.

Rousseau also said the constitution has finally been drafted by the famous commission presided over by Joseph Barthélemy and including Bardoux,[34] who, one might add, is an anti-collaborationist. The main idea is to have two chambers composed exclusively of people appointed by the government and of others chosen by its appointees. This procedure, which has been used in the academies, the universities, etc., has never produced anything but ridiculous results. At the Banque de France, it ended in catastrophe. But in politics, what a disaster! Public opinion will immediately revolt. This famous constitution will never take effect.

Joseph Barthélemy, in all of his books over the last forty years, said he favored the parliamentary system energetically and with "conviction!" Treason by the intellectuals! Fortunately, this is all more grotesque than dangerous. He who laughs last, laughs best. Once again, military events will be the deciding factor. How all of these people fear true popular opinion!

More humiliating is the cession of Indochina to the Japanese. Vichy has declared that the Japanese are "cooperating with France" to defend Indochina against the English! This headline in *Paris-Soir* must have made the Chancellor-Führer laugh deliriously.

34. Joseph Barthélemy: Pétain's minister of justice (1941–1943); Jacques Bardoux: French senator, academic, and a member of Vichy's National Council. [TF]

On Friday I received one of Léonard's fellow prisoners, a man named Klein, bringing rather good news. Léonard's impatience is growing, and he dreams of escaping. In Vichy, Klein was told that the recall of naval officers (he is a chief administrator in the navy) for the stated purpose of putting them back into service is just for show; the true purpose is to send them back home for reasons such as illness. He seems to be convinced that this is true and that Vichy is sincere. I say nothing, though deeply convinced, alas! that when the occasion arises they will be sent to fight the English on the pretext of English aggression of some kind. Every dirty trick is in order today.

SATURDAY, 2 AUGUST 1941 On Thursday I was visited by Wagemann.[35] He has been charged with finding out if the economic institutes' international meetings can be resumed. He is equally interested in resuming those of the Institut International de Statistique. "We shall restore," he said, "a European scientific community of some sort – and if England and the United States continue to keep their distance, well, then, we will do without them." Such stupidity is disarmingly naïve. He explained all of this with some discomfort but great volubility. He had come from Rome and Spain, and he intends to pass through Brussels and Amsterdam. I told him that the moment is not appropriate, as we are in a war economy, which hardly lends itself to international studies. I believe he would especially like to use the institutes to keep up to date on the food situation, which he is required to study for Germany. I turned the subject to Russia. He turned to the topic with gusto. The impudence of his declarations was entertaining. *"Militärisch,"* he begins, *"ist eine leichte Sache."*[36] (I could not help smiling to think that we were ending the sixth week of the Russian campaign and the Germans had yet to advance beyond Smolensk!)

"Yes," I said, "but how do you imagine you would govern Russia?"

"I don't know what the thinking of our authorities is on this topic," he said, "but here's more or less how it appears to me. Take South America. There the Indians were completely conquered by a few Spaniards. Why? Because the war completely destroyed the Indian elite. Well, now the Bolshevik regime has completely destroyed the Russian elite. A very small number of Germans will therefore be sufficient to administer all of Russia."

---

35. Ernst F. Wagemann: German economist, friend of Rist, and director of the *Institut für Konjunkturforschung* (economic research institute) in Berlin; he collaborated with ISRES between the wars.

36. "Militarily, the thing is easy." [JNJ/TF]

"Yes," I said, "but there are many more Russians than there were Indians."

"Certainly, but the *proportions* are the same. The Indian population was around six million. The Spanish population at that time, I estimate, was more or less three million. That is the same relationship that exists between the Russian population and ours."

And there you are! He then told me about a 1922 book that he promised to send me – very curious, he said – in which current events and the rise of the Führer in Germany were already foreseen! "And that is absolutely consistent," he said, "with the doctrine of historical crises that I have developed." Mysticism and philosophy of history!

The same day, a curious conversation with Jean Boissonnas, so typical of the Protestant conservatives' state of mind. "The Russian resistance is not owing to good Russian organization but uniquely to the spirit of resistance on the part of civilians."

"However," I said, "there are many tanks and planes playing a role!" But that did not impress him. Acknowledging that the dreaded Bolshevik regime was capable of organizing an army would have been too distressing. On the other hand, any argument that does not blame the French collapse on the French population and the awful Republican government rather than on the army must be avoided. So they have come up with a theory according to which the Russian people, and not the Russian army, is the true source of resistance. But, then, this Russian people is defending at once its country and its dreadful regime! Where does this patriotic fervor come from? And how is it that they do not profit by events to overthrow the regime they supposedly abhor, as has been predicted for years? And yet we do not see it happening; rather, to general amazement the opposite is occurring. But to acknowledge this truly astounding fact, one must have an open mind. Thus the French civil war persists in people's minds through all events, even those that cause rejoicing by patriots on both sides of the barricade. J. Boissonnas has one or two sons fighting with de Gaulle, and he is proud of them. But he does not want to hear any criticism of the army.

Yesterday Millerand, whom I told of plans for a constitution drawn up in Vichy, said to me: "Those people are preparing a civil war."

All the German military vehicles now bear the *V,* encircled by two laurel branches.

SUNDAY, 3 AUGUST 1941 In the general chaos that will follow this war, there hardly seems any possibility for France other than a military government, but one entrusted to a *victorious* general. Only such a regime can revive unity in this country – based on patriotic feeling, the only link uniting men of opposing views who can agree only on this point. Such a regime would be perfectly compatible with adequate freedom of expression internally and representation of the country externally. It must necessarily rely on the support of a segment of the popular classes and impose a peace in which the worker makes himself heard. It must bring to heel all of those who advocated defeatism. Supported by England and America abroad, such a government could reconcile necessary freedoms with an equally necessary firmness in disarming all of those imbecilic reactionaries beating the drums of civil war. Such a government could have the Church on its side, without being itself subjected to it. It is already clear that no one can come up with the name of a single "civilian" having any authority whatsoever. That is what the royalists are counting on in order to push their merchandise.

WEDNESDAY, 6 AUGUST 1941 Well-off Protestants generally consider themselves to be the salt of the earth; most often they are just the vinegar.

Today they announced Darlan's decision to call on the Germans to "collaborate in the defense of our African colonies." This infamous dereliction brings home to us the immensity of the defeat and the cowardice of those who signed the armistice. The political idiocy that consists of falling out with England and the United States at a time when chances of a German victory are diminishing each day strains belief.

SATURDAY, 9 AUGUST 1941 A revealing note about the sentiments of middle-class Frenchmen during this war: R. A.,[37] freed from a relatively painless captivity within France itself, tried to go back to his cotton firm. Asked if he had made any progress, he replied, "No, not yet; these gentlemen have become *very pessimistic* since the Russian campaign began!" So what causes the patriots to vibrate with hope causes the merchants, comfortably settled into defeat and satisfied with the Germans' protection against communism, to tremble. And suddenly the enemy's victory is no longer certain! What a disaster!

Today marks the end of the seventh week of the Russian campaign! – which was apparently supposed to end in fifty days. We wait patiently and impatiently. Only yesterday the radio seemed to be preparing us for the fall of Kiev.

---

37. This must be René Amphoux, Rist's nephew.

Read Tarle's book on the Russian defense of 1812.[38] Kutuzov, the target of animosity on the part of his emperor and the other generals, was hostile to the English, who hoped the Russians would hand them a cheaper victory. The Russian soldier, even then, was admirable. The nobles were haunted by fear that after the war the peasants would demand their freedom.

Laurent-Atthalin tells me that N., when he was a manager with the Banque de France, received a substantial commission from Mannheimer[39] to keep him up to date on decisions made there. "It is costing me a bundle," Mannheimer told him, "but I am well informed." What a hue and cry by "respectable people" when Blum got rid of the old managers! And what noble protestations on the part of the latter!

MONDAY, 11 AUGUST 1941 The Russian battle still has everyone on tenterhooks. The German advance on Kiev is worrisome, but the fact that the eighth fruitless week of the offensive begins today inspires hope. Eight weeks! It seems this is the period the Germans had given themselves to be done with Russia.

Contrary to general opinion, I am convinced that all the economic development of the nineteenth and twentieth centuries is leading us to a growing need for individual *liberty*. Prosperity has increased dramatically. Life for the peasant, the laborer, is infinitely happier than a hundred years ago. Life for the bourgeois, the office worker, is infinitely easier. Advances in material well-being have led to the growth of individualism. Each individual wants not just to be well-off; once he prospers materially, he also wants to know more, to live a more well-rounded intellectual, emotional, and artistic life. The individual feels more like a *person*. Under these circumstances, how could one not insist on feeling free to choose one's activities, one's readings, one's opinions, and to voice them as well?

Totalitarian governments have only been able to persist thanks to two things:

---

38. Eugene Tarle, *La Campagne de Russie, 1812* [The Russian Campaign, 1812] (Paris: Nouvelle Revue Française, 1941). Translation of a book by Yevgeny Viktorovich Tarle, a Russian historian and author of books on European and Russian history. Mikhail Kutuzov headed the Russian army that defeated Napoleon. Kutuzov was promoted to head the army in spite of Tsar Alexander I's dislike for him and the fact that Kutuzov was Russian, as opposed to the mostly foreign generals in charge of Russian troops at the time. [JNJ/TF]

39. Fritz Mannheimer: powerful financier during the interwar years.

1. The need for security or for revenge on foreign enemies, legitimizing in the eyes of their citizens the measures of constraint necessary to ensure national defense. We see today that this preoccupation has dominated not only Germany but also Russia. In Italy such patriotic propaganda made no sense – it was just empty words, incapable of organizing an army;
2. An irrational fear of the communist specter on the part of the ruling classes. But communism's appeal is dimming with the rising prosperity of the working classes; it was able to flourish only because of the postwar crisis and the collapse of currencies and price levels. A visionary social policy will go a long way toward weakening the virus. On the other hand, the military will be strongly disparaged after this war: in the countries so far conquered, for incompetence and routine methods; in Germany – if, as one can expect, it is finally beaten – for their very insatiability and lack of political sense. We will need either a mechanized, professional army, or a much more closely controlled national army. The real soldiers will be civilians.

TUESDAY, 12 AUGUST 1941 Last night on the radio, a speech by the marshal. From his shapeless jumble I have retained this: (1) I shall save you from the great capitalists as the kings of France saved you from feudalism (this passage inspired by Bergery); (2) I shall double the police force; (3) workers, I shall save you from yourselves. The whole thing crowned by handing off all powers to Darlan. Not a word about Indochina, about the collaboration with Germany in the colonies, etc. – that is to say, about the only things that matter to the French. The "parties," he says, must disappear. But an exception is made for the "Legion," an Action Française organization bent on terrorizing non-occupied France. These contemptible words, dictated half by Doriot and half by Darlan, but all in accord with Germany's wishes, were delivered in a quavering voice, lacking conviction, in any case, as if by a child who is repeating something learned in school. To try to make the French believe that the country can be restored by putting an even stronger gag on it than exists now is a bit naïve. The intent is to put an end to "Gaullism." In fact, the great majority of the French are, if not Gaullist, at least pro-English, and the two views are tending more and more to merge. The marshal's words will not change this one whit. They will just make him lose a little more of his already damaged prestige.

In Henri de Man's memoir *Après coup,* I read: "In no profession (as in that of the military) have I seen such an abundance of bad judgment based

on unfounded dogmatic assurance, routine conservatism, indifference to
new experiments, scorn for imagination, and intolerance of opposing views.
There are certainly exceptions, but they prove the rule because of the harsh-
ness of their milieu."[40] He was talking about the Belgian military. But this
applies perfectly to the French as well.

Curious, this book of de Man's. His long sojourns in Germany have de-
sensitized him to the fact that Germans are the least capable of teaching others lessons in civilization. Wherever they go, they sow hatred. The unification
of Europe is a beautiful dream; but if there is a nation incapable of realizing
it, that is precisely Germany. It is curious that de Man does not see this.

SUNDAY, 17 AUGUST 1941 Reread Vaihinger's little book on Nietzsche.[41]
What wretched philosophy the Nazis extracted from this great writer – so
naïve in some ways. Darwinism, once it leaves the realm of natural history,
is childish in the extreme. To take no account of suffering, to let the strong
triumph over the weak, what idiocy, even from their own point of view. Medicine as a whole, and surgery, these magnificent arts, what did they arise from
if not the desire to lessen suffering? And is there not also a struggle for life
among states, nations, and races? Is there anything more fatal to the survival
of a state than internal conflicts, which today all derive from the permanent
struggle between the weak and the strong, the "rich" and the "poor"? To
attenuate this struggle, giving the weak as well as the strong the idea of a
community to defend, is the best way to strengthen the State in its struggle
with others. This is the origin of all "democratic" institutions. Applied to
world politics, the term "struggle for life" has no meaning other than to give
the "strong" a *pretext* for continuing their abuses and demands. They all
want to belong to the "elite." But what is an "elite"? The artists, the scientists,
the wise – or the sleepwalkers of Berchtesgaden? Is it young men with billy
clubs, or workers burning the midnight oil to make a discovery or develop
an invention? Darwinism has succeeded so well only because it is a form of
anticlericalism. As for "natural selection" among human beings, let it operate "naturally." To pretend to do it in nature's stead – choosing in advance
those who will be declared the elite and keeping the others in positions of
inferiority – is precisely to *oppose* natural selection, which operates in subtle
ways that only nature, which can turn the son of a poor tanner into a Louis
Pasteur, knows. To make people believe that their instincts for justice, pity,

40. Henri de Man, *Après coup* (Paris: Editions de la Toison d'Or, 1941), 114. [TF]
41. Hans Vaihinger, *Nietzsche als Philosoph* (Langensalza: Hermann Beyer & Söhne,
1930). [JNJ/TF]

and kindness must be suppressed in the name of the "struggle for life" is to artificially suppress some of our most profound feelings, the most spontaneous that nature placed in the heart of man precisely to guarantee the "survival of the species," which otherwise would be destroyed by the brutes who from time to time proclaim themselves the "elite."

A joint proclamation by Roosevelt and Churchill – who met at sea – on their war goals: no territorial conquests, but disarmament of aggressor nations. Agreement discussed with Stalin for pooling the resources of the three great states.

This will no doubt discourage those who think the war will be short or that we are on the brink of a compromise peace.

The fundamental inability of most French people to understand Anglo-Saxon tenacity, as well as their illusion that the latter are clamoring for peace (like themselves), is unalterable. Among those of the "elite" there is a secret sympathy for Hitler, which they suppose exists also among the English. But the English, who for seventy years refused to believe in the German danger, have finally awakened. An Englishman who has seen the light sees it for a long time.

For two months a curious reversal has been taking place, even among the "resigned" or "collaborating." They are beginning to believe in an English victory. Result of the Russian resistance.

The Germans are requisitioning potatoes for the eastern front. It seems the administration is resisting a bit.

Eight

Pétain's Ambassador
to Washington?

30 AUGUST–26 OCTOBER 1941

In August 1941 Rist was told that Pétain wanted him to be Vichy's ambassador to Washington. For the next few months, discussions between Rist and Vichy primarily focused on two conflicting notions: Pétain wanted Rist to persuade the United States not to invade North Africa; on the contrary, Rist wanted Vichy to guarantee the United States that should it invade North Africa the French colonies would not put up a fight.

SATURDAY, 30 AUGUST 1941 Trip to Vichy and to Fraisses to see Jean. Left on Wednesday, 20 August, passed through Vichy the next morning, arrived in Fraisses that Thursday evening, and stayed until Sunday. Then to Vichy from Monday to Wednesday. Returned on Thursday morning. My only aim was to see Jean, but the unexpected happened. In a conversation with Matthews on the twenty-first, he let me know in passing that it had been decided to recall Henry-Haye from Washington and that my name had been pronounced by Darlan as a replacement. I did not attach much importance to this, but then on Monday, Romier,[1] whom I ran into at a restaurant, asked me to come see him. He received me on Tuesday morning in his Council office and right away asked if I would accept the post of ambassador to Washington if the possibility arose. According to him, it was especially important to keep the United States from landing in Dakar with all the disastrous consequences that would entail. I answered by saying what I knew about the American attitude and that in principle I was ready to consider the offer if it should be made. Saw Matthews again for a moment on Wednesday

---

1. Lucien Romier, a journalist and personal friend of Pétain, served as minister of state from 11 August 1941 until he resigned on 31 December 1943. He was viewed as a kind of *éminence grise* behind Pétain. [JNJ/TF]

morning to ask him what the American government would think about this. He answered that the American government would certainly be favorably disposed. To his knowledge, the other name being entertained was that of General Réquin. Returned then to Romier, who told me that two candidates were under discussion: Weygand (whom they wished to get out of Algeria) and myself. I got him to clarify that in my case this was a simple suggestion and not a firm proposal. I asked him if the suggestion had come from Darlan or Pétain. He answered: from both of them. I left Vichy that evening after having learned the news of the attack on Laval.[2] I had seen Rochat briefly and shared with him my optimism regarding the outcome of the war.

I received general confirmation that nothing important has been conceded to the enemy in regard to North Africa. Matthews attributes the Resistance to the attitudes of Weygand and the United States.

Returned here perplexed and ambivalent. My position in Washington would be extremely difficult, what with an entirely Gaullist French colony, a suspicious entourage at the embassy itself, an American government trusting the ambassador but mistrustful of his government, and uneasy relations with the government in Vichy. On the other hand, there is hardly a better post from which to exercise influence on Vichy by informing it of the real situation.[3]

Here terror reigns. Three convicted by the "special tribunal" were guillotined as soon as their sentence was pronounced. Arrest of a great number of Jewish lawyers.

SUNDAY, 31 AUGUST 1941 Yesterday, a notice in the newspapers and red posters on the walls announcing the condemnation to death by German court-martial of, on the one hand, three "spies" (of whom one was a forty-year-old navy lieutenant, Comte d'Estienne d'Orves), and on the other, five "communists" who had taken part in a demonstration against the occupying power. Thus eleven murders in only a few days.

---

2. Laval was shot, along with Déat, by French resister Paul Collette during the course of a military parade for the delivery of a French flag to the first contingent of the Legion of French Volunteers against Bolshevism, a collaborationist militia. [JNJ/TF]

3. A telegram by Leahy, U.S. ambassador to Vichy, dated 27 August, confirms this narrative precisely – notably, the interview with Romier and the perplexity of Charles Rist. Rist would not accept "without knowing first if his friends in Washington truly felt he could render some service to both countries or whether they would think that by aiding the Vichy government he would become a collaborator." Department of State Archives, 701. 5III/817.

TUESDAY, 2 SEPTEMBER 1941 For a month the "Secours National"[4] has filled the empty houses that surround us with children organized into summer camps – girls and boys. Excellent idea. They have chosen to complement this with the latest educational methods, of which the main one consists in never letting them go out without singing. Also a nice idea. But what do they have them sing! The oldest, most useless regimental songs: "Ah! If Papa Knew That," "He Did Not Have to Go!" etc., etc. And in what piercing, out-of-tune voices! Never a choir with more than one voice part, never doing something over again, or a correction of off-key notes. The young monitors who are guiding them are as ignorant of music as the children. And the latter (who gather here in the morning, but return to their families in the evening) are not even washed! National Revolution!

WEDNESDAY, 3 SEPTEMBER 1941 Ran into Clément Moret[5] as I got off the train. He was thrilled by the Russian resistance. "But," he added, "the Russians must not go too far. That would be very dangerous." I told him I do not believe in the possibility of Bolshevism in France and that after the war the Russians will absolutely require English and American aid to restore what has been destroyed.

He spoke to me of the "Anti-Bolshevik Legion." Members were recruited from the prisons by promises of freedom. They are only dreaming of escape. On a train transporting four hundred, the conductor (from whom he obtained the information) lost one hundred before reaching Paris.

THURSDAY, 4 SEPTEMBER 1941 A frightful increase in prostitution and venereal diseases according to Mme Pesson-Deprêt.[6] This is how the principle so often repeated by Wilhelm II – *"Am deutschen Wesen wird die Welt genesen"*[7] – works in practice.

A German officer chatting with a merchant in Versailles, who reported the conversation to Germaine, declared that the Germans have already lost the war. It is what is going on in Russia that is depressing them.

In his book *French Patriotism in the Nineteenth Century* (1923), which I have come upon in my library, Paul Desjardins, speaking of 1813–1814, quotes characteristic passages demonstrating the royalists' attitude – not just anti-

4. Secours National: aid organization created during the First World War. [TF]

5. Clément Moret: former governor of the Banque de France (1930–1934).

6. Madame Pesson-Deprêt: militant member of the Abolitionist Federation and of the Union against the Trafficking of Human Beings.

7. "German character will heal the world." [JNJ/TF]

Napoleonic (which is natural), but anti-patriotic. Here is a passage from the *Mémoires* of the Comtesse de Boigne:

> I very much regret to confess it, but the Royalist Party is the one that least loves our country for itself; the quarrel that has arisen among the various classes has made the nobility hostile toward the soil where its privileges are unrecognized. And I fear it is more in sympathy with someone of foreign nobility than with a Frenchman of the bourgeoisie. The loss of common interests has led to affinities among the classes and broken up nationalities.[8]

It is the same situation today. Except that part of the bourgeoisie has sided with the nobility for fear of communism.

FRIDAY, 12 SEPTEMBER 1941 At four this morning heard Roosevelt's speech announcing, in the aftermath of a German submarine's attack on the *Greer,* that from now on American planes and ships would attack German ships and submarines in all waters that "the Americas" deem necessary for the protection of their commerce – and would protect other merchant marines as well as America's. This is the Anglo-American maritime alliance. The declaration also targets the Italians. "When you see a snake, you crush it before it strikes," he said. He considers this measure to be a defense against pirates and recalls the precedent set by President Jefferson when he decided to pursue the Barbary pirates.... Thus, not a declaration of war, but war.

What is Germany going to say and do? What is Vichy going to do? Break off diplomatic relations? In any case, Henry-Haye has become impossible. They say he is under fierce attack because of spying maneuvers that have benefited Germany. How could I succeed him under such conditions! Impossible to accept unless it means turning Franco-American relations in a completely new direction, implying the gradual abandonment of "collaboration." That is the question I shall pose to Vichy if I am called.

SATURDAY, 13 SEPTEMBER 1941 If the war had been short, and if England had been conquered in September 1940, the coup d'état that carried the marshal and his henchmen to power could perhaps have succeeded. But the band of "revolutionaries" has now been in power for a year, and the country has been able to see their value and that of their ideas. The result is a profound disgust for them and for anything related to them. In regard to the Germans, they have conducted themselves with complete cowardice. The occupied

---

8. M. Charles Nicoullaud, *Récits d'une Tante; Mémoires de la Comtesse de Boigne, née d'Osmond* (Paris: Plon, 1907–1908), 1: 291.

country will not pardon them for it. As for "National Renewal," it has come to mean vengeance and terror. The only practical problem the country cares about, the provision of fresh supplies, is going as badly as possible. The law courts have become revolutionary tribunals. Financial and economic measures have exasperated all those who oversee or manage companies. As for finances, printing more money is not a policy. This government thus finds itself tied to the German occupation. English victory will signal the end. The only ones to regret it will be the small group of reactionaries from *Gringoire* and the Action Française. The rest of the country will spit them out in disgust, which is exactly why they are now installing a police force to help them stay in power the day Germany is defeated. But that will be in vain.

SUNDAY, 14 SEPTEMBER 1941 Everyone recognizes that the Germans have not won and can no longer win. But neither can the English. And how could they?

I see only two roads by which they could achieve victory. First: via the terror and discouragement procured by uninterrupted and much more devastating air raids on Germany. But will the English have the courage, and will they have enough planes? Second: by the conquest and destruction of Romanian oil fields, which would make continuation of the tank and air war impossible.

The English blockade always stupidly turned a blind eye to the fact that a military power can always seize embargoed resources by military force. Whether a matter of iron from Briey or Sweden or oil from Romania or Baku – they can always go get it. This is a contingency the English never wanted to foresee. After this war, when people try to discover what role the blockade played in the German defeat, they will find it mattered little. An Englishman deprived of his breakfast is unhappy. But he supposes that others are as well. Serious mistake.

TUESDAY, 16 SEPTEMBER 1941 Brouillet,[9] back from Montpellier, tells me that all "upright" citizens there are overjoyed to see France governed well at last. The National Revolution pleases them no end. Their sentiments are well represented in this dialogue he overheard as he left church. One of his friends was addressing a young woman: "What's wrong with you today? You seem sad." "How could I not be, seeing the Bolsheviks resist the German army the way they're doing?"

9. René Brouillet: junior official at the revenue court, former chief assistant for Senate president Jules Jeanneney, and former colleague at Rist's research institute.

In Radio Paris broadcasts, the German army in Russia is referred to as the "European" army.

Brouillet tells me: "Here we can speak much more freely than in the free zone. And in the prohibited zone, it's even better."[10] Informants are plentiful in the free zone. High-level bureaucrats and private individuals take it upon themselves to report to the government on people's "state of mind."

SUNDAY, 21 SEPTEMBER 1941 A busy week. Responding to a telegram from Bouthillier, on Wednesday morning I went to the finance ministry. He had me brought from Versailles by car. Leroy-Beaulieu, whom I saw for a few minutes before being received, told me I was going to be entrusted with a mission to the United States of an economic – in fact, a political – nature. I was ushered in to see Bouthillier, who explained what it was all about. Of this rather vague and incoherent account, I have retained the following: Marshal Pétain is anxious to stay on good terms with the United States; moreover, he has a personal relationship with President Roosevelt, who sends him messages. He would like to have someone close to him explain his position to the president. According to Bouthillier, this amounts to explaining (1) the armistice, without which France would have been reduced to complete impotence; and (2) the marshal's desire to prepare a strong, well-led France for the postwar period. Having given this explanation of domestic policy, Bouthillier passed on to foreign policy: "Between complete adherence to Germany and an Anglo-Saxon victory, there are various possible solutions – for example, regarding such ports as Casablanca and Dakar, one could envisage a kind of neutrality. A peace concluded now with Germany is not impossible. One might then, thanks to America, obtain certain advantages."

This is all quite vague. What sticks in my mind is their desire to negotiate with Germany, their preoccupation with politics, especially the domestic variety, their belief, more or less clearly expressed, that they could win the support of the United States for this policy, and that I could help them do it.

I replied to Bouthillier (1) that I was not interested in domestic policy; (2) that I did not at all see what Germany could give us in a negotiated peace and that any promise on the part of the Germans seemed to me pure illusion; (3) that to my knowledge the United States is entirely committed to the English side, not just for reasons of sentiment but for reasons of immediate political interest; and (4) that it is absolutely essential to have the

---

10. Areas contiguous with the external borders of the occupied zone, including the Atlantic coast and large stretches along the North-East Line, were declared *zone interdite* – that is, off-limits to ordinary people. [TF]

Americans with us when the peace treaty is negotiated. I told him I have been approached regarding an ambassadorship. He answered that the recall of an ambassador is a dramatic event, but if I were over there, I could more easily replace Ambassador Henry-Haye[11] after a few months. It is clear that they fear Germany's objection either to my departure or to Henry-Haye's replacement and that they would rather I went on the quiet.[12]

Afterward, long conversation with Couve[13] and Leroy-Beaulieu. I sketched out for them all the difficulties I foresee with such a mission – all of Vichy's illusions with regard to the United States. Couve told me that the important thing is first of all to convince Vichy – then to exert influence on Vichy from New York.

In short, Pétain wants me to persuade Washington to follow the Vichy agenda (in which concern for domestic politics predominates), whereas my goal is on the contrary to bring Vichy over to America's way of thinking.

I asked in any case that measures be taken to have Léonard return so that he could accompany me.

Two days later Jaoul let me know he wanted to see me. He told me that a week ago, lunching with the marshal, the subject of Henry-Haye's recall came up. Perrin took advantage of the moment to remark, "In that case, M. Rist must be sent." "That's a very good idea," said the marshal. And a bit later Du Moulin returned to the subject, repeating, "That's a very good idea."[14]

A long conversation with Couve the next day in which I recounted to him all the problems of such a mission if it were not clearly defined, if I did not have a personal letter of accreditation from the marshal and Darlan, if I

11. In his memoirs, *La Grande Éclipse franco-américaine* (Paris: Plon, 1972), Henry-Haye gives no details about the mission proposed to Rist and mentions him only to place him on the list of pretenders to the ambassadorship in Washington in July 1940.

12. This interpretation is confirmed by Leahy in his telegram of 26 September 1941. He explains that it is probably German opposition to the recall of Henry-Haye that had led Vichy to come up with this new project of a special mission for Rist – with "rather broad powers" and the probability of being named ambassador after some two months. A second telegram, dated the next day reports the information "conveyed by a mutual friend" that Rist is hesitant and will not make a decision until after "thorough discussions with authorities in Vichy" and having obtained Weygand's "assurances as to the future foreign policy of France." Department of State Archives, 701.5III/839 and 846.

13. Maurice Couve de Murville was currently director of foreign finance at the finance ministry. He told Noël Rist that he remembered nothing of this episode of the proposed ambassadorship.

14. Du Moulin de la Barthète: Pétain's chief of staff. [TF]

were not completely independent of Henry-Haye, etc. He agreed completely. "Your most difficult negotiation will be with Vichy," he told me.[15]

Bouthillier was so afraid the Germans would find out about the project that he asked me to obtain my pass to the free zone on my own. I turned to Matériel Téléphonique.

SUNDAY, 28 SEPTEMBER 1941 Last week a four-day visit from Jean, who had not been back here for a year! Stories of what is happening in the free zone – and of the efforts of Marion, the propaganda minister, to "Nazify" the youth.

TUESDAY, 30 SEPTEMBER 1941 Yesterday sudden news that Léonard would be returning in the afternoon. We went to his place to welcome him home. He has not changed. We suppose he was liberated through the intervention of Grosskop[16] and Wagemann.

New executions of so-called communists ordered by the special *French* tribunal.

Vichy has had its spokesman say that there is no intention to recall Henry-Haye and that reports claiming it has asked Washington to approve of "Governor Rist's" appointment were false. There you have it, the government's own indiscreet revelation of the news that it was intent upon keeping secret.

WEDNESDAY, 1 OCTOBER 1941 There are only two avenues open to French foreign policy: entente with England and the maritime countries – Holland, Belgium, perhaps Norway, and including Italy – or else a permanent entente with Germany for the formation of a continental bloc, from which Holland and Belgium would naturally be excluded (by their own decision) and with which Italy most probably would not want to be associated.

---

15. Emmanuel Mönick, a finance inspector who had just been dismissed from his post as general secretary of the French Protectorate of Morocco, but who maintained some friends in Darlan and Pétain's entourage, was meanwhile actively lobbying to have Rist sent to Washington as soon as possible. Leahy, 27 September 1941 telegram, Department of State Archives, 701.5III/840, and Emmanuel Mönick, letter to Noël Rist, 11 February 1983. According to Leahy, Mönick's view was that Vichy would finally have reliable information "coming from a *French* source whose integrity was unquestionable" on the situation in Washington "instead of the complex and deceptive picture that Henry-Haye is constantly providing."

16. Not identified.

There is only one problem with the first group: England may perhaps persist in its refusal to take upon itself permanent military responsibilities; these responsibilities must be fairly distributed among France and the other neutral states in the group. France cannot continue indefinitely as the west's bastion against Germany while waiting for the others to get ready.

From all other points of view this grouping would correspond to the needs of France. A maritime power open to two seas, France cannot expose itself to having to fight the world's greatest maritime powers one day; on the other hand, it cannot give up the immense advantage of having free maritime communications in time of war, nor the advantages of its ports and its situation of accessibility to America (North and South) and to the Mediterranean in time of peace.

From the point of view of public opinion, the support of which is essential to a policy of this kind, the democratic aspirations and traditions of this country coincide with those of western nations. They are the only ones with whom we share a certain kinship of feeling.

From the perspective of economic development, France's interest in first reaching understandings with nations having all the raw materials is obvious; her industrial problems can be more easily solved with them than with any other country.

Permanent entente with Germany is a condemnation to perpetual war. For a century, Germany has dreamed of unity with a view to expansion. This dream will endure. Germany will want to drag France along with it or lean on her to realize the dream. To lean on France means, above all, using her maritime resources against the Anglo-Saxon world. We shall become the battleground of this struggle.

Psychologically, nothing is more different than the spirit of the two peoples. The one is individualistic, rebellious, intent on having its say in everything, impatient at any superiority, jealous of those who have power or wealth, all the while passionately desiring power and wealth. The other is submissive, faithfully carrying out duties that are imposed on it, full of respect for its leaders and its guides, uninterested in political battle, but full of a mysticism that is deeply opposed to French positivism and, moreover, individually focused on material interests. They are opposites in everything: traditions, methods, beliefs, tastes, sympathies, and intellectual and artistic gifts.

Besides, the true interests of Germany go in two different directions. Politically, its expansion aims toward Central and Eastern Europe. There it can gain influence. Commercially and industrially, it is oriented toward America and the British Empire. There it will encounter a lasting antagonism. This double orientation makes it constantly hesitate between two paths of conquest. It wants to pursue both at once, and that is its downfall.

France has no need to expand either to the east or to the west. She has her natural expansion to the south across the Mediterranean. She must thus keep the peace with her two neighbors, England and Germany. She has no quarrel with the first. She has no business getting mixed up in quarrels of the second. England is turning more and more to the west as it gradually finds wider prospects for export outlets and a linguistic and political community in its dominions. The danger of a Germany that dominates France and threatens her coasts is huge. The France-England link is thus the natural one to pursue.

SATURDAY, 4 OCTOBER 1941 Saw Couve on Thursday and Friday. He told me of Vichy's worry at seeing the United States, under public pressure, recognize de Gaulle's new government and of his haste to see me leave for the United States to combat this tendency.

Upon reflection, Bouthillier's suggestion seems to me less and less acceptable. This feeling was strengthened by an unexpected visit from Reibel,[17] newly returned from Vichy, where the marshal had spoken to him of the mission he wanted to entrust me with – and by a conversation on Thursday with Millerand, in which the latter insisted that I clearly state my conditions. I therefore drafted a letter to Rochat in which I declared that I could not consider the mission to the United States under the conditions in which it has been presented to me. I could only accept a mission on condition that I were assured complete independence vis-à-vis Henry-Haye. I gave the letter to Couve.

Here is the text of the letter, taken from the draft kept by Rist, in which some words are indecipherable.

3 October 1941

My dear minister and friend,
    I know that you are aware of recent conversations I have had with the finance minister and his collaborators. I am taking advantage of M. Couve de Murville's kindness to share my reflections with you; it would be invaluable to me to have your comments when I next travel to Vichy.
    It goes without saying that I am extremely pleased to see the importance attached by the government to preserving good relations with the United States.

17. Charles Reibel: senator from Seine-et-Oise; undersecretary of state, 1920–1921. [JNJ/TF]

I have always maintained, as you know, that in this terrible conflict their role would be decisive and that a falling out with them would mean disastrous, incalculable consequences for France. This is to say I am ready to lend my full support, if you judge this useful, to a policy aimed at retaining the goodwill of a country that is going to be the greatest naval and air power in the world and asks only that we not reject that goodwill.

But I do not believe it will contribute to the desired result, given the form my participation would take. An unofficial mission of such a vague nature raises two sorts of problems vis-à-vis the American government and vis-à-vis the ambassador.

As for the American government, my position will be very poorly defined. Will I be there to strengthen the position of the ambassador or to implement a policy that is parallel and necessarily a bit different and independent? It will be impossible for the American government to know. In order to assure the State Department that I am in contact with the embassy, my requests for an audience must be made through the latter, meaning some of the coolness with which the ambassador is viewed will rub off on me.

If my mission consists of conveying a personal message and ends there, it will have only a narrow impact, and, besides, such a message can be carried by others. If it is to last a few weeks, it will quickly give the impression of being either an extension of the embassy or, on the contrary, the center of a less open opposition to it, which would be unfortunate for French prestige. In both cases, what personal credit I enjoy with members of the government and certain other important Americans would be undermined, for they will understand neither my coming as an understudy for M. Henry-Haye nor my apparent attempt to diminish his authority in the country in which he represents France.

As for the ambassador, my position will be even more difficult. I have experienced numerous missions in which I always benefited from the utmost cooperation from our representatives abroad. That was particularly the case for my last mission to Washington. But I know by that very experience how much such cooperation is necessary for the decoding of telegrams, setting up contacts, or arranging hard-to-get meetings. How could I expect similar cooperation from M. Henry-Haye when he can only see my mission as tinged with mistrust of him? How can I be assured of the secrecy of my communications with your department, since I must submit my telegrams to the coder? I cannot, I confess, envisage being in any position other than one of total and complete independence, both materially and morally, with respect to M. Henry-Haye. My personal relations with him have always been perfect. But the situation would overpower the best intentions. I could not accept a mission that did not give me the most absolute security in this regard. Even if I had this security, the difficulties of a mission on the margins of the embassy would still be significant, as contacts would be inevitable, resulting necessarily in ambiguities and misunderstandings vis-à-vis the American government and important Americans with whom I would be meeting. These, then, are the ambiguities that I wish to avoid at all

costs. I understand Americans well enough to know in advance that the success
of my mission would be gravely compromised by such misunderstandings.

After having examined the question in all its aspects with the strong desire
of understanding the government's point of view, I do not see the possibility of
usefully fulfilling a mission such as that which has been proposed.

It goes without saying that as soon as I have my pass I shall go to Vichy, as agreed
with M. Bouthillier, and will ask for a meeting in which to explain my position
to the marshal. But I wanted to let you know now the conclusion I have reached.
I shall be very happy to have your comments on all this, and in closing, please
accept, etc.

We are still passionately following the Russian resistance. The taking of
Kiev is glorified in all the German newspapers published in French. Leningrad's resistance, emphasized on the radio, seems increasingly energetic, like
that of Odessa. Not a hint of the Russian army's destruction. This resistance
impresses the most timid among us and worries the collaborators, who wish
France would make haste to ally itself definitively with Germany.

New executions of hostages. Panic among the Jews regarding rumors of
general internment in the concentration camps.

SUNDAY, 5 OCTOBER 1941 A certain prisoner's wife, who came to inform me of her husband's plans to escape, told me this, word for word: "If my
husband escapes, he won't be able to return here to the occupied zone. Well, I
don't want to leave my apartment. If he gets to the free zone, I won't join him.
And anyway, why escape? Isn't he like the other one and a half million who
are waiting to be freed?" This woman is playing her role as an inconsolable
widow everywhere and demanding to be pitied.

Léonard, here with his wife for dinner last night, told us stories about his
camp. The camp's main captain, Commandant P., *one week* after his internment in Saint-Lô – barely a few days after the taking of Cherbourg – composed a letter to Marshal Pétain telling him of his desire to fight against England alongside the Germans, then tried to gather signatures. He found only
six! The same commander sent an emissary to Léonard to ask if he were not a
Freemason. Because, of course, his great fear was to see France fall again into
the hands of the "Jews and Freemasons." It is with such superior officers as
this that France had to defend herself! What is so surprising about her defeat?

I wonder if Hitler is not indulging in Mephistophelean joy simply to see
how low men can go – if he were not sent by a sardonic God to bring out into
the open all of the cowardice, pettiness, and idiocy that in ordinary times
are hidden in the depths of society and whose revelation the conventions of

a well-ordered community normally prevent. If that is truly the experiment he is attempting, one may say it has succeeded. Let us hope that in the future there will be a historian courageous enough to write about it. Otherwise, the game of illusions, thanks to which a nation manages not to be too ashamed of itself as it contemplates the past, must continue.

THURSDAY, 9 OCTOBER 1941 Our little granddaughters came back from the countryside (La Bouffource) at the end of last week to return to school. Their mother writes that they look wonderful and have gained weight. They had all the milk, butter, and eggs they wanted! This is what most French families – those who could – have done. In some places, the peasants have so many deliveries to put together for people in the towns that they refuse to accept new orders, no matter what price they are offered.

The Germans have announced the beginning of their great drive to take Moscow. Yesterday they were already in Vyazma. We are once again in a state of suspense. Based on figures obtained from engineers coming back from Berlin, Wibratte estimates twelve million troops mobilized against Russia: five million combatants and seven million for transport and supplies, etc.

FRIDAY, 10 OCTOBER 1941 My pass for Vichy is not yet ready. They tell me it will take another ten days! That will make one month all told!

The great attack on Moscow announced by Hitler has already produced substantial results. But decisive? That is another question. Already the Germans are trying to make an impression here by declaring the Russian question settled and Germany victorious. It is early days yet. And England and America have not gone away. One would be tempted to believe, on the contrary, that this haste to proclaim the end suggests uncertainty about it.

My colleague G. tells me that two of his engineers now back from Berlin, having been shown assembly lines for airplane construction, estimate the Germans' monthly output at eight to ten thousand planes! A formidable figure in contrast to which the two thousand a month announced by the Americans, even including the English output, are small change. But how was the calculation made? On the basis of one or two factories?

Auboin, here the day before yesterday, says that Swedish experts estimate, on the contrary, that equality between Germany and the Anglo-Saxons will soon be achieved.

MONDAY, 13 OCTOBER 1941 No more leather for resoling shoes. No more cloth for a new garment unless one brings in *two* old ones! People are making shoes with wooden soles. Lunch at Larue, 75 francs without wine or beer or coffee. People travel to Normandy to find butter and eggs. Orders for firewood are banned. The prefect has forbidden taking wood from Seine-et-Oise (where there is no more wood). The Noëls may take 2 *steres* of wood from our place, but no more. Trains are rarer and slower. I am going to buy 2,000 square meters of woodland in order for us to have fuel in the winter of 1942–1943, for one must think ahead. Thanks to Matériel Téléphonique, we have some pasta and a little rice; otherwise, these items are unobtainable.

19 TO 25 OCTOBER 1941 First trip to Vichy for my mission. Left on Sunday morning, 19 October, arrived early in the afternoon and went straight off to an orientation session with Rochat. He insisted that I accept, emphasizing the poor reputation of Henry-Haye even among the French. Then I met with Romier, who outlined the role he sees for me in Washington. Above all, he said, we must prevent the Americans from entering the war (!), making it clear to them how important they could be as mediators and how awful it would be for a humanitarian nation such as theirs to exacerbate the disaster for civilization that this war is. I was aghast at such naïveté. I told him that the Americans *are* in fact already in the war, that they will support the English to the end, and that if I say the things he suggests when I am in Washington, I will become an instant laughingstock to people who once had confidence in me. The only serious basis for my mission is to assure the Americans that we will defend North Africa at all costs. To my shock, he did not say a word but simply accepted my thesis. No doubt he thinks the important thing is to get me over there and then see what happens.

At six o'clock I was escorted to Darlan, who took it for granted that I had already accepted the mission. He held forth at length with bitter statements about the Americans, who, he said, do not understand a thing. "I asked Leahy, can you deploy a million men to Marseille? No? Then let me do my job without interference. Have I given anything away in Africa? No, so get off my back." This is what I must explain to the Americans.

The marshal, told of my presence, sent me an invitation to dine with him. After dinner he took me aside to say he wanted me to be his "ambassador to Washington," that President Roosevelt had asked for me. "Have Rochat give you my correspondence with him, as well as the telegrams of Henry-Haye, then see the foreign minister, and we'll talk again. I'd like you to set off as soon as possible. Meanwhile, have dinner with me whenever you like."

Thus have I been able over five days, sometimes at lunch, sometimes at dinner, to judge the extraordinary atmosphere of a small court forming around the marshal and his wife. At his table I saw the minister of agriculture (Caziot); Joseph Barthélemy and his wife; General Laure, longtime guest (who let me read part of his private journal recording negotiations and important transactions); Ménétrel, golden boy favored with the informal "*tu*" form by Marshal Pétain; Perrin, the engineer from Ugine; Bernard Faÿ; Rueff; Claude-Joseph Gignoux, who never opened his mouth; General Réquin and wife; Romier and wife; lesser lights such as Garrone[18] (Berthier's son-in-law) from the École des Roches; and minor provincial nobles who believe the happier days of 16 May and that other marshal, defeated at Sedan, have returned. I rarely saw anyone from the admiralty, for relations between Pétain and Admiral Darlan's circle were clearly tense.

It was the next day with Rochat that I read the correspondence between Roosevelt and Pétain. It was mostly about the armistice. Roosevelt was simply asking that the terms of the armistice not be violated. Pétain's replies were generally positive but couched in vague language that reeked of uncertainty and hypocrisy. As for Henry-Haye, his letters reported State Department reaction to frequent incidents in which French ships carrying banned merchandise were boarded and inspected by the English. It was impossible to imagine anything more humiliating to a Frenchman whose only defense was quibbles and lies.

Afterward, I spoke to Rochat about the best way to organize my mission. It was my intention not to undertake it unless I could assure President Roosevelt that North Africa would be respected and that Bizerte was in no danger. Then I learned from Rochat that *an agreement had already been signed in May of 1941* allowing German entry. It seems this desire to throw a bone to the Germans and to protect France from the English followed upon the initiative of Piétri, Vichy's ambassador to Madrid. He quickly spread the word, after conversations between Samuel Hoare and Rudolph Hess, that the Germans and the English were preparing an agreement at our expense. Two days later the deal was confirmed to me by Moysset, who felt obliged to obscure the issue in a tide of historical philosophizing and muddled language. It was clear he would very much have preferred to keep me in ignorance.

In consultation with Rochat, I therefore decided to prepare a letter to be signed by Marshal Pétain assuring Roosevelt in formal and precise terms that we would not allow North Africa to be invaded. Armed with such a personal letter, I would be completely independent of Henry-Haye. If, moreover,

18. Louis Garrone was in charge of education at the Secretariat-General for Youth, a government department established by Pétain to encourage quasi-fascist youth movements and counteract what he viewed as a corrupt system of education. [JNJ/TF]

there were any delay in recalling him and naming me to his post, I would return to France at the end of three or four weeks. In any case, if the promise made to Roosevelt were violated, I would resign and consider myself a free agent in Washington. (My intention would be, in this event, to use my influence in Washington to support General de Gaulle.)

That very day I learned that Weygand was in Vichy. I let him know I was there too and asked for an urgent meeting. He sent word that he would be dining with Marshal Pétain.

Immediately after dinner I approached him to ask his advice about the mission I was being asked to undertake. Without beating around the bush, he encouraged me to accept. I told him briefly of my intentions. Then he spoke about Bizerte: "You know, the Vichy government has signed an agreement with the Germans without even asking for something in exchange. When I found out, I rushed here to tell them it was disgraceful, and I raised quite a ruckus. I got them to agree that the accord would not be put into effect and that things would be dragged out until the Germans had undertaken a certain number of commitments." I then informed Weygand of my intention not to take on the mission without formal assurance, in the form of a letter to Roosevelt, that Bizerte and North Africa would be respected. At that point Marshal Pétain approached and took us aside. I explained to him the conclusions I had reached and said I would be submitting a letter for his signature. Weygand backed me completely, and Pétain stated that he was in perfect agreement.[19]

I spent part of the next day composing the letter. This was the heart of it: "M. Rist's mission is to assure you, on behalf of myself and of Admiral Darlan, that I am resolved not to go beyond the terms of the armistice, most particularly with regard to North Africa." (I have not been able to find the exact text of the letter among my papers.)

I showed my letter to Rochat, who expressed concern that my language was too precise and could not be accepted by the marshal. My response was that this passage constituted the touchstone whereby I would know whether I could accept the mission.

Romier raised no objection. He showed the letter to Darlan, who had no problem declaring it acceptable.

19. In his memoirs, *Rappelé au service* (Paris: Flammarion, 1950), Weygand does not mention this meeting of Monday, 20 October, and says, seemingly in error, that he had left Vichy on Monday morning (522–25).

SUNDAY, 26 OCTOBER 1941 My negotiations over the course of the week were prolonged because of the tragic hostage crisis in Nantes and Bordeaux. Admiral Darlan had rushed to Paris to try to save the fifty hostages remaining after Stülpnagel had a hundred of them shot. That is why I did not see him again until Friday, the day Pétain had proposed to the Council of Ministers that he would go to the Demarcation Line and offer himself as a hostage. He was prevented from doing so by Pucheu and Darlan.

I had obtained an interview on Saturday with the marshal at which Darlan was to be present. I had hoped to see them both together. But at the last minute, Darlan, detained by Pucheu, who was leaving for the occupied zone, excused himself. Thus I saw Marshal Pétain alone. I found him reading the letter agreed upon with Darlan and Romier. I stressed the importance of the passage regarding adherence to the terms of armistice, pointing out that what this meant was protecting Bizerte. "Yes," he said, "that's fine . . . unless there's a *diktat* from the Germans, but I told Leahy that I would warn him if my policy changed." He signed the letter, then spoke of my mission. "*We must gain time.*"

He also said, "The English have become our enemies, so we must remain on good terms with the United States."

I said, "It is the English, however, who will save us."

"This must not be said."

I asked him how I would correspond with him. He said, "Everything that goes through the admiralty is known to the Germans. You can keep me informed by letters passed via the American diplomatic pouch."

Then he showed me the book with his collected speeches. "You will give one copy to President Roosevelt on my behalf. The other is for you. Before you leave, come by and I'll sign it for you." He appeared to attach great importance to some aphorisms about government that conclude the book. "I wanted to commit my deepest thoughts to paper, *like Pascal and others.*" Then he got up and led me to a table bearing an album of Épinal prints.[20] The album, made in his honor, features the great stages of his life. He leafed through it, showing me the cartoon-like illustrations one by one, commenting on each. "I'm going to send it to Pershing," he told me. The whole thing was painful, oppressive, an extraordinary display of senile vanity and childish remarks at a time when we should have been speaking solely of French policy, to which I tried in vain to lead him back.

---

20. *Images d'Épinal*: colorful prints that became synonymous in France with naïve traditionalism and a rose-colored view of the world. [TF]

I left Pétain and went looking for Darlan, who was still in conference with Pucheu. Commandant Guichard, Darlan's chief of staff, came to apologize on behalf of the latter. I asked again if Admiral Darlan had found my letter acceptable. He confirmed that he had. I told him what Pétain had said to me: "The admiral must also sign it." (In the end, this did not happen.)

Upon leaving Pétain I said to him, "I'll do my best to succeed, but I can't guarantee it." His answer: "My friend, if you don't succeed, it won't be your fault." He accompanied me to the door and asked, incidentally, if he should declare the money he has on deposit with Morgan Bank in America!

Thereupon I sent word to Matthews that "the die has been cast,"[21] and it was not without misgivings that I took the train back to Versailles. I had asked to see Admiral Auphan, with whom I spent half an hour begging him to use all of his influence to prevent Franco-American policy from changing in the slightest over the course of the next few months, thereby allowing my mission to proceed.

But Darlan (threatened by both Laval and Pucheu) had decided to follow his own path.

---

21. Two telegrams from Leahy, dated 20 and 27 October, corroborate Rist's account, his anxieties upon arrival, and his final decision to accept, which led the American ambassador to think "that he is satisfied with the assurances given by Marshal Pétain and Darlan regarding foreign policy." Leahy insisted upon the extreme importance of secrecy. State Department Archives, 701.5 III/848 and 851.

Nine

"End of My Mission"

11 NOVEMBER–15 NOVEMBER 1941

Rist returned to Vichy in November only to find the government in the midst of a political crisis. After conferring with Marshal Pétain, Admiral Darlan, and others, he concluded that he could not accept the mission to the United States after all and reflected on "the completely inane conversations" of "that little clique of idolatrous reactionaries who surround Marshal Pétain."

TUESDAY, 11 NOVEMBER 1941 End of my mission to the United States.

Upon leaving Vichy on 25 October, I had obtained Darlan's support and Marshal Pétain's signature on the letter of introduction I was to present President Roosevelt on the marshal's behalf. According to the letter, I was charged with reiterating assurances that the French government, in so far as Africa was concerned, would respect conditions laid down in the armistices. It was understood that I would return to Vichy two weeks later and depart on my mission. Meanwhile, Couve would see the Americans in order to work out plans for my arrival, my passage on the Clipper, and my reception in Washington.

However, I knew much could happen in two weeks. Admiral Darlan, who saw me on the twenty-fourth, had expressed exasperation regarding General Weygand. He told me that upon Weygand's departure he intended to question Weygand's trustworthiness[1] and accused him of putting collaboration with the occupier in jeopardy because of his anti-German statements. I then informed him of what Admiral Leahy had told me the previous evening, Thursday, 23 October, regarding the probability of a serious crisis vis-à-vis the United States if General Weygand were to be recalled. In fact, he

---

1. Darlan was concerned about Weygand's trustworthiness with respect to his command in North Africa.

spoke of a "break in diplomatic ties." I had immediately alerted the marshal, who said to me, "You must tell Admiral Darlan," which I did the next day. Darlan appeared to be unmoved. I was left feeling that the conflict could erupt at any moment. Romier, whom I had also warned, remarked a bit naïvely that this was a purely French affair.

It was in these circumstances that I boarded the train on 9 November, arriving in Vichy at 3:30 in the afternoon. My primary concern was to see Rochat. The first thing I asked him was whether the conditions for my undertaking had finally been established – whether, in particular, there had been any decision regarding the transformation of my "personal" mission into an official ambassadorship. It was essential, in fact, to know the length of my stay, as my *Ausweis*[2] was going to expire on 15 January. If I came back after that, I had no means of reentering the occupied zone and would find myself cut off from both family and business affairs for an indefinite period. Rochat replied that they had not considered these aspects of the matter, and as he personally had no information and had not even seen Pétain's letter to Roosevelt, I should discuss these things with Marshal Pétain.

I then asked about the status of the Darlan-Weygand conflict. There, too, Rochat was in the dark. He let me know, however, that just a few days before he had had a visit from Matthews, who conveyed American uneasiness over rumors that continued to circulate regarding the general's departure, saying a crisis would not fail to follow. Rochat had forthwith informed Darlan of Matthews's visit. The admiral had waxed indignant over this interference, but Rochat observed that, as extraordinary as it was, it revealed a state of mind that we had no right to ignore. Under these conditions I needed to see Marshal Pétain as soon as possible to get some clarification. Du Moulin, upon my request for a meeting, replied that Marshal Pétain would receive me immediately.

Finding him in his office, I told him right off the reason for my visit. I asked where things stood with the question of Weygand, which could have serious repercussions for my mission. I reminded him of the letter he had signed, which he had clearly forgotten. He even said at one point, "We forgot about you." He sent Du Moulin to fetch the letter, read it attentively, rediscovered the essential paragraph, and immediately said, "But that's no longer relevant to the current reality." He rose, visibly shaken, and walked around the room for a bit, saying, "Things are going badly." Then he sat down again and said, "You must see the minister of foreign affairs" and had a meeting set up for me at 6:30 with Darlan. He then said, "I've asked the Germans to

2. *Ausweis*: ID card. [TF]

fulfill certain conditions before Weygand's recall." I reminded him of my conversation with Admiral Leahy and of the report I had made to him and to Admiral Darlan. I also mentioned the rumor circulating in Paris on the preceding Monday that Admiral Darlan was being replaced by M. Pucheu. This seemed to upset him even more. He insisted that I tell him who was spreading this rumor; I said I could not name him. "From what party?" he asked. I answered that this person did not belong to a party. He declared that the rumor was absurd and asked me to come back after I had seen Darlan.

In the vestibule I said to Du Moulin, "You know these people better than I do. Can I be blunt with the admiral?" He replied, "That's the only way you'll get anywhere here. I don't even know what's going on myself. All the conversations having to do with General Weygand have taken place between the marshal, the admiral, and Romier. They're the only ones who know what's been decided."

I passed by Romier's office and filled him in on what I had just heard and on what I was going to tell the admiral. Without prompting, he declared, "It would be better to put off your mission till January."

Having been introduced into the admiral's office, I conveyed what Marshal Pétain had told me upon rereading the letter signed by him, and I pointed out that my mission was now irrelevant. I could not leave for the United States in the middle of a crisis. The admiral proceeded to lecture me at length. He began by repeating that Weygand is physically young but intellectually old, that he is not master of his ideas, and that he must go. Then he launched into a general exposition:

> There are two vanquished parties in this war, France and Russia. Germany will shortly be their master and can exploit them as it wishes, which will allow the creation of a continental Europe. France must be part of this Europe. We cannot die of hunger waiting for the war to be over. In another month the victorious Germans are going to head back in our direction and seek to become masters of the Mediterranean. They can succeed, passing across Spain and the Caucasus. I shall be happy to see the Mediterranean free of the English, who, in any case, can do nothing. Their army, whose soldiers sleep at home every evening, is worthless. It's in the same shape ours was in behind the Maginot Line. It's not even certain they can resist a German attack on England.
>
> As for the Americans, they're barbarians. They don't understand the first thing about the situation. They have no army. They're trying to build an enormous navy so they can free themselves of the English. England will become the platform from which the Americans can keep watch over Europe. Here, they'll take Brest and Dunkirk, which they'll use as advanced bases. The war will become a duel in which the United States will be incapable of attacking Germany on the ground and the Germans will be incapable of attacking Americans on their own turf. The war may thus go on indefinitely.

The intelligent thing would be to try to stop it. But instead the English are being pushed to keep on fighting. Under these circumstances I must think of France before it has been ground to dust. That's why we must become part of the new Europe. The Germans are driven only by economic motives. Their homeland is too poor. From the beginning we should have turned them toward Russia. Once they're in control there, we'll be left in peace. The peace will be one of compromises. For now we must become part of Europe. If not, there will be nothing left of us.

He complained as well that the Americans make fun of Marshal Pétain. He showed me a newspaper in which Pétain was depicted as a senile old man. "I protested to Admiral Leahy. He replied that the press is free in the United States, an absurd idea."

I made an attempt to reply in kind to this long harangue. "As an economist," I said, "I can assure you that it will be a long time before the Germans will be able to exploit Russia. It will be years before the Ukraine can produce more. The Russian peasant is a poor worker; he will work even more poorly under the German whip. As for the Americans, I can assure you it is counter to their interests and to their traditions to install themselves in Europe. You say they want to be rid of the English navy. They have even stronger reasons not to tolerate a German fleet." I reminded him of the ideas Roosevelt had discussed with me, his fear for South America and for Greenland, and, seeing the skeptical look on the admiral's face, I assured him that this fear was real and reasonable. "We must have the Americans with us when peace is declared, especially if it is a negotiated peace, and for that reason we must do nothing to undermine their trust."

"They don't trust me," said Darlan.

"All the more reason," I said, "to shore up the points of trust they do have."

"That point is called Weygand," he said.

"Yes," I said, "but it's not the person who matters; it's the principle he represents: the integrity of North Africa. From there, their confidence will spread. As for the Germans, their motives are not primarily economic, they're political. They can be summed up like this: in the sixteenth century, Spanish hegemony; in the seventeenth, French hegemony; at the end of the eighteenth and in the nineteenth, English hegemony; and now they want the century of German hegemony. Their idea is purely political, and their goal, which as an Alsatian I'm well aware of, is to crush their hereditary enemy."

I left him and returned to Marshal Pétain, to whom I related the main points of our conversation. He spoke once again, this time more forcefully, of his intention to set conditions for the Germans. The first would be to obtain their authorization to further fortify North Africa, a request that the

Germans have so far denied. "I shall not allow Weygand to leave before this has been done, and I don't believe they will agree." I got the impression that over the past hour, while I was talking to Darlan, Pétain's resolution had hardened, that he was more in battle mode, readier to fight. He asked me to stay for dinner.

At the table were the Romiers, the Rueffs, and Admiral Fernet. A rather puerile conversation, with remarks such as "authority comes from above" and comments on American democracy. I tried to explain the difference between republicans and democrats. "I don't like the word 'republic,'" said Marshal Pétain, "because it implies that the masses will take part in government." Attention shifted to the word "love," which the French Academy was currently attempting to define. This subject had the advantage that it always cheers the marshal up. He rose, visibly relaxed, and declared that it is nice to ease one's cares by chatting with friends. We gathered in a circle, and Romier, Rueff, and I reeled off stories about Poincaré, Briand, and Waldeck-Rousseau, demonstrating that the Third Republic had, after all, some great characters. As he left, Marshal Pétain asked me to come back the next day.

I summarized my conversation with Admiral Darlan for Romier, expressing my shock at some of Darlan's opinions. "As for General Weygand," I said, "you had better at least prepare the Americans for his ouster and make sure his successor will give the same guarantees. That way you can avoid a crisis with America. After all, it's not Weygand himself that's important, if the admiral can't abide him; it's the principle that he represents and that America is counting on, the integrity of North Africa." I added that my decision had been made, that my departure for the United States was not in the cards, and that I would be heading back to Paris the next day. I invited him and his wife to join me for dinner on Monday evening.

On Monday morning I had my ticket picked up, then I went to find Couve at the finance ministry to explain why my mission would not take place. I told him I would not go to America on behalf of Vichy, as I did not wish to be seen as their interpreter. It was he who must go. He was worried about reactions to this decision in Washington, where my arrival was expected. A seat had even been reserved for me on the plane. In his opinion, sending me there was to be a sort of compensation for the dismissal of Weygand (a truly simplistic tactic, and one that takes the Americans for idiots). At eleven I saw Rueff, who shared my impression regarding the childishness of the previous evening's dinner-table conversation. He added, "These people don't realize the strength you bring to them. They suspect you because of your ideas. The marshal likes you, but his wife is wary."

"She takes me for a Red."

"Exactly."

At four in the afternoon I returned to Rochat, brought him up to date, and asked for an appointment with Marshal Pétain. It was set for six. Rochat was in effect kept out of things, but had had a strong enough whiff of what was going on to put me on guard with his silences and question marks.

At six the marshal received me. He repeated his decision to set conditions to the Germans for the departure of General Weygand. He had sent a telegram to Weygand telling him to come to Vichy. "I will ask you to come back while he's here." He leafed through some papers on the table. "I have received a report," he says, "a most remarkable one. I want you to read it and give me your observations. But it's top-secret. You have time between now and dinner. Come back when you've finished reading it."

I went off with the report. It was a long exposition by Darlan demanding the departure of Weygand, whom he sees as an obstacle to French-German collaboration, offering to resign if this departure does not occur, and providing his arguments for collaboration. In this document I saw repeated, but organized and polished, all of the ideas that Darlan had expounded to me the previous evening. The whole is a monument of political absurdity, presented as logical deductions. Even after having read them, I still wondered whether these ideas represented Darlan's real convictions or whether this was a "provisional" doctrine designed to give the impression of complete adherence to German policies until something else became possible. Three words underlined in the report – "for the present" – may allow one to think he is reserving the right to change one day. Meanwhile, one cannot imagine anyone more completely aligned with the conviction that Germany is winning and that resistance is futile.

The main points are those he laid out for me in our previous conversation: Germany will crush Russia, then will turn toward France for support in conquering the Mediterranean and evicting the English. This undertaking can be realized without great difficulty via Gibraltar and other points. The conquest of England itself is not out of the question. That done, Germany can organize Europe and Africa as a viable union. England is already defeated, or partially subject to America. Consequently, there will be a negotiated peace between Germany and the United States. In this peace, France must be on the side of Germany.

The chancellor told Darlan he was not interested in territorial conquests as long as France put an end to her hostility toward Germany; what the latter is always afraid of is a change of government that would place France once again in the enemy camp. If Germany were satisfied on that score, its support for France would be assured and Germany would focus on defeating Russia.

What role would the United States play in all this? According to Darlan, it could be of no help to France. In any case, the Americans are solely concerned about their own purely selfish interests – notably, the enslavement of England, which is already at their mercy. They would not even be averse to taking over French bases, such as Brest or Dunkirk, in the event they were victorious. But they cannot be, because they are just as incapable of managing a landing as the English, whose abstention during the four months of the Russo-German War demonstrates their impotence. The conclusion is thus clear: we must continue the policy of collaboration that has already shown results – in regard to prisoners, for example – and remove the obstacle to this collaboration whose name is General Weygand.

Obviously, one of the conclusions not expressed in the report is that France must support Germany in the conquest of the Mediterranean basin! Between this policy and that advocated by Marshal Pétain lies an abyss. What is the point of keeping on the good side of the United States in such a scenario? And how could we continue to protect North Africa?

At around seven thirty I carried the document back to Marshal Pétain. He kept me in his office until eight o'clock. I summed up my impression of the report by saying, "To equate keeping or not keeping the general with keeping or not keeping the policy of collaboration is a position that cannot be defended. Besides, the careful deductions concerning the unfolding of events in the future are contrary to all reality. There is room for the unknown, for the increase of American and English armaments, for example."

But the marshal was more interested in talking than in listening. His ideas, delivered in a monologue, convinced me that he was already prepared to give in on essential points. He wants to fortify North Africa. But against whom? Against the English. What he fears is that the Germans will judge us too weak to defend Algeria against the English and will take over the command. "They already tried to do that in Syria," he said. "I protested, but they didn't want us to send reinforcements. If we had been better armed, we would have defeated the English." He envisions the possibility that we ourselves might call in the Germans to defend us against the English. I listened to all of this in amazement. I asked if he really sees such a quick victory of Germany over the Russians that they can already be thinking about North Africa. He replied that the Germans will finish the Russian campaign when they wish by establishing themselves on an Arkhangelsk-Petersburg line, and then their attention will turn to the Mediterranean. He envisions submarines blocking both the Atlantic and the Mediterranean, subduing the English through hunger. He has visited Gibraltar. He believes it can be taken easily by using gas. I was astounded by this general defeatism. I said, "But that will all take time; if Germany returns to Africa, it will not be tomorrow." I repeated what I had told Admiral Auphan: "Wait six months before you decide to choose one side or the other." Marshal Pétain agreed and said, "Yes, we must gain time."

"Meanwhile, Weygand must not be sacrificed."

"I sent a telegram today telling him to come," he says. "But the general is not easy to deal with; he is capable of handing me his resignation."

It was time for dinner, so he accompanied me to the door. I made one last remark: "If you keep the general, you won't only gain time, you'll have the gratitude of the occupied zone, which would view his departure with great apprehension!"

The marshal insisted that I stay for dinner and said I should invite Romier and his wife to come too. Which I did. That evening I saw General Le Rond and his wife, Engineer Perrin (from Ugine), an admiral with whom I was not acquainted, and the Romiers. Conversation languished. As he left, Romier told me, "General Weygand is going to arrive soon – what an awful week for me!" For he is the buffer between Weygand and Darlan.

All of these conversations have convinced me that if Marshal Pétain wanted to send me to Washington, Admiral Darlan saw the move as nothing more than a polite gesture, without envisaging any real policy of rapprochement with the United States. To go under such circumstances would be sheer folly. Besides, they now have to start from scratch, as Marshal Pétain himself considers the letter (which was to be my safeguard) no longer in line with reality. If I am asked for again, it would thus be on a new basis. Between now and then so many things could happen! These conversations, however, may have served to strengthen Marshal Pétain's resistance. We shall see. But what a frightening gap between the feelings of the French and their wishes in the occupied zone and what I have been able to observe of the ideas of "Vichy," all directed toward Germany, against England, and toward new capitulations. We are in fact in the hands of the enemy.[3]

3. Du Moulin de la Barthète mentions the aborted ambassadorship in his memoirs. After Weygand was recalled, he writes, "the storm subsided. But Charles Rist, former deputy governor of the Banque de France, who had been approached by Pétain about possibly replacing Henry-Haye in Washington and had made it clear he would not accept unless the situation in North Africa remained unchanged, declined the offer, saying he would not go to the United States." *Le Temps des illusions – Souvenirs (juillet 1940–avril 1942)* [*The Time of Illusions – Remembrances (July 1940–April 1942)*], 401–402.

FRIDAY, 14 NOVEMBER 1941 I went to see Millerand to explain why I had given up on going to the United States. He expressed satisfaction that things turned out as they did before I found myself in an impossible situation. He also shared my disgust at the spectacle provided by Vichy – France fallen into the hands of such cowards and incompetents! I reminded him of General Buat's pronouncement regarding Pétain: "He only organizes retreats." We agreed that it is up to the Russians to save us. He wondered what is going on in England and if their inertia masks a wish for a negotiated peace. This would be unthinkable. Debates in the British Parliament, reopened several hours later, vindicated our faith.

The Germans remain bogged down in the mud and snow a hundred kilometers from Moscow.

The Americans have voted (at last!) to repeal the law of neutrality, which will allow them (at last!) to use their own merchant ships to transport goods to England. Roosevelt was elected for a third term a year ago. It has taken a year for this stupid law, a monument to resentment and fear, to be overturned. Meanwhile, the Americans have zealously castigated the French and the English for their weak resistance to Hitlerism!

SATURDAY, 15 NOVEMBER 1941 I am mulling over the completely inane conversations I was privy to these last few days. That little clique of idolatrous reactionaries who surround Marshal Pétain have reached the height of folly with their allusions to Freemasonry, their aversion to the word "republic," and their general lack of culture. This suggestion of holy secrecy, this hatred of anyone who does not rally round the new cult, it is all grotesque. These people do not have a single new idea, a single original perspective that might penetrate the confusion of the time to provide a vision of the future. Who has noticed the rise of military demagogy that typifies Hitlerism? How is it that this little court, in which the stale ideas of French conservatism have found refuge with an old soldier, cannot see that it will perish at the first shock? The impression of unreality that emerges is incredible. And yet Marshal Pétain is the only one here who has attempted to resist the enemy's stranglehold. He is the only one who has not completely folded. Unfortunately, he no longer has the will or the memory. He forgets recent events. He no longer puts facts together in order to draw conclusions. But the Germans need him. Without him the odiousness of this whole new system would appear intolerable. That is why he is stronger than he seems. The Germans will not easily let him disappear. They have no marshal or admiral with whom to replace him. It is just a question of Pétain himself deciding to exercise his power – does he even know he has it?

Ten

The Wind Shifts

16 NOVEMBER–14 DECEMBER 1941
Relying on foreign radio broadcasts and news from his own informants, Rist recorded in his diary the war's dizzying twists and turns – the German advance on the Don, but impasse before Moscow; the English offensive in Libya that caught Rommel by surprise; and the 7 December bombing of Pearl Harbor and declaration of war by Japan on the United States and Britain, resulting in the United States' declaration of war on Japan, Germany, and Italy.

SUNDAY, 16 NOVEMBER 1941 A curious phenomenon, especially for an economist, is the growing role played by tobacco as a "third commodity," much like the role played by gold in the early days of money. Even those who do not smoke sign up to buy tobacco, because they can offer it to smokers in exchange for favors, such as a rationing coupon for another item. Packets of tobacco or cigarettes assure the goodwill of those who have desirable items to offer. Tobacco has become rare, and thus precious, though in reality it does nothing more than produce smoke. The same with gold, which according to cynics serves only to gild picture frames and fill teeth but is desired by everyone. Tobacco has thus become the means to acquire *other things*. In the barter economy to which, for all practical purposes, we have returned – and in which paper money is no longer a sure way to obtain goods, as they are hidden – tobacco becomes the way to make merchandise suddenly pop out of its hiding place. Official money no longer serves to produce this miracle.

The Germans are still pinned outside Moscow. If they remain so for a month, the prophecies of Darlan will prove false, and the position of Pétain and Weygand will be strengthened.

FRIDAY, 21 NOVEMBER 1941 Once more we are witnessing great events: the English have unleashed an offensive in Tripoli. Let us hope that this time, finally, they will not disappoint those who are counting on them.

Meanwhile, in Vichy, Weygand has been dismissed. America immediately let it be known via Cordell Hull that its entire foreign policy regarding France would be reviewed. I had warned Pétain and Darlan. If they paid no attention, it is because the former is too weak to react and the latter utterly determined to side with the Germans. To think that I might already have left (I was to take the Clipper on the nineteenth!), only to learn about the change when I arrived in New York!

The Germans are advancing very slowly toward the Don – and spinning their wheels outside Moscow.

Our electricity has been reduced. That intended for heat is completely cut off. That for light, greatly diminished.

People no longer have food for the rabbits and poultry on which they depended so much last year. Today they have to sacrifice them.

I am buying 1,500 square meters of woodland at Glatigny to keep us warm next winter. Luckily, this year's supply is still sufficient.

Pastor Monod, whose daughter is a Red Cross nurse at the Drancy barracks where five thousand Jews have been confined, tells us horrible stories about the sanitary conditions: no food, no blankets, no trash receptacles. Serious illnesses for which German doctors have had patients taken to the hospital. Scurvy! The director and the doctor managing the camp are *French*.

Anglo-French radio, which has been scrambled for several weeks, is now broadcasting long-wave. One can hear perfectly. Just today there was an attempt at breaking it up, happily without result.

SATURDAY, 22 NOVEMBER 1941 I am reading in Renan's *Questions Contemporaines* these lines written in 1868:

> The Revolution threw France into a state of heroic crisis that at times left her lower than all other nations, depriving her of the advantages of right-thinking people, but marking her for a mysterious destiny. I would not want *this divine fever that constitutes our greatness to disappear....* In the heart of our country, as in that of Rebecca, two populations are at war, the one wishing to suppress the other. Must one abdicate, surrender to the other? No, they must support each other, and, in spite of their differences, make common cause – that of justice and the common weal, inseparable from that of the nation. Divided into four factions[1] of which three are always hostile to the one in power, France can never

---

1. Here Rist adds in brackets, "the legitimists, Orléanists, Bonapartists, and republicans, no doubt."

really call on more than a fourth of her strength; and yet those permanent interests that transcend dynastic change should never suffer. (Preface, xxviii)

THURSDAY, 1 DECEMBER 1941 On Thursday at the Suez Company
board meeting I was astonished to hear Humbert de Wendel strongly criticizing the Vichy government: "Even the good they try to do is doomed to
failure."[2] He told me that Louis Marin has broken off relations with Marshal
Pétain. He expressed regret that I was not sent to Washington. It is curious
that even these men on the extreme right are solid in their opposition to the
"collaborators." In the future, one hopes for a degree of understanding in this
regard, making unity easier.

Russian victory at Rostov-on-Don, where they threw out the Germans
and retook Taganrog. At Tripoli the English seem to have underscored their
victory with an extraordinary tank battle. Will Vichy get it? Or, sticking to
the notion that "the Russians are going to be the great victims of the war,
along with us" (Darlan), will they really open the door to the enemy in North
Africa?

Growing threats from the Japanese in the Pacific. Without a doubt, that
will be key to America's entry into the war. As Walter Lippmann told me
almost two years ago.

WEDNESDAY, 3 DECEMBER 1941 Émile Borel and the other members
of my institute arrested with him a few weeks ago have been released. For
one month Borel was kept in solitary confinement, without interrogation,
without talking to a soul, even to those who brought him food. Today he is
free but plagued by nightmares. What a disgrace for a savant in his seventies
to be treated this way. Who denounced him? What was he accused of? No
one knows.

Pétain (accompanied by Benoist-Méchin) has met with Marshal Goering at Saint-Florentin! What went on? What is going to happen? Anxiety has
us all in its grip.

SUNDAY, 7 DECEMBER 1941 I read in the second volume of the Duke
of Broglie's *Memoirs*, which were sent to me by his grandson Duke Maurice
de Broglie, the following passage: "Ancient wisdom had it right. One should
not try to rule over one's peers beyond a certain age. The mind and the body

---

2. The Lorraine steelworks tycoon here expresses the feelings of his family, at least
those of his brother François, senator and close associate of Louis Marin, president of
the Republican Federation (see Jean-Noël Jeanneney, *François de Wendel en République*
[Paris: le Seuil, 1976]). Theirs was an assuredly minority attitude in this ambiance.

may remain, or appear to be, intact. Courage and strength of will bend with the weight of years. Only heroic characters resist this slow and stealthy decline. M. Thiers has never been mistaken for a hero" (180). If one substitutes "Pétain" for "Thiers," these lines, so unjust for the great statesman, become justice itself when applied to his so-called successor.

I hear on the radio that President Roosevelt has sent a personal message to the emperor of Japan in a last attempt to avoid war. So far his messages have had little effect.

Two days ago England declared war on Finland, Hungary, and Romania, German allies on the Russian front. Four days ago the United States finally announced that it would extend the Lend-Lease Act to apply to Turkey. Has Turkey, then, chosen sides?

The idea of integrating France into the "new order" is the greatest imaginable economic folly. It is in fact already integrated. The result is clear. The nation has been pillaged by Germany and deprived of raw materials and food by the English blockade. If instead of being occupied, France were allied with Germany, the result would be the same. Germany's current allies, including Italy, are not in any better economic shape than France, and we know what state Austria-Hungary was in during the last war. On the other hand, if France were allied with the maritime powers, even though partly occupied by Germany, we would have access to more supplies of food and textiles, among other things. Yes, but if Germany occupies France completely! We come back to the same old problem. As long as France is not defended militarily against Germany, we will always be in a precarious economic position. There is no arrangement that can save us from the pillage that will take place, no matter whether France is an ally or an enemy of Germany. Defended, however, we will be in a position to carry on economically, as long as we retain freedom of the seas. The problem is thus military, not economic. Moreover, it is the same for Belgium, for Holland, and for Italy. One is thus led to imagine a common military defense for these countries. The problem can be resolved as long as its solution is not in the hands of the military, who should be simply the agents of a common plan prepared and conceived by civilians, engineers, and statesmen.

What has partly saved France from famine is the decentralized nature of its agriculture, its system of varied crops and small farms. A backward state of things, if you wish. But as war constitutes a return to primitive conditions – that is, to a "closed" economy – the economy best suited for these conditions is precisely a relatively primitive one. The more modernized our agriculture becomes – that is, the more it becomes part of the international economy via specialization and rationalization – the more necessary it will be to keep the nation's maritime routes, as well as its links to maritime powers (which are also the great agricultural powers) free in times of war. We are thus always led back to the same military policy.

France cannot have *simultaneously* a navy strong enough to defend it against a much more powerful British navy *and* an army strong enough to defend it against a superior German army. We must thus make a choice. This choice is imposed by the existence of Algeria and our colonial empire – impossible to protect against a British fleet at the same time that we would be fighting on the Atlantic coast. The other side of the coin is the risk of invasion by Germany. Can this risk be avoided? Absurd to think so. The only way to avoid it would be for Great Britain to organize a strong enough army, in cooperation with the small and great powers threatened by Germany. In that case, the threat on land could be averted.

Some will say that Great Britain may not be interested in the continent and, consequently, may not be interested in the fate of France. That seems impossible, because in that case Germany would be free to build an air force and a navy that sooner or later would threaten England. In a word, of the two hypotheses – that which leaves France isolated on the continent so that England can dedicate itself exclusively to its empire and withdraw to the west, or that which makes of France a bastion for the Atlantic powers – it is the second that is conceivable. The future and the peace treaty will demonstrate England's choice.

I have finished the Duke of Broglie's *Memoirs*. No more candid and sincere demonstration can be given of the imbecility of reactionaries, of their childish attachment to simple words (for example, the horror they profess at the word "republic"), and of their unbelievable ignorance (thanks to their parochial upbringing and society) of the deep feelings and real conditions of life in France. That was true seventy years ago. It is still true today.

MONDAY, 8 DECEMBER 1941 This morning (and last evening) we learned by radio that Japan has attacked the United States and England. These simultaneous strikes in the Philippines, Hawaii, Siam, and Shanghai were carried out by air and by sea. Let us hope that the Americans and the English have prepared their responses. Germany used to describe the yellow race as the greatest threat. That vulgar noncommissioned officer Emperor Wilhelm II proclaimed this discovery. Today it is the Germans who have unleashed the yellow race against the white race, preparing a Japanese hegemony in Asia that can only be sustained at the cost of bloody and frequent wars with North and South America. All of this in order to enhance their own bloodstained attempt to conquer Europe. Once again German strategy has led to a rebirth of savagery.

This morning the Parisians have been given a 6:00 PM curfew because of new attacks on the occupying army. This will complicate everything.

THURSDAY, 11 DECEMBER 1941 Two large English battleships sunk in the Gulf of Siam; the Japanese are landing everywhere, even on Luzon; Wake Island (center of undersea cables) and Guam have been taken. President Roosevelt has declared that the news is generally bad and that Americans must be prepared to see all their foreign bases taken! Beautiful start. This will, I hope, stir Anglo-Saxon ardor! Can the United States allow Japan to win this war? What a humiliation! The war will be a long one.

The Germans have announced that the Russian front is no longer of interest and that operations must be suspended because of a rough winter. Ruse or reality?[3] In any event, Moscow has not been taken, nor Leningrad. The whole thing is a failure.

SATURDAY, 13 DECEMBER 1941 Yesterday Germany and Italy declared war on the United States. Unbelievably vulgar speeches at the Reichstag and Piazza Venezia.

The Russian business remains puzzling. Are the Russians advancing and pushing back the Germans? Or are the Germans adjusting their front line? In any case, it is clear that the Germans have failed to take Moscow. The Russians are not defeated, and the consequences may be serious. Darlan's assertions that they were bound to lose were rash, to say the least.

The Japanese continue to pile up victories. Unbelievable lack of preparation on the part of the British. Now we hear of a military pact between Japan and Indochina!

Mlle Spitzer's Jewish father was arrested at his home yesterday morning. He worked with Géraldy, who seems to have declared that the German

---

3. In *A Short History of World War II*, William L. Stokesbury confirms the reality: "The [German] hand froze before it could clutch. Winter arrived early, the earliest and the hardest winter in half a century. The Germans had expected to win by now; they had summer uniforms, summer equipment.... Overnight the temperature dropped and kept on dropping; it finally clunked to the bottom at forty degrees below zero, with the wind blowing straight from the North Pole. A last spastic effort carried the German 3rd and 4th Panzer Groups to within twenty-five miles of Moscow. That was as close as they ever got." (160) [TF]

victories amount to an Iliad and that a magnificent era is opening for Europe! Saw Gidel to ask for his support. He tells me that other arrests were made the same day.[4]

Last Tuesday, conversation with Moreau as I left the Paribas board meeting. I learned that for four years before the war, Pétain was taking classes in administration with Alibert, his future minister of justice *and Action Française partisan*! Thus, this former marshal of the French Republic, which showered him with honors, had been preparing to betray her for a long time. What more perfect circumstance for a marshal than defeat – one he perhaps did not arrange directly, but did nothing to avert?

SUNDAY, 14 DECEMBER 1941 Visit from the Millerands yesterday afternoon. We agreed there is not currently a single politician in France around whom a simple majority of Frenchmen could rally. And so, I said, that leaves only a general – at least one of those who have fought and whose name will mean something to the popular imagination! I mentioned a letter from my son Jean suggesting that the marshal did not give anything away to Goering during their recent meeting in Saint-Florentin and that Darlan had been given the runaround by his superior. Let us hope it is true.

4. Janine Spitzer was the secretary at Rist's research institute. Her Jewish father, Robert Spitzer, collaborated on plays with Géraldy (the pseudonym of Paul Lefèvre). René Gidel taught at the Paris Law Faculty and served as a member of Vichy's National Council (notably, on its committee charged with drafting a constitution). [JNJ/TF]

Eleven

"A War against the Jews"

15 DECEMBER 1941–27 FEBRUARY 1942

Facing attacks from within France and setbacks in Russia and elsewhere, Germany reacted with drastic reprisals – hostages were shot, Jews rounded up en masse – and extermination of the Jews became official Nazi policy.

MONDAY, 15 DECEMBER 1941 The announcement that a hundred hostages will be shot in reprisal for the attacks carried out in Paris have filled us all with ominous dread. Even Vichy felt obliged to protest. Nothing could have been better designed to upset plans for increased collaboration. Doctor Bloch committed suicide as he was being arrested on Friday during the roundup of Jews. Yesterday a phone call from Mlle Spitzer, very upset about her father.

All this comes at a moment when Germany's defeat has become a certainty. The failure in Russia and the United States' entry into the war are two vital, decisive facts. Those who do not see this are blind. But how many twists and turns still to go before the end!

SATURDAY, 20 DECEMBER 1941 A week of horror, filled with executions and the roundup of Jews. One hundred people were apparently shot on Monday at Fort Mont-Valérien on the outskirts of Paris. Every day we learn more names of those arrested last Friday: doctors, engineers, etc. Impossible to know where they are – maybe Drancy, maybe Compiègne. They say that trains have already been sent east from Compiègne, doubtless to Russia, in accordance with General S.'s warning of reprisals. Count C. assures me that the French government agreed to allow these reprisals to target the Jews so as to spare the rest of the French. Some articles even more disgusting than usual by Abel Bonnard and Jean Luchaire sounded the bugle call for the kill. The depths to which some of our people have fallen confounds the imagination.

Tried to discover the whereabouts of Mlle Spitzer's father. Impossible to learn anything. The poor fellow should have fled long ago. He has allowed himself to be taken through a kind of inertia. Met Max Lazard at the Statistics Society. He says he wants to stay, in spite of the urging of all the committee members, who are begging him to go underground. Courage? Fatalism? Pride?

I have spent the last three days taking steps to keep Françoise from suffering possible consequences for not having declared herself. From now on notaries and bankers must report the Aryan or non-Aryan status of beneficiaries! Saw the notary, then Mettetal.[1]

Meanwhile, news of the war gets better each day. English victory at Tripoli seems assured. The German retreat from Russia has resulted not just from the harsh winter but from aggressive Russian attacks. I find it hard to believe that the Germans will keep on trying. Pro-Germans say, "It's only a six-month postponement of the German army's victory. Meanwhile, they'll attack London." Foolishness, in my opinion. These things do not happen twice.

The defeats in the Far East are humiliating for the Allies. But for the war against Germany they have only secondary importance. The prestige and the strength of the United States are at stake. It will not accept defeat.

The French military, of course, had foreseen none of that. The incompetence of the military is particularly striking with regard to military matters. In civilian affairs their stupidity is limited by the atmosphere of civilian common sense within which they operate; but in military affairs it is the whole atmosphere they have created that pushes them beyond the limits of ignorance and vanity. In light of these events, Darlan's remarks barely four weeks ago take on stupefying, macabre dimensions. He could already see the Mediterranean in German hands.

SUNDAY, 21 DECEMBER 1941 Excellent news from Russia and Libya.

The admirers of Mussolini and Laval are cut from the same cloth: they are the ones who are afraid. They are the same conservatives who, in succession, hated the revolutionary Briand and applauded him when he stopped the strike by railway men in 1910. Such people only admire those who can deliver them from their fears of the moment. That is how they judge statesmen. It really does not matter to them that a man has the gift of leadership,

---

1. Françoise, the wife of Rist's son Claude, was of Jewish origin, and Maître Mettetal, a lawyer well regarded in the Vichy camp, was enlisted to protect her from persecution.

generosity, character, or nobility. He will not be judged on that basis. They look at one thing only: Does he or does he not serve our current interest, or, rather, our permanent interest – that of our property, our fortune, and our peace of mind? What does it matter that Laval is rotten, corrupt, diplomatically incompetent, capable of all acts of perfidy and treachery? They have sensed that he will defend them, and they applaud. The same with Mussolini.

Between these two men, moreover, the similarities are striking. The one a lycée proctor, the other a low-level schoolteacher. Both eaten up with ambition, resentment, and envy. Both understanding that the only way for them to become rich is through politics, for they would be brushed aside in economic circles. Both aware that scruples about means are only allowed to those who have already attained certain heights of fortune or reputation. Both devoid of general culture and vision. Both trusting only in the forces of intrigue, envy, and fear. The one, Mussolini, believing in force, the other, Laval, believing in trickery as a primary means, but neither having faith in any means of government except the police – that is to say, precisely the instrument dearest to conservatives – and thus winning the latter's support. The one making use of a very Italian theatrical eloquence, seasoned with brutality, to secure his following. The other not speaking in public but meeting people in corners, sowing lies, calumny, and rumors, silently acquiring the support of individuals who believe in his star – and thus finding himself at the head of a faction comprised of the needy, of cynical journalists and corrupt businessmen, who draw the naïve along with them. Both misjudging the forces of courage and loyalty, in which they do not believe and whose possibilities they discount; both failing lamentably in the face of powerful nations whose continuity and traditions, bolstered by the forces of morality and conscience, they ignore or scorn; both of them particularly incapable even of understanding (owing to their complete lack of education) what Anglo-Saxon Protestantism with its narrowness, but also with its greatness, represents in the world; and finally, both defeated by this Anglo-Saxon world which they ignore and disdain. It will be to the eternal shame of French conservative parties and a faction of the French bourgeoisie (indeed, of the Protestant bourgeoisie) to have made of these two men – whose every trait should have repelled them – objects of admiration and trust.

Bellet, back from Vichy, tells me of the following conversation between Behiç Erkin, the Turkish ambassador, and Joseph Barthélemy, Pétain's minister of justice. The latter said to him: "If the English win, they'll take all our colonies." Behiç replied: "If you do not mind, M. le Ministre, we shall wait until the end of the war to discuss that point." To think that in this moment the opinions of a man like Barthélemy, perfectly ignorant of all matters of foreign affairs, can count in the vital decisions our government will be making!

Others will tell you: "What we need is for the Germans and the Bolsheviks to destroy each other so neither wins!" A typical opinion of the "right-thinking" French bourgeois and of the European bourgeois in general, as Ortega y Gasset describes him in his remarkable *Revolt of the Masses*. The bourgeois does not want to choose. He believes that opposites can coexist. He wants to satisfy both his petty patriotism and his massive fear of communism. It goes without saying that, if there were really no way to enjoy both at the same time, it is the petty patriotism that would fall by the wayside.

MONDAY, 22 DECEMBER 1941 Great news on the radio last night. Hitler is dismissing Brauchitsch from his duties as general in chief and is taking over the Supreme Command of the war himself. I have an urge to say: "Lord, let your servant depart in peace, for my eyes have seen your salvation." No more doubt today about the outcome of the war. It is lost for the Germans. What a somber drama à la Wallenstein underlies this decision! Resistance on the part of some generals? Discouragement, or refusal to obey, on the part of some military units? Defeats and losses greater than can be admitted? Gasoline shortages after efforts that took longer than expected? What one can guess is that the decision to retreat, after reiterated proclamations that the Russian army had been destroyed, could not have been made without difficulty, arguments, altercations, and fits of rage. It is a confession of impotence at the very moment when the German-Italian army in Libya is collapsing.

THURSDAY, 25 DECEMBER 1941 Yesterday young S.,[2] back from Vichy, brought me echoes of the various comments being exchanged there. They are worried about the Germans' possible entry into Spain. England has supposedly been holding back supplies to the country for the last two weeks. Franco, uneasy about his increasingly precarious internal situation, would not be displeased to see German troops enter Spain. From there they would continue on to Morocco. In such a case the response would be limited to a feeble protest and that would be that. The marshal, in his meeting with Goering, is said to have declared that France would defend Africa against "whomsoever." Goering apparently became very angry at such a proposition. It seems that Pétain, as he had told me he would, asked permission to fortify North Africa. Goering supposedly replied: "If I pass your memorandum on to the Führer, France will be demolished." Moreover, it appears there is talk in Vichy of a second government to be established in the occupied zone in competition with that of Vichy.

2. Not identified.

All these suppositions rest in part on an interpretation of the Führer's instruction to his troops in which people think they perceive big plans. I only see in this communication a sort of *plea* to discouraged and exhausted troops asking them to hold on until the spring. In such a situation can the Führer make any serious move in the Mediterranean? It would seem unlikely. All of his efforts seem aimed at camouflaging the disaster in Russia. We shall soon see.

Today a party for the children and grandchildren, all gathered here. Léonard among us. A sumptuous feast with two chickens! Christmas tree, singing, violin and piano – children's skits. Hopes for a better year!

FRIDAY, 26 DECEMBER 1941 Fall of Hong Kong and the taking of Benghazi. The latter news is far more important than the former. The successes of the Japanese are secondary compared to the Mediterranean victory. That is where the great danger must be confronted. And the English troops seem determined this time to maintain their pursuit all the way to Tripoli. In that case, what will France do? One has the impression that it will not be a party to the entrance of the Germans or the Italians into Tunisia. It was doubtless to encourage Pétain's resistance that Cordell Hull has just protested the handing over of Saint-Pierre-et-Miquelon to the so-called government of the Free French forces. An important and significant step. The United States is maintaining its ties with Vichy.

The United States is losing in the Philippines. Landing of 150,000 Japanese there. What a humiliation for the Americans! The Japanese stranglehold on the Malay archipelago could inhibit the transport of American arms via the Red Sea and the Persian Gulf to Egypt or to the Caucasus. That is the greatest risk. And if they triumph in the Dutch Indies and in Singapore, will they not turn back again to confront the Russians in Siberia? All of this would be very serious. Once again the Anglo-Saxons believed that speeches and threats were useful substitutes for armed force against well-armed countries! Will the inevitable reaction of American public opinion in the face of these bloody defeats be in time to provoke defensive or offensive measures? Or are they going to trust once again "in time that is on our side?" A nice topic of conversation for Roosevelt and Churchill, who will be meeting in Washington over Christmas.

SATURDAY, 27 DECEMBER 1941 During the first weeks after the armistice, at the moment of our greatest despair, I was reading Chateaubriand's *Napoléon*, Sainte-Beuve's *Lundis*, and Montaigne. I renewed myself in the beauty of the French language, and one of the reasons I felt confident was precisely the splendor of this language, so perfect in its sonority, so capable of expressing the simplest and the most common things, as well as the most subtle, the most noble and profound. There is no sentiment of the human soul that cannot be represented by words whose sound is pure and clear – or by the harmony of a phrase and its music. And I said to myself: a people capable of creating such a language will never perish. . . . But the convoluted literature of these last twenty years must be done away with in order to pick up the thread of tradition.

A speech by Churchill to the American houses of Congress announcing the common will of the United States and England to remain united after the war in order to organize the peace and prevent new aggressions. A great vision. Anglo-Saxon hegemony. A curiosity yet to satisfy: to see how they will go about it. Will France understand her role? A place for geographic communication – a place of historic communication between the old European civilization and the novelties of industry? France, *at the same time* Mediterranean and Atlantic, and *almost not* continental, being separated from Central Europe by the Alps and the Jura, and linking up with it only in the northeast, from which all invasions have come.

Today we have proof in the Russian campaign; Germany will have all it can do in the future to protect itself from the Slavs. That is its historic calling. Still *it must accept this* and not always be looking toward France or Italy. The day Germany wishes, France will be its friend. But Germany has never desired this. Its bitterness, its jealousy, its envy, were too strong. In order for France to renounce her fears, it would suffice for Germany to tell her: "The danger and the future for me is in the east." But what has happened, on the contrary? It is always on its Russian flank that Germany has sought reassurance *against France*. This is not just hatred of a country that is militarily strong; it is hatred of a civilization and a system of liberty. Czarist Russia seemed a guarantee of Germany's own system of tyranny. But what about the U.S.S.R.?

WEDNESDAY, 31 DECEMBER 1941 This morning comes the announcement that the Russians have taken Kerch. This is their reentry into the Crimea, where Sebastopol is still holding out. What a noise the Germans made when they took Kerch! Their "friends" already saw them occupying the Caucasus. And now! The conquest of Russian oil will not happen anytime soon.

FRIDAY, 2 JANUARY 1942 Yesterday all the children were together except for Jean and Claude. Léonard and Marie provided music. Games with Isabelle. Everyone in better spirits than last year!

It must never be forgotten that most people experience nothing like the exaltation that seizes us when faced with the great events of history or the splendors and miseries of our country. For the vast majority – especially those of the middle class who no longer react instinctively as do common people in the presence of "foreigners" – the defeats are physical calamities, like an epidemic or a flood, as a result of which everyone is out to save himself. Those same people, moreover, are incapable of imagining that same exaltation among other peoples. Hence that perpetual misunderstanding of what is mystical and fantastic in Hitler's projects and imagination. One always wants to steer him toward "reasonable" proportions – that is, "wise" and "moderate" ones that a French or English (for the English have sinned as much or more than we have in this area) member of the middle class would readily assign to historic transformations. Thus this refusal to believe in the enormity of his pretentions, in the gigantic scale of his projects and preparations, in what there is of *"uferlos,"* of "no limits," of the indeterminate in Hitlerian psychology. Thus, too, this belief that one will manage with some concessions and arrangements, and this refusal to face at once the tragic grandeur and the *complete absurdity* of current events. For to recognize this tragic absurdity would be to recognize that the absurdity can only be vanquished by force and by an effort commensurate with that absurdity, which their laziness refuses to accept.

The same misunderstanding exists, moreover, of the indomitable will of those who in England and in the United States have taken the measure of all the grandeur and all the dreadful danger of the situation: Churchill or Roosevelt. Thus the belief that the Anglo-Saxons are willing to accept a "compromise peace" or to make arrangements behind the scenes, and the refusal to recognize that they grasp the *unique* character of events that, if allowed to develop in the direction Hitler would like, will change the whole course of British and American history. Equally impossible for such people to understand the clash of civilizations that is in play, the conflict between concepts inherited from the Austrian Middle Ages and those on which is founded all the grandeur of the Anglo-Saxon communities, who have turned toward the future and toward a new "humanism," still somewhat puerile in its expression but singularly salutary in its results, envisaging not just the glory of an "elite" but a joie de vivre accessible to all. This is shocking to some "artists" for whom history is only interesting if it is presented to them as a beautiful tragedy and who measure the grandeur of an epoch by the "artistic" satisfaction it gives them. But history is not an opera. And it is curious to note that these "artistic" minds are in fact incapable of seizing the superhuman tragedy of this immense conflict.

The law against the Jews is a scandal and an absurdity. To be recognized as Aryan it is not enough to have two Aryan grandparents out of four. One must also have made an "act of adherence" to another religion before 25 June 1940.[3] This act of adherence, in practice, means "having been baptized." Thus those whose parents wished to raise them as agnostics or "free thinkers" will still be Jews, but those who have been baptized as Protestants or Catholics will be Aryans. So race will depend upon religion, and yet a child who was not baptized before 25 June 1940 may well, after that date, adopt Christianity but will not on that account stop being legally Jewish. Mettetal tells me that there are priests and nuns who, having three or four Jewish grandparents but whose parents had converted, are considered Jewish and have registered as such with the police. Hence, there will be children who are Christian by belief and practice and whose civil status will be Jewish, meaning they will be forbidden to practice a whole series of professions simply because they were not baptized in time. Needless to say, from now on, in order to avoid such consequences, all children of mixed marriages will be baptized immediately after their birth. Only those who did not have their papers in order as of 25 June 1940 will be persecuted. Maxime Leroy[4] tells me that he obtained a certificate of "provisional Baptism" from a good woman for his son, who without it would have been dismissed from his job, since he was born of a mixed marriage. From now on, the marshal has said, there will be no more "lies."

Many French people today justify their "collaboration" or their "acceptance" of events by Hitler's "genius." One more example of these breathtaking misunderstandings of men on the other side. If one could compare Hitler to someone in history, it would be Philip II much more so than Napoleon. Underlying all of Napoleon's ruses and lies was an extraordinary foundation of bourgeois common sense, which was expressed in everything he said. Believing his military genius to be all-powerful and his army to be invincible, he let his political imagination extend beyond the real and the possible, but

---

3. These are precisely criteria that Rist's three granddaughters (ages twelve, ten, and seven in 1942) could not satisfy. The girls were brought up in the Reformed Protestant Church of France, the church that their mother, raised in a non-practicing Jewish family, had been attending; however, the custom in that church was to baptize children between the ages of fifteen and seventeen at the time of first communion, so the children had not yet made an "act of adherence." E-mails from Antoinette Rist Constable, 2 December 2010, and Isabelle Pinard Rist, 13 October 2011. [TF]

4. Maxime Leroy: sociologist and historian who taught at the École Libre des Sciences Politiques.

he established the civil organization of France. Nothing like this with Hitler. He is a mystic, out of touch with normal human life. Supported by an army that outranks all others but whose formation had nothing to do with him, he believes he is in a position to realize dreams forged during his time as a common soldier in the trenches and during a youth that was nourished with memories of the Germanic Holy Roman Empire. He speaks of intuition, of an inner calling, just as Philip II found his primary inspiration in prayer and faith in Catholicism. The one persecutes Jews just as the other persecuted Protestants. The call of "race and soil" echoes the belief in a divine calling. Philip II also had an army that seemed invincible, an infantry that had never been beaten. Philip II and Hitler represent all the ideas of the past. Napoleon is still the symbol of the French Revolution. No doubt Hitler, like Napoleon, scorns routine-minded governments suffocated by outdated methods. But Hitler also misunderstands all that is alive and new in popular governments, whereas Napoleon's hatred targeted forces of the past. Besides, Napoleon thought only of himself. His egotism absorbed everything. Hitler thinks he is an instrument destined by Providence to realize German dreams. Napoleon never thought about France. He was too realistic. He knew and he said he was unique. "After me people will say: whew." Philip II was not a genius. He was an inhuman dreamer. Later the same will be said of Hitler. Both misunderstood the real march of civilization, which no longer tolerates hegemony and refuses to believe that any military or ideological hegemony can last.

SUNDAY, 4 JANUARY 1942 A New Year's message from Hitler. He declares that the war was caused by Jews and Freemasons, of whom Roosevelt is the puppet. The whole message revolves around this theme and his regret that he cannot dedicate himself to social and cultural works! The message was addressed "to the German people and the National Socialist Party." Certainly more so to the latter than to the former, for one dares not think that this political philosophy has become that of all the German people. On the contrary, it makes better sense as a rallying cry to the party in difficult times.

Metternich said something about Napoleon that is quite curious to reread in the current situation: from Paris, in 1807, he wrote that there was nothing to do except wait for "the great day when Europe would put an end to this essentially precarious state of things because it is against nature and against civilization" (cited by Georges Lefebvre, *Napoléon*, 246). And Talleyrand, in 1808: "France is civilized, but its ruler is not" (Lefebvre 263).

What could one say today of Napoleon's imitator? And what of the prodigious nature of Napoleon's culture compared to Hitler's barbarity? But "civilization" in the mouths of Talleyrand and Metternich refers not to individual culture but to normal relations between men and states, which the Napoleonic era utterly transformed. And that is also what is happening today.

FRIDAY, 9 JANUARY 1942 Went to Ugine on Monday. Jaoul and Perrin are making great efforts to get me to see the marshal and to encourage him in his desire not to fall out with the United States. It is curious that Germany up to now has not demanded that we break off relations with them. By mutual agreement the United States continues to supply North Africa.

Overheard in the mouth of the conservative T.:[5] "What idiots these French bourgeois who rejoice in Bolshevik successes! They'll come down to earth when the Russians have Bolshevized Germany." A typical example of conservative ideas. Bolshevism is the only true enemy. The Bolshevization of Germany, this is the threat that has been brandished at us for the past ten years. The fact is that Germany is *un-Bolshevizable* – and the Germans know it best of all. German Bolshevism is precisely Nazism. It is even more frightening than its counterpart.

The Germans, they say, are looking for hospitals in Paris where they can lodge soldiers who have come back from Russia with typhoid fever.

SUNDAY, 11 JANUARY 1942 Saw Mettetal on Friday: Françoise problem taken care of.[6] But the children! He hopes Protestants will do what the archbishop of Paris did: declare that only ministers of the religion are judges of whether or not there has been, as the law decrees, "adherence" to the Protestant or Catholic faith. I shall see Bertrand.[7]

The widespread advance of the Russians is looking more and more serious for the German army. A German newspaper has opined that it is very wrong of them to pursue and attack the German troops since, in any case, the latter have decided to withdraw!

TUESDAY, 13 JANUARY 1942 Yesterday, discussing the probable duration of the war, a "collaborator" declared that it will soon be over, "because the Americans will quickly tire" and the Germans will be successful in their spring offensive. Always the same attitude, the same ignorance or lack of comprehension of the Anglo-Saxon will. Having got everything

---

5. Not identified.

6. Presumably arrangements had been made to change the date on which Françoise declared herself Jewish. [TF]

7. Bertrand: pastor for the Church of the Oratorio during the war, charged with resolving all problems concerning Protestantism in the occupied zone.

wrong – about the invasion of England, about the United States' entry into
the war, about the Russian resistance – these same people now cling to the
same illusions as the Germans themselves. It will be interesting to see what
they say in six months. As of now they foresee a major air attack, either from
England or from Italian Africa, to relieve Rommel.

SUNDAY, 18 JANUARY 1942 Icy cold for several days now. The Marios
no longer know how they can keep warm and are thinking of moving to
an apartment in Paris. Their supply of wood is diminishing so rapidly that
they switch off their stove. Ours will scarcely last more than a month. Food
is more and more reduced to potatoes and carrots. The markets are empty.
The merchants are reserving their goods for clients who pay black market
prices. Isabelle has come here for a few days on the pretext that her sisters
have the mumps.

There are some aspects of Christianity so obsolete that attempts to revive them are futile. Modern man respects two great virtues: a concern for
the truth and courage (including, and especially, military courage). Now
the concern for truth is not compatible with Christian dogma or myth,
nor is "turn the other cheek" compatible with patriotic pride. On the other
hand, there is in Christianity an element that is essential to a modern man
of breeding: a respect for the equal dignity of every human being – poor or
rich; intelligent or stupid; black, yellow, or white. If this respect were not
felt, cultivated, and developed by education and maintained by laws, life
in society would be nothing but a lawless free-for-all. Is it not curious that
contemporary defenders of a return to faith are interested only in dogma
and in Christian humility, neither of which has any chance of conquering
souls, and take a kind of fearful distance from the only Christian sentiment
that can attract people today – that of the fraternity of men before God and
of their equal dignity? The explanation is, alas, all too obvious: it is the only
aspect of Christianity that would cost the bourgeois something. Then, too,
is the Gospel not in this regard a bit "Bolshevist"?

General von Reichenau has died of a stroke upon returning to Berlin.
Decidedly, the history of modern Germany cannot be understood without
rereading that of the Thirty Years' War. Only Wallenstein and his generals
can give one a clue. All of these Frenchmen who are blissfully ignorant of
German literature understand nothing of what is going on in Germany.

THURSDAY, 22 JANUARY 1942 Suez Company meeting and lunch.
Baron de Benoist, our general agent in Cairo, has had his French citizenship
taken away. His crime is to be a Gaullist. It is this attitude alone, however,

that has permitted the safeguarding of French interests in the Suez. Otherwise the English would have thrown out all French personnel. Darlan is seriously irritated by Egypt's breaking off of diplomatic relations with France. He has declared that the Suez, like Egypt, must suffer the consequences. The idea that this is a matter of great material and moral interest to France does not faze these gentlemen. On the contrary, they have given a warm welcome to Doriot, back from Russia, where his anti-Bolshevik legion has suffered enormous losses because of the cold. Wherever an enemy of France must be defended, Vichy is there. Wherever Frenchmen must be defended, dereliction. Example: the Merlier affair in Athens.[8]

What I read disgusts me. What I hear sickens me. The French today are settling international matters with incredible shamelessness. Hardly any of them have traveled. Some know a little German or English. But the vast majority of those who express an opinion would be incapable of understanding one column of a German or English newspaper. They know nothing of the literature or history of these countries. Thus they judge everything according to their petty political ambitions. With no shame they express their simultaneous mistrust of the Russians, the Germans, the English, and the Americans. They dream of a world in which all foreign countries would remain calm and unchanging in order that the French bourgeoisie, which has a horror of all movement and of all change, could continue to lead their petty lives in peace; they would like to immobilize the world around this sleeping, frightened, and uncomprehending axis – the bourgeois Frenchman.

SUNDAY, 25 JANUARY 1942 I spent the weekend doing what I could with and for Françoise. We shall know only after several days whether our efforts have been successful.

MONDAY, 2 FEBRUARY 1942 I saw Pastor Bertrand on Saturday regarding Françoise's children. I suggested a general course of action to him. He told me that Boegner[9] has already interceded in the free zone. He added that a bureaucrat at police headquarters came to tell him of his disgust at the things he is obliged to do and to ask him to back him up at the Office for Jewish Affairs. He agreed with Bertrand to get in touch with Mettetal and

---

8. Octave Merlier: administrator of the French Institute in Athens; suspended from his duties for having proclaimed his Gaullism too loudly, then imprisoned upon his return to France.

9. Pastor Marc Boegner: president of the National Council of the Reformed Church of France and member of the National Council of Vichy. [JNJ/TF]

will try to do something similar to what the archbishop did. As of now he is doing his best to facilitate the proofs of "adherence" required by law. All this, he told me, is just a way to encourage liars.

The bronze statues are disappearing one by one. Condorcet and Voltaire have disappeared from the Quai Conti. Gambetta is still there, but the bronze geniuses who surrounded him are gone. Likewise, the two pharmacists, Caventou and Pelletier, have been sent to the foundry, giving a rather embarrassing idea of the enemy's resources. That is the main impression left with the general public.

The pessimists are once again using American failures in the Sunda Islands as a pretext to see all as lost. The siege of Singapore leaves them in despair, and even more so the new defeat of the English at Benghazi. This weakness of the English army is staggering. What do they lack? Intelligence or foresight? Or discipline among the men? No one knows, but there is much shaking of heads. Churchill's last speech upon his return from the United States was somber. The Japanese blow to the American fleet has reduced the latter to impotence for some time. But these things are just the vicissitudes of battle. Of greater importance are the Russian victories. And the Americans will make up for their losses rather quickly. The way things are going, the only certainty is that the war will be prolonged.

WEDNESDAY, 4 FEBRUARY 1942 New attacks on the Germans. The latter let it be known that in retaliation they are sending "to the east" a hundred "communists and Jews" and that they have shot four "Jews or communists." The poor Spitzer woman is afraid for her father.

Conversation with Moreau as we left the Banque de Paris. Because he did not vote for Laurent-Atthalin's reelection as president, the two have fallen out. When Laurent-Atthalin asked him to explain, Moreau said he disapproved of his policies and thought he was deceitful. Moreau has put himself in a false position: he should either have left the bank when Laurent-Atthalin passed him over or, if he stayed, kept quiet about his personal grievances. He told me that Madame Romier, who had come to see them while she was in Paris, exclaimed that an English victory would be disastrous for France. Well, what does Vichy want? A German victory? Are they foolish enough to expect some advantage for themselves?

I have been given the text of the declarations made by Pétain to Goering at their Saint-Florentin meeting. In it the marshal says that as the policy of collaboration has not resulted in Germany's giving any advantage to France, he "will stick to the terms of the armistice." (This is the formula that I had

had him use in the letter he gave me for Roosevelt.) How can this attitude be reconciled with that of Romier, Barthélemy, or Darlan with regard to the English?

SUNDAY, 8 FEBRUARY 1942 Yesterday American radio announced that Pétain is leaving for Madrid in order to form a "Latin bloc." If the news is true, it is surely the stupidest initiative the French government could take. France united with those two corpses – namely, the Spain and Italy of today. No army, no navy, and public opinion in revolt against incompetent regimes. A fine force to resist Germany or England! The three Catholic states, all three impotent, forming a league! Inspired by what? Hitler, evidently, whom they expect to make things difficult for England in the Mediterranean. But the inspiration of Hitler has certainly found an echo among the obtuse and ignorant clericals who have led France to embrace the reactionary fantasies.

SATURDAY, 14 FEBRUARY 1942 It has been a week now since René Parodi[10] was arrested. We still do not know anything about him except that he is probably in the Santé prison. They say he is accused of having been involved in an anti-German organization. His wife is very courageous. The search carried out at his house by the German military police yielded nothing. Having shown up at 2:00 in the afternoon and learning that he was at the Palais de Justice, the police said they would come back in the evening. Meanwhile, he could either have fled or secured his papers. He preferred to return home calmly, having nothing to hide. His children are in Évian with their grandmother, who does not yet know anything. What a nightmare.

All the news right now is bad. The battle for Singapore will be over in a few days, perhaps in a few hours, for the radio announced this morning that the Japanese have taken over the water supplies. In Libya combat has temporarily halted, but the Germans are not far from Tobruk. This English retreat after the initial hopes has shocked everyone. Meanwhile, it seems certain that Darlan helped to resupply the Italo-German forces via Tunisia. All of this makes people wonder whether English military incompetence will not in the end discourage them, making their tenacity count for naught. The pro-German cohort in London has not laid down its arms. And now we see that

10. René Parodi: deputy prosecutor in Paris; active in the "Libération Nord" Resistance movement alongside Robert Lacoste, Albert Gazier, and Christian Pineau. Parodi was arrested at the same time as the leaders of Combat Zone Nord and died in prison a few months later. See Rist's journal entry for 17 April 1942. [JNJ/TF]

three German cruisers, the *Scharnhorst, Gneisenau,* and *Prinz Eugen,* have managed to leave Brest, where they were trapped for a year, and returned to Heligoland, the German naval base, under the very noses of the English. Of the United States we know little. Radio Boston (which one can hear admirably well) is sticking to generalities for the present. One does not any longer get a good feel for reactions of the American press. One only knows that General MacArthur is holding on in the Philippines and that what is left of the American fleet made a successful attack on a Japanese squadron in the Marshall Islands. Surely the lesson the United States will draw from events is that they must carry on to the end. They have definitively emerged from splendid isolation and would lose face with South America and with themselves if they did not make the gigantic effort required. But how can one persuade people here who do not know anything about America and who regard with dread the now inevitable prolongation of the war and the increasing difficulty of providing food and heat?

News from Yugoslavia by way of Engineer J. de Trifail. The Croats, who in the beginning made a distinction between the Italians and the Germans, today hate them both. On the other hand, the Bulgarians in Yugoslavia – now occupying certain regions in place of the Germans who were sent to reinforce troops in Russia – are looked upon "fraternally." The Pan-Slavic idea is advancing rapidly, spurred on by Russian victories. All the Serbs have weapons, and Mikhailovich exercises great authority. In retaliation the Germans are machine-gunning and burning down entire villages. Their troops temporarily on standby in Romania and Bulgaria will probably be withdrawn in greater and greater numbers to face the Russians.

The Italians are sick of the war. Apparently it is considered bad taste to bring up the subject in polite Italian society. Besides, they know that in no case will they remain in Croatia. If the Germans win, Trieste will become German. If they lose, the Yugoslavs will drive the Italians out of Istria and Dalmatia.

In the rags devoted to Germany we are constantly reminded that this war is a "revolution," and Déat berates France for not realizing it. Of course, it is a revolution – but a purely technical one. The art of war has been transformed, and the revolutionary is the German High Command. Apart from that, this ideologically inspired war is nothing but a great *reaction.* A revolution must have an idea or an emotion. Here the idea is simple: German supremacy. What is revolutionary about that? What does it contribute to the world of hope and ideals? Persecution and violence. The European union? It has become more impossible than ever. Such things are founded on a basis of collective feeling. Yet the only feeling common to Europe today is hatred.

Is it the purpose, then, of this great military effort to arrive at an economic union? What good would it do, since economic progress, the forging of relations in spite of appearances, was necessarily brought about by economic methods and the inevitable and continuous growth of trade? If there were a revolution, it would be only a social revolution – an attempt to put an end to certain social privileges for the benefit of the masses. But who will believe that the enrichment of the "masses" can come about as the result of general impoverishment? What remains, then, of the "revolutionary" idea? Military government for the benefit of some leaders. The economic and technical revolution of the nineteenth century, one of the greatest ever known, took place thanks to peace and in peace.

SUNDAY, 15 FEBRUARY 1942 Germaine visited old Mme Bloch, whose son, a hospital surgeon, drank potassium cyanide, long since prepared, when the Germans came to arrest him in November during the great roundup of Jews. He was Protestant, having been baptized nearly thirty years ago. The funeral service took place at the Church of the Holy Spirit. He had even walked out of the apartment with his two Huns, then toppled over at the bottom of the stairs. A colleague who lived in the house and had gone down to see the concierge snatched him away from the policemen and had him taken to a hospital. His elderly mother (a Protestant herself) said he had done well. His disgust with the French government's abandonment of suffering Jews and his horror at the way Nazism was being accepted and spread had made life seem unbearable. He had warned his mother that he would not fall into "their" hands alive. Mme Bloch's sister was married to General Lévy. Mme Bloch herself had married a member of the military, and her father-in-law was a prosecuting attorney for the Cour des Comptes. It is all these servants of the French State that the present government is treating like pariahs.

Restrictions on gas and electricity are becoming increasingly severe. The Versailles-Paris train service has been cut by half. The official line is to blame the drought, which has cut electric power to a minimum. But everyone knows that in the past coal substituted for hydroelectric power. It is the coal that is gone; we all know where.

After several trips to the prefecture we obtained authorization for the conveyance of 10 steres of wood, which General S. is willing to grant us. The truck driver who is to make the delivery asked us for 2 steres in addition to the price of transport! Which we are gladly doing! In exchange he promises to keep himself available to us if we have need of transport – on the condition, of course, that he can obtain the fuel, which is drip-fed to us.

MONDAY, 16 FEBRUARY 1942 Last night at ten on English radio the speaker announced: *"Ladies and Gentlemen, Mr. Churchill."* We then heard the somber, sad, and deep voice of Churchill. He spoke of his speech broadcast a year ago. He recalled that they were alone then. Now Russia and the United States have joined England. But there is a downside to this immense improvement: Japan has declared war. England could not fight on all fronts at once. Japan's treacherous attack has decimated America's Pacific fleet and opened the way to a flood of Japanese troops in the Sunda Islands. *"Singapore has fallen."* (The cease-fire occurred at ten, just minutes before he spoke.) And now England, in this the greatest crisis in its history, must once more show its tenacity and spirit. He is calling above all for national unity. Whoever might try to weaken it today, "it were better for him that a millstone were hanged about his neck and he were cast into the sea."[11] Courage of a great man who wanted to tell the country himself of a disaster that, if not rectified, will put an end to English prestige in Asia and to its role in the Far East.

A few days ago Chiang Kai-Shek, invited to Delhi, saw Gandhi and Pandit Nehru. Evidently to persuade them not to abandon England at this time. The defeatists here are already seeing the collapse of the British Empire and the revolt of India. It is a little early. It is now up to the United States to "show what they are made of."

WEDNESDAY, 18 FEBRUARY 1942 American radio recounts that Japanese officers, rather than be taken prisoner, are committing suicide. It has never been said that any French officer committed suicide during the German invasion or after the armistice.

Death of Edgar Bonnet.[12] His son took me into the mortuary chamber. Beautiful calm face, rejuvenated – a strange thing, making him seem forty years younger!

SUNDAY, 22 FEBRUARY 1942 The Riom trial began on Thursday. It is a judicial travesty – an unpardonable political offense. At the bottom of all this once again one finds Laval. In the panic of June 1940, he saw the means to get rid of one of his political adversaries. As Blum said, what they are actually doing is putting the republic on trial. A trial managed by people who would never have amounted to anything without the republic on behalf of a reactionary party that is now loathed by the vast majority of French people.

---

11. Luke 17:2. [TF]

12. Edgar Bonnet, former inspector of public finances, was the father of Georges-Edgar Bonnet, managing director of the Suez Company.

Gamelin has declared he will say nothing. This great chatterbox has become the "great mute." Calculation? Condition of a deal?

Relentless freezing cold. Today–8°. One shudders to think about those who have been imprisoned. We now know that Parodi is in Fresnes under conditions of absolute secrecy.

I am rereading Siegfried's history of Panama.[13] The treason of the reactionary party is ever present; it is revenge for the defeat of Boulangism. Little do they care about defaming a great Frenchman – or a great French work – provided one can get at the republic and Parliament through a few corrupt members. Who will finally write the history of this party, which pursued its vengeance and its resentments via 16 May, then via Boulangism, Panama, and the Dreyfus affair, yet was always beaten? Its greatest defeat came with the victory of 1918, which it swore to avenge. Finally, firing up partisan aggression, it succeeded in breaking France apart with the Stavisky scandal and 6 February, triumphing at last thanks to the defeat. How damning for these men who, as the Comtesse de Boigne has said, are no longer interested in a France where they have lost their privileges, and who refuse to understand the future in any form at all.

At R. B.'s yesterday I had lunch with some people. Collaborators. R. B. believes or pretends to believe that "Eurafrica" is the beginning of a new era when companies will be rationally divided up among the principal countries without any loss of strength and that only the Germans can achieve this masterpiece. I asked if he really believes that a war like this was undertaken for the sake of a little free trade. And what would the new Europe consist of? Is England included? Russia? The best part is that R. B., as far as I know, made his fortune thanks to monopolies in Indochina. These sudden conversions to free trade on the part of French colonials are rather disturbing. But can one be astonished by anything today?

WEDNESDAY, 25 FEBRUARY 1942 At Maxime Leroy's for lunch, Ledoux[14] repeated to me what J. said upon returning from Lisbon the other day: that everyone in Spain is expecting the prince of Asturias to return. Ledoux saw the prince. Franco, having been asked for his consent, said: "Yes, but first I must judge the three hundred thousand who are still in prison." I fear, under these conditions, that the restoration will be somewhat delayed.

---

13. André Siegfried, *Suez, Panama et les grandes routes du trafic mondial* (Paris: Colin, 1941).

14. Frédéric Ledoux: businessman and trustee of the mining company Société Pennaroya and of the Casa de Velasquez in Madrid.

The three accused Museum of Man[15] members have been condemned to death. It seems that the president of the German military court congratulated them on their patriotism. Thereupon, it is said, he shook the hand of the first of the accused, Vildé, son-in-law of Ferdinand Lot. One hopes for a reprieve.

The filth and desolation in Paris are unbelievable. On the streets, apart from military vehicles and a few civilian ones, all the trucks that have not been repaired or repainted over the past three years have become foul rattle-traps. In the shop windows, practically nothing. In the food stores, excluding some bakeries that never run out, empty boxes have replaced the produce that was once on display. Some stores still have lovely fruit at incredible prices. Some tarts and cookies made with buckwheat flour and covered with a sort of chestnut concoction. On the train between Paris and Versailles, men and women have suitcases or bags to transport the rare bits of food they have discovered and are carrying to their families. Shoes almost all have wooden soles now. Leather is a luxury. Children with emaciated faces. Old people, thin and bony. Some women loaded down with packages have faces etched by sadness. Lines in the snow in front of food shops. People have an astonishing patience.

Social, political, and national hatreds are piling up, one on top of the other. But all in silence.

The Japanese have just demonstrated once again the naïveté of the English-style blockade. The English have specialized in waging war without soldiers. Financial, commercial, and industrial means are sufficient for them. They rely on other peoples to furnish them with arms and on their own navy to deprive the adversary of primary goods necessary for war production. But the enemy *with its armies* is frustrating this excessively naïve strategy. Already the Germans, by seizing Romania and Norway, as well as northern and eastern France, have guaranteed their supplies of oil, iron, and coal. A serious defeat for the blockade. And here the Japanese are seizing the oil of Borneo, the tin of Malacca, and the rubber of the Dutch Sunda Islands. Now who is thus deprived of rubber and tin? The United States, lacking these two essential products, had them brought from Malaysia. The blockade has backfired on them and on the English, thus demonstrating that a well-conducted military operation *breaks through the blockade* and that war – even "economic warfare" – is waged with armies. If the Germans now manage to seize oil wells in the Caucasus, the demonstration will be complete. As for

15. The Musée de l'Homme [Museum of Man] group was the first Resistance network set up in France in response to de Gaulle's 18 June 1940 radio appeal. [TF]

the food blockade, it is a joke, because a man can tighten his belt indefinitely and because there will always be enough to feed the soldiers – and feed them well – the sine qua non in time of war.

FRIDAY, 27 FEBRUARY 1942 The English are clearly shaken by their repeated defeats, as this week's debate in the House of Commons attests. The reassuring speeches on the radio are an attempt to calm the public. It appears that above all the high command is being blamed – both the army's and the navy's. For the first time this people is wondering if perhaps, after all, it is *not* the salt of the earth. The danger is seeing the Germanophiles reappear. But the Americans are there to keep them from surrendering. The fact remains that for twenty years a great empire was able to believe it would endure without doing what was necessary to defend itself.

Everyone is discussing the "spring offensive." The Germans have announced total victory over Russia. The Russians have announced that they will free their land. Here some people think the offensive will be against England and that the offensive against Russia is just a ploy. Others already envision the German armies joining up with the Japanese in India. Meanwhile, the Russians are continuing to deal heavy blows south of Leningrad.

The French government has forbidden the Suez Company all communication with Egypt. We are an "Egyptian" company, and Vichy has not forgiven the Egyptian government for the discourteous manner in which it broke off diplomatic relations last January. Thus they will bully the Suez, an essentially French company with French capital. Negotiations to lower the charges for occupation costs were on the point of coming to an end over the last few days. It was the Führer himself who brought them to a close by refusing any reduction. Swiss newspapers say it is not just Brauchitsch but thirty other generals who have apparently been forced out. In a communiqué to his party on the anniversary of its founding, the Führer has declared he will exterminate the Jews. This world war, is it not really just a war against the Jews?

Young Spitzer has news of her father at last. She has the right to send him clothes but not food. He is in the same room as Pierre Masse, the lawyer, and René Blum, brother of the minister. Forbidden to write him.

Twelve

War Hits Close to Home

4 MARCH–15 JULY 1942

The war hit close to home for the Rist family in 1942, with area bombardments and unnerving sirens at night, Charles Rist anonymously denounced, and increasing danger to Françoise and her daughters. Whether through fear of becoming part of an official file or from pride as a converted Protestant, Françoise had not registered as a Jew (see 20 December 1941) and refused to wear the yellow star when doing so was made mandatory in June 1942.

WEDNESDAY, 4 MARCH 1942 Last night violent aerial bombardment announced by sirens. It lasted from 9:30 to 11:30 in the evening. It seemed to be happening very near here. We learned this morning that it was at the Renault factory in Billancourt (we heard this on English radio!).

The condemned Museum of Man resisters were shot three days ago. Among them Vildé of the National Library, son-in-law of Ferdinand Lot. They say they had distributed leaflets. The *Kommandantur* has announced that it shot twenty hostages for the murder of a German guard who is being buried today. If within a week the guilty are not identified, another twenty hostages will be shot. Death sentences are handed down daily and not just for known hostages. All those with family members in prison are fearful.

Visit from Jean yesterday. Very colorful stories about informing methods and Nazi propagandizing in the factories by agents of Marion and Pucheu. The lowest kind of riffraff signed up as propagandists. Creation within the "legion" of so-called order units, more realistically, "assault" units, armed to maintain domestic order. They are thus preparing civil war in the free zone while we here are in the clutches of the enemy.

René Auboin, with whom I had lunch, tells me that Laval went to see Herriot to suggest they work together to reestablish a "parliamentary" regime – the absence of Parliament seeming dangerous for the country to this self-styled "republican." It seems Herriot replied that he was not interested. "You," he said to Laval, "have based your policies on Italy; I have chosen Russia and the United States."

SUNDAY, 8 MARCH 1942 Everyone is talking about the bombardment. The details are becoming known little by little, amid massive exaggerations and inaccuracies. The certain fact is that the Renault factory was 90 percent destroyed and will be out of service for several months. The tank works was the worst hit. The English made a dive-bombing run. The German inspectors prevented the remaining personnel (luckily very few) from leaving and decreed that work would continue. The antiaircraft batteries barely functioned. There is no talk of any English planes being downed. There were no sirens in Paris, to everyone's disgust. The English had dropped leaflets during the preceding days to announce their coming. The dead (from three to five hundred) are civilians. Neighboring apartment buildings, which suffered the greatest damage and where the most victims were found, should have been evacuated plenty of time in advance.

The indignation of the Germans' French-language newspapers is touching. Their concern for the victims and that displayed by Vichy are moving. Jean Luchaire demands that we go to war with England immediately – an excellent way, no doubt, to avoid new factory bombings in the region of Paris! The government has decreed that yesterday, Saturday, would be a day of national mourning: banks, schools, etc., closed. Regarding the Germans' shooting of twenty hostages a week ago for one sentry killed, or their threat to shoot twenty more this week if the authors of the attack are not identified, Vichy and the newspapers are silent.

This sort of charade is repugnant but has become so commonplace that it almost makes one laugh in disgust. In contrast, among the public there has been not a word of criticism of the English raid. Silence on the trains. Silence in the boardrooms. One speaks about the raid as one speaks, in times of real war, of an operation with a high cost. One counts the dead, but one knows they are an inevitable part of any military action.

The Claudes had a bomb in their yard. Impossible to visit them because of complications and the scarcity of trains.

These last few days I have been reading Commandant Rollin's book on the Russian Revolution, lent me by Admiral Durand-Viel. A prophetic work. It shows the role that reading Clausewitz played in the formation of Lenin and in Russian military doctrine. The foundations of industrial and military organization, the results of which we see today, were put in place at the beginning of the Russian revolution. The thought of revenge for Prussia after

Jena ever present in the minds of the army heads. The idea of the orthodox "Russian mission" simply replaced by that of revolutionary Russia. Russian pacifism during the twenty postwar years was indispensable for giving time for industry and the army time to prepare. When Rollin's book appeared, no one could deduce its true consequences. Or, rather, people always thought that Russian war would be waged against the capitalist west. People did not recognize the power it could bring to bear against Germany, or else they did not wish to make use of the knowledge for fear of Bolshevist "contagion." As always, social or religious ideology complicates relations between states. "The victors are pacifists," Clausewitz was already saying. Therein lies the explanation of the Anglo-French inadequacies and blind spots of the postwar period. It must be added: "In times of war as in times of peace, the military are blind. They are not to be trusted."

SUNDAY, 15 MARCH 1942   Jean left without having been able to obtain any coal for his factory, which operates two weeks out of four. He was almost killed by two "very correct" drunken German soldiers who, revolvers in hand, forced him – because he was looking at them – to go down into a subway station with them (at 11:00 at night). Luckily, he got away and was able to jump on a train just as it was pulling out.

On Wednesday morning a police inspector paid me a visit. He was sent by the Office for Jewish Affairs to ask if I were Jewish! *"Ist Charles Rist Jude?"* The Germans had him ask this.

It was very probably a Frenchman – there are some who do not like me – who had alerted them, no doubt to please me. The police officer did not seem very proud of his mission. Three years ago my Gess ancestry would have been used by the same people to mark me as a German and not "national" enough. Today it serves to protect me, because, regardless, a Lutheran *Generalsuper-intendant* can hardly pass as Jewish. So goes the world.

Saw Mettetal on Friday to try to do something about my granddaughters' situation. We agreed to see Boegner in the free zone at the end of the month.

Last night Mlle Spitzer phoned to tell me her father has left Compiègne. Germaine Lubin, the opera singer, intervened, as did Stülpnagel[1] himself. It was high time. People are dying of hunger there.

A radio broadcast addressed by Australian prime minister Curtin to the United States declared Australia ready to fight to the last man. Curtin appealed to America to defend the Pacific and Australia, the last bastion against

---

1. Karl-Heinrich von Stülpnagel: commander of the German occupation forces in France.

the Japanese tidal wave before it sweeps over South America. Everyone is dumbfounded by the appalling impotence of the United States. This nation that was complacently carrying its "big stick" and speaking as if the Pacific belonged to it has not one ship, not one plane to defend the ocean and block the advance of the Japanese. This three-month invasion of all the Sunda Islands and Burma, threatening India, resembles the German invasion of Holland, Belgium, and France. One looks on but sees nothing that opposes it. What do the Americans think today? I mean, the ones who do think. To move the masses, they need only wave the flag of racial warfare. And that is what is going to give this conflict its true character, making it inexorable and interminable. The United States seems like Gulliver tied down by pygmies. But to build an army and rebuild a navy, how much time will they need? Today with twenty years' hindsight, how mad appears the Anglo-Saxon policy, with its idea of a peace-loving civilization irresistibly imposing itself yet undefended by armies, relying only on a navy to protect its trade routes. And yet what a paradox: in order for peace to be maintained one must be the mightiest, and there is no example of a people who, having become the mightiest, did not seek to disrupt the peace.

Meanwhile, we are sinking in the mire. In vain do we look for seeds to grow some potatoes and vegetables in the garden. Without them, how will we eat next winter? Well, there are no seeds, or else they are kept hidden.

MONDAY, 16 MARCH 1942 The bombardment of Boulogne, in the popular view, has now taken on its definitive legendary form: the bombs dropped on the Renault factory were English; the others, those that destroyed houses and killed civilians, *were German.* There you have the admirable reaction of national feeling in the face of efforts after the bombardment to stir up anger against the English. What a lesson!

WEDNESDAY, 18 MARCH 1942 Went to see Moreau yesterday. He tells me that the Comte de Paris, when he came incognito to the capital, was provided lodging by the House of Worms. The role of this company will decidedly require careful study by future historians. It was tied to Doriot, to the Comte de Paris, etc. This is the company that now supplies France with Pucheu, Barnaud, etc., just as it once supplied her with coal.

Barnaud? With what aims and under what inspiration? More and more, he seems somber and narrow-minded, with repressed ambitions, always silent, perfectly enigmatic. No one knows his intentions or his thinking.[2]

2. Jacques Barnaud was at the time chief delegate for Franco-German relations. Charles Rist had known him well as an efficient negotiator at the finance ministry when the franc was being stabilized in 1926.

SUNDAY, 22 MARCH 1942 Lunch on Friday with Falkenhausen and Windelband, a German academic. A rather meaningless conversation. I avoided everything that might touch on the current situation. We limited ourselves to literature and to occasional remarks about *earlier* politics. Windelband told me he has been dismissed from the University of Berlin for not being sufficiently "partisan." He has been taken on here at Foreign Affairs; now charged with examining the documents of the Quai d'Orsay, he says great pressure was exerted by the French military to occupy the Ruhr. The operation in the Ruhr will certainly have been one of the catastrophes of our postwar policy.[3] After lunch I asked Falkenhausen if he could tell me what has become of René Parodi. He promised to do so in the next two weeks.

WEDNESDAY, 25 MARCH 1942 The Riom trial[4] is becoming embarrassing for the marshal. The revelation that the non-continuation of the Maginot Line was advised by the Supreme War Council in a letter signed by the marshal himself confirms what we already knew about the outdated doctrines of that council and of the marshal's role in the defeat. This is the man who "hates lies." The marshal was Doumergue's minister of war at a time when Germany had just reestablished obligatory military service. What did he do in response? Nothing. Thus there is a move on to stop the trial. No mention has been made of the displeasure evident in Hitler's last speech, in which he expressed astonishment that responsibility for the defeat rather than for the war was in question. The press in the occupied regions is becoming more and more offensive toward Vichy. Joseph Barthélemy is in the process of seeking legal arguments that would permit a postponement of the trial.

Received a visit yesterday from Ferdinand Lot, an eminent historian and member of the Académie des Inscriptions et Belles-Lettres.[5] His son-in-law, of Russian origin but a naturalized Frenchman, was shot along with six others four weeks ago for having participated over a year ago in editing a clandestine newspaper, *Libération*. He came to thank me for the note of condolences and admiration I had sent him. He told me about the judgment and spoke of the magnificent attitude of the condemned man. He read me the letter written two hours before the end. Simplicity, courage, heroism. He

---

3. French and Belgian forces occupied the Ruhr in 1923 and 1924 as a result of the German failure to pay reparations after World War I, triggering outrage in Germany. [TF]

4. The Riom trial was authorized by the Vichy regime with the intent to prove that leaders of the Popular Front government, elected in 1936, were responsible for France's defeat in 1940, and that France, not Germany, was responsible for the war. [TF]

5. The Académie des Inscriptions et Belles-Lettres: a learned society devoted to the humanities; one of the five academies of the French Institute. [TF]

showed me his son-in-law's photograph. An expression of rare nobility and will. I was unable to contain my emotion before this elderly gentleman as he described the young man's imprisonment and death with the objectivity of a historian and the simplicity of a great soul.

The appeal, signed by all the German judges, was rejected by Berlin without explanation. His condemnation – for an act committed in 1940 – was based on a decree of 1941. The minister of Finland, asked to intervene, was particularly ignoble. The Russian origins of the condemned man served as a pretext for his refusal to intervene, even though two years ago the young man had asked to fight with the Finnish troops against Russia.

Benoist-Méchin, whose mother is linked to the Lot family, did intervene, but to no avail.[6]

SATURDAY, 4 APRIL 1942 A period of little movement in which we are all waiting and watching. The English have resumed their bombardment of the factories in the region of Paris, and we have had alerts these last three nights. The Matford factories in Poissy really took a bad hit. They manufacture trucks. The radio talks a lot about the English and American fighting spirit. But when will that translate into results?

5 APRIL 1942, EASTER SUNDAY Our granddaughters are with us; they make a show of not being scared by the bombings, but they hate the sound of the planes.

This week I had some wood cut on the Glatigny land, bought to keep us warm. Our yard is filling up with wood, which will dry until autumn. Will they not come to requisition it between now and then? Everyone around here is cutting down their trees. We all fear for next winter. I am having to deal with woodcutters and cart drivers. Knowing they have the upper hand, they lay down conditions, allow no argument, and treat you like an incompetent man of leisure. At the least remark they threaten to drop you! Yesterday the local policeman came along during the delivery. He announced that I must pay 5 francs per cubic meter as the fee for transporting wood in Versailles. The tax is due even for trees cut down in one's own yard!

MONDAY, 6 APRIL 1942 Violent bombardment around four this morning. The most annoying part is the sirens that announce the beginning and end of the alert. Their noise wakes everyone up, whereas one could very well go back to sleep when the bombs are far enough off. According to the

---

6. Martin Blumenson's book *Le Réseau du musée de l'Homme* [The Museum of Man Group] (Paris: Éditions du Seuil, 1979), recounts the whole story in moving detail.

radio, the factories targeted were Gnôme and Rhône in Gennevilliers, which manufacture spare parts for airplanes.

Two political negotiations are the focus of attention now. Though not on the same scale, they are both important for the fate of France: the English negotiation of Stafford Cripps with India, and that of Laval with Pétain. The first depends upon the meeting up of the Japanese and German armies in Iran and, afterward, the fate of Egypt and to a certain extent Russia. The Japanese have bombed Colombo. Their advance in the Indian Ocean would be a disaster for American transports. Impossible to judge the result, but the English, the only armed presence in the Indian theater, will always be able to lead the defense.

As for the second, one hardly knows anything – except for the conversations and indiscretions of sidewalk radio, as Frerichs puts it. According to Frerichs, with whom I had lunch on Friday (and who was recently imprisoned by the Germans for having refused, as president of the University of Brussels, to appoint one of the traitors of the preceding war to a professorship), the marshal supposedly told Laval: "I will gladly take you back into my cabinet if you get me something from the Germans, such as the release of prisoners." This was calling his bluff, and negotiations were broken off. On the other hand, according to the radio it was a question of taking on Monzie as president of the Council, with Laval at Foreign Affairs. That Monzie would reappear amid the rot of the collaborators could have been expected. Whether he will succeed is another matter. The marshal knows very well that among all these sharks he will be destroyed. That is in fact one of the only things he knows.

In the astonishingly perspicacious work on the Russian Revolution written by Henri Rollin in 1930, I have come across the following lines – most apt for our current situation, with a few changes in wording:

> In countries shaken by revolutionary fever, the question must always be asked, if defense of the regime must trump that of the country, if, in fact, respect for principle must not trump everything. As has been said: in times of revolution the difficult thing is not to do one's duty, but to know what that duty is. For some, it is to go to Koblenz (like today's collaborators), placing the regime at the top of the hierarchy of ideals; for others, it is to run the risk of undermining the country by according primacy to new principles. But what makes revolutionaries strong is the great number of people who, faced with a foreign threat, repeat the words of Blake, the great admiral from the time of Cromwell: "Our unalterable duty is to fight for our country, without bothering about who heads the government. I would have preferred the contrary of what has occurred, but in our profession we have only two virtues: obedience and victory." (1: 86)

WEDNESDAY, 15 APRIL 1942 Yesterday we heard on the radio that Laval had returned to Vichy, that he would figure as "head of government" *with* Darlan, and that the cabinet would be reshuffled. At the same time, it was announced that the Riom trial has been suspended and will no doubt be transferred to another jurisdiction, that Vichy protested to the American government against the nomination of a United States consul in Gaullist territory – that is, in Equatorial Africa – and that in response Washington said it is determined to support all those fighting against the powers of aggression.

The return of Laval is the sign that Marshal Pétain has given in to German threats. What threats? Impossible to know. The word making the rounds is that France would be carved up, dismembered, etc. But clearly these rumors are spread by the collaborators. Is it not they themselves, at least as much as the Germans, who have pressed for this solution? This is without a doubt an attempt to get France involved before the results of the spring campaign are known. What campaign? Will it take place in Russia or in the Near East, as some would have it? No one can guess. This is also about cutting France off from the United States. Later they may demand our participation alongside Germany.

That is all madness. I see "reasonable" people who are convinced that the war will be over in August, with a German victory. The great disappointment caused by American setbacks has completely discouraged them. They already see India conquered by the Japanese and the latter blocking American supply routes through the Persian Gulf and the Red Sea. I am completely certain that somewhere the Anglo-Saxons are readying a response – that in any case they will continue to fight without stopping until they have regained the high ground. Yet the only point on which reason sustains my conviction is the strong fight the Russians are putting up. As for the strength of Anglo-Saxon resistance and attack, we are reduced to guessing games. Regarding German means of attack, we know only one thing: that they are powerful. As I cannot demonstrate or provide reasons, I hold my tongue, hoping that the near, or at least rather near, future will avenge those who have "faith."

The *Idée générale de l'histoire de France* by Edme Champion (dating from 1886 and reissued in 1906),[7] which I have come upon by chance in my library, demonstrates to a tee the idiocy of the reactionary policy they are trying to impose upon us today. It goes against all of French history. It repudiates the profound tendencies of our people. The "nobility" have too often

---

7. This book by Edme Champion was issued first in 1882 as *Philosophie de l'Histoire de France*, then in 1907 as *Vue générale de l'histoire de France*. [TF]

acted *against* France. They are still doing this, even after having absorbed part of the bourgeoisie. "Common people" have always *felt* French. Champion is right when he says that revolutionary ideas, with their "optimism," truly constitute a new "religion." This is also what Bourde says.[8] It is true. When one has witnessed the Dreyfus affair, and then the last ten years, one is obliged to recognize that such civil hatreds can only arise from opposing *religious* feelings. The abject embracing of the victor's knees today is the logical conclusion of the hatred of 1789, which bursts forth in everything the "collaborators" write. The following passage quoting the Comte de Ségur is particularly apt:

> Meanwhile, let us contemplate the "shocking surprise" of the Comte de Ségur upon his return to France at the end of 1789 after an absence of five years: "At a distance of 800 leagues from my country, I could not imagine the extraordinary changes that our laws, our characters, our minds, our manners had undergone. . . . Along my route everything that met my eyes became an unforeseen spectacle: the bourgeois, the peasants, even the women showed me in their bearing, in their gestures, in all their features, something sharp, proud, animated that I had never seen before. . . . If I questioned individuals of the lower classes, they replied with a proud look. When I departed from France, I had left behind a people bent under the yoke, and now I found they were standing tall!" The people of France standing tall! If we had nothing but that to oppose the critics of the Revolution, would it not be enough? (Champion 301)

We have come to such a point of tension, of expectation, and anxiety in regard to the near future that the mind refuses to think about what will be required for this country to recover when the storm has passed. For all hangs upon the military outcome. Depending upon whether it goes in our favor or not, the path to follow will be completely different. In the case of defeat, we will not be the ones deciding our future. The problem will require no further effort – at least for the men of my generation. Let us first know if we are beaten. But what is not in question is that even if we come out on the winning side there will be an authoritative government relying on the masses and trying to please them. Reactionary feudalism will be swept away. Is that not in any case the meaning of the National Socialist revolution? And is that not precisely what the masters (master-slaves!) of the hour do not understand? Will we then have a French version of National Socialism?

---

8. Paul Bourde: author of *Essai sur la Révolution et la religion* [Essay on Revolution and Religion] (Paris: Hartmann, 1939).

FRIDAY, 17 APRIL 1942 The day before yesterday at 7:00 in the evening, a member of the public prosecutor's staff asked to see us. He had news of René Parodi. For nine weeks we had heard nothing. We wasted no time getting there. He looked deeply moved. He told us Parodi had committed suicide in his prison. It took only nine weeks to make of this generous, tender, patriotic, idealistic man a corpse.

We found it hard to believe he had killed himself. That is the German story accepted by the public prosecutor's office. Yesterday I saw his wife and his father; it is clear from what they know that it was *not* suicide. But how was his death brought about? He had seen the German chaplain four days earlier and complained about weakness caused by the lack of food, but he was thinking clearly. Afterward there was an interrogation. And it was after this that he was found – say the Germans – hanging from a bar of his cell by his long underwear. The chaplain himself is certain that it was not a case of suicide. But what happened? Did they drug him, as we are told is the custom during interrogations? Did his weakened body not tolerate the drug, or were his emotions, the moral resistance required to endure the interrogation, too strong? We will never know. We will only know that in nine weeks of moral torture they destroyed him.[9] The ignominy overwhelms one. Hatred for this regime of brutes, as well as the need for revenge, is building. It seems certain he was denounced by the maid of one of his friends, at whose house he sometimes had lunch and with whom he talked freely. The maid was also arrested. He was accused of espionage. Which is absurd.

On the radio there is much talk about the return of Pierre Laval to power. The Boston announcer cites the interview given by Pétain to an American journalist in *January 1941* – two months after Laval's dismissal. The marshal was fierce in his disparagement of the heir apparent. He declared he was sold to the Germans, and he added, in these precise terms: "Even physically, he disgusts me." And now he takes him back! And this is a trio, Pétain-Laval-Darlan (who hate one another), a trio composed of a weak man and two ambitious, unscrupulous cynics to whom the fate of France is entrusted. The United States has ordered its consuls in the free zone to evacuate all Americans. The two supply ships due to depart for North Africa have been held back in New York. Do they think war is about to break out? According to their radio, the Germans want France to provide military support in the case of an English landing in France. We would thus be fighting with

---

9. According to the book *Combat, histoire d'un mouvement de résistance* [Combat: History of a Resistance Movement] (Paris: PUF, 1957) by Marie Granet and Henri Michel, it was murder.

Germany *against* the Allies, and the former would have fresh troops available to fight Russia. Pétain's complete capitulation has not gone unnoticed by the Americans. The perfectly successful English landing of several hours' duration a couple of weeks ago at Saint-Nazaire has no doubt made the Germans uneasy. But to go as far as entrusting the defense of German ports in France to the French, that seems pure fantasy. The risks for Germany would be too great, for the new French army might capitulate to the English, and German leaders like to be certain of things.

Later people will say of those in the Vichy regime: some acted shamefully, others treacherously, and all of them, abjectly.

It is curious that in times of great distress one always seeks consolation in the past. It can be found by reading the introduction to Edme Champion's book. For each century of our history he cites observers who assert that France has never stooped so low. One must also reread the chapter by Montaigne in which he expresses the same idea.[10] Or contemplate the fact that the history of all countries is nothing but a long comedy of errors and horrors, of aggressions and lawlessness, of the crushing of the peace-loving by the impassioned and the unscrupulous, and that in the end all comes back around again. Between the division of Europe two thousand years ago and that of today there is not much difference. One need only compare maps from then and from today. Gaul was always Gaul in spite of Julius Caesar, and it has become increasingly that again. Neither India nor China has borders that differ greatly from those they had in the past. But these commotions leave corpses in their wake, and some of the noblest. After all, what counts if not individuals, their dreams, their inventions, their creative genius? Who can say how many noble souls have perished during this war who might have furnished new Mozarts or Newtons or Poussins?

MONDAY, 20 APRIL 1942   This morning we buried poor René Parodi. Service in Notre-Dame-des-Champs, then at the Père-Lachaise cemetery. His mother was not there, having been arrested at the Demarcation Line. One more cruelty. Beautiful wreaths and flowers on the martyr's coffin. When we are free to speak, we must honor the memory of this great spirit, so generous and forthright, who almost joyfully sacrificed his life.

The inanity of Laval's chosen collaborators is stupefying. Joseph Barthélemy is of course loyal to his position, which amounts to creating more special courts. For Finances they could find no one but a certain Cathala. Of

---

10. See Montaigne, "Of Vanity," in *Essays*, vol. 17, chap. 9, trans. Charles Cotton, ed. William C. Hazilitt. [JNJ/TF]

course the shady Guérard is back, along with the even shadier Barnaud. But Laval must have come up against a not inconsiderable number of refusals to have settled for so many second-rate people. Abel Bonnard is at the national education ministry. If this odious, effeminate fanatic imagines his task will be easy, he is deluded.

MONDAY, 27 APRIL 1942 According to conversations coming from the right and from the left, it seems increasingly plausible that Laval himself took the initiative to return to power. The Germans intervened only *after-ward* in order to support him. When negotiations were first cut off, Laval had the German government put pressure on Pétain. To what extent and in what form? The stories vary. Some say they threatened Italian incursion into Savoie and complete closure of the Demarcation Line. Darlan suppos-edly announced that the United States was threatening to break off relations if Laval came back, and the Germans would have taken offense at this. It makes little difference. It is done. But in setting up the cabinet, Laval clearly ran into trouble and numerous refusals. His idea would have been to form a cabinet "from the right to the left." An absurd idea, moreover, given the country's complete indifference to factions. He was unable to have Herriot or Paul Faure or Gignoux, etc., and is left with his "specialists," who represent nothing.

Radio programs are announcing the escape of General Giraud, who had not wanted to subscribe to any of the German conditions for his liberation. An escape that may have serious consequences. Will he join the Free French Forces?

Seven members of the French embassy in Washington have resigned because of Laval's coming to power. The military attaché is joining the Gaullists.

On Friday evening I attended the lecture given by Falkenhausen's fa-ther at the "German Institute" regarding the French Huguenot colony in Brandenburg. He concluded by saying that the best way to win the loyalty of "minorities" was to treat them as well as Prussia had treated the French Huguenots. A rather curious contrast with the policy his government is fol-lowing elsewhere. An intended criticism or an unthinking lapse.

Big speech by Hitler in the Reichstag. He is demanding full judicial power! Might there be wavering inside Germany?

WEDNESDAY, 6 MAY 1942 They tell me that the tombs of Englishmen buried in the Gonnards cemetery are covered with flowers every day. The paratroopers who get injured when they fall and are arrested by the Germans become the object of sympathetic gestures by the populace, who present them with cigarettes, flowers, cookies, etc.

Yesterday it was announced that the English have occupied Diego Suarez.[11] There will be shock waves in Vichy. What will come of this? War with England? Vichy keeps saying it does not want trouble with the United States. It is always the same old head-in-the-sand policy. They live with the illusion that the United States is not behind England. Or is it the Germans who are using us to keep open a channel of communication with the United States?

MONDAY, 11 MAY 1942 A big speech by Churchill on the radio the night before last. A completely different tone from his last one. Without being optimistic, much less triumphant, he is considerably more confident. He declared that the Allied aviation is now superior to Germany's. He brought up the passage in Hitler's latest speech in which the latter spoke of spending a second winter in Russia. He threatened that if the Germans use gas in Russia, England will use it on German cities. He ended by saying: "Cheer up, but good cheer or bad, we shall do our duty."[12] He announced that France, including Alsace and Lorraine, would be restored. He called Mussolini "the miscalculator."

Nevertheless, we live in a state of strong tension. For the German attack is being prepared *somewhere*. Where? And what will the first effects be?

The Americans appear to have won a victory against the Japanese fleet in the Coral Sea. The Japanese are proclaiming victory, but so are the Americans, who declare they have prevented a landing in Australia.

Yesterday General Watteau, a judge at the Riom court, came to the Ottoman Bank to ask me to give evidence – or to draft a statement – regarding the part that bad financial policy has played in the catastrophe. I accepted in principle but did not hide my opinion that a military defeat can generally be attributed to the military. He seemed little disposed to acknowledge this truth. He gave me the impression that the Riom court will not reconvene. My statement will thus remain buried among many other papers for the delight of future historians. But in fifty or a hundred years, who will be interested in this story?

11. The Battle of Madagascar (Operation Ironclad) began with the invasion of Diego Suarez (known as Antsiranana after 1975) at the northern tip of Madagascar on 5 May 1942. [TF]

12. In fact, the evening before, 10 May 1942, Churchill declared: "Tonight I give you a message of good cheer. You deserve it, and the facts endorse it. But be it good cheer or be it bad cheer will make no difference to us; we shall drive on to the end, and do our duty, win or die. God helping us, we can do no other." [JNJ/TF]

Laurent-Atthalin told me this morning that the Banque de l'Europe Centrale is going to cooperate with the Germans in Ukraine and asked how I felt about it. I told him that as far as I was concerned, if this collaboration were to occur very soon, I preferred not to be a part of it and that I would leave at once so that my departure did not seem to be motivated by this new policy. Besides, I said, as he knew, my views on the outcome of this war are not the same as his. I did not say what I was thinking, as Laval is a friend of his, and it would have seemed pretentious, but Laval's belief in German victory is enough for me to believe that this victory has already become impossible.

WEDNESDAY, 13 MAY 1942 Yesterday saw Mettetal, along with the pastor. We are hoping to arrive at some solution for the children.

Death of Seignobos. He was my best teacher. His was not a *great* mind, but a mind devoid of all prejudice and always suspicious of stock notions. His concern for objectivity was amazing; he was essentially curious about facts for their own sakes, and the way they linked up independent of any preconceived doctrine; he enjoyed their reality, their reciprocal and surprising repercussions. He was peerless as a teacher of critical thinking, and he did not believe in any work that was not grounded in original documents. Always moving against the tide of current ideas, yet not very constructive and lacking all passion. His devotion to his students was admirable. No other teacher has given so much of his time to each of them on a personal level. Teaching was his sole passion. An old republican, a somewhat naïve Radical-Socialist. Very intelligent.

FRIDAY, 15 MAY 1942 Laroche, former ambassador to Warsaw, tells me that in 1931 Count Zaleski, Poland's minister of foreign affairs, ended his stay in London with a visit to King George V. The latter, after having spoken of many things, said to him: "There is still a matter about which I wish to speak to you, but off the record and on a completely personal, confidential basis. We are quite uneasy about France's current efforts to create an air force, and we want to know against whom it is being prepared." Zaleski naturally recounted all this to Laroche upon his return to Warsaw.[13] A really astonish-

13. Jules Laroche, in his memoirs, reports the episode in the following manner: "Warsaw's government was equally worried about Anglo-French relations. Zaleski (minister of foreign affairs) had made an official visit to London at the end of 1931. The English, depressed by the economic crisis, struck him as being somewhat humiliated by the prosperity that France continued to enjoy. In political circles, France was spoken of unkindly and even with mistrust. Had he not even been confronted with worries over the strength of French aviation? 'But surely you know well which possible enemy it is

ing example of traditional English mistrust and misunderstanding of French intentions and German danger. (It is true that at the time Brüning was in power.) Were there not also some memories of the invasion of the Ruhr, so disastrous for all our subsequent policies?

THURSDAY, 21 MAY 1942 A Suez Company lunch. I was seated between V. and D.[14] The former, on my right, said to me: "Bolshevism is much more to be feared than Hitlerism; it's on the rise in the countryside." The second, on my left, said: "The bourgeoisie are sickening; no matter what happens, they are guided by only one sentiment, fear of communism, and they think only of their 'hard cash.'" I believe these two opinions sum up current French divisions. This morning I was told of something Thomasson said, apparently aimed at me: "Only imbeciles believe in Anglo-Saxon victory." To be remembered for future reference.

We are once again experiencing anxiety. Timoshenko's Russian offensive. Southern German offensive in the south of Ukraine. We will not know the results and consequences for several weeks. Until then, it is futile to speculate.

SUNDAY, 24 MAY 1942 The other day Germaine, standing in the crush of travelers on the Versailles-Paris train, overheard two workers talking. The older said to the younger: "I'm pretty upset; London radio has been so scrambled that the boss lady gets irritated and doesn't want to let me listen anymore. Well, I get mad, shut it off, and don't get anymore news." Germaine looked at him and said in a low voice, glancing at the Jerries filling the car: "Then listen to the 1,500-meter broadcast; the Bourges pylon used for scrambling was blown up; now you can listen again." The worker's face lit up: "Ah! Well, then, many thanks, madame, I'll have a fine evening doing just that." Alas! The long-wave broadcast has been scrambled again for three days. We cannot hear anything anymore except by shortwave or else in English. But all of these good people are clinging to London radio as the only thread of hope. The role played by the *radio de Londres* is significant and truly new – the only common link among the French, who refuse to despair. Squeamish souls cringe when someone mentions London radio. But that is what is keeping popular fervor alive.

---

intended to combat?' he had objected. His interlocutor shook his head and persisted in seeing it as a threat to the security of Great Britain. Was this state of mind not reflected in the attitude of British diplomacy toward questions of disarmament?" *La Pologne de Pilsudski – Souvenirs d'une ambassade 1926–1935* (Paris: Flammarion, 1953), 107.

14. Perhaps Louis de Vogüé and Georges Durand-Viel.

We hardly know anything of events in Germany. And yet one can guess that discontent is growing. Three days ago Goering gave a speech addressed to the workers, only some of which has been published in the papers here – evidently on orders. Judging from the digest broadcast by Boston, one can know only that he spoke of new sacrifices, of the need to strengthen the home front, etc. In short, one understands that the war will be long and that victory is far off.

The Nazi minister of agriculture, Darré, has been replaced, according to an announcement. And countless posters, with growing insistence, are calling upon the French to work in Germany, sign of a labor shortage. News, too, of the execution of a dozen people in Mannheim. All of this indicates greater and greater anxiety. The papers here are full of news about the lack of unity among the Allies, resistance of American popular opinion, etc., etc. – just foolishness when one knows that Americans have unanimously supported the war since the Japanese attack. The whole problem is to know if German anxieties will have practical consequences. Not much can be expected from German public opinion. As everywhere, it reacts with a certain weariness in the face of a drawn-out war. Nothing more. The army alone is in a position to put an end to hostilities if the outcome begins to look uncertain. But it will do nothing before bitter setbacks occur in Russia. It always comes down to this: will the Russian peasant hold out? Salvation depends upon him alone.

The very immensity of the German enterprise, the expression of a gigantic and impossible dream, will be its downfall. The Japanese enterprise, an attempt to create a yellow thalassocracy in the Pacific, is much more rational. It is the "gigantism" that dooms the Germans to failure; by arousing fear and horror around the world, Germany is herself creating the forces that will kill her. This is why waiting and endurance are the only means of survival available to France – a passive policy that upsets the leisure classes more than the workers and peasants, who are more accustomed to a life of hardship and privation.

Since Laval regained power, signs are growing in many circles of a certain impatience to push for more economic collaboration. They feel their fate is more or less tied to that of Laval. They do not wish to have their initial defeatism refuted. They want to hold on to the power they gained only because of the defeat. Therein lies the danger for the next six months and for as long as the outcome of the Russian war is uncertain. The coming months will be the hardest for us to bear, morally speaking. One can hardly breathe surrounded by people who subordinate the survival of their country to maintaining their financial or social advantages, and who for ten years have lived in terror of workers' demands. "Conserve" is the true motto for conservatives of all stripes. They are not capable of envisioning a future in which their social privileges would no longer assure them of an advantage over other citizens who have only their work and their intelligence to carve out a place for themselves in the nation's economy. This impossibility to believe in the future, this terror in the face of struggle and adaptation through effort – these are the true signs of conservatism in the word's deepest sense. "Conservatives of the world, unite": this is the slogan underpinning Hitlerism's power outside Germany. Those who believe in this slogan are weak-minded. Hitlerism is more revolutionary than anything they could imagine. German conservatives realized this long ago. But who among us knows anything about Germany?

New executions of hostages in Paris. The pretext: an attack on a German soldier.

A pregnant woman asked the "Secretariat of the Family" for the woolens officially promised in her case. She was told that there were none, and the person appointed to this post added: "This is no time to be having babies." Work, family, fatherland – the slogan of the new regime!

MONDAY, 1 JUNE 1942 The English have announced an air raid on Cologne by a thousand bombers, accompanied by two hundred fighter planes. The biggest ever. Nothing in the papers here this morning. Meanwhile the battle in Libya is raging. The one in Karkoff has stopped.

Lolli is still at La Bouffource to fatten and fortify the expected baby. All one speaks of now is food supplies, of the eggs and butter being sent in packages from Saint-Germain-de-Coulamer. We anxiously watch over our three fields of potatoes, so too the green beans.

TUESDAY, 2 JUNE 1942 The English have not resumed their air raid, citing "unfavorable atmospheric conditions." But the sky has never been clearer, the wind dropped three days ago, and the moon is shining. Is this another brave sally with no tomorrow?

As of yesterday, Jews must wear a special badge. They say this is the welcoming gift of the new commissioner, the infamous Darquier "de" Pellepoix.

Yesterday I was at Marcel Monod's to see what sort of documents prove my Protestant ancestry[15] – for purposes of the certificate required for the granddaughters.

---

15. Marcel Monod: pastor of the Reformed Church of France in Paris, later Versailles. [TF]

On Saturday Laval apparently convoked the presidents of organization committees to tell them to send workers to Germany. He supposedly said, "The government has assumed its responsibilities, you must assume yours." The only problem is that the workers do not want to go – and some of those who are already there want to return at any cost. Will this man find the means to add social conflicts to everything that is already tearing us apart? Clearly he has promised Germany a contingent of workers. What has been promised him in exchange? Nothing, no doubt.

Our neighbor, the veterinarian, has just been sentenced to death after six months in prison, during which he was not even allowed to see his wife. His assistant, an Alsatian, was sentenced to five years in prison. They say his long months of preventive detention have already completely destroyed him, physically and morally.

WEDNESDAY, 3 JUNE 1942 A massive new air raid by the English, this time on Essen. We still do not know the results. This is a truly new and powerful tactic. It opens up a vast panorama of hope. It seems this is the only form of offensive currently available to the Allies. Landings are probably too dangerous and futile. I see only one place where they could occur successfully: Italy. That would give the Allies greater control over the Mediterranean, end the Libyan affair, and put them in proximity to the Balkans. But this is idle speculation.

Up to now the Libyan battle has been a failure for Rommel. But it is not over. The French troops seem to have played a brilliant role.

The more I think about it, the clearer it seems that once the war is over, all those with fascist or Hitlerian tendencies must be reduced to *impotence*. These are the elements that have systematically demoralized our country in its struggle against the foreigner. These are the ones who saw the foreigners' presence as a way to safeguard their interests. These are the ones who have always confused the safeguarding of their interests with patriotism. For them this word only applies to internal politics. They were proud of being patriots when they fought against the "Popular Front" or the "Republic" in the name of what they called "patriotism." They threw themselves at the feet of the enemy the minute patriotism meant running risks to defend French territory. Words do not have the same meaning for them as for us. For them a bad citizen is not one who betrays his country, who cheats and abuses his neighbor, who lives by con games; rather, it is someone who does not hold sacred the interests of conservatives. No matter if he is loyal, courageous, and intelligent, he will be shamed, vilified, and dragged through the mud

because he committed "sin against the holy coffers." They have long practiced this method of polemicizing, vilifying, sullying, and slandering all
those who do not share their narrow-minded, biased, shabby little views. It
was practiced under the Restoration and the Second Empire, just as it was
under the Third Republic. And it is from them that communism borrowed
its cynical, lying ways.

The strength of Protestant countries lies in the fact that public sentiment forbids certain outbursts of party politics that would go against the
conscience of *everyone*. The inner feelings of *all individuals* forbid the violation of such bounds. They are brought up to believe that the lack of a certain
minimal human respect is "indecent." In our country no such limits exist,
and everything becomes permissible.

FRIDAY, 12 JUNE 1942   Came back yesterday from the free zone. Left
on Saturday the sixth, stayed with Jean on Sunday and Monday in Saint-
Étienne, then spent Tuesday and Wednesday in Vichy. I am summing up my
impressions before they have faded. Events fly by so quickly that from one
day to the next one's memories are replaced by new ones.

Visited Jean's farm. It has been so hot that there is no fodder at all in
the region, and cattle are being sold for slaughter. Cows that were selling
for 6,000 francs six months ago are now selling for half that. He and his ten-
ant farmer are discussing which of his nine animals to sacrifice. The dairy
is producing 10 liters of milk instead of the expected 50. But he has planted
lentils and potatoes, and with that he can make do during the winter. The
children are looking well and get enough to eat, but he is thin and careworn.
He showed me the issues of the weekly *Weltwoche* that he gets from Zurich.
Objective and very encouraging articles. As for Jean, the need to take a more
active stance at any given moment weighs on his conscience.

In Vichy I saw several people: Tuck from the U.S. embassy, Rochat,
Romier, Stucki, Behiç. A generally optimistic atmosphere in contrast to the
black pessimism of six months ago.

Stucki gave me a carefully vetted and verified account of Laval's return.[16] Laval presented himself to the marshal on his own initiative, *with
no pressure or intervention from Germany*. He explained the need to take
the side of "Europe," given the complete success of the Germans in Russia (this was in April-May). The marshal then asked Laval what he could
offer in exchange for his return to power. Laval went back to Paris, talked

16. This passage may be compared to telegrams of the period sent by Stucki to the
Swiss government, extracts of which are cited by Raymond Tournoux in *Pétain et la
France* (Paris: Plon, 1980), 376–77.

things over with the Germans, and returned completely empty-handed. Notice that the talks had been suspended appeared in the papers. Meanwhile the Americans, alerted, said they would break off relations with Vichy if Laval returned to power. Darlan, delighted, showed the American message to the marshal. There was talk, and the echo of the chatter reached the Führer, who made it a matter of prestige, demanding Laval's return. Laval was recalled, with the inevitable consequences. Stucki did not say whether Italian pressure to occupy Savoie and Nice immediately is linked to the business. But now Laval is back in power, and everyone is astonished by his conciliatory attitude toward the United States. He is thought to be much better than Darlan at maneuvering. Stucki, who would represent American interests in Vichy if relations are broken off, was taken into Laval's confidence in a long conversation. He told me, "He's a statesman," and repeated what Laval had said to him: "Everyone will be amazed by my policies."

What these policies will be, I have an idea from having talked with Romier, who seems to have lost weight and looks depressed. He has stayed on, he said, "to be the marshal's man." He asked me questions: How much prestige does the marshal have in the occupied zone? I did not hide the fact that his prestige has greatly diminished. He asked: Couldn't someone put an end to this odious English propaganda? I replied that the state of mind in the occupied zone is determined by the occupant. I described the effect produced by the massacres of hostages and by the imprisonment of so many people who are our relatives or the relatives of our friends.

"Who, if not the English," I asked, "can deliver us from such horror? It's this feeling alone that makes English propaganda."

He asked, "How can one be sure that France will be represented at the peace table by a Frenchman who is not in the pocket of the English?"

I replied: "One must first be sure that France is represented by a man who really represents France; given domestic policies of the past two years, how can you expect France to support the government? Come on, now! The slogan 'Liberty, Equality, Fraternity' applies more aptly to the French spirit than 'Work, Family, Fatherland'; even the ancien régime had its Estates-General. Today's petty policies have destroyed one of the rights most treasured by the French."

Romier blamed Alibert for this.

I said, "In his speeches, at least, the marshal needs to make it clear that if he accepts German demands, he doesn't approve of them.

Romier replied, "The Germans don't tolerate the slightest qualification or nuance." And he added, "Their demands have never been stronger than they are today."

From this conversation I conclude that the main idea is to make peace at the expense of the English, while looking to both the Germans and the Americans for support. This completely mad idea is certainly in the Laval tradition. He once steered a course between Italy and England with well-known results, and today he thinks he can manage the affairs of France by steering a course between Germany and England, while isolating the latter from the United States. This is the vainest of games and the most dangerous.

Stucki himself thinks that the United States may give up the fight in the Atlantic in order to concentrate exclusively on Japan. Leahy had told him, "We want to crush Japan, you understand, *crush it*. As for Germany, we shall see." He concluded from this that the United States might vacillate at some point and let England fend for herself. I assured him that in my opinion America would never abandon England, because the Atlantic is just as important to the United States as the Pacific; the words of Leahy may well apply to the peace treaty, but not to the war.

My conversation with Tuck[17] (whom I saw first) left me strongly impressed by the United States' resolve to fight to the end. He spoke to me of attacks in the west as a very real possibility. They will be carried out, in his opinion, by paratroopers. He also appeared more satisfied with Laval than with Darlan. The negotiations regarding Martinique, in which an effort is being made to achieve a simple disarming of merchant ships (instead of scuttling them to suit the Germans or ceding them to a South American company to suit the Americans), strike him as evidence of the Council president's skill and sangfroid. I spoke to him of sympathy in the occupied zone toward downed English parachute troopers or aviators. He was quite amazed by this. I begged him to do everything he could to keep the U.S. embassy in Vichy open. He expressed the opinion that his department had shown itself to be maladroit on various occasions owing to its intransigence. They had obtained absolute assurance, he stated, that France would cede nothing in regard to the fleet or to North Africa or to supplies of wheat or oil passing through Tunisia.

All agree that the biggest trouble spot right now is the maritime war, in which English losses have been considerable.

SATURDAY, 13 JUNE 1942 Yesterday and the day before, the conclusion of the Anglo-Russian treaty of alliance signed in London on 26 May by Molotov and Eden was reported on the radio. A similar accord is in the works with

---

17. Pinckney Tuck: chargé d'affaires at the American embassy in Vichy during most of 1942. [JNJ/TF]

Washington, doubtless in a form adapted to American traditions. The treaty is for twenty years. It includes the renunciation of all territorial acquisition. Which is probably going to reassure the Turks, who may fear the Russians' entry into Constantinople. It excludes all interference in internal affairs, meaning the Russians are renouncing communist propaganda. Which is going to reassure the English and American conservatives. The importance of the treaty is underlined by the complete silence of the German papers here, which hardly mention it except to say it is laying the groundwork for the creation of a second front over the course of the year 1942. Strangely enough, they mention it only with regard to the United States, whereas it is the English who are talking about it.

They say Msgr. Chaptal,[18] whose mother is a Russian Jew, has insisted on having a yellow badge.

THURSDAY, 25 JUNE 1942 The battle of Libya lost by the English . . . as usual. Churchill is in the United States. It has now been a year since Roosevelt was reelected. American troops are not visible on any front except in the air. The Libyan front is the only one in which English troops are fighting, and they have not managed to hold it. What do the Russians and the Americans think? Fortunately, the Russians are still holding out. But where will prestige lie after the war? With the Russians or with the English?

I have witnessed the reactions of the French bourgeoisie on three grave occasions: during the Dreyfus affair, after the war of 1914–1918, and after the defeat of 1940. In the three cases, reaction has tended toward the idiotic or the cowardly. Who has more to gain from legality than the bourgeoisie? Yet the majority of our good middle class, along with almost all conservatives, saw the Dreyfus affair as a way of overturning the republic and thus sided against legality. After the Peace of Versailles, it remained to establish the peace; those same people, by stirring up an imbecilic and risk-free nationalism against the wishes of the country, prevented a reconciliation that probably would not have endured on the German side but would not have distanced us from England and the United States. There again it was a matter of exciting "national" sentiment against the republic. Finally, after 1940 . . . the same people seized upon the defeat as the dreamed-of means to strike at the heart of "the regime."

In all three situations, the "people" – that is to say the peasants, the workers, the common people – acted in the interests of the country. It was

---

18. Mgr. Emmanuel Chaptal: auxiliary bishop in Paris.

Clemenceau's greatness to have been in tune with "the people" in the first two cases and Briand's in the second. Both of them would have been in tune with the mood of the country in 1940. How clear-sighted was Michelet's interpretation of French history!

On the radio this evening, the fall of Tobruk. This will give heart to the collaborators.

Laval's speech sickened everyone. His allusion to General Giraud, whom he blames for the non-return of the prisoners, is especially odious. The antipathy he is trying to arouse between workers and farmers is unequaled for ignominy. His whole tone is that of a scoundrel advising his perceptibly hostile listeners to do something underhanded.

FRIDAY, 3 JULY 1942 Left last Friday (26 June) with Marie and Antoinette for La Bouffource. Conversation with Pécate[19] and some local people. Pécate told me: "It's curious, but the few collaborators in the village are all reactionaries. Around here they're still called 'Chouans.'"[20]

No one listens to anything but French radio from London. People do not like England's recent announcements of landings. They say the English should act without warning. In spite of requisitions, country people have all they need. They willingly make up packages of food for folks in the city. We have profited greatly from this. Since January Mme B. has sent more than two hundred packages to the Claudes, to their friends, and to the friends of their friends. What they are upset about is the surveillance and the controls. In fact, Pécate tells me, despite the threats, sanctions are never carried out. Of course declarations of cattle or horses or pigs never give the true figures. Eggs are requisitioned at so many per hectare, not per chicken! But the amounts demanded leave plenty to spare. The women are again spinning wool on old abandoned spinning wheels.

I gave the woman who owns the tobacco shop one of the new aluminum francs. She eyed it scornfully and said with disdain, "French State!" I replied, "Yes, French Republic was worth more."[21]

On the train returning to Versailles, a young man with the look of a thug was taking up two or three seats in the compartment all by himself. From

19. Pécate: village blacksmith and a neighbor of the Rists in La Bouffource.

20. The Chouans were late eighteenth-century counterrevolutionaries concentrated in western France. [TF]

21. "French State" coins, which remained in circulation for a considerable time after the war, were issued by the Vichy regime during World War II. The motto on these coins read "Work, Family, Fatherland" instead of "Liberty, Equality, Fraternity." [TF]

his briefcase he pulled out *Le Pilori*,[22] which he read with attention, and his whole bearing seemed to say: "The thugs are in power now. I'm a thug and I'm the one who rules."

SUNDAY, 5 JULY 1942 The catastrophic news from Egypt has cast a shadow over our last days in La Bouffource. What is disconcerting is the persistent lack of preparation on the part of the English, their inability to assess the adversary's strength. "It's only thanks to catastrophes," said an important banker the other day, "that they'll end up winning."

MONDAY, 6 JULY 1942 Jacqueline Parodi asked to see me urgently. She had been warned that Jewish women between twenty-five and forty-five were going to be arrested and sent to Poland – with no distinctions. I hurried to Mettetal. He reassured me. Three days ago he had met with the commissioner for Jewish Affairs and asked him what truth there was in the rumors going around. Answer: "We are going to arrest twenty thousand stateless people in the occupied zone and ten thousand in the free zone. They'll be sent to Poland. *I hope the French will have their turn!*" Mettetal added, "It was the kind of thing you'd hear at a political rally." I said, "So I don't need to warn my daughter-in-law." He answered, "No; besides, if she were threatened, I'd intervene right away; you've nothing to fear."

The next day, I saw Doctor Tisné on behalf of poor Bourowsky.[23] He told me that all the sick and those who had undergone serious operations at the Rothschild hospital have been transferred, in handcuffs, to Drancy. He himself feels threatened and thinks he is going to be replaced by an anti-Semitic doctor.

WEDNESDAY, 8 JULY 1942 Bellah[24] has broken her hip and a rib walking in her room. Immediately bedridden and immobilized. Germaine has a new patient to watch over.

SATURDAY, 11 JULY 1942 Yesterday I read Pagès's book on the Thirty Years' War. A remarkable effort to clarify that extraordinary period. A few outstanding conclusions deserve to be more often remembered: (1) The idea that France broke up Germany in the Treaty of Westphalia, as Maurras and

22. *Le Pilori* was an anti-Semitic newspaper published in Paris during the war and funded by the Germans. [TF]

23. Not identified.

24. Referring to Bellah (Isabelle) Monod, Germaine Rist's aunt. [TF]

his friends repeat, is absurd. Germany split itself apart. Saxony, Brandenburg, the Palatinate, and Bavaria were not French inventions. These regions
existed, and it was they who did not want administrative unification by the
emperor. (2) When France entered the war, it was not prepared militarily,
and the French generals were beaten everywhere. In 1636 (the year of Corbie[25]) the enemy almost penetrated as far as Paris. The successes came only
afterward thanks to a close understanding with the Swedes. Richelieu's reforms consisted of putting *civilians* into the military administration. A good
model to emulate. (3) Finally, the grandeur of France, her diplomatic victories, came about only when she was fighting against tyranny or the hegemony
of a European nation. As a Catholic country, her role was to form an alliance
with the Protestants against the intensification of Catholic sectarianism.

Richelieu is the father of this policy. It corresponds to that hatred of
intolerant dogmatism at the heart of French feeling which keeps France at
an equal distance from ultramontanism and Huguenot Protestantism. In the
eighteenth century the only war that brought us anything was the one we
fought alongside America, a youthful power with reserves to draw on in the
future. Every time France's internal fears and taste for conservatism lead her
into an alliance with aging or decadent powers, she suffers. The wars of Louis
XIV profited us nothing – likewise that of Louis XV. Still today our political
fate is tied to the success of the great powers of free economic expansion
against the soulless methods of the Central European powers. Bainville favored the reversal of the 1743 alliances and of the entente with Austria. Grave
error on the part of that lucid mind.

Reread the second volume of Stendhal's *Le Rouge et le Noir.* I had forgotten its bitter emphasis on reactionary stupidity.

In chapter 22, "The Discussion," there is a curious passage. "In England," says the Marquis de la Môle in a political meeting attended by Julien
Sorel, "its noble lords, at least, hate these despicable Jacobins as much as we
do. Without English gold, Austria, Russia, and Prussia can fight only two
or three battles. Will that be enough to conduct *a felicitous occupation, like
the one M. de Richelieu squandered so stupidly in 1817?* . . . It is not to foreigners alone that we may owe *a new* military occupation." He then proposes
to install a force of five hundred dedicated men in each department: "And
that's when you'll be able to count on a foreign occupation." And further on:
"Between freedom of the press and our existence as gentlemen, it's a fight
to the death" (add universal suffrage to freedom of the press and you have
today's state of mind).

25. The Spanish took Corbie, a northern French commune, on 15 August 1636. [TF]

Thus for Stendhal the great grievance was the *desire* for foreign occupation. The same situation in 1830 as today. The same state of mind among reactionaries then and now: the desire for foreign occupation in order to suppress the Jacobins of yesteryear, the "communists" in our time – not to mention the republicans. The same liberal disgust at this state of mind. The same organization of an internal army destined to introduce the enemy. The Marquis de la Môle's idea has been realized by the C.S.A.R.

To confirm how clearly Stendhal saw things, I reread the third volume of Caulaincourt's memoirs and his disgust at the spectacle of young noblemen and members of the upper bourgeoisie applauding the Allies upon their entry into Paris.[26]

Who will write "The History of Reactionary Parties from 1815 to 1940"? That would be more fascinating than all the histories of republican parties. And the true history of the interwar period will be one in which what is true seems most untruthful.

TUESDAY, 14 JULY 1942 I never get tired of looking for the continuity since 1789 of this anti-France, as well as the continuity of the revolutionary ideal. In Edme Champion, as in Paul Bourde (those real flesh-and-blood Frenchmen), I find a deeply anchored feeling that the religion of France is really belief in the perfectibility of man and his institutions. Let no one say this idea is *false*. That has nothing to do with it. The question is whether this idea is an active myth, a force for the good. The idea at the heart of Christianity – salvation by Christ – is it *true*, in the sense in which scholars speak of truth? Certainly not. Is it a powerful idea? Has it been beneficial? Certainly, yes. In the same sense, the ideal of the revolution – that of a common effort among men who are free and equal to create a better society – is *true*, beneficial, and religious. For Bourde and Champion that religion is the antithesis of Christianity. I think they are confusing Christianity with Catholicism – or even with clericalism. But that would require too many pages. This passage from Champion sticks in my mind: "People believe they can embarrass us by asking what we will put in the place of Christianity. As if the religion of the future still had to be found!" For all those who witnessed and understood the revolution (Tocqueville, Mme de Staël, André Chénier), its religious character is beyond doubt, a fact the positivists have forgotten.

The current war is being waged against that religion. French reactionaries hid behind the invader precisely to abolish it. To the horror that the

26. This is a reference to the occupation of France by nations allied against Napoleon. [TF]

very word "republic" has for them may be added the terror of communism. This is the new fear that has led to the defection of the bourgeoisie. As if the social question did not arise in every age!

WEDNESDAY, 15 JULY 1942   Yesterday, 14 July, little Jean-Franklin, Mario's second son, was born. He is our eighth grandchild.

Bad news everywhere. Though the English appear to be resisting near Alexandria, the Russians are retreating on the Don, and the advance of the Germans toward the Caucasus seems almost unstoppable.

Thirteen

Certificates of Not Belonging to the Jewish Race

24 JULY–23 OCTOBER 1942

With the persecution of Jews accelerating, Rist worked hard to obtain a "Certificate of Not Belonging to the Jewish Race" for each of his three granddaughters. As of 2 June 1941 and the promulgation of the second anti-Jewish law, the girls were legally vulnerable. Under the first Anti-Jewish law they were not considered Jewish, as they had two non-Jewish grandparents. Under the second, this exemption applied only to those who could prove they had been baptized before the armistice. Rist's efforts to obtain exemptions for his granddaughters obliged him to maintain a relationship with Maître Mettetal, a lawyer in favor with the Vichy regime, to swallow his disgust at having to deal with the likes of the notorious Darquier de Pellepoix, and to ask the Protestant hierarchy to issue false certificates of baptism.

FRIDAY, 24 JULY 1942 Last weekend was marked by the roundup of thousands of Jews. The women are being kept at the Vel d'Hiv. Children from six to fourteen are taken from their mothers and grouped under the watch of gendarmes. The men are to be sent to the eastern front. They say that only stateless Jews are being arrested. In fact, it looks as if some French citizens were also swept up in the net. Everyone is stunned by these horrific and terrifying measures.

At the same time, the head of the German police has had posters put up everywhere in the occupied zone announcing that any act of sabotage will be followed by the execution of all male relations of the guilty party, including descendants over the age of eighteen; that all female relations over the age of eighteen will be sent to do forced labor; and that children under the age of eighteen will be sent to a "house of supervised education."

Jean, who has come from the free zone for a few days of vacation, told us that Poincaré's memoirs have been removed from the public libraries there because of his criticisms of the marshal. A crime of *lèse-majesté* before the fact.

In Marseille there were Gaullist demonstrations for the fourteenth of July. People wearing the tricolor cockade were beaten up by members of different leagues mobilized for the purpose. Four were killed.

Invited to lunch yesterday by M. von Falkenhausen, along with bankers Georges-Edgar Bonnet, Union Parisienne president Paul Bavière, and Neuflize. Sieburg,[1] Tirpitz (son of the admiral), and a certain Kreuter (intelligent face) were also there. According to Sieburg, rumors have been spreading among the editorial bureaus that the Russians are asking for an armistice.

WEDNESDAY, 5 AUGUST 1942 On behalf of my little granddaughters, I tried all of last week to obtain a certificate good enough for the Jewish Affairs commissioner, who, after some formal promises, declared he could not give his consent and demanded more unambiguous statements. All the scandalous illegality and grotesque arbitrariness of these procedures have been visited upon us.

News of the German advance in the Caucasus continues to be alarming. More than ever we are reduced to "believing" in the future, having no positive reason to hope for an improvement except faith (so often disappointed already) in energetic action on the part of the Anglo-American allies. What is more reassuring is that they are saying nothing, whereas German newspapers and German radio are full of warnings regarding the second front! For us it is, as always, the situation in the Bluebeard tale: "Anne, sister Anne, do you see anyone coming?" How long will this go on?

The potato crops have been ravaged by mildew because of the constant humidity. What will winter be like? For the first time since the beginning of the war, we are facing a real famine. The Ministry of Agriculture has forbidden sending parcels of butter – our last resource.

SATURDAY, 8 AUGUST 1942 Oppressive and oppressing days. The Germans' push to the Caucasus continues. The concept of the English blockade, in the face of an army determined to conquer the sources of supplies, appears increasingly imbecilic. The English never imagined that the Germans might amuse themselves by "taking" Danish butter, Swedish iron, Romanian and Russian oil, which the British fleet was supposed to cut off! What intellectual decadence in this "imperial" people. It was revealed on American radio last

---

1. Friedrich Sieburg: German journalist and author of *Dieu est-il français?* [Is God French?], trans. Maurice Betz (Paris: Bernard Grasset, 1930). [TF]

night that up until two months ago, American naval losses surpassed the reconstruction of ships. Only for the last two months has the curve changed directions. What would become of the English without the Americans? There is no doubt that the blockade of England by Germany has been and remains at least as effective as that of Germany by the English.

The German press and radio speak constantly of the "second" front. Is there a serious intention on the part of the British to establish one? Or is all of this journalistic noise just meant to provoke the English into making some declaration that would put the Germans onto their plans? I do not see the possibility of a real second front – a landing in Holland or France – given that the English are having such a hard time in Egypt. If only their bombardments of German cities were effective and frequent! But in spite of all their grandiloquent declarations, this hardly seems to be the case. The English have become Gascons, all talk and no action! Another transformation caused by the war.

TUESDAY, 18 AUGUST 1942 Léonard has me reading Élie-Joseph Bois's recollections of the days of the armistice. They appeared in the *Times*[2] – and *Cassandre*, a pro-fascist Belgian paper, published it alongside expressions of horror at this supposed "thug." I have once again been impressed by this man's gift for sharp journalistic observation, representative of what remained of the most intelligent (and I think also the most corrupt) in French journalism. His narrative more than confirms what we suspected: the shameful role of the Comtesse de Portes and of Baudouin,[3] the cowardice of Weygand (who has since tried to pull himself together); the petty politicking of all those people; and the spinelessness in the end of Reynaud, saddled with a role that was too big for him. One is sickened and very deeply saddened that a country like France could have fallen so low.

The news continues to be bad. Retreat of the Russians. One fears the conference in Moscow has had mediocre results at best. Only the air raids on Germany give some hope. When they multiply, that will be the true beginning of the war.

WEDNESDAY, 19 AUGUST 1942 Reread the history of the Thirty Years' War – Pagès's and Friedrich von Schiller's. Schiller's focuses on two great

2. Élie-Joseph Bois's recollections were published in London in 1941 as *Truth on the Tragedy of France*, trans. of *Le Malheur de la France* by N. Scarlyn Wilson (London: Hodder and Stoughton, 1941). [TF]

3. Paul Baudouin was considered to be a protégé of the comtesse. [TF]

figures: Gustavus Adolphus and Wallenstein. His narrative conveys the spectators' passions and the profound antagonism of Catholics and Protestants, laying at their door the violence, suspicions, and hatreds, both personal and popular. Pagès's history shows the political positions of the leaders. But it was the passions that made the war last longer than people believed a country could endure. The two protagonists aside, all the other participants were hateful nonentities driven by self-interest. The Germans were as savage toward one another as they have shown themselves to be toward foreign peoples. It is perhaps in this war that their true character best appears. The only man of great spirit was the foreigner, Gustavus Adolphus. The imbeciles in the Action Française, who recast the teaching of history in our poor country by falsifying everything, would have the French believe that Mazarin's cleverness in the Peace of Westphalia consisted in dividing up Germany! Which of course gives a false idea of the ancien régime's foreign power! But Germany divided itself. We had nothing to do with it. At most we helped to make the division endure. That division was based upon the multiplicity of territorial sovereignties. It is once and for all defunct. And one must look for something else.

FRIDAY, 21 AUGUST 1942 A great undertaking two days ago by the Canadians and the English, who attempted a landing at Dieppe. The German communiqués have been gloating since yesterday, qualifying the English attempt as a "dilettantish operation." It was never intended to be more than a reconnaissance mission, a show of strength. The withdrawal occurred at the appointed time, after nine hours of combat in the streets of Dieppe and surroundings. The point is that they were able to land. An enormous air battle took place in which the English announced ninety-five of their planes downed, an equal figure for the Germans, plus two hundred put out of action. This was probably the greatest air battle of the war. The fact that the English immediately seized the two batteries defending the coast made the landing possible. Unfortunately, the arrival of their flotilla could not be kept completely secret. An encounter with two German boats forced an engagement and allowed the Germans to be alerted. Two years ago people were talking about a German attack on England. The situation is no longer the same.

SATURDAY, 22 AUGUST 1942 The lawyer telephoned last night, giving me high hopes that the matter of my granddaughters is going to be satisfactorily resolved. I will believe it when I see it. Isabelle left us yesterday after a ten-day stay. More silent and preoccupied than usual.

I too am making prophecies. People are talking about the death of the British Empire. In actuality, after this war we are going to witness an increasingly tight coalition of all the Anglo-Saxon countries, one in which the role of America (including, no doubt, the Americas) will be decisive. With Canada it will constitute a compact and influential group. The other dominions, whose independence will have become still greater, will look favorably upon this group. South Africa and Australia will be politically attracted to it, but Great Britain will be deeply involved in the coalition, and London will remain the great financial and commercial trade center. Three nations will pay court to this Anglo-Saxon coalition: Germany, France, and Russia. And if France does not hurry, Germany will be the first to win the coalition's friendship.

If one looks to the past, one sees that Germany's desires for hegemony have always existed. First with the Hohenstaufen. Then the empire of Charles V, dominating both Spain and Germany. In the next century Ferdinand II, to assure his hegemony, unleashed the Thirty Years' War.[4] The Peace of Westphalia, and even more, the rise of Prussia and the slow decline of Austria, created a respite from these endeavors until 1870–1871. Then after 1900 they began again. We are living through a new effort, which this time extends beyond Europe. For the first time, Germany is aiming not just at the continent but at England and America, too. The great mistake is to have forgotten the Thirty Years' War, in which the obscurantist stranglehold on all of Germany was prevented only by Swedish and French intervention. It must be noted that today's neo-obscurantism also comes from Austria.[5] The origin is always the same: the fundamental restlessness of the German soul (what they call their dynamism), which is never satisfied except by the spectacle of its own power and which always wants to transcend itself.

SUNDAY, 23 AUGUST 1942 Joseph Barthélemy has just had Vichy adopt a law punishing by *death* those who make radio broadcasts contrary to the national interest! This same man has dedicated forty years of his life to pro-

---

4. Hohenstaufen: German dynasty of kings (1138–1254) that produced three Holy Roman emperors. Charles V: member of the House of Habsburg; King of Germany, Italy, and Spain; and Holy Roman emperor, 1519–1556. Ferdinand II: member of the House of Habsburg, King of Germany, and Holy Roman emperor (1619–1637); his imposition of counter-Reformation policies led to the Thirty Years' War. [TF]

5. The House of Habsburg became entrenched in Austria in 1276 when the Archduchy of Austria became the family's nucleus. Hitler was born in Austria, but his family moved to Germany when he was three. [TF]

claiming in his books and in his courses the sacred principles of safeguarding individual rights and freedom of expression![6]

A decree of the *Militärbefehlshaber* once again forbids the sending of any money from the occupied zone to the free zone. One wonders why.

Again this week I have experienced the wearying frustration of being on governing boards in these appalling times. On Thursday I returned to the Ottoman Bank and the Banque de Paris. Business is nonexistent or else tied exclusively to the war. It is clear that nothing matters, that everything can be overturned by military events from one instant to the next, that banks and companies are dominated by the outcome of the war, regarding which we can do nothing. Nothing else counts. People want to keep things the way they are, looking toward an unknown future. Thereupon minds clash – envisaging that future with hopes, fears, and desires that differ from one person to another and are only indirectly expressed. The majority, however, wait and hope for the Allies' victory. The rest consider themselves better informed and more intelligent.

Reread Loisy's *Mémoires pour servir à l'histoire religieuse de notre temps*.[7] The purified and rationalized religion he expounds and to which he came after a long intellectual and emotional crisis is meant only for an elite. Religion-as-passion or religion-as-safeguard or religion-as-habit, these suit the masses who do not have time for reflection. It is a fact, however, that the masses are completely detached from dogma, be it Catholic or Protestant. Already, Stendhal, in his *Promenades dans Rome* (1826), wrote that no one in France was interested in religion. And it is another fact that the masses demand to *believe* in something. If a "purified" religion is not accessible to them, they will take up *another*. That is what we are witnessing today, a time when "socialism," "communism," and "nationalism" are not just parties or political stances, but "religions." It is thus not a matter of indifference to know which religion is being adopted by the masses. From the sixteenth century on, Protestantism proved superior to Catholicism because of the *education* given to successive generations and the cult of conscience and sincerity as opposed to the cult of dogma, ritual, and ceremony. A religion must form *character*. Could we not imagine a religion that is purified but made simple and concrete for the masses, one that would be different from the political

6. Joseph Barthélemy, Vichy's *garde des Sceaux* (minister of justice), had been a professor of constitutional law before the war. [JNJ/TF]

7. *Mémoires pour servir à l'histoire religieuse de notre temps* [Memoirs to Contribute to the Religious History of Our Time]. 3 vols. (Paris: Nourry, 1930, 1931). [TF]

passion-religions left us by the nineteenth century as a consequence of the universal criticism of Christianity?

At one time the French Revolution was such a "religion." Today religion cannot be separated completely from the nation. Could one not, however, imagine a religion that would be "humane" and would stir the heart for the great things of humanity? By that I mean things transcending nationality and coexisting with "patriotism," which would itself be taught and cultivated by the state, with its holidays and rituals – alongside the holidays and rituals of religious worship. Why not?

French radio has finally overcome the scrambling. We can hear it again on different wavelengths.

TUESDAY, 25 AUGUST 1942 Constant came to see me on Sunday with his friend D.,[8] whose wife has just been sentenced to death by the military tribunal in Arras for having sheltered, over a period of months, a Polish aviator who had come down in the vicinity. They have five children. The older girls (twenty-two and twenty years old) have been sentenced to two years in prison for complicity. The husband, who was away during the period in question, was acquitted. The final decision rests with Falkenhausen, the governor-general of Belgium. I told this poor fellow (who has plenty of guts, like his wife, who showed admirable courage throughout the trial) that I would see the general's nephew, our commissioner at the Suez Company, about it. In effect, I saw him yesterday morning. I knew he was a decent man. But I was surprised by the speed and zeal with which he assured me he would speak to his uncle about it. He asked me to give him a note that he would pass on that very day. The general is to come to Paris on Thursday. I told the nephew that I was ready and willing to see General von Falkenhausen if that would help, or even to go to see him in Brussels. "What is appalling about war," I said, "is that the very acts that seem criminal to some are considered heroic by others." He responded: "Yes, you are right, and doubtless if I had been in that woman's place, I would have done the same thing." The Prince de Ligne, president of the Red Cross, is expected to intervene in Brussels.

The German push toward Stalingrad is becoming more violent. The Germans have crossed the Don and are advancing at the same time in the Caucasus. We are following these events with growing anxiety. Will we see Russia crushed once again before the Anglo-American coalition has arrived?

8. D.: Duval, an engineer in Saint-Gobain.

And will we see the battle between the Horaces and the Curiaces[9] begin all over again, the Germans freed up in the east and able to devote themselves without fear to maritime warfare, with all the oil they want, and, as they will no longer need so many tanks, the unlimited construction of submarines and planes?

Léonard tells me that when Weygand left in 1935, the government wanted to name General Maurin as the chief of staff. Pétain is said to have intervened to prevent it on the pretext that Maurin "believed in tanks," and he is the one who supposedly assured Gamelin's nomination. This remains to be verified. If true, it completes the portrait of the "hero of Verdun," herald of the "National Revolution."

SATURDAY, 29 AUGUST 1942 Alerted by an anguished card from poor Mme B.,[10] I asked for a meeting with the assistant to the director of the Sûreté Générale.[11] I was courteously received by M. Léger. Upon learning that Mme B.'s son was a naturalized citizen who had fought for France and was now a prisoner, he immediately declared that she should be exempt from the measures being taken. "Only," he said, "you've come a little late. The measures are already being carried out. Besides, for reasons you can understand, I cannot telephone or telegraph in such a case, nor even send a note to Vichy, as all such notes are being inspected at the Demarcation Line. We must wait for M. Bourguet to arrive in Paris – that is, until Monday or Tuesday of next week." I told him I had been informed of what was brewing only two days earlier. He answered: "Indeed, we have kept all this very secret." I insisted that he act as energetically as possible. The unfortunate thing is that B.'s mother is German. I told Léger she must be nearly sixty years old, if not more. He said, "That is not enough to protect her." I understood from his remarks that all of those unfortunates were to have been carted off to the occupied zone and, once there, would depend solely on the occupying authorities. I have only one hope left: that they will have managed to escape or at least to hide her grandchild. Thus in the space of a week I will have had to undertake measures to save from death or a still worse fate two wretched women. This gives an idea of the tragic atmosphere in which we live each day.

9. According to Livy, in the seventh century BCE Rome and Alba Longa agreed to allow the outcome of their war to be determined by a battle between two sets of male triplets: the Horaces from Rome and the Curiaces from Alba Longa. [TF]

10. Madame Bamberger: mother of Marc Bamberger, a colleague of Rist's at ISRES.

11. Sûreté Générale: civil law enforcement agency. [TF]

They say the marshal sent a telegram congratulating General Stülpnagel for having pushed back the English who landed at Dieppe! His portrait is becoming increasingly clear.

Bellet, having returned from Dieppe, told me that from his point of view the English operation was a success and that the Canadians who had landed, after penetrating 4 kilometers inland, were saying at noon: "It's too late to re-embark. Our return was set for 11:30." So it was in fact, as the English said, a reconnaissance operation.

WEDNESDAY, 2 SEPTEMBER 1942 Augé-Laribé, who came to see me last night, and who has accepted a post at the Ministry of Agriculture, is quite somber about the food situation. He is sure we will experience a famine, at least for bread, in April–May next year. The drought in the south of France has wiped out vegetables and hay and made it impossible for cows to give milk. Le Roy Ladurie, Vichy's minister of agriculture, was able to bridge the gap this year but only by taking reserves intended for next year.

The ban on sending packets of butter or potatoes has become much more rigorous. This is the old system of forbidding communications in order to avoid famine. History shows that it is by easing communications that famines have gradually been reduced in the world. But these examples are worthless.

He told me they were preparing to force Jews in the free zone to wear the yellow star!

SATURDAY, 5 SEPTEMBER 1942 On Thursday I saw Mettetal about my granddaughters. He was furious that Darquier de Pellepoix has refused to sign after having promised Mettetal that the thing had been done. But he assured me, "We will bring them around"! According to a decision of the court in Aix, in a case like ours it is up to the accusers to show that the children *adhered to the Jewish religion.* A reasonable solution, for the presumption is that the children belong to the Christian religion if the two parents are Christian. Let us hope that with a little energy we will have the desired result. Mettetal assures me that new measures against French Jews are not envisaged.

Last Sunday the archbishop of Toulouse gave a sermon protesting the measures taken against foreign Jews and regretting that the churches no longer enjoy the right to offer them sanctuary.

We received a letter from Noël in Libourne. He was not able to cross the Demarcation Line and says the thing is difficult at this time. He is thus separated from his wife, who left on Monday on a student train and is patiently awaiting her husband in Aix.

We gather our potatoes and at night we shell our beans. The potato harvest will be smaller than we thought. At most we will have 300 to 350 kilos. This is what our large household will have for three months. The official allocations – if they are carried out – will give us 34 kilos a month for the whole house!

The cook, who returned this morning from Brittany (she found abundant food in Finistère), says they are inspecting all parcels at the railway stations, as well as postal packages, to see if they contain butter.

On Thursday I submitted my deposition regarding the role played by monetary policy in the defeat! Good General Watteau was hoping that it would strengthen his thesis that on all fronts prewar policy weakened the country. He will be disappointed. If Reynaud should read the document, he will have reason to be pleased. But he will not read it, because my deposition will be buried in the files of the Riom trial, which will certainly not reconvene. I am keeping a copy of the deposition as evidence of my thinking on the question. I concluded by saying that the problem lies in knowing if the credits accorded – and they were quite substantial – were sufficient to cover military needs. In other words, military preparation alone is implicated. A police officer, armed with a Letter Rogatory, came to collect the document.

I am reading Charléty's volume on the Restoration from the great *Histoire de France* by Lavisse. That age gives us an idea of what French life would be like if those now in power remained after the war. The ultra-royalists of that time are the nationalists of today. Scorn and hatred for true public opinion in the country. An appeal to foreigners to suppress the "revolutionary" spirit, as, today, to suppress "communism." But it is ever the spirit of 1789 that is the target. Fundamental inhumanity on the part of the privileged, born of an intense fear. Complete lack of patriotic feeling.

MONDAY, 7 SEPTEMBER 1942 It is becoming harder and harder to take a real interest in work that has no direct relation to the war. The impression that everything we do is meaningless – without importance or consequence, unrelated to the struggle that is going on without us – dominates and gives to our daily acts, and to all our occupations, a ghostly air of unreality. "Waiting is the greatest of all evils," and we live in a state of waiting: waiting on military events; waiting on the evils that may befall our threatened friends; waiting on battles in the ocean, in the Mediterranean, in the Black Sea, or in Egypt; waiting for cards or letters telling us what our children are doing or whether they have successfully crossed the Demarcation Line; etc. Added to this, uncertainty over the availability of clothing and food. Yesterday Mario and I discussed the clothing that can be arranged for him this winter! European countries are just living off their inventories. How long will they last?

Rommel's attack in Egypt seems to have been momentarily repelled. But for how long? The bombarding of German cities is increasingly frequent. But what are the true results? And what is the effect on morale?

A card from Noël leads us to think he must have crossed the Demarcation Line on Saturday. We are impatiently awaiting the phone call that will reassure us.

TUESDAY, 8 SEPTEMBER 1942 Yesterday a phone call from the Banque de Syrie let us know that Noël is in Aix. One less worry.

Millerand tells me that one of his friends, back from Vichy, had a conversation with the marshal during the course of which the latter assured him that he had nothing to do with the congratulatory telegram sent to the Führer after the Dieppe affair and that Laval informed him of the telegram only after it was sent. Poor marshal!

SATURDAY, 12 SEPTEMBER 1942 Much news, both good and bad. Astonishing resistance by the Russians at Stalingrad, but they have definitively evacuated the port of Novorossiysk on the Black Sea. Churchill has given a great speech to the reconvened House of Commons in which he outlined his relations with Stalin, who, he says, is complaining that the Allies are not giving him enough help. As for Egypt, he let it be known that the pushback eight days ago against Rommel's attack was a great English victory. He asserted that the security of Egypt was guaranteed for several weeks – and even several months.

Jeanneney and Herriot have protested nobly and energetically against the dissolution of the Senate and the Chamber of Deputies by Laval. They told the marshal that he has violated all the commitments he undertook in the month of June 1940, when the chambers voted to give him exceptional powers. This protest was greeted by Cordell Hull as an act of great courage. Simultaneously, Herriot resigned from the Legion of Honor after two "anti-Bolshevik legionnaires" killed in Russia were posthumously decorated at Les Invalides[12] in front of German troops. An indignity that has not revolted General Brécard (Protestant!).

---

12. Les Invalides: collection of buildings in Paris that includes museums relating to military history and a burial site for war heroes. [TF]

In the free zone, multiple protests of the Catholic clergy (and I suppose of Boegner as well) against the barbarous treatment inflicted on the wretched Jewish refugees, rounded up and delivered to the occupying authorities. Cardinal Gerlier gave a speech. The archbishop of Toulouse regrets that he can no longer, by the right of sanctuary, make the churches available to them. General Saint-Vincent, the commander in Lyon, resigned in order not to make the troops participate in these dreadful operations. Slowly but surely universal disgust is mounting against the government, which, in the name of National Revolution, is reverting little by little to barbarism and to all that was odious under the ancien régime. It will not have taken long for the revolution's promoters (a mix of reactionaries, Action Française, and members of the bourgeoisie frightened by Bolshevism) to show their true face and disgust all of France. But how will the awakening come about, the day when the country is delivered from the occupiers?

I have resigned from the Banque des Pays de l'Europe Centrale, as Laurent-Atthalin told me he wanted to collaborate completely with the Germans. He claims to still believe in their victory. He thinks the Turks will side with them, lured by territorial bait. I made my contrary conviction clear to him, both in regard to the Turks and to the Germans.

I often repeat to myself the admirable verses of Victor Hugo's "Napoleon II" (probably the finest thing he wrote):

> Mil huit cent onze. Au temps où les peuples sans nombre
> Attendaient prosternés sous un nuage sombre, etc.[13]

How could one express in more gripping terms what people today are feeling? Except we are not waiting for Heaven to say, "Yes." We are waiting for Heaven to say, finally, "No"!

Admirable late summer days. I cannot remember a warmer September or a clearer sky. Le Très-Clos must be incomparable. One feels the return of a certain optimism.

SUNDAY, 13 SEPTEMBER 1942 From time to time people tell me that this demoniac Hitler is a great man. I do not agree. The two greatest political figures of the nineteenth century were Napoleon and Bismarck. One has only to reread their speeches, their letters, their memoirs. First of all, they

---

13. Eighteen hundred eleven, when numberless crowds
     Were waiting, prostrate, 'neath a somber cloud.
        – from Hugo's *Les Chants du crépuscule* [Translator's footnote and translation]

had a sharp sense of human reality – not of humanity's vileness and villainy (though Napoleon in particular had a very low opinion of men), but of the human being, the same in his simple daily reactions as in his official role; in his peasant or bourgeois character as when wearing the uniform of a general or prime minister. There is something Balzacian in their clear-sightedness. With Hitler, there is something Mephistophelean.

Then, too, with Napoleon and Bismarck there was a permanent sense of the historic continuity that they represented. They both saw themselves in the lineage of the Alexanders, the Caesars, the Charlemagnes, or the Fredericks. They belonged to a family of great men. They felt carried along by the spirit of history, which gave their words an unforced, entirely natural grandeur arising from the fact that they were on the same level as all that is greatest in history. As for Hitler, there is only his "ego," swollen with resentment and with his perpetual wonder at having arrived so high after starting so low. His speeches are the venting of bilious spleen as well as happiness that he can crush the noblest among us. No vision of the future, nothing of the universal ideology of a Napoleon, nor of the Bismarckian sense of what is always at risk in a great political undertaking. In the demoniac there is a mix of Wallenstein and Philip II, a mix of the adventurer and the mediocre, types who cannot transcend their personal ambition – or transcend the vision of a parvenu.

MONDAY, 14 SEPTEMBER 1942 In that bizarre and amphigoric poem of Hugo's called the "Épopée du ver," there is this stanza full of sense, if not beauty, that applies marvelously to the history of today:

> Hommes, riez. *La chute adhère à l'apogée*
> L'écume manquerait à la nef submergée,
> L'éclat au diamant,
> La neige à l'Athos, l'ombre aux loups, avant qu'on voie
> *Manquer la confiance et l'audace et la joie*
> A votre aveuglement.[14]

14. Laugh, my friends. *The fall adheres to the apogee.*
    Sunken ships would have no brine,
        The diamond no shine,
    Athos no snow, no shadow the wolf, before you
    Would lack presumption and bliss
        In your blind oblivion.
            – from Hugo's *La Légende des siècles* [Translator's footnote and translation]

TUESDAY, 15 SEPTEMBER 1942 Yesterday a talk by Walter Lippmann on London radio about Anglo-American relations. He said these relations have become so close and so intertwined that they cannot be broken and that after the war the union of the two countries will be an essential and permanent factor in world politics. This is evident, in fact. Any French policy that ignores this certainty is doomed from the start. He also stated that isolationism in the United States is definitely finished. Americans are now deep in world politics and will stay there. Without saying so explicitly, he meant that the Monroe Doctrine is dead.

The inhabitants of Dieppe are very happy. They say, laughingly, that having obeyed General de Gaulle's orders, they have been congratulated by Marshal Pétain, thanked by the Führer, paid 10 million, and had their prisoners returned. They ask only to do it all again.

The latest bombardment of Rouen by America's Flying Fortresses, from a height of 4,000 meters, killed more than 150 people. This has cooled the ardor of many people with regard to the Americans.

We are following the siege of Stalingrad with growing anxiety. The question of time has taken on excruciating importance. Depending on whether the fortress holds for two weeks or a month, the fate of the entire German campaign, given the proximity of winter and cold, will be decided one way or another. It is truly a race against the clock. However, even if Stalingrad were taken, it is hard to see how Russia could be crushed before winter. But the Allies' difficulties would be notably aggravated.

In Victor Hugo's *Légende des siècles*, there is a piece called "1453" containing this little gem:

> Mon nom sous le soleil est France.
> Je reviendrai dans la clarté
> J'apporterai la délivrance,
> J'amènerai la liberté.[15]

A new Vichy law gives the government the right to require all men and women between eighteen and fifty years old to work "*in the national interest.*" Everyone knows what that means. It means they will be sent to Germany. Cordell Hull has declared that the American government will consider the

---

15. My name under the sun is France.
    I will return to the light,
    I will bring deliverance
    And freedom from night.
        – [Translator's footnote and translation]

sending of workers to Germany to be a hostile act on the part of Vichy, as it is a direct aid to the enemy. The jailer is becoming increasingly ruthless with his prisoners! We feel we are at the mercy of his every whim.

SATURDAY, 19 SEPTEMBER 1942 Attacks on the occupying troops are multiplying, and Stülpnagel has had 120 hostages shot in Paris. That is what we heard on the radio this morning. Meanwhile all the local radio stations, cinemas, public gathering places, etc., are closed today and tomorrow. Terror, which is surely preparatory to the application of the obligatory labor law.

A certain Charles Vallin (former Croix-de-Feu) and Pierre Brossolette have arrived in England. The former said on the radio that when he saw the marshal in June 1940, he was told that the English were going to ask for an armistice and that consequently he, the marshal, was going to make peace quickly to obtain good conditions. A lie or naïveté? In any case, Charles Vallin's eyes have now been opened. Disgusted with the marshal, he is going over to the Resistance.

On Thursday de V.[16] told me that Laval is having the Comte de Paris (who currently resides in Morocco) come to Vichy and that the latter has declared himself ready to assume all necessary duties. Naïveté? Childishness? Congenital ignorance of the situation? And as for Laval, what a Machiavellian plot to hold on to power – combining with a young simpleton, as he had previously done with a vain, enfeebled old man.[17]

Sir Samuel Hoare, England's ambassador to Madrid, made a speech in London to tell the English that winning the war (which they were sure to do) was not enough; they must win it *in time* – and not wait until Europe had become an economic and moral desert. Wise words coming from a man who has not shown himself to be particularly wise. They express very well the way we all feel, those of us in the thick of things who have heard the Americans and English over the past two years announcing great events that never happen.

MONDAY, 21 SEPTEMBER 1942 Yesterday, on Stülpnagel's orders, we spent the afternoon and evening confined at home. The Marios came over just before three. We read and made music. In Stendhal's *Mémoires sur Napoléon* we saw all kinds of connections with the current epoch. I had forgotten how much Stendhal loved the revolution and everything that made it

---

16. Rist was probably referring to Louis de Vogüé of the Suez Company.
17. The Comte de Paris was the Orléanist pretender to the throne of France.

great. The same degradation experienced by conquering leaders after Napoleon's first campaigns was repeated after the victory of 1918. All the pretense one finds in Barrès's portrayal of Napoleonic enthusiasm is absent in Stendhal's, where there is only the simplicity of true passion and unlimited scorn for reactionary stupidity.

Stalingrad is still holding out. English planes bombarded Munich on Saturday night.

I have learned from a letter that Marc Bamberger's mother was able to take refuge in Switzerland with her daughter and grandson.

WEDNESDAY, 23 SEPTEMBER 1942 On Monday General Hellot called a meeting at Morgan's of Le Matériel Téléphonique's governing board. He informed us of the new situation created by the government's decisions to send workers to Germany. Each company is taxed with supplying a certain number of specialists. The Renault factories, with 10,000 workers, must supply 400; L.M.T., with 5,000 workers, must supply 652. A strange disproportion. The government will undertake to select the workers. What they want from us is a list of single people and married workers with one or two children. The maximum age for men is fifty; for women, thirty-five. But no one wants to send women. We are stunned by this new blow. What can we do? Drag things out? Protest? The workers have not yet been told of the decree that appeared on Saturday in *l'Officiel*. Nothing in the local papers. In meetings on Saturday and Sunday at which Minister Bichelonne communicated the news to factory heads, he declared that the government is expecting "great political results" from this decision, especially the reopening of the "closed zone" in northeastern France (which for all practical purposes was reopened six months ago!). The total number of workers he wants to send is 300,000. Of these, 135,000 specialists. For every three specialists sent to Germany, one prisoner will be returned – in all, at most 44,000 prisoners for 300,000 workers!

THURSDAY, 24 SEPTEMBER 1942 Lunch yesterday with Falkenhausen, Vogüé, and Georges-Edgar Bonnet. Falkenhausen spoke to me right off about the Duval affair. He said his uncle the general will do all he can to grant a pardon. I asked him to let me know as soon as a decision has been taken so that these poor people will not be suspended between life and death as they are now. With the group, conversation about agriculture, Romania, Caillaux's memoirs, the Dreyfus affair. No mention of the events and possibilities wrenching our hearts. Falkenhausen said in passing that several of his friends have lost their houses. So the bombings have not been without effect!

FRIDAY, 25 SEPTEMBER 1942 It has been announced that Blondel, the French minister in Bulgaria, is joining the Gaullists! After Helleu, ambassador to Ankara (where he was replaced by Bergery), this is an interesting sign. Because these men must be rather well informed about the situation in the Near East and the true leanings of Turkey and Bulgaria.

Staggering resistance at Stalingrad, astonishing everyone.

Terray, de Vogüé's son-in-law, has resigned as Barnaud's assistant for "Franco-German relations." They say Barnaud himself is starting to feel fed up. The German demands for labor are evidently the cause.

A law forbidding workers to resign from their factory has just completed the system of worker conscription. But the workers are nevertheless disappearing, escaping to the countryside. Seventy hostages have been reported shot in Bordeaux.

MONDAY, 28 SEPTEMBER 1942 Stalingrad is still holding out. It seems the whole world is hanging on news of the siege. Wendell Willkie, who has just been to Moscow as Roosevelt's personal emissary, has issued an appeal to the American people stressing that the Russians have lost *five million* men in the common struggle and that they must be helped with all possible energy. German papers are doing their best to explain the prolongation of hostilities. One of them supposedly said, "A lesser genius than Hitler would not have hesitated to take the city. But the Führer wants to spare German blood." Everyone knows that the attacking troops are being sent to their deaths in countless numbers!

Autumn has made its presence known for eight days now: rain and cold everywhere.

Benoist-Méchin[18] has been given his walking papers by Laval. The wolves are eating one another. They say he acted as Doriot's pawn against Laval.

Echoes of the feelings of some Germans in France have reached our ears: extremely pessimistic.

FRIDAY, 2 OCTOBER 1942 This morning Germaine left for the free zone so she could see our grandchildren, whom she has not seen for two years. Obtained a pass thanks to Matériel. We had to get up at 5:00 in the morning, actually 3:00 according to the sundial. Night softly illuminated by the moon. Léonard was waiting for her at the Saint-Lazare station to take her across

18. Jacques Benoist-Méchin was appointed in June 1941 as secretary of state in the Vichy foreign ministry. He was ousted by Laval in September, 1942. [JNJ/TF]

Paris and see her to the train, where she had a reserved seat. She will still need to change trains at Saint-Germain-des-Fossés without being assured of finding a seat. She may need to stand all the way to Saint-Étienne.

Coming back from Paris at 7:00 A M, I saw German officers on the train. One of them, drunk, had lost his military cap somewhere and was looking for it under the seats. This is the first drunk German I have encountered since the occupation began.

A speech by Hitler calling Eden, Roosevelt, and Churchill idiots and madmen. Terrible threats against the Jews – and threats of reprisals against England. He announced the fall of Stalingrad and the taking of the oil fields. He compared his great victories to the Dieppe affair and spoke of the union of Allies of greater Germany. All this scarcely differs from the language of certain proclamations of Napoleon.

Yesterday the Social Service School reopened. I had to give a short speech. The children were all cheerful, their faces bright. Delighted to be getting back to work.

MONDAY, 5 OCTOBER 1942 Moreau tells me that in the interview between Laval and the Comte de Paris, it was the latter who took the initiative. Moreau supposes it had to do with suggestions for peace coming from Italy, as the Duchess of Aoste is the sister or cousin (I no longer remember) of the pretender.[19] Let us hope they will not be so stupid as to go down that path. But rumors of negotiations with the English are also coming from all directions. These rumors are evidently started by the Germans, who find the Stalingrad affair is dragging on too long. I reply to everyone that even if the English wanted to make a deal, the Americans would not permit it.

An interview in which a barely polite Stalin responded harshly to an American journalist, saying that the second front is essential to Russia and that to establish it the Anglo-American allies need only keep their promises – meaning evidently that in his opinion they are not doing so. However, English air raids are continuing nonstop.

A speech by Goering at the *Sportpalast* saying he is doing his best to defend Germany, but that as long as German aviation is needed on the Russian front, it cannot be available on the others! Cold comfort for those who have been bombed! He summed up the war by calling it a war against the Jews!

Herriot arrested, or at least confined to his house.

---

19. The duchess was the Comte de Paris's sister, in fact.

FRIDAY, 9 OCTOBER 1942 Saw Mattioli[20] at the Banque Française et Italienne, all of whose Brazilian branches were seized after Brazil declared war on the Axis. He is the first Italian I have seen since the war began. He shares our state of mind. We stuck to generalities by tacit agreement. He noted that the great victor of this war will be the United States. He declared that no system will be viable except one based on liberty. He insisted on having been "pure," saying that fascism already existed when his generation reached the age of reason (he was twenty-five then), so in effect they are not responsible at all. No one, he said, suspected Russia's strength, which shows me that in Italy, as in Germany, the Russian affair has upset all plans and shaken opinion. He spoke bitterly of the financial and political support that America and England had given to fascism. He remarked that all the concessions that might have been made to Germany would not have prevented this war. But of Italy itself he spoke little. However, he foresaw an end to the war next spring. I did not push him very much about his country's future. I would have been obliged to tell him that the great loser of this war will be Italy.

All conversations revolve around Germany's labor conscription. Agitation is great among the workers. What will happen if the occupiers themselves make it their business to take the workers?

Gaussel,[21] having returned from captivity, says German morale is low and that many think the war will end like the preceding one: a great debacle after great, useless victories. Mattioli himself pointed out that Hitler, in his speech, declared the Allies would not be victorious but did not say he would be.

SUNDAY, 11 OCTOBER 1942 Stalingrad is still holding out in spite of Hitler's prophecy, which amounted to an order for his generals. Last year at this same time we were saying if the Russians can hold out until 15 September, the Germans will be attacked by the English and by winter their luck will turn. Nothing of this came about except for the defeat of the English at Tobruk. This year once more we are saying if the Russians hold out until 15 October, the Anglo-American coalition will have time to get involved before winter, and their luck will turn. But the English are doing nothing. Their raids on Germany are too spaced out to produce a real blow to morale. Their fate in Libya is not even certain. Thus at the beginning of the fourth year they are incapable of any action, even with American support. And those people were dispensing their diplomatic protection to all the little countries! Who will

20. Mattioli: head of the bank.
21. Georges Gaussel: head of Crédit Coopératif's central branch.

still want to be allied with them? The imbecility and laziness of their middle class are on a par with our own.

The Germans have announced that they are going to handcuff the English prisoners caught at Dieppe. How they scorn the English! Churchill's response is that he will handcuff an equal number of German prisoners.

WEDNESDAY, 14 OCTOBER 1942 Stalingrad has not yet been taken. A month ago we thought that if the city held out one more month, the German campaign in Russia must be considered a failure. Here we are! And what we thought then is still true! But will the Allies know how to take advantage of the situation?

Yesterday on the radio a new English warning to the French: in the case of a landing, we are advised to take shelter in preparation for new bombings near railways, stations, and factories.

The nearly simultaneous speeches of Roosevelt and Churchill did not really say anything new. Their reasons for hope are the same we have given ourselves for some time now. No further news was added. Churchill noted that Goering's speech emphasized the Führer's sole responsibility for military strategy and the generals' simple role in carrying it out. Are the Germans already looking for those responsible? It is a bit early, and it is not among the generals that one must look for opposition! The other day von Falkenhausen, speaking to me of Caillaux's memoirs, was particularly taken by something MacMahon said to one of his friends, who had advised him to have a general head the government: "My dear fellow, do you not realize how little courage generals have?"[22] Why was Falkenhausen so struck by those words? Did it seem to apply to his own country?

This morning brought news of an American naval victory over the Japanese in the Solomon Islands.

FRIDAY, 16 OCTOBER 1942 Big news: Halder, the German general chief of staff, has been dismissed, as was von Bock some time ago. So Hitler is not happy with his generals. The interesting thing is that Halder had been singled out to me before the war by Goerdeler as the general who would be at the head of "military opposition." And he is the one leaving.

22. Joseph Caillaux, *Mémoires*, vol. 1: *Ma jeunesse orgueilleuse* (Paris: Plon, 1942). Marshal Patrice de MacMahon was himself a general and the first president of France's Third Republic (1873–1879); M. von Falkenhausen was related to the notorious General von Falkenhausen. [JNJ/TF]

Under these conditions the Stalingrad affair is taking on an even more dramatic aspect. For two days now the assault has intensified in a supreme effort to accomplish the Führer's will in spite of all. If the Russians resist, it is not just a defeat for Germany but also a personal defeat for the Führer.

Mettetal has phoned to tell me that Darquier de Pellepoix has given the green light for my granddaughters. He still has not signed. I am impatient to receive the letter and will believe it only when I see it.

The papers are hinting at a prospective American attack on Dakar and urging the Vichy government to resist, saying that the French army will not be alone. All this shows the German desire to get a foothold there. It would also be an advantage, though not a great one – even if they intended to attack Algeria. Passage through French Equatorial Africa is hardly less convenient. I conclude from all of this that the Americans will not attack if the Germans do not move first. Now, there is a prediction that will be amusing to reread sometime later.

People are beginning once more to talk about the future. A liberal government must be formed again, but one cannot simply repeat what existed before. Too many people have come to loathe the pre-1940 government. Rightly or wrongly. It matters little; that is a fact. The government will have to be parliamentary but modified and simplified. Supported by a party, the government must be truly able to lead, but only on the great issues – the military, foreign affairs, and social laws. For the rest, maintain order and oblige people to listen to one another. With regard to economic matters, people will inevitably go back to their old ways. But who will organize a party? As of now, only the communists are organized. The others have broken up. A republican party of "reconstruction" will be needed. With no talk of "restoration" or of anything "national." There is too much nonsense attached to those two words. To "reconstruct" means to have accurate techniques for gathering information and to establish precise goals for the policies one wishes to follow: technical advances in the army, agreements with maritime powers, etc.

SUNDAY, 18 OCTOBER 1942 Yesterday Mettetal phoned to tell me that the signature has been affixed to the commissioner's approval, saying that the little girls shall be Aryan! What a relief! It has been exactly a year since I began to work on this. How many alleyways I have gone down and how much worry I have experienced in the process.

The radio has announced the landing of American troops and planes in Liberia. Now, here is something that is going to thicken the plot in Dakar. The game is becoming more closely contested.

Trouble in Ambérieu and Lyon following the departure of the railway workers for Germany. They say blood has been shed. A little more blood on the hands of Laval and Joseph Barthélemy.

I have come across the following passage in Albert Sorel's examination of the Directory's politics. We are in 1797. Sorel is writing of royalist intrigues on the eve of Fructidor.

> They feel so unpopular, so condemned by the vast majority of the French that they do not dare to show themselves. . . . Nothing better reveals the impotence of the royalists than their inability to conceive, even if successful, the hope of a return to favor in the public eye. They could only count on external alliances, a play for power which they would surreptitiously join in, and a revolution that was *republican in appearance*, the only way to get the people to accept the coup d'état which they would later try to turn to their advantage. (*Europe et Révolution française*, 5: 219)

The situation has not changed. The royalists and reactionaries in general are still the same. In 1940 they seized on the defeat because in 1936 they had once again sensed that public opinion was against them. Who will write the history of the reactionary parties since the revolution and demonstrate the astonishing continuity of their methods?

MONDAY, 19 OCTOBER 1942   Two days ago at 6:00 PM an English raid on Le Creusot lasting seven minutes. According to the BBC the factory was completely destroyed. German papers have announced forty deaths and thirty injured among the civilian population.

I am still reading Sorel, the volume about the Directory's politics. The Directory's inability to conceive of reasonable agreements with Europe; its delight in the most extravagant dreams, believing the most foolish schemes to be possible; its methods of destabilizing from within the countries it wanted to conquer or "protect" – all that provides the prototype for what we see in Germany today. Only the proclaimed ideologies differ. But the methods are the same. A crisis of megalomaniacal delirium caused by the initial ease of victories and by the belief in a superior human being.

The result is admirably summed up in a memoir about the negotiations of Campo-Formio, presented by Talleyrand to the Directory and cited by Sorel on page 282 (vol. 5 of his *History*):

> In the situation of a republic that has newly arisen in Europe despite all the monarchies, and upon the debris of several among them, one that dominates through the terror of its arms and its principles, can one not say that the treaty of Campo-Formio and all the other treaties that we have signed *are nothing but military capitulations of varying attractiveness? While hatred subsists, the quarrel that*

is temporarily laid to rest by the astonishment and consternation[23] of the conquered cannot be definitively ended by weapons of the moment. Because of the extreme heterogeneity of the two contracting parties, our enemies do not consider the treaties they sign with us to be anything but truces similar to those that the Muslims are content to conclude with the enemies of their faith without ever taking such engagements as a definitive peace. . . . They continue not only to be secret enemies, but remain in a state of coalition against us, and we are alone in Europe with five republics that we have created and which for these powers are a new source of worry.

Replace "republic" by "Nazi State" and "monarchy" by "democracy," and you have exactly the situation in which the German Reich finds itself after all its victories in Europe. Talleyrand wrote this in 1799. It took sixteen years for the European coalition to triumph over the French dream of hegemony. How long will it take this time to triumph over the German delirium?

FRIDAY, 23 OCTOBER 1942   Yesterday I received our new Ottoman Bank colleague. He assured me he knows that it is via Morocco and Algeria that the second front will be established. He was advised to keep his bank liquid in case of a panic. Preparations around Dakar are supposedly a feint. I am always a little bit shocked by information of this sort, which must be known by the enemy! On the other hand, it is hard to see another place where a second front could usefully be opened. One could attack Rommel's army and at the same time relieve Egypt and threaten Italy. But can one materially succeed in landing enough troops all at once? Would there not be a bloody confrontation with French troops? The response is that the population of North Africa is quite ready to take up resistance and that Spain has made its choice and gone over to the English camp.

Wednesday the lawyer sent me the three certificates of "not belonging to the Jewish race" for each of my three granddaughters. I believe nothing has aged me more over the past two years, especially this last one, than the anxiety I have suffered for these three children. There they are, safe and sound. But how shameful to have need of those papers signed by the infamous Darquier de Pellepoix. I asked the lawyer what became of children born *after* 20 June 1940 of a mixed marriage. He answered that such children did not fall under the weight of the law, because they were not born when it was promulgated. Thus a trap was set for all those born *before* the law and who were counting on the previous law. Who committed this infamy? Mettetal replied, "Xavier Vallat, *a good Catholic*," whom the free thinkers tried to

---

23. Charles Rist added a note here saying, "These two expressions apply admirably to the conquered today."

vilify. Look where that got us. How right Renan was to say, "Do not speak ill of M. Homais; without him we would all be burned!"[24]

I have read the speech delivered on the radio three days ago by Laval to encourage workers to leave "voluntarily" for Germany. Few things so abject have ever been said by a French minister. This man very naturally finds arguments that are so base no one else could even imagine them. Nothing better reveals the ignominious circle in which this man's brain revolves. He threatens France with the dangers of a Bolshevik victory that would submerge Europe! He tells the workers, "If you do not go voluntarily, Germany will very well force you!" He paints the necessary Franco-German alliance in glowing colors. And more: "The French left for war in 1939 without having been asked their opinion; do you likewise." These arguments, without exception, set the workers' teeth on edge. But is he at all aware of it? For this man who is incapable of feeling *à la française* and gathers ideas in his brain that a Frenchman would never have had, it is war itself that is bad. Little does it matter for what cause or against which enemy: all means are thus appropriate to avoid it. Germany is the most dangerous, so let us help it. This is not just base; it is an unprecedented lack of clear thinking. For he is the only one not to see that the game is being lost by Germany and that he himself will not survive the dishonor of his words.

Meanwhile the workers are doing everything they can to avoid leaving.

By seizing power so eagerly after the defeat of 1940, the reactionaries in league with Laval and Pétain made a huge error. Believing the war was over, they thought they would control the levers of power in the coming peace. But the war goes on. And they are the ones who are accumulating on their heads all the unpopularity of and disgust at the methods inspired by the Germans, by themselves, and by the necessities of war and occupation. It is with this baggage that they hope to win over public opinion when the war is over! They are preparing their own defeat.

---

24. Monsieur Homais: a pretentious bourgeois in Flaubert's novel *Madame Bovary*. [TF]

Fourteen

"Coup de Théâtre":
A Turning Point
in the War

24 OCTOBER–13 DECEMBER 1942

Charles Rist was able to draw back occasionally from the pain and horror of the moment to see the war as part of something larger – "the second act of a drama in which the war of 1914–1918 was only the exposition" (17 January 1943). For him, the good news coming from North Africa in November 1942 constituted a coup de théâtre.

SATURDAY, 24 OCTOBER 1942 The English have taken the offensive in Egypt, while the Germans have resumed their attacks on Stalingrad with new urgency, but apparently without success. Bombing of Genoa.

We are at a phase in which the drama has intensified and become more focused. The battle in Egypt has resumed, and preparations are under way for Casablanca and Dakar. What orders has Darlan given to those in charge there? With what forces will the Americans land? Will there be a useless shedding of French blood and supreme shame for France? What is happening meanwhile in Germany? What will Hitler demand of the French government? Will he want to back it up with German troops? If the Allies are victorious, what turmoil will result in Germany? And not long afterward, what turmoil in France? How can one not foresee a dreadful clash between an exasperated French people and a French government that has failed in all of its plans and is supported solely by the police? Only the French Revolution offers a similar spectacle of unleashed passions. And if the Allies fail in their undertakings or just do not manage to advance, how long can the appalling current situation remain stable?

The dramas are multiplying. Mme Picabia is in the free zone.[1] In her absence, her daughter and son-in-law have just been arrested. In view of her

---

1. The wife of the famous painter Francis Picabia lived in Versailles.

son-in-law's service during the last war he is being released, but on condition that he bring back his mother-in-law. He has been promised that his wife will be released when his mother-in-law has returned to her place in Fresnes. But is it certain that his wife will be released? Will there not be two prisoners instead of one?

Poor Bourowsky, whom I got transferred to the hospital last year after his arrest, has been sent to Poland. His panic-stricken parents have had no more news of him for a month. The Drancy doctor confirmed his departure to me yesterday. What can one say to his unhappy parents?

Doctor Veslot tells us that a woman just watched her second child die at the hospital. Her husband is in a concentration camp. It was arranged that he could come say good-bye to his child's corpse. He arrived accompanied by two gendarmes. The doctor says *every day* a call goes out for some of his colleagues. He watches them leave. He knows they will be shot. He awaits his turn. The gendarmes confirm his story.

A German told Mettetal: "Culturally, we have lost the war. We are nothing but armed thugs."

FRIDAY, 30 OCTOBER 1942 I have accepted Cangardel's proposition to serve on the board of Air France Transatlantique. This will be a means, after the war, to keep up or renew my contacts with the United States. There is an enterprise that can do us honor. They also intend to ask André Siegfried to serve or, if he cannot, Laboulaye.

During the conversation, Cangardel told me they now have only one ship at their disposal, the *De Grasse* – all the others have either been lost or taken by the English.

All kinds of rumors are circulating about Anglo-American intentions. Some say the Americans will move directly from Equatorial Africa to Chad, and from there to the rear of Rommel's army, passing through the oasis of Koufra, which is already occupied by the French. This is the hypothesis that seems least extravagant to me.

Morgan Bank's Pesson-Didion begged me to see him on Tuesday. The Germans want him to entrust them with hundreds of millions in deposits. Of course he refused. He asked me if he should break off relations, or go away, or liquidate his bank. I told him he is covered by the fact of war, since his German commissioner has full powers. He replied that what is good enough for France is not so for the United States, which expects you to be a "martyr." I advised him to stand up to his commissioner and that the latter, whose name is Caesar, would eventually give in.

The curious thing is that at this point the Germans, rather than demand an increase in France's daily indemnity, prefer to take the money from American and English banks. Their expenses in France are over 300 million a day. They are rapidly emptying the reserves they had built up at the bank, and even that is not enough! What are they doing with this money? Fortifications, apparently. In any case, they are several billion in the red in every country – and intend to quit while they're ahead. In all neutral clearing agreements, they owe money.

MONDAY, 2 NOVEMBER 1942 I have often observed that the collaborating reactionaries to whom one cites the example of Prussia, defeated in one week in 1806, crushed by Napoleon and back on its feet seven years later in 1813, profess to be particularly offended by this. "There is no comparison," they will say, "between that case and France's." For these gentlemen, everything that does not show France to be a definitively sick country requiring a *prolonged* reactionary cure is extremely disagreeable.

On Saturday, at lunch with Maxime Leroy, we were wondering how far back preparations for the marshal's coup d'état went. Someone who seemed well informed indicated the years 1934 and 1937 as the time when Alibert and the marshal got together. It was also stated that Laval, told of these talks, finagled his way in so that by 1940 the trio was all set to take advantage of events. Knowing this, the tremulous emotion of Pétain's first speech, in which he made the "gift of his person" to France, is all the more repugnant.

The genius of Tolstoy's *War and Peace* shines even brighter in the light of current events. He highlights the fact that popular patriotism is somehow superior to the calculations of the cleverest strategists. Barclay de Tolly, a German,[2] does not understand that once the struggle has been transported to Russian soil, the resistance of the Russian people takes on new strength. The same is true of this war. People like Pétain and Weygand, completely isolated by their political opinions from popular sentiment, did not believe the country would resist. Already during the last war the American Leffingwell said to me, "The sole reproach I have for your statesmen is their lack of faith in your people's readiness for sacrifice."

And what can one say of the prodigious resistance of the Russians? Each morning the radio announces, "Stalingrad is still holding out." It will soon be three months since the attack began.

2. Prince Barclay de Tolly, a German-speaking Russian field marshal during Napoleon's 1812 invasion of Russia, is included as a character in Tolstoy's novel. [TF]

A week ago I received a card from Jean saying he is having problems with Joseph Barthélemy's people for having aided some foreign Jews to escape the great roundup. I hope the poor boy does not have to suffer for his generosity. He told me he had written to Barthélemy. I have had a ticket purchased so that I can return to Vichy. We will doubtless have details from Noël, who is coming back from Switzerland today and has passed through Saint-Étienne.

TUESDAY, 10 NOVEMBER 1942 Left on Wednesday morning, 4 November, to see Jean and together decide what must be done to extricate him from the fix he is in. On the train I read *Journal de la France, 1939–1940*, a curious book by Fabre-Luce that is completely oblivious to events and basic patriotic feelings. His predictions of the future, so prodigiously belied by today's events, disqualify him as a writer. Noël was waiting for me at the station in Saint-Étienne and took me to see the good family of Charles Trocmé in their new home.[3] On Thursday morning at breakfast he shared with us the latest radio news: the German and Italian troops in Egypt have taken a beating and are on the run. We all sensed that this marked a turning point in the war. Noël briefly brought me up to date on Jean's affair.

I called Potut, the prefect for the Loire. A former student of mine, he received me quite amicably and offered to go with me by car the next day to Vichy – or to have a seat reserved for me. I spoke to him of Jean, to whom he could be of service if the need arose. Then I left for Fraisses.

At 2:00 PM the radio confirmed and completed the morning's good news. Jean, home from his factory at 6:00, told me all the details of his adventure, his arrest at Saint-Julien, his forty-eight hours in jail. He has shown a truly admirable courage and generosity. We agreed on what I would say to Joseph Barthélemy. The next morning he went with me to the train. He told me everyone at the factory was wearing a smile. Back in Vichy, I went to the

3. Charles Trocmé was the son of Charles Rist's sister Ève and Henri Trocmé. In addition to being first cousins, Charles Trocmé and Jean Rist were particularly close friends for having cohabited in Paris during their university years (1918–1921) at their uncle Édouard Rist's. In the course of their professional career Jean Rist (at the steelworks near Saint-Étienne,) and Charles Trocmé (at the Seyssel Sanatorium, near Vienne) lived only 60 kilometers apart and kept in close contact. During the war and the occupation years they were of like minds, making decisions that led them to change jobs and live even closer to each other. Charles Trocmé, dismissed from his sanatorium for employing Spanish republicans and Jewish refugees, made the first move and in 1942 established a private medical practice in Saint-Etienne. Hence Charles Rist's mention of "the good family of Charles Trocmé in their new home." Charles Trocmé and Jean Rist from then on combined their efforts to protect and assist Jewish individuals and families. Email from André Rist, 13 September 2010. [TF]

American embassy around 5:00 PM. Tuck and I had a long talk. He seemed rather distracted and preoccupied. At 6:00 he had me listen to the radio, along with the embassy staff. We were all there, our hearts full of hope. But I had no inkling of the *coup de théâtre* I was about to witness.

On Saturday morning I went to the Swiss legation. In Stucki's absence, the first secretary immediately put me in contact with Bousquet[4] regarding Jean's two protégés, who had been given Swiss visas. Immediately received by Bousquet, who promised to give Rivesaltes the order to free them.

Next I went to Joseph Barthélemy, who had Jean's file on his table and promised to do "everything possible." He said the marshal had told Cardinal Gerlier, "You're helping me." He also told me that the government has forced *Le Temps* to publish articles by a certain Boissy demonstrating that American industrial power is a myth![5]

Reuter arrived in the afternoon.[6] We only talked about events in Egypt. At 6:30 I went to have tea at Behiç Erkin's. I have never seen him so happy and animated. He recited to me the most important bits of President Ismet İnönü's speech, especially his declaration that small nations must be allowed to exist and that no hegemony is possible in Europe. He agreed with me that Italy would be the great victim of the war. He foresaw imminent consequences of Rommel's defeat and arranged to meet me soon in Paris, where he already imagines himself to be and where he says he will pay back the visits I have made to him in Vichy. During the course of the conversation, in response to a question I put to him, he said that in Turkey no more than elsewhere did people have any idea of the strength of Russian arms.

On Sunday at 7:30 in the morning Planque rushed into my room with his radio and announced the landing of the Americans in Algeria and Morocco! We listened to Roosevelt and Eisenhower's proclamation. After lunch we took a stroll through the park along the Allier River. Already police and riot squads were everywhere. This is Vichy's normal reaction. At 11:00 AM I met with Tuck. He told me about his interview with the marshal – the handing over of Roosevelt's proclamation, of which the marshal already had the translation, then the marshal's declaration that he was obliged to give North Africa the order to defend itself. And Tuck added: "But this is for you *alone*:

4. Under Laval's interior ministry, René Bousquet was general secretary for police (April 1942–December 1943), playing an important role in Vichy's collaboration with Germany. [JNJ/TF]

5. Cardinal Gerlier was honored by Yad Vashem as "Righteous among the Nations" for his efforts to save Jews during the war. *Le Temps* was France's major newspaper under the republic; it ceased publication at the end of November 1942. [TF]

6. Paul Reuter: professor at the Law Faculty in Aix-en-Provence.

after his official words, the marshal took both my hands, wished me bon voyage, and began humming a song with a satisfied air."

I caught the two o'clock train and arrived back in Paris at ten.

Naturally, everyone is focused on the big news. But on the train people looked at one another without daring to speak. Arrived at Noël's at 10:30. We talked until midnight.

WEDNESDAY, 11 NOVEMBER 1942 Announcements of the fall of Algerian and Moroccan defenses are coming in quick succession. Darlan's role is mysterious. Did he go to aid the defense? Does he want to associate Vichy with it? And Giraud? We learn he has left for Algeria. Is this a sign of dissidence, or will he remain tied to Vichy?

This morning news came that the Germans are going to occupy the free zone! A double proclamation by Hitler. He has offered to have the government come to Versailles! Hitler is demanding the aid of the French army!

Just now a phone call informed us that Marie rejoined Noël last night. We were afraid that events might have stopped or delayed her.

Leaflets with Roosevelt's proclamation to the people of France are being dropped from airplanes. I picked up four of them in the potato patch in my yard.

The question is no longer *if* the Germans will be defeated, but *how*. The Mediterranean problem seems to have been resolved in favor of the Allies. What can the Germans do to save Rommel? Nothing. The American occupation of Tunis means control over the passage between the two sides of the Mediterranean as well as the possibility of attacking the Italians on their own soil and supporting the Balkan States. But then? One sees only the systematic aerial bombing of German cities. The only other hypothesis would be a general retreat of the German armies from Russia. But that possibility is terribly far off.

THURSDAY, 12 NOVEMBER 1942 Today and yesterday, all sorts of grave news. The Germans have crossed the Demarcation Line and occupied our borders. Pétain has solemnly protested this violation of the armistice. But Darlan is in Algiers. It is on his orders that we had a cease-fire. What role is he playing? His constant concern has been to prevent "dissidence," which is much more important to these wretches than defending France. This morning they say he has given the troops orders to maintain the strictest neutrality.

Meanwhile the Germans are landing troops in Tunis, where British and American forces are also heading in a hurry. Who will move the quickest?

Marie returned to Paris yesterday, or rather the night before last – just in time, for we learned this morning that the Germans have closed the Swiss border. She and Noël came to see us last night. We shared our hypotheses, our hopes, our fears. It is now up to France to show whether she still wants to fight. Are we to witness the shameful spectacle of the army and navy continuing to keep the country in the state of lethargy into which they have plunged it in order to assure their political ascendancy in the future? Imbecilic and puerile calculations.

FRIDAY, 13 NOVEMBER 1942 Here we are again, waiting anxiously.... But for the first time since the war begin, we are not expecting catastrophes, but rather are impatient for good news. There is a race between the Americans and the Axis to see who reaches Tunis and Bizerte first. What will Admiral Esteva do?

I suspect that there are conflicts among the generals and admirals in Algiers. Darlan? De Gaulle? Giraud? Who will take charge? Will there be a new rebellion? Will we see Algeria under one government, Equatorial Africa under another? Clearly Darlan is out to save his skin and his future. According to an announcement today, he suggested that the fleet in Toulon head out to sea. (?)These people should unite as quickly as possible.

Except for English radio, no one is speaking to France. Radio Vichy is keeping quiet and is in the hands of the Germans. There has been no response by the government to Hitler's appalling proclamation. It is urgent that someone be communicating regularly with France from Algiers.

SATURDAY, 14 NOVEMBER 1942 On the radio the marshal has condemned General Giraud as a traitor to his word and to his country! A proclamation no doubt ordered by Laval, who imagines he can, with the marshal's authority, set the French against Giraud. Just another example of those psychological errors that only this wretch, whose every reaction is anti-French, is capable of committing. As if from this day forward every French person were not saluting the name of Giraud with a frisson of hope.

Yesterday read the second volume of Fabre-Luce's *Journal de la France*, which goes up to April 1942. In it he reveals that Laval, as far back as September 1940, wanted to set out for the Gaullist colonies to reconquer them with Germany's help! This would have been the origin of the conflict with Pétain and was the "policy of Montoire"![7] So on the pretext of the empire's unity, this man was leading us straight into conflict with England and into military alliance with Germany. This man was ready to have France fight against

7. A meeting at Montoire-sur-le-Loir between Laval and Hitler (22 October 1940) was followed two days later by one between Hitler and Pétain, signaling the beginning of formal collaboration. [TF]

itself and against England. The shame and the insanity of this policy could only have been fathered by this wretch. Today the *event* that, according to Thiers, "is the judge of public men" shows the sinister imbecility of this man who, with astonishing consistency, is in all places and all cases wrong. But failing victory over England, he will try to defend himself and find a way to take over France. Except French patriotic feeling at this juncture is too wide awake, the opposition of the entire country, too strong. The wretch will be swept away. But when and after what upheavals?

As for Fabre-Luce himself, this spoiled child's lack of any French sentiment is equally typical. His overly honed political intelligence, his refinement of all feelings, his allegiance to the new Europe at the expense of France and of her honor – all of these attest to political rancor and a misunderstanding of his own nation. This overly refined dabbler is as much a failure as those Bernanos denounced. Fabre-Luce passed through all the parties. His adhesion to Doriot came about after his rejection by the voters of Touraine in the elections of 1938, in spite of the book in which he proclaimed the Radical-Socialist Party as the true representative of French opinion. That book no longer appears on the list of his publications.

How Fabre-Luce must be sulking today, faced with the defeat of Rommel and the American occupation of North Africa, as he rereads the last pages of his book. For these people lacking all conviction, with no ambition except to be on the latest bandwagon, it is a supreme humiliation when they realize that they have made a mistake!

SUNDAY, 15 NOVEMBER 1942 Mario, back from Vannes, where he went looking for potatoes for Ugine, told us of the following incident. The German troops left Brittany in a kind of panic in order to rush toward the south and occupy the Côte d'Azur. A young soldier (very young) stayed behind in a village, but the departure was so hurried he was not left any food. The poor boy asked everywhere for bread. But people jeered at him. One said, "Go look for bread in Egypt"; another, "Go look for some in Moscow"; another, "Go look for some in Algeria." Finally the unhappy fellow, exhausted, sat down on a boundary stone in front of an inn, crying from hunger. The woman who runs the inn, taking pity on him, ended up giving him food. And he, grateful, found nothing to say but "Us, fucked." Obviously, nothing could have pleased his hostess more.

Just now at 10:30, we heard on the radio the bells that Churchill had ringing in England this Sunday in honor of the victory in Egypt. Germaine and I were both quite moved. I thought of René Parodi strangled in his cell for having wished to hasten this day. The bells had not rung in England for two years except to warn of air raids.

I cannot manage to work these days. How can one concentrate one's thoughts on the history of economic doctrines when our whole future hangs upon the outcome of military actions? One wonders anxiously if the Allies' victories are lasting, if the German High Command will not have some devastating response. Optimism prevails, however. The dispatch of troops to the south is a proof of nervousness. The Allies are not threatening Marseille. It is Italy that is the target. And the more widespread the occupation, the more patriotic feeling will spread throughout France. Already Vichy no longer matters, and Laval is dragging the marshal down with him.

FRIDAY, 20 NOVEMBER 1942 Very little is known about operations in Tunisia except that the Germans are making a big effort there and, no doubt, occupying Bizerte and Tunis. What is the attitude of the French troops? Have they all gone over to Giraud? Roosevelt has declared that the arrangement with Darlan was just temporary. French radio from London says nothing about the Darlan-Giraud-de Gaulle controversies. The German papers in France are making fun of these conflicts "among traitors." Yesterday Beltrand, the engraver, spoke to me indignantly of the generals who have gone back on their word. It is Giraud he is talking about. Well, precisely, Giraud has always refused to give his word. But Beltrand is just a specific case of the blindness of some Frenchmen. Besides, he is a royalist and mildly mystical. He said, "I have a horror of the Germans, but I detest the English and the Americans." One would like to ask him, "Anything else, Monsieur?" The most disparate rumors are making the rounds. The one about the death of Doriot (killed in a fight) keeps resurfacing.

Regarding the Toulon fleet, we are in the dark. Some think it went to sea and was destroyed by the English. Others believe Laborde (the admiral) declared he would fire on any German who penetrated the harbor of Toulon, which is why the Germans have left the port alone. This appears the most likely hypothesis. Meanwhile, decrees giving full powers to Laval were published yesterday. He alone will sign laws and decrees from now on. Is it the marshal who wanted to distance himself from a policy he disapproves of and thus lessen his responsibility? Is it Laval who pushed him into a corner like a piece of old furniture? We do not know. But one wonders what new power Laval can require, since he already has all he needs, and the police forces are at his beck and call.

Rumors are also spreading of a French mobilization on behalf of Germany and of a peace treaty (?) with the latter. A ridiculous story but one that shows people believe Laval is capable of anything. In reality Vichy has ceased to exist for most French people. Since Algeria has been freed from the enemy's grip and one foresees the liberation of the Mediterranean and the collapse of Italy – already bombed at Genoa and Turin and soon to find itself at the mercy of North African and Maltese airfields – everyone senses that this is where the fate of France is being decided. In the light of this great event, the intrigues of Vichy to maintain its prestige no longer matter. An announcement this morning of a Russian victory at Nalchik: securing the oil fields of Grozny. The day before yesterday a great American naval victory against the Japanese was reported, definitively freeing the Solomon Islands. News is that a great number of Foreign Affairs staff (they say some thirty) have resigned. This is heading in the right direction.

A week's curfew has been imposed on Versailles. Everyone must be home by eight PM. It seems a German officer was killed by one of his comrades over a woman. It is we who drink to that.

Moreau tells me he received two letters from the Comte de Paris telling him about his stay in Vichy. He was treated like a prisoner, constantly escorted by two policemen. Moreau advised him to enlist in the American army.

A curious state of mind among our sailors: a naval officer, the son of Mme B.[8] (an ardent patriot), came to see his mother a few weeks ago. "Salvation can only come from an American landing in North Africa," he told her. "We all know it and we want it. But we also know that we'll be given the order to fire on these saviors and we'll do it." (Recounted to Germaine by Mme B. herself).

SATURDAY, 21 NOVEMBER 1942 Last night once again (it is the third or fourth time this week) we heard antiaircraft guns firing on English planes as they headed toward Italy. The guns first go off around eight PM, then again when the planes return after midnight. Hearing them fills us with joy.

Last night and this morning, Laval's appeal to the French. He says he wants to unite France with Germany because he believes the latter is going to win the war, but he would not change his mind even if Germany were going to lose! (*Quos vult perder, Jupiter dementat.*[9]) He adds that he is going to form a legion to help Germany defend itself!! A proclamation by the marshal telling the French that they need only "obey"! The poor man is talking like a corporal to his men. The French are quite determined not to "obey" a man who derives his authority only from himself and his perfidy.

---

8. Not identified.

9. *Quem Jupiter vult perdere, dementat prius*: "Whom Jupiter would destroy, he first drives mad." [TF]

MONDAY, 23 NOVEMBER 1942 Yesterday went to Vésinet to see Françoise, whose sister Hélène died in Clermont-Ferrand.[10] The impossibility of communicating in these times of family mourning adds to the sadness. Claude and she complained of the difficulty of feeding our granddaughters, who are looking jaundiced and thin. Marie-Claire is having health problems caused by the lack of fat and meat. They also have little heat. Pretty drawings by Isabelle.

Airplanes overhead tonight around 8:00 PM and again at two in the morning. More antiaircraft thunder. It is the English planes going to Italy and returning.[11]

The Russians have resumed the offensive in the Caucasus and near Stalingrad. They have announced great victories.

An English cabinet shuffle. Stafford Cripps is turning over leadership in the House of Commons to Eden and leaving the war cabinet to take over airplane production – a purely administrative responsibility. What is behind this business? Disagreement with Churchill? Another question we will not learn the answer to. Stafford Cripps is a proud and irritating utopian idealist who hardly inspires confidence.

TUESDAY, 24 NOVEMBER 1942 Last night on the radio, *coup de théâtre*. Governor Boisson, along with Dakar and the entire federation of French West Africa, has gone over to the Allies! He is teaming up, not with de Gaulle, but with Darlan. But the military result is the same: landing facilities, extra help from the troops in Dakar, etc. The effect on morale will be equally huge. This morning there was not a word about this on Vichy radio. Laval is being gradually abandoned by everyone. Today's results could have been attained much earlier, we could have avoided all the threats against Egypt and long since have conquered Italian Africa if in June 1940 the French government had moved to Algeria. We see clearly today all that the cowardice of Pétain, Weygand, etc. lost for us. But they were obsessed with profiting from the defeat to make their "National Revolution."

This error was preceded by an even worse one: the refusal to ally with Russia in 1939. That error was committed especially by Chamberlain. The alliance dictated by circumstance of England, Russia, France, and America will come to pass. But it could have been realized three years earlier and per-

10. Hélène Lagache. According to Françoise's daughter Antoinette, she died of undiagnosed diphtheria. [JNJ/TF]

11. Rist added a note here, saying, "We later learned they were headed to Stuttgart." [TF]

haps war would have been avoided. The appalling danger had to become clear to everyone before they could decide. And "everyone" was mentally obtuse.

Napoleon said to Talleyrand, "You are nothing but shit in a silk stocking." One might equally say to the false Talleyrand of Châteldon, "You are nothing but shit wearing a white tie."[12]

Weygand has been arrested by the Germans and taken to Germany. He was leaving Vichy, where the marshal had summoned him!

FRIDAY, 27 NOVEMBER 1942 As I was about to board a second-class car on the train to Versailles, an "anti-Bolshevik legionnaire" in a French uniform tried to get on ahead of me. The conductor came by and pointed out that soldiers travel in third class. The legionnaire showed his card and said, "German soldier." The intimidated conductor let him have his way. Thus a wretch in a French uniform flaunts his status as a "German soldier." Such is the shame that Laval's policies have wrought.

Yesterday lunch at the Suez Company. We had not met for two months. I was curious to note reactions to the latest developments. Everyone was rejoicing except for two people. One was the president, who was certain that the Americans would give Tunis to the Italians. He said, "In six months the Germans will be in Egypt. The English are incompetents." He was exasperated by Roosevelt's having intervened to restore the Crémieux Decree[13] for the Jews of Algeria and to liberate imprisoned Gaullists. The other exception was Lesseps.

One of our colleagues living in Brittany told me that already in some places lists of "collaborators" have been posted to expose them to public condemnation. Naturally, these lists contain many errors. A foretaste of the formidable tidal wave that will wash over this poor country when our land is liberated.

The radio of "fighting France" has gone silent in London. Explanations have been demanded of Eden in the House of Commons. Eden replied that the English government had asked for General de Gaulle's silence for a while in order not to endanger the military operations under way. But he added that the English government was keeping the promises already made to de Gaulle. The English continue to mistrust Darlan, whose attitude toward them is known.

12. Châteldon: where Pierre Laval was born. [TF]

13. Adolphe Crémieux granted full citizenship for Jews in French-ruled Algeria through the 1870 *Décret Crémieux*. [TF]

For some days all eyes have once again been turned toward Stalingrad and toward the new Russian offensive between the Don and the Volga, which has just driven the German and Romanian troops from the field. Several tens of thousands of prisoners. The liberation of Stalingrad would be the most formidable blow so far against the prestige of the Führer, who promised to take the city two months ago. Simultaneously, the Germans have been repulsed at Nalchick and barred from the oil fields at Grozny for a long time. If the Germans were deprived of the Romanian oil wells without having been able to seize the Russian ones, the war might be over sooner than expected. The Turks could accomplish this. Will they decide to do it? That is the great question mark.

A little while ago the radio announced one hundred thousand Germans and Romanians killed or taken prisoner since the beginning of the offensive between the Don and the Volga. German communiqués are becoming increasingly muddled, carefully hiding the facts from the public.

The papers have yet to utter a word about French West Africa joining Darlan's rebellion. (For we continue to have several rebellions, of which the papers make much ado. This replaces the absent German victories in their columns.) But all French people know what is going on. What we do not know is to what extent the French troops are participating in North African operations. If we continue to abstain and do not join the Americans, our role at the peace conference will be minimal, and our moral situation after the war, unbearable.

A letter from Jean telling me that the friends for whom he took risks have in fact been freed.

SATURDAY, 28 NOVEMBER 1942 Jean's birthday, he is forty-two!

Last night we were shocked by news that the fleet in Toulon has been scuttled to keep the Germans (once again violating the armistice) from getting their hands on it. An act of magnificent and tragic heroism that will trouble the souls of all Frenchmen but will help to unite the country. It proves that the navy has at last understood in which direction the enemy lies; it will encourage the fleet at Alexandria; it demonstrates the weakness of Germany, which suddenly decided to use those ships to restore the situation in the Mediterranean; it shows all Frenchmen their duty; and it definitively shames the sordid wretch whose policies have led us to such results when a timely order to put out to sea could have saved the fleet. This act has been hailed by English and American papers as a great victory. But how different this victory could have been, how much more effective and still more glorious.

News has come this morning that Germany is demanding the disarmament of the entire French army. The officers who were not collaborators will be investigated! We are now completely in the hands of the enemy and of our own traitors. We still do not know the number of victims. The survivors will be imprisoned. I phoned Édouard to find out where his son Bernard was. He does not seem worried!

Last night Françoise called to tell us of her aunt's arrest. This sixty-five-year-old woman has been transported to Drancy. Françoise is quite worried. This morning she called again to say they had succeeded in having her aunt put in Drancy's infirmary. No one knows why she was arrested . . . (probably yellow star . . .). Three days later we learned that she was freed thanks to the energetic intervention of her husband, old M. Eyrolles. This eighty-year-old stood up to the *Sturmführer*, who called in one of his subordinates and said to him, "Take a look at an eighty-year-old Frenchman" (Eyrolles himself told this story).

SUNDAY, 29 NOVEMBER 1942   I am rereading Quinet. Better than any other, this man understood the French reactionary party. He plumbed the depths of their stupidity, rancor, and incomprehension. And he asked the overriding question to which one must always return: is a change of religion not required to assure a free system of government in France? In effect, the Revolution committed France to a new religion, as Bourde saw so well. But that religion (in which the majority of French people, deep down, believe) is officially neither expressed nor preached. It regains its vigor only in great crises but is constantly under threat. For its formulas are essentially political; its grip on the soul fluctuates along with political vicissitudes. And a part of the nation is always prepared to destroy it, whereas in England, in the United States, in Switzerland, and in Holland there are common principles born of the Reformation that constitute a common ground for all parties and to which even the most conservative are attached, setting limits to any reaction. Such a community of fundamental principles does not exist in France, with the result that there is no limit to the excesses of parties on both sides. Civil war is possible at any moment.

In *L'Enseignement du peuple*, a book written by Quinet in 1849, one reads on page 5 these profound lines:

> Where religious revolution precedes political revolution, there are certain moral victories that no one dreams of undoing. (This is the case of England, the United States, etc.) By contrast, everywhere that political revolution was accomplished without any modification of the national religion, you find, simultaneously, incredible progress and even more incredible reverses. In the calmest of times you

discover that beneath the most liberal government the former absolute government persists. You cannot say of any reform, even the most insignificant, that it is irrevocable. . . . I know of states like this in which one spends the day wondering if one will be governed that night by Babeuf or by Gregory VII.

All this was true of France from 1930 to 1940.

But Quinet did not believe in a new "religious revolution" in the old sense of the term, and he was right:

Why? He (the Frenchman) does not need it anymore. Each person has won the right to an inner vote in the city of divinity. What good then are riots in the infinite? . . . This is why no movement will come about among them to replace an old clergy with a new one. (180)

But how, then, can respect for the idea of freedom and the ways of liberty, respect for the person and for human dignity, be maintained in France? Schooling is not enough if the family is pushing in the opposite direction. In fact, however, in most families of the "people," school and family, more or less unconsciously, follow the same principles and the same beliefs, not with regard to dogma, but to life. Their indignation is the same when faced with certain examples of cowardice or injustice; likewise with their hatred of lies. And it must not be forgotten that seventy years of the Republic and freedom have caused this country to acquire new habits.

It is the bourgeoisie – and only a part of it – that forms the opposition and is ready to go back on all the freedoms that have been won in order to be socially secure. But after all, is this true only in France? Do we not see in Switzerland, in England, in the United States a similar reaction? The answer is, "No, not in the same measure, nor with the same fanaticism as in France." Even when those countries are most oppressive toward the lower classes, they never dream of suppressing freedom itself. In France it is the opposite. It is through the prior suppression of freedom in all areas that one hopes to achieve security.

I believe therefore that a religious reform is necessary in this country in order to safeguard freedom – but a reform in which the State would not be involved, a reform that would arise spontaneously from the grass roots and would, for example, reflect the thinking of Loisy as expressed in his book on religion,[14] a reform that would sanction this gradual transformation of Christianity into a human religion (I am not saying into a religion of humanity) toward which three centuries of history have led us.

14. Alfred de Loisy, *La Religion* (Paris: Nourry, 1917).

MONDAY, 30 NOVEMBER 1942 Last night a speech by Churchill at 9:00 PM. Short, serious. He talked about the results obtained over the course of this eventful month. He also observed that nothing permits him to believe that "the war will thereby be shortened." He urged England to continue its efforts, which must not let up. Clearly, at a time when American radio speaks insistently of a "turning point" in the war, he wants to warn against premature optimism. He foresees the case in which the European war would be over but the Asiatic war would still be going on. He almost seems to desire this in order to maintain the necessary cohesion among the Allies at the peace conference rather than letting them break up as they did at Versailles. Threats made against Italy, which, believing England's defeat a foregone conclusion, thought it could betray both France and the United Kingdom. All Italy's misfortunes are owing to the will of a single man.

SATURDAY, 5 DECEMBER 1942 Last night we learned of the arrest and imprisonment of Herriot, Jouhaux, and François de Tessan. We had learned shortly before that Reynaud and Mandel were handed over to the Germans. The government continues to obey the orders of Germany, and the latter continues its pursuit of vengeance, in line with Hitlerian methods. Arrests are taking place everywhere. Never before have we fallen to this degree of powerlessness. But neither has unanimity of feeling ever shown itself to the same degree. The sabotage in Toulon crystallized French sentiment into irreducible opposition to the enemy. In all milieux the talk one hears is unanimous. Everyone is counting on the Americans and the English. The blatant collapse and the uselessness of Laval's policy is there for all to see. I do not hear anyone defending him now. People view him as Germany's agent. And the impotent marshal's prestige has vanished.

These past few days rumors have been flying that Laval was forming a new cabinet with Doriot and Déat. But we have heard this so often it is hard to believe.

The new Russian offensive between Rzhev and Velikiye Luki – that is to say, at a point where a break in the German front would oblige Germany to retreat – is creating new hope. The Germans' own communiqués are even more encouraging. They systematically falsify all news to attenuate its seriousness or to have people believe, despite all, in their success. They no longer bother to disguise their anxiety and rage.

Speech by Mussolini responding to Churchill. More ridiculous than odious.

Noël and Marie, who went to La Bouffource at the beginning of the week, have brought back provisions for everyone! Butter – even cream – and a chicken! The potatoes requested for weeks have finally arrived! Great relief for the coming months.

SUNDAY, 13 DECEMBER 1942 The means of transportation have returned to a primitive state. Outside the cafés and train stations one finds bicycles to which little two-seater carts are hitched. They call them "taxis." Their price makes them prohibitive except for those who are very fortunate or very tired. The cyclists are like the "coolies" of India or China – or the ancient bearers of sedan chairs. Man has reverted to being a beast of burden for man. Those who own bicycles in any case are fortunate. A small cart mounted on rubber wheels and attached to the bicycle also allows the cyclists to transport packages or provisions. As gentlemen and ladies today do their own shopping, this is a precious aid for those still young enough to pedal. Some automobiles are provided with huge steel containers shaped like elongated bombshells for storing gasoline. Others are equipped with large tanks for converting charcoal to gasoline. But these vehicles are reserved for the transport of goods. Private cars with an S.P. seal[15] are rare. In these December days, despite the general penury, people want to do some shopping for Christmas or New Year's in the empty stores. The trains from the suburbs and the subway are jam-packed, and most people have to stand, crushed against one another even more than usual.

L. R.,[16] having returned from the free zone, says Herriot is not in prison but in a closely supervised private detention. The police came to take him, along with Mme Herriot, at four in the morning.

Numerous arrests on all sides: the brother-in-law of P. D.[17] and the daughter-in-law of Hottinger. No one knows why.

15. According to André Rist, the initials S.P. stood for "Syngas [Synthetic Gas] Production" in German. The Germans, who had no oil on their territory but who had plenty of coal and were expert chemists, became leaders in the chemical combustion of coal. [TF]

16. Not identified.

17. Possibly Rist was referring to Maurice Pesson-Didion.

Fifteen

Internal Gangrene

16 DECEMBER 1942–6 FEBRUARY 1943

Rist's diary reflects the rollercoaster of emotions experienced by the French as they awaited the war's end. In December 1942 Rist describes his visit to Lucien Romier, who is suffering from "internal gangrene." Romier's condition, coupled with his explanation of why he stayed at Pétain's side so long, seems from Rist's viewpoint emblematic of France as a country that was rotting away internally. But in January 1943 the news coming from Russia was exhilarating, "as if the whole world were feeling the first stirrings of deliverance."

WEDNESDAY, 16 DECEMBER 1942 Yesterday went to see Romier, who had phoned to ask if I could stop by. He is prostrate, his face ravaged, having just come out of a three-week stay in a clinic – for "internal gangrene" (?). He is no more than a shadow of his former self. He said to me: "By staying, I can still save some people. I have saved ten or so from the firing squad. This regime of army officers" – did he mean the Germans or the French? – "who have lost the war is appalling. But the marshal has begged me to stay. If I go, there's no one else. They make him write and publish letters that he hasn't even read." (He was referring to the marshal's response to Hitler, a monument of platitudes and abdication in which a marshal of France declared himself prepared to work with General de Rundstedt on organizing a French army!) "I wish he would go off in some corner and keep himself in reserve for later. Laval is a man who makes greatly persuasive speeches based on nothing. Laval says, 'I'll eventually be rewarded for lying.' What do you think of the situation?"

I answered that in my opinion the die has been cast, the triumph of the Allies is certain, and even the Italians will arrange to be on the right side before we do. He listened distractedly. His sole concern: should he stay in the cabinet? I told him not to. "Most of my friends are telling me to persevere," he said. I understood what he wanted of me and said, "Yes, if you can save some people, stay." He is a poor fellow with no willpower who started on an adventure without having considered the impact or the consequences and who, still today, is trying to create the illusion that his presence is justified. He asked, "Do you think the Allies will let us keep our colonies?"

"There's no question," I replied. "The English have just demonstrated that they can't even defend their own, so they're not going to add more." And I added: "You're lucky that Churchill and Roosevelt are *personal friends* of France; it is they and it is that which will save us at the peace conference." He thanked me, held out his hand, and I left.

FRIDAY, 18 DECEMBER 1942 Jean came yesterday for two days, responding to our alarm over Claude's health. He told me the story he had already recited about the prewar reactionary plot. Alibert had told the story to V.[1] with astonishing insouciance. Jean got it directly from V. In agreement with the C.S.A.R. and financed by the Synarchists at the Banque Worms, Alibert was preparing a coup. There was an understanding with Hitler that he would intervene at the appropriate time to assure the success of the affair and, acting as an arbiter, would impose his conditions. When the war broke out, the conspirators continued to count on Hitler. They pushed for the armistice, believing that the desirable terms previously agreed to by Hitler would thus be introduced all the sooner. They quickly discovered that Hitler did not give a damn about the Synarchists but set draconian conditions for France. Great astonishment on the part of these gentlemen. Indignation. Return of patriotism (!), but too late. Meanwhile Laval played his hand, believing that if he threw himself at Hitler's feet, his personal charm would seduce the ogre. Hence the inevitable conflict between the Synarchists and Laval, and 13 December.[2] Meanwhile, they assassinated Marx Dormoy, who, as Blum's interior minister, knew about the whole plot and had to be got rid of.[3]

Having listened to this dark history of treason, imbecility, and reactionary fanaticism, V. said to Alibert: "Do you know the name for what you've

1. Rist is probably referring to Vergniaud, president of Jacob Holtzer Steelworks, where Jean Rist worked as an engineer. At the end of the war the version of this story of treason related in Jean Rist's own diary was offered in evidence at Pétain's trial by Alexandre Parodi, Jean Rist's friend. [TF]

2. The thirteenth of December 1940 was the date on which Pétain dismissed Laval as his vice-premier. [TF]

3. On 26 July 1941, Dormoy was killed by a bomb placed in his house by Cagoule terrorists. [TF]

done? It's called treason." And he received this stupefying answer: "But after 1870 didn't the republicans profit from the situation to take power?" V. had no trouble pointing out that (1) the republicans had not conspired with the enemy before the war, and (2) after 4 September they headed up the defense.

There is still worse. It appears that if the Sedan army gave up on 10 May, it is because its commander, Huntziger, was in on the plot. And thus is explained the military's general cry after the first defeats: "The communist teachers are to blame!" The same old alibi.

What role did Pétain play in all that? Did he conspire himself, or did they simply tell him that he would be chief of state once the "revolution" was accomplished? Hard to say. What is clear is the role of the Comtesse de Portes (mistress of Le Roy Ladurie), who found the means to surround Reynaud with the very traitors who were to strangle him and bring about his downfall – B., B., and Co. Almost as preposterous as the story itself is the fact that the republican government was so paralyzed it could not defend itself against such a band of traitors: spineless men like Chautemps became accomplices to defeatism, and the "Popular Front" did not react against the military conspiracy.

"The truth can sometimes be implausible." It is under this sign that the entire history of these last fifteen years must be written, and not just in France but also in Germany (where no one believed Hitler would triumph), in England (where imbeciles like Chamberlain were courting Germany), and in the United States, where all the "right-thinking people" and the pacifists – except for Roosevelt, who decidedly rose above all those pygmies like a truly great man – believed they were protected from Germany, Japan, and the war.

SATURDAY, 19 DECEMBER 1942 Lunch yesterday with Hillaert, Béguin, Préault. All these fine men, good patriots, are overjoyed by events but are already worried that the "old regime" will raise its head! Always internal politics.

SUNDAY, 20 DECEMBER 1942 In Goethe's *Sprüche in Reimen* [Rhyming Proverbs] I find the following stanza, which will no doubt be often quoted in the future. It contains a condemnatory forewarning by one of Germany's greatest men of the current mad, fanatical undertaking.

EPIMENIDES ERWACHEN

(last stanza)
Verflucht sei wer nach falschem Rath
Mit überfrechem Muth

Das was der Corse-Franke that
Nun als ein Deutscher thut.
Er fühle spät, er fühle früh,
Es sei ein dauernd Recht;
Und geh es, trotz Gewalt und Müh,
Ihm und den seinen schlecht.[4]

The line "Es sei ein dauernd Recht" is magnificent; for all the petty realists who believe only in force, the appeal to eternal law by the great realist, the great believer in nature, must set their teeth on edge.

Announcement of a major Russian attack on the Don, south of Voronezh. A considerable stretch of the German front line appears to have been broken.

In Goethe's *Sprüche in Prosa*, part 6, I read this brief but bitter thought: *"Mit den Jahren steigern sich die Prüfungen."*[5]

SATURDAY, 26 DECEMBER 1942 Christmas party yesterday. All the grandchildren gathered around the tree. Isabelle and Antoinette put on a scene from *Le Bourgeois gentilhomme*. Only the Claudes were missing – and of course the Jeans. The radio brought us all the messages addressed by the Allied heads of state, George VI and Roosevelt, to the fighting troops and to their people. France said nothing. The marshal has nothing to say, and the wretch who is supposed to be in charge would only have words of treason. But in the messages to free people, the words are confident for the first time. The pope also addressed the world. He condemned totalitarians. He enumerated the essential elements of a civilized life and in first place: the establishment of regular courts and judgment according to laws. This is indeed the hallmark of civilized countries. France no longer possesses this foremost of the rights of man.

---

4. EPIMENIDES' AWAKENING
   (last stanza)
   Damned be he who, following bad advice,
   With daring insolence
   Now does as a German
   What the Franco-Corsican did.
   Let him realize soon, or let him realize late
   That an eternal law prevails;
   And that he and his will fail
   Despite their power and might. [TF]

5. "With the years grow the trials": one of Goethe's "Proverbs in Prose," taken from *Wilhelm Meisters Wanderjahre* [Wilhelm Meister's Journeyman Years]. [JNJ/TF]

The radio has brought news of Darlan's assassination in Algiers. By whom? Mystery. Today we heard that his assassin, sentenced by a court-martial, was shot. Personal vengeance? Political crime of a Doriotist? We will not know. But this changes nothing. The important thing is that French troops are continuing the fight.

In his speech the pope proclaimed the right to work. Goebbels, in his, agreed, and declared that the idea of the right to work originated with the National Socialists! When the Revolution of 1848 proclaimed this right, the French bourgeoisie was up in arms! Today the idea still frightens them. Poor French bourgeoisie, living in terror and afraid for their wallets. Fear makes people stupid and malicious. This war has shown that it also leads to treason.

SUNDAY, 27 DECEMBER 1942 Giraud has replaced Darlan as high commissioner for North Africa. He has announced his intention to consult with de Gaulle. Now we have, finally, the common defense of the empire. Which is what could and should have happened instead of the armistice. Why didn't it? Because the English and the Americans were not ready. Who knows if at this moment the Germans have not penetrated into North Africa via Spain? This is what Darlan affirmed. Responsibility for the disaster is shared so heavily by England that France cannot be condemned at the peace conference. What saved England in 1940? The sea. English courage came in only second place.

Great Russian victories in the loop of the Don. Their luck seems decidedly to be turning. Are we about to witness the German Poltava?[6] A great disaster there would necessitate a partial evacuation of the Balkans and undermine Italian loyalty. (?) All of this may be nearer than we think. But who yet dares to hope for happy surprises after all we have suffered?

MONDAY, 28 DECEMBER 1942 Decidedly, in this war I am seeing once again that my reactions are always those of the people. In the Dreyfus affair, I felt "people." During the previous war, I felt "people." After the war, confronted with the stupid nationalism of the *Chambre bleu horizon*[7] and Poincaré's boastful bluster, I felt "people." During the Stavisky affair and again on 6 February 1934, I felt "people." And now, during this new war, I again feel "people," and, like the people, I believe the military and the reactionaries have committed treason. It is the peasants and the workers in this

---

6. The question is a reference to the Russian victory over the Swedish Empire in 1709. [TF]

7. The *Chambre bleu horizon* ("sky-blue" chamber) was elected in 1919 and named for the color of French uniforms, the color of the political right. [TF]

country who have a proper sense of their national obligations and duties, of the honor and true glory of the nation; in momentous circumstances, they are the ones who truly represent the "national spirit" in contrast to the spirit of caste and party. Michelet, in his *Révolution*, was justified in wanting to erect a monument to that just and profound sense of what constitutes the grandeur of France in the world, and he chose the common people as the hero of his book. Those who do not understand such sentiments will never understand the power and profundity of the book. It portrays the common people with a truth and insight that no historian has ever attained and helps one understand what is still going on today in the depths of the national soul. Nothing false and artificial à la Barrès, but the exact reflection of the common sense and spontaneous generosity of the simplest and sincerest people of this country. They quickly perceive the barest hints of insincerity and cowardice on the part of those who govern.

SATURDAY, 2 JANUARY 1943 The Russians have announced the taking of Velikiye Luki, north of Smolensk, and of Elista on the Kalmyk steppe. The first marks a great advance that might force the Germans to make a general retreat along their whole central front. Last year the Russians tried in vain to take this staging area, which opens the way to Smolensk.

Claude has been at the François clinic since Wednesday. Treatment for his collapsed lung was successful. Isabelle and Antoinette are going to stay with the Noëls. We are keeping Marie-Claire. Despite all the sadness, the children celebrated Christmas with joy and yesterday were all here together – except for the Claudes – to bring in the New Year.

WEDNESDAY, 6 JANUARY 1943 Saw Mettetal yesterday to consult him about Françoise's change of domicile. His advice: better to avoid going to the S.S., who are normally responsible for such things. He is back from Montélimar, where he saw the occupying Italian troops. He confirms that they are miserable, in rags, poorly nourished, a sorry lot. The soldiers work in the vegetable gardens to earn a little something, and there is nothing they will not sell to have some food. They cannot wait for the Americans to deliver them from the Germans!

One of the countless forms of backward, cantankerous stupidity on the part of the French bourgeoisie is its disdain for all things American. Some criticize Americans for their jazz, others for their "naïveté," still others for their "materialism." All to avoid having to admire the tremendous enthusiasm, the zest for life, the pride in invention and production of this people whose role in the world is growing at an incredible pace. He who has not seen

New York cannot know the creative power of Americans. The same snobbery can be found in the English disdain for the Yankees. But from today it is clear that their role at the peace table and afterward will be immense. With Wilson it was a question of whether the United States would extend its "benevolence" and "generosity" to Europe. Today the question is entirely different. The Americans have felt themselves threatened – and from two sides at once. Now they must decide whether, under the pretext of an outdated Monroe Doctrine, they will allow external threats to grow to the point of becoming real dangers or whether they will exercise their formidable industrial and military power in the world, in Europe as well as in Asia. The answer cannot be doubted. If France misses this chance to come to an understanding with the United States, it is her entire future that will be sacrificed. As for Germany, Russian power has made it plain that the Germans must treat France with care if they do not want a repeat of the famous war on two fronts. With Russia to contain Germany, France can finally devote herself to her colonies and to the sea.

FRIDAY, 8 JANUARY 1943 Opening address by Roosevelt to the new Congress. He announced an imminent aerial attack on Japan. He noted the building of forty-nine thousand planes by the United States last year – without mentioning those built in England. He promised a second front.

The question of the second front's location will generate a lot of ink. I am betting on the Balkans, in the form of an attack on Bulgaria, aided by Turkey, with an eye to taking over the Romanian oil fields and thus bringing a quicker end to the war. In the spring I will know if I have won my bet.

SATURDAY, 9 JANUARY 1943 It is amusing to watch people arguing over which is best, democracy or totalitarianism, as if it were a matter of opposing abstract principles that can be decided by logic and reasoning. This issue, which has already been settled by experience, cannot be judged by abstract concepts. Democracy *lives* in the United States, in France, in Switzerland, in Belgium, in Holland, in Great Britain, and this democracy is no longer that which flourished in the small towns of ancient Greece or of medieval Italy. Modern democracy is grounded in great populations whose support of the government is essential if the latter wishes to survive, and that support, in countries with universal education, necessarily implies participation. Democracy, with its back-and-forth of views that trade off taking the lead, prevents any one view from becoming completely dominant and imposing itself by force. This greatest experiment of the past century, carried out in all the European democracies (including the French democracy) and that of the United States, has given proof of the continuity and effectiveness of democracy – the best guarantee, the best insurance against extremes. Democracy should thus be hailed by *conservatives* as the only means to save them; individual tyrants, by contrast, given unlimited power, must depend upon a kind of mass enthusiasm and thus are pushed to perform passionate acts to keep the passions, both internal and external, alive. To maintain the unity of thought and action of many millions, tying them to the fate of one individual, one must set the most sensitive strings vibrating, the most violent interests. Experience shows that this system inevitably leads to war, for only war offers free rein to passion, fear, enthusiasm, and hatred. But nothing is so destructive of conservative interests, of the material and moral values of a country, as war – especially in the "total" form it assumes today.

WEDNESDAY, 13 JANUARY 1943 Never have French journalists in German pay – or, simply, fascists voluntarily serving Germany – displayed their baseness with more cynicism than today. The theme in all the papers is as follows: "The French colonies have been delivered to the Anglo-American enemy; if we had sided squarely with Germany after the armistice, today German troops would be in North Africa and the enemy driven back. The only French colony remaining to us is Indochina, thanks to our understanding with Japan. Will the French people at last understand their true interest?" That such madness could flow from French pens is truly the shame of partisan passion. But that those people could imagine the French will ever forget the attitude they have taken, at the very time when all of France can see at last the door to salvation, owes more to profound stupidity than to villainy.

North Africa's internal problems are evidence of the confusion caused by two years of Vichy propaganda and the marshal's wretched pronouncements disavowing all patriotic actions. Under the circumstances, one might have expected a united front. Instead, what one observes is divided opinion – without our even knowing precisely what is happening. And this divided opinion, which is observable in the military as well, prevents French troops from acting. To the very end the "conspiracy" that is at the root of our disasters will have delayed France's defense and liberation. This is what must not be forgotten.

The German retreat from the Caucasus is the chief military event of these last few days. There is no better sign of the state of disarray in which their high command finds itself than the fact that German propaganda has been slow to acknowledge it.

Swiss radio has announced that Laval had a conversation with the Führer in Ukraine and was roundly rebuked by Goering. What could this wretch have promised his masters or asked them for? Today he is condemned to bear the burden of his treason, and he must bear it to the end. He is no longer the master of his fate.

FRIDAY, 15 JANUARY 1943 Yesterday received the former minister of agriculture, Ricard. He told me he is working on a specifically French economic plan that would situate French commercial policy in the new Europe – that is, in Hitler's continental Europe. This plan, he said, would be useful "no matter the outcome of the war." He wants me to study the "financing of large-scale European public works." He sees the marshal every month, and the marshal has shown great interest in his work. I listened a long time in silence, flabbergasted that a man could spend his forced leisure time on such perfectly useless tasks. I replied that the Germans were losing the war, that there would be no continental Europe, that, moreover, the Germans were the last to believe in this notion conceived for suckers, and that they would be the first to reach an understanding with England and the United States. He told me that "several eminent men" had spoken to him as I had.

The war with Russia is going to influence German policy for a long time. The horrors and the terrors, like the revelation of Russian industrial power, will dominate the German political imagination. Fear of a war with Russia will be the beginning of wisdom, and the preparation of a new war with her the secret desire. Under these conditions, Germany may be of two minds regarding future dealings with France: whether to reach a generous understanding with her to avoid a second front and assure her neutrality or to crush her outright and reduce her to impotence for fifty years. The *furor germanicus* condemns Germany to choose the second solution. The first would be too subtle. If Germany is finally victorious, we can be sure that its Russian experience was our death sentence, pure and simple. If Germany is defeated, this same experience, by orienting Germany to be on the defensive against the Slavs for a long time, will give France a long respite and the possibility of political autonomy, which she can use to her advantage even vis-à-vis England and the United States, as France can lean on Russia or on the Anglo-Saxons or on both at once. The wise course for her will be to develop her colonial empire and her navy and to make certain that the Germans and Russians do not form an alliance against her.

Doctor V.[8] has told me of an amusing rumor that is making the rounds: "General Georges is apparently now in Russia"; hence a French general is to be thanked for the great Russian victories! A similar tall tale circulated dur-

---

8. Rist is probably referring to Doctor Veslot (see 24 October 1942).

ing the last war: for every success carried off by the Russian general Brusilov, one would say mysteriously, "You know, Brusilov, he's actually the son of Prince Victor" (the one who was a general in the Russian army).[9] French generals, having been unable to avoid defeat, want to claim the victories of others as their own. This rumor has an undertone: if General Georges (regarded as a reactionary) is the author of these resounding successes, de Gaulle's glory (and that of the republicans who surround him) is totally eclipsed! And that is what had to be demonstrated.

Pastor V.'s[10] daughter got herself arrested in the following circumstances: on the subway she found it amusing to take a German soldier's sword; as the soldier was leaving, he realized it was missing, turned around, and, seeing her next to him, figured she was the culprit; he seized her by the arm and found the weapon. She pleaded that it was just the lure of danger! A rather childish heroism.

SUNDAY, 17 JANUARY 1943 Lunch yesterday with the Moreau family. Peacetime menu: eels, roast, pâté! They regularly receive parcels from their place in the country. Lucky people!

This morning, news of great Russian victories: on the Voronezh front the German line was penetrated, with an advance of 50 to 60 kilometers; great stretches have been taken along the Rostov front line; the German army between the Don and the Volga, violently attacked after refusing to surrender, is suffering losses of men and materiel; the Russians say the Germans have been reduced from two hundred thousand to eighty thousand men. Hitler's recent appeal to Bucharest, Budapest, and Sofia for new reinforcements risks falling on deaf ears. And if the Bulgarians move against Russia, will it not be the Turks' opportunity to go into action? Already the king of Iraq has declared war on Germany, Italy, and Japan!

Historians may come to label the past four years as the "reign of rogues" – the *rusé*, the zealot, and the jackal.[11] For the "rogue" is an individual who

9. Prince Napoléon Victor: pretender to the French throne; his brother Prince Louis, not Prince Victor, fought with the Russian army. [TF]

10. Pastor V.: Pastor Vergara, an Oratorian. Oratorians belong to the Congregation of the Oratory of St. Philip Neri, founded in Rome in 1575 and comprising independent communities of secular priests under obedience but without vows. Merriam-Webster online. [JNJ/TF]

11. *Le rusé* is Rist's common nickname for Laval in the diary; Mussolini was labeled a "jackal" by Churchill when Il Duce followed Germany's lead and invaded southern France; the "zealot" clearly refers to Hitler. [TF]

willfully separates himself from the social norms of decency, generosity, and
courtesy, who cynically proclaims that he is only out for himself and that he
is determined to have his own appetites triumph through force, wiles, brutality, cruelty, and crudeness, having no other means to succeed. That these
rogues are the unconscious instruments of history, as Hegelian philosophy
would have it, can hardly be believed – unless it is because of the contradic-
tion they pose and the opportunity they thus provide to the true forces of
history to manifest themselves. What we are seeing today is the entry onto
the world stage of two great powers: Russia and the United States. It is the
second act of a drama in which the war of 1914–1918 was only the exposition
and in which these two central characters appeared one moment only to
disappear the next and withdraw into their solitude. What adulation will
surround them after the current war!

TUESDAY, 19 JANUARY 1943 Rereading some of these notes, I have been
struck above all by one thing: how difficult it is for us to guess, amid the silence and lies that envelop this unhappy country, what is really going on and
what really happened at the moment of crisis and during the period preceding it. Groping our way along, we can catch a few glimmers that permit us
to divine that secret and abominable history whose protagonists are hiding
today as one hides from a shameful disease but whose effects continue to be
felt in the spiritual disarray of those who believe or say they are our leaders.
What is remarkable in this almost total darkness is that the people, the simple
peasants and workers, by a sure instinct have been unhesitatingly on the side
of hope and faith, which was also the side of reason.

WEDNESDAY, 20 JANUARY 1943 Spoke yesterday with L. and J.[12] at the
Société d'Ugine headquarters. The former advocates waiting (until after the
enemy's evacuation) to let the French people have their say. He is certain
that the first chore will be negotiating a treaty. For this, there must be men
who are already prepared. Then these same men must be supported by an
elected assembly, which will settle on a definitive constitution and ratify the
treaty. But to L.'s way of thinking, elections right after a peace treaty must
be avoided, as they would mean a large majority voting for left-wing parties.
L. is from the Action Française, though he is truly and profoundly patriotic.

FRIDAY, 22 JANUARY 1943 Talk of the Comte de Paris is on everyone's
lips. People who have always been strongly anti-parliamentarian will whis-

12. J.: Jaoul.

per in your ear: "The only way to save our parliamentary institutions is to reestablish the monarchy!" The history of the Restoration and that of Louis-Philippe demonstrate that the royal game has always consisted in altering parliamentary institutions. According to the papers, when Lord Eden was asked by an English member of Parliament if the presence of the Comte de Paris in North Africa threatened to cause complications, he replied, "I do not believe the Comte de Paris is important enough to create complications anywhere."

Three days ago the siege of Leningrad was broken after more than a year, and Schlüsselburg was captured. German communiqués no longer contain geographical names. In the Caucasus, Russian troops have taken Voroshilov[13] and are approaching Maykop, the only oil field held by the Germans up to now. Clearly the German troops are staging a "voluntary" withdrawal that has been "imposed" upon them by the threat of Russians advancing on several sides. The English are in Tripoli, and Rommel's army is trying to meet up with the German and Italian troops from Tunisia.

The other day de Vitry, back from Germany, was telling me that the German army consumed 18 million tons of gasoline in its 1942 campaign, that 4 are produced in its factories, and 8 (a figure that appears greatly exaggerated to my eye) come from Romania. The deficit would thus be 6 million. One can see why they are fighting in the Caucasus. And if Germany were to lose Romania?

Four or five trees have been felled on the grounds of the Avenue de l'Amiral-Serre villa. We shall have an extra 7 steres of wood. Luckily this winter has been as mild as last year's was harsh.

TUESDAY, 26 JANUARY 1943 Today it is as if the whole world were feeling the first stirrings of deliverance. The German disaster in Russia is the cause. This is like the hope that seized the world after the Battle of Berezina, presage of the "Ogre's" downfall.[14] The Germans admit that their troops are trapped between the Don and the Volga. We are told their defense is the most heroic feat of arms in history! In the Caucasus and near Maykop the situation seems scarcely better. German radio has announced that the front lines will be shortened. The pope, on the radio, referred to the recent speech of the Hungarian primate, declaring that there are no superior or

13. Voroshilov: now known as Luhansk, or Lugansk, the city was called Voroshilov-grad from 1935 to 1958 in honor of Soviet military commander Kliment Voroshilov. [TF]

14. A reference to Napoleon's disastrous retreat from Russia. [TF]

inferior races, no master people, that all men are equal, and that a crime is a crime, even when committed for ideological reasons against the enemy of your ideas! Stalin, in a dispatch to his troops, enumerated the cities retaken, the tanks, cannon, and rifles collected. He exhorted his troops to escort the enemy all the way to the border. I remember what Laval said to the American journalist Knickerbocker in June 1940: "You exaggerate the importance of what's happening in France. What matters is that Hitler is preparing to crush Bolshevism!" He is now getting his just desserts.

In any case it seems clear that Stalin will not cross the Russian border and will not enter Germany. In all of his speeches he talks only about "German fascism."

In the Balkans the unease of Germany's allies is growing. Bulgaria does not want to march against the Russians; Hungary and Romania are growing desperate. Is this where the collapse will come?

WEDNESDAY, 27 JANUARY 1943 This morning a meeting of Roosevelt and Churchill in Casablanca was announced. "Conference on unconditional surrender." Giraud and de Gaulle met there and reached an understanding. At the same time, we learned of the total destruction of German troops encircled at Stalingrad – foreshadowed by German communiqués speaking of their super-heroic resistance. So much great good news. We are starting to believe the war may not last as long as feared.

FRIDAY, 29 JANUARY 1943 The board of the Banque de Paris met yesterday. The "collaborators" have sensed a change in the political winds. Some are already preparing their about-face and now speak of the Russians with respect. According to Augé-Laribé, ministerial offices have received a circular from Joseph Barthélemy saying that "in the current state of the law" there is no reason to replace the words "French Republic" with the words "French State" in official documents! Is it the de jure or the de facto state of things that has suggested this gross mischief to Barthélemy? Oudot said that Mattioli, here for a meeting of the Franco-Italian Bank for South America, is sure the end of the war for Italy will be next April!

In Germany total mobilization of men from seventeen to sixty-five and of women up to fifty-five years old. A spectacular measure and a measure of their impotence.

In France the conscription of workers is becoming increasingly widespread. All you hear is women talking about the departure of their husbands, sons, brothers, and brothers-in-law. It is a veritable roundup.

On the stock exchange for the past week, a sharp drop in all the stocks that have been inflated up to now by fears for the franc. People are cashing in because they foresee the end of the war and the happy ending that will stop the franc's fall.

The Russians have surrounded the German troops at Maykop. The one oil field gained by the Germans' 1942 offensive is now lost. What will happen if they lose Romania?

In their Casablanca communiqué, the Allies said – or rather, Roosevelt said in his declaration – that what they want to destroy is the "philosophy" of the aggressor countries. Enormous difference from the declarations of the coalition formed in 1813 to oppose Napoleon. What they wanted was to destroy the hegemony of the emperor and of France. A pure question of politics. No one at the time dared to say that they wanted to destroy a philosophy, which would have been that of the French Revolution. And once the emperor had fallen, the philosophy of the Revolution, at least that of 1789, was bound to endure. It was shared by a good part of France's adversaries, if not by their sovereigns (but the latter and their ministers, beginning with Metternich, did not dare express their secret doubts). Today, on the contrary, everyone senses that what would triumph with Hitler is the anti-civilized regime he put into effect at home, which is counter to the ideas of 1789. Oddly enough it is precisely those ideas that Hitler and Mussolini are against, like all those in other countries (including France) who wished them to be victorious. It is thus the clash of two "religions," as Laval said several weeks ago. Only today everybody shares the religion of 1789 – even the pope. By destroying German hegemony, a political and military operation, one will also be destroying the new German religion, which is just a perfected form of the old feudal system in which the sovereign was everything but in which the multiplicity of sovereigns constituted a brake. Today, on the contrary, the sovereign state enjoys complete tyranny, its power multiplied tenfold by the great nations under its sway.

SATURDAY, 30 JANUARY 1943 A new Russian victory on the Voronezh front, where they have taken twenty-five thousand German and Italian prisoners, and on the Caucasian front, where they have taken Kropotkin.

The Führer has forbidden Germans to celebrate the tenth anniversary of the seizure of power by the "party."

Speech by General Giraud in Algiers, saying that an understanding has been reached with de Gaulle and that he is administering Africa in the name of the French nation and not constituting a government. This is the doctrine of Roosevelt, who said from the beginning that he would aid all of those French people who fought and that their administration of territories would be in the name of the French nation, thus refusing to judge in advance the wishes of the latter. It is in this way that Roosevelt's influence prevailed at the Casablanca talks and will prevail again at the peace table – a fact we had better remember!

Last night I read to Germaine the next-to-last chapter of Hölderlin's *Hyperion*. A chapter that should be translated and included in a book called *The Germans Speak of the Germans*.

SUNDAY, 31 JANUARY 1943 News last night of two air raids on Berlin during Goering's speech for the anniversary of the Third Reich. Scheduled for 11:00, the speech was postponed to midnight. A parade of buffoons who feared being booed by the public were announcing new stunts, sure to be more successful. The maniacs were crying that the *Judenthum* are responsible for everything. Poorly disguising their uneasiness, they recalled to their listeners the most desperate moments of France and England in the last war in order to show that Germany in its turn will finally be victorious if it can just get through this critical juncture. Meanwhile, Admiral Raeder has been dismissed and replaced by someone else, and one gets the feeling that things are not going so well between the generals and the party.

This time German leaders will not be able to say that it is weakness on the "home front" that led to the military disaster. They are experiencing a military defeat that cannot be disguised. The odds are, however, that the German military will once again lay the blame on others! They need only say they were just following Hitler's orders. And the famous "Prussian militarism" will once more be safe and sound. The trick will be played, and the Germans will regain their fetish. Since Arminius[15] they have never given it up!

This morning new Russian advances. Maykop has fallen, saving Russian oil fields from the Germans. The advance from Voronezh to Kursk has been equally fast. The whole German front appears weak, and their leaders seem to fear even greater disasters. Could we be closer to the end than we think? I am telling the children they shall return to Le Très-Clos this summer!

In a *Paris-Soir* article of 25 January, the author, waxing indignant, declares that nothing in France has changed and that the National Revolution has convinced no one. "The French would rather die than renounce their democracy, the ballot, alcohol, Jews, members of parliament, Masons, ra-

---

15. Arminius: German tribal chieftain who in 9 CE destroyed a Roman army in the Teutoburg Forest. [TF]

pacious bureaucrats – in a word, everything that has pulled them down so
low. . . . They still expect to flourish and thus do not want to hear anything
about revolution or National Socialism. So long live America and England,
right?" It is signed by one Jean Bosc. Similar passages can be read from time
to time in all the traitors' newspapers. What a frank acknowledgment that
the French have remained republicans and patriots and that those who have
profited from the enemy and once again counted on returning to power in his
battle wagons[16] have not won over the public. Those preparing our postwar
government will do well not to forget this.

I have received a wedding announcement for Taittinger's son. His father was careful to put his title as a deputy.[17] Thus does this imbecile, who
has made a career of being anti-parliamentarian, insist today on reminding
people of his participation in Parliament. A sign of the times!

MONDAY, 1 FEBRUARY 1943 This morning General von Paulus (made
a marshal by Hitler three days ago) is reported to have surrendered to the
Russians along with sixteen other German and Romanian generals. This
marks the end of the tragedy of Stalingrad. German generals surrendering
to the Russians! When has such a thing been observed in history? Not since
the Seven Years' War. They say there were three hundred thousand Germans
engaged at Stalingrad! There is not one who has not been killed or taken
prisoner! The capitulation of General Dupont at Bailén with his ten thousand
men[18] pales by comparison. And yet those whose ears were attuned could
already hear the bell tolling for the empire. We shall not wait so long to see
this one crumble. Will the Germans pardon Hitler for this appalling and
futile massacre? They are certainly capable of it. But the new recruits, not
yet twenty years old, are no substitute for the seasoned troops destroyed at
Stalingrad.

Massigli's arrival in England and adherence to General de Gaulle has
been announced.

People whose philosophy consists of judging a government by its military successes or reverses will be obliged to affirm the superiority of the

16. An allusion to the return of the émigrés and the Bourbons "*dans les fourgons de
l'ennemi*" [in the enemy's battle wagons] in 1814 and 1815. [TF]

17. Pierre Taittinger, a deputy representing the first arrondissement of Paris since
1929, founded the Jeunesses Patriotes [Patriotic Youth] in 1924 and between the two
wars became one of the leaders of aggressive right-wing opposition to the Third Republic. [JNJ/TF]

18. In 1808, during the Napoleonic Wars. [TF]

Bolshevik regime over Hitlerism, just as they affirmed the superiority of the latter over the French Republic! This will be a bitter pill for them to swallow. Or if it is a question of the superiority of one people over another, then it is the Russians who are superior to the Germans and the Russian civilization to that of the Germans and the French! To speak truly, is war not a barbarity, and can a barbarian not always find someone more barbaric than he? But then must we say that the Allies, when they have triumphed, are more barbaric than the Germans? All these classifications are stupid, though even a Renan allowed himself one day to make war the sovereign judge of the merits of a people, as if they were a Napoleon. Power changes hands, and the combinations of power at a given moment can force the most civilized to admit defeat. The whole history of wars is nothing but the chronicle of these shifts in power. It is not by the variable and momentary successes of these power games that the moral and intellectual quality of a people can be judged. At most they determine a people's sphere of influence and prestige for a few decades. But lasting influence and prestige are grounded in other elements. The French Revolution did more than the empire or Louis XIV for France's prestige in the world. And in the world of ideas and feelings, what remains today of the prestige acquired by Germany after the war of 1870? Practically nothing. What German political idea has spread throughout the world? None. Its scientists, its musicians and writers have not been more numerous after than before. Its technical and economic abilities are not superior to those of America or England. The only wars that are great and fruitful are those that save the individuality of a people, its moral and intellectual originality, its particular civilization. But for this to happen, the people must have a distinctive individuality, originality, and civilization. The judge of that is not the changing fortune of arms.

TUESDAY, 2 FEBRUARY 1943 More big news: a meeting in Adana of Churchill, Ismet İnönü, Saradjoglou, and their chiefs of staff. This signals Turkey's entry into the war at an as yet unknown date. Rid of her worries in regard to the Caucasus, she now feels free to fight. It is the Romanian oil fields in Ploieşti that will be under threat and whose fate will perhaps determine when the war will end. What will be the attitude of Bulgaria, which must be crossed to reach Romania? Will she allow her borders to be violated? Will she abruptly switch sides? Will she resist?

FRIDAY, 5 FEBRUARY 1943 Yesterday, lunch at Maxime Leroy's. A sign of the times, Germain-Martin was there. This collaborator has seen the light after Stalingrad's liberation! The admiral[19] thinks the second front will be created at Adrianople[20] – and here I am in agreement with the military! There was talk about Darlan; his assassin was evidently a mentally disturbed person who wanted to avenge his father, a navy officer fallen in fighting with the Americans when they entered Morocco.[21] No one doubts any longer the outcome of the war. Just the date, with optimists predicting six months.

Received Cangardel, who came to talk to me about Air France Transatlantique. He would like to get his planes in the air as soon as peace comes, beginning with the Antilles and northern South America, reserving for later routes to the United States, which, he says, will want to monopolize Atlantic air travel. There is much talk of "postwar American imperialism." Some people are more afraid of this than of German imperialism.

The Germans have decreed three days of mourning in honor of Stalingrad. To read their papers, you would think it was a great victory. Meanwhile the scrambling of radio signals has become a real problem. It is increasingly difficult to hear the news.

SATURDAY, 6 FEBRUARY 1943 My niece Florence,[22] a teacher at the École de la Légion d'honneur de Saint-Denis, tells me that General Brécard, a high-ranking officer in the Legion of Honor, spoke at the school the other day, saying that this period is worse for France than that of June 1940, for she has now lost her entire colonial empire. Thus does a French general (Protestant!) feel and speak at a time when 80 percent of French people are anticipating at last their deliverance thanks to the Russian and English

---

19. Possibly Alfred Edouard Richard. [TF]

20. Adrianople: now known as Edirne, in western Turkey. [TF]

21. The assassin, Frenchman Fernand Bonnier de la Chapelle, was actually a twenty-year-old student-patriot who had once been a member of the anti-Vichy Singers of Youth. He hated Admiral Darlan "as a traitor to France in 1940, a toady to Hitler thereafter, and at last, if allowed to play out his opportunistic game, a double turncoat capable of discrediting the very idea of liberation." Tried summarily, Bonnier was hastily executed. Roosevelt and Churchill publicly lamented Darlan's death and condemned the assassin. The Americans, in particular, had found Darlan a useful counterweight to de Gaulle and a welcome source of authority who "could save the lives of countless American and British soldiers by instructing his fellow countrymen to cooperate with the Allies." Yet his death was also seen as a gift, as it freed America from "entanglement with hastily converted collaborationists." Franklin L. Ford, *Political Murder: From Tyrannicide to Terrorism* (Cambridge, MA: Harvard University Press, 1985), 279–80. [TF]

22. Florence Schaller: Italian teacher.

victories, a time when the French flag is in the hands of dissidents in all the French colonies and the English and American leaders have given their word that they shall remain French. General Brécard is either an imbecile – which seems the most likely hypothesis – or he is an arriviste paying court to the Germans and to Laval by making such statements. He is probably one of those Frenchmen who found their political aspirations finally satisfied by the German victory.

Today, according to the radio, Mussolini has sacked all of his ministers and replaced them with second-string backups. Ciano himself has been ousted, as has Grandi, the former ambassador to London, the one who told me when I was in Rome that he would not give a penny for all the artistic treasures of Italy! Even those fascists are now suspect.

Sixteen

Growing Doubts and Hardships at Home

10 FEBRUARY–6 JULY 1943

As the war dragged on, Rist became increasingly worried that liberation would not come in time to save the French people from starvation. An exacerbation of their hardships was the levy (la relève), Laval's naïve scheme by which one French prisoner of war would supposedly be sent back for every three Frenchmen sent to work in Germany.

Then, too, Rist was alarmed by the role that French generals, particularly de Gaulle and Giraud, might play in a postwar government. Equally troubling to him was the danger posed by some members of the Resistance: the hotheads, whose deeds of sabotage or assassination led to horrific reprisals; the idealists, who wanted to create "a 'pure' political climate" with "nobody from the old parties"; and the informers, whose denunciations led to many in the Resistance movement being arrested and shot.

WEDNESDAY, 10 FEBRUARY 1943 The Russians took Kursk yesterday. The whole Orel-Kursk-Kharkov-Rostov line has been penetrated, and the Germans are threatened in the Donets Basin. One wonders whether the Russians really have a crushing superiority or whether the Germans are just discouraged. In the first case, all the frenetic efforts of the Germans to get back on an equal or superior footing are in vain: the Americans and the Turks have passed them up. In the second case, it is hard to see what would reinvigorate them.

Here, registration of all men between eighteen and thirty-five; they must present themselves at the town hall with their registration forms. This abominable roundup is a sign of desperation. What suffering yet remains for us? However, everyone can foresee the end.

SUNDAY, 14 FEBRUARY 1943 All French people must hand over an amount of copper proportional to their property tax! A great proof of the enemy's penury. A terrible trial for our peasants' beautiful pots and pans. I await the sheet of paper detailing the number of kilos we will have to hand over!

Lunch yesterday with Ledoux and Quiñones.[1] Ledoux put forward the idea that the cause of the Americans' entry into the war was "economic imperialism." My answer is to repeat what Roosevelt said to me three years ago. It is alarming to see intelligent, cultivated men explaining events in such contemptible generalities. As if the Americans, had they wanted to exercise "economic imperialism," would not have done much better by peacefully waiting for the end of the war, when, faced with a shattered Europe and a diminished England, they would be the only ones left standing. Fears of communist unrest were also discussed. I declared such fears absurd. Quiñones did not open his mouth. I shall find out why!

Visited Claude in the Bon-Secours hospital. Still a little shaken by yesterday's operation.

MONDAY, 15 FEBRUARY 1943 Last night it was announced that the Russians have taken Rostov-on-Don. A triumphant victory that may precipitate a debacle for the German army as their troops are encircled in the Donets Basin.

In his speech last week, Roosevelt declared that the Allies were not fighting to keep the Quislings and the Lavals in power. A word to the wise is sufficient. Yet people here still whisper in your ear that Laval "is really in with the Americans" and that we must therefore keep him.

Strange turnabout: the English, hostile toward the French Revolution, and the Americans, quite cold toward it, returning to France at the end of this war to reestablish the principles of the Revolution, which have been betrayed and held in contempt by the very country that proclaimed them! What better demonstration that these principles were adopted by the whole world, except in the always hostile countries of Central and Eastern Europe. And yet! Even there, these principles have made some headway with public opinion and only await (at least in Germany) the end of the war to become manifest.

Last night, violent antiaircraft fire. This morning we learned that some English planes had flown over Italy and Germany.

---

1. Quiñones de Léon: Spanish diplomat, former Spanish ambassador in Paris, personal friend of Pétain and Alfonso XIII.

WEDNESDAY, 17 FEBRUARY 1943 The taking of Kharkov by the Russians was announced last night.

SATURDAY, 20 FEBRUARY 1943 Lunch on Wednesday with François de Wendel, General Serrigny, Edme Sommier, and Castellane. It is amusing today to hear the first of these: Wendel no longer fears the Bolsheviks. He told us, "If the Germans win, we'll have them here for fifty years; if it's the Russians, well, then, we'll elect a few more leftists." General Serrigny told us about his visit to Vichy on 12 November to persuade Pétain to resign or leave for Algeria. Nothing would move him. The marshal's entourage believes the English will be victorious, but they are not happy about it.[2]

Yesterday Mario presented himself for the registration of men between twenty-two and thirty that was decreed a few days ago. He says he does not need to fear being sent to Germany. This registration is combined with the convocation of young people between twenty and twenty-two for forced labor. No one knows how many of these children will be sent to Germany. The government has had all kinds of false reassuring rumors published in the press. But everyone remains uneasy.

MONDAY, 22 FEBRUARY 1943 All the German papers published in French are raising the bogeyman of Bolshevism. "Germany is defending western civilization against the savagery of the steppe that is sweeping over Europe." This campaign is just the reflection of the one being waged in Germany itself. I would like to know with what degree of success. Are there many people disposed to do forced labor in order to free themselves from the Bolshevik nightmare when they have so much suffering to endure from the Nazi nightmare? In France only some fanatics – those who fear the "return of the Jews and the Freemasons" – are afraid of the "Red tide." The great English demonstrations in honor of the twenty-fifth anniversary of the Red army, the proclamation of the Anglo-Russian entente as a basis (for twenty years) of the reorganization of Europe, and, lastly, the sword of honor offered by

2. General Serrigny was head of the Chambre syndicale du pétrole [Petroleum Federation] and a friend of the marshal. In his book *Trente ans avec Pétain* (Paris: Plon, 1959), he recounts in detail his interview of 14 November (not the twelfth) with Pétain and the failure of his efforts (224–27). Stanislas de Castellane was a former moderate senator from Cantal. As for François de Wendel of the Lorraine steelworks dynasty, he does not mention this lunch in his journal, but his general notes regarding this time confirm his changed state of mind (see also the meeting with Humbert de Wendel, younger brother of François, mentioned in the entry for 1 December 1941).

the king of England to Stalingrad and accompanied by a dispatch from the king to Stalin, show the English government's decision to reduce to silence all those who still believe in the Bolshevik bogey. Eden has made a mockery of Hitler, the "defender of civilization."

Meanwhile the Americans are losing in Tunisia. The American radio program *America Calling Europe* has declared that this defeat is inexcusable and must be immediately redressed. The English general Alexander has been called on to take charge of operations. Here many are sniggering. Most are pleased to see the Americans given a chance to realize that war is not easy.

FRIDAY, 26 FEBRUARY 1943 The roundup of laborers and office workers requisitioned by Germany continues. Yesterday at the Ottoman Bank and at the Banque de Paris everyone was filled with dismay. Up to now nothing has been demanded of us at the Ottoman Bank. The Germans are indiscriminately taking bachelors and fathers of families, young people and fifty-year-old men. They are asking for 350 employees from the Banque de Paris.

The speech sent by the Führer to his Munich faithful for the anniversary of the party's founding on 23 February has been published. He wrote from his general headquarters. It is a diatribe against the Jews as well as a declaration that he will ruthlessly draw on the occupied countries' populations to defend civilization against Bolshevism and capitalism. He is fighting for a *Weltanschauung* that will get the better of the "capitalist-communist" system in league against it. If he has risen, he who was unknown twenty years ago, to the place he occupies today, that can only be by the will of Providence, and it is impossible that it not continue to protect him. The puerility and baseness of these statements recall the speeches of Wilhelm II.

Meanwhile the game in Russia is getting rougher as the Germans fight tooth and nail to defend their position in the Donets.

Baumgartner[3] tells me of a visit he had from Baudouin, who came to tell him that he has always been pro-English and that from the very beginning he foresaw the turn events would take! Barnaud himself abandoned Laval's ship two months ago, and Legueu is complaining that the generals who advise him are always wrong! What splendid conversions!

Sat with the board of Air France Transatlantique for the first time on Tuesday. The Germans have threatened to take our three planes! We cannot even make test flights. Paralysis everywhere, in industry, in transportation, in agriculture.

3. Wilfrid Baumgartner: inspector of Public Finances, head of Crédit National.

However, people are full of confidence. "It won't last much longer" – that is what you hear repeated ten times a day. Let us hope all these good people are right!

MONDAY, 1 MARCH 1943 The American papers are pointing out that the "ides of March" has always been fatal for Hitler, as it is always on that date he has been hit the hardest. Is this a way of announcing in veiled terms that the famous landing is about to happen? Shall we see it take place this very month? Soon enough to avoid consequences from the dreadful roundup of workers in occupied countries?

One would like all the more to believe it, as life is becoming more difficult every day. To tell the truth, this winter has been remarkably mild and continues to be so. The prospect of cold after the rigors of last winter terrified everyone. In the end, the number of days in which the thermometer fell below freezing is insignificant. But it is food that is becoming increasingly monotonous and insufficient for the young. Potatoes, carrots, pasta, and sometimes spinach constitute our basic nourishment. Meat is in short supply. One can find some once every week or two. There is not enough sugar. Or salt. No one knows why. We have recently had the good fortune to receive, from various quarters, enough to feed us for several weeks. Butter and lard have almost completely disappeared or reach us in minuscule amounts. As the days lengthen, electricity rationing is less noticeable. But gas is still reduced to the point that cooking is very difficult. In many regions the production of butter has been so closely supervised that people in the countryside do not want to send any more. Even exchanges for cigarettes (three packs for a pound) have become increasingly rare.

SATURDAY, 6 MARCH 1943 Yesterday I went with Bellet to take the list of our Ottoman Bank staff to the German agent in charge of registering workers. A sinister measure. The argument that we are a Turkish bank did not faze him. He retained the names of seven men and four women. His assistant assured us that the four women will not be taken. In any case, they would go somewhere in France. The others must in theory remain in France. But the German gave the impression that they would leave for Germany – despite the assurances of the banks' organizing committee. Back at the Ottoman Bank, I convened the social committee that represents our personnel and explained what had been done. I told them, "Never over the course of our careers have I or Monsieur Bellet taken a more painful step." One of the committee members was among those singled out by the German. He had tears in his eyes; already one of his brothers has been called up for the levy, and the other is being held prisoner. He is the only one his mother has left at home. In spite of all, these good people were almost relieved, having expected even more would be taken. We too. Bellet himself is anxious for his son in Marseilles, who is being pursued by the Gestapo and whose whereabouts are unknown. Another of his sons is in London; the third has just been sent back because of the dissolution of the youth camps and is threatened by the levy. All married.

The Russians have taken Rzhev and are advancing along the entire Rzhev-Kharkov line. They can now take Vyazma and Smolensk. The very line followed by Napoleon.

MONDAY, 8 MARCH 1943 One lives in the feverish expectation of "something." The more the English and the Americans appear confident of the future, the more impatient one gets to see them strike a decisive blow. All events seem insignificant: Ribbentrop and Mussolini meeting in Rome, the American air victory over the Japanese squadron in New Guinea, the German army setbacks in Tunisia. Only the Russian advances appear meaningful. But Europe is waiting for something else. Not just occupied Europe, but also Germany, whose fortifications in France are becoming increasingly hasty and whose troops, they say, are multiplying along the coasts. The Anglo-American bombing raids on Lorient, Brest, Saint-Nazaire, Tours, etc., are becoming more numerous and bloody.

Claude still in the Bon-Secours hospital in Paris. A room has been found for him at the Durtol Sanatorium. He is waiting for Jean to come pick him up. The disappearance of the Demarcation Line since 5 March will facilitate things, let us hope.

FRIDAY, 12 MARCH 1943 Yesterday morning Bellet went along with our employees who have been designated by Germany to have a medical checkup. He found himself there with many others. After an hour of comings and goings and much conferring, they were all sent away. Decisions have changed. There is talk of negotiations between Laval and the Germans. It seems the draft of three classes of young people between nineteen and twenty-two will take the place of workers taken from industries and banks!

At the Suez Company, nothing has yet been asked of us.

The Germans have reportedly retaken a certain number of towns in the region of the Donets. Meanwhile the Russians have advanced on Vyazma.

Auboin, with whom I had lunch, says the Swiss are quite optimistic and expect the end to come this summer. On the radio this morning the Americans announced they will have nine million enlisted men by the end of the year, and with the English and the Russians, a force of more than two hundred thousand planes. This is magnificent, of course. But here we see our men leaving, the labor shortage growing worse, and food increasingly hard to find.

SUNDAY, 14 MARCH 1943 Lunched on Thursday with Hillaert and Prételat.[4] Among other things, Prételat told me that his friend General P.,[5] who commanded an army at the beginning of the war, was asked by Doriot to head up the Doriotists! There you have the generals of the Third Republic. They think only of a coup d'état, and all believe they are qualified to carry it off! Hillaert asked me my opinion, and I told him that if the general wants to sink himself definitively he has only to go along with the tempters, whose fate after the war will be quickly settled and whose ties go unnoticed by no one. The general, he said, was apparently impressed by the very personality of Doriot! Clearly, faced with de Gaulle and Giraud, Doriot's partisans want to have a general of their own! We are looking more and more like China.

They have announced the death of old Morgan at seventy-six.[6] He always treated me charmingly and in particular gave me an unforgettable welcome three years ago at his country house in the United States, showing me his paintings, his conservatories, his library, and talking to me with a touching confidence.

FRIDAY, 19 MARCH 1943 Jean, having arrived Monday, spent Wednesday with us. He has resigned from his factory in order not to work for the Germans. Now he is looking for a job.

The Germans have retaken Kharkov. The military situation is stable. We live in waiting. Here unrest caused by the forced labor is growing day by day. Some of the rebels who refuse to work for the Germans have taken refuge in the mountains of Haute-Savoie and are waging an armed struggle against Italian troops and the French Mobile Guard. Meanwhile everyone lives in the hope of a landing somewhere that would give a boost to military operations and relieve the Russians.

Claude arrived in Durtol with no problems.

MONDAY, 22 MARCH 1943 A splendid spring accompanied by a drought such as has not been seen for a long time here, threatening disaster for farmers. Jean no longer knows how he is going to feed his cattle. The milk and

---

4. General Gaston Prételat: member of France's Supreme War Council in 1940 and commander of the armies in the east.

5. Not identified.

6. J. P. Morgan, Jr.: wealthy banker and philanthropist. [TF]

butter on which he was counting have fallen off. The restricted diet we are experiencing, almost entirely vegetarian owing to the shortages of fat, meat, and sugar, has had some curious effects that people feel free to comment on in their conversations. If not discussing the tragic subject of the levy and the multiplying requisitions of men, one hardly talks about anything anymore except supplies, food, and transportation problems. Diphtheria is spreading again. The anti-diphtheria serum is no longer working. Noël brought back a new strain of the bacillus that has allowed him, after many experiments, to obtain once again an effective anti-diphtheria serum for the Pasteur Institute.

One has the impression that the delays in Allied action must have something to do with the powerful German submarine offensive, since Admiral Raeder and all those admirals loyal to him have been replaced by Admiral Doenitz. In a recent speech the English minister of agriculture said, among other things, that submarines had never been so dangerous. Churchill, in an important speech broadcast last night, made a similar remark. It is the last chance for the Germans, a way they can prolong the war still further, for their success in the Donets is not likely to last.

Long conversations with Jean (who leaves tomorrow for Fraisses) regarding his future projects.

Churchill announced last night at the end of his speech that General Montgomery has taken the offensive in Tunisia and that he is "satisfied" with the preliminary results. This will cool our impatience for some time, though renewing our anxiety.

In a speech ten days ago in which Giraud spoke of his rapprochement with de Gaulle, Giraud advocated unity, proclaimed himself the servant and not the head of the French nation, and promised to reestablish the laws of the republic and the equality of Jews and Muslims (without reestablishing the Crémieux Decree) in North Africa. General Catroux has been charged with organizing a meeting of the two generals. Giraud announced the formation of a French army of three hundred thousand men provided with modern weaponry. Noguès has rallied to the ideas expressed by Giraud. General Bergeret, in contrast, has resigned as Giraud's assistant. Giraud announced that the French nation, once it was liberated, would freely choose the government it preferred.

TUESDAY, 23 MARCH 1943 Morin,[7] back from Haute-Savoie, gave me some specifics about what is happening there. In Chablais and Faucigny

---

7. Jean Morin: worked with Charles Rist at ISRES.

some fifteen hundred young people have rebelled against the work levy. They are armed and commanded by reserve officers. The population is exasperated by the Italians and is now beginning to be exasperated by the Germans. The Italian troops tried to put down the business at gunpoint. But after having advanced into the mountains, they realized that the operation was more difficult than they had imagined and perhaps even dangerous. This last consideration, in keeping with their national tradition, deterred them from continuing, and they turned instead to French authority. The latter brought together the mobile guards from three departments, giving them the order to surround the Savoyards without firing. But the whole population is helping to supply the "rebels" as small vans go in search of food in the villages. In this way the Resistance can go on for a long time. The Germans have therefore decided to intervene, but so far have apparently not acted.

THURSDAY, 25 MARCH 1943 Yesterday, lunch at Bolgert's. Mange, whom I had not seen since my work on the blockade, gave us specifics on the increasingly numerous attacks on trains. At first they were sporadic; today it is clear they are being organized according to a general plan. Right now there are some fifteen derailments a day, aimed at transports of troops and goods. He also said that the bombings of railroads and train stations, even when they are done from a high altitude, are remarkably precise and effective. Transports are going to be hindered by this from now on. The S.N.C.F.[8] has maps on which the effects of these bombings are recorded.

In regard to possible landings, it is presumed they will take place in several spots at the same time, and Mange believes the first result of this will be an almost complete suspension of the transport of goods destined for private use. The countryside will not suffer much, but cities will be seriously affected. His advice is to have as many provisions as possible at home in view of this possibility.

Couve de Murville and Leroy-Beaulieu escaped a few days ago. The former, according to Algiers radio, was named general secretary for all of North Africa. Leroy (without escaping, however) had already abandoned his post as general secretary of the finance ministry. Simultaneously it was announced that a large number of consuls have resigned in Spain. It seems Piétri has only two clerks with him at the embassy. The abandonment of the Vichy government by anyone with a conscience is accelerating.

---

8. S.N.C.F.: Société nationale des chemins de fer français (French National Railway Company). [TF]

Léonard tells me that a general roundup of Jews is expected on the first of April.

An attack on the Mareth defensive line by the British Eighth Army, launched a week ago, has made no headway. Positions occupied on the first day have all been retaken by the Germans. American and English officials have issued a flood of declarations saying that the Tunisian operation will be long and difficult.

WEDNESDAY, 31 MARCH 1943   The Mareth Line breached; the English at Gabès. Rommel's army in retreat at Sousse.

SATURDAY, 3 APRIL 1943   The subway has reduced its ticket books by half to save paper. Each ticket can be used twice!

Everyone is wondering where the Anglo-American invasion will take place. The Germans, Laurent-Atthalin tells me, are amassing troops in the Pyrenees and say the invasion will come through Spain! Always the same story. *They* are the ones who would like to occupy landing areas in Spain, and perhaps some ports for their submarines, thus replacing the lost African ports, while at the same time threatening Casablanca, which has become a center of operations for the Americans. People who are not under the influence of German propaganda are thinking more and more of the Balkans. An invasion there would permit the taking of Romanian oil wells. Clearly Germany fears this most. One must hope they drag the Bulgarians along with them. If they do that, it will provide a pretext for the Turks to enter the war. As for France, people believe partial attacks will take place from several sides. I think entry into France will be put off for much later and that at most some diversionary incursions will be made. Amid these various hypotheses, France once more lives in hope and anxiety that deliverance is more or less imminent. Impatience is growing, as well as the fear of soon experiencing a food shortage caused by a breakdown in the means of communication. The unseasonable heat has caused the seed potatoes kept in cellars to sprout too soon. People do not dare plant them yet for fear of the late April freezes.

SUNDAY, 4 APRIL 1943   Yesterday at the Academy, Germain-Martin congratulated me on Noël's successful work on the anti-diphtheria vaccine. An effective vaccine has been made possible thanks to a strain Noël brought back from Switzerland. Germain-Martin is on the Pasteur Institute's board, which decided the day before yesterday to promote Noël to the post of deputy section head. A well-deserved compensation for his long perseverance.

MONDAY, 5 APRIL 1943 On Saturday at the Academy, Bardoux told me that elections must not be held right after the Liberation. He would like the Senate to be entrusted with running the government[9] and wants me to pass this idea on to the Americans. . . . These "moderates" are amazing. They always fear their own fellow citizens. Do they really believe they can prevent the country from bringing its will to fruition once this oppression has ended? Do not they see that in order to avoid the uncertain risk of a Chamber of Deputies too far to the left, they run the *certain* risk of a revolutionary explosion against those who, after these years of silence, would like to put a new gag on the country? Do not they see, moreover, that we must return to the only existing legality, that which existed before the "National Revolution"? Well, that legality comprises the Chamber as well as the Senate.

Yesterday around 2:00 PM, while we were walking in the woods with the children in marvelous spring weather, sirens began to wail, and the noise of explosions could be heard. We could not see any planes, but we did see little puffs of smoke at a great height in the sky. After five minutes it was all over. Upon returning we learned, and it was confirmed this morning on the radio, that American planes had bombed the Renault factories in Billancourt. The radio spoke of nine German planes downed and four American Flying Fortresses lost.

WEDNESDAY, 7 APRIL 1943 Sunday's raid resulted in some 250 deaths. Bombs fell on the Longchamp Racecourse in the Bois de Boulogne while there were races going on – also on the Saint-Cloud subway station, where many people wait for the bus to Versailles. A disastrous combination.

SATURDAY, 10 APRIL 1943 The lessons of history! Is there really anyone who believes in them? In every age, attempts at hegemony begin anew: Wilhelm II and Hitler learned nothing from Napoleon; Napoleon learned

---

9. The result of Bardoux's efforts along these lines is reported in his journal, published under the title *La Délivrance de Paris, séances secrètes et négotiations clandestines, octobre 1943–octobre 1944* [The Liberation of Paris, Secret Meetings, and Clandestine Negotiations, October 1943–October 1944] (Paris: Fayard, 1958). The journal describes a later conversation with Charles Rist (19 June 1944) that seems to have signaled something of an evolution in Rist's ideas: "He experienced a veritable repulsion at the prospect of reviving the Chamber. He seems to favor Menthon's solution: a provisional senatorial assembly, elected in two stages. I am beginning to believe . . . that we will have a great deal of trouble in gaining acceptance of our idea: the continuation of the National Assembly." Charles Rist does not mention this encounter.

nothing from Charles XII. In any case, how could a world that includes giants like the United States, Russia, and the British Empire learn anything from periods when these states did not exist? Today as always it is the passions – the same passions as long ago – that govern the course of history, only with different weapons. War is waged in another way, so people think everything has changed and examples from the past are no longer relevant. And we start all over again.

In Tocqueville's *Souvenirs*, page 92, I find this astute remark: "Louis-Philippe had been disappointed by *that deceptive gleam cast by the history of past events on the present*" [Rist's emphasis]. And he gives examples. And the *meaning* of history? Another word with no significance. When one skims through events of the past two thousand years, it is always the same tiresome spectacle of battles, of rivalry between peoples, of states and governments that come and go. If there were not a real life beyond these struggles, a life that little by little transforms customs, improves social life, increases well-being, and opens the mind to science and to art, history would be the most disappointing of all spectacles. Yet only a small minority profit by this expansion of the soul. The rest are doomed to begin the adventures of life again and again, just as nations and empires begin the adventures of history again and again.

The slow advance of British and American forces in Tunisia is exasperating to everyone.

SUNDAY, 11 APRIL 1943 Last night two alerts and heavy bombardments coming very close together. We could not find out where. Later we learned these came from planes on their way to bomb Germany.

Rommel's army in full flight beyond Sfax, but the Americans have not managed to cut it off. It remains to be seen if the French and American forces now near Kairouan will have more success at turning the retreat into a complete rout and preventing reembarkation.

A few days ago the wife of one of our Suez engineers returned from Tunis, via Naples, in a German plane and said everyone in Tunis is for Pétain and Laval. This is the work of that imbecile Admiral Esteva and his Doriotist henchmen.

WEDNESDAY, 13 APRIL 1943 Yesterday at the Banque du Maroc our Italian colleague Petrelli insisted that the shareholders' meeting should take place on the seventh rather than on the seventeenth of June, because, he said, we risk not meeting at all if we put it off too late. Then he left without speaking to anyone. Clearly he is expecting things to happen in Italy or France that will make it difficult for him to come to Paris (he lives in Lausanne). I find it amusing to compare his crestfallen look of today with the carefree air he had three or four months ago.

Sousse abandoned by Rommel's army, which is still on the run, but the Americans took Kairouan too late to attack their flank. Rommel is going to join forces with von Arnim and shore up defenses in Bizerte and Tunis. Exactly what the Americans were trying to prevent! The Americans have announced they are downing a great number of transport planes between Sicily and Bizerte. Are these planes organizing the evacuation or bringing in reinforcements? The first hypothesis is the more likely.

FRIDAY, 16 APRIL 1943 Laval's whole policy can be summed up by this refrain from a ditty of some fifty years ago: "I piddle in the deep blue sea to fuddle the English fleet."

His imbecilic hatred of England is the only explanation for Laval's clownish behavior.

Jean arrived on Monday with news that he has been asked to draw up plans for the establishment of a new national research laboratory for the steel industry. A huge task and an honor that shows his colleagues have understood his gesture of resignation and approve.[10]

Yesterday Lolli left for La Bouffource with her two children and Isabelle. The train was so packed it seemed about to burst, so we passed the children in through the window.

Yesterday morning the anniversary mass for René Parodi. Lots of people at Notre-Dame-des-Champs.

Jean tells me that Champetier de Ribes[11] has been imprisoned by the marshal because he would not give back a letter sent by Pétain before the war in which the latter announced in clear terms his intention to organize a coup. These gentlemen are beginning to fear the High Court. It is the only thing about the Anglo-American successes that interests them.

---

10. After Jean resigned from the Holtzer Steelworks in order not to have to work for the Germans, he was asked by the Comité d'Organisation de la Sidérurgie (CORSID) to make plans for a national research laboratory, of which he was to be the first director. He accomplished this in one year in Paris, even as he was carrying on with his Resistance work. Jean's recommendations for organizing the laboratory were delivered to CORSID in 1944. His ideas were not only accepted and implemented, but the laboratory he founded still exists today. André Rist, "Jean Rist, (1900–1944), Le Fils, Ingénieur et Résistant," in *Charles Rist et les Siens*, 23–24; Jean Rist, *Projet de Laboratoire de Sidérurgie* (Paris: IRSID, Imprimerie Tancrede, 1948), 1–3. [TF]

11. Auguste Champetier de Ribes: Popular Democrat deputy from the Basses-Pyrénées since 1934 and secretary of state at the Foreign Affairs office during the Phoney War.

The other day on the streets of Versailles I witnessed an outrageous spectacle. About a hundred French soldiers in khaki uniforms were singing while they marched behind a German officer; meanwhile some French officers were bringing up the rear. Next came a similar formation of German soldiers. They were all coming back from exercises. The French no doubt belonged to the anti-Bolshevik militia or to one of the numerous militias of the kind created by Laval. Passers-by looked at them with amazement and disgust. Who would later be able to believe that such a disgrace had been possible? And that in a region occupied by the enemy, at the very moment when workers were hunted down to be sent to Germany, some wretches in French uniform were singing, led by enemy officers?

SATURDAY, 1 MAY 1943 A proclamation by Stalin denouncing German attempts to make a separate peace, either with Russia or with the Anglo-Saxons. He has taken up the rallying cry of Casablanca: unconditional surrender for the Nazis. This will surely – at least for a time, let us hope – put an end to the murmurings of collaborators (ex-collaborators today, but whose true feelings have not changed) who whisper in your ear that the Russians and the Germans are close to an agreement.

SUNDAY, 2 MAY 1943 I am reading in Tocqueville's *Souvenirs*, written in 1850 and published in 1893, this passage that still rings true today:

> Amid this languishing of political passions, brought on by weariness with revolutions and their vain promises, a single passion remains alive and well in France: hatred of the ancien regime and mistrust of the old privileged classes who still represent it in the eyes of the people. *Like the water of those marvelous springs that, according to the ancients, passed through the ocean waves without mixing in and without disappearing into them, this feeling passes through revolutions without dissolving* [Rist's emphasis]. As for the Orléans dynasty, experience did not leave people with much taste for going back to it so soon. It would only push the upper classes and the clergy back into opposition, and would separate itself from the people as it had done before, leaving governmental plans and concerns to those same middle classes whose inability to govern well I had observed for eighteen years. In any case, nothing was ready for its triumph.
>
> Louis-Napoleon alone was prepared to take the place of the Republic, because he was already in power. But what could result from his success if not a bastard monarchy, scorned by the enlightened classes, hostile to liberty, and governed by schemers, adventurers, and lackeys? (311)

The opening sentence of this passage is still true. It continues to be the basis for political sentiment among France's common people. It is this sentiment that accounts for the durability of the Third Republic. As for the other parties – Orléanists and Bonapartists, together with "schemers, adventurers, and lackeys" – today they also form a single great party successively known as nationalist, Boulangist, or national, and united under the sign of anticommunism by that schemer and lackey called Laval. The middle classes signed on, too. The genius of true statesmen of the Third Republic, from Waldeck-Rousseau to Briand and Poincaré, was to give the bourgeoisie sufficient social security and a strong enough guarantee of property to prevent them from interfering violently or by military means in the life of the democratic republic and, little by little, to educate the working classes in the ways of freedom.

The problem remains the same today. But in favor of France's democratic regime there is an argument of another kind, and that is not of a political nature, but of a rather *physiological* or *ethnological* kind: true intellectual capacity can no longer be found in conservative milieux or among the sons of social-climbing bourgeois. It is rather to be found among the sons of peasants, workers, or industrious bourgeois. These are the people who alone are sufficiently devoid of artificial traditions to enjoy a free spirit and a taste for technical and scientific progress. If France is not to decline, we must have a regime that makes room for such men and lets the others fall back into the inertia of their old intellectual and moral routines. That is what is important, and up to now only the Republic has demonstrated the ability to guarantee the rise of such men. The penetration of conservative, hidebound elements into the army, industry, and schools over the past twenty years, thanks to the scheming and weakness of republican leaders themselves, was one reason for our disaster.

SATURDAY, 8 MAY 1943 The American and English armies took Tunis and Bizerte by storm yesterday! This is tremendous news! This is the first bell tolling for Germany and Italy. Stalingrad marked a shift in the winds. Russian power made itself felt. But this time it is Anglo-American power! This is even more serious.

How much time does Italy have left? Not much longer, especially if there is a landing in Sicily. And has not Turkey's time come as well?

Aviation seems to have played the decisive role. Anglo-Saxon superiority now seems crushing.

WEDNESDAY, 12 MAY 1943 If one believes an English broadcast, the purpose of Rudolf Hess's arrival in England two years ago was to obtain the English government's consent to Germany's attack on Russia! If that is true, this episode in German diplomacy is really quite amusing – operatic melodrama and the belief that their adversaries are imbeciles. After having admirably penetrated their weakness before the war, Germany is incapable of understanding their strength during the war! This is yet another example of a psychology that scorns imponderables. First among these imponderables must be the terrible *fear* that Germany inspires in England and in the United States and that Germany does not suspect. It is that fear, however, and the sudden illumination of the abyss to which their laziness and their weakness were leading them that have made the Anglo-American allies implacable. Nor is this understood any better by people here, who still believe that a compromise peace is possible. Their faint hearts make it impossible to understand more passionate ones.

General Franco, the genius, has just made it plain in a speech that because events have proved none of the combatants could achieve a complete victory, there is nothing left to do but begin peace negotiations. This executioner of his country, whose every speech includes some monumental stupidity, was truly qualified to serve as the intermediary for German – or French – peace initiatives. I would like to know by which intermediary, which Piétri or which Pétain, Franco was led to make his speech. Yet another enigma of history whose secret we will later learn. What is clear is that for Laval and his friends a compromise peace is the only way to solve our problems. It is thus surely they who pushed the poor general to make this speech, which is all the more ridiculous because only Anglo-American support has allowed him to survive. But what a peculiar idea to let the Germans know that even in Spain no one (not even Franco, one of the stupidest of Spaniards) believes in their victory anymore.

Churchill on his way back to Washington. One can expect decisive action on the part of the Allies in the not too distant future.

It seems Herriot, who was being taken to Germany, fell gravely ill on the way and was hospitalized somewhere in Burgundy.

A Vichy law freeing delinquents who have performed services "in the national interest." This amounts to making inmates available for the militia or for the "work in Germany" program. What a disgrace!

SATURDAY, 15 MAY 1943 In Joseph de Maistre's diplomatic correspondence I find this passage, quoted by Sainte-Beuve in volume 15 of his *Causeries du lundi* (the article is from 1860):

> Why could two great powers not just once, for the benefit of humanity, make the most beautiful and most useful of experiments, that of a free trade of good faith, agreed upon for a certain period and without any intention of getting round each

other? But perhaps that is too much to hope for. Either I am badly mistaken, or that experiment would uncover a great truth. (80)

The experiment was made in 1860. It united France and England. The result was conclusive. It was the Germans – in particular, the Prussian squires, great property owners – who interrupted it in 1870. But the occasion will present itself again at the end of this war. And this time it will be England and the United States that will make the experiment. Will they want to? And if they do, will it be "without any intention of getting round each other"? But if they really wanted it, what a great thing they could accomplish!

FRIDAY, 21 MAY 1943 The bombing by an English squadron of two large dams in the south of the Ruhr and to the south of Kassel, with the resulting floods and destruction, has made a strong impression. The Germans are not talking about it in their newspapers and dedicated only three lines to it in their communiqué. But everyone understands this was an act of war of the first importance.

Visited by Robert Merle d'Aubigné and, yesterday, by Seydoux.[12] The latter was threatened by Abel Bonnard with serious disciplinary action for supposedly having given bad advice to his students at the École [Libre] des Sciences Politiques. Abel Bonnard is a wretch. His threat is part and parcel of Laval's policy of "purging" and "terrorization," which has been applied with renewed strength since his last trip to Germany.

Received and read the two monetary plans of Keynes and White. The former's is absurd from start to finish. Aimed at the United States.

SUNDAY, 23 MAY 1943 Admiral Esteva, supposedly out of loyalty to the marshal, surrendered the Bizerte front to the Germans, when it was so easy with the troops of General Barré to keep it for the Allies and thus avoid the bloody combat that was necessary to retake it. Then when he came to Paris, he was saluted by a German honor guard and honored by letters from both Ribbentrop and Pétain. All of this has been reproduced in photographs by the newspapers, wherein one sees, facing Germanic giants, a small man with the mien of a country doctor and the expression of a well-behaved schoolboy, saluting and being saluted. It is completely disgusting. The admiral comes off as pure and innocent. People call him a saint. Strange praise for a man of war.

This reminds me of the conversation between Napoleon and Marmont shortly before the latter's act of betrayal. I am reproducing here the version

12. Roger Seydoux: director of the École Libre des Sciences Politiques.

found in Sainte-Beuve's *Causeries du lundi* of 5 April 1852 (6: 17), where three fine articles are devoted to Marshal Marmont. The emperor received Marmont at one o'clock in the morning:

> [Napoleon] complained about his allies and about his father-in-law, the Emperor Francis, and thereupon launched into an explanation of the difference between *the man of conscience* and *the man of honor*. With the man of honor, with the person who purely and simply keeps his word and his commitments, one knows whom to trust, whereas with the other, with the man of conscience, who does what he thinks best, one depends upon his wisdom and his judgment. And he continued, "My father-in-law the emperor of Austria has done what he believed was in the best interest of his subjects. He is an *honnête homme*, a man of conscience, but not a man of honor. You, for example (here he took Marmont by the arm), if the enemy had invaded France and was on the heights of Montmartre and you believed, even rightly, that for the sake of the country you must abandon me and you did, you would be a good Frenchman, a fine man, a man of conscience, and not a man of honor." Marmont continued with understandable emotion: These words pronounced by Napoleon and addressed to me on 11 October 1813, do they not bear the imprint of an extraordinary character? Is there not something supernatural and prophetic in them? They came back to me after the events at Essonne and impressed me in a way that you may imagine and which I have never forgotten.

Time passed, and after 1830 Marshal Marmont found himself in Vienna instructing the Duke of Reichstadt on events in Napoleon's life, and here the subject came up again:

> In a conversation with the marshal touching on various subjects, he eventually brought up an abstract, or rather moral issue, and comparing the man of honor to the man of conscience, he expressed a clear preference for the latter, "because it is always the best, the most beneficial outcome that he wants, whereas the other can become the blind instrument of a bad or crazy person." (Sainte-Beuve [*Causeries du lundi*], 56)

How interesting it is to reread these passages today. Esteva is perhaps, according to this definition, a man of honor (!), but certainly not a man of conscience. The curious thing is that during this war most of our generals, admirals, and marshals, including Pétain, have been men of conscience when it came to betraying the republic and men of honor when it came to obeying Marshal Pétain, who set the example for betrayal.

MONDAY, 24 MAY 1943 According to the radio, Giraud's latest proposal to de Gaulle is for an executive committee to be presided over by both generals and four members, two of whom would be appointed by Giraud and two by de Gaulle. This committee would appoint commissioners and must have the support of a legislative council (appointed how?). As soon as possible this committee would submit its powers for approval by the Assembly of General Councils appointed according to the law of 1872 – that is, the one doing away with the houses of Parliament.[13]

This project is the height of absurdity. The two generals will constitute a *directoire* destined for impotence or for a coup d'état. And as for the application of the law of 1872 (repealed by Vichy), it is incomprehensible, given that the chambers of Parliament still exist, though suppressed by Vichy. If one accepts this latter suppression, why would the law of 1872, equally suppressed by Vichy, still be in force? And, conversely, if the law of 1872 remains in effect, all the legislation of Vichy is null and, consequently, so is the de facto suppression of the chambers of Parliament.

One would like to know the de facto reasons that lie hidden beneath these judicial proposals.

FRIDAY, 4 JUNE 1943 Today at last the agreement between de Gaulle and Giraud has been announced. The communiqué leaves considerable room for uncertainties regarding the future. They say the "Liberation Committee" will be replaced, once the enemy has vacated the territory, by a "provisional government" appointed according to the laws of the republic. These laws to my knowledge do not provide for a "provisional government." So what does that mean?

The committee includes four generals: de Gaulle, Catroux, Giraud, and General Georges, springing up out of nowhere for the occasion. The civilians are André Philip, Massigli, and Jean Monnet. The latter no longer knows anything about France, as he has not lived here for eight years. Two others must be appointed to round out the committee to nine members. Let us hope there will not be more generals. This is all very murky and scarcely reassuring.

It has been announced that Puaux will replace Noguès as France's resident general in Morocco.

Jean just spent three days here. He has been given the mission of creating a national research laboratory for the steel industry. But his thoughts are elsewhere. He is asking himself where his duty lies.

Saw two or three people who spoke to me about some so-called Resistance groups. They are the carbonari[14] of the Liberation. They start off full

---

13. Paris was under martial law for five years following repression of the commune in 1871. [TF]

14. This diary entry is intriguing. These "carbonari of the Liberation" remain unidentified. [JNJ] Carbonari: persistent but feckless provocateurs. [TF]

of enthusiasm. Soon they are on somebody's payroll making a career out of it. Their ideas are simplistic and absurd: make something new, nobody from the old parties, creation of a "pure" political climate, etc., etc. People with the outlook of a La Rocque and the lingo of the Popular Front. Neither judgment nor ability. To top it off, the movement is rife with informers. When the Germans entered the free zone on 11 November, many who had been denounced were arrested and shot.

C.[15] has asked if I did not want to go over to the other side, saying my name has been mentioned several times. I answered that at my age I have too many responsibilities, too many children and grandchildren who depend partly on me, that some men must stay in France. (The truth is that I don't know what I would be doing over there, what purpose I would serve; I know in advance I would be disgusted by all the political hot air.) I told him there is only one place where I could be of service and that is in Washington. But for now it is the military, and they alone, who have a say.

I come back to a 1914 book by Edmond Théry, which has statistics relating to Russia. Théry estimated the 1912 population at 171 million and foresaw (at the growth rate from 1900 to 1912) a population of 272 million in 1936! In point of fact, after its foreign and civil wars and various famines, Russia must have more than 200 million today. How is it that Europe could have been stupid enough to believe that it could just boycott such an immense population? How did it not understand that such masses necessarily have a despotic government and, sooner or later, a powerful military? French and English conservative parties have demonstrated their blindness in this regard. Théry also predicted the rapid settlement of southern Siberia and its penetration "by a network of railroads that has already been planned" and calculated a quarter of a century for this transformation to be achieved. That is exactly what happened. And it is probable that with or without the Russian Revolution this miracle would have taken place. He concluded that observers "taking into account what has occurred since the beginning of the twentieth century . . . will infer that . . . around the middle of this century Russia will dominate Europe, both politically and economically." On this pretext Germany invaded Russia, precipitating the catastrophe that it wished to avoid. This is the great fact that faces us now and will dominate the postwar years.

FRIDAY, 11 JUNE 1943 A period of waiting, impatience, and anxiety. The adversaries are all watching each other; the Germans do not dare attack

---

15. Rist was probably referring to René Courtin, professor of economics at the Montpellier Law Faculty and former colleague of Charles Rist. [JNJ/TF]

before knowing on which side the Allies are going to fall upon them. Even air attacks on Germany have been suspended. The only action is in Pantelleria, which refused to surrender and is still being bombarded. The world is in suspense. There is not a word from the Allies to indicate where the event that has been expected and announced will take place. The only thing one can guess is that Russian operations and the Allied landing will probably be coordinated. Will the latter begin in Italy or in the Balkans? I lean toward the second alternative. Who knows? Perhaps it will start with a strong attack in the Balkans followed, once all the German forces have massed on that side, by an attack in Holland or in Scandinavia? Or even in Corsica and Sardinia? Lately many Allied ships and planes appear to be operating in those regions.

I have been told of the death of poor Raymond Philippe, interned by Laval in a concentration camp and killed by a stroke. He received no treatment and was refused a shroud in which to be buried. They say that in his camp he was befriended by General La Laurencie, interned likewise by Laval for the crime of lèse-majesté.

FRIDAY, 25 JUNE 1943 The war has been reduced to air raids on Germany and Italy. On the eastern front the Russians seem to have air superiority. Moreover, the Germans have announced they are withdrawing their submarines from the Atlantic because of England's new methods of attack. One is thus reduced to guesswork as to the possibility or impossibility of a landing. Certain soothsayers (citing remarks made by Payot of the *Journal de Genève* at a lunch with the queen of Spain) declare that a landing is impossible. On the other hand, on a visit I made to Behiç, back in Paris to prepare his definitive move to Constantinople, he indicated that he expects important events to occur over the course of the coming weeks.

WEDNESDAY, 30 JUNE 1943 Arrests everywhere. Daniel Trocmé arrested in Le Chambon.[16] Jean has been here with Marcel for the past week.

16. Daniel Trocmé, son of Charles Rist's sister Ève and her husband, Henri Trocmé, was in charge of two shelters for young refugees, mostly Jewish and Spanish children, in Le Chambon-sur-Lignon. According to Daniel's niece Françoise Nicolas Trocmé, on 29 June 1943 the Gestapo arrived to arrest the children in one of the shelters and sent for Daniel from the other. Daniel, when asked if he was Jewish, replied, "*Si vous voulez*" ("If you wish"), in order not to be separated from the children. After spending some time in jail with his young charges, he was transferred to Compiègne, then to the Majdanek death camp near Lublin, Poland, where he died the following year. Philippe Boegner recounts his arrest and the atmosphere at the time in Le Chambon in his book *Ici, on a*

He has been working enthusiastically on planning his national research laboratory. But his thoughts are elsewhere.

TUESDAY, 6 JULY 1943   German offensive at Kursk, which the Russians say was repelled. Do the Germans want to rid themselves of the Russian front before the Allied offensive is ready? And afterward, swoop down on the Allies in the Balkans? Are the tactics of the Horaces and Curiaces beginning all over again?

---

aimé les Juifs [Here, the Jews Were Loved] (Paris: Lattès, 1982), 157–58. Interview with Françoise Nicolas Trocmé, 12 November 2010. [JNJ/TF]

Seventeen

Good News from Italy,
Perils on the Home Front

12 JULY–5 SEPTEMBER 1943
The Allied landing in Sicily and subsequent resignation of Mussolini once again brought hope that the war would soon end. There was, however, an ironic and poignant contrast between good news on the Italian front and the danger of starvation and death at home.

As the Rists came under increasing pressure to protect the Jewish members of their family, they allowed ten-year-old Antoinette to cross over the Alps on foot with her aunt Marie. This dramatic crossing, a journey fraught with peril, receives only circumspect mention in the diary.

MONDAY, 12 JULY 1943 The Anglo-American landing began in Sicily on Saturday. The little being said about it in the newspapers and on German and Italian radio indicates utter confusion. This augurs well. They say there are three hundred thousand Italians and one hundred thousand Germans garrisoned in Sicily. But the Allies have reportedly deployed two thousand ships for the landing. At one hundred men per ship the landing of a big army can be fast. The radio recalled the expedition of Belisarius.

TUESDAY, 13 JULY 1943 Once again we are hanging on every radio broadcast. One would like to follow developments hour by hour. The English and Americans have declared they are quite pleased. But they add that the real difficulty will begin *after* the landing. Meanwhile ten coastal cities have already been taken with hardly a blow struck. One wonders if the Italian resistance will be serious and if the army will not seek to surrender at the first chance, then join the British and Americans to drive out the Germans.

MONDAY, 19 JULY 1943 Excellent military news. The British are about to take Catania and already occupy a third of Sicily. They have taken thirty thousand prisoners, a fact that does not indicate great enthusiasm for combat on the part of the Italians. It seems the Sicilians have welcomed the Allied troops with open arms. In Russia the German offensive has failed and the Russians themselves have retaken the offensive around Orel.

Fabre-Luce has presumably been arrested following distribution of the third volume of his *Journal de la France* (not for sale), in which he envisages the possible defeat of Germany, and in which he declares that the real advocates of the "wait-and-see" policy were the "collaborationists," of whom he was one of the most publicly avowed. A magnificent reversal, but one that has strongly displeased the Germans. In *l'Opinion* Gignoux, another collaborator, declares that whatever may happen, the "National Revolution," which he adds has not even begun, must become a reality. This is another reversal, but what ignorance of the situation if he thinks that after the war he can salvage principles (!) that will be forever marked by the seal of the invader.

In Sainte-Beuve's articles on Mme Desbordes-Valmore, I find an 1856 letter from Raspail, then in exile in Belgium, addressed to Mme Valmore, whom he used to call his "muse." In it he expresses admirably the sentiments of a Frenchman for France in one of those moments in which history brought the country to its lowest depths:

> Oh! What a beautiful country is mine! A land rich in miracles even in times of temporary torment and waywardness! Here people just pass you by; where you are, people exist, love one other, appreciate one another, understand and respect one another, even after death. Oh! if France were to be wiped off the map, the universe would lose its head and heart; this little corner thinks and acts for everyone. All is renewed as soon as it understands it must change clothes; everything under the dome of heaven trembles once this Jupiter frowns. The mere memory of its sun could warm you even on polar ice. Good mother or wicked stepmother, France is adored; one would have oneself killed twenty times over, even if she were ungrateful, provided that she were more beautiful still. *Though history has seen France possessed by idiots and scoundrels, no one has been able to humiliate or enslave her* [Rist's emphasis]. Sing, my muse, of this admirable France, heroic, witty, kind and affectionate, thrifty and liberal, a bit coquettish and fundamentally loving, a bit sardonic, but always just and impartial, great mistress of endless progress who carries in her turbulent wake even the Cossacks and Hurons. Sing of this mother, you her adoptive daughter, who understand her so well. (*Nouveaux Lundis*, 12: 251)

In response to this letter Sainte-Beuve writes the following lines (we are in 1869), which foresee the collapse of 1870–1871 and which could so well apply to the years preceding this current war:

> Already in the Middle Ages people spoke of *la douce France*; the knights, the valiant Rolands who died far from her, saluted her thus. *The children of the*

Revolution enthusiastically and proudly renewed this filial cult and this love [Rist's emphasis]. Has it weakened since then, as so many signs indicate? Has it altered or dried up? That France of our fathers, the one of '89 and '92, that France of Manuel, of Béranger, of Raspail, that of our youth, is she thus no longer the France of today and tomorrow? I do not dare to press the future or to force the omens; I do not want to look at the greater or lesser resemblance; I will stick to that pious and enthusiastic invocation by which a faithful believer saluted the absent homeland at the new year. (250)

And we too, could we not ask: has it then disappeared, that France of our youth, that of Zola, of Picquart, of Clemenceau, that of our mature years, that of Foch, that of Clemenceau, that of Briand, and even on certain days, that of Poincaré?

THURSDAY, 22 JULY 1943 The Hitler-Mussolini meeting in northern Italy, at the very time when Allied aviation was bombing Rome for two and a half hours, must have been the most dramatic of the war. The communiqué states that they viewed the military situation "with no illusions." It was evidently the German High Command that dictated those words, which for Italians are the equivalent of *"Lasciate ogni speranza"*![1] How much longer can they last? How long will the army agree to fight in vain? Already we hear of forty thousand prisoners. It seems the troops defending Catania are mainly German. American troops have occupied Enna, at the very center of Sicily.

FRIDAY, 23 JULY 1943 The speed with which the Allies are advancing in Sicily is amazing everyone and is giving rise to the greatest hopes. The Americans are already in Palermo. Everyone is wondering what direction the army will take after Catania falls. The advance of the Russians toward Orel is perhaps even more important. Meanwhile the American government is urging the public not to entertain illusions or believe the war is already won. The tone of papers here is ever more curious. They are no longer trumpeting Laval's praise. They restrain themselves to ask, "In his place, would you do any better?" And this defense of the government, when not a line can be written against it, shows well enough that he knows everyone despises him.

MONDAY, 26 JULY 1943 This morning at 8:30 the radio announced Mussolini's resignation. What this news means for the world is huge! Not that

---

1. *"Voi ch'entrate, lasciate ogni speranza"* (You who enter here, abandon all hope). This is the famous inscription that Dante placed over the gates of hell in the *Divine Comedy.* [JNJ/TF]

this character was great, but he had inaugurated the governmental regime of permanent fear. And that regime is falling. One cannot prevent the entire world from seeing in this event – through one of those certain intuitions that are known by their very intensity – the prefiguration of another event that from now on will appear to be certain: the fall of Hitler. And he himself cannot fail to see this as a bad sign – not to mention the henchmen of Hitler and Mussolini, the Lavals and the Francos, who derived all of their confidence from imitation.

Now we will see how much political sense the Anglo-Saxons have and if they have understood events. They might forgo demands of unconditional surrender, thus inviting Germany to make a sacrifice similar to Italy's, replacing Hitler with a member of the military in order to obtain the same advantage. Or they might demand that the Italian king and Marshal Badoglio capitulate, assuring them of certain guarantees, and then one can hope the Allies would pursue the war until Germany is defeated and the Allies enter Berlin.

Badoglio has declared that "the war goes on." That is also what the Lvov government declared after the fall of the czar, which did not stop the Russians from laying down their arms. The Italian soldiers are no more eager to continue the war than were the Russian soldiers back then. This expression makes sense only with regard to the Germans, whose reactions can be troublesome as long as they have troops in Italy and must be reassured.

Once Italy is out of the game, the Balkans will be freed of the Italian garrisons. We may see Turkey enter the war and setbacks for German troops in Russia. In that case the war could end much sooner than expected. Instead of six months or a year, it could be three or four months. What hope all of this will give the French!

The Germans will be able to say that in 1917 the fall of Russia did not prevent the Allies from winning and consequently the fall of Italy does not compromise the Germans' triumph today. But analogies of this sort mean nothing. The Americans had arrived to aid the Allies in 1918, replacing disabled Russia. From whom can the Germans expect similar help today?

I have just heard on American radio that Mussolini's resignation is only an incident, that it does not mean fascism is dead, and that the Allies will continue to demand "unconditional surrender" as long as a democratic revolution has not taken place in Italy. It hints that the event may have been prepared in Verona at the time of the meeting with Hitler. Clearly the message for Americans is that they should not let their guard down, as the war has not been won.

FRIDAY, 30 JULY 1943 Since Monday the only news that interests us concerns the repercussions of Mussolini's fall. As of now we have only rumors. Every country, especially Italy, seeks to conceal what is going on within its borders. In the papers controlled by Germany the name Mussolini no longer appears. One would think he had vanished. The only commentaries allowed consist in declaring that Italy is still in the war and that Germany is very strong. Vichy persists in believing that at the last minute the English and Americans will turn against the Russians. This is a measure of the profound stupidity of the Vichy people. Earlier their hope was that the United States would prefer an end to the war rather than to enter it themselves. All of this indicates a bizarre confusion. As for the Balkans, English radio talks of great shifts of opinion in Bulgaria, Romania, and Hungary. But all this is, of course, premature.

Here everyone is rejoicing. Even people you do not know share their optimism with you. The feeling everywhere is that something very important has happened, and very few still doubt a happy outcome.

Scorching heat, disastrous drought, threatening the potato and bean harvests.

Antoinette and Marie (Noël) crossed over the Cornettes de Bise and have arrived safely in Vevey.

Noël is still in Aix. His supervisor, Doctor Lafaye, called me to say that the passport he was waiting for will not be delivered. All passports for Switzerland have been suspended owing to political and diplomatic events.

The news filtering in from Germany indicates that the air raids on Cologne, Aix-la-Chapelle, and Hamburg have left tens of thousands of victims.

SUNDAY, 1 AUGUST 1943 Noël arrived yesterday from Aix. He came to get his passport to Switzerland, but we told him he had been refused. He has therefore decided to leave by his own methods. Then, lo, this morning a phone call informed him that the Germans believe they can provide him with one anyway. He will thus spend a few more days waiting for it! But with no guarantees! He told us of Antoinette and Marie's eventful journey crossing the Cornettes de Bise.[2] Only we fear that now German guards will

---

2. Behind this circumspect summation lies a poignant story. Antoinette, Rist's Jewish granddaughter, made this harrowing crossing of the Cornettes de Bise, a mountain on the border between France and Switzerland, at the age of ten. The journey, made on foot, marked her profoundly: "I remember very well crossing the Swiss border with Marie. . . . It must have been a bit of an ordeal for her, a Swiss citizen, to smuggle a child

replace the Italians at the border. And all will be more difficult. How complicated and how frustrating!

According to the radio the Germans have occupied Fiume and Trieste! They have lost no time, whereas the Allies have suspended raids on Italy to give the Italians time to reflect. This is what one learns from a new proclamation by General Eisenhower. The Anglo-American forces are thus always going to be outflanked! They do not see that the best way to get the Italians to surrender is a vigorous pursuit of the war.

We know nothing at all about what is going on in Italy. Clearly the new government has only one thing in mind and that is to save the position of the king, to maintain the House of Savoy at all costs – just as Darlan thought only of maintaining the Vichy government when the Americans entered North Africa! But what will be decisive is the attitude of the troops and their refusal to fight. And if they refuse, they will no more fight against the Germans than against the Allies. The fact is, the Germans can occupy Italy much more easily than the Allies can. It is the latter, once again, who will find themselves trumped! The fall of Mussolini will backfire against them.

MONDAY, 2 AUGUST 1943 According to the radio, American pilots have made low-altitude bombing raids on Ploeşti, the heart of Romania's oil refineries. This area is practically the only source of natural petroleum accessible to the Germans, as they were unable to seize Russian oil fields. Until now the Allies could not reach those fields from available bases, but problems of distance have been overcome, and the result may be significant. Such a move has been long awaited; I always thought the aim of the Allied offensive in the Middle East had to be Ploeşti. If the raids have the desired effect, they will mark an important step toward shortening the war.

A proclamation has issued from the Allied High Command in Egypt demanding that Crete prevent the Germans from disarming the occupying Italian troops, as rumor has it they want to do throughout the Balkans! A new paradox of this war! But are the Allies sure that the armed Italians will no longer be a danger to them? Do they think the Badoglio government is already ripe for capitulation? Do they not fear the treachery that is natural to any Italian government? Are they counting on Italy's current turmoil to

---

illegally across that border. It was traumatic for me, terrifying when bullets rang around us, as Italian guards shot at us, maybe intentionally missing, I do not know, but then, I felt they wanted us dead. It was then that I understood the full extent of the fury against Jews." Email to translator, 11 March 2011. [TF]

force the hand of the government despite the presence and resistance of the Germans?

Jean left this morning for Saint-Étienne. Still anxious to know if he has fulfilled his duty. I advised him strongly to remain in France, where he will be able, when the time comes, to render great services, whereas he might be immobilized in Switzerland for an indefinite period.

FRIDAY, 6 AUGUST 1943 Yesterday the radio announced the taking of Orel by the Russians and of Catania by the British. Today the Russians have announced that Belgorod has been retaken. Everyone realizes the importance of this decisive news. Soon we will know what choice Italy has made. Radio Paris and the papers bankrolled by Germany are silent on these events; on the contrary, they have invented a German victory at Isim in Russia. This is becoming almost as comical as it is odious. Nor is there a word in those papers regarding the appalling devastation rained down on Hamburg by the air raids. We are really on the way to liberation! No longer do we suffer anxiety, just impatience.

One must read Quinet's book *La République*, in which he gives us the thinking of conservatives after the defeat of 1870–1871 in its stark purity. Quinet's description is just as relevant today as those of Béranger or Stendhal were in 1815. In all three periods one finds the same cowardice, the same lack of national spirit, the same hatred of the system of free government! The continuity is alarming. Here is a passage, on page 255, that applies word for word to the reactionaries who gave us the "National Revolution," and whose heroes are Laval and Pétain:

> In every nation one can measure the vitality of a class by the energy and stubbornness its members exhibit in defending the nation against foreign invasion. This rule is as certain as any of the laws of physics.
>
> In our time the opportunity has arisen to demonstrate what the retrograde parties still retain of national energy. When they pounce on those who would wage all-out war on the enemy (Gambetta) and fight to the end for the soil of the fatherland, how can they not see that it is they themselves who will suffer the greatest wounds?
>
> By repeating constantly that after the first loss France must bow her head, surrender her arms, and place herself in the hands of the enemy, do they not realize they are breaking with the French nation? Has any other people ever experienced such talk?
>
> The English aristocracy has stayed in power because it did the complete opposite: it took the lead in the great war against France from 1792 to 1815; it desired *all-out war* for the grandeur of old England. That is why the English aristocracy has endured.

Those who in 1940 constantly repeated, "We are beaten," concluding that the sole option open to France was resignation, thus had their forerunners in 1870–1872, and they have not changed. Let us not forget, however, that in our time many socialists did the same. And that, conversely, de Gaulle and d'Estienne d'Orves have numbered among the Resistance fighters.

Quinet continues:

> One must not suppose, however, that a nation will perish because the so-called upper classes collapse or lose their raison d'être. The nations that count in the world have all changed heads several times. If the crown withers, the sap will continue to circulate through the rest of the tree. What we are seeing today appears to be the crisis whereby the weakening upper classes are replaced by those classes that have maintained their vitality. (257)

WEDNESDAY, 11 AUGUST 1943 A victorious advance by the Russians on Kharkov. After the Orel crisis, they have marched on without stopping. This offensive power has astounded everyone. Roosevelt is in Montréal with Churchill and Mackenzie King to discuss the Allies' next military moves. Will they take place in the Balkans or in Italy? On the radio we hear of various rumors circulating in the neutral capitals regarding the uneasiness of the Balkan governments and their desire to change allegiances. All depends upon how fast the Italians capitulate. But Italy is dragging its feet, though the Italian army's desire for peace is no longer in doubt. The Italians garrisoned in Nice, Cannes, Aix, and Chambéry have been replaced by Germans.

The Franco-German papers are an ever greater curiosity. They complain of the stupidity of French public opinion. They urge unity under the aegis of Laval. Many of these journalists who have been in the pay of the enemy for three years declare they have only followed and supported the policies of the legal French government, which was, they say, the duty of any good citizen. One can already see their line of defense and their fear of reprisals. Meanwhile Laval is preparing his Praetorian Guard in the form of various "legions" and the new French army, of which one regiment, it seems, has already been set up. He will not leave the scene without having first set off civil war. The poor marshal in a speech has declared that everybody "talks too much" and that "everything would be fine" if people said less. Does he not realize that no newspaper has said anything for the past three years?

Noël, returning yesterday, told us that Baumgartner, Escalier, and other public finance inspectors have been arrested. Bertoud, warned in time, managed to escape. Simultaneously the arrest of a great number of *French* Jews apparently took place in the 13th Arrondissement. Why?

Noël is still waiting for his passport for Switzerland. Jean is coming this evening. Françoise has written to say it would be wiser for her not to come here. The Trocmés are still in the dark regarding the fate of Daniel, who, it seems, must stand trial. For now we think he is in prison in Moulins. When will this all end?

Yesterday saw Falkenhausen, who is thinner and seems somber, and asked him to see what he can find out about poor Mme L.,[3] who still has no news of her husband, imprisoned somewhere in Germany.

An hour of antiaircraft fire, first at 11:00 PM, then at four in the morning. We presume they were firing on the bombers that, according to radio reports this morning, raided Nuremberg during the night.

FRIDAY, 15 AUGUST 1943   Russian attack on Kharkov.

Rumor has it that the marshal already sees Hitler overthrown and the Wehrmacht in power. In that case, they say, he would reach an understanding with the latter, promising to oppose any English landing. In exchange he would get some major concession from the Germans – for example, the repatriation of prisoners – thus restoring his prestige with the French. The operation would be preceded by Laval's ouster. As a result, Spain, Italy, and France would all have a military figure as their head. The Franco-Badoglio-Pétain trio would cut a fine figure in the history books. Three generals without an army! These it seems are the foolish dreams of this poor man.

They say Mény, the best man in the oil industry, has been arrested by the Germans. He is one of the most energetic and efficient Frenchmen I know. Protestant, like Baumgartner and Escalier.

New antiaircraft fire during the night. This time the American or English planes were flying toward Italy.... As I write, there goes the air-raid siren again. It has become an almost daily occurrence.

At bottom this test of strength that the war amounts to is between militarist and industrial powers. It is a matter of ascertaining whether the latter are the most likely to win, given modern conditions, and to triumph in all domains over countries that rely solely on their army. If this is indeed the meaning of the conflict, we might be able to move toward a rather long peace after the Allied victory. But that peace does not rule out future wars *between industrial powers* themselves – a rivalry between the Germanic, Slavic, and Anglo-Saxon worlds! Or between the three greatest empires in the world. We pale in comparison to these enormous forces; our only role will be to keep the

3. Not identified.

peace and to "civilize" our empire *and ourselves*. Harmony with neighboring small peoples and with England will protect us from the closest dangers. And as in the past with the Turks against the Hapsburgs, we shall side with the Russians against Germany. Russia's future is formidable.

TUESDAY, 17 AUGUST 1943 No one is talking about anything but the finance inspectors' having been sent to Germany. They were quite properly treated, grouped, and dispatched in second-class cars. We can only guess at the reasons for their arrest. Doubtless to exert pressure on Laval or to have hostages.

Bombing of Turin and Milan. The Italians have declared Rome an open city. But the Allies have responded that a simple declaration is not enough and that they must prove that Rome will no longer serve any military purpose. Badoglio is decidedly in an uncomfortable position.

The American radio commentator one hears on Saturday evenings complains that Stalin is taking initiatives that endanger the Allies. A certain committee calling itself "Free Germany" has supposedly published in *Pravda* a proposal for peace with Germany that indicates the Russians are disposed to leave the German army intact after the fall of Hitler. The Americans point to this as an unsettling sign. English and Franco-English radio broadcasts do not mention the incident. This "free" Germany with its committee based in Moscow, would it not be a "communist" Germany? Is Stalin making overtures to the German generals? Shall we see Prussian militarism kept in the saddle by Russian militarism under the guise of communism? Yet another surprise!

SUNDAY, 22 AUGUST 1943 Litvinov has left Washington and been replaced as ambassador. Given Maisky's departure from London, is this a sign of Marshal Stalin's unhappiness? Is there some new Allied decision or some new Russian about-face in the wind? We continue to live in the dark, reduced to conjectures based on fragmentary news. The other day Wibratte told me that Stalin has opposed the Balkan landing. But on what information is Wibratte relying – and coming from whom? Are the Allies going to renounce the most efficacious military operation? Where, then, would they come down? On the radio "the representative of the inter-Allied command" asks the French to be ready! Is it plausible that such a statement would be made to the enemy – if it is not a ploy? The Quebec Conference continues. We shall know in a few weeks, perhaps sooner, what truth there is in all these conjectures.

Jean left again last Tuesday for Fraisses. Somber and preoccupied by what he must do for Marcel.[4]

Noël finally left on Friday evening, armed with his passport. He waited for four weeks for it and had to endure the insults of an embassy bureaucrat who asked him, "Do you want my fist in your bloody face, or do you want to spend time in the bloody clink?" It seems he is a former boxer, representing his party at the embassy. Always "correct," these gentlemen.

WEDNESDAY, 25 AUGUST 1943   Yesterday a great cannonade of antiaircraft fire. At 7:00 PM we saw at least a hundred English planes pass overhead, surrounded by a mass of little jet plumes marking the explosions of antiaircraft fire. The group of English planes crossed through this storm with calm majesty, never getting out of formation. This morning we learned via radio that they were in Villacoublay.

SATURDAY, 28 AUGUST 1943   The Quebec Conference has concluded. Roosevelt has declared that the Germans, if they knew what awaited them, would immediately and unconditionally surrender.

Great raid on Berlin at the start of the week.

Recognition of the Liberation Committee in Algiers by England, the United States, and Russia. Russia states it is going to send a diplomatic representative to the committee.

In Germany, Himmler has been appointed minister of the interior.

Reading Quinet – his correspondence during the years of exile and just after the second of December – I am struck once again by the similarity of the periods and the states of mind. But to think that after seventy years of

---

4. That summer Jean Rist was anxious to ensure the safety of his wife and children. He was not just undertaking to design a new research laboratory for the steel industry, but would soon be resuming his activities in the Resistance. It was too dangerous for the family to remain in Fraisses, as the Jacob Holtzer Steelworks nearby, now in the service of the Germans, would become a target for Allied bombing, and Jean's Resistance activities might trigger police raids. The decision was made to have his wife, Jeannette; André (sixteen); and Simone (twelve) move to Le Chambon-sur-Lignon. Marcel, who had recently turned eighteen, risked being forced to join one of Vichy's youth movements unless he could get a job or continue his studies (he had just completed his baccalaureate). After working for the summer in Saint-Etienne, he was able to return to his lycée in the same town for a new second-year preparatory course, "established that year as if by a miracle," for entry into the École Normale Supérieure. Marcel would live in Saint-Étienne with Charles Trocmé. André Rist, email to translator, 16 November 2011. [TF]

republican government a group of Frenchmen could be found who would try to restage the coup d'état, inspired by the same ideas that made it succeed some ninety years ago! It is beyond belief. Even to the point of reusing the same old words! Dufaure, in a speech for which Quinet criticizes him strongly, calls the republicans "demagogues." This is precisely the term used today by reactionaries when referring to republicans.

No doubt this war was necessary to make it crystal clear that a police state is *impossible* in the modern world. This is what will be blindingly apparent once the war is over. All those who have supported such a state will go to ground. The more moderate have at last understood the meaning of political freedom. For some – for example, Quinet – and for me in large part, the word "freedom" had a certain mystique. But what will make it triumphant is the impossibility of doing without freedom in the world in which we live, if that world is to achieve the minimal well-being and efficiency that the less mystical and more positive citizens wish for. Freedom is the condition without which – given our enormous populations, in which each class and each profession is compartmentalized, knowing almost nothing of the others – it would be impossible to know anything of what others are doing and thinking. The worst sentiments, the worst professional deficiencies could be ignored forever if there were no freedom to discuss and to publish. A government can thus incur its own ruin, preparing its own internal tidal wave or else horrendous foreign catastrophes without realizing it, without anyone being able to call out to warn it. One man or even several men, though they be wise and well-intentioned, are unable in this immense and complicated modern world to understand and master what they must of people and of events. But of course if they are wise and well-intentioned, they will hold fast to freedom. Only the strong and the wicked dream of settling for force.

TUESDAY, 31 AUGUST 1943 King Boris of Bulgaria died on the way back from a visit to Hitler in Berlin. Doubtless assassinated by a Macedonian.

Yesterday the Russians took Taganrog.

State of siege proclaimed in Denmark. The Danish fleet scuttled. They say the king has been taken prisoner. Fighting between Danish troops and the Germans.

SUNDAY, 5 SEPTEMBER 1943 On Friday Anglo-Canadian troops crossed the Strait of Messina into continental Italy, landing in Reggio. According to the radio, they were acclaimed by the Italian people, and the Italian soldiers surrendered en masse.

The Trocmés came to see us yesterday. They have just been informed that Daniel was transferred to Compiègne. Under what conditions? Why? With what possible new transfers, perhaps to Germany? They never lose heart. They are going to Compiègne on Tuesday to try to see him and are prepared to do whatever is necessary to free the poor boy. It seems he was denounced by someone in the Belgian consulate in Vichy, with which he had had some dealings.

It has been announced today that the Holy Synod in Russia has been reestablished!

Provisions are becoming harder to get by the day. Nowhere has the potato harvest not been ruined. If we do not come up with the 1,000 kilos we had last year, there is no way we can feed our extensive family this winter.

A speech by Churchill in Quebec in which he talked sympathetically about France in a very long, seemingly important, passage.

Last Tuesday Courtin came to see me, and we talked about his economic report.[5] He was keen on the idea of freezing some bank deposits to prevent a rise in prices after the war. I told him why that is absurd. All the ideas of his group favor unchecked interventionism. He is doing the best he can.

On Saturday the English made a raid on Paris in broad daylight.

More and more frequently now we are awakened by antiaircraft fire aimed at the English planes heading to or from Germany.

5. The *Rapport sur la politique économique d'après-guerre* [Report on Post-War Economic Policy], which René Courtin drafted for the General Studies Committee of the Resistance, was published secretly in November 1943.

Eighteen

Twilight of the Rogues

9 SEPTEMBER–20 NOVEMBER 1943

In Charles Rist's view, Hitler the zealot, Mussolini the jackal, and Laval the rusé were simply rogues whose time was running out. In late October, however, the rogues' reign of terror came very close to home. According to Rist's diary entry for 31 October 1943, his daughter-in-law Françoise was summoned by the Gestapo in Maisons-Laffite for an interrogation regarding two denunciations that had been received against her: one for not wearing her yellow star, the other for traveling between her home in Le Vésinet and Paris.[1]

THURSDAY, 9 SEPTEMBER 1943 Romier came to see me yesterday. Supposedly at the marshal's behest he had come to consult me on the following point: the marshal is anxious to rid himself of Laval; he can no longer tolerate his physical presence. The minister would be sent packing to be replaced by civil servants; the current general secretaries would be in line; the marshal would surround himself with a directory of three to five members. What did I think of this? My immediate response: "Keep Laval. He wanted to do this job, let him continue. Who, at this stage of the game, will want to take on the responsibility of replacing him? Or else have the marshal go."

"I'm not just thinking of the marshal," Romier replied, "I'm thinking of France. *If he goes, it is civil war.* There are plenty of generals who ask nothing more than to lead this gang. It's the marshal who commands their respect." I did not ask where these generals would find men to follow them. I just asked

---

1. The paragraph regarding Françoise's ordeal has been restored from Rist's manuscript entry for 31 October 1943 (see "A Note from the Translator"). See also chapter 3, footnote 6, for daughter Antoinette's recollection of her mother's nocturnal bicycle trips. "As Many Stars," a poem written by Antoinette many years later, recreates the horror of a Nazi raid on their house (see appendix 3). [TF]

whether the marshal, if he let go of Laval, would not have Doriot shoved down his throat. He answered that the marshal would not have Doriot under any circumstances.

"Are you sure he has enough willpower to avoid it? In any case, better Laval than Doriot."

"But what if Laval resigns?"

I admitted that this would be more problematic, but I still thought the marshal had better try to keep him on – or let the Germans govern.

What I did not say, but what I was thinking, is that Laval or Pétain, it makes no difference, as I consider them both to be hopeless; they will be forcibly removed the day the Allies land. I simply told him that the marshal's authority in the occupied zone is nil, and I do not think his presence or absence will make much difference to the Germans. Romier assured me that, according to Brinon, if the Germans are defeated they will attempt to end with a great *Gotterdämmerung*² and already have a list of forty thousand people to arrest in the case of an Anglo-American landing. (Always the same technique: fear of the German is evoked in order to prop up the Vichy government as the only lifeboat in sight. That is how all of those poor people assuage their guilty consciences. Or do they really believe that something from the Vichy way of doing things can be salvaged?) Romier asked in passing if I preferred the generals in Algiers to those in France. My answer: I detest any military government, period. But it is not hard to see what is worrying him. They fear de Gaulle much more than they do the Germans.

After his visit, I wondered what he really came to see me about: adhesion to a Pétain government without Laval? Was he putting out feelers to see if I was a Gaullist? Or was he looking for a way they can save their skin, testing the waters to find out if they still have some popular support? What is amazing is that they seem to think they still exist. They apparently have no idea of the degree to which they are nonexistent.

At 7:30, while we were at dinner, Jacques Millerand showed up to tell us Italy had capitulated. We turned on the radio and heard Eisenhower's announcement coming from Algiers, stating the terms of the surrender and saying that it was signed on Friday – that is, the day the British landed in Reggio. This morning it was announced that during the night the Americans had landed near Naples and elsewhere. A speech by Roosevelt seems to indicate that the Allies are preparing to drive the Germans out of Italy. That might take a long time! Fortunately, the Russians have taken Stalino and seem to have purged the Donets Basin of the enemy.

2. Twilight of the gods. [TF]

I have been interrupted by the sound of antiaircraft guns firing on American planes that one can see passing in the most majestic calm above the smoke from shell bursts. Impossible to know where they are coming from.

On Tuesday Lamson[3] stopped by to tell me about de Gaulle's problems in Africa and how at first everyone (bureaucrats, Giraud, colonists, etc.) was against him. The Americans, getting their information from Murphy and Leahy, were apparently not at all favorably disposed toward him and rather more positively inclined toward Pétain. It was de Gaulle's very intransigence that finally assured him respect and success. I stressed two points in response: (1) the importance of political continuity; and (2) the need for immediate reestablishment of the law in all its forms and *with* all its forms. The law and juridical guarantees, I said, are the heart of the republic. If you do not reconstitute them right away, there is no need to change regimes. We have no preference among despotic systems, we do not want a despot. My advice is to call the National Assembly back into session in order to appoint a government, then to dismiss that assembly and convoke a Constituent Assembly or a new National Assembly.

I am reflecting on the fall of Mussolini and the collapse of Italy. I remember saying to myself when he came to power that I did not want to die before seeing how the affair ended. I have lived and have seen it: nothing sensational, just the classical end to a dictatorship amid foreign wars and defeats. None of the cretins in France who admired Mussolini had foreseen that. There may not be any "laws" of history, but there are a few *rules* that in our time even the most foolish should not have the right to ignore.

There is a sordid quality to this whole war, a stench emanating from the lowlifes who wanted it and conducted it. The first and the oldest of these rogues has just disappeared. There are others whose fate will be the same. What Élie Halévy called the rise of "tyrannies" could just as easily have been called the rise of "rogues." We are now witnessing the twilight of the rogues, of those whom the bourgeoisie in all countries (especially the rogue-loving French bourgeoisie) had acclaimed. Are they to be replaced by other rogues, this time acclaimed by the people? Or are we at last to see some *men* at the head of our government? It is about time.

The Germans are beefing up their antiaircraft defenses. At the Issy-les-Moulineaux station the trains are loaded with antiaircraft guns and enormous searchlights. In the park, guns have been stuck in every nook and cranny among the trees. The fight against the bombardments is evidently

---

3. Doubtless a reference to André Lamson, of the Ministry of Native Affairs in Morocco from 1936 to 1943.

going to become the Germans' great, unique preoccupation (as the fight against submarines was for a long time the English preoccupation). It is to be expected that it will become increasingly deadly for the Allies. Another pressing reason for them to move quickly. From this point of view the taking of the Italian airdromes is of capital importance. They are now in striking distance of the cities in central Germany, Bulgaria, and Romania.

General Smuts's recent speech predicting that the war would not be over for another year seems far too pessimistic to me.[4] Let us say six months. Even that is way too long.

FRIDAY, 10 SEPTEMBER 1943 Today's papers are full of German imprecations against the treason of Badoglio and the king of Italy. In *Le Matin*, journalist Robert de Beauplan does his best to cast the Germans' retreat from Russia in a good light. It seems they knew the troops would soon be needed in Italy. And thus the invincibility of the vanquished is salvaged. What an admission!

But what a strange situation for Italy, which is going to serve as a battleground, its adversary yesterday's ally. And what a situation for the Germans, who find themselves occupying yet another of the European countries. With the exception of Spain, Switzerland, and Sweden, all of them in turn will have fallen into their clutches.

The landing of the Americans south of Naples is no secret. Now the second front has been established.

The Germans are disarming the Italians where they can and are having the Croats replace the occupying Italian soldiers in Albania and Yugoslavia. Wherever they can they try to foment civil war, the better to bring a country to its knees.

Meanwhile the Russians have retaken Stalino and the whole Donets Basin, which is probably more important than anything else.

Read Nietzsche's *Unzeitgemaesse Betrachtungen* [Untimely Thoughts]. Remarkable language. It took courage after the victory of 1870–1871 to tell the Germans publicly and so vehemently that they had no culture at all. What he said is even truer today than back then. And do not come telling me that Nietzsche is the father of National Socialism. His invective against the role of the State and its omnipotence belies any idea that he would pay the least deference to the current system. Moreover, he saw barbarism on the rise and predicted wars in the name of nationalism more terrible than any previous

4. General Jan Christiaan Smuts: South African prime minister. [TF]

wars. He must be read to appreciate the prophetic power that allowed him to divine, amid the exhilarating victory of the German Empire, the seeds that were to barbarize the Third Reich.

"In fifty years, all able-bodied men in Europe will be familiar with weapons and military maneuvers, and the most gifted will even know something of tactics. Anyone who then wishes to impose his opinion can be sure he has a trained army backing his ideas. That is what will determine the history of opinions" (Nietzsche, *Complete Works* in German, vol. 11, p. 66, ca. 1880).

What else have we seen happening in Italy, Russia, Germany, and even in France, with the La Rocques and Doriots?

SUNDAY, 12 SEPTEMBER 1943 The Italian fleet has headed for Malta and Gibraltar. It will be in the service of the British. Meanwhile the French fleet in Alexandria remains anchored. The Anglo-Saxons will pay us back for this at the peace treaty. The Italians will be better viewed than we will.

The king of Italy and Badoglio have left Rome, which has been occupied by the Germans. Milan also is in their hands. But Anglo-American forces have Salerno, Taranto, Bari, and Brindisi.

The Germans have replaced the Italians as occupiers between Toulon and Nice. What anguish we would be suffering if we had allowed our granddaughters to leave for Cannes!

But the greatest coups are going to come from Russia.

We are here like buried miners who hear the noises of the rescuers getting closer yet are still far off. There is only one thing we think about: how long?

This problem of "culture" that haunts Nietzsche is a false problem. We only notice *after the fact* that a people in such-and-such a time, in such-and-such a place, had a culture, because by this time there has emerged a Pléiade of great writers (under Louis XIV or Louis XV) or a Pléiade of great painters (France in the nineteenth century and Italy in the sixteenth) or a Pléiade of great architects (France from the twelfth to the fourteenth centuries). But no one had considered forming or preparing those people. Doubtless they would not have been able to emerge and to work if there had not been people around them who could understand them and whose soul, eyes, and ears were ready to receive them! But souls, eyes, and ears were formed spontaneously. It was not the state that had prepared them. It was some great enthusiasm, some taste or powerful interest like that experienced by the French in the seventeenth century for the human soul, its innermost reaches and its passions. Cultures are not made. They are only discovered afterward. The only thing one can create is an *education*, which is good at best for the average mind, and in which taste or virtue or ideas of beauty or grandeur will have their place. But that depends upon those who teach. During the hundred years that Latin and Greek have been taught, has the sense of Greek beauty and Roman grandeur been cultivated? It has not, because our teachers are ignorant of them and because one cannot admire Bossuet and Sophocles at the same time, which is the task to which they are condemned! Education must be a physical and moral *discipline* in a context of *freedom*; the rest will come of itself.

THURSDAY, 16 SEPTEMBER 1943 Yesterday's bombardment – of Renault, Citroën, etc. – hit the Saint-Lazare line. At Courbevoie the train stopped and emptied. I went on foot with Homolle, who was there also, as far as Neuilly, where we took the subway. I arrived half an hour late at the Ottoman Bank. Everyone saw the planes, of which five or six went down in flames. We had seen them from our windows, returning after the raid in admirable order, surrounded by artillery shells.

The Germans are proud of having carried off a minor victory in Salerno, where they have delayed a widening of the British bridgehead. They are making haste to celebrate without waiting for confirmation of their success (which, as of this evening, appears precarious). This is a new method that demonstrates their need to throw a bone to public opinion, which is increasingly disillusioned. To cap it off, they have blown up out of all proportion the spiriting away of Benito Mussolini by their parachutists! A great coup, they say. Onlookers here are quick to cover them in glory. Nevertheless, it is clear that the Allies must not have been eager to make a martyr of him . . . like Napoleon. What a sad sight, on the contrary, this "great" Italian taking refuge with his country's enemies – and what a comedown for a dictator to resign and then flee. While the other one, by trying to patch up the Italian's prestige, is revealing how fearful he is for his own.

This evening the radio announced the taking of Novorossiysk! Great news. The eastern side of the Black Sea is once again freed up for the Russians, and the Germans have been chased out of the Kuban region. The Russians are advancing all along the front and are no longer far from Poltava or Smolensk. They still have not announced the taking of Bryansk, which the Germans say they have evacuated.

FRIDAY, 17 SEPTEMBER 1943 This morning the Salerno bridgehead seems assured, and it is the Germans who appear to be doing badly. Yugoslav guerrillas have occupied Spalato on the Adriatic. Will that be the port of entry for the Anglo-Saxon armies?

France, after having exhausted all the glories that royalty could bestow – the creation of a civilization and a literature – seemed to be at an impasse, revolting the rest of Europe with its corruption, religious intolerance, and rhetorical emptiness. It was at that moment that she was completely renewed by the revolution, which provided an inventive impetus, instilling institutions, hearts, and minds with a modern soul, one that was full of energy and an insatiable curiosity, and pulling the whole world in its wake. That is what reactionaries of all ages have not pardoned her for. But that is precisely what makes her beloved by an elite that is scattered throughout the world.

SATURDAY, 25 SEPTEMBER 1943 I have done no writing this week, as I have been much too busy. Events, however, have been significant: the retaking of Smolensk today after rapid Russian advances all along the front; the consolidation of the British landing at Salerno; the arrival of French troops in Corsica; and the taking of the Dalmatian coast by the Yugoslav army, helped by the fact that the Italian army stopped fighting. In the House of Commons, big optimistic speech by Churchill on his return from Washington.

Here, of course, the most contradictory rumors are circulating secretly: the Germans are supposed to be contemplating an entente with the Russians as soon as the latter near their border; anti-Hitlerian Germans are supposedly negotiating in Lisbon with the Allies! Meanwhile English air raids are multiplying, as are the alarms day and night. The trains are back in operation on the Saint-Lazare line. The destruction one sees at the Bécon stations and in the city is terrible.

Letter from Marie Bonnet telling us that the Rives are safe and sound in Nantes, but that the bombardment was frightful.[5]

Roussel, the director of Matériel Téléphonique, told me he had traveled from Lyon to Paris on the same train as François-Poncet and President Lebrun, both under arrest. From three in the afternoon until ten at night they remained with two German NCOs, without speaking and without being offered anything to eat. After they arrived in Paris they were conducted through the crowd, Lebrun carrying his own suitcases (without anyone recognizing either man or paying any attention to them), and ushered into a gray car by a police commissioner. Taken where? Who knows?

The schools will not reopen before the eighteenth of October. At this juncture the prefects in each department fix the date for the start of the school year. Why the eighteenth of October?

---

5. Marie Bonnet: old friend of the Rist family and founder-director of the Maison des étudiantes on the Boulevard Raspail; the Rives: cousins of Germaine Rist.

I have finished the "Louis XV" article in Michelet's *Histoire de France*. After having read it, I am convinced that Michelet is the only historian who ever existed. This reconstitution of thoughts and feelings, and from them the chain of events, is a unique phenomenon of retrospective intuition. The depths to which that era had sunk can be understood only in the light of our present abjection.

THURSDAY, 30 SEPTEMBER 1943 News of the Noëls' arrival in Aix-les-Bains. So they were able to cross the border with no problems. One worry the less at least.

The Russians are on the Dnieper. Almost everyone is convinced that the Germans' hasty retreat was not planned, as they are pretending, but forced. In that case their situation is no doubt much worse than outward signs such as the number of soldiers would indicate. At the same time, the taking of the Foggia airfields has put all of southern Germany as well as the Balkans within reach of heavy bombers. All this brings the end of the war a step closer, perhaps before next spring.

Reading Michelet one realizes that the history of the eighteenth century is incomprehensible unless one's point of departure is Catholicism's ambition to recover its lost status, combined with resistance on the part of Protestantism and those Catholic nations less fanatical than France, which constantly vacillates between the two groups. Without this thread as a guide, the wars of the period seem to be frivolous chess games played to shift some borders to no useful purpose. The situation is similar to that of today. Conflicts between nations do not sufficiently explain these renewed battles. Deeper sentiments lie beneath them. People would not have tolerated the miseries of war if they had not believed it was the only way to save something precious. Moreover, dynastic interests and the placement of the offspring of royal families on thrones big or small were at stake. The two motives overlap. Meanwhile a new popular movement was on the rise, its aspirations translated by the *philosophes* and the Encyclopedists, aspirations that triumphed with the French Revolution. In our time the aspiration for social equality seeks to cut a path for itself across all political struggles.

SATURDAY, 9 OCTOBER 1943 A very busy week during which I was not able to write. I should be writing every day; otherwise many things of importance slip by.

The Noëls have arrived. Marie came to see us on Tuesday and Noël spent Sunday here; he arrived before her and took Antoinette back to Le Vésinet, where she was picked up by her mother.

A new offensive by the Russians after a lull of three or four days. They are crossing the Dnieper at three points. Hitler has called the Gauleiter together to discuss the domestic front, and Goebbels and Himmler have announced that defeatists will be executed.

Attacks on trains are multiplying. On Tuesday evening the Paris express climbed up onto a derailed freight train, whose oil tankers caught fire. There were already thirty dead as of Thursday.

Meanwhile the killing of hostages by the Germans is accelerating. They say some are shot every day. The Noëls were delayed the other day by a grenade launched on a German detachment on the rue de l'Odéon.

Lunch a week ago Friday with Edme Sommier and his friends. They think the previous Parliament will have to be convened but would like to put off convening a new one for as long as possible. A serious mistake in my opinion. Always the same mistrust of the country.

SATURDAY, 16 OCTOBER 1943 Yesterday Isabelle returned to Le Vésinet, escorted by her grandmother. On Monday she will take her exam. This frees me of my Latin lessons. But the house is now empty of children!

Yesterday an unexpected visit from Bamberger,[6] who had come from Lyon to see me. He spoke in detail of his leaving Germany and of his life there. He saw many factories and workers, spoke to many of the bosses. Since Stalingrad, he said, morale has been falling steadily. The ousting of Mussolini after that had a huge impact. A foreman said aloud in his presence, "We'll know how to get rid of ours, too." Today, by his estimate, there are 25 percent fanatic partisans of Hitler, 25 percent equally fanatic opponents, and 50 percent moderate malcontents ready to turn against him. In the detention camps, intense hostility toward Pétain and Laval. Portraits of the marshal distributed by Scapini disappear the next day.[7] According to him, the intervention of the state in all economic fields has removed any initiative from the industrialists and merchants, who await government orders to do or not to do. The workers' greatest fear is being sent to Russia. Everyone listens to London radio.

Signs of fatigue and discouragement among the troops here are multiplying. Germaine visited the Winters' house, which was once again emptied and is to be reoccupied. The young soldier with whom she spoke told her, in

6. Marc Bamberger: Rist's colleague at ISRES.

7. Georges Scapini: Vichy's envoy to Berlin, chief of the Diplomatic Service for Prisoners of War, ostensibly responsible for improving prisoner conditions (1940–1944). [TF]

regard to the war, *"Wir haben die Nase voll."*[8] In Fraisses the military officer who came to inspect factory production told the French Alsatian employee who received him, "You are no longer fighting and you are going to win. We are still fighting, and we are going to lose."

Bellet saw Turkey's new ambassador to Vichy. Perfectly confident about the war's outcome. But, he said, the Germans still have considerable defensive strength. The peace settlement will be satisfactory for all. No need to fear the Russians, but evidently they will play a big role in future politics. Not a word about Turkey's possible entry into the conflict.

SUNDAY, 17 OCTOBER 1943 Two great events this week. The first is the Russian battle to cross the Dnieper, the Germans' last line of defense, which, once penetrated, will expose the Balkans, obliging Hungary, Romania, and Bulgaria to abandon Hitler. It is not yet won, but success seems close. The taking of Kiev will be the visible sign of victory. Second is Portugal's ceding of the Azores to England for the duration of the war. Portugal no longer fears Germany! That is the great political fact that must make all neutral nations pause to reflect; England's access to this airbase threatens all submarines in the Atlantic. A huge political and naval victory for the Allies.

The French Revolution appears all the greater when viewed against the backdrop of the whole eighteenth century. It was truly a watershed in French history, marking a turn toward modernity. It was revenge for the failed Reformation, a French version of the revolution of ideas that made Prussia, England, and the United States the great nations of the nineteenth century. I have just reread the whole confusing history of the eighteenth century. Michelet does a marvelous job of elucidating it. For its political representative, France had the vile Louis XV. During that time Germany had Frederick the Great, while England had its great Whig bourgeoisie, with William III and the great Pitt, its immense colonial expansion, and, finally, its most beautiful creation, the United States. Politically, France was dominated by Hispano-Austrian intrigues and sectarian Catholicism. After Louis XIV, Catholicism emerged as all-powerful, considering itself to be the master of souls and of the future. In this, the most disgraceful period for our foreign policy, France's decadence and diminution (noted by Goethe in *Dichtung und Wahrheit*) were clear to the whole world.

During those degrading sixty years a new way of thinking took shape in opposition to the clique in Versailles, a new middle class grew rich, and

8. We're fed up. [TF]

Montesquieu, Voltaire, Diderot, and even Rousseau conquered minds not just in France but in the whole world. The Revolution was the political explosion that brought these triumphant new forces to light. The generation that gave its men to the Constituent Assembly, to the Convention, and to Napoleon issued from that long preparation and saved France politically and morally, bringing it into the fold of progressive Protestant nations, with its own character, its deep hatred of intolerance, and its belief in science and progress, or, as Michelet so magnificently puts it, in "action." And that is exactly what the imbeciles of today want us to see as decadence and intellectual inferiority. Clemenceau was right. The Revolution must be seen as a whole. It rehabilitated us after the "disgraceful" eighteenth century – so great intellectually, so wretched politically. And that is precisely why the Gaxottes, the Action Française and their ilk, not to mention the Hitlers, the Mussolinis, and their henchmen, detest the French Revolution. They are truly the counter-revolution, today's equivalent of the appalling Hispano-Austrian politics of the eighteenth century.

The day before yesterday, on London radio, the speaker, addressing the French magistrates whom Laval had called to Vichy, ended by saying, "It is Laval who will speak to you, but you will hear Parodi." This sudden evocation startled us. Then we trembled with fear for Alexandre.

Quinet's greatest book is the one titled *La République*, which he published in 1872. Nearly every page pertains to the situation today. Sainte-Beuve was right to say he sometimes had the insights of genius. Nowhere does one find such a perfect understanding of the "anti-France," the stupid reaction that from time to time raises its head, or of what lingers of the old hidebound Catholic upbringing, even among republicans themselves. And with regard to the military, his chapters on capitulations in the middle of nowhere, what prescience, what foresight into the disgrace we have lived through!

TUESDAY, 19 OCTOBER 1943 Important speeches in the United States by Sumner Welles (who is resigning for unknown reasons[9]) and Wendell Willkie, the Republican candidate. Both of them advocate American postwar interventionism in world affairs with a view to keeping the peace. This marks an abandoning of the Monroe Doctrine. It will be the great new international development in years to come. It is around this issue that American public opinion will crystallize.

9. Welles resigned from his post as undersecretary of state because of tensions with Secretary Hull. [JNJ/TF]

Meeting in Moscow by Eden and Cordell Hull with Molotov. What will come of it? Moses in triplicate on the Muscovite Sinaï. We will be hearing the voice of Jehovah next.

Visit from Moreau-Néret, candidate for the Academy. He tells me how the 400 million-a-day tribute was obtained in spite of his and Deroy's resistance. It was General Huntziger who came one day from Wiesbaden and convinced the hastily convened Council of Ministers to grant the amount demanded. Three months later the issue was brought up again with the same result. That is when Moreau-Néret resigned.[10]

THURSDAY, 21 OCTOBER 1943 Mettetal, consulted, gives me vague hopes for Daniel.

We are waiting for Jean, who had said he was coming but has not arrived. We fear some incident.

Stupid rumors. People tell you in great secrecy that when you hear among the "personal ads" on London radio the words "the key is turning in the lock," it will be a signal for the landing. We have heard those words for the last two days!

FRIDAY, 22 OCTOBER 1943 I have finished reading about the eighteenth century in Michelet's three-volume *Histoire de France*. That amazing man turns history into a unified drama in which events are all tied to one another through personal influence, character, foreign pressure, domestic financial worries, etc. This is life itself. It is precisely thus that historic events come about and decisions that affect the fate of peoples are arrived at. When one has read him, one understands what history really is, a chain of "accidents," as Seignobos, who in his dry way applied the same method, said. One needs only to have been involved in some events to know that history really works this way. Only Michelet adds passion and spirit to the mix.

SATURDAY, 23 OCTOBER 1943 The eyes of the world are fixed on the Dnieper Basin, where the Russians are advancing toward Krasnyy Rog and Melitopol. The crossing of the Dnieper was in itself a huge victory. They are now forcing the Germans to retreat deeply on the right bank and threaten to cut off the Germans who are entrenched in the Crimean Peninsula,

10. General Charles Huntziger commanded French armies in the Ardennes, 1939–1940, and negotiated the armistice with the Germans. Olivier Moreau-Néret was general secretary for economic matters at the Ministry of Finance in 1940. He quit in 1941 to work for Crédit Lyonnais. [JNJ/TF]

particularly around Sevastopol, from their bases. These days are decisive for the more or less imminent end of the war. We each feel this and remain in a state of suspense. If one is to believe the radio, the mood of the German public is at a low ebb. The fact that Anglo-American forces are making no headway on the Volturno River is frustrating to everyone.

Naturally, the yellow-bellied Bolshephobes among the bourgeoisie are beginning to tremble at the thought of communist victories. They had dreamed that the Russians and the Germans would demolish each other. And here we see that the operation is not at all mutual. They are obsessed by this fear of the Russian, a fear that in fact conceals fear of those Frenchmen who do not think as they do, which is to say, the vast majority of their fellow countrymen. I collect the echoes of these fears at each meeting of the Ottoman Bank and of the Banque de Paris, but this week I felt it growing in everyone. People no longer bother to conceal it.

Here is a fine page from Quinet, truer today than it ever was:

> Reactionaries in France have always been the same: swimming against the tide, unable to adapt to new laws, *their very language having become a perpetual trap.* Conservatism means destruction of the progress achieved by the French nation; by moderation, understand anger, passion, unleashing of the dead mind versus the living mind; by ruling class, the inability to be enlightened by a single ray of universal truth. . . .
>
> *Among foreign peoples I found that the most resolute conservatives had a great number of points by which the modern mind is illumined.* (How true that is!) Conversation was what it should be, an exchange of views from soul to soul. *In France one can find almost nothing of the sort.* Too soon I sense the spirit of routine, or rather the spirit of death, which condemns life in all its forms. This spirit has acquired only one thing, the art of disguising itself by means of conventional wisdom; it knows how to hide, to change its name. . . .
>
> All is well provided it can escape our own time; *the only one in which it cannot live is our own.* Fear of the present throws it back upon the past, the farther the better, where it is swallowed up, fossilized. . . .
>
> Knowingly and stubbornly, French reaction in all areas, political, religious, and philosophical, has become an accumulation of retrograde, decrepit ideas *that one would not find combined in such a way in any other place in Europe;* it represents the ashes of all that has died in the human mind. Elsewhere reactionary thinking is mixed in with a few glimmers of light and is contradicted now and then. Here one has arrived at a complete system which denies modern life in its entirety. Under pressure of ultramontanism, that great machine, a perfect vacuum has been achieved; *not a glimmer of rebirth has escaped it.* (La République, chapter 28, 135–38 [Rist's emphasis])

Never has one characterized French conservatism with more accuracy. Thus it was in 1871; thus have we observed it in Vichy since the armistice.

The same attitude toward domestic policy as toward foreign policy: submission and collaboration, seeing anyone who resists as a bizarre maniac. All of this can be found in Quinet. Decidedly, someone must write a history of "reaction."

SUNDAY, 24 OCTOBER 1943 Melitopol has fallen. The Crimean route is open.

Yesterday on the train I was sitting opposite a gentleman who, during the whole journey, was busy doing the following: from a box of matches he would carefully take out the cigarette stubs he had accumulated, open them up, and place the tobacco in a metal box that he was thus gradually refilling. His patience and fastidiousness were touching. Symbol of all the economies everyone must make! And of the concerns of most French people.

I am reminded by the radio that this is the anniversary of the Battle of El Alamein, which, along with Stalingrad, changed the course of events. A year to change the course of events. How long now to the final seal of victory?

SUNDAY, 31 OCTOBER 1943 On Tuesday Françoise was summoned by the Gestapo in Maisons-Laffite for an interrogation regarding two denunciations that had been received against her: one accused her of not wearing her yellow star; the other, of traveling between Le Vésinet and Paris. I went with her so that she would not have to face these worrisome characters alone. But I was not allowed to be present at the interrogation. I had to wait in the hall. After she came out, she told me she had been able to clear herself on all points. She had signed a record of the interview and was told that she would be summoned again once her statements had been checked.

On Thursday lunch with Maxime Leroy. One of our friends affirmed that negotiations are under way. The Germans, alarmed by the Russian advance, are supposedly ready to surrender to the Anglo-Saxons, preferring an Anglo-American occupation to a Russian one. We remained skeptical. That is too good to be true.

Someone quoted these words of Tristan Bernard, transferred as a Jew to Drancy: "So far we have lived in anxiety, now we shall live in hope."

I was also told of this witticism regarding the Vichy regime: "White terror, black market, and pink library."[11]

If one can believe English commentaries, the Moscow conference ended satisfactorily for all. Roosevelt declared he was delighted with the results.

---

11. In other words, "Counter-revolutionary terror, black market, and juvenile books." [TF]

The encounter between the aging Cordell Hull, looking like a Presbyterian minister, and Stalin, former Orthodox seminarian, must surely have been picturesque. Cordell Hull represents the Mayflower tradition, everything that is best about the United States, and one of the best things there is in this wretched world. And now shall we witness the invasion of the Balkans? Or must we wait until next spring?

According to J.,[12] two hundred people have just been arrested, betrayed by a "militant," who thus managed to save his skin! A noble zeal. He cited the total number of hostages shot since the beginning of the occupation as fifty-seven thousand; this must be Vichy's official statistic. Many French people know nothing of these executions and hide behind their ignorance to continue their self-interested support of the occupier.

Terrible famine in Bengal. According to an official communiqué yesterday on English radio, seven thousand people have died of hunger in Calcutta in a single week. The problem is a lack of shipping capacity to provide enough food.

WEDNESDAY, 3 NOVEMBER 1943 For two days radio broadcasts have been analyzing the terms of the Moscow accords: the constitution of a European commission (of which France would not be a participant); liberation of Austria; the promise of continued Anglo-Russian-American entente after the war. All of this quite vague and verbose. The important thing was to make clear to Germany the impossibility of pitting the "united nations" against one another. It will try anyway, but in vain. Here, Laval is spreading the rumor of an imminent Franco-German accord. For want of the Russian thrush, Germany would supposedly forge an entente with the French blackbird. Naïveté.

Meanwhile the Russians have just closed the Isthmus of Perekop and landed in the Crimea. The German troops are now surrounded on the peninsula. But how much longer will it be? The Russians have also seized the mouth of the Dnieper. That is not far from Kherson and even Odessa and Romania. Will the British and Americans at last make a landing in the Balkans?

SUNDAY, 7 NOVEMBER 1943 The Russians continue to astonish the world. Last night the radio announced the taking of Kiev. Huge victory, whose moral and strategic impact will be incalculable. And this morning American radio announced that the Turks have granted air bases to the English under the same conditions as those under which the Portuguese granted

12. Jean, perhaps.

them in the Azores! Is this a preliminary step for entry into the war? Doubt-less no. It is just maintaining pro-Allied neutrality! There too the impact will be great, especially in the Balkans. That is evidently where the second front (which Stalin in last night's speech declared imminent) will be established. It has been precisely a year since the British and Americans landed in North Africa! What a change in the situation since then. Yesterday the Russians celebrated the twenty-fifth anniversary of the founding of the Soviet Social-ist Republic. Congratulatory telegrams from all the heads of state. What a change in the world's political situation. Napoleon said, "In a hundred years Europe will be either republican or Cossack." Are we going to see a Europe that is *both* republican and Cossack?

In France there are more and more arrests, and attacks on collaborators, trains, town halls, etc., have become shockingly widespread. Arrests every-where of "terrorists," as the newspapers call them, of "patriots," as the public calls them. This government of "order," aided by that man of order Hitler, will have created, following the constant rule of history, a state of anarchy.

The cold arrived three days ago. The idea of facing a fifth winter in dark-ness, with insufficient heating and problems obtaining supplies, chills us in advance. But one at last sees the end of the tunnel. That is the main thing.

SATURDAY, 13 NOVEMBER 1943 On Tuesday I was visited by Jean-Mar-cel Jeanneney.[13] Above all, I was anxious to know his father's state of mind. It is rather curious. He dreads the reconvening of the National Assembly – too hard to conduct, he declares. Moreover, he thinks too many deputies have been disqualified and no longer have the necessary authority. He also dreads the convening of a Constituent Assembly, given current uncertainty as to the mood of French voters. He would favor a kind of dictatorship of the Algiers Committee for a few months. This committee would appoint a commission with limited powers whose job would be to draft a constitution, and once the latter was adopted, the chambers of Parliament would be convened in accordance with the newly established rules.

I objected that France could not be left so long in uncertainty. It is this uncertainty in all areas, judicial, legal, and political, that is troubling. I sug-gested that on the contrary the chambers should be convened as soon as possible, even if under the old system. His reply: "If you did that, you'd never

---

13. Son of Jules Jeanneney and professor of political economy at the law faculty in Grenoble (where Jules Jeanneney, the Senate president, settled after Pétain dissolved Parliament in 1942).

achieve constitutional reform." To which one might answer that the chambers could be obliged in advance to revise the constitution.

In short, one finds among these republicans the same mistrust of the country and of universal suffrage as among the reactionaries. Jeanneney's concern is evidently to put a lock on the chambers' powers from the start. I, on the other hand, remain convinced that after these trials the voters will have more collective good sense than any constitution drafters.

Jeanneney is equally concerned about the military danger. And he is right to be. There again, the convening of the chambers is the best way to create a barrier.

On all these points, in any case, Jeanneney's views appear to diverge from those of the legislators in Paris.

On Wednesday I had lunch with Mario and his boss.[14] The speed with which the Algiers Committee has proceeded worries the latter. As for the marshal, he supposedly wants to rid himself of Laval. His close associates Ménétrel and Jardel would like to isolate him from Laval's unpopularity. They have prepared a statement for him in which he would tell the country he is against the police state, informers, etc. One would hope someone will encourage these tendencies on the part of Pétain and will, above all, suggest men to replace Laval. The marshal is leaning toward Bouthillier, Georges Bonnet, and Bonnafous – in other words, the most corrupt and despised men he could possibly think of. His attention must be directed away from them, I am told. But who, if not precisely people of that ilk, would link his fate to the marshal's at this stage of the game? To all of this I simply respond, "Let the dead bury their dead." Besides, the occupiers would never allow it, and the marshal will never have the courage to do it.

What is most important is to make plain the suspicions aroused in many by the political atmosphere surrounding the Algiers government. The constant friction, most recently the exclusion from the committee of Giraud, whose authority has been limited to the command of troops, leaves a bad impression and is worrisome. And then there are those who would, after all, like to save something of the "National Revolution," which seems increasingly threatened. This is a great illusion. The people who brought about the so-called revolution have lost the game. It is high time to say "*Bonsoir, Messieurs*" to these clever characters, as Arthur Meyer said to the Boulangist leaders after their "*brav' général*" took flight.[15]

14. André Lebreton.
15. When a warrant was issued for General Boulanger's arrest in 1889 on charges of conspiracy and treason, he fled from France and ultimately committed suicide in 1891 on

SUNDAY, 14 NOVEMBER 1943 It was announced last night that the Russians have taken Zhytomyr, some 125 kilometers to the west of Kiev. The advance took one week. The Petersburg-Odessa railway line's been cut. The separation of the German armies in the center and in the south is well under way. I am beginning to believe that four or five months will probably be enough to end the war. Provided that the Anglo-American allies decide to do something in the Balkans. They will cut a sorry figure if the Russians arrive in Romania before they do and thereby gain an even stronger say in things than they have today.

Last Thursday Mettetal told me he had some hope in regard to Daniel Trocmé and that new efforts are being made to free him.

WEDNESDAY, 17 NOVEMBER 1943 The great fear of communism has revived. The advance of the Russians on the one hand and the role attributed to the former communist deputies in Algiers on the other have again frightened those who, more or less consciously, counted on the war to rid them once and for all of this specter. I hear the echoes from all directions. But this is not just a matter of opinions and feelings. Various signs indicate that those who feel most threatened are already preparing to resist and are attempting to recruit *active* partisans in diverse quarters – former sailors, former officers, etc. All hinges, therefore, on how, at the critical moment, the Anglo-American troops and Giraud's French troops will enter France and take sides. Giraud is perfectly capable of using his forces to maintain and consolidate Vichy. On the other hand, one can expect the Anglo-American allies to demand free elections. In that case France's choice is not in doubt. But it is the interim period that will be decisive.

Yesterday at the Banque de Syrie, discussion of events in Lebanon. No one knows exactly what happened or why Helleu staged his coup.[16] Here people still believe the Bolsheviks exercise a critical influence. But no one can explain how and why. This phantom haunts everyone here, and our good French bourgeoisie imagine that the whole world shares their terror. As a result, their ability to make sound judgments has become distorted.

---

the grave of his mistress. Arthur Meyer, a newspaper publisher, had supported Boulangism's right-wing tenets. [TF]

16. After consultation with de Gaulle, Jean Helleu, delegate general of the French Committee of National Liberation, had the president of the Lebanese Republic and several ministers arrested on 11 November 1943 and set up a provisional government in their place. This followed moves by the newly elected Lebanese leaders to assert Lebanon's independence from France. [TF]

SATURDAY, 20 NOVEMBER 1943 English radio has been saying for two days that the marshal has resigned and left the Hôtel du Parc, that he is being guarded in a private villa by occupying soldiers, and that Laval and the Germans are doing everything they can to make him change his mind. He supposedly wanted to convene the chambers in order to have them name his successor. He was to announce this via radio on Thursday evening. At the last moment Laval is said to have kept him from speaking. Hence the resignation.

The puerility of this idea exposes the naïveté of the marshal's crafty move. To convene the chambers under the watchful eye of the occupant! And return to the republican constitution in order to designate a new head of state who would thus be the child of that same Parliament so scorned by the National Revolution. As events have frustrated all his expectations, he is really just trying to shed the responsibilities that have become so burdensome. He has no idea how low his prestige has fallen.

Nineteen

The Old Man's Wall

21 NOVEMBER–31 DECEMBER 1943
As the war dragged on, seemingly interminable, Rist's spirits sank to a new low. The weather was "uniformly gray . . . under a ceiling of fog that no sun has managed to penetrate," contributing to the almost unbearable oppression of enduring "this material and moral regression." Adding to this sense of gloom, Rist wrote of a kind of wall facing old men who know that "the end – their end – is coming" (21 November; 6, 11 December 1943).

SUNDAY, 21 NOVEMBER 1943 I am reading Sainte-Beuve's "Monday chat" on the Restoration (14: 368) in which he comments on Napoleon's return from Elba: "After so many affronts and so much stupidity, I am swept along, *I am people, I feel like the people*, and with no further theorizing, 1815 is explained to me." Somewhere in these notes I wrote that in all the great national dramas – the Dreyfus affair, the wars of 1914 and 1939 – I felt and was still feeling "people." So I am in good company. And to Sainte-Beuve I could add Michelet.

Like all of those who are aging, I am rereading history. I understand why this is common. Old men know that the end – their end – is coming. They face a wall beyond which they know they cannot go. What happens beyond the wall no longer interests them. When one is young, one does not see the wall. Space is wide open, and one believes the part one will play in what happens in that space is limitless. By contrast, life has revealed to the old man all that the world contained in the past and still contains of wondrous things one did not suspect existed in one's youth: landscapes, cities, monuments, books, works of art, the lives of brilliant or noble men.

Goethe says somewhere in his *Conversations with Eckermann*, "When I was young, if I had known about all the masterpieces written before me, I would have given up writing" (magnificent modesty from one of the world's greatest writers). At twenty, we too are ignorant of the splendors already achieved in the world before our time. As we age and approach the final wall, we are seized by a growing desire to know all that is still within our reach of the beautiful, noble, and grand that our short life has not allowed us to see, admire, and touch. Before reaching that fatal wall, we want to fill our eyes, heart, and mind with all of those admirable creations, and we thirst to know all that is still within our reach of those things that our life's activity has condemned us not to know. As we reluctantly approach the wall, we want to turn around, and through our eyes, through reading, through the imagination, encounter all of that human past that we have known in only bits and pieces. That is why the old man gives others the impression he is living in the past. He is only trying, before he disappears, to take once again, and in his own way, "possession of the world."

I am reading in Huizinga's Dutch book *Incertitudes* and in Röpke's *Die Gesellschaftskrisis der Gegenwart*[1] – the first published in 1939, the second in 1940 – essays diagnosing the mental confusion that followed the war. Both agree with the older but remarkable book by the Spaniard Ortega y Gasset, *Révolte des masses*.[2] One sees in all of these books that the same changes occur at the same time in all European or American countries. The moral crisis is widespread, as was the economic crisis. For example, the pages devoted in each of these books to the disintegration of the family are almost identical. In Holland, in Germany, in Spain, one hears the same complaints as in France or in the United States. This gives one pause for thought. For the common cause of these pathological phenomena is always the equally common conditions that our transformed material life imposes today on families around the world.

When one can go in twenty-four hours from Paris to New York, and in twelve hours from Paris to Marseilles, the possibilities of expansion for each individual are entirely different from what they were when one could range no farther from home than the 50-kilometer maximum of a day's car ride. Everything today is accessible to everyone. Geographic limits have disappeared. Space is no longer an obstacle. And each of us learns via radio, telegraph, and newspapers what is happening in the world every day. If the

---

1. Johan Huizinga, *Incertitudes, essai de diagnostic du mal dont souffre notre temps* (Paris: Librairie de Médicis, 1939); Wilhelm Röpke, *Die Gesellschaftskrisis der Gegenwart* [The Social Crisis of Our Time] (Rentsch: Erlenbach-Zürich, 1942). [JNJ/TF]

2. A translation by Louis Parrot (Paris: Delamain et Boutelleau, 1937) of "La rebelión de las masas" (*Revista de occidente*, Madrid, 1930).[JNJ/TF]

family is to survive as a unit, its hearth must be warmer and more spiritual than in the past, when families were maintained at once by material ties and geographic limits. Besides, in those families, so closed in upon themselves, what frightful dramas, what hidden hatreds, what crimes never revealed. Someone who lives in Saint-Gingolph and has observed its inhabitants for a long time was telling me that domestic crimes were frequent and never punished by the law. Under the old order in Russia, a special law was needed to legitimize the children resulting from the father-in-law's coupling with his daughter-in-law during the son's tour of military duty. And I have never been able to contemplate without a shudder the measure of virtue and patience needed for a harmonious, decent family life on isolated farms or in the tiny apartments of big-city workers. I remain therefore a skeptic in regard to this so-called disintegration of the family. In England family spirit survives only because all the families are dispersed. Affection persists, but no one, not the parents nor the brothers and sisters, intervenes in the decisions of the separate couples, who remain completely independent in their own homes. Fifty years ago Henri Becque, thinking of certain families that tyrannically confined their members in suffocatingly close quarters, asked, "Where can one be better off than within one's family?" and gave this cynical reply: "Anywhere else."

FRIDAY, 26 NOVEMBER 1943 Yesterday Romier's private secretary came on his behalf to tell me about events in Vichy two weeks ago. The marshal had carefully prepared a decree by which he restored constituent rights to the National Assembly in case he should die before having been able himself to draft the new constitution he was charged with creating. He read it to the Council of Ministers and announced that he would read it that evening on the radio. After the Council meeting, he summoned Krug von Nidda, Germany's consul general in Vichy, and communicated it to him "by way of information." At 6:00 PM the Germans let him know that they were against the broadcast and if necessary would take over the radio by military means. The marshal summoned Krug von Nidda once more and declared to him that no clause in the armistice permits the Germans to interfere in purely internal matters in France (discovered a bit late) and that because they were making it impossible for him to carry out his duties, he would abstain from then on from all acts as head of state – presiding over the Council of Ministers, signing decrees, receiving government officials, etc., etc. That is where things stand. The Germans have said they will try to find some "formula for compromise," but so far nothing has been done. In short, the marshal is on strike.

Romier had his secretary tell me that if a different decree were to be published, I should understand that it is against or independent of the marshal.

The marshal has had the text of his decree taken to all the senators and deputies in Paris and elsewhere. That is his method of propaganda, already used in other circumstances. I noticed at the Suez Company lunch that many there already knew about the text. One of them had the following rather euphoric reaction: "It's very clever. It's directed against Algiers, not just against Laval." An accurate observation; the maneuver is too transparent to fool even the most naïve. As Algiers has attracted some deputies and senators, the marshal wants to draw them to him by telling them: but I am quite disposed to return to you (upon my death!) the powers you invested in me and that I used to abolish Parliament. It remains to be seen whether the legislators (with the exception of a very small number) will be won over by a promise contingent upon such an uncertain day of redemption. The odds are in fact that the marshal's cunning will serve to discredit the idea of convening the former Parliament as soon as France has been liberated. This idea, which I support in spite of everything, is energetically opposed by those in the Resistance. The marshal's action is going to strengthen them in their opposition. Once again the marshal will have served to divide France and to cause reasonable views to be dismissed. The total silence of French radio in London regarding this incident (which English radio has mentioned but without giving any details or incorrectly referring to the marshal's "resignation") shows pretty clearly that the Gaullists do not want to fall into the trap of publicizing, by the only means that exists in France, the marshal's apparent return to "republican legality."

Romier's secretary assures me that all the other ministers are with Laval and that Romier alone is with the marshal. He tells me, moreover, that the loyalty of the "militiamen" to Laval is more than doubtful and that he can hardly count on any real force to defend his position should the Germans leave.

Horrible story about the regional prefect in Rouen, a certain Parmentier, going to the German commander after an attempt on the life of a German officer – one that took place at midnight, when all the inhabitants of Rouen were in their houses – to offer "not just apologies, but compensation: the handing over of 250 Jews." The offer was accepted. The individual is a lawyer from Cherbourg (or Dunkirk) who offered his services to Laval after the defeat and was rewarded by this local post as a petty tyrant.

Growing hostility toward Algiers in "right-thinking" circles, strengthened by the momentary lull in Allied military advances. The taking of the Dodecanese Islands by the Germans, their more or less successful offensive against the Russians' left flank, and their recovery of Zhytomyr give the impression that they are still stronger than one thinks. But now this morning comes the announcement of a great new Russian offensive between Gomel and Vitebsk and an advance of more than 50 kilometers. Decidedly, the Russians will not cease to astonish us.

Fearsome bombing of Berlin. The Germans claim that their morale is only strengthened by it. But Goering supposedly told the miners in the Ruhr that they must "not yet" consider the war as lost and that "just a few days' patience" would show them what Germany was capable of. Are these really the terms he used? If so, it would indicate that morale is truly low, even among their highest leaders.

MONDAY, 29 NOVEMBER 1943 In vain have we waited three days for Jean. He told us he would be here at the end of the week. One always wonders if some "accident" – railway or "other" – has not held him up.

MONDAY, 6 DECEMBER 1943 Jean finally arrived last Monday, in good shape. But on Friday he suffered a sprain and had to go to bed. Full of stories of the hunting down of Jews in the formerly free zone. Françoise's mother, Mme Gorodiche, had to leave La Vignasse. She saw Jean in Durtol at Claude's bedside (Claude returned to Le Vésinet on Friday). Her son and daughter-in-law also had to leave Mandelieu. How right I was not to allow my granddaughters to leave for the south! What torments we would be suffering if we had learned they were in danger and had had to flee.[3]

3. For a time Françoise had wanted her daughters to leave for the south with a Red Cross convoy. Because her husband, Claude, was very ill with tuberculosis, Charles Rist became closely involved in decisions made regarding the couple's three Jewish daughters.

La Vignasse was the property acquired by Françoise's parents, Léon and Fanny Gorodiche, in 1934. Located at Mandelieu–La Napoule on the French Riviera, it became a refuge for members of the Gorodiche family until Germany took over the free zone in November 1942. Françoise's brother Philippe, who had been imprisoned at Dunkirk, then in eastern Prussia, had escaped in March 1942 and made his way to La Vignasse. When that was no longer safe, he made his way through Spain to England, where he joined the intelligence service. Brother Jean met up with Philippe in Spain and likewise left for England to join de Gaulle. Their brother Pierre, who had taken refuge at La Vignasse with his wife, Kathleen Parker, was similarly obliged to flee. Sister Rose-Marie fled to the United States with her Jewish husband, Louis, and their two small children. Mme Gorodiche and her daughter Élisabeth fled to Lyon, where they took refuge for a time in a brothel. Mme Gorodiche would attend pro-Vichy gatherings in Lyon for the coffee and warmth, saying, "There at least no one will look for me!" Élisabeth, a stenographer, carried messages to Resistance groups, traveling by motorbike. Isabelle Rist, emails to translator, 11 to 19 August 2011. [TF]

This week the radio broadcast a speech given in London by General Smuts two weeks ago. In his estimation, France will not regain her position as a great power for a very long time; Italy and Germany have lost it forever; and a triumvirate consisting of Russia, England, and the United States must dominate the world for at least twenty years if peace is to be maintained. He said that political entente between the United States and England will be difficult, that the latter will be considerably weakened and will have to depend upon the western powers (France, Belgium, and Holland) in a kind of federation. He did not mention China's role. The speech has caused lively protests in England itself, where people are saying that it is in England's interest to have a strong France and that the silence maintained in regard to China is astonishing.

The longer the war goes on, the more the fundamental baseness that has characterized it from the beginning is apparent, with all of its consequences. This material and moral regression would have seemed unbelievable a few years ago. No more materials for making basic repairs, no leather, no steel, no wood. Food is reduced to its simplest terms. Morally unscrupulous middlemen are in control. Everywhere denunciations, arrests, terror. Fear is the arbiter of opinion. Those who fear today frighten those who, still triumphant a year ago, shudder to think of tomorrow's reprisals. Uncertainty about the aftermath of peace makes people delirious; they all want to shape tomorrow's world according to their little personal image of the world of yesterday. Only one point in common: people trust nothing but force, constraint, and violence to achieve their goals. How can anyone impose order in such an environment!

Meeting of Roosevelt, Churchill, and Stalin in Teheran after the meeting of the first two with Chiang Kai-Shek in Cairo. We do not know what decisions were made. Today we learned that Ismet İnönü was at the Cairo meeting. Will we at last see Turkey unleashed?

FRIDAY, 10 DECEMBER 1943 Some weeks ago a German general named Jodl, speaking after Goering to a gathering of Gauleiter, made this magnificent statement, which the German papers reported: "*Wenn wir den Krieg verlieren, so hat die Weltgeschichte keinen Sinn*"![4] It is a symbol of German mental deficiency that this character – doubtless a good military man – could claim to know the meaning of world history. This imbecilic exaggeration of the national ego that lies at the heart of all their ills is fed by so-called phi-

---

4. "If we lose the war, world history has no meaning." [TF]

losophy of history, surely the most inane occupation of mental defectives. That is the "political education" that National Socialism claims to have given its adherents and that is nothing more than a romanticization of brute force.

SATURDAY, 11 DECEMBER 1943 For the last month or so we have been living under a uniformly gray sky and under a ceiling of fog that no sun has managed to penetrate. This adds to the oppression of our wait, which is becoming almost unbearable.

One learns via the radio that the Turks have come back quite satisfied from the conference in Cairo, where they were apparently reassured regarding Russia's intentions. What is more, there are clear signs, such as the resignation of the minister of foreign affairs and the sending of a military attaché to Moscow, that the Bulgarians want to change sides. A Swedish newspaper reports that in a secret session of the Chamber the majority party was asked to change the government's foreign policy. These are promising omens for the end of the war. The declarations in Teheran regarding the union of the three great Allies were primarily aimed at shaking up the Balkan countries by leaving them in no doubt as to Russo-English supremacy in that part of Europe. If Bulgaria and Turkey form an alliance, what will become of Romania? It will be the sacrificial victim of the peace treaty.

With no army and no unity, the position of Algeria in all of this seems precarious. What can one say of Vichy's, which is even worse?

TUESDAY, 14 DECEMBER 1943 Yesterday Romier's secretary came to my office to tell me about events last week in Vichy. The Germans sent the marshal a long, contentious missive, accusing him of having never really collaborated and demanding that he appoint a sincerely collaborationist minister – Déat, Bonnard, perhaps Doriot. At the same time, they continued to insist that he not publish the decree on his succession. Thereupon Pétain took a middle road: he would resume his duties and not renounce his decree, but simply would not publish it. A document has been drafted in which he states that the decree targeted neither the *Reichswehr* nor the "person" of Laval. It seems the latter was quite miffed and demanded that "powers" be substituted for "person." He came to Paris last week, doubtless to reshuffle his ministry. The importance Pétain attaches to his decree derives primarily from its emphasis on his *legitimacy*.

It so happens that a few weeks ago the Foreign Affairs Committee of the U.S. House of Representatives apparently voted to require the president not to engage in peace negotiations with governments whose legitimacy was in question. Pétain is still counting on Roosevelt's support and, by means of his decree and the exposition of his motives, wanted to give advance notice that "legitimacy" is his middle name. The maneuver was all too transparent.

MONDAY, 20 DECEMBER 1943 The papers have announced that the marshal has again shown up for the ceremonial raising of the colors. So now his strike is over. How disgusting.

No important war news for the past two or three weeks, though the announcement of Churchill's pneumonia has caused us to shudder. What would happen if this man, the great hero of the war, were to die? Today's news is fortunately better. But militarily nothing encouraging has occurred. The British are bogged down in Italy. Here, meanwhile, arrests are multiplying and material hardships are getting worse by the day. The prospect of waiting till spring for something decisive to occur is depressing to everyone.

CHRISTMAS DAY, SATURDAY, 25 DECEMBER 1943 According to rumors circulating in Paris the day before yesterday, Laval has recruited Marcel Déat and Jean Luchaire for his new cabinet. This is the "improvement" won for us by the marshal with his little protest. Fortunately, Laval is too clever to be manipulated, and we have often had rumors of reshuffling that have proved false.[5]

Still other rumors are making the rounds: the English and the Americans were not actually able to reach an agreement with Stalin in Teheran and are supposedly abandoning the idea of an invasion through the Balkans. What is driving these rumors is clear enough: if true, they would favor German victory owing to discord among the Allies – and thus justify Laval's wait-and-see policy. But it is inconceivable that the Allies could have told such a lie to their people regarding the success of the Teheran accord; propaganda based on such a scandalous lie would one day backfire violently against Roosevelt and Churchill. Governments that only have to deal with a muzzled public opinion will never understand this.

The Noëls have arrived here for the Christmas festivities, still shaken by the arrest of Noël's lab assistant. She was summoned to Gestapo headquarters and held for transfer to Drancy.

WEDNESDAY, 29 DECEMBER 1943 Two important Allied victories: the *Scharnhorst*, one of the last three German battleships, has been sunk by the English fleet near North Cape, and near Kiev the Russians are breaking

---

5. Three months later, on March 16, 1944, Déat was in fact appointed to Laval's cabinet as minister of labor and national solidarity. [TF]

through the troops of Marshal von Manstein, who for the past month has been trying to reach the city. They are also advancing on Vitebsk. Churchill has recovered his health.

The murder of Maurice Sarraut[6] seems to be clearly attributable to Laval's Milice. We are back in the era of the C.S.A.R. and murders committed by "men of order." Nothing in common with the acts of vengeance committed in response to denunciations. Murdering a public figure because of his domestic politics or executing someone who has delivered French people to the enemy are both crimes, but they are not comparable. The second is an act of vengeance that can lay claim to a sense of justice and that eliminates someone who is himself a criminal. The first is gratuitous violence, which targets an honest man because of his ideas.

The Allies have announced Eisenhower's appointment to head the armies that are to attack the European fortress. Eisenhower, speaking to journalists, has predicted victory in 1944. All this drum beating is disagreeable. One would prefer to see action. Or is this intended to demoralize the enemy?

The Algiers Committee has made known its plans for the hour when France has been liberated: general reelection of city councils and selection by the latter of delegates who in turn will appoint a Constituent Assembly of some four hundred members. They will choose the head of government, who will appoint a ministerial cabinet that the Assembly will approve or reject en bloc. The Assembly will also appoint a committee of eighty members to draft the electoral laws. The chambers will meet once the prisoners have returned.

From the judicial point of view, collaborators will be tried according to articles of the penal code that punish consorting with the enemy. The military courts have jurisdiction. But civilian judges will be added to them, along with guarantees of the right to a defense. Flandin, Pucheu, and a few others have been arrested in Algiers, but their trial will be postponed until France has been liberated.

Yesterday I thought I heard on the radio that poor Berthod, Radical senator from the Jura and former philosophy professor, has been murdered.[7] Yet another!

6. Maurice Sarraut: journalist and important leader of the Radical Socialist Party under the Third Republic; suspected of being a Freemason, he was assassinated on 2 December 1943 by Laval's Milice. [JNJ/TF]

7. An active Resistance fighter and former minister of national education, Aimé Berthod actually escaped this assassination attempt by the militia but was later arrested by the Gestapo. He died in June 1944 from a pulmonary illness contracted during his imprisonment.

FRIDAY, 31 DECEMBER 1943 Numerous alerts today. The fog lifted, and flying conditions were magnificent. Young Blot, arriving from Paris to visit us, said the Saint-Lazare line has once more been cut by the bombings. It took her three hours to get here.

On a walk in the woods with our granddaughters, we saw a plane flying very high but recognizable by the trail of smoke behind it. The shells of antiaircraft fire were exploding around it, but much too low. It raced toward the Marly forest at top speed. In the woods, a great many *Courrier de l'air* propaganda leaflets had fallen to the ground.

Announcements yesterday of the Russians' rapid advance on Korosten and the deep retreat of von Manstein's army along a 100-kilometer front. Sensational victory, full of promise and sure to discourage the adversary.

Twenty

Reign of Terror

2 JANUARY–23 FEBRUARY 1944
Civil war threatened in France as Vichy's Mobile Guard and the French police followed the dictates of Darnand and Laval to round up members of the Resistance, rebels who refused to work in Germany, Freemasons, and personal political enemies – "all under the protection of the occupier" (14 February 1944).

SUNDAY, 2 JANUARY 1944 Several alerts over the past three days. The bombs fell on ball bearing and truck factories in Ivry and Courbevoie. The rail line has been cut at Bécon, and the Saint-Lazare station is no longer usable. The little ones, who were supposed to return to Le Vésinet today, will leave by bus early tomorrow morning for Saint-Germain. In spite of that, the children were all here with us yesterday afternoon, except for Jean and Claude.

The contrast between the tone of Goebbels's speech on 31 December and that of Attlee's, both of them heard via radio broadcasts, was most encouraging, but the general mood is one of despondency. People are disappointed by the Algiers deputies and the committee's impotence, and they hold de Gaulle responsible. They are even more disappointed by the slowness of military operations and daily promises of invasion that remain unfulfilled. Some are more worried than heartened by Russian victories. The old divisions are reappearing. The collaborationists are starting to be afraid. Monzie's book *La Saison des juges*, which came out three months ago, is revealing.

The only thing the machinations of Pétain and his entourage have earned us is the appointment of M. Darnand, a known stooge and scoundrel, to head up the main police force. Moreover, he now has at his side a special envoy officially approved by the Führer. The marshal, according to London radio, has promised sincere collaboration with the Germans in 1944.

Romier has been sacked. Poor fellow; that is all he got for trying his hand at big-time politics! This could at least help later in his defense. If he calls me as a witness, I will say he was hypnotized by the marshal – that is his main excuse – but that he tried to extricate himself when he could. The question remains whether a certain mental weakness was not a precondition for being hypnotized by a man like Pétain!

There are more and more murders. The dean of Grenoble's science faculty and his son[1] were found on a road some distance from the city. It is unsure whether this was the work of the Milice or the Gestapo. They were viewed as socialists.

SUNDAY, 9 JANUARY 1944 The day before yesterday a telephone call informed me of Romier's sudden death. Heart attack, they said. Death came in time to spare him further painful reversals.

When this war is over we can all say: "We find ourselves five years older, after five years during which we have not lived."

Confined to my bed since last Tuesday by an acute case of tracheitis.

The Russians have taken Kirovograd. Great hopes are pinned on their advance west of Kiev, combined with their movement in the Dnieper loop. One can already visualize them on the Bessarabian border. Comments from the German military are veiled in mourning.

WEDNESDAY, 12 JANUARY 1944 François Trocmé's hands were ripped apart (one of them amputated) when he tried to keep a bomb placed in his factory at Lannemezan from exploding. Ève has left for Tarbes. They had just learned a few days ago of Daniel's departure from Compiègne for Germany. What anguish for these unhappy parents.

Some people's attitude toward "terrorism" is rather curious. They disregard the motives, which they pretend ignorance of, and condemn "terrorism" outright. They make no distinction between reprisals against those who have betrayed French people to the enemy and murders such as those of Sarraut or Aimé Berthod committed by political enemies. This perversion and confusion of ideas is the most telling sign of France's moral decadence. Deep down many people find it natural to eliminate one's political enemies *because of their ideas*. To their way of thinking, the fact of having ideas they hate is equivalent to having delivered or denounced Frenchmen to the enemy. The

1. René Gosse and his son Jean, a lawyer. See *Chronique d'une vie française, René Gosse, 1883–1943* [René Gosse, 1883–1943: Chronicle of a French Life], written by René's wife, Lucienne Gosse (Paris: Plon, 1963).

two things are on the same level. The act that rids you of one or the other is "terrorism." This suffices to explain and excuse everything. An act that is a human disgrace and a political idea that displeases you – two things between which these people can see no difference and for which murder is justified.

SATURDAY, 15 JANUARY 1944 Yesterday a radio announcement of the murder of eighty-year-old Victor Basch and his wife.[2] He had been a great Dreyfusard and president of the League of the Rights of Man. It is the Radical republican that was targeted, as with Berthod and even Sarraut. The event is horrible. It is related to the promotion of Darnand to chief of police. The marshal, with his ridiculous strike, seeking to save himself, will have obtained only one thing: the reinforcement of the reign of terror under which we were already living. This is what I had predicted to poor Romier when he came to talk to me about the marshal's plans for "independence."

The Russian advance on Pinsk, from the east and south, opens perspectives full of hope. Today what remains to reconquer in Russia is insignificant compared to what has already been retaken. It will not be long now until the Dnieper Basin has been evacuated. Bulgaria and Romania are directly threatened. English radio has announced evacuations from cities in Bulgaria following air raids on Sofia. The Turks are taking measures for the return of their Jews who are in France and, by radio, are advising their students in Berlin to go to Switzerland.

How long must we still wait before the general attack is unleashed? Impatience here grows daily. Tension, too. Every day the stranglehold of German and French police becomes more atrocious. Problems obtaining provisions are getting worse. One runs terrible risks with each train ride. Allied air raids are multiplying. The one a week ago interrupted traffic flow at Saint-Lazare for several days. The damage in Bécon-les-Bruyères is worse than the last time. Yesterday once again we saw the planes moving overhead. There were three alerts during the day. Any intellectual work has become difficult. Everything seems futile as long as one remains ignorant of the dénouement, which one feels is near but which is still fraught with so many unknowns.

The domestic situation in France grows ever darker. According to certain reports, the situation of the Gaullists in Algiers vis-à-vis the United States and England gets tenser by the day. The authority of de Gaulle's people appears to have greatly diminished on account of their close relationship with Moscow. In France favorable opinion toward them – at least in

---

2. Victor and Hélène Basch were murdered by the Milice.

bourgeois circles – has become increasingly reserved. The communist question trumps all in the minds of most people. It is impossible to estimate exactly the strength that diverse political groups will command at the critical moment. All depends upon the army's loyalties. If the army vacillates, the different armed bands organized here under the name of "leagues" will be able to play a certain role. If the army is well in hand, there will be neither communism nor Pétain-Lavalist reaction. But whom does the army obey?

SUNDAY, 16 JANUARY 1944   The radio has announced a meeting of de Gaulle and Churchill in Marrakesh. They probably focused on the status of the Algiers Liberation Committee when the Allies land in France. De Gaulle must have insisted – as the Algiers Committee already did two weeks ago in an appeal to Allied governments – on immediate recognition of his government by the Allies as the sole legitimate French government. If this is not done, the French will be once more divided into two camps, with the risk of civil war breaking out along with the foreign war. Let us hope de Gaulle has made his case with Churchill. It is the only reasonable and practical solution. The rest will follow.

Persistent fog, making this period of anxious waiting and moral obscurity even more painful.

WEDNESDAY, 19 JANUARY 1944   Jean left again this morning for Saint-Étienne. He lives in fear of being separated from his children if some act of war should occur. Someone spoke to him of the possibility of a landing this weekend. He does not want to risk being out of their reach.

Only events in Russia continue to be of interest. Today a new double offensive was announced to the north of their front at Oranienbaum and near Lake Ilmen. Meanwhile the German effort to keep them from approaching the Bug River appears to have been thwarted. That was the nerve center of the front these last few days. But how can one explain the Russians' isolation and the Allies' inertia? The day before yesterday *Pravda* announced negotiations in Cairo between Ribbentrop and the English. The latter responded with a categorical denial published by *Pravda*. But what is at the root of these suspicions, accusations, etc.? German probes? Russian concerns that a separate peace might be made? Or, on the contrary, similar plans on the part of the Russians?

TUESDAY, 25 JANUARY 1944   On Radio Paris, the announcer Robert de Beauplan stressed that around 1935 General Giraud was part of the same clandestine group as Joseph Darnand. If the information is true – and there is no reason it should not be, coming from one who would like to compromise Giraud – it paints a curious picture of the general. It is clear today that his prewar halo owed to his status as a militant reactionary. This is the origin of all military reputations in France so long as the officers have not been tested in time of war. This character must be watched when he returns to France leading the Gaullist troops.

The British landed three days ago at Nettuno, on the coast south of Rome. They are trying to outflank the German army, which is farther south – provided they are not crushed by unknown German reserves!

WEDNESDAY, 26 JANUARY 1944 In his *Cahiers* [Notebooks], Sainte-Beuve cites an astonishing passage by Thiers in which there is a curious mix of prophetic and erroneous predictions. The future of Germany is as poorly divined as the futures of Russia and America are accurately foreseen. And France? She was obliged to play the role of Greece, but against Germany, three times in a row – and the last time, alas, by betraying her past, without a trace of heroism! Here is the passage from the *Cahiers*:

> Sunday, 19 December 1847. Thiers says that our old world is finished, that the time for great things has passed for old Europe, that it had its day and that the decadence of the French language is the surest sign that ruin has set in. There are now only two young peoples, he says. On the one hand, Russia – it is still barbarous, yet it is great and (except for Poland) respectable; old Europe will sooner or later have to come to terms with this youth, for Russia is *youth*, as the common folk say. The other *youth* is America, a drunken, adolescent democracy that knows no obstacles. The future is there, between these two great worlds. One day they will clash, and then one will see struggles beyond anything known in the past, at least in terms of size and physical shock, for the time of great moral things has passed. France is left with only one role that I would envy, but I have come fifty years too early. After Alexander, Greece had only one role; it was to be Philopoemen, to die with his country while heroically defending it. France still has that great moment to experience before ending under blows from the North. As for Germany, it is finished. (65–67)

THURSDAY, 3 FEBRUARY 1944 Russia's advance toward Estonia is the great event of these last few days. Will the Russians be able to cut off German communications with Finland? And what will result? Or are we going, once again, as with the Balkans, to form premature hopes?

In the future it will be incomprehensible that England could have declared war in spite of needing four years to be ready for it – and during those four years left her allies and those under her protection to suffer the appalling yoke of the invader.

FRIDAY, 4 FEBRUARY 1944 Moscow's 250 cannon thundered the day before yesterday to announce the meeting of the two Russian armies in the Dnieper loop and the encirclement of nine German divisions. We are once again living in feverish expectation.

Yesterday Noël told us that he has bacilli again and that his old cavity has reappeared. Tréfouël[3] had just left after appointing him to head the laboratory. One more consequence of insufficient nourishment. These poor children are facing difficult decisions. And what anxieties before seeing the outcome! Luckily there are two of them, both full of courage.

SATURDAY, 5 FEBRUARY 1944 Saw the Noëls when I left the Academy. Édouard is advising thoracoplasty. On Wednesday they will attempt a pneumothorax at the Pasteur hospital. But the chance of success is one in a hundred.

Frerichs, passing through, told me that in Belgium Paul-Émile Janson, Senator François, and a general were sent to Compiègne and from there deported to Germany in a cattle car. People in Belgium are also being murdered. The Rexists have killed the man whom the patriots were holding in readiness to be mayor of Anvers.

For the first time, one reads articles expressing great alarm in the traitorous newspapers here. In contrast to German military communiqués, they openly discuss the German divisions' encirclement.

Meanwhile, under the aegis of Laval and the marshal, there is increasing momentum for civil war in France. The Mobile Guard have been sent against the Maquis in Haute-Savoie, and thirty-nine rebels who refused to work in Germany have been killed. A big roundup of Freemasons is in the works. A so-called conspiracy against the wretched Darnand, chief of police, provoked the arrest of some thirty people.

Jean has left again for Saint-Étienne. Very worried about his two sons, given the law authorizing the requisition of men between sixteen and sixty.

SUNDAY, 6 FEBRUARY 1944 I have just reread in Michelet the history of the uprising of 10 August 1792. Remarkable similarity to the present. The uprising was not just Parisian, having been fomented by committed provincial volunteers; it resulted exclusively from the conviction, which corresponded with reality, that the enemy had entered France at the request of the court. It was the nobles grouped around the king who became the accomplices of

---

3. Jacques Tréfouël: director of the Pasteur Institute.

foreigners; it was the patriotic heartland that reacted against treason. We have now seen once again the same positions: on one side the reactionary fifth column, calling for, desiring, then supporting the enemy's invasion of France; on the other, the feelings of the great majority of the country. There is no way to express those feelings, however, and the "patriots" are being slaughtered – killed off one by one on pretexts of communism or criminality or else gunned down by the Germans. But when will the uprising take place, and how? This is the question everyone is asking. Laval has formed his leagues and militia of hatchet men and bullies, composed of the most appalling hoi polloi. Yesterday on the train sitting across from us were two of those sinister-looking bullies, talking about their plans with no concern for who might be listening.

The marshal is circulating Ribbentrop's letter criticizing him for his "resistance" to collaboration and demanding a truly obedient ministry. It was subsequent to this letter that Joseph Darnand was called in to collaborate with Laval. The letter will provide an admirable shield for the marshal in the future. He is making use of it with his usual hypocrisy. But in vain. He is already doomed. And there is no doubt that as a result of the Churchill–de Gaulle meeting in Marrakesh, England has sided with the general.

As I write, alarm and cannon blasts. Yesterday there were two of them, and Villacoublay was set on fire. Great thunder of bombs this afternoon, with all the window panes shaking.

I have heard these two variations on Pétain's name: Philippe-Éteint and Philippe-Illégalité.[4]

SATURDAY, 12 FEBRUARY 1944 The Anzio bridgehead seems to be in great danger. People are once again shaking their heads when speaking of the British army.

The Germans occupying the Winters' house next door have had a trench dug in front of the gate, from which they could supervise the five roads that intersect there and machine-gun them all in turn. Uneasiness about possible trouble in the event of a landing? Or a decision to machine-gun anyone who walks out into the street?

Noël is about to get his passports for Switzerland. Obtained without any problem, thanks to Édouard. He will come here on Monday and stay a week before leaving.

---

4. Philippe-Extinct and Philippe-Illegality. The first is a play on sound (Philippe Pétain/Philippe Éteint), the second a play on sense with reference to Philippe-Égalité ("Philippe-Equality"), Duke of Orléans, who supported the French Revolution. [TF]

Jean has come back from Saint-Étienne. He tells us that the daughter of the German general commanding in Haute-Savoie was taken as a hostage by the Maquis. This will contribute admirably to cooling the initial ardor of Joseph Darnand's men.

MONDAY, 14 FEBRUARY 1944 Laval is apparently taking advantage of the occupier's presence to get rid of his personal and political enemies. This is a despicable policy. This is terror under the protection of the occupier for the sole profit of the gangs.

The Russians are appealing to Finland, Hungary, and Romania to move quickly to abandon their German ally if they do not want to be caught up in the coming catastrophe. Cordell Hull has made a similar appeal to Finland. Evidently their strategy amounts to sounding the trumpets around the walls of Jericho. That would be a resounding victory, to see Germany abandoned before any combat, and the Russians are now near enough to all those borders to speak with authority. Yesterday the taking of Luga was announced, which leaves them in control of the whole region, all the way to Lake Peipus.

One senses that in London as here there is concern over the fate of the British army at Nettuno. Churchill issued a communiqué two days ago saying that generals Alexander and Wilson had both reported to him, affirming their confidence in the success of the "battle for Rome" in spite of the inevitable vicissitudes of combat.

Bolgert's small property has been occupied. In conversation with a German, the latter said to him, "In France you think we are beaten, do you not?" Bolgert cautiously replied: "That's what most people believe, but how about you, what do you think?" The other replied: "We shall win thanks to the secret weapon!" A miracle of propaganda.

Noël arrived today to spend a few days before leaving for Leysin.

WEDNESDAY, 23 FEBRUARY 1944 I was told the following anecdote about an incident that took place at the Saint-Étienne lycée. The teacher was reading aloud from the "Billiard Game" in Daudet's *Contes du lundi*. After reading the story, in which French marshal Bazaine seems quite happy to have won at billiards while the army is being beaten at Sedan, the teacher had only one comment: "Well, you see, my children, in this story Bazaine is Marshal Pétain, and the billiard game, that is the National Revolution." The students were delighted!

Noël is leaving this evening for Switzerland. He must wait twenty-four hours in Bellegarde for a connection to Geneva.

Huge American and British raids on Leipzig and Stuttgart. More than two thousand planes involved. Churchill announced in the House of Commons that these raids will only increase, warned against exaggerated optimism, and hinted that the Germans may start some new bombardments of London using new techniques such as radio-controlled aerial torpedoes.

The Russians have taken Krivoy Rog. Great, very great, victory.

Twenty-One

All-Out Civil War

29 FEBRUARY–25 APRIL 1944
In spite of having obtained the Certificates of Not Belonging to the Jewish Race, Rist continued to worry about the safety of his Jewish granddaughters as France found itself in the chaos of civil war.

TUESDAY, 29 FEBRUARY 1944 I am trying to summarize for myself the current state of mind of all types of people.

One group eagerly awaits the English and is ready to do anything for them. Some people of modest means long for the arrival of a parachutist in order to be able to hide him. Some have already prepared the civilian clothes to disguise him. In the north, photographs of those who were sheltered during the first part of the war are surrounded by flowers. To these fine folk can be added all those who harbor hatred of collaborators and a desire for reprisal. For them – and they are numerous – it is less a matter of love of the English than of their personal humiliation and suffering. Then, too, one must add to this group all those who hate Hitler's system of government – among them, all the socialists, communists, and still faithful republicans. With them there is a mixture of patriotism and republicanism. Domestic and foreign politics are as one. De Gaulle's partisans will all come from this group.

A second group is composed of people who detest the Germans as occupiers but have not stopped admiring their strength, their discipline, and their "correctness." They are not crazy about the prewar French, especially not the "regime." But the horrors of the occupation are making them more indulgent for the past, though not enthusiastically so. One could say that their dominant characteristic is anti-Germanism, but that for the rest they are neutral. They would be ashamed not to call themselves anti-German. But they are mistrustful, worried about what might well happen after the departure of the occupier, frightened of communism and Bolshevism, though not denying that the Russians and their military might are necessary for victory. They are the eternally fearful.

Finally, a third group includes all those who, without loving the idea, believed German victory was inevitable. They easily became accustomed to it because of their inveterate mistrust, both of the Anglo-Saxons and of whatever in France is, as a matter of taste, attached to Anglo-Saxon ideas. Now that they no longer believe in German victory, they are coming back to their hatred, above all, of "Jews and Freemasons." They are preparing to fight them, and their method of combat is to sow mistrust of the Anglo-Saxons. They do not dare to express regret for German failure, but starting now they are preparing to struggle against tomorrow's victors solely by way of conservative ideology.

In contrast to these three anti-German groups, of which the first is by far the most numerous, there are the collaborators, toward whom all three are hostile. The collaborationists are clearly pro-German and regret the eclipse of the German victory that they had not only accepted, as did the third group, but applauded and desired. They fear for their own skin.

SATURDAY, 4 MARCH 1944 A week ago the Finns entered into negotiations with the Russians. The latter are proposing to return to the borders of their 1940 treaty. This is a great moral blow to Germany. Strategically, if the Gulf of Finland and the Baltic Sea are open to the Russian fleet, the consequences may be grave for transports from Sweden to Germany. Politically, the Balkans will open their eyes.

Yesterday, 3 March, was the moment Laval chose to proclaim in *Paris-Soir* that Germany "will not be beaten." "I am not saying it will be victorious," he said, "but it will not be beaten." This man's prophecies are incredible. In 1940 he declared that England was already defeated, then that the United States would not enter the war, later that the only important thing was the struggle against Bolshevism, and later still that Italy would be victorious. Now he is playing the compromise-peace card. Just as he played it in Stockholm and Zimmerwald during the last war. Events once again will prove him wrong. Neither the Russians nor the English will accept a peace without victory. And we, even less so. He understands nothing of unleashed passions. He completely ignores Germany's true feelings toward us. He imagines there is a role for him as arbiter in the future peace conference. He does not realize that the Anglo-Saxons will never tolerate his presence at the same table.

Grave news from Turkey: the English have stopped providing it with arms, because, they say, they intend to provide them only to those who are actually waging war. What does that mean? That the Turks have definitively taken a neutral stance until the end of the war? Or is it a feint to trick Germany? Or, rather, do the Turks mistrust English power? Or do they think that victory is so certain that they have no need to contribute to it, having no territorial ambition? Or are the English blackmailing the Turks? It would be interesting to be in the wings at this juncture.

The *Pariser Zeitung* of 2 March contains a curious call to England to return to her traditions and reject Bolshevism. Another attempt to divide. It also contains an article titled "*Völkerfamilie aus Raum und Rasse*,"[1] reproducing a lecture given at the German Institute in Paris, "*Die Wiedergeburt Europas aus dem Lebensgesetz der europäischen Völkerfamilie*,"[2] which deserves to be passed on for posterity. The aberrations of the philosophy of history have never been more outlandish. The Germans resort to delirious imaginings to justify their spirit of conquest.

Our Romanian colleagues in the Bucharest Law Faculty have sent us a special shipment of soap, sugar, oil, and flour! Great joy for everyone. Two weeks ago the Ottoman Bank's Garelli had sent me some bacon and raisins. For our fortress under siege, the role of food is ever more important. We are stocking up on supplies for the eventuality of a landing and the possible interruption of rail transport.

SUNDAY, 5 MARCH 1944 One of the strangest impressions of this war is the silence that reigns over the country at night. From midnight (or even sooner) to 6:00 AM, no Frenchman has the right to be outdoors. The roads, the streets, and the countryside are open to Germans alone. Not a single vehicle, not one French car. It is sinister. We no longer hear anything passing by. Just the footsteps of the sentry stationed at the Winters' house, coming and going in the street.

There are many signs of German anxiety about an Allied landing. Everywhere small fortifications are being set up for defense in the event of street fighting. They can be seen in Paris as well as right next to our house here in Versailles. The day before yesterday, posters (*Bekanntmachung*) of the German High Command made it known that anyone who conceals a soldier or officer belonging to an enemy army, or aviators or paratroopers, or fails to report downed planes, etc., will be tried by the war council and may be sentenced to death. In the papers a general campaign aimed at demonstrating the perfidy of the English, how absurd and silly it would be to pay attention to

1. "Family of Nations Tied by Territory and Race." [TF]
2. "The Rebirth of Europe According to the Natural Law of the European Family of Nations." [TF]

their radio propaganda. French newspaper editors outdo one another in their zeal to demonstrate that Germany is invincible and that the arrival of the English will be the worst possible catastrophe for the French. Laval's speech the other day is just one aspect of this orchestration. It all feels like the night before a battle. The S.N.C.F. has announced that many trains will not be running as of tomorrow and that it will later announce the resumption of normal service. Travelers are asked not to use the trains except in cases of urgency.

In Brussels, Galopin, president of the Société Générale de Belgique, was murdered by the Gestapo.

The cold returned several days ago, with intermittent thaws.

MONDAY, 6 MARCH 1944 Claude visited us yesterday afternoon. There have been roundups of Jews in Le Vésinet, and he came to talk about Françoise. The Léonards also came. They recounted the adventures of a young American who is more resentful of the English than of the Germans.[3]

Veslot tells me that even his hospital unit has been searched; they were looking for a sick Jew in order to transport him to the Rothschild hospital, where he can be watched.

WEDNESDAY, 8 MARCH 1944 Claude brought Isabelle to us. The good Baume had advised him to get his children to a safe place. The two others will be lodged elsewhere.

Yesterday at the Suez Company the president told us of his son's trial in Reims. It is expected to end today. The poor father has little doubt as to the outcome. His son[4] was taken to the court in handcuffs. During the pretrial investigation he endured eight hours straight of interrogation while standing with his hands handcuffed behind his back.

We are in all-out civil war. "Terrorists" are being arrested everywhere. Battles in the Maquis and condemnations by the special courts are killing off members of the Resistance ten and twenty at a time. And we are still waiting for the English!

Monday evening, bombing of the rail yard in Trappes. We heard the noise of the bombs and saw the glare of the rockets. The next day at the prefecture I learned there were a hundred victims. The radio declared that the German aircraft offered no resistance and that all the Allied planes returned

---

3. This was an aviator that Léonard and his wife had sheltered.
4. Bertrand de Vogüé: administrator with Veuve Clicquot in Reims.

safe and sound. At the prefecture I was given useful advice regarding possible roundups in the region.

SATURDAY, 11 MARCH 1944 I am reading Chardonne's book *Voir la figure – Réflexions sur ce temps*.[5] Chardonne is a Protestant. He belongs to a family of porcelain manufacturers in Limoges. The well-to-do son of big industrialists, he has written overly refined, effete novels in which the tenuous threads of worn-out sentiments have been sliced four ways. Suddenly the defeat made him a Nazi sympathizer after having been the opposite up to then. Types such as this do not feel they are part of the "people." But there is more. For all their literary culture, they do not understand and in fact know nothing about Germany. The difference between the political-military Germany and the bourgeois hail-fellow-well-met Germany escapes them completely, as does the meaning of this ardently nationalist reaction of the petite bourgeoisie that constitutes Nazism. These men who believe themselves to be highly cultured, super-intellectuals fall for the most inane arguments of the most ignorant of the Germans and are incapable of penetrating German deceitfulness. They allow themselves to be taken in by the fiction of "one Europe." The silliness of Chardonne's reflections is unbelievable. I cite only three of them. One on Pétain: "France would literally no longer exist if she had not been incarnated in Marshal Pétain" (54). Another on German economic ideas: "The entente with Germany means we accept its principles regarding currency, trade, the economic unity of Europe – in short, a revolution. *To renounce the gold standard, that is a great leap!* [Rist's emphasis]." Yes, exactly, for those who understand nothing about modern economic life, that is a great leap. And this last one, which caps the others: "We are indebted to Marshal Pétain for the notion of good government. He is not responsible for whatever flaws there are" (36). That is the best by a long shot. The profound reason for this attitude? An appalling intellectual, social, and political laxity. A desire for the knout . . . to thrash others, believing that will be to one's advantage. . . . But what does he think now that the Russians are beating the Germans everywhere?

Yesterday I visited poor Mme Quesnay at her old boardinghouse on the Boulevard de Port-Royal.[6] Her third son, Eric, just died there, asphyxiated

---

5. Jacques Chardonne (real name, Jacques Boutelleau), *Voir la figure – Réflexions sur ce temps*, memories of the year 1941 in Paris (Paris: Grasset, 1941). [TF]

6. The widow of Pierre Quesnay, Rist's trusted colleague and the former head of economic services at the Banque de France during the time when Charles Rist was deputy governor.

by a bad gas stove. He was seventeen. She is still the same. She speaks with the same tranquility as before. From the height of happiness she has been plunged into grief by the death of her husband, who drowned before her eyes, and by the fate of her unhappy Finland, divided as she is between her French sentiments and affection for her former country. Her son Pierre, the eldest, was liberated from Fresnes two days ago, thanks to the intervention of Ribbentrop, who responded to the request of her brother Ramsay, Finland's foreign affairs minister. But what can the poor boy do, now that he is threatened by France's compulsory labor service? She is distressed. She read me a letter from her brother, who spoke of the immense power of Russia. He is the one negotiating with Germany now.

According to the radio, Pucheu has been condemned to death by the military court in Algiers. A grave political error in my opinion, which will only incite reprisals against the "Resistance" and the "Maquis." Or will it perhaps cause Laval's gang to pause for thought? Who can say?

TUESDAY, 14 MARCH 1944 The Russians have taken Kherson. Romania increasingly under threat.

Saw Baume yesterday. We talked at length about what must be done. He thinks the most important thing is for the children to be in a safe place. Isabelle, fortunately ill, is staying here for the time being. Jean returned last night.

FRIDAY, 17 MARCH 1944 Saw a Russian on Tuesday, a friend of Michelson.[7] He said Stalin supposedly remarked in Teheran, "I want to destroy Germany's military might, but I don't want it to become communist, because communist countries become too strong militarily."

We live in anxiety. Everyone expects something to happen within a couple of weeks.

The German retreat in Ukraine appears to be turning into a debacle. The departure of Prince Stirbey for Cairo seems to indicate that Romania is considerably shaken. Whose case is he going to plead? What position will he take, he who was hated by King Carol and who is basically just a businessman?

Jean Pillet-Will told me the other day that forty years ago, when his father was a Banque de Paris director, no decision was taken without first

---

7. Alexandre Michelson: French economist of Russian origin; general secretary of the Institut International des Finances Publiques.

consulting Rothschild. Moreover, the president was the former business manager for the Rothschilds and the Griolets. Through him, thus, they controlled the Compagnie du Nord and the Banque de Paris. As for the Treasury, it made no issues without consulting Rothschild. When we[8] arrived at the Banque de France, we found a similar situation. Poincaré was constantly consulting Rothschild. We put a stop to that.

WEDNESDAY, 22 MARCH 1944 Yesterday I received a visit from Georges-Picot, the former ambassador. He told me that Pucheu had offered to have him preside over the "State Court," which Pucheu (along with Joseph Barthélemy, I believe) had created by decree. Georges-Picot asked him, "What will be the role of this court?" Pucheu's reply: "To condemn to death as many people as possible without having to take the law into account." When Georges-Picot expressed his indignation, Pucheu said, "You're an odd duck." Such is the man who has just been shot in Algiers for complicity with the enemy and whom some people today want to turn into a martyr for the cause of anticommunism. As a matter of fact, Pucheu's role has for a long time consisted of collecting funds from large and small industrialists to support Doriot's anticommunist campaign.

The Russians have crossed the Dniester and entered into Bessarabia. The German line seems to have been penetrated along a large stretch. Decisive stage of the war. The Germans are reportedly occupying Hungary.

Finland has refused Russian conditions for an armistice.

Have reread Alfred Loisy's last book, *La Crise morale du temps présent*.[9] A remarkable effort on the part of this old man who devoted his life – astonishing for the continuity and immensity of his labor – to studying the history of the Christian religion and religions in general in order to define the faith he arrived at and the beliefs he affirmed with admirable clarity. I share this mysticism, this belief in the spirit that he considered to be indispensable for morality. There is within us an active force that comes from the depths of our being and that we cannot define for ourselves until *after* having experienced

8. In 1926 Finance Minister Joseph Caillaux dismissed the governor and deputy governor of the Banque de France and replaced them with Émile Moreau and Charles Rist, respectively, to oversee the devaluation of the franc. [TF]

9. Alfred Firmin Loisy, *La Crise morale du temps présent et l'éducation humaine* [Human Education and the Current Moral Crisis] (Paris: Nourry, 1937). Accused of "modernism" by the Catholic Church, Loisy was excommunicated. A professor at the Sorbonne and the Collège de France, he continued to write books of biblical criticism until his death in 1940. [TF]

it over the course of our whole life – and that is the profound force behind our actions and our intellectual pursuits. It is the origin of faith for the scholar who spends his nights in research, just as it is the origin of faith for the man of action who strives to turn an ideal into reality; it serves as a guide to the mass of men who, in spite of appearances, have in their daily lives – no matter how they make their living – a certain ideal of life and of conduct. To define this force is difficult, and the definition is never completely satisfying. But there is no education possible without a certain definition of this faith so that it can be inculcated into young souls who need to believe in something. The definition he gives – devoted love – is the most appropriate to form souls. It is a religion. It can be adapted to all the higher religions. The problem faced by all non-dogmatic parents – that is to say, most cultivated parents – Loisy resolves in a way that can appeal to all those who are dogmatic, can enliven traditional religion, and can fit in with that grand humanist religion that is believed in to greater or lesser degree by most people in the world today and that no barbarism can now destroy.

FRIDAY, 24 MARCH 1944 The arrival of the Russians in Bessarabia and near Lvov has led to a new German offensive action: the military takeover of Hungary and replacement of its government with Nazi loyalists. No doubt it will be Romania's turn in a few days. The Allies seem once again to be surprised. They are lavishing advice on Hungary, Slovakia (also occupied), and Romania to resist. But they send them no help. This is a new phase of the war, with the Balkans as the theater of hostilities, and probably the Carpathians as the line of resistance. Will the Russians make do with their own forces? Will the Allies try to land in the Balkans? Here we are once again hanging on events, fearing an indefinite prolongation of the war.

The death penalty for Vogüé's son has been commuted to imprisonment. Yesterday it was not clear whether this would be in Germany or in France. Vogüé told me he preferred Germany, because in France they take prisoners as hostages to be shot.

MONDAY, 27 MARCH 1944 Everything we learn about Pucheu reveals him to be the cynical agent of his backers, having no other motivation than the anticommunist, materialistic goals of the *patronat*. The struggle of this capitalist elite against communism is perfectly legitimate. The stupidity begins when it becomes a political battle, pushing into power men with no program other than this struggle. In their blindness, the capitalist bourgeoisie have sought to sustain themselves with a Doriot, paid by the Germans.

Pucheu was the intermediary between them and Doriot. Here again is a curious chapter to be written regarding prewar reactionary politics. And once again one runs into the Banque Worms et Cie.

MONDAY, 3 APRIL 1944 A suspenseful week, hanging on the rapid advance of the Russians across Bessarabia and toward the northern passes of the Carpathians. Today it was announced that Russian troops have entered Romania proper – that is to say, beyond the Prut. Molotov has declared that he does not intend to annex anything or to make any changes in the Romanian government.

Last Thursday afternoon I had tea at the house of Claudel's son-in-law. Claudel, who was present, is raging. He says we are being governed by "gangsters." He is furious about the newspaper campaign against the Comédie Française, where his play *The Satin Slipper* is being performed. On the way back, stopped by a derailment in Chaville. It took me two hours to return to Versailles.

L.[10] filled me in on the arrest in Lyon of poor Marc Bloch.

The papers here are in total disarray. They reiterate in spite of everything that Germany is going to win and that it has maintained all of its reserves intact. But at the same time, they write that it will not be able to resist the Russian advance for a few weeks yet. Clearly the great breach that the Germans had successfully fended off until now has been achieved. The troops in the Ukraine have lost their cohesion. The consequences are incalculable. If the Allies make a strong enough strike in Yugoslavia or in Scandinavia, if the Turks get going, the end of the war may come in six months.

MONDAY, 10 APRIL 1944, THE DAY AFTER EASTER A magnificent spring. The fruit trees are in bloom. But we live in an anxious state of expectation. Material difficulties are getting worse by the minute. One can no longer find a nail or a spool of thread. Train travel has diminished, and train trips are dangerous. The papers talk about nothing but arrests and the fights between Maquisards and the militia or the Germans. In Paris a week ago, the French police entered the École Normale Supérieure. The head of the school, though disabled, tried to stop them and was arrested. They demanded to see identity cards and arrested a number of the students. The same at the Sorbonne, where neither the dean nor the rector felt he could oppose the entry of police officers. The police have erected barriers at subway exits or at train stations. Everyone is searched, and both young and old are detained.

10. Léonard, probably.

The Russians have arrived at the Czechoslovakian border, surrounded Odessa, and are threatening Jassy. The English have still not begun to move except by air. They are advising the Balkan peoples via radio to rise up against Germany. It is easier to say that from the safety of their island than to do it under the threat of the Gestapo.

WEDNESDAY, 19 APRIL 1944 We are living in anxious expectation. It is like being in the dentist's waiting room before he calls you in to pull a tooth. It is impossible to focus one's attention on anything. The English have suspended the right of foreign diplomats to communicate freely with their governments. So something is going to happen. What events will we find ourselves faced with from one day to the next? What material difficulties, what moral anguish?

The Russians are nearing Sevastopol. The Germans are counterattacking in the Lvov sector.

SUNDAY, 23 APRIL 1944 This week heavy bombardment of Paris – the Chapelle station, Juvisy. For two hours on Thursday evening we heard the explosions of bombs and antiaircraft fire. The casualties were considerable, five hundred to six hundred. English inaction continues to be incomprehensible. Yes, it is clear that these bombings are intended to prevent German communications. But when will they need to use them? Four months of activity remain until September – and we shall be entering the sixth year of the war! Today the radio reminded us that today marks the anniversary of the attack on Zeebrugge during the preceding war. General de Gaulle spoke of the coming offensive. There was also talk on the radio of the regrouping of Russian troops behind their front lines in preparation for a direct march on Berlin! Meanwhile, people here are dying, hiding, or being arrested.

TUESDAY, 25 APRIL 1944 Renewed heavy bombing last night. Rather far away. Impossible to know where it was happening.

Yesterday the Marios greatly upset. The Germans have requisitioned their villa. They must leave within three days. The children have whooping cough. We deliberated last night. We decided, Mario and I, to go to the town hall, then to the Kommandantur this morning to seek a postponement. At the town hall the fool of a military man in charge of the bureau, an officer from Saint-Georges, told us there was nothing he could do. Finally they gave us an Alsatian interpreter, a good man. After a period of waiting at the Kommandantur, the officer told us that the requisition had been withdrawn. The Alsatian told us that the *Luftwaffe* had opposed allowing the Kommandantur to set up shop in the Château de la Maye, as it had wanted to do. The Marios' house, which is opposite the château and would have provided useful office space, thus no longer interests them. The Alsatian's name is Ritz. He is from Colmar and served as a volunteer for the entire 1914–1918 war.

The English are not allowing anyone to leave England except those serving Her Majesty. Yet another part of the prelude.

Gustave-Adolphe called to tell us that his sister Germaine has been arrested and taken to Dijon.[11] We do not know why, or where to turn for help.

11. Germaine Monod (1887–1957) was a nurse with the Red Cross.

Twenty-Two

"Poor France!"

27 APRIL–6 AUGUST 1944

The war was now in the Rists' backyard. Whereas once Charles Rist would describe Allied planes flying overhead as "majestic" and "magnificent," the din of war was becoming painful, the hardships more critical, and anxious hopes for liberation all the more poignant. After so many disappointments, even news of the long-awaited landing in Normandy would cause more anxiety than joy. Rist repeatedly asks the question, How long can all of this go on?

THURSDAY, 27 APRIL 1944 Yesterday at the Air France lunch, Laboulaye announced that the marshal had spent the morning, in uniform, at the Notre-Dame ceremony honoring the victims of the Anglo-Saxon bombings. General surprise. It was unannounced. A well-guarded secret that spread all over Paris during the afternoon. This morning the papers announced that he had spoken from the balcony of the Hôtel de Ville, that *schoolchildren were led there* by their teachers, and that he was roundly cheered. There you have it, they say, a true plebiscite! It is not the general in Algiers that France wants. Let the Anglo-Saxons get that through their heads.... The maneuver is obvious! It is one of the most indecent that this indecent old man has yet attempted. They have him show up on the sly. Then they round up "schoolchildren" and doubtless also the pro-Doriot gangs and police squads dressed in civilian clothing, they have him cheered by these people without anyone in Paris knowing of his presence, they have photographs published showing the crowd in front of the Hôtel de Ville, then they have him quickly disappear. And they have pulled it off. Once again this eighty-eight-year-old man, manipulated by Laval, has stooped to duping public opinion with cheap campaign tricks, haunted as he is by the fear of being knocked off his pedestal by his rival, the man in Algiers, and furious at the decision of the English and American governments to entrust civil administration to de Gaulle as the liberation progresses. But people here are not falling for it. Not a soul who does not shrug his shoulders in scorn.

Enormous bombardment last night in Villeneuve-Saint-Georges. The explosions could be heard from here. This morning I was told that several train stations – du Nord, de l'Est, du P.L.M., and Austerlitz – have been obstructed. Only Saint-Lazare and Montparnasse remain in service. The English have announced they are going to bomb all the railway yards. All of this clearly portends the imminent resumption of operations. At least in the east, where the Russians are not doing anything right now but are obviously regrouping. In the west? One remains skeptical.

The evening subway trains are full of people leaving vulnerable areas to spend the night elsewhere. The authorities are doing all they can to increase panic and create chaos. Nothing has been organized to provide people with temporary housing. The Secours National is doing its best to help. From one minute to the next, after the bombings of Juvisy, they had six thousand people to clothe and feed. That is according to Laboulaye.

SATURDAY, 29 APRIL 1944 Another nighttime bombardment.

Yesterday I went to the finance ministry to arrange for a loan for the Statistics Institute. The budget director, very friendly. He spoke indignantly of the arrest of old M. Rucart, more than eighty years old, as an act of vengeance against Minister Marc Rucart in Algiers. The place where they are keeping this old man, along with other hostages taken at the same time, is crawling with vermin.

MONDAY, 1 MAY 1944 The bombardment now comes nightly, with constant alerts during the day. Last night the bombs fell on Achères. Jean and Mario watched the spectacle from my office windows,[1] but I fell back into a deep sleep. The English papers explain the bombings as having passed from a strategic to a tactical phase. Admirable military jargon! If the English had only passed to the tactical phase a little sooner, we should have been most grateful. For here at the beginning of May 1944, we are still in the same hole. The radio regularly announces that we will be liberated by the first of May next year. But if things keep on the way they have been up to now, one wonders if this prediction is not very optimistic.

---

1. Rist's office was a corner room on the third floor of the house, with tall windows on two sides. [TF]

FRIDAY, 5 MAY 1944 Jean left us today to go back to his children.

The Marios left this morning to look for provisions in la Mayenne; they say they are out of food. Their two children are with us.

The radio no longer talks of anything but bombings. Nothing about military operations. The Yugoslavs, supported by Allied ships, have laid siege to Split. Is it here that a landing will be attempted?

Forty-five of sixty employees have been taken from the Morgan Bank. We tremble for Léonard.

MONDAY, 8 MAY 1944 Lunch on Saturday at Lambert's.[2] A certain engineer by the name of Ducast showed himself to be the perfect stereotype of the reactionary bourgeois who realizes that it would be shameful to defend Vichy but does not want to have anything like what came before! "This country no longer has traditions or ideals; it doesn't know which way to turn." I replied that one thing is sure, it wants the Republic! "Of course," he answered, "we're all republicans (!), but which republic?"

"The republic that will provide judicial guarantees, freedom of discussion, and parliamentary elections," I said. Ambassador Léon Noël, who was there, added, "You must admit that the parties on the right have been the strongest supporters of the current government." This Ducast is the epitome of Colonel de la Rocque's friends. Poor country! Poor bourgeoisie!

Frequent bombings and sirens going off. Yesterday at least four or five, the same during the night. The planes, most of them heading for Germany, are greeted by a few blasts from the antiaircraft guns.

WEDNESDAY, 10 MAY 1944 Everyone is talking about the marshal's transfer to the Château de Voisin (belonging to de Fels), near Rambouillet. According to well-informed sources he has been there since yesterday, guarded by militia and for all practical purposes a prisoner. Why? And for whose benefit? People are getting carried away making wild guesses. To tell the truth, it is not very important.

Sevastopol taken. That does matter.

Night before last, at 10:00 PM, Mario and Lolli returned from La Bouffource with supplies. It took them twenty-eight hours to go and twelve to return. It is normally a four-hour trip. They managed to catch a freight train on the way out.

2. Perhaps Marcel Lambert, a member of the board of the Banque de France and administrator with Ateliers et Forges de la Loire, or perhaps Alfred Lambert-Ribot, former general delegate of the Foundries Committee.

Those who have seen the destruction at the Chapelle station say it was dreadful and terribly efficient. The station will be out of commission for months.

Alerts last night and this morning.

FRIDAY, 12 MAY 1944 I spoke with Laurent-Atthalin yesterday about Moreau's objections regarding the distribution of dividends by the Banque du Maroc. Atthalin insists this is just a way for Moreau to annoy him. He complained vociferously about Moreau and said that when French treasury bonds were issued in Holland, where Mannheimer was the partner of Banque de Paris, Moreau asked him for 500,000 francs on behalf of the Conte de Paris!

At the board meeting of Air France Transatlantique, Laboulaye repeated that negotiations were going on in Lisbon and that we were about to witness a "reversal of alliances." The Americans are supposedly anxious to get the war over with in Europe so that they can go after the Japanese and sever ties with the Russians. I told Laboulaye, "What a fine strategy for Roosevelt, leaving the Russians free to form an alliance with the Japanese just when the United States wants to attack them!" These people, who feel they can now save themselves only by a "reversal of alliances" – upon which no doubt the Germans are counting – have mistaken their hopes for certainties. They come up with the most absurd notions to reassure themselves that they have not taken a wrong turn.

SATURDAY, 13 MAY 1944 I have been reading in Walter Scott's *Peveril of the Peak* this passage, which must be remembered after the war:

> The English nation differs from all others, indeed even from those of the sister kingdoms, in being very easily sated with punishment, even when they suppose it most merited. Other nations are like the tamed tiger, which, when once its native appetite for slaughter is indulged in one instance, rushes on in promiscuous ravages. But the English public have always rather resembled what is told of the sleuth-dog, which, eager, fierce, and clamorous in pursuit of his prey, desists from it so soon as blood is sprinkled upon his path.[3]

3. Rist read the passage in Defaucompret's translation of the novel, page 502. Sir Walter Scott, *Peveril du Pic*, trans. Jean-Baptiste Defauconpret (Paris: Furne, Charles Gosselin, et Perrotin, 1835); published in English as *Peveril of the Peak* (London: Routledge & Sons, 1879). Source of Walter Scott's text cited here: Project Gutenberg website. [TF]

SATURDAY, 20 MAY 1944 Growing tension. Intolerable wait. No one thinks about anything but the landing; they say it will be for the fifteenth or the twentieth or the twenty-fifth and end up believing their own predictions. Radio appeals for people to evacuate the big cities are multiplying. Everything we hear from the provinces shows the increasing nervousness of the Germans, their violence against those suspected of hiding weapons, etc.

Constant alerts from the moment the sky is clear. Bombings last night and again this morning.

Lunch on Tuesday with a representative of the Turkish National Bank who had come to discuss settlement of the debt. He spoke repeatedly of Turkey's desire for neutrality. However, he has been told to return, along with his entire delegation, this weekend.

WEDNESDAY, 24 MAY 1944 French victories in the attack on Italy have been systematically ignored by the papers here. The local Franco-Germans are denying their own fellow soldiers.

"Believe in France." This does not mean believe in an abstraction defined by centuries past. It means believe in the French of *today*. Believe that today's descendants of that past still have enough force, energy, enthusiasm, and courage to free themselves from foreign oppression, build a viable social and political organization, and defend themselves against the enemy. That is precisely what the defeatist reactionaries cannot do. They speak about the France of the past. They hate the France of today, which is to say the French of today, because 90 percent refuse to listen to the same old tune and have forever destroyed what the reactionaries still adore. The latter do not believe in France, because they detest and mistrust it. That is why they have betrayed it without scruple and delivered it with pleasure to the enemy. This conceit of limiting the notion of France to that of the past is the very negation of patriotism, a denial that France still exists.

FRIDAY, 26 MAY 1944 This morning I went with Bellet to the German "carding" office.[4] We took with us a list of all our employees, who must now pass the medical exam, during which in all probability they will be declared unfit. The German was effusive in his attempt to be friendly. The reason is simple: the Turkish consul general intervened on our behalf with the German military, and the Germans are anxious to please him. Now is not the

---

4. This was Operation "Peignage des Entreprises," a process by which workers were culled for the S.T.O. (Compulsory Work Service). [TF]

time for them to fall out with the Turks. Especially after Churchill's speech three days ago revealing that the Turks were about to join the Allies and make their airfields available when the German landing in the Dodecanese Islands scared them off.

A little while ago at the barber shop I overheard some farmers assessing the harvest. The uninterrupted drought over the last few weeks is scorching the wheat and other crops, especially in sandy areas where the clay does not retain water. As there has been no fertilizer for three years, the land is starved for organic nourishment. They say that if the drought continues we are in for famine, given the lack of transport. "People have no idea of the situation," one of them next to me said.

Four or five alerts during the day.

Churchill's speech in the House of Commons has given rise to all sorts of interpretations. Friends of de Gaulle see promise of a closer understanding; his enemies see a new desertion of de Gaulle. But as Churchill has made it clear that in no case will he deal with Vichy, one may well conclude that the government in Algiers is the only one with which he is planning to deal. And that is what galls all the undecided and the collaborators, whose predictions are being undone.

WEDNESDAY, 31 MAY 1944 Germaine's Aunt Bellah went peacefully in her sleep at noon on Sunday. The funeral will take place this morning.

The alerts have multiplied over the past five or six days. Often they follow on one another after short intervals. This morning we received a letter from Jean reassuring us about the bombing of Saint-Étienne. He and Marcel safe and sound. We had been worried about them for three days. But he writes that this was really a massacre. The Americans were bombing from 3,000 or 4,000 meters. Well, there are no antiaircraft guns in Saint-Étienne. They could have made dive-bombing runs. The station was scarcely touched. It was the working quarter that got hit, with eight hundred dead. The details are horrible. A public garden where schoolchildren had taken refuge was hit by bombs that flattened everything.

I saw Wenger[5] on Tuesday afternoon. He assured me that, given the withdrawal from their lines in the east, the Germans would compensate for the loss of Romanian oil by a reduction of their needs. Around 4 million tons would thus be unnecessary, and that is what Romania produces. When he told this to a friend of Laval's, the friend exclaimed, "Ah! I will tell the

---

5. Léon Wenger: director of the Comptoir Européen de Crédit; responsible for purchases of Romanian oil, which remained in German hands till the end of the war.

president; it will please him." Laval is clinging to the smallest hope of an Allied failure.

THURSDAY, 1 JUNE 1944 An alert of almost an hour and a half last night, with deafening antiaircraft fire. This morning we learned that, once again, Trappes was the target. Horror at the number of victims during these days of Pentecost is on everyone's lips. A new reason for division and uncertainty for this poor country. Up to now there was one certainty: the arrival of the English and, thanks to them, liberation. And now there is growing doubt about their effectiveness and humanity! Will France become the victim of the other nations? Should she consider them all as her enemies? Can she only rely on herself, withdrawing into isolation after the war? These are the reflections of many simple souls. Naturally they are exploited every day by the German rags signed by Luchaire and company[6] and by everything anti-English in France.

Guy Crouzet has stopped writing for Luchaire's *Nouveaux Temps*. They say he was abducted by members of the Resistance! (He has since reappeared.)

SUNDAY, 4 JUNE 1944 Ève Trocmé[7] telephoned to say that her son Daniel, arrested last June in Le Chambon, has died in a German camp; she does not even know where it is. This was murder. Poor parents. They never had any news from him.

Continuous alerts yesterday. During the evening the bombing was so violent we ran and opened the windows to keep them from shattering. A great cloud of smoke has risen in the distance. This morning word is that the Allies bombed the Gare des Matelots, Versailles's freight depot. Two bombs fell in the Saint-Louis quarter. One of them fell on the area shelter, killing everyone.

The Allies' entry into Rome was announced this morning! What revenge for the French troops to occupy the capital of Italy after Italy's abject backstabbing. What drama will be made of these events: Mussolini, exalted in 1940, believing he had seized the hand of destiny, then run out of his capital in 1944 and hidden in who knows what hole, with the haggard, crumpled face one sees in the latest photographs. But where will the Anglo-American army turn next? Is it going to lend a hand to the Yugoslav army? That seems

6. Jean Luchaire: supporter of Vichy's National Revolution; founder of the collaborationist paper *Les Nouveaux Temps* in 1940. [TF]

7. Rist's sister.

to be the thing to do. But via what route? Crossing the Apennines again to reach Venice and Trieste? Or heading for Genoa? All this remains a mystery.

In Sainte-Beuve's fine article "De la connaissance de l'homme au XVIIIe siècle" (*Nouveaux Lundis*, 3: 237), I found this quote from Duclos: "The French are the only people who may become depraved without becoming fundamentally corrupt or losing heart." This is true, but it may well not last.

WEDNESDAY, 7 JUNE 1944 I learned about the landing yesterday from J.,[8] who came to have lunch with me at the club. He said, "The great day has arrived." I asked, "What great day? The taking of Rome?" Then he gave me some rare bits of news. During the evening the radio had broadcast a summary of Churchill's two declarations to the House of Commons; speeches by the king of England, General de Gaulle, and General Eisenhower; and the few results announced by the communiqué. Our household staff came to listen with us. Already the most diverse rumors had reached them via the market and the shops. Anxiety is foremost. What is going to happen? How long will the struggle go on? How far will it extend? Will it reach us here? What will those dear to us do? We have had so many disappointments! And there are so many uncertainties in any military operation! Already French radio in London is broadcasting absurd instructions, impossible to carry out and dangerous for those who listen to them. Individual attacks only result in awful retaliation against innocent people. Mario gave me the example of what happened near Ugine two days ago: after a mine planted along the road blew up a passing German patrol, three workers' houses were immediately set fire to and twenty-eight hostages shot!

This morning I went to the Franco-German "carding" commission, to which I had been summoned on behalf of the research institute. The good Lucien[9] went with me. It ended well, as no one was taken. But what a sight, those sons of small shopkeepers and manufacturers filing past the tables, explaining their small business, trying to save part of their personnel. You would have thought they were a herd of sheep[10] on their way to the slaughterhouse. The transformation of a whole population into simple numbers, the suppression of all individuality and all humane considerations – what a sad sight. Meanwhile on the walls of Paris and in the subway stations we could

8. Not identified.

9. Lucien Héritier: odd-job man at Rist's research institute.

10. Rist plays here on the meaning of *"peignage"* (carding) that applies to sheep: combing out wool preparatory to spinning. [TF]

see great white posters bearing Pétain's proclamation to Frenchmen, urging them to obey the occupiers' orders. No one was reading them.

FRIDAY, 9 JUNE 1944   A deafening roar of planes above us on Wednesday night. The blasts from cannon and machine guns lasted nearly an hour and a half. This morning we learned that German troops had been on the march the whole night, protected by some planes and attacked by English air power.

I went to repay Pastor Ullern's visit.[11] He talked about some significant aspects of bourgeois psychology. On the Avenue Villeneuve-l'Étang he had run into an engineer, a director of a large corporation and former officer, who commented to him regarding the English landing: "This means the return of the Jews and the Freemasons. Anything is better than that. I have made my choice. I like the Germans better." This character is a Protestant.

A letter from Jean, received yesterday, telling us that he is going "to help Uncle Loulou harvest potatoes."[12]

News of the landing is scarce. We have learned that the English are occupying Bayeux and threatening Caen on one side and the Cotentin Peninsula on the other. Meanwhile the situation here is becoming increasingly difficult. The sending and receiving of packages has been suspended. Replenishing supplies is thus going to become almost impossible. Travel beyond the Gare des Chantiers to anywhere in the west has been halted. Only the suburban lines are operating. This morning telephone communications with Paris ceased. We are now almost out of gas, and there are electricity cuts for several hours a day. The lack of coal, which no longer reaches us on trains coming from the north, has led to the laundries' closing. We are doing our own washing at the house using the wood we chopped during the spring, which we are also using for cooking. How long can all of this go on?

I read in the *Deutsche Allgemeine Zeitung*, which one can buy at the Rive-Droite train station, that "several million" Germans are now eating every day in "soup kitchens." The reporter adds that many people are wondering if it would not be a good idea to continue this system after the war and to extend it! He timidly objects that the family table was not without advantages and that it would perhaps be regrettable to have it completely disappear! While these grave questions are being asked with seriousness and humility in the land of culture, in the rest of the world, including the United States, England,

11. Pastor Ullern: pastor in Versailles.
12. Louis de Glehn: Cambridge professor; first cousin of Germaine Rist. Among the Rists, "going to see Uncle Loulou" meant going to England. In fact, Jean met up with his Resistance group in the Loire.

and the dominions, there are millions of people peacefully enjoying their freedom to come and go, to organize their lives as they think best, and as they please!

MONDAY, 12 JUNE 1944 Constant alerts. Yesterday there were at least six. Fortunately people no longer pay attention. But it is making communications very difficult. Here the trams stop as soon as the sirens start up. In Paris the subway comes to a halt and does not resume until half an hour after the end of the alert. Under these conditions one is never certain of getting to a meeting on time.

The gales have not let up, causing anxiety about the success of the landing. The extraordinary thing is that the Germans' immense coastal fortifications have proved to be useless. The Allied forces have leapfrogged over them with disconcerting ease. The papers here are doing their best to explain that all those forts were built to fire not toward the sea, but toward the land, into the rear of the landing troops! In any case, we will not know how the Allied troops have fared for several days.

The Russians are attacking in Karelia. At last the two fronts are in sync.

THURSDAY, 15 JUNE 1944 Significant conversations this morning at the Ottoman Bank and at Paribas. One can guess the worries and leanings of all those who, during the war and the defeat, saw nothing but a new chance for their reactionary hopes. Vogüé declared that Stalin is master of the game and is now going to sit back and let the British and Americans muddle through alone. He will not make another move and will refrain from attacking in the hope of joining forces with Germany! I objected that this would be a curious strategy, to shore up Germany after having been on the receiving end of such agonizing blows. But this argument has no effect on those for whom Stalin and communism were the sole concern for the past ten years and who judge accordingly.

At the Banque de Paris they say de Gaulle has been abandoned by the Anglo-Saxons, that he is no more than a puppet in their hands. The single hope of these former collaborators rests with Camille Chautemps. As a matter of fact, according to the English press and Churchill's latest declarations, the English support de Gaulle and hope to bring the United States around to their point of view. For reasons that are not yet clear but that must have to do with fear of putting a military man in power, opposition to de Gaulle comes only from Washington. The near future will show that these collaborators have once again got it wrong and misread the power of popular feeling.

The alerts recur almost at two-hour intervals. Our minds are at rest now regarding the success of the landing. But the Allied advance in Normandy is slow and apparently very costly.

SATURDAY, 17 JUNE 1944 Two pieces of military news. The Americans, taking off from China, have bombed Japan from aerial "super-fortresses." The Germans have sent unmanned airplanes over England. It is not surprising, says an English commentator who calls himself "the man in the street," that this pilotless country should send us pilotless planes.

No letup in the bad weather. After weeks of blue skies, wind and rain hit with the Normandy landings!

Laurent-Atthalin tells me that treatment of the national railway directors (Fournier, Le Bennerais, etc.), arrested a few days ago then released, was extremely rough. A Gestapo agent, accompanied by a member of the French Milice, pushed the directors around and addressed them in crude language. They went twenty-four hours without eating. It is the reign of hooligans, led by Laval and protected by Pétain.

I have tried to reread Joseph de Maistre's *Les Soirées de Saint-Pétersbourg*,[13] which I came across in my library. It amounts to intellectual dementia. No brain that has not been roused to fanaticism by the horror of the modern world could indulge in this bias of declaring everything that is incomprehensible obvious, and everything that is contrary to all experience, rational. It is the cheek of a man who knows he would be discredited from the start if he made the least concession to good sense and who resolutely clings to the opposite of good sense – total absurdity. He is clearly convinced that this stance will stupefy his adversaries. As Hitler later proclaimed, the bigger the lie, the more believable it is. De Maistre's essays on the misfortunes that strike the just, which are always deserved, or on prayer, which is always efficacious, would be intolerable if one took them for anything other than a firm commitment to absurdity so as to defend a notion to which one is attached. "I know nothing about it, but I am certain of it," as Maurras says. Everything Quinet says about reactionaries applies marvelously well to de Maistre. He represents, as Quinet says, "the residue and ashes of all that is dead in the human spirit." I quote at random from de Maistre's pretty sayings, this one from a note at the end of the First Dialogue:

---

13. *Les Soirées de St. Pétersbourg, ou Entretiens sur le gouvernement temporel de la Providence* [The Saint Petersburg Dialogues], first published in 1821. In these dialogues, de Maistre critiques rationalism, focusing on the existence of evil. [TF]

> We have no trouble understanding the opinion of those who are convinced that the most important quality of a doctor is piety. As for me, I infinitely prefer to the impious doctor the murderous highwayman against whom one can at least defend oneself and who at least from time to time is hanged.(!)

He also anticipated the Christian Scientists in the following magnificent sentence:

> As every evil is a punishment, it follows that no evil can be considered necessary and, as no evil is necessary, it follows that all evil can be prevented either by suppressing the crime that had made it necessary or by prayer, which has the power to forestall or mitigate punishment. (1: 57)

His reasoning is magnificent: "The whole human race comes from one couple. This truth, like all others, has been denied: so? what difference does that make?" (1: 68). What a marvelous bit of cheek and absurdity. And it is all of a piece.

SUNDAY, 25 JUNE 1944 Yesterday morning between 8:15 and 8:30, while we were finishing our coffee (so-called), there was a series of bomb blasts ending with a particularly violent one that seemed nearby. But it was only at 9:00, as we left for Paris and saw people in our street and in the neighboring streets, that we learned our neighborhood had been bombed. There are craters in de Magenta and de Montebello streets, two in Albert-Joly, and several bombs in neighboring yards. The tram depot has been destroyed. One bomb hit a German train at the de Rive-Droite station. It is evidently this train that was targeted. Bombs also fell on the Gare des Chantiers, where, we have been told, there were two hundred victims. The antiaircraft fire did not work. Everyone was taken by surprise. Since trains leaving from Versailles were not functioning, I walked with Mario to Chaville, where I took the train to Paris. By evening the trains were back in service.

The offensive has now been launched everywhere. The Russians have announced operations in the central region around Vitebsk at the same time as they are advancing in Karelia. The Americans are drawing closer to Cherbourg, which has been cut off, and in Italy fighting is taking place 200 kilometers north of Rome. The Allies are 80 kilometers from Livorno and 40 from Ancona. It is on the Russian front that we are expecting the most decisive victories.

SATURDAY, 1 JULY 1944 For some time we have been able to hear a clandestine German radio broadcast addressed to the troops, whom they call *Kameraden*. It is rather curious. With no commentary, this broadcast details all German losses and presents the situation of the Reich armies in the bleakest light. But above all it gives news from the home front. Among other claims, these two recent ones: first, the Führer is supposedly collecting Japanese objects, had a room furnished à la Japanese, and has immersed himself in the "doctrine of sacrifice" of a Japanese sect whose name I have forgotten, under the guidance of a professor specializing in Japanese studies; second, the government is said to be in the hands of a triumvirate led by Himmler. This triumvirate is supposedly the real master, making decisions in Hitler's place "when the latter goes into a depression."

This week I received a visit from someone who came in the name of a group numbering, he said, nearly six hundred people between the ages of twenty-five and forty-five who support Monzie, Izard, and Camille Chautemps, with whom the group is in touch. Their watchwords are no reprisals, no communism, no corporatism. They claim to be at one with American views of the French government and describe themselves as a group of "politicians." National reconciliation by the wheeler-dealers.

People are calling the murder of Philippe Henriot an "execution." At the very time when the English landing raised such hopes here, this born liar had provoked French feelings by spending the past few weeks in Berlin to proclaim his faith in Germany and his hope that it would be victorious. He was a Jesuit version of Ferdonnet, and Ferdonnet was a depraved Henriot.

Last Thursday I found everyone at the Ottoman Bank and at Paribas extraordinarily optimistic. The speed with which Cherbourg was taken and the catastrophic advance of the Russians has many believing that peace will arrive in three months.

Ismet İnönü has gone for a stroll in Thrace. Is this a sign that Turkey is at last launching operations? Meanwhile the Finns are still allowing themselves to be seduced by the Germans. For the Germans to make these efforts, so clearly inadequate to blunt Russian victories, they must dread the effect that Finland's abandoning the war would have on opinion within the Reich!

MONDAY, 3 JULY 1944 I find in Balzac's *Ursule Mirouet* this astonishing analysis of grandfatherly love:

> When old men love children, there is no limit to their passion; they adore them. For the sake of these small creatures they silence their manias and recall every detail of their past. Their experience, their indulgence, their patience, all the acquisitions of life – this treasure so painfully amassed – they dedicate to those young souls who in turn make them young again; thus by intelligence they make up for their lack of maternal qualities. Their wisdom, ever alert, is as good as a mother's intuition; they remember the sensitivity which in her amounts

to divination and apply it with a compassion whose strength is in proportion to their great weakness. The slowness with which they move takes the place of maternal gentleness. And then, for them as for children, life is reduced to its simplest terms; if a mother becomes the slave of her feelings, the detachment of all passion and the absence of all other interests permits the old man to give himself completely. This is why it is not unusual for children and old men to get along well together.

We have taken in seven refugees from the bombed Chantiers district and set them up in the outbuildings of Mario's villa. One might think these people would be furious at the British and Americans. On the contrary. Not a complaint. They understand we are at war. They are suffering, but their hatred of the occupiers is such that they are ready to endure anything to see them leave. The father is a worker at the Renault factory. Another is an accountant. Anyway, many common people express the conviction that the bombs being dropped are German!

Yesterday all the Versailles-Paris trains were taken out of service. During the week all midday trains are canceled. The last leaves here at 8:35 A M, and one must wait until 5:30 P M to return from Paris!

We are following with growing impatience the lightning advance of the Russians on Minsk. One tries to keep one's heart from bursting with hope.

No one speaks of anything anymore but supplies and provisions. Private stores of potatoes are almost all gone. Packages from the countryside no longer arrive; the trains are out of service. Those who go off on bicycles in search of food are machine-gunned on the roads, as the British and Americans think they see Germans everywhere. Meanwhile, butter, eggs, and meat are going for next to nothing in the countryside, as they can no longer be sold in the cities.

MONDAY, 8 JULY 1944 The drama grows more intense. De Gaulle has been in Washington since Thursday. His reception has been primarily as a soldier. But that reception prepares his recognition as head of government. His prestige will be enhanced because of this. The Russians are within sight of Vilnius, just 200 kilometers from eastern Prussia. The German generals are letting themselves be taken prisoner. Rundstedt has been sacked.[14] English radio claims this followed upon disagreement with Hitler. The Ger-

---

14. Marshal Gerd von Rundstedt was to redeem himself, however, by serving on the Court of Honor that expelled hundreds of officers after the 20 July attack on the Führer. [JNJ/TF]

mans are transferring their files from Paris to Nancy. Meanwhile everyone here fears going hungry in a few weeks. Communications are increasingly problematic. Every day the Paris train schedule changes. The Allies are making no headway in Normandy. If they do not liberate Paris in the next two months, we will no longer know how to feed ourselves. We must wait until the Cherbourg port is functioning again to permit massive new troop arrivals. In Washington de Gaulle has predicted that the French nightmare will be over by year's end, when he says the last German in France will have been driven out.

Last night a major alert and heavy bombardment, but we do not know where the bombs fell. This morning there were four or five alerts.

Mario took a truck to the Orléans area on Tuesday in order to find food for his company. We will not know if he has come back safe and sound until today or tomorrow. Jean is alone in Fraisses, completely cut off from his family in Le Chambon. Marcel has found a job with the gasworks in Saint-Étienne. We live our lives clinging to the radio news.

A big monetary conference in the United States. France was represented by Mendès France and Istel. Georges Boris, of regrettable memory, invents his memoranda on money. All of those people dream only of reprisals.

SUNDAY, 16 JULY 1944 The Russians have taken Vilnius and are in the suburbs of Grodno – 75 kilometers from eastern Prussia.

Here the horror of civil war is mounting. In Versailles during the night of the seventh to the eighth of July, a group of people woke up the police *intendant* (a creation of the new regime) and brought him the body of Georges Mandel. They gave some vague explanations, then withdrew. It seems Mandel was being driven from La Santé Prison to one of the camps, and along the way some people tried to free him. He was supposedly killed during the ensuing fight. None of that seems plausible. Most probably he was murdered by the Milice. The *intendant* had the body sent to the hospital morgue. There were two bullets in his neck, one of which had entered from behind. Some papers were on the body, among others a notebook with personal notations. Various people were allowed to go through the notebook, including the person who told me all this. My informant has ties to the judicial system, but others who went through the papers did not. He was buried on Monday. The original idea had been to put him in the communal grave! An examining magistrate was charged with investigating!

Rumors that Jean Zay has been murdered have been circulating for two weeks.

Laurent-Atthalin assures me that Reynaud and Blum are in La Santé Prison.[15] According to him, the German government asked the French government if it wanted to see these two people return, and Laval apparently said no but learned a few days later that the two former presidents were in La Santé. Now Laval is supposedly quite worried that they are in danger of being murdered. In any case, rumor has it that a revolt at La Santé on Saturday, 15 July, resulted in a hundred dead and a hundred escapees. Does this have something to do with the presence of Reynaud and Blum?

Clearly, power is in the hands of the Darnand-Déat gang, who are committing murder before the German defeat results in their ouster. Atthalin says the ministers attached to them have even addressed a letter to the German government asking it to replace Laval, not Germanophile enough, with Doriot!

Meanwhile, dreadful news: the Waffen S.S. has massacred the population of a village near Limoges.[16] Eight hundred inhabitants perished in the flames, women and children having been shut up in the church where a box of explosives was set off.

Indirect news of Jean. A cause for worry.

The German guards placed at the Winters' house allow us to follow the concerns of the occupier. Up until four weeks ago, just one was enough to keep watch on the intersection. Since the landing, two have been placed there. For the last week, instead of holding their guns on their shoulders, they are holding them under their arms, with the barrel aimed horizontally at the bellies of passersby.

Mario has left again in a truck to find food for Ugine in the Deux-Sèvres. He will be ranging abroad the whole week, running the risk of being machine-gunned on the road.

WEDNESDAY, 19 JULY 1944 Yesterday, a visit from D.[17], quite upset by rumors that once de Gaulle enters Paris, bills of 1,000 and 5,000 francs will need to be stamped. For a year everyone has been hoarding bills. He tells me of someone who has 8 million, someone else, a more modest 250,000. But what can one do if they must be stamped, which in reality means confiscated? D. declares that the absurd rise we have witnessed in the stock market over the past four weeks has no other cause. People are getting rid of their bills in exchange for gold or stock certificates. It seems the napoleon has spiked from

15. The rumor was false.
16. Oradour-sur-Glane, a commune in the Limousin region. [JNJ/TF]
17. Not identified.

2,300 to 4,000. All of this rests on the so-called stamping of bills in Corsica by de Gaulle's government.

The truth is that this stamping is a fiction. But how would the public know that, since the decrees signed by Couve de Murville have never been published here, and those who have seen them have only done so in secret? What a magnificent position for the people betting on panic over the franc against whose machinations no countermeasures are possible – because they have all the controlled press with them!

But behold, on Tuesday evening a rumor made the rounds at the Bourse: armistice between the Russians and Germany. Suddenly the stock market collapsed! A nice market coup for the bears. And loads of simpletons fell for this silly rumor, a rumor suited to the mentality of many bourgeois who see Stalin and the Bolsheviks as deceitful characters bent on tricking the capitalists rather than on defending the interests of their country.

An incident last week showed once again the stranglehold that thugs, the lowest of the low, have on France, and the government's lack of will to do anything about it. This goes back ten years, when a former officer named Bucard founded the "Francist" party.[18] This Bucard and some of his henchmen had entered a house in which there were precious jewels. The owner had time to call the emergency police services. Some policemen arrived and asked Bucard if he had a requisition order. When he responded negatively, they attempted to arrest him. Bucard got away in his car. They chased him. A traffic jam ensued. Cornered, Bucard fired, killing two policemen and wounding a third. Bucard was arrested. The police prefect telephoned Laval, who told him not to hold Bucard. The prefect replied that if he could not keep the man in prison, his agents would not obey him anymore. As of now we do not know if Bucard is still in prison or not. Just a few months before, this same Bucard was publicly embraced by Pétain as one of the purest representatives of French patriotism.

Dormoy, Alexis Léger's brother-in-law, has told me what happened when Léger was discharged in 1940, which explains Léger's hatred of Reynaud and Baudouin. He learned that he was being ousted from his post as general secretary of Foreign Affairs from colleagues who brought him the morning's *Journal Officiel*. Léger went straight to Lebrun, who greeted him by saying, "Well, you must be happy, M. Léger." Stunned, the latter explained to Lebrun that he had just learned of his discharge. "How can that be?" replied Lebrun. "They brought me the decree to sign after midnight as a matter of urgency. I

---

18. Marcel Bucard: founder of the Francist party, an extreme right-wing group; executed for treason after the war. [TF]

was already in bed. Reynaud told me you were in total agreement." Energetic protests by Léger. Lebrun then called for Reynaud, whom Léger reproached vigorously for his deed and his way of going about it. Reynaud raised his arms to heaven and said to Léger: "At a time when we have so many serious matters to deal with, how can you be so concerned about yourself?" Léger was offered the ambassadorship to Washington, but he refused it. Behind this coup were Mme de Portes, who detested Léger, and Baudouin, who had not forgiven Léger for refusing to heed his advice regarding rapprochement with Mussolini.

FRIDAY, 21 JULY 1944 Big news: an attempt on Hitler's life. Some dynamite blew up near him, wounding those close to him. Hitler spoke on the radio, declaring that the attack had been planned by a "clique" of generals. Of course one must be on one's guard against believing blindly what these people say. But the fact that Goering also spoke on the radio to say that the air force should obey only him clearly proves that the army is involved. This is the Wallenstein drama all over again. I said as much in these notes a few months ago. It is the only way Germany knows when there is opposition to the government. Nothing in that country ever comes from the people. The thing must have been serious for them to feel obliged to talk publicly about it. According to Hitler, the perpetrator of the attack was a colonel bearing the aristocratic name of Count von Stauffenberg. The one consolidating power over not just the army but the civil administration as well is Himmler.

One hopes that tomorrow at the latest Russian troops are going to enter East Prussia. A new offensive starting from Kowel is bringing them very close to Lublin. An invasion of German territory and of German Poland has begun along the whole front. The debacle is under way. In Normandy the English are rapidly advancing south of Caen.

Tojo's Japanese cabinet has resigned. A general and an admiral have been charged with replacing it. They belong to the military clique. But they have declared they could not manage to form a new cabinet. In the end it was decided to create a cabinet presided over by a general alone. This says much about cordial relations between the Japanese army and navy.

SATURDAY, 22 JULY 1944 One hears nothing on the radio but talk about the military coup d'état in Germany. In spite of the interruption of all communications between Germany and the neutral countries, as well as the dearth of information, we can be certain of the following:

1. If Hitler felt obliged to publicize the attack, it is because the importance of the putsch and the need to advertise the fact that he was not dead were great.
2. The fact that many generals have declared the war lost cannot fail to have a disastrous effect on the others, as well as on the troops. The disintegration of the German army is under way, especially, it seems, on the eastern front.
3. Goering and Doenitz have spoken on behalf of the air force and navy to assure Hitler of their loyalty. But Keitel, who was present, did not give such assurance in the name of the army. Thus the army must be in a state of defiance, if not revolt.

All of this will rapidly come to a head as the Russians advance.

They say that last night in Paris the *Wehrmacht* tried to disarm the Gestapo and the S.S. There is also talk on the radio of naval mutinies in Kiel and regimental mutinies in Latvia and Estonia.

What are our *bons bourgeois*, who counted on the German troops to maintain order at the end of the war, going to say?

It is time to repeat with Henri de Jouvenel, "A dictatorship generally begins well and always ends badly. A revolution generally begins badly, but often ends well."

What a blow to the French establishment, which has been dreaming of a Hitler and a Mussolini for us and refusing to see in Stalin anything but a bandit. This same ruling establishment insulted Roosevelt when he rose to power! Useless to hope they will do some soul-searching regarding their own stupidity.

SUNDAY, 23 JULY 1944 News on the radio of continuing troubles in Germany. This is filtering through despite the suppression of communications between Germany and other nations.

All those generals would not have revolted if the head of state had been their legitimate sovereign. Such a sovereign would no doubt have yielded to their leadership. But usurpers cannot give in to men who are not their creatures. That would be a sign of weakness. Therefore the generals revolted, not having the reverence for Hitler that they had for Wilhelm II.

This revolt broke out only as the Russian front was collapsing. It is a sign that this front no longer holds. The Prussian military want it said that the homeland never experienced war when they were in charge. Now that the land is going to be invaded, however, they are turning against Hitler and declaring, "If we had commanded instead of him, this would not have happened." So once more they are proved innocent. Hitler's great mistake was to take over command of the army two years ago. He laid himself open to the rancor of the generals, who will declare him to be responsible before the nation, as in the last war they blamed the "home front."

TUESDAY, 25 JULY 1944 I went to see Falkenhausen yesterday to ask him to intervene on behalf of Mme Guerpillon, the mother of Léonard's friend who has been in captivity for four years. Falkenhausen received me cordially. He simply said, "Yes, but my name at this point is scarcely a recommendation." I took advantage of the moment to ask if he had any news of his uncle, the governor of Belgium, who the papers say has been dismissed. He said he did not know anything. He will try to find someone whose name is better viewed than his to undertake the mission I requested of him. We exchanged a few general remarks. I said, "This is the moment to reread Wallenstein."

"Certainly," he said, and as I was comparing our time to that of the Thirty Years' War, he added, "No, it is different. In the two camps there was still a common language. They still understood each other. The Duke of Saxony wavered between the two camps. Today it's a different language being spoken." He told me he reads Ronsard and Montaigne and that his wife reads Pascal – "God would be very unjust if we were not guilty."

I can guess at all the soul-searching and thoughts on the German situation reflected in that sentence. As I left, I said, "I would enjoy a conversation with you when the war is over and we're no longer inhibited by the limitations imposed by the war."

"So would I," he said.

During the afternoon I touched base with the Suez Company board after I left the Banque du Maroc. Georges-Edgar Bonnet told me of his nephew's arrest by the Milice. He is worried because there has been no news of his whereabouts for two days.

Last night I received a telephone call announcing the arrest of Mme Campinchi![19]

Three arrests announced in three days!

The appalling reprisals in Saint-Gingolph were recounted on the radio.

Stülpnagel victim of an assassination attempt. How many French people will be executed in retaliation! The Maquis are causing more casualties

---

19. Hélène Campinchi: appeals court lawyer; widow of César Campinchi.

among the French than among the Germans. Afterward they said he tried to kill himself.[20]

The Russian troops are not yet in East Prussia. They are first ridding the Baltic provinces of German troops. The party of imbeciles is making the most of this, telling everyone that the Russians do not intend to enter Germany. They still cling to the hope of an armistice between Germany and Russia and of supposed negotiations in Lisbon between Laval and the United States. These wretches will believe to the end that they will be spared the arrival of the Allies and, above all, that of de Gaulle. This is their nightmare. Meanwhile the Russians are in Lublin, and just 100 kilometers separate them from Warsaw.

SUNDAY, 30 JULY 1944 The house has been invaded by floor fleas. This seems to be happening to everyone in Versailles. We can no longer clean the floors with bleach, which is not available, nor with wax, equally unavailable. These fleas lodge in the gaps between floorboards.

The Russians have begun bombing Warsaw.

SUNDAY, 6 AUGUST 1944 Events of the past week have been breathtaking. The Americans are in Rennes, Fougère, and Mayenne. They are nearing Saint-Nazaire and Brest. We expect them to advance along the Loire in the east, and perhaps the decisive battle will be waged at Chartres. The communiqués and radio commentaries give us no idea whatsoever as to their intentions. The English are advancing more slowly south of Caen. So the biggest threat is to the Germans' left flank, which will presumably be attacked from the rear by Americans coming from the south.

Warsaw is still holding out, but the Russians are advancing quickly toward Krakow. They were expected to enter East Prussia, but they are moving most rapidly toward Silesia.

Meanwhile we are in ever greater danger of dying of hunger.

The "National Revolutionaries," looking for forerunners to anti-Semitism, have rediscovered the old book by Toussenel, *Les Juifs rois de l'époque* (1845).[21] I was curious enough to search for it. Here is what one reads on page 4:

---

20. In fact, Stülpnagel shot himself in the head but did not die of the wound. [JNJ/TF]

21. Alphonse Toussenel: nineteenth-century anti-Semitic Utopian socialist who wrote *Les Juifs rois de l'époque: histoire de la féodalité financière* [The Jews, Kings of the Epoch: A History of Financial Feudalism] (Paris: Gabriel de Gonet, 1847).

I warn the reader that this word is generally taken here in its popular sense: Jew, banker, money merchant. No one recognizes more readily than I the superior character of the Jewish nation. The Jewish people have played an immense role in the history of humanity. . . . No race has been richer in brilliant individuals. It seems they were endowed by nature with all the talents. . . . Unfortunately, all readers of the Bible, whether they are called Jews or Genevans, Dutch or Americans, must have found written in their prayer book that God had conceded to the followers of his law the monopoly on global exploitation, for all those mercantile peoples bring the same fanatical religious fervor to the art of fleecing mankind. This is why I understand the persecutions that Romans, Christians, and Muslims have carried out against the Jews. The universal revulsion inspired by the Jew for such a long time was but a legitimate reaction to the hatred he seemed to harbor toward the rest of humanity.

And that is all. Toussenel aims his accusations at bankers in general, Protestant bankers, those he calls Genevans, and industrialists. His conclusion is that the State should take over the insurance companies, as well as trade, transport, banks, and sugar. Socialism of 1848.

He appeals to the king to oppose Jewish feudalism so that he will side with the people, and to support his case, cites anti-Jewish statements by the Duke of Orléans.

Twenty-Three

State of Siege:
The Allies Advance

11 AUGUST–24 AUGUST 1944
As the world rejoiced at General Koenig's announcement that Paris had liberated itself, Rist told quite a different story. In contrast to General Koenig, who was not present, the occupier still was, and the fighting and indiscriminate firing on innocent bystanders continued as Paris and environs remained under siege.

FRIDAY, 11 AUGUST 1944 Dominating everything is the lightning-fast advance of the Americans. Yesterday they were at Beaugency near Orléans. Today the radio says they are at Chartres. Many reasonable people expect them to be in Paris on Monday. But where will the Germans engage them? Some say near Paris, between the Loire and the Seine – that is, between Chartres and Orléans. Yesterday General Pujo told me the Germans must have about ten divisions there. Others say they are going to pass the Seine and fight in the Somme (where they are supposed to have forty divisions), the Oise, and the Aisne. Ferocious fighting continues around Vire and in Mortain, and they are trying to cut off the corridor between Avranches and Vire through which American troops are passing from the Cotentin Peninsula into Anjou.

Last night a sudden halt to all trains on the Paris-Versailles lines from 6:00 PM on. Luckily I had taken the 5:20 train from Montparnasse, which arrived without problems. Service resumed a bit later, and it is functioning today, but the station has announced that there will be no trains tomorrow. The subway is back in service, but with no trains between 11:00 in the morning and 3:00 in the afternoon.

The Germans, apparently in total disarray, are moving their offices to Nancy. The newspapers have been ordered to move to Gérardmer. Only *Le*

Matin has refused. Old Bunau-Varilla has just died.[1] He was a scavenger. His son is said to have come to the paper and removed Hitler's portrait, resulting in tantrums and squabbles. Châteaubriant's paper *La Gerbe* has declared that the defeat of the Germans would be the death of socialism. These reactionaries, who hate the working class and inflicted 6 February 1934 on them, claim today to be the only true socialists and vilify the German generals who revolted as country squires and aristocrats! But their rage and hatred, directed against the Anglo-American alliance, overshadow everything else. Their "day of glory" arrived in June 1940 and is now being snatched away. A spectacle of base stupidity.

At the Banque de Paris they are preparing to welcome de Gaulle and to renew ties with the English, whose empire Laurent-Atthalin regarded as lost two years ago. He says he is anxious to resume conversations with the Ottoman Bank in London. He wants to send B.,[2] but I have told him I am the one to resume relations after four years of war.

According to Anglo-American reports, the American troops, after having headed toward the south of Avranches, are turning back to close on the Germans' rear by way of Alençon and Argentan, which the radio says they reached this morning. American and English radio broadcasts are already drawing enthusiastic conclusions regarding the possibilities thus opened up. Some twenty divisions will be surrounded; they could escape by only one route, that of Lisieux, and would then risk being driven back to the Seine, all of whose bridges have been destroyed.

For two days here we have heard shelling toward the north – that is, beyond Paris and in the direction of Rouen. The most absurd rumors are circulating. It was announced on Saturday that the Americans would arrive in the evening. That night some of the German contingent moved out, making a noisy exit. At 10:30 last night the Schallers called, urging us to stock up on water. We have done so without much conviction. During the day many siren alerts and some loud bomb blasts. Magnificent weather and quite hot. The hottest days of the year.

No news from Falkenhausen. His secretary remains silent. Édouard V.[3] told me he has been given the choice of leaving for the front or entering La Santé Prison.

1. Editor of *Le Matin*, Maurice Bunau-Varilla (1856–1944) had long been favorable to Nazi Germany.
2. Possibly Félix Bellet, one of the managers of the Ottoman Bank in Paris.
3. Surely, Édouard Vernes.

The Gustave-Adolphe Monods have lost their nephew,[4] charming boy, father of five children, killed in a guerilla skirmish in Aude.

TUESDAY, 15 AUGUST 1944 Last night we were warned that the Germans intend to round up all males over the age of ten. The bishop of Versailles has excused the men from attending today's Mass of the Assumption. Of course these are all just false rumors, and this morning nothing happened. The day before yesterday we were warned by telephone of a water shortage and urged to lay in a supply. The simplest thing is to take precautions and hope they will not be necessary. We are cut off from everything, and too many people have an interest in sowing panic.

Poissonnier[5] explained to me what is going on in Cherbourg, where people are paying top prices for the occupation money brought in by the Americans. There are two reasons for this: first, they believe its buy-back value is better; then they think it cannot be demanded if an inventory is made of bills. This is equally foolish.

The bread ration has been reduced to 150 grams. People are lining up at the bakeries.

We heard on the radio that a French division under the orders of General Leclerc has joined up with Anglo-American troops in Normandy. Our eyes filled with tears.

The Allies speak of the progressive encirclement of the one hundred thousand Germans spread out between Mortain and Falaise as a practical certainty. False hope, optimistic illusion, or reality? We are in suspense. Everyone is on edge because of this anxious waiting, which has lasted now for weeks.

THURSDAY, 17 AUGUST 1944 Everything is happening at once. Yesterday Mario, who had gone to Paris and back on his bicycle, told us: (1) that the police have disappeared, having gone on strike to protest against the arrest of some of their own by the Germans; and (2) that Herriot (who was believed dead) is negotiating with the Americans to have Paris declared an open city. Mario found the road jammed with German vehicles, some on their way to Paris, others heading from Paris toward Versailles and the west. I begged him not to go to Paris today, as bicycles can be requisitioned by any officer or soldier.

---

4. Jacques Monod (1903–1944): professor of literature.
5. Poissonnier: stockbroker in Paris and neighbor of the Rists in Versailles.

This morning great unrest in Versailles. During the night we heard some strange explosions. This morning we were told that the Germans had been blowing up their stores of explosives at the Château de Beauregard. Again, all this morning and afternoon explosions have been going off. They say the Germans are blowing up their storage depots in Satory. Around 3:00 PM great billows of smoke, mixing with the clouds, darkened the sky. The Germans are scattering in all directions. They have evacuated the Château de la Maye and the hospital they had set up facing it. The Gestapo have left the house they occupied on Avenue Villeneuve-l'Étang. I walked with Germaine along the rue du Maréchal-Foch and the Avenue de Paris. Many German automobiles, but, above all, inhabitants of Versailles everywhere, communicating the news. They are waiting for the Americans who were, they say, in Rambouillet and are about to enter Versailles. In truth, no one knows anything. At 2:30, as I was leaving the house, I ran into Leyendecker,[6] who was leaving police headquarters. He told me that the Germans are requisitioning all men between sixteen and fifty to go dig trenches tomorrow. They want seven thousand, and if they do not show up, they threaten to go into houses with grenades. I am going to see Lolli to ask her to call Mario and warn him not to come back late tonight. Mario, who wanted to go to Paris in spite of everything, will spend the night there on Lebreton's advice.

SATURDAY, 19 AUGUST 1944 Completely contradictory rumors reach our ears. What was true yesterday is no longer so today, or is no longer so in the same way. The only certainty is that yesterday Paris had no police, no mail service, scarcely any electricity or gas, and no subway service, since the railway and postal workers have stopped working. No more papers and no more Radio Paris. But here is what is not certain. Morin and Mario (back last night) told us that an agreement has been reached for Paris to be evacuated by the Germans along two routes that would not be bombed; that Herriot, after having negotiated this agreement, was again taken prisoner by the Germans and sent back east; that the cabinet is resigning and in flight; that only Cathala is still at the finance ministry; and that Déat has been put in charge of the government! According to Mario, some white posters were put up on Thursday night by the Resistance. These posters carry the heading *République Française, Liberté, Égalité, Fraternité.*

We spent the evening and the night waiting to see the Americans arrive, all the more assured of welcoming them tomorrow by London radio's an-

6. Leyendecker: architect in Versailles.

nouncement that they are near Versailles. According to the prefecture, the Americans are known to be in Épernon and Rambouillet.

But this morning all has changed. The Germans are still in the Winters' house. I called Gustave-Adolphe, who told me there was no agreement. According to the radio, nothing will be said about the Americans' movements around Paris. Leyendecker, whom I saw outside the prefecture, told me that Pétain, Laval, and Herriot are prisoners in Belfort and that no one can understand why the Americans, who are so near Paris, have not yet arrived. I went past the Borgnis-Desbordes barracks on the Avenue de Paris; the policeman on duty said it blew up by accident last night when a store of grenades exploded too soon. In the Passage Saint-Pierre the window behind which the sad face of Philippe Henriot was on display (and which was guarded by a policeman) is in a thousand pieces, and the face has disappeared. Not a single German on foot in the city. But on Avenue de Saint-Cloud I came across several trucks covered by foliage and full of soldiers and barrels of benzene. They turned onto rue Georges-Clemenceau – headed where? Toward Saint-Cyr or toward Paris?

On the Avenue de Paris a few automobiles pass by, coming from the direction of the Gare Rive-Gauche and taking the rue des Chantiers (to continue toward Buc and Villacoublay?). Above us, planes are firing at one another. So this is the battle. In the city people question each other on their doorsteps. They look up in astonishment at the planes, and the inhabitants of Versailles wonder whether they will be in the line of fire.

As German troops head out of Paris and the suburbs, I suppose the Americans must be moving toward Corbeil to attack them from the rear. That the Germans are withdrawing is the only thing not in doubt. Yesterday we continued to hear the explosions coming from Satory. I encountered four P.P.F. (Doriot's party) in their blue shirts.[7] Why are they showing themselves? Do they still want to create havoc? As for the soldiers of the anti-Bolshevik militia who were lodged on our street, they disappeared the day before yesterday, as did the young woman who had offered them her generous hospitality.

The weather is splendid and hot. It seems we can already breathe the air of freedom. We look once again to the future. Life, *real* life, is opening up again after this long nightmare. But we are like people who have been starved for a long time and cannot tolerate heavy food. We open our lungs only halfway.

---

7. P.P.F. (Le Parti Populaire Français): fascist, anti-Semitic party headed by Jacques Doriot. [TF]

Mario has told us about Léonard's adventure last week: arrested at the Morgan Bank along with one of his colleagues, a disabled veteran from the Great War, by a Gestapo brute who had come to demand 300,000 francs, which they refused to give him without authorization. They were dragged to the rue des Saussaies, shut up for half an hour in a room that measured 2 square meters with no air but that coming in under the door, then led before an elegant gentleman who apologized for the brutality of his agent and released them.

Positive news of the landing on the Mediterranean seaboard that took place a week ago. German resistance appears to be quite weak. In Haute-Savoie it appears the lakeshore has been cleared and the Maquis are in control. We are breathing a sigh of relief for the Schneiders[8] and for Le Très-Clos.

We can hear shelling again, coming from the northwest. Let us hope Saint-Germain is protected.

At noon Mme Bolgert called to tell me that the French flag is flying above the Banque de France and over the town hall in the Second Arrondissement. She went to the town hall, where people were singing the *Marseillaise* in chorus. A little later I learned that the tricolor had been raised above the Hôtel de Ville. Paris has been put under a curfew to take effect after 2:00 PM this afternoon, evidently so the Germans can leave without any skirmishes taking place (as apparently happened at the Place de la Concorde). The police went back on duty at 1:30 and are patrolling the streets of Paris.

The Americans are said to be in Sens. Their movement is becoming increasingly clear.

At 9:00 PM, Mme Barbey,[9] who lives near the Quai de l'Horloge, called to say there is a fight going on at police headquarters, that the Resistance fighters are cooperating with the police, but that the Germans are attacking them with machine-gun and artillery fire and that no one knows how to resupply them or to care for their wounded. We are confounded, no longer understanding what is going on or who is in charge.

SUNDAY, 20 AUGUST 1944 We notice that the Germans are far from being all gone.

Colas's birthday.[10]

---

8. The family of Georges Schneider whom the Rists sheltered at Le Très-Clos during the war. (See the note for 19 October 1940.)

9. Mme Barbey: aunt of Noël Rist's wife.

10. Colas Rist (1940–2014): grandson of Charles Rist, son of Mario and Lolli Gaede Rist.

Finally at 4:00 PM in a call to Léonard we had some direct news. Yesterday morning the F.F.I.[11] took over some town halls and raised the French flag. They also took control of police headquarters and the Seine prefecture. Hence some incidents with the Germans. But at three today an agreement was reached. The Germans are leaving, they recognize the F.F.I. as belligerents, and they will treat their prisoners as soldiers. But the German troops will take more than three days to evacuate. Until then the German and French flags will be left where they are.

I went to the Kommandantur – people packing, camouflaged trucks and cars full of suitcases outside the Hôtel Vatel, about to leave. But yesterday people were already saying they had left.

The Americans are in Pontchartrain, sunbathing on the grass. They have no orders. This was reported to me by an eyewitness. American radio continues to speak as if the Americans have reached Versailles. People call to know if it is true or to congratulate us. But we can only say no.

The radio has announced the capture of Goerdeler,[12] the former burgomaster of Leipzig who headed the revolt of the generals. A bounty of a million marks had been put on his head. I am despondent. I saw him many times before the war, the last time in Fribourg, Switzerland, in strict secrecy. I had taken him to see Daladier and Léger. He always said that if war broke out, Germany would revolt at the first setback of the German troops. What illusions he lived under! Like all Germans, he misunderstood his country. Though he acted in good faith – a confirmed conservative – he had no real influence. Conservatives, no matter in what country, understand nothing of what is going on. He had shown me, in a newspaper photograph, the picture of General Halder, at the time chief of staff, saying, "He is the one who will rebel." He did not lift a finger.

The absence of any French radio addressing France or Paris is terribly annoying. This silence on the part of the leaders leaves one with the impression that any absurd initiative is possible. The prolongation of the silence and of the absurd lingering of the Germans in Paris while the Americans have yet to arrive is very dangerous. Only the presence of the F.F.I. is saving us.

MONDAY, 21 AUGUST 1944 Léonard called to tell me that Courtin has been named to National Economy, Mönick to Finances, and Alexandre

---

11. F.F.I. (French Forces of the Interior): name given Resistance fighters in 1944. [TF]

12. Goerdeler was hanged a few months later.

Parodi, general delegate. He is the one who signed the agreement with the Germans yesterday. But the Germans still control the bridges of Paris.

Last night the exceptional curfew of 9:00 PM was still in effect, and we had to go home instead of going for a walk, as we wanted to.

Still no French newspaper or poster or radio. Without London radio, which seems poorly informed about what is happening in Paris, we would know nothing. Still no indication from that source as to the position of American troops. Was the armistice signed with the agreement of the Americans? All this is mysterious. They say the Germans need to bring three armored divisions that are supposedly stuck in Maules through the streets of Paris. Will the Americans allow them to do this?

I am rereading Maupassant's "Boule de Suif," where I find a passage that still today depicts the mentality of "decent" people: "the countess and the factory owner's wife, who harbored in their souls the *unreasoning hatred of respectable people for the Republic* [Rist's emphasis]."

In *Grandeur et Misères d'une Victoire,* in which there is so much nonsense side by side with some fine and telling pages, Clemenceau, addressing Foch, wrote (and it applies equally to people today who, not having despaired, foresee victory): "I can at least tell you *that there is no defeat of the law which does not contain the seeds of a triumphant reaction in the future,* so it is enough to be on the right side of the barricade to find oneself justified in the end" (218).

At 11:00 Germaine and I left to see what was happening in the city. A red poster of the Feldkommandantur: *Bekanntmachung.*[13] All the business of a state of siege – forbidden to go out from sundown to sunrise, no groups of more than three people, take shelter in the cellars if the enemy appears, etc. In a word, they are getting ready to fight: so the Americans are coming, but not with flowers at the end of their rifles. It is a battle that is approaching. One can hear shelling in the distance.

At the Kommandantur one sees many soldiers and cars; they are far from being gone.

Thus the outlook is changing daily.

The F.F.I. in Versailles have put up white posters in the streets to remind everyone that they are the only legitimate authority and that they are the ones who are to receive the Allies. But they have yet to make a move to take over the town hall or the prefecture. It is said they have taken the town hall of Chesnay. They put up the flag, then took it down.

13. Proclamation. [TF]

One wonders now if the F.F.I. in Paris have not begun too soon, if they would not have done better to wait for the Germans to leave Paris. That would have avoided any bloodshed. The blood continues to flow.

There appears to be combat on the outskirts of the city. All day we could hear distant shelling. And now we are experiencing violent explosions that shake the house (6:50 PM) without knowing where they are coming from. Are we in the line of fire?

TUESDAY, 22 AUGUST 1944 Charles de Gaulle landed in Cherbourg along with Juin, d'Argenlieu, and Koenig. Koenig has been named governor of Paris. In the south it is de Lattre de Tassigny. Here we are, in full military rule. Only madmen are not worried about our future. For all of these people come more or less from the Action Française and hate the Republic.

Telephone calls from Paris. The fighting continues. It is stupid and useless.

The Germans are still in Versailles's Kommandantur. Camouflaged trucks with not many men – but those few armed to the teeth – are heading for the front. But what front? According to the communiqués, the Americans have crossed to the right bank of the Seine at Mantes and at Fontainebleau. Meanwhile the Germans in Normandy are being backed up to the Seine and slaughtered on all sides. Triumphant orders given by Montgomery to his troops.

I no longer think, I no longer reflect, I wait. Everyone is so tense they do not even talk about food anymore. We are cut off from everything, no trams, no trains. Without the telephone, all contact would be lost. We are like a prisoner four days before the end of his sentence. He still acts like a prisoner, but his mind is focused on conflicting feelings of imminent liberation and worry about his cloudy future.

I had a telephone call from Morin asking for news. He tells me a communist has been named to Education, that is Wallon, a professor at the Collège de France, and another to Justice (a lawyer, Willard). Gustave-Adolphe will supposedly head up Secondary Teaching.

Léonard calls from time to time to find out if we are still alive and if the Americans have not shown up yet. He says clandestine newspapers are appearing freely.

WEDNESDAY, 23 AUGUST 1944 Up until 3:00 or 4:00 AM we could hear the shelling coming closer. This morning we did not hear anything more. The radio news is the same as yesterday's.

On Tuesday I read volume 8 of Barrès's *Cahiers*. Curiously false position of this beacon of the Church. He declares he is a nonbeliever. Simultaneously he reproaches the Republic for not teaching Catholicism and for not having a secular moral doctrine to give children. At least the Republic made an effort to provide an education, whereas Barrès, for lack of anything better, recommends the teaching of things that he knows to be false. Besides, the Church exists; no one is preventing children from following its teachings. One could begin to criticize secular education if it served to attack religion. But that is what the Republic always prohibited. And then the Catholics and conservatives are astonished at their lack of influence on public opinion and at being increasingly rejected. To those who lack faith, they offer their own absence of faith as a cure. This was always the position of Chateaubriand, "republican" in private, Catholic and royalist in public. Such a lie corrupts those who speak it and those to whom it is spoken. Most people turned away from these clowns a long time ago and do not listen to them anymore.

This is the day of the Koenig "Ems Dispatch." Telephone calls from Paris tell us that the fighting continues in many streets and that the Grand Palais is burning, attacked and set on fire by the Germans. So the German troops are still there. And yet suddenly at 10:00 English radio announced: "Paris has been liberated," citing a dispatch from General Koenig, military governor of Paris (but who is not there), declaring:

> On Saturday, on the order of representatives of the provisional government, the F.F.I. – consisting of fifty thousand armed men, along with hundreds of thousands of unarmed Parisians – rose up against the enemy. Public buildings have been occupied by the F.F.I. Paris has been liberated by the Parisians.

Well, we know full well that it is nothing of the sort, that the occupier is still there, and that there is fighting just about everywhere! How can one explain this good news in view of the facts? Does he believe what he says? Or is this a bluff to make the world believe that Paris liberated itself all alone, without Allied help? We can only guess, and find a bitter contrast between what we know of reality and what the world is being told. For it is the rest of the world that is now raucously rejoicing: dispatch from the mayor of London to the mayors of France; dispatch from the mayor of Manchester, the ringing of bells in that city; a speech by Eden in the evening; dispatch from the United States ambassador in London, Wynant; a visit from the English ambassador in Spain to the F.F.I. in Hendaye, etc., etc. We are proud to think that "Paris's self-liberation" has produced such enthusiasm. But meanwhile we find ourselves in a full state of siege. As I write, the thunderous shelling is coming ever closer. In Koenig's whole dispatch there is only one truth: that the public buildings and administrations are in the hands of the French. The papers – the real ones – are reappearing in Paris. It is the French who administer provisioning and mount posters in Paris. But at the same time everyone is being ordered to put up barricades to impede the enemy.

During the afternoon we were given some details by Zambeaux,[14] who had returned from Paris on foot. It appears the communists set things off while the F.F.I. was taking over the town halls. He found the justice ministry in the hands of Willard, a communist, who made haste to put communists everywhere and did not bother to hide his desire to insist upon the "will of the people" without waiting for the return of the prisoners and workers from Germany. Zambeaux explained Koenig's dispatch as an attempt to put the communists out of the game and put the spotlight on the F.F.I., who are commanded by well-disciplined, professional army officers.

THURSDAY, 24 AUGUST 1944 The artillery fire is coming nearer. Yesterday evening around 6:00 we had another Allied bombardment (where it landed we do not know) with a violent reaction by German antiaircraft fire.

This morning on the radio a new sensational American announcement: General Leclerc supposedly entered Paris yesterday! (Word is there is nothing true in this information.) The American correspondent said the delegate of the provisional government in Paris went to see General Bradley yesterday to tell him that the "truce" expired on Wednesday at noon and that it was urgent to send in troops.

Meanwhile we hear the machine guns and artillery coming ever closer. Where are they firing? And upon whom? Olivier[15] called to tell me he finds the announcement of Paris's liberation a "bitter" one, for he could hear the artillery fire from his apartment in the des Ternes district. The same old bluff.

At last we are getting regular broadcasts from the Eiffel Tower radio, giving orders to Parisians! At least one French voice is reaching us. Yet at the same time it announces fierce fighting on the Boulevard Saint-Michel. From various quarters we hear of skirmishes, and people who call are dumbfounded and rather disgusted by announcements from London radio showering us with all the manifestations of American enthusiasm for the "Liberation of Paris." Everyone is rejoicing except the Parisians, who know the sad truth: the Germans are firing on innocent bystanders in the streets, everyone

14. Charles Zambeaux: assistant district attorney in Versailles; friend of Mario Rist. [JNJ]

15. Olivier Rist: Charles Rist's nephew, son of Édouard and Madeleine Rist.

is asked to stay home; all private and public offices are closed. Meanwhile it has been announced that the American troops are marching on Troyes – that is, to the east – doubtless to meet up with the troops from the Rhône valley, who are advancing rapidly toward Lyon. But Paris plays no role in all that, much less Versailles – though there have been two telephone calls asking me if it is true that the Americans have arrived here! Some people even assure me that they have seen them! What I have seen this morning is German trucks and tanks covered by foliage going up the Avenue de Villeneuve-l'Étang.

The Romanians have just made peace with Russia, England, and the United States, and King Michael has proclaimed he is going to win back Transylvania from the Hungarians. Maniu, that fine old man, is supposed to replace Antonescu in the new cabinet, and the king says he wants to return to democracy. The European fortress is crumbling on all sides. At any moment we can expect the Bulgarians to switch sides, and the radio already sees the Allies entering Yugoslavia, and from there, southern Germany. In the interim, the Germans in Normandy are trying to cross the Seine or, according to more recent information, to set up new positions south of the river. Could that be toward Évreux? In that case, we would soon be in the thick of the battle.

Torrential rains during the night and this morning. Allied planes are going to find themselves reduced to impotence.

This morning I heard Alexandre Parodi's speech at the Seine prefecture in his capacity as Algiers' general delegate. He certainly deserves the honor.

At this very moment (2:00 PM), the rattle of machine guns or rifles almost on our doorstep. Then all afternoon artillery and machine guns, apparently in Satory.... New bursts of gunfire, this time quite near. The Germans are taking anything they can as vehicles. I just encountered some in a funeral car, the kind that families use to follow a hearse. A truck full of Germans just passed down our street, machine-gunning anything in its path. Luckily, no casualties. We heard bursts of firing on all sides. Later we were told that they claimed to have been fired on from the town hall and took their revenge by terrorizing the city.

Twenty-Four

The Ransom for
Deliverance

25 AUGUST 1944–27 DECEMBER 1945
Joy reigned as de Gaulle finally entered the city of Paris and greeted the French people with a welcome "Vive la France!" The sweet taste of liberation soon palled for the Rist family, however, as they confronted a series of bitter revelations.

FRIDAY, 25 AUGUST 1944 A very difficult night. The continuous thunder of artillery fire not far from us – from the woods above? Or from Satory? And on whom and what?

But this morning all had ceased. Word was that the Germans had left and the Allied troops were arriving. We headed for the city. As we approached the rue Clemenceau, we saw more and more flags bedecking the houses. People already had bits of tricolor ribbon in their buttonholes. We arrived on the Avenue de Paris in front of the town hall. The crowd was already dense. We waited; it was about 10:30. Suddenly the first trucks emerged, coming down the rue de Grandchamp. Huge cheers. The *Marseillaise* burst forth from the town hall's loudspeakers.... This lasted all day long. The passage of the troops continued without interruption, and the crowd only grew larger.

During the evening we learned that the last German troops in Paris had surrendered to General Leclerc.... At last we are truly liberated!

Léonard called to say that Parodi asked him to serve as an interpreter with the Americans and that he had lunch with Leclerc at the Hôtel de Ville and was present at de Gaulle's arrival in the evening. He is ecstatic, full of enthusiasm about everything that has happened.[1]

---

1. In some journal entries prepared for his brother Noël, this is how Léonard Rist described de Gaulle's arrival:

It is a pleasure to see the population so joyful. Good humor, kindness, unanimity. Everyone is wearing a tricolor cockade. It is a way to show one's joy.

SUNDAY, 27 AUGUST 1944 Paris is delirious with joy. General de Gaulle appeared on the balcony of the Hôtel de Ville and needed only to shout *"Vive la France!"* This day crowns one of the grandest and most beautiful efforts that a man has ever made to raise his country up from humiliation. The whole country is cheering him today. Last night there was a brief rumor that he was the victim of an attack while attending a *Te Deum* mass at Notre-Dame. The Germans (or members of the Milice?) fired on the crowd. In the end, as there is no more about it on the radio, we suppose the rumor was false.

What is surprising is the quiet and complete fade-out of anything related to Vichy. No one knows anything about the former government. But neither is anyone asking to know. The nothingness of those men is manifest. That mix of pious reactionaries, stupid Colonel Blimps, ambitious politicians, and embittered losers, that foul-smelling nest of crafty and cruel cynics who

---

Around 5:00 PM it was announced that General de Gaulle was at the war ministry. A curious idea to go there. He imperiously waited for the general secretaries of the National Resistance Council. However, they were waiting for him at the Hôtel de Ville. The first symbolic conflict. We learned the next day, moreover, that he was fired on as he arrived at the war ministry. Alexandre Parodi, minister without portfolio, hurried to the war ministry in an open car (!) and with great difficulty brought us the general. He put in a brief appearance at police headquarters, then went on to the Hôtel de Ville.

Humph! A bit disappointing, this first contact. One would have preferred more harmony. And his curt, authoritarian speech at the Hôtel de Ville. Fine, perfect, but still he could have thanked the Resistance Council and Alexandre, who gave him so much support.

Tall, imperious, with an impassive face and restless, disquieting eyes. Not the smiling charm of Leclerc, rather a man who is anxious to produce a certain effect. But being aloof does not exclude his being morally upright; people willingly grant him this, for it seems to be his nature. It is just that, returning to Paris and seeing that crowd crazy with curiosity, hearing the crowd sing the *Marseillaise* in chorus when he appeared on the balcony, sensing their effusions of joy and hope, he could have shown a little emotion. He said only, "Mr. Prefect, please introduce to me those who were your principal collaborators in this effort," then he turned toward the forty people in the salon and the crowd on the stairs and added: "I only want to say, 'Long live Paris, Long live France!'" The response: "Long live de Gaulle!" Why would I rather they had cried "Long live France"? And yet I am wearing the Cross of Lorraine in my boutonniere and on my arm band!

sought to obtain from the enemy the playthings of power denied them by a free nation – all of this has disappeared as if swept away by a great storm of good sense and trust in the future. Of course we can already spot other politicians, no less denuded of scruples, seeing this country's great wave of gratitude for those who took away their shame as a springboard for new tyrannies and new frauds. The communists are already at it, their political morality precisely modeled on that of the Nazis. But nevertheless a breath of fresh air has replaced the others' shameful dungeon smell, which was suffocating France.

Meanwhile the collapse of Germany moves on apace. And this is truly high drama, one of the great tragic spectacles of history – a whole country caught up in mass hysteria or a sleepwalker's dream. A country that has long ceased to experience the feelings by which others live has abruptly awakened from that dream and fallen into the political abyss. Romania has turned its weapons on Germany. Bulgaria has locked up the German troops on its soil. In France the Allied armies are preventing any further German resistance to the north or to the east. The American troops are about to meet up with troops advancing up the Rhône valley. Marseilles has been liberated. The taking of Toulon is in its last stages. We are now going to see Greece and Yugoslavia serve as springboards for the invasion of southern Germany, while Belgium and Holland will serve the same purpose for the occupation of northern Germany. The backward surge is under way. The great armed robbery, so long prepared for, so admirably executed, has collapsed under the size and weight of a superior industrial power. Industry is no longer the hallmark of peaceful powers. It is the greatest instrument of bellicose power. The spirit driving it is all that will matter from now on. It will not be in itself and by itself, as the Saint-Simonians believed, the instrument of peace.

Bernard Faÿ, the sinister puppeteer directing the persecution of Freemasons, has been arrested. This sorry scribbler taught at the Collège de France and served as a librarian at the Bibliothèque Nationale! He was haunted by Freemasonry. He saw Masons everywhere. He even claimed some bishops were Masons, as General Laure told me at Marshal Pétain's table. And the good general defended his bishop, the one in Orléans, who fell prey to Faÿ's accusations. Faÿ is the typical product of a clerical education and the vicious stupidity of Paris's bourgeoisie. He is the son of a Parisian notary. He had masses of minor officials, who had only their salary to live on, arrested and fired as supposed Freemasons. He is a malicious, dishonest man. Everyone had forgotten Freemasonry; it no longer mattered. He renewed its luster and prestige.

MONDAY, 28 AUGUST 1944 All night long the guns thundered. Telephone communication with Paris was suspended as of yesterday afternoon. What is going on? All we know is that on Saturday de Gaulle was shot at while attending the *Te Deum* mass at Notre-Dame, just after he had returned from the Unknown Soldier. He came down the Champs-Élysées on foot and by car. He did not want to parade on a white horse or on a black horse. Good for him. On Saturday night German bombardment of Paris. Many deaths. Did it start all over again last night? We were hoping that the trains to Paris would be running again. Nothing of the sort. And no mail either. Thus no way to know anything of the Léonards.

Looking at events, one can only think that the taking of Paris was not in the Allied plans; that the city was supposed to fall automatically and without combat as a result of being encircled to the north and south; that it came as a great surprise when the communists took up their weapons on Saturday the nineteenth; that the F.F.I. had to follow suit; that they tried to put a curb on things by signing an armistice; and that, feeling overwhelmed by Wednesday, they called for help from the Allies, who would rather have dealt with other matters (today people are saying it was the return to work by the police in solidarity with the F.F.I., whom the Germans would have attacked at the prefecture, that set things off). Today, as the Germans have not yet been pushed out of the area north of Paris, they can shell the city with no problem and inflict the meanest kind of vengeance.

TUESDAY, 29 AUGUST 1944[2] Still neither mail nor railway nor telephone links to Paris.

Yesterday morning terrible news reached us, telephoned officially by the prefect's chief of staff: the twentieth of August, during the Allies' arrival in Verneuil, Ève received a head injury at the École des Roches.[3] The young Schaller girls went to Paris to inform Édouard, who, on getting word from Henri, left with an ambulance. Her condition evidently worsened on Friday, and we know poor Henri must have lost all hope. She was in a shelter, and the shrapnel came in through a crack between two boards that covered the shelter. It was Monday before she was transferred to the Verneuil hospital,

2. As the entries for 29 and 30 August were left out of the French edition, their translation is based on Rist's original manuscript. [TF]

3. Ève Trocmé, Rist's sister, had been hit in the head by a bit of shrapnel during the bombardment of the École des Roches, which the Americans believed to be occupied by the Germans.

where there was neither surgeon nor doctor. So for six days now she has been in danger without our being able to learn anything. That heart full of love, generosity, and devotion has no doubt stopped beating. And we are completely separated! It seems as if a great void has opened in our life. She is the only person in Verneuil who was wounded.

WEDNESDAY, 30 AUGUST 1944 Mario, having gone to Paris on his bicycle, was able to see Édouard, who had returned from Verneuil with Ève by ambulance. Her condition is less serious than one could have believed. She was well cared for, but the hospital in Verneuil lacked everything. Thus they could not X-ray her, and it is not known whether there is a piece of shrapnel in her brain. She did not lose consciousness. Some functional problems, in particular, paralysis of her left arm. No fever. A critical condition, but not hopeless. She has been taken to the Léopold Bellan hospital. Guillamant is the surgeon.

After the great days of friendship and brotherly love among the French, friction is already breaking out again. The Algiers faction want to keep all the positions for themselves and the F.F.I., resulting in unhappiness on the part of the Resistance fighters, who they think they have a right to a say even if they did not suffer. Here in Versailles some sort of communists have been placed on the Municipal Council, presided over by that madman Labeyrie.[4]

The exchange rate has been set at 200 francs to the pound, which is quite high for the franc. Right now that is not very important, because we import nothing from England except through official channels. But this rate cannot last.

Still no telephone link to Paris, no rail or postal service. We are completely cut off – back to the condition we were in right after the armistice, when people in France could not communicate with one other. But today we accept this state of affairs with hope, whereas back then each day brought only new humiliations. The press is reemerging. The same abrupt about-face in the newspapers. They are all praising freedom. After the armistice all the newspapers (even and perhaps especially in the so-called free zone) were praising servitude and bemoaning the puerility of the old slogan: *Liberté, Égalité, Fraternité.*

---

4. Émile Labeyrie, of the French Communist Party (P.C.F.), was mayor of Versailles from 1944 to 1947. [TF]

The Germans are still north of Paris, hanging like ripe fruit. We could hear the shelling all through the night. Montmorency and Le Bourget were only liberated yesterday.

WEDNESDAY, 6 SEPTEMBER 1944 Still no telephone communication with Paris, no mail (even within Paris), no trains except for three convoys before 7:30 A M and three returning in the evening; for a single meeting one must spend all day in Paris, where there is no subway. We feel cut off from everything. The telephones are cut off for military reasons, but the train and subway outages are technical problems – lack of electricity and coal. Paris is going to have one hour of gas starting tomorrow. Here we have always had this minimum. But the electrical blackout begins at 9:00 PM! Fortunately, Germaine had put aside a lamp and a little kerosene in September 1940.

The head of Electricity here lent us a car on Tuesday so that we could go visit Ève in the Léopold Bellan hospital. She could not see us. But they say there has been a slight improvement.

Yesterday Léonard came for dinner and spent the night. He talked about the friction between the Algiers group and the Resistance.[5] The former want to have it all. But he has wonderful memories of those first days. He is resuming his work at the Morgan Bank.

---

5. Léonard wrote about this in the notes for his brother Noël, dated 3 September:

All appears to be going well. Seen from the wings, however, the drama is as we had feared. Algiers sent us its ministers, who arrived with their ready-made plans, a "few details" of which can be changed, according to what André Philip told me yesterday.... In their wake three thousand people are in a hurry to be the first to get to Paris. In France six or seven hundred thousand members of the Resistance. Those whom the general characterized as "good people" in his radio speech, they too have their little ideas, which are not any more foolish than those of Georges Boris and M. Ardant. The struggle is on, and the France of the home front feels snubbed by the France of Algiers. There is one incident after another. Yesterday a decision had to be reached on a cabinet reshuffle.... What is it? Already, the rise in salaries proposed and promised by the Resistance has been strongly rebuffed by the high command. Already the F.F.I. High Command has been decapitated, already the union leaders and the communists are protesting vigorously (and their troops make up a large part of the F.F.I.). So they have suppressed those who were holding in check a crowd that is armed and will soon consist of malcontents. We shall know shortly whether de Gaulle is the symbol we thought he was or if he believes he is an incarnation. But this matters little. Alsace and Lorraine will soon be free.

Lunch at Fouquet's, where Behn[6] held a meeting of Matériel Téléphonique's board. I went in a car sent by the company. I learned from Pesson-
Didion that Laurent-Atthalin has resigned as president of the Banque de
Paris; the finance minister had let it be known that there would be no relationship with the bank as long as Laurent-Atthalin was president. I am
eager to learn more from Wibratte as soon as it is possible to travel again.
What a comedown! Strange that a man so shrewd could have been so badly
mistaken.

Behn was in a buoyant mood. He told me that the Americans do not
trust de Gaulle; that after Casablanca, Roosevelt did not want to see him
anymore, since de Gaulle had said he represented both Joan of Arc and Napoleon; that if it took so long to arm the Algerian troops it was because they
did not trust him; and that the Americans' man was Giraud. He wondered
if France would manage to recover from this fall, if she had the necessary
resilience. I promised to send him a note describing the French state of mind
vis-à-vis the general and his predecessor, the marshal.[7]

THURSDAY, 7 SEPTEMBER 1944 It was announced this morning that
letters can once again circulate within the Seine department. We do not yet
have this freedom, and the telephone remains cut off.

Belgium liberated yesterday. It is expected that Holland will be freed
today. Germany has yet to be entered, either from Russia or from the west.

Dreadful weather. Rain, wind, storm.

TUESDAY, 12 SEPTEMBER 1944 Ève passed away Wednesday night. We
learned the news from the little Schaller girls, who had returned from Paris
by bicycle. Nothing now will remain of that radiant life but a memory in the
hearts of those who loved her. What selflessness, what humility, what grandeur of soul in all circumstances! How painful to think we will never again
find her echoing all our feelings and thoughts, and always full of acceptance.
The thought of her Daniel haunted her to the end.

Ève's funeral took place on Monday, the eleventh of September, at the
Temple de Plaisance. Pastor Maury spoke, quoting passages from a book

6. Sosthène Behn, president of ITT (International Telegraph and Telephone). On
his role, see Maurice Deloraine's book *Des ondes et des hommes – Jeunesse des télécommunications et de l'ITT* (Paris: Flammarion, 1974).

7. The text of this interesting letter appears in appendix 4, a good synthesis of Rist's
interpretation of the French situation at the time.

by Wilfred Monod that Ève used to reread with pleasure. Extremely well attended, a sign of how well she was liked and respected. We, along with my brother Édouard; Ève's husband, Henri; and her daughters, accompanied her mortal remains to the Bagneux Cemetery.

That evening at eight o'clock, as we spoke of Ève, we saw Mario, Léonard, and Léonard's wife come into the living room with somber faces. Léonard said, "We have some bad news." We looked at them and guessed the horrible truth. Our Jean killed by the Germans on the twenty-first of August, the day after Ève was wounded.

The next day Madeleine came to see us. She had no sooner left on her bicycle to return to Paris than the secretary to the prefect arrived. I thought he was coming to express his condolences, but he read me a note: Olivier Rist killed on a flying mission!

What a ransom for deliverance!

At the end of June, Jean had written this sentence to our friend Marguerite des Gouttes: "Each of us must feel both solidarity with others and detachment from himself." That sentence, Jean in a nutshell, sums up his life and death. What an example for his children!

There is nothing more now but silence.

"Greater was he than his father" people will say of him, as Hector in the *Iliad* prays men will say of his son.

SATURDAY, 16 SEPTEMBER 1944 The emptiness of all the chatter regarding "leaders" is clear today. To become a "leader" a man must have been misunderstood, hated, scorned. Such a man knows what it means to command and to resist. It is not Pétain, the Épinal cartoon, but rather the "traitor" de Gaulle, condemned to death, who is a leader. It is not the smooth-talking Poincaré; it is the scorned Clemenceau. Jean, alone, struggling in his personal and professional life, had the stuff of a leader, though unrecognized and uninterested in taking center stage. In this country in particular, people recognize leadership in someone only when he has triumphed. Then everyone showers him with praise, after having discouraged him! A leader is not made, but revealed.

SUNDAY, 15 OCTOBER 1944 For a month now I have written nothing. The shock was too much. And I asked myself if I would ever again have the heart to take up these notes, written in large part for his eyes. It seemed so useless to continue, now that part of our life will be meaningless except to honor his memory. Nevertheless I am beginning again in order not to allow my days to fall into oblivion, but to record them as they drift by. And then, too, current events are too gigantic to ignore the reactions they provoke. In vain are we affected by the awful emptiness of the present time; life goes on around us. It is not right to isolate oneself, to watch it pass by as if one no longer had any part to play. Perhaps others one day, children or grandchildren, will take an interest in what we have felt and thought during this great upheaval; the French cannot isolate themselves from France.

The loveliest testimonial and the truest Ève received is in these lines written by a young Englishman, a teaching assistant at the École des Roches in 1909 who was later killed at Hébuterne in the Pas-de-Calais, on the fourteenth of September 1915. After the war his family published his letters and his diary in a small book. His name was H. S. Wilson. He was twenty-three. Here is what one reads in his letter of 18 June 1909. I had remembered it, and Henri has sent me the text:

> The book (*Jean-Christophe*) was lent to me by Madame Trocmé, a relation of Lewis von Glehn and one of my great joys in life here. Perhaps the only gentle person in the place: a lover of books and music and all beautiful things. I lunch in their house four days a week, nominally to talk English at table with the boys. But as they know, I have refused to do this at all in the other houses, and the real reason is that I may sit in their peaceful drawing-room after lunch for half an hour in the middle of the day and savor not only coffee but also real civilization. And when I rise to finish the day's work, I am always the better for having spoken with her and for having been in her presence: though, as is always the case, she would be very much astonished, I think, to hear it said.

How many others must have experienced the same simple charm; she was so enthusiastic and passionate, with a delightful and humble goodness.

SUNDAY, 28 JANUARY 1945 Cold, snow, ice for the last two weeks. This winter recalls the first two of the war, so brutally harsh, especially the first. But one still had heat. Whereas today there is no more coal or wood. People are working in unheated offices at temperatures of 5 or 6 degrees Celsius. Meetings at the ministries take place with everyone in overcoats.

Fortunately, the news is good. The Russians are flooding the German borders with their troops. That takes the place of meat, butter, and vegetables. That compensates for the disappointments of justice. Some think too few are found guilty. But most are disgusted by the arbitrary arrests without cause, keeping innocent men behind bars. The French do not worry about judicial guarantees. They must be constantly reminded of them. Special courts, as well as "administrative internments," are as prevalent as they were under Vichy. Drancy is functioning as it was under the Boches.

Everything is worn out during this sixth year of war: things that can no longer be replaced or altered – and patience. The end is in sight, and the ups and downs seem endless. Exasperation is growing against the absurd resistance of the Boches, and one begins to pity the wretched populations fleeing the German state, including, as here in 1940, women and children. And all of this in subfreezing temperatures. All one sees now is the appalling stupidity of the war. One burns to emerge at last from the universal anarchy it has created.

However, people who think they are profound have already predicted war between Russia and the United States within ten years!

21 APRIL 1945 I have read in Madame de Staël (*Considérations sur la Révolution française*, 298) this profound sentence: "The social order, the secret of which lies in the patience of the majority, suddenly seemed threatened."

During the evening I dined at Murphy's[8] with Douglas Bullitt, who was wearing a French uniform. He is attached to de Lattre de Tassigny's army.

This afternoon I testified before Bouchardon, the examining magistrate in the Pétain affair.[9]

7 DECEMBER 1945 In the last pages – so much calmer – of *Will to Power*, in which Nietzsche anxiously seeks the path that will lead him out of pessimism, allowing him to go beyond it and to say "yes" at last to life and to the universe, I find this thought, which is truly admirable and conceived to reconcile one with life – a simple, almost humble thought, moreover, for in linking it to a completely deterministic view of the world, he did not elevate it to the heights of a philosophical argument:

> The first question is by no means whether we are content with ourselves, but
> whether we are content with anything at all. If we affirm one single moment, we

8. Robert D. Murphy, the U.S. consul in France from 1939 to 1941, was the American representative in Algeria at the time of the landing. He was now General Eisenhower's political adviser.

9. According to Benoît Klein, Charles Rist was there to authenticate the note written by his son Jean that had been presented in evidence at the trial by Alexandre Parodi. Jean's journal note, dated 20 November 1942, describes in detail the conversation with Alibert discussed in Charles Rist's journal entry for 18 December 1942. [TF]

thus affirm not only ourselves but all existence. For nothing is self-sufficient, neither in us ourselves nor in things; and if our soul has trembled with happiness and sounded like a harp string just once, all eternity was needed to produce this one event – and in this single moment of affirmation all eternity was called good, redeemed, justified, and affirmed.[10] §1032 (1883–1885)

Who, in certain circumstances of his life – friendship, love, tenderness for a child, the joy in intelligence or in art – has not experienced those instants in which feeling suffices in itself, appears truly to be an "absolute," with no other meaning for us but the illumination it gives us, allowing us to dispense with all super-terrestrial "eternity" and yet belonging to eternity?

9 DECEMBER 1945 This winter, after a year and a half of liberation, is as painful as all those that preceded it. It is the seventh since the start of the war. And as we were occupied in 1940, it is the sixth since Germany plunged us into misery. The Americans, who entered the war in 1942 and who never suffered more than insignificant restrictions, which disappeared several weeks ago, cannot understand this. Here problems with heating and electricity are the worst. The "rotating power cuts," as they are referred to by the engineering-school graduates in charge, are worse than ever. Naturally, they come at the most inconvenient times: meals, the evening. Nor can one have new clothes. As for food, aside from fish, which has reappeared, and a little meat now and then, the situation is only slowly getting better. Above all, the odious authorizations that one must request for everything – driving permits, for example – are intolerable. We are the slaves of an administration that has not changed any of its habits, including bad humor and inertia.

In the midst of all these material nuisances, a political atmosphere of absurdity, violence, self-centeredness, ignorance, and vulgarity surpassing anything imaginable.

27 DECEMBER 1945 The revelations of the Nuremberg trials have put the final seal on this horrible war. An entire people possessed by the delirium of conquest and allowing themselves to be led by a band of characters devoid of all scruple (as we had already seen) and pushing ignominy, inhumanity, and deliberate cruelty beyond anything seen in previous ages. The Germany of Christmas trees hides a Germany of gross lustfulness, bestial sadism, and

---

10. Rist quotes the passage, which he labels §478, in French. The Kaufmann-Hollingdale English translation (*The Will to Power* [New York: Vintage, 1968]) has been used here. [TF]

passive obedience whose equivalent exists nowhere else. One should reread what Nietzsche has to say about the German ethic of obedience when it is transformed into the ethic of domination.

Two small symbolic facts: the seat of the new League of Nations will no longer be in Europe, but in America; and the pope has just hatched a brood of mostly non-Italian cardinals. In the name of "geopolitics" and the "philosophy of history," Germany has precipitated Europe into decline vis-à-vis the United States, South America, and Russia.

The historical period we are now entering is completely different from the previous 150 years. The small nations have disappeared. The power of the three great ones will be felt everywhere. Asia will be the new battleground – removing war from the European theater. Germany will have disappeared for a long time as a political force. I thus foresee a European peace – as one saw peace among the Greek cities after the Roman Conquest. The atom bomb will replace the Roman Empire.

The style of civilization will be decidedly Anglo-Saxon: organization of the family; sports; economic criteria for deciding on the value of peoples and individuals; complete indifference to religion, with some local renewal of mysticism. Overall, the "masses" will be happier and less wretched than in the past or today. But as they will not make this comparison, their envy with regard to the more fortunate will only increase. The compensation will be the rapid growth of science, to which noble minds will be attracted. One must also hope there will be some real and great artists.

Appendix 1:
Timeline of Rist's
Travels during the War

1939

2 September. France and England give Germany an ultimatum.

Charles Rist is living in Versailles and working in Paris, where he oversees his research institute and serves on government committees as well as on the boards of various banks and corporations.

1940

24–30 January. Rist travels to London to discuss the possibility of a joint Franco-British blockade mission to the United States.

24 February. As part of the blockade mission, Rist travels to the United States, where he holds numerous meetings with top officials, including Franklin Roosevelt, in New York, Washington, Ottawa, and Montreal.

Timeline for the 1940 blockade mission:

24 February. Unable to fly because of bad weather, Rist sails from Genoa.

4 March. Arrives in New York and travels to Washington, D.C., by train. Stays at the Mayflower Hotel.

15 March. Flies to New York, stays at the Waldorf Hotel.

20 March. Flies back to Washington.

27 March. Flies to New York.

29 March. Takes the train back to Washington.

1 April. Flies to Ottawa and Montreal, meeting with top government officials.

5 April. Flies back to Washington.

10 April. Meets with President Roosevelt.

19–29 April. Waits in New York for favorable weather to return to France.

Early May 1940. Arrives back in Versailles.

17–18 May. Turning point in the focus of Rist's concerns: worried for their safety, Rist takes his Jewish granddaughters to La Bouffource.

19 May. Returns to Versailles.

9 June. Having been warned by French general Weygand to vacate Paris immediately, the French government leaves en masse to Tours. The presidency is temporarily installed at the Château de Langeais, a few miles outside of Tours.

9 June. Rist arrives in the city of Langeais to see if there is anything more to be done with the Blockade Committee.

11 June. Rist and his wife leave by car for Le Très-Clos, their country house in Haute-Savoie, near Lake Geneva, where the family's women and children have been converging since late May. They spend the night in Bourges.

12 June. The Rists arrive at Le Très-Clos.

14 *June. As the Germans enter Paris the French government retreats from Tours to Bordeaux.*

16 June. Rist and his wife set off for Firminy, where their son Jean lives.

17 June. The Rists then head for Vichy, where Charles Rist verifies that his banking duties are not required, and as "I do not know anyone in the new ministry," they once again head for Le Très-Clos.

18 June. Arrival at Le Très-Clos.

23 June. Fearing the region will be occupied, Rist and the family members with him become "refugees" and head to Switzerland in several cars.

25 *June. Hostilities between France and Germany officially cease.*

26 June. Learning that Haute-Savoie is not occupied, the Rists return to Le Très-Clos.

1 *July. The "French State" sets up its capital in Vichy.*

10 *July. Parliament grants full powers to Marshal Pétain.*

12 July. In response to a telegram from an Ottoman Bank official saying there is talk of relocating the banks to Paris, Rist and his wife head to Vichy.

15 July. The Rists return to Le Très-Clos.

20 August. Rist begins an arduous thirty-hour journey to Vichy.

21 August. Rist arrives in Vichy for discussions with representatives of the Suez Company and of banks whose boards he serves on; has lunch with Harrison Freeman Matthews, a U.S. embassy official, and also sees the Turkish ambassador.

30 August. Returns by train to Évian, from there to Le Très-Clos.

20 September. Leaves Le Très-Clos by car with his Jewish granddaughters and spends four days in Vichy en route to Versailles.

25 September. Returns to Versailles.

26 September. Rist resumes business meetings in Paris.

19 *October 1940. Anti-Jewish decree issued.* Charles and Germaine Rist pick up their Jewish granddaughters in Le Vésinet.

1941

26 February to 6 March. Trip to Vichy, Saint-Étienne, Évian.

In Vichy Rist sees Vichy contacts on behalf of the prefect Roger Langeron and regarding Mme Le Verrier's case; also sees Harrison Matthews and Admiral William D. Leahy, the U.S. ambassador; Robert Marjolin, a colleague; Behiç Erkin, the Turkish ambassador; and Jules Jeanneney.

1 March. Visit to Jean's family in Fraisses via Saint-Étienne and Firminy.

3 March. Arrival in Évian, finds the Marios in good health.

10 March. Back in Paris, goes to the Société d'Ugine about "Mario's affair" (Mario evidently resigned as judge when Vichy took over and needed another job).

2–9 July. Charles and Germaine spend the week at La Bouffource with Noël Rist and his wife.

20–30 August. Trip to Vichy and to Fraisses to see Jean.

21 August (Thursday A M). Sees Matthews in Vichy. Talk of Washington, D.C., ambassadorship.

21 August (Thursday P M). Fraisses.

25 August. Vichy. Runs into Romier, Pétain's minister of state.

26 August. In Romier's office, Romier asks if Rist would accept ambassadorship.

28 August. Returns to Versailles.

19–25 October. First trip to Vichy regarding ambassadorship.

9 November. Returns to Vichy regarding ambassadorship.

11 November. Returns to Paris.

1942

29 May 1942, *enforced as of 1 June: Jews ordered to wear a yellow badge.*

6–11 June. Trip to the free zone.

6, 7 June (Sunday, Monday). Stays with Jean in Saint-Étienne. Visit to Jean's farm.

8, 9 June (Tuesday, Wednesday). Vichy. Sees Tuck from the U.S. embassy, Rochat, Romier, Stucki, Behiç.

12 June. Returns to Versailles.

26 June. Goes with Marie and Antoinette to La Bouffource

4–8 November. Travels to Saint-Étienne, Fraisse, and Vichy to help Jean, in trouble for helping two Jews.

20 November. Goes to Le Vésinet to see Françoise, whose sister Hélène died in Clermont-Ferrand.

The 20 November 1942 trip to Le Vésinet is the last mention in the diary of travels by Charles Rist away from Paris/Versailles.

Appendix 2:
The Anti-Jewish
Laws of Vichy

ACCORDING TO THE ARMISTICE SIGNED ON 22 JUNE 1940, FRANCE retained sovereignty over all of its territory, but the government was required to collaborate with the occupying power when asked.

After the Germans issued several anti-Jewish decrees in the occupied zone, the Vichy government, without having been obliged to do so, promulgated its own similar laws that were now valid throughout France, including the free zone.

In October 1940 these laws were consolidated in the first *Statut des juifs*, excluding Jews from most public posts, the army, education, the press, and company management echelons. Prefects were authorized to lock up non-French Jews.

In June 1941 a second *statut* went further, excluding Jews from the liberal, commercial, and industrial professions.

A Vichy law of "Aryanization" in July 1941 confiscated the property of Jews who were absent or who had disappeared, and a great number of companies run by Jews were placed under the administration of non-Jews (a measure that had been taken in the occupied zone in 1940).

As these measures of exclusion broadened, so did the legal definition of "Jewishness":

FIRST *STATUT DES JUIFS* (3 OCTOBER 1940)

Any person with at least three Jewish grandparents – or if the spouse is Jewish, only two Jewish grandparents – shall be considered Jewish.

SECOND *STATUT DES JUIFS* (2 JUNE 1941)

The following shall be considered Jewish:

1. Those having at least three Jewish grandparents – or only two Jewish grandparents if the spouse also has at least two Jewish grandparents. Grandparents who belonged to the Jewish faith shall be considered Jewish.

2. Those belonging to the Jewish faith, or who did so as of 25 June 1940, and who have at least two Jewish grandparents. Not belonging to the Jewish faith is established by proof of adherence to one of the other religions recognized by the State before the law of 9 December 1905. Those having two Jewish grandparents could not simply declare themselves agnostic. They had to prove that they had received a Catholic or Protestant baptism before 25 June 1940 – that is, before the armistice – a devious trap. (See Rist's entry for 23 October 1942.)

It is this second *statut* that suddenly put Rist's three granddaughters in danger, as they had not been baptized at all.

Appendix 3:
Poem by Antoinette
Rist Constable

THE POEM THAT FOLLOWS BRINGS TOGETHER SEVERAL MEMORIES *of Antoinette's life under the occupation. As her father, Charles Rist's son Claude, was tubercular, and her mother Jewish, the story and poem give a glimpse into dark corners that Rist's diary could only hint at for reasons of prudence.*

As Many Stars . . .
Under Nazi Rule, 1943
by Antoinette Rist Constable

Tonight, the phone rings and stops ringing, telling her
they are only three blocks away. In her apron, she rushes
out the back door. By the corner at the front of the house
lined with boxwood, she starts to crawl between the wall
and the shrubs into the dog house opening
under the stoop, grazing her hips. Long ago,
when they had owned a dog, she had thrown
an old blanket inside. Finds it hard with frost.

Sits because there's no room to stretch. Hidden. Girls . . .
Children of an Aryan father. His name saves them. But that's all
he's done for them lately, lying in his hospital bed for months.
How dare he be sick? Hears thuds above. Refuses to guess, afraid.
Afraid of hearing cries. Counts to a thousand. Twice.
No mistakes, or else. Counts obediently, skipping numbers.
Rub your sides. More. Rub your thighs, your knees.

Dizzy from the dark, she transforms herself, shrinks
into less than a cat, less than a cricket or a minnow.
She's a barnacle clinging to the hull of Europe.
Prays, *do not forsake me.* Asks, *how much longer?*
Hears stomping like hooves at a gallop inside the house.
Wills *them* away: *be gone. Soon.* Sounds on the landing

just above, as if she were under an avalanche of rocks.
Then, inches away, the crunch of boots on gravel

decreases. Ceases altogether. She frames her face
into the dog house opening. Listens, listens to the night.
She crawls out, stiff, bruised, not caring
what she may leave behind. She stands. *I won,*
I beat them at their game! She feels some degree
of exultation as she walks alone around the house
to the back door, merging with the night
full of harmless stars. As many stars as Jews.

Appendix 4: Postmortem

AMONG CHARLES RIST'S RARE DIARY ENTRIES AFTER 1945, HERE
*are two that give an idea of his reactions after 1945, as well as a letter dated 12
September 1944 in which he explains the evolution of French public opinion in
regard to Marshal Pétain, why the French people have now acclaimed General
de Gaulle, and a consideration of the problems the general and France will face.
(Diary entries from 1914 to 1915 that were included in the French appendix have
been omitted here.)*

LETTER TO AMERICAN COLONEL BEHN REGARDING
THE SITUATION IN FRANCE[1]

12 September 1944

(See the diary entry for 6 September 1944)

Dear Colonel,

You asked me to tell you briefly how I see the political situation at the present
time and particularly that of General de Gaulle. I will try to do so, in very broad
brush-strokes. Naturally, the impressions I convey to you are only *impressions*.
For four years the French have been separated from each other. For six months,
most especially, communications between Paris and the rest of the country have
been virtually cut off. The press did not exist until a week ago. Freedoms, even
of conversation, except with a few trustworthy friends, disappeared. The normal
means for forming an objective opinion are thus scarce. Hence this *subjective*
and personal opinion. I will add, nevertheless, that in this great drama, despite
the distances and the silence, there has been an extraordinary unanimity of
feeling among completely isolated people who, though separated by hundreds of
kilometers, had identical reactions. That is what happens in great crises.

---

1. This letter was sent on the twenty-sixth of October to the State Department by
Selden Chapin, a diplomat with the American embassy in Paris (American Archives 851-
00 / 10-644).

In a nutshell, the situation can be described in two sentences:

On the one hand, 80 percent of the French people have acclaimed General de Gaulle.

On the other, as of yesterday they knew almost nothing of his political ideas or of his true character.

The almost unanimous acclamation with which General de Gaulle was greeted is simply explained. Here are the three essential reasons:

1. In the midst of the most appalling humiliation in our history, when each French individual was physically isolated from the others, General de Gaulle, in an unforgettable radio speech, affirmed his faith in France and in the future. While humiliating and discouraging words (such as no statesman in history has ever pronounced after a military defeat) were issuing from the mouth of Marshal Pétain, General de Gaulle proclaimed his carefully thought-out confidence in the power of our allies and in the forces that one could still muster within the French Empire and his refusal to accept defeat. He expressed the general will to resist on the part of a people who understood nothing of that sudden defeat and to whom the French radio and newspapers offered only lies. Over the course of these four years his continuous, persistent action, the growing effectiveness of the forces grouped around him, the part played by French units in the great British victories in North Africa, then the reconstitution of a true French army in Algeria demonstrated that those words pronounced by him expressed not just a powerful emotion but a strong will. Thus, *from the beginning*, the hearts of the vast majority of French people were with General de Gaulle. With the exception of a small minority, all of our farmers, our laborers, the majority of the bourgeoisie, stopped listening to any but Radio London. It was the only one they could believe. Among so many people who remained silent for fear of spies or informers, there existed a common thought, a deep unity, that was rekindled every night by listening to the BBC. No one believed Vichy radio, which most people did not listen to. Hence the unanimity of feeling that nothing could render visible, hence too that unanimous acclamation when General de Gaulle returned to France. No wonder that people outside of France had trouble perceiving that internal ferment, that real unity of the French even as all official acts and speeches made it seem that France was hostile toward the Allies and had abandoned her most traditional national sentiments.

2. The second reason is the hatred and disgust inspired very quickly by the Vichy government. There again it was almost impossible for a foreign observer to realize the depth and breadth of that feeling, for there was no way to convey it abroad. Sheltered by the foreign occupation, Vichy organized in France a so-called revolution, which its authors called "national," but which in reality resembled the worst of all the reactionary regimes we had in France during the nineteenth century. It must always be remembered that since the uprising of 6 February 1934, organized by the Action Française, the country was for all practical purposes in a state of civil war. In spite of popular opinion in France, a small active minority tried to take advantage of her enormous financial difficulties and of the mediocrity of most politicians to destroy the republican form of

government. Whatever people outside the country may imagine, the vast majority of French people are and remain profoundly republican. They understand by this word a government based on the principles of the Revolution of 1789, which today are those of all civilized countries.

The royalists, divided among themselves, are politically insignificant. Aside from royalists, one sees only the personal regime of this or that adventurer or party – a solution that France views with horror, having experienced it twice in the nineteenth century. Though socially and economically conservative, the most moderate statesmen to grace the history of the Third Republic, from Gambetta to Waldeck-Rousseau and M. Poincaré, always stayed true to republican ideas. None of them could have relied on public opinion to the extent they did without having recognized the inviolability of such principles as freedom of thought, freedom of speech, freedom of association, and universal suffrage, the foundations of French public life. And then suddenly we had the Vichy government declaring that these principles were no longer valid; that since 1789, France had been living on lies; and that fascist ideas, colored by those of the Action Française, would now serve as its guide. Thereupon a regime was created à la Franco and Mussolini, a regime that, on the one hand, bowed to all demands of the enemy, and, on the other, brought the full-to-bursting prisons back into the Middle Ages, introduced racist laws, suppressed the motto *"Liberté, Égalité, Fraternité,"* raised the ire of all French farmers by organizing requisitions in the countryside, and prohibited any expression of opinion that ran counter to its own views.

You cannot imagine the deep disgust that these policies of Vichy inspired in most French people, from Catholics to unionists. A few well-intentioned souls thought they could take advantage of the authoritarian regime to introduce economic or social reforms they had long advocated. Some of those reforms – for example, with regard to health centers or relations between workers and employers – were not bad. But in the context in which they were presented, they lost all value. "Even what Vichy does well," M. Humbert de Wendel, who's certainly no revolutionary, said to me, "is useless in the political system it has created."

Nor could this deep opposition by the great majority of French people to Vichy's government, represented first by Laval, then by Darlan, then again by Laval, be expressed in any way perceptible to foreigners. And yet, nonetheless, it existed at all levels of society – employers, workers, priests and pastors, farmers, intellectuals. The motto *"Liberté, Égalité, Fraternité,"* which President Roosevelt justly repeated in some of the letters he sent to the marshal, has never ceased to be the motto of the French people, in contrast to Vichy policy. Many, moreover, were convinced that this policy had been prepared far in advance and that a plot had been hatched even before the war to take power with external support. This opinion, which I share, can be supported by overwhelming evidence.

3. But, you will ask, what about Marshal Pétain, who everyone knew did not agree with M. Laval and whose personal prestige had won the approval and admiration of many of the French? The evolution of the French people's feelings toward the marshal would require a long analysis. I will try, however, to explain

briefly why the marshal, acclaimed by many when he came to power, was eventually consigned to oblivion.

The indisputable popularity enjoyed by Marshal Pétain during the first months after the defeat derived from two very different sentiments that are not easily understood by outsiders unacquainted with the deep internal divisions that marked the prewar years.

For a certain group of French people, Marshal Pétain's coming to power represented first and foremost the triumph of the opposition to the republican system of government. He was the symbol of opposition to the Third Republic, which this group viewed as responsible for all the country's woes. He embodied the ideas of the rather weak but active minority that for ten years had been clamoring for a new system of government. The most typical representative of that minority was M. Maurras, who was able to write shortly after the defeat that it had brought him the "divine surprise" of seeing his ideas come into power. It is this minority that, from the beginning, has remained loyal to Marshal Pétain throughout all his palinodes. This loyalty is thus explained solely by reasons of internal politics.

But another group, *much more numerous,* saw in Marshal Pétain both an embodiment of military virtues that had been momentarily eclipsed and the hope of their rebirth. For this group – inspired by indisputable patriotism – Marshal Pétain for a time symbolized the *continuity of the French State* and the *wish to resist* the enemy. They believed he was playing a patient and skillful waiting game that at the right time would allow him to call on what remained of France's fighting forces to face the enemy. The cheers he received on his visits to cities in the non-occupied zone were for the man who embodied that possibility of resistance. The crowd was applauding that *symbol* of French continuity. Those outside of France might have believed for a time that most French people were "Pétainistes"; it is certain that if the marshal had really followed the policy attributed to him despite his retrograde domestic policies, he would still have been popular in much of the nation, even with those who disagreed with his ideas.

Unfortunately, from the beginning the marshal's actions belied all such hopes. Not only did his speeches and conversations suggest that he attached much more importance to domestic policy than to foreign policy, but we saw him give way before pressure from the foreign occupier when resistance would have been possible. We saw him defer to the personal ambitions of Laval and Darlan. We watched with amazement when he took Laval back after having unceremoniously dumped him. We saw him publicly approve all of Laval's police strategies for pursuing Resistance fighters; accept all political condemnations, pronouncing some of them himself against former ministers who had been imprisoned without trial; intern a man like Herriot; and organize an anti-Bolshevik militia that wore the German uniform (!), then a fascistic Milice, the very one that murdered Mandel, to chase down France's own patriots. The great distancing between public opinion and the marshal dates from German entry into the "free" zone on 11 November 1942. His refusal at that moment to leave French territory and go to Algeria (in spite of the urging of his closest friends); his passive attitude regarding the fleet in Toulon; his public praise for the officers in Casablanca, Algiers, and Bizerte who resisted the landing of the Allied fleet; his acceptance of despicable men such as Déat and Darnand into his cabinet – in the end, too many deeds to enumerate demonstrated his growing impotence and weakness of will and gradually repulsed all those who had seen in him the symbol of French hopes. The only ones to remain loyal are those who had placed in him their hopes regarding domestic policy and who feared more than anything the threat of Bolshevism, or whose reaction to the landing of 6 June 1944 was (as I myself heard it said): "Better the Germans than the return of Jews and Freemasons."

How could one be surprised, then, that the vast majority of French people, especially those whose opinion is most pure and objective, those who have from the beginning refused to accept defeat – those who risked their lives to struggle against the occupier (don't forget that a few months ago Vichy itself put the number of French people shot by the occupier at eighty thousand) – how could one be surprised that such people have long seen in General de Gaulle the only authentic representative of the will for renewal and for patriotic resistance against the enemy? In any case, who today besides him enjoys prestige and authority? There's not a single civilian who isn't controversial. General de Gaulle alone enjoys an authority capable of uniting all well-intentioned French people.

But who is General de Gaulle? What are his intentions? What are his leanings, his visions of the future?

This is where interpretation becomes difficult. France is making a great act of faith in the general. She is trusting his unshakable patriotism to restore dignity to the country and to support her efforts at renewal.

But France today is faced with widespread political problems of the gravest kind. What position will the general take with regard to them? How will he go about solving them? This is what we do not know. Only those who have been close to him in London or Algeria could say.

But one can say that General de Gaulle's political future will not depend solely on his character and personality. It will depend above all on the way he solves the political and economic problems facing France today. The French people are determined to take back control of their destiny. In six months, when the new chambers are appointed, French public opinion as a whole will be making pronouncements on the government and on the men it will trust. I see no sign that the French people are willing to accept a personal government. To the contrary.

Nor do I see any sign that General de Gaulle is disposed to attempt such a government. He has always declared that he intended to reestablish republican freedoms. I know several of the men he has around him, all of whom have long-standing, solid republican convictions. Right away he has called on one who embodies the French republican tradition: M. Jeanneney, president of the Senate and former colleague of Clemenceau. He is a man of absolute integrity, and I am proud to call him my friend. It is he who will be the best guide for the constitutional reform that is under way. One may count on him to maintain the two-chamber system of government and to consolidate the role of the Senate, which for fifty years has been the pillar of a moderate republican regime.

On the other hand, I see no one but the general capable of dealing with some of today's urgent problems. I'm not talking about immediate or far-off problems such as supplies, reestablishment of communications, monetary issues, or international trade. Such problems will be dealt with by his ministers. We can expect to see all the big debates that followed the last war resurfacing. Allow me to emphasize in passing that the attitude of the United States will play a large role in their resolution. Washington will be able to exert a big influence on the more or less reasonable answers that will be given to these questions. And I fervently hope that no "debt problem" will arise, as after the last war, to poison Franco-American relationships and pose an insurmountable barrier to all attempts at mutual understanding.

It is rather to the solution of political problems that the general's personality will be able to contribute very effectively over the next few months. The greatest – the one that will determine the direction the crucial elections of 1945 will take (the first electorate poll after five years of war and silence) and consequently the direction of French policies for a number of years – is the unification of France.

There will be no lack of difficulties. Here are the main ones. There is not complete unity between the Gaullists of Algiers and French Resistance fighters. Each of the two groups claims to have played the major part in recent events. Between these two groups and the calmer mood of the rest of the country there has not yet been a meeting of minds. Whether or not public opinion will accept the "Resistance fighters" as leaders will depend upon their success over the next six months in solving problems of resupply, industrial reconstruction, and prices. There is another viewpoint that is as yet unknown: that of the prisoners and workers who were deported to Germany. They, too, will return to France with demands and resentments. Mutual understanding will not occur overnight. Finally, there is a party that is hard to define but that is quite prepared to lay traps for General de Gaulle; it is composed of businessmen and former politicians who had to a greater or lesser extent colluded with the Germans and Vichy from the beginning and would like to return to public life by attracting all the fence-straddlers. This is the self-styled party of "politicians" – that is, men who will be guided not by sentiment, but rather by "realities" and interests. It is this party that will try to exploit the mistakes and failures of the current government with an eye to the elections. It includes men belonging to the former Radical, Socialist, and moderate parties and appeals to all the "independents," those for whom material interests take priority. Finally – last but not least – the future stance of the Communist Party, whose influence grew with Russia's military victories, remains a mystery; no one knows whether it will or will not play a lone hand.

If General de Gaulle wants to further his prestige, play a lasting role, and prevail in the elections of 1945, he must merge all of these currents, combining energy with moderation and inspiring confidence in his fairness and impartiality. I know of no one more qualified than he to succeed in this task. And one must never forget that in the aftermath of France's disasters of 1870–1871, the great politician Adolphe Thiers, the "Liberator of French Territory," was ousted after three years of government; that the great patriot Gambetta was only a minister for three months; and that after the war of 1914–1918, the "Tiger" Clemenceau did not succeed in becoming president of the Republic.

As for me, I am convinced that the hope of lasting friendship among France, the United States, and England – an essential relationship for future peace – rests in large part on the success of General de Gaulle. And I pray for that success.

Please excuse, dear Colonel, the length of this letter, which I meant to make quite short but which has expanded in spite of me. You will thus see proof of the importance that I attach to your opinion, as well as evidence of my high esteem and affection for you.

THE "TYRANNY OF THE MILITARY"

6 August 1946 at Le Très-Clos

If historians have the courage to tell the truth, these last two years will show France under the tyranny of the military. They dispose, they decide. Parliament is just a farce. General de Gaulle has imposed an infantile foreign policy, fed by anti-English and anti-American rancor, and a domestic policy that led to a burst of energy on the part of the electorate against the scandalous constitution that was put to the vote on 5 May. General de Gaulle is above all a soldier. For a century the army has been the scourge of France. It has become a cancer eating away at the country. The officers believe they can do anything they want. The generals act like satraps. Their behavior in occupied Germany has brought disgrace on France. Their permanent rebellion against anything that might reduce their prebends has resulted in five hundred thousand men in uniform when one hundred thousand would suffice. Our powerless Parliament does not dare to say anything. The press no longer has any influence. The Radical Party has given way to the Catholic party and the Communist Party, both of which foment fanaticism and foolishness inspired by religious dogma. Meanwhile, money is hemorrhaging away. No one has noticed that this flight of capital is ruining our economy.

CRUELTY EVERYWHERE

13 May 1948

I am resuming these notes for my personal satisfaction. Time flows less quickly when one tries to retain the memories.

And my recollection is so imprecise that after a certain time, the facts become distorted in my mind. I measure that deformity when I refer to these notes. And that is a rather healthy exercise.

My strongest impression today and over the last few months is one of growing sadness in the face of widespread cruelty. Of course much time must pass after the savagery unleashed by war before public opinion can regain enough strength to bar the way to certain brutalities that seemed natural during wartime. The legal massacres of communists in Greece recall the shooting down of *communards* after 1870. As for the Palestinian war, it is the result of racial and religious hatreds that have not gone away.

Einaudi has become president of the Italian Republic.[2] What poetic justice! Under Mussolini he had asked me to serve as the intermediary for his correspondence with his son who had taken refuge in America (and whose letters were compromising). I can still see him with Mme Einaudi, seemingly exhausted in an armchair, a few years before the war. Though conquered and persecuted as a teacher, his liberal faith remained undaunted.

The Cotnaréanus have strongly insisted on my becoming board chairman for *Le Figaro*. I have energetically refused. At my age one does not take on responsibility for a big newspaper. And what a hornet's nest that editorial staff is!

2. Luigi Einaudi: anti-Fascist Italian economist; after the Liberation, he was elected president of the Italian Republic. See his article "L'homme. Un témoignage" in the special issue of the *Revue d'Économie politique* dedicated to Charles Rist.

Appendix 5: Members of Rist's Extended Family Imprisoned or Killed

(*Relevant diary entries are given in parentheses.*)

bomb placed in his factory from exploding. (12 January 1944 entry)

IMPRISONED OR WOUNDED

Amphoux, André. Charles Rist's nephew, son of Germaine's sister Jeanne. Imprisoned in Koblenz. (23 November 1940 entry)

Amphoux, René. Charles Rist's nephew, son of Germaine's sister Jeanne. Imprisoned in France until mid-1941. (9 August 1941 entry)

Cestre, Louis. Jeannette Rist's uncle. Deported to Buchenwald, rescued 23 April 1945.

Eyrolles, Mme. Françoise Rist's sixty-five-year-old aunt was taken to Drancy in November 1942 but freed after her eighty-year-old husband stood up to the *Sturmführer*. (28 November 1942 entry)

Monod, Germaine. Red Cross nurse related to Germaine Rist; arrested and taken to Dijon. (25 April 1944 entry)

Rist, Léonard. Son of Charles Rist, prisoner of war, captured after the armistice. (19 July 1940 entry)

Trocmé, François. Charles Rist's nephew, son of Rist's sister Ève and Henri Trocmé. His hands were ripped apart, one amputated, when he tried to keep a

KILLED

Monod, Jacques (1903–1944). Professor of literature. Nephew of Gustave-Adolphe Monod, related to Germaine Rist. Father of five children, killed in a guerilla skirmish in Aude. (11 August 1944 entry)

Rist, Jean (1900–1944). Eldest son of Charles Rist. Head of Liaisons and Transmissions for the Loire Maquis. Killed in action during the battle of Estivareilles (Loire) on 21 August 1944. (12 September 1944 entry)

Rist, Olivier (1914–1944). Charles Rist's nephew, son of Édouard and Madeleine Rist. Killed in action on a flying mission in Algiers. (12 September 1944 entry)

Schaller, Marc (1909–1940). Son of Constant and Gabrielle Schaller, nephew of Charles Rist. Killed on 15 June 1940 in the bombing of Neufchâteau. (27 December 1940 entry)

Sueur, Jean. (1905–1939). A cousin. Killed in a plane crash during an air raid, September 1939. (20 September 1939 entry)

Trocmé, Daniel. (1912–1944). Son of Charles Rist's sister Ève. Arrested in

June 1943 by the Gestapo at Le Chambon-sur-Lignon (Haute-Loire) when they came for the young refugees he was sheltering. Died in a German camp (Maidanek) on 2 April 1944. (30 June 1943 entry)

Trocmé, Ève (1875–1944). Charles Rist's sister, wife of Henri Trocmé. Killed by ill-targeted American bombardment in September 1944. (29–30 August and 12 September 1944 entries)

Trocmé, Henri (1873–1944). Husband of Charles Rist's sister Ève. Knocked down on a road in Normandy by an American military truck, 10 December 1944. Died from his injuries eighteen days later.

Glossary

Descriptions of people generally relate to the context in which they appear. Birth and death dates have been supplied for those who died before the war. In some cases identification came only from the diary itself and thus may include only a last name.

*Names marked with an asterisk appear in the "Brief Who's Who of the Rist Family."

6 February An anti-Parliament riot in Paris, 6 February 1934, thought to have been inspired by Fascism. (See Stavisky affair.)

Abetz, Otto Nazi Germany's head diplomat in France (November 1940–July 1944).

Action Française Right-wing movement and periodical led by Charles Maurras.

Adler, Hans Otto Anti-Nazi German, naturalized French citizen, and brother-in-law of one of Rist's colleagues at ISRES. In a concentration camp near Blois, September 1939–January 1940. (See C. Rist, *Papiers Charles Rist*, 79.)

Aldrich, Richard S. U.S. Representative from Rhode Island.

Alexander, General Harold British general.

Alexander the Great (356–323 BCE) Created the Macedonian Empire.

Alibert, Raphaël Pétain's notorious éminence grise during 1939 and 1940. Drafted the first anti-Jewish law of October 1940.

Alphand, Hervé Inspector of public finances and director of commercial agreements at the Ministry of Commerce.

Alphonse XIII (1886–1941) Exiled Spanish king.

Alsthom A power and transport firm. (See Detoeuf, Auguste.)

Altschuhl With the Lazard Bank.

Amiel (Villa) The house where Charles Rist and his family lived in Versailles. It belonged to his mother-in-law, Olga Monod, née Herzen, who lived with them.

Amphoux, André Charles Rist's nephew, son of Germaine's sister Jeanne.

Amphoux, Jeanne Charles Rist's sister-in-law, mother of René and André.

Amphoux, René Charles Rist's nephew, son of Germaine's sister Jeanne. Imprisoned in France till 1941.

Anthoine, General François Paul World War I veteran.

Antonescu, Petre Romanian brigadier general during World War II; appointed to the Ministry of Defense in 1941.

Ardant, Gabriel Part of Pierre Mendès France's circle. Together they authored *La science économique et l'action* (1954).

Argenlieu, Georges Thierry d' Priest, French navy admiral, and major contributor to de Gaulle's Free French Forces.

Arragon, Allan Trustee of the Morgan Bank in Paris.

Ashton-Gwatkin, Frank Rist's British counterpart on the blockade mission to the United States in 1940.

Assemblée du Musée du Desert (Mialet, Cévennes) Annual assembly of thousands of Protestants. Charles Rist delivered the first postwar speech there in 1945.

Atatürk See Kemal, Mustafa.

Attlee, Clement Wartime coalition deputy prime minister under Churchill, then postwar prime minister.

Aubin, Élisabeth Rist's niece, daughter of Ève and Henri Trocmé, and wife of Robert Aubin.

Auboin, Roger Council of State attorney; accompanied Rist on his Romanian missions in 1929–1932. (See his article on the subject, "Les Missions en Roumanie, 1929–1932," in the 1955 issue of *La Revue d'Économie Politique* dedicated to Charles Rist, 927–43. Also see the homage Auboin pays him with regard to those years in his book *Les Vraies Questions monétaires*, 42–43.)

Auboyneau, Jacques Inspector of public finances; member of the French mission on economic warfare in Great Britain.

Audiffret-Pasquier, Etienne d' Moderate deputy from the Orne department.

Augé-Laribé, Michel Agricultural expert; former student of Charles Rist in Montpellier.

Auphan, Gabriel Paul French admiral who gave the orders that led to the scuttling of the French fleet in Toulon.

Babeuf, François-Noël, known as "Gracchus" (1760–1797) Political agitator during the French Revolution.

Badoglio, Marshal Pietro Fascist follower of Mussolini named to replace him after Il Duce was arrested in 1943; signed an armistice with the Allies that led to civil war in Italy.

Baeyens, Jacques Consul general of France, Washington, D.C.

Bailby, Léon Right-wing journalist who founded *L'Alerte*, a pro-Vichy periodical, in September 1940.

Bailey Chase Bank director, Paris.

Balbo, Italo Heir apparent to Mussolini.

Baldwin, Stanley British Conservative prime minister in the 1920s and 1930s.

Ballande, Laurence Roger Langeron's niece; future countess of Bourbon-Busset; worked on economic chronology at ISRES.

Balzac, Honoré de (1799–1850) Nineteenth-century French novelist, author of *La Comédie humaine*.

Bamberger, Marc Rist's colleague at ISRES. *Les Chômeurs*, his study of unemployment, was published in 1941 with a foreword by Charles Rist.

Bamberger, Mme Marc Bamberger's mother.

Bank for International Settlements The first international financial institution, created in 1930 to facilitate the transfer of money for reparations. A bank for central banks.

Banque de France France's central bank.

Barbey, Mme Aunt of Noël Rist's wife, Marie.

Barclay de Tolly (1761–1818) Prince Michael Andreas Barclay de Tolly was a German-speaking Russian field marshal during Napoleon's 1812 invasion of Russia.

Bardoux, Jacques French senator and writer; member of Vichy's National Council.

Barnaud, Jacques Inspector of public finances; managing partner of Worms et Cie.

Barnes, Maynard B. First secretary; chargé d'affaires in the absence of U.S. Ambassador Bullitt.

Barré, Georges Edmund Lucien Senior French military commander in Tunisia as of January 1942.

Barrès, Maurice (1862–1923) Nationalist and anti-Semitic French author and politician.

Barthélemy, Joseph French politician; Pétain's minister of justice (1941–1943).

Basch, Victor Dreyfusard and president of the League of the Rights of Man; murdered by the Milice along with his wife, Hélène, in January 1944.

Baudouin, Paul Conservative banker; inspector of finances; Banque de l'Indochine director; undersecretary of state for the Council presidency as of 30 March 1940. A protégé of the Comtesse de Portes.

Bauer, Otto (1881–1938) Leader of the Austrian Social Democrats. After the party's failed uprising in February 1934, he went into exile.

Baume Manager at the Lyonnaise Waterworks, where Claude Rist directed the lab. According to Claude's daughter Antoinette, the primary place where her mother, Françoise, would hide out was at the Baumes', going "at night, without a light on her bike, in black streets."

Baume, Robert Renom de la Minister plenipotentiary; deputy director of political and commercial affairs at the Quai d'Orsay; managing director for the blockade ministry.

Baumgartner, Wilfrid Inspector of public finances; CEO of Crédit National.

Bavière, Paul President of the Banque de l'Union Parisienne.

Bazaine, François Achille (1811–1888) French marshal imprisoned for sur-rendering the Army of the Rhine to the Germans at Metz (subsequent to the surrender at Sedan) during the Franco-Prussian War.

Bazard, Saint-Amand, "Armand" (1791–1832) A leader of the Saint-Simonian movement.

Beauplan, Robert de Fiercely anti-Semitic French journalist who contributed to collaborationist media during the Vichy years.

Beck, Lieutenant Colonel Josef Poland's foreign minister; conducted an anti-Russian and pro-German policy from 1934 to 1939 and did not object to Hitler's annexation of Austria (March 1938) and Czechoslovakia (March 1939).

Bedaux, Charles Colorful millionaire; proponent of Taylorism-style scientific management; friend of British royalty during the 1930s and of the Nazis during the war.

Béguin Paper manufacturer.

Behn, Sosthène President of ITT.

Belin, René French union leader; minister of labor under Pétain.

Belisarius (500–565) General of the Byzantine Empire.

Bellah See Monod, Isabelle.

Bellet, Félix One of the managers of the Ottoman Bank in Paris.

Beltrand, Jacques French wood engraver.

Benech, Pierre French naval attaché in Washington, D.C.

Beneš, Edvard Czechoslovak president-in-exile during World War II. Opposed German claims to the Sudetenland and was forced to resign under German pressure.

Benoist, Baron Louis de Local agent of the Suez Canal Company in Cairo.

Benoist-Méchin, Jacques Appointed in June 1941 as secretary of state to the Council vice presidency, he oversaw foreign affairs, notably Franco-German matters. Ousted by Laval on 29 September 1942.

Béranger, Pierre-Jean de (1780–1857) Prolific nationalist French songwriter whose songs helped to bring about the Revolution of 1830.

Bérard, Maurice President of the Banque de Syrie et du Liban and trustee of Paribas.

Berchtesgaden Site of an extensive Nazi retreat in the Bavarian Alps.

Bergeret, Jean Marie Joseph French general who first supported Vichy, then joined General Giraud's forces in North Africa. From December 1942, when Darlan was assassinated, until March 1943, Bergeret was deputy high commissioner for North Africa. Later arrested in a Gaullist purge.

Bergery, Gaston A one-time pacifist Popular Front deputy, in 1940 he called for a new authoritarian, anticommunist order. Helped compose some of Pétain's addresses and served as Vichy's ambassador to Moscow (1941) and Turkey (1942–1944).

Berle, Adolf A., Jr. U.S. assistant secretary of state.

Bernanos, Georges French writer who spent the war years in South America; sharply critical of French society, particularly the Vichy regime.

Bernard, Maurice Manager, Eaux d'Évian (mineral water from the French Alps).

Bernard, Paul ("Tristan") Jewish writer and lawyer. Released from his internment at Drancy in response to public protest, he died in 1947.

Bernex, Jean A medical doctor, Bernex was elected in 1936 as the Popular Front deputy from Haute-Savoie. He later joined the Resistance but was arrested by the Gestapo in 1944 and deported to Dachau. Liberated in 1945.

Berthier, Georges Headmaster of the École des Roches; Louis Garrone's father-in-law.

Berthod, Aimé Active Resistance fighter and former minister of national education. Arrested by the Gestapo, he died in June 1944 from a pulmonary illness contracted during his imprisonment.

Bertrand, André-Numa Protestant leader in the occupied zone during World War II and active opponent of anti-Jewish persecution.

Bichelonne, Jean French minister closely associated with the conscription of young Frenchmen to work in Germany during the occupation.

Billecart, Léon Prefect of la Seine-et-Oise, site of one of the internment camps for German and Austrian refugees.

Billy, Count Robert de (1869–1953) Friend of Marcel Proust and former French ambassador; served on the boards of numerous companies.

Bineau, Henri-Marie-Auguste French major general, retired in 1940.

Bion, Commandant Ship captain with Matériel Téléphonique.

Bismarck, Otto von (1815–1898) Creator and chancellor of the German Empire (1871). Bismarck unified the German states and encouraged balance-of-power diplomacy in Europe.

Bizot, Jean-Jacques Deputy governor of the Banque de France.

Blanc One of three delegates who replaced the city council of Maxilly in March 1941.

Bloch, Dr. Drank poison rather than be arrested in a roundup of Jews (1941).

Bloch, Marc French historian. An Alsatian Jew, Bloch was active in the Resistance. Arrested and shot by the Gestapo in 1944.

Bloch, Mme Elderly mother of Dr. Bloch.

Bloch-Lainé, François Inspector of public finances, later finance minister.

Blondel, Jules François French minister in Bulgaria who joined de Gaulle in London in 1942.

Blum, Léon First socialist and first Jew to serve as prime minister of France (1936–1937 and March–April 1938); arrested by the Vichy regime and imprisoned in Germany.

Blum, René Imprisoned brother of Léon Blum.

Blumenson, Martin American military historian.

Boche French slang for a German.

Bock, Fedor von German field marshal during World War II.

Boegner, Marc Pastor; president of the National Council of the Reformed Church of France; member of the National Council of Vichy.

Boigne, Comtesse de, Adèle d'Osmond (1781–1866) Comtesse by marriage. Her memoirs of the July Monarchy provided inspiration for Proust's fictional Madame de Villeparisis.

Bois, Élie-Joseph Editor in chief of *Petit Parisien* since 1914, Bois was a power in the world of journalism. His account of the 1940 armistice was published under the title *Le Malheur de la France*.

Boisanger, Yves Bréart de Deputy governor of the Banque de France, then governor as of September 1940.

Boissière, Gustave Manager at the Ottoman Bank in Paris.

Boisson, Pierre Governor general of French West Africa.

Boissonnas, Jean Former diplomat and banker (Protestant); on the board of the Ottoman Bank in Paris.

Boissy Mentioned in the diary as having published articles in *Le Temps* demonstrating that American industrial power was a myth.

Bolgert, Jean Chief inspector for the Banque de France who accompanied Charles Rist on his Romanian missions.

Bolgert, Mme Wife of Jean Bolgert.

Bonn, Dr. M. J. German professor of political economy; at Bowdoin College in Maine during Rist's 1940 visit to the United States.

Bonnafous, Max Member of the Vichy cabinet in various roles, including secretary of state under Laval.

Bonnard, Abel Appointed to the national education ministry by Laval in April 1942.

Bonnefon-Craponne, Louis Honorary director at the commerce ministry.

Bonnet, Edgar Former inspector of public finances; father of Georges-Edgar Bonnet, managing director of the Suez Company.

Bonnet, Georges Minister of foreign affairs from April 1938 to September 1939.

Bonnet, Georges-Edgar Chief operating officer of the *Compagnie du canal de Suez*. Rist was appointed to the Suez Company's board of directors in 1933. Bonnet wrote about him in the 1956 issue of the *Revue d'Economie politique* dedicated to Charles Rist.

Bonnet, Marie Old friend of the Rist family and founder/director of the Maison des Étudiantes on the Boulevard Raspail.

Bor, Yugoslavia (now Serbia) Site of one of the largest copper mines in Europe.

Borduge, Marcel President of the Banque d'Indochine; accused of being a Freemason and dismissed by Bouthillier.

Borel, Émile One of several members of Rist's research institute who were arrested and kept in solitary confinement for a month (1941).

Boret, Victor Senator from La Vienne beginning in 1927 and twice minister of agriculture (1917–1919 in Clemenceau's cabinet and 1930–1931 in Théodore Steeg's).

Boris, Georges French journalist, politician, and economist influenced by Keynes and the New Deal; advised Léon Blum and, later, General de Gaulle in London.

Boris III Tsar of Bulgaria and reluctant German ally. His death in 1943 led to various conspiracy theories.

Bosc, Jean Contributor to *Paris-Soir*.

Bossuet, Jacques-Bénigne (1627–1704) Seventeenth-century French theologian, writer, and court preacher to Louis XIV who supported the divine right of kings.

Bouchardon, Pierre Examining magistrate at the trial of Marshal Pétain.

Bouffource, La A small farmhouse in Mayenne (a department in northwest France) that served as a refuge for the Rists. Given to Noël Rist for as long as he lived by the Pasteur Institute in recognition of his research on sulfones, used in curing leprosy.

Boulanger, Georges (1837–1891) An anti-republican general whose Boulangist movement advocated revenge on Germany, revision of the constitution, and restoration of the monarchy. When a warrant was issued for his arrest in 1889 on charges of conspiracy and treason, Boulanger fled France and ultimately committed suicide.

Bourde, Paul (1851–1914) Author of *Essai sur la Révolution et la religion*.

Boure, Maurice Met with Rist in Washington, D.C., in March 1940 to discuss financial matters.

Bourguet, Monsieur Mentioned on 29 August 1942 in connection with Rist's visit to the Sûreté Générale.

Bourowsky, Monsieur Apparently a Jew in ill health on whose behalf Rist tried to intervene.

Bousquet, René Under Laval's interior ministry, Bousquet was general secretary for police (April 1942–December 1943), playing an important role in Vichy's deportation of Jews to Germany.

Bouthillier, Yves Finance minister under the Vichy regime (as of 16 June 1940).

Bovet, Pierre Swiss psychologist interested in educational reform.

Bradley, Omar U.S. army general; senior commander during World War II.

Brauchitsch, Walther von Promoted to *Generalfeldmarshall* in 1940, Brauchitsch played a key role in Hitler's blitzkrieg.

Bréart de Boisanger, Yves Replaced Pierre Fournier as head of the Banque de France (1940).

Brécard, General Charles Théodore Pétain's secretary general in 1940; removed for his anti-German sentiments and made chancellor of the Legion of Honor.

Briand, Aristide (1862–1932) French politician and pacifist active in international diplomacy. Served eleven terms as French prime minister from 1909 to 1929.

Brinon, Fernand de Leading proponent of French collaborationist policy; named secretary of state in 1942.

Broglie, Maurice de French physicist.

Broglie, Duke of (Victor) (1785–1870) Author of *Souvenirs*.

Brossolette, Pierre French socialist and Resistance martyr.

Brouillet, René Junior official at the revenue court; former chief assistant for senate president Jules Jeanneney; one-time colleague at Rist's research institute.

Bruce, Stanley Melbourne Australian high commissioner to the United Kingdom.

Brüning, Heinrich German chancellor (1930–1932) who tried to fend off Nazism and communism while imposing unpopular economic reforms.

Brusilov, Aleksei (1853–1926) Russian general whose innovative offensive tactics during the First World War were copied by the Germans in the Second World War.

Buat, Édmond (1868–1923) French World War I general, long acquainted with Marshal Pétain. General Buat's voluminous but unpublished diaries cover the period 1914–1923.

Bucard, Marcel Former officer who founded the Mouvement Franciste, an extreme right-wing party; executed for treason after the war.

Buisson Perhaps François Albert-Buisson, senator, president of Rhône Poulenc, and a colleague of Rist's at ISRES.

Bulletin quotidien, Le An influential mimeographed newsletter of the Foundries Committee, founded in 1920.

Bullitt, Douglas Mentioned in the 21 April 1945 entry as serving in the French army.

Bullitt, William C. American ambassador to France (1936–1940).

Bunau-Varilla, Maurice Pro-Nazi newspaper editor.

Buresch, Karl (1878–1936) Christian-Socialist chancellor of Austria (1931–1932); assassinated in 1936.

Burgess, Warren Randolph Vice chairman of the National City Bank of New York.

Burthe, Claude Parisian notary for the Rist family.

Butler, Nicholas Murray President of Columbia University, diplomat, politician, and philosopher; awarded the Nobel Peace Prize in 1931. His reputation was somewhat tarnished by Columbia's anti-Jewish policies.

Caesar, Julius (100–44 BCE) After leading military campaigns that made Gaul a province of Rome, Caesar assumed control of the Roman government and was given the title "Dictator in Perpetuity."

Cagoule, La See C.S.A.R.

Caillaux, Joseph French politician; published volume 1 of his memoirs in 1942. (See 14 October 1942.)

Caix, Robert de Journalist and diplomat; Middle East specialist.

Cambó, Francesc Spanish minister of economy and finance (1921–1922).

Cambon, Paul (1843–1924) French prefect during the 1870s, then diplomat. His *Correspondance, 1870–1924* was published in the 1940s.

Campbell, Sir Gerald British high commissioner to Canada (1938–1941).

Campinchi, César Minister of the navy under Blum, Daladier, and Reynaud.

Campinchi, Hélène Appeals court lawyer; widow of César Campinchi, who died in 1941; arrested in 1944.

Candide Literary weekly (1924–1944) that covered politics and Parisian culture.

Cangardel, Henri Shipowner; CEO of the Compagnie Générale Transatlantique (1940–1945).

Canning, George (1770–1827) British foreign secretary and, for a few months, prime minister (1827).

Carbonari Secret revolutionary cells that formed in Italy during the early 1800s. They borrowed their initiation rituals from the charcoal sellers, hence the name. Largely failed provocateurs.

Carcopino, Jérome French historian; Vichy's minister of national education and youth (February 1941–April 1942).

Carol II King of Romania (1930–1940).

Carsow, Michel Embassy attaché, then oil exporter.

Carter, Bernard S. ("Bonny") Director of the Morgan Bank in Paris.

Casa de Velazquez Complex in Madrid dedicated to the training of French artists. Completed in 1935, it was partially destroyed during the Spanish Civil War.

Cassandre A pro-fascist Belgian newspaper.

Castellane, Stanislas de Former moderate senator from Cantal.

Cathala, Pierre Longtime Laval associate; minister of finance and national economy (1942–1944).

Catroux, Georges Commander in chief of de Gaulle's Free French Forces (1941–1943); governor general of Algeria (1943–1944).

Caulaincourt, Armand-Augustin-Louis, Marquis de (1773–1827) French general and diplomat whose memoir *With Napoleon in Russia* was published in 1933.

Caventou, Joseph-Bienaimé (1795–1877) Celebrated chemist who, with Pierre-Joseph Pelletier, isolated numerous pharmaceutical compounds, including quinine and strychnine.

Caziot, Pierre Minister of agriculture in Pétain's cabinet.

Cerjat, Charles de Like Rist, a trustee for the Banque de Syrie et du Liban.

C.G.T. (Confédération Générale des Travailleurs) France's national trade union.

Chalkley, Sir Owen British commercial attaché.

Chamberlain, Neville British prime minister (28 May 1937–10 May 1940).

Chambon, Le (Chambon-sur-Lignon) Protestant enclave in south-central France; became a haven for Jews and other refugees during the war under the leadership of Protestant minister André Trocmé and his wife, Magda. Charles Rist's son Jean and his family had strong connections with Le Chambon and often spent the summer there. During the school year 1943–1944 Jean Rist sent his wife, Jeannette, and his children André and Simone to be sheltered there, and the children attended Chambon's Collège Cévenol.

Chambrun, René de Son-in-law of Pierre Laval. Like all the Chambruns, he inherited dual American and French citizenship.

Champetier de Ribes, Auguste Popular Democrat deputy from the Basses-Pyrénées and foreign affairs secretary of state during the Phoney War.

Champion, Edme (1766–1852) French author and philanthropist.

Chantilly According to daughter Isabelle, Claude Rist worked in Chantilly until, for health reasons, Charles Rist helped him find a job in Le Pecq, closer to his home in Le Vésinet.

Chapin, Selden Diplomat with the American embassy in Paris, 1944.

Chaptal, Msgr. Emmanuel Auxiliary bishop in Paris.

Chardonne, Jacques French novelist; author of *Voir la Figure – Réflexions sur ce temps*; open supporter of Pétain and the Vichy regime.

Chargueraud-Hartmann, Paul Legal adviser for the French foreign ministry and appointed to the Blockade Committee in this capacity.

Charles V (1500–1558) Ruler of the Holy Roman Empire (1519–1556). Born in Flanders; member of the House of Habsburg.

Charles IX (1550–1574) King of France from 1560 until his death.

Charles XII (1682–1718) King of the Swedish Empire (1697–1718). A brilliant military leader, his campaigns in the Great Northern War nevertheless ended in the defeat of Sweden and the end of its empire.

Charles-Roux, François Léger's successor at the Quai d'Orsay. (See his memoirs, *Cinq mois tragiques aux Affaires étrangères.*)

Charléty, Sébastien French historian. Published *La Restauration (1815–1820)* in 1911.

Charmeil, Pierre Advising magistrate with the Revenue Court, honorary commerce ministry director.

Chateaubriand, François-René de (1768–1848) Nineteenth-century French writer, historian, and diplomat.

Châteaubriant, Alphonse de French writer who founded the pro-Nazi newspaper *La Gerbe* in 1940.

Chatou A town west of Paris, a short distance from the home of the Claude Rists in Le Vésinet. Claude Rist's boss, M. Baume, the Swiss manager of Lyonnaise Waterworks, lived in Chatou. Claude's Jewish wife, Françoise, sometimes took refuge with the Baumes, riding to their house on her bicycle at night.

Chautemps, Camille French prime minister during the 1930s; close ally of Pétain in arguing for an armistice with Germany in 1940.

Chénier, André (1762–1794) French poet guillotined in 1794. Robespierre, who had not forgotten the satirical verses of this believer in constitutional monarchy, sentenced him to death.

Chiang Kai-Shek, Generalissimo Chairman of the Nationalist Government of China (1928–1931 and

1943–1948); chairman of the National Military Council (1932–1946).

Chiappe, Jean Former prefect of police whose replacement by Daladier unleashed the events of 6 February 1934. Chiappe was on his way to the Levant, where he was to be Vichy's governor general, when his plane was mistakenly downed by Italian aircraft involved in the Battle of Taranto.

Christie, Loring C. Canadian envoy to the United States from 1939 until his death in office, 1941. Canada's Washington legation became an embassy in 1943.

Christin One of three delegates who replaced Maxilly's city council in March 1941.

Churchill, Winston British prime minister during World War II. Led the British Empire to victory by his persistent exhortation to "never surrender."

Ciano, Galeazzo Italian minister of foreign affairs; Mussolini's son-in-law.

Claudel, Paul Conservative Catholic dramatist and poet.

Clausewitz, Carl von (1780–1831) Prussian general who wrote *On War*, a treatise on military strategy and philosophy.

Clauzel, Count French ambassador to Austria in the early 1930s when Charles Rist was there as a consultant for the reorganization of the Kredit Anstalt, a bank sunk by the monetary crisis.

Clemenceau, Georges (1841–1929) French liberal politician (Radical-Socialist) and journalist; ardent Dreyfus supporter and defender of the republican government; French prime minister (1906–1909 and 1917–1920); nicknamed "Le Tigre" (the Tiger) and "Père-la-Victoire" (Father Victory) for his leadership during World War I.

Cochran, H. Merle First secretary (Financial), U.S. embassy, Paris (1932–

1939); technical assistant to Secretary of the Treasury Morgenthau (1939–1941).

Codreanu, Corneliu Zelea (1899–1938) Founder and leader of Romania's ultranationalist, anti-Semitic Iron Guard.

Collette, Paul Fired on and wounded Laval and Déat in August 1941.

Colson, Clément (1853–1939) French economist.

Combes, Émile Director of the territorial police.

Compagnie Générale Transatlantique, aka the French Line French shipping company established in the nineteenth century.

Condé, Prince de (Louis de Bourbon), formerly Duc d'Enghien (1621–1686) French general known as "le Grand Condé" for his military victories.

Condorcet, Nicolas de (1743–1794) Enlightenment philosopher and political scientist.

Cooper Journalist with the Associated Press.

Corap, André Georges French general blamed for letting the German army break through at Sedan, 1940.

Corbin, Charles French ambassador to London (1933–1940).

Corelli, Arcangelo (1653–1713) Seventeenth-century Italian composer and violinist.

Cortot, Alfred Denis French pianist who supported the German occupation and served on Pétain's National Council.

Cotnaréanu Mme Yvonne Cotnaréanu, ex-wife of François Coty, was majority shareholder in *Le Figaro*.

Coty, François Right-wing perfume magnate whose Solidarité Française movement participated in the riots of 6 February 1934.

Coudenhove-Kalergi, Count Richard Co-founded the Pan-European Union in 1922 with Prince Otto von Habsburg.

Coudert Perhaps a member of the New York–based Coudert Brothers law firm, which represented France in the purchase of American planes in the buildup to World War II and also represented the Banque de France.

Coulondre, Robert French ambassador to Bern for a few weeks in 1940.

Courtin, René Professor of political economics at the Montpellier Law Faculty and former researcher at ISRES; consulted Charles Rist about the economic program that Courtin drafted for the Comité Général d'Études (General Studies Committee) of the Resistance; the report was published secretly in November 1943.

Couve de Murville, Maurice French finance inspector; deputy director for general fund transfers.

Crémieux, Adolphe (1796–1880) Author of the Crémieux Decree granting full citizenship for Jews in French-ruled Algeria (1870).

Crémieux Decree The 1870 decree by which Adolphe Crémieux granted full citizenship for Jews in French-ruled Algeria.

Cripps, Sir Stafford British Labour politician; member of Churchill's War Cabinet; ambassador to Moscow; sent to India in 1942 to negotiate support for the British war effort in exchange for postwar self-government.

Croix-de-Feu (Cross of Fire) Far-right league of World War I veterans led by Colonel François de la Rocque; dissolved in the 1930s.

Cromwell, Oliver (1599–1658) Military and political leader of the Roundheads, who overthrew the monarchy of Charles I; the latter was tried and beheaded in 1649.

Cross, Sir Ronald Chamberlain's blockade minister.

Crouzet, Guy Collaborationist journalist who wrote for *Les Nouveaux Temps*.

C.S.A.R. (Comité Secret d'Action Révolutionnaire) Secret extreme-right organization known as "La Cagoule" (hood/cowl/mask).

Curtin, John Joseph Australian prime minister (1941–1945).

Daladier, Édouard Prime minister of France (10 April 1938–21 March 1940).

Dard, Émile French diplomat and historian of the French Revolution.

Darlan, Admiral François Head of the French navy at the beginning of World War II; head of Pétain's government (10 February 1941–April 1942); assassinated on 24 December 1942.

Darnand, Joseph Key Vichy collaborator; founder and leader of the Vichy Milice; joined the S.S. and became head of the police; executed in October 1945.

Darquier, Louis (aka de Pellepoix) Vichy's commissioner for Jewish Affairs.

Darré, Richard Walther Nazi minister of food and agriculture (1933–1942).

Daudet, Alphonse (1840–1897) French novelist.

Daum Perhaps Paul Daum of the Daum Glassworks family.

Dautry, Raoul French armaments minister (September 1939–16 June 1940).

Dayras, Georges Council of State attorney; Georges Pernot's chief of staff.

Déat, Marcel Déat founded the collaborationist Rassemblement National Populaire (RNP) in February 1941. Minister of labor and national solidarity in Laval's cabinet (1944); after the war, convicted in absentia of collaboration.

Degrelle, Léon Belgian (Walloon) founder of Rexism; fought with the Germans against the Soviet Union and became a lieutenant colonel in the Waffen S.S.

Delachaux, Lt. Guard at Saint-Gingolph on the Franco-Swiss border.

Delbos, Yvon Radical Party legislator and minister of national education under the Republic who left for North Africa aboard the *Massilia* on 21 June 1940.

Delenda, Antoine Undersecretary for commercial affairs at the Quai d'Orsay; ex-officio member of the Blockade Committee.

Deloraine, Maurice Researcher at Le Matériel Téléphonique, subsidiary of I.T.T.

Denis, Pierre Financial expert with the Blair Bank.

Dentz, Henri Fernand French army officer in charge of defending the French mandates in Syria and Lebanon under the Vichy regime.

Deroy, Henri General secretary for public finance (1940–1943).

Desbordes-Valmore, Mme Marceline (1786–1859) French Romantic poet, singer, and actress; friend of Balzac.

Desjardins, Paul Writer; Dreyfusard; founder of l'Union Pour la Vérité (Union for Truth) and the intellectual gatherings of the Décades de Pontigny.

Detoeuf, Auguste President of Alsthom, a power and transport firm; best known for his *Propos de O. L. Barenton, confiseur*, a collection of aphorisms written at the end of the 1930s.

Deutsch, Julius Radical Austrian social democrat.

Deutsche Allgemeine Zeitung German newspaper (1861–1945).

Deuxième Bureau France's military intelligence agency (1871–1940).

Dewey, Charles U.S. financial adviser to Poland (1927–1930).

Dewey, Thomas E. Governor of New York (1943–1954); Republican candidate for president in 1944 and 1948.

Diderot, Denis (1713–1784) French Enlightenment philosopher and writer.

Doenitz, Admiral Karl Germany's senior submarine officer in the early years of World War II; replaced Grand Admiral Erich Raeder as commander in chief of the German navy in 1943.

Dollfuss, Engelbert (1892–1934) Austrian chancellor; executed in Vienna in July 1934 during the course of an abortive coup attempt fomented by the Nazis.

Doriot, Jacques French politician and journalist.

Dormoy, Marie François Abel Husband of Marguerite Léger, sister of Alexis Léger (Saint-John Perse).

Dormoy, Marx Léon Blum's interior minister; killed by a bomb on 26 July 1941.

Douaumont Village near Verdun; site of fierce anti-German resistance; destroyed during World War I.

Douglas, Lewis Williams American diplomat, academic, and politician who lobbied Roosevelt to aid the Allies.

Doumergue, Gaston (1863–1937) Prime minister of France (1913–1914 and 1934); president (1924–1931).

Dreyfus, Alfred (1859–1935) Alsatian Jew who was falsely accused as a traitor in 1894, dishonorably discharged, and condemned to solitary confinement on Devil's Island in French Guiana. The Dreyfus affair became a cause célèbre that profoundly divided French society. Charles Rist worked actively with other Dreyfusards to protest the injustice.

Drouin Possibly Oscar Drouin, Canadian politician who, when the Liberals came to power in 1939, served in Adélard Godbout's cabinet, in charge of commerce and municipal affairs.

Ducret One of three delegates who replaced Maxilly's city council in March 1941.

Dufaure, Jules Armand (1798–1881) French prime minister during the 1870s.

Dulles, John Foster Supporter of Hitler in the 1930s; close adviser to Thomas E. Dewey.

Dumaine Possibly Cyrille Dumaine, Canadian legislator.

Dumont Secretary of the Comité France-Amérique who met with Rist in New York, 17 March 1940.

Du Moulin de la Barthete, Henri Pétain's chief of staff.

Dunan, Marcel Historian specializing in the study of Napoleon; cultural attaché in Vienna from 1919 to 1938.

Dunn, James (Jimmy) Political adviser to the U.S. secretary of state.

Dupont, Pierre (1765–1840) French general of the Napoleonic and Revolutionary wars, defeated in the Battle of Bailén, Spain (1808).

Durand Charles Rist's chauffeur. (See 17 June 1940.)

Durand, Julien Former minister of commerce in Paul-Boncour's cabinet (June 1932–January 1933); former deputy from Doubs.

Durand-Viel, Admiral Georges Navy chief of staff and president of the navy's high command (1931–1937).

Duval Friend of Constant Schaller, Rist's brother-in-law.

École des Roches Famous French private school created in 1899, the first French "new school." Charles Rist's sister Ève and her husband, Henri Trocmé (vice principal), worked there.

École Libre des Sciences Politiques School of Political Science (aka Sciences Po).

Eden, Anthony British foreign secretary during World War II.

Einaudi, Luigi Anti-Fascist Italian economist.

Einaudi, Mme Wife of Luigi Einaudi.

Eisenhower, General Dwight David November 1942, appointed Supreme Allied Commander for North Africa; December 1943, Supreme Allied Commander in Europe.

Ems Dispatch A communication edited by Otto von Bismarck that is seen as the reason France declared war on Prussia in July 1870.

Enfantin, Barthélemy Prosper (1796–1864) Entrepreneur and leader of the Saint-Simonian movement.

Erkin, Behiç Turkish ambassador to France.

Escalier Public finance inspector arrested in 1943. (See 11 August 1943.)

Esterhazy, Ferdinand (1847–1923) French officer whose passing of information to the Germans was attributed to Alfred Dreyfus. (See Dreyfus, Alfred.)

Esteva, Jean Pierre French admiral, Vichy's resident general in Tunisia.

Estienne d'Orves, Henri Honoré d' Right-wing French Resistance hero.

Europe nouvelle, L' Political journal created in 1918 to which Rist contributed articles.

Eyrolles Mme Eyrolles was Françoise Rist's aunt, arrested and sent to Drancy. Her eighty-year-old husband managed to convince the *Sturmführer* to let her go. (See 28 November 1942.)

Fabre-Luce, Alfred French writer and journalist.

Falkenhausen, General Alexander von Repressive German military governor of occupied Belgium.

Falkenhausen, M. von German civilian commissioned to oversee French banks during the occupation; the notorious General von Falkenhausen was his uncle.

Farnier, Charles Finance inspector; former deputy governor of the Banque de France.

Faure, Paul Former left-wing politician and pacifist who supported the Vichy regime.

Faÿ, Bernard French historian who wrote a book to prove that the Freemasons were behind the French Revolution (1935). During the occupation was head of the Bibliothèque Nationale and director of Vichy's anti-Masonic bureau.

Feis, Herbert Economic adviser for international affairs to the Department of State under Roosevelt.

Fels, Edmond de French historian; publisher of *La Revue de Paris*, a literary journal; wealthy owner of the Château de Voisin.

Ferdinand II (1578–1637) Born in Austria; head of the German Catholic League; member of the House of Habsburg; King of Germany and Holy Roman Emperor (1619–1637). His imposition of counter-Reformation policies led to the Thirty Years' War.

Ferrasson, Louis President of Paris's chamber of commerce.

Fey, Major Emil (1886–1938) Nationalist commander of Austria's right-wing paramilitary *Heimwehr*; vice-chancellor (1933–1934) under Dollfuss; active in the bloody suppression of the Socialist Party.

F.F.I. (French Forces of the Interior) Name used by Charles de Gaulle for Resistance fighters on the soil of occupied France.

Figaro, Le Important French newspaper founded in 1826; bought by François Coty, perfume tycoon, in 1922.

Finlay, Lord William British magistrate; chair of the Contraband Committee since the beginning of the war.

Firminy Industrial town nearest to Fraisses and to the steel plant where Jean Rist worked.

Flandin, Pierre-Étienne Conservative French politician; prime minister (1934–1935 and 1940–1941); finance minister under Laval (1931–1932). On 13 December 1940 was appointed by Pétain to replace Pierre Laval as foreign minister, but was replaced by Darlan soon after under pressure from the Germans.

Flouret, Marcel Senior magistrate at the Cour des Comptes (Court of Audit).

Foch, Marshal Ferdinand (1851–1929) Distinguished military leader of the French army during World War I.

Fougère, Étienne Former deputy from the Loire; president of the National Association for Economic Expansion.

Fournier, Pierre Head of the Banque de France (1937–1940).

Fraisses Village where Jean Rist lived with his family.

France-America Committee The Comité France-Amérique, which evolved into today's Cercle France-Amériques, was founded in 1909 and originally intended to inform French public opinion about the importance of the United States in world affairs.

Franco, General Francisco Spanish dictator who provoked and defeated the republicans in the Spanish Civil War with aid from Fascist Italy and Nazi Germany.

François-Poncet, André French ambassador to Rome.

Frankfurter, Felix U.S. Supreme Court justice.

Frederick the Great (1712–1786) Eighteenth-century king of Prussia.

Free French Officially, the Free French Forces (Forces Françaises Libres, aka F.F.L.) were those who enlisted with de Gaulle's organization in London after the Franco-German Armistice of 1940 and before August 1943. In mid-1943 the Free French Forces merged with the French forces in North Africa, becoming the "Armée Française de la Libération."

Frerichs President of the University of Brussels; collaborated with Rist's research institute before the war.

Fritsch, General Werner von (1880–1939) Commander in chief of German ground forces (1934–1938); killed during the siege of Warsaw.

Galopin, Alexandre Influential Belgian businessman murdered in 1944 by a Nazi collaborator. His Galopin Doctrine posited that it was acceptable to produce goods for the occupiers so long as they had no military purpose.

Gambetta, Léon (1838–1882) Fierce opponent of the 1851 coup d'état and the resulting empire. In 1870 he proclaimed the establishment of a republic at the Hôtel de Ville. Prime minister (1881–1882).

Gamelin, General Maurice Gustave Commander in chief of French forces in 1940; succeeded by Maxime Weygand; tried for treason during the Riom trial and imprisoned.

Gandhi, Mahatma Mohandas Leader of India's nonviolent independence movement.

Garde des Sceaux Minister of justice.

Garelli, Philippe Turkey's general director of the Ottoman Bank.

Garr, Max Viennese journalist who kept Charles Rist informed about Austrian problems at the time of his missions to Vienna.

Garreau-Dombasle, Maurice French commercial attaché in New York.

Garrone, Louis Educator at the École des Roches; in charge of training at the Youth Secretariat.

Gascon A native of Gascony; a boastful person.

Gaulle, Charles de French general who led the Free French Forces during World War II.

Gaussel, Georges Head of Crédit Coopératif's central branch.

Gaxotte, Pierre Right-wing French journalist and historian.

Gazier, Albert Active in the Resistance (see Libération Nord); represented the C.G.T. (Confédération Générale des Travailleurs) with de Gaulle in London.

Gentin, Fernand Radical deputy from l'Aube; trade minister in Édouard Daladier's cabinet.

George V (1865–1936) King of the United Kingdom (1910–1936).

George VI King of the United Kingdom during World War II.

Georges, Alphonse-Joseph French commander of the north/east forces in 1940.

Georges-Picot, François French diplomat. During World War I he and Englishman Sir Mark Sykes signed the Picot-Sykes Agreement dividing up the Ottoman Empire.

Georges-Picot, Jacques Director-general of the Suez Canal Company.

Géraldy (pseudonym of poet and playwright Paul Lefèvre) Co-wrote Son mari, a comedy (1936), and Si je voulais . . . (1946) with Robert Spitzer.

Gerbe, La Pro-Nazi French newspaper.

Gerhardt Acquaintance of Charles Rist in Switzerland.

Gerlier, Cardinal Pierre-Marie Honored by Yad Vashem as "Righteous among the Nations" for his efforts to save Jews during World War II.

Germain-Martin, Louis Law professor; former finance minister under the Third Republic. In the diary Rist calls him an "unprincipled mediocrity" (31 January 1941) and a "collaborator" (5 February 1943).

Gide, Charles (1847–1932) Mentor and co-author with Charles Rist of the enduring *Histoire des doctrines économiques* (1909).

Gidel, René Professor at the Paris Law Faculty. As a member of Vichy's National Council, he served on the committee charged with drafting a constitution.

Gignoux, Claude-Joseph French politician, economist, and journalist; member of Vichy's National Council.

Giraud, Henri Honoré French general who escaped from a Nazi prison and joined the Free French Forces.

Glehn, Louis de Cambridge professor; first cousin of Germaine Rist.

Goebbels, Joseph Hitler's minister of propaganda.

Goerdeler, Carl Friedrich Anti-Nazi ringleader of the generals' revolt (20 July 1944) against Hitler; hanged in February 1945 by the Nazis. He played an important role as an informer for the western democracies, notably Great Britain, for which he represented the idea of a "national opposition" to Hitler.

Goering, Marshal Hermann Commander in chief of the German air force.

Gorodiche, Fanny Hertz Wife of Dr. Léon Gorodiche; mother of Françoise Rist.

Gosse, Jean Lawyer; son of René and Lucienne Gosse.

Gosse, Lucienne Wife of René Gosse and author of a book about him.

Gosse, René Dean of the Science Faculty in Grenoble.

Gouttes, Marguerite des Rists' oldest friend in Geneva.

Grady, Henry F. U.S. assistant secretary of state during Rist's 1940 mission to Washington, D.C.

Graham, Sir Ronald U.K. ambassador to Rome, 1921–1933.

Grandi, Dino Italy's ambassador to the U.K. (1932–1939) and leading member of Mussolini's government who turned against Il Duce in July 1943.

Gravière, Raymond Banque de France inspector, later Vichy's general discount manager.

Graziani, Marshal Rodolfo On Mussolini's orders, Graziani moved against British and Commonwealth forces stationed in Egypt on 9 September 1940. The Italians dug in at Sidi Barrani but were defeated there on 10 December and surrendered on 6 February 1941.

Greene, Wilfrid England's master of the rolls (1937–1949).

Gregory VII Pope (1073–1085).

Griffith, Colonel Mentioned 31 January 1940 as having been sent from the U.K. to France to discuss plans for the blockade.

Gringoire Right-wing weekly newspaper allied with the Vichy regime. Curiously, during the war it published, under a pseudonym, the work of Irène Némirovsky (author of *Suite Française*), a conservative writer of Russian Jewish origin, until she was arrested by the French and handed over to the Nazis.

Grosskop Mentioned 30 September 1941 as having presumably helped obtain Léonard Rist's release from German captivity.

Grünfelder, Jean-Georges-Henri French general; former student of Charles Rist.

Guérard, Jacques Appointed general secretary by Pierre Laval on 18 April 1942.

Guerpillon, Mme Mother of a friend of Léonard Rist on whose behalf Charles Rist asked M. von Falkenhausen to intervene.

Guichard, Louis Darlan's chief of staff (1941–1942).

Guillemin, Henri French historian and literary critic who often wrote of the class struggle between the elites and the common people.

Guimier, Pierre Leader of an anti-Blum newspaper campaign in the 1930s; head of the Havas news agency, then political editor of *Le Journal*.

Gwatkin See Ashton-Gwatkin, Frank.

Haakon VII Elected king of Norway who defied Nazi occupiers.

Habsburg, Prince Otto von Son of the last Austro-Hungarian emperor-king, Charles I; opponent of Nazism and communism; co-founded the Pan-European Union with his mentor Coudenhove-Kalergi in 1922.

Halder, General Franz German general who often disagreed with Hitler but refused to overthrow him in 1940 as Goerdeler urged.

Halévy, Elie (1870–1937) Author of *Era of Tyrannies,* a book of essays.

Halifax, Lord (Edward Frederick Lindley Wood) Conservative British foreign secretary from 1938 to January 1941, when he became the British ambassador to Washington; advocate of appeasement prior to the war.

Hankey, Lord Maurice Minister without portfolio under Chamberlain. (See S. Roskill, *Hankey, Man of Secrets.*)

Hannotin, Edmond Council of State lawyer; senator from the Ardennes.

Harcourt, François-Charles, d' Deputy from le Calvados (1929–1942); distant cousin of Charles Rist.

Hargrove Possibly Marion Hargrove, an American journalist and author of *See Here, Private Hargrove*, a popular World War II book.

Harrison, George L. President of the Federal Reserve Bank of New York (November 1928–December 1940).

Hartman, Lee Foster Editor of *Harper's* magazine (1931–1941).

Havas World's oldest news agency; today known as Agence France-Presse.

Heinemann, Dannie (1872–1962) President (1905–1955) of SOFINA (Société Financière de Transports et d'Entreprises Industrielles), an important Belgian energy and financial company.

Helleu, Jean Delegate general of the Algiers Committee who had the rebellious president of the Lebanese Republic and several ministers arrested on 11 November 1943 and set up a provisional government in their place.

Hellot, Frédéric Retired general; board president of Matériel Téléphonique.

Henderson, Sir Nevile British ambassador to Germany (1937–1939). Advised Chamberlain to appease Hitler and support the Munich Pact, but on 3 September 1939 delivered the ultimatum that led to Chamberlain's declaration of war against Germany.

Henriot, Philippe Vichy's minister of information and propaganda; assassinated by the Maquis in 1944.

Henry-Haye, Gaston Senator-mayor of Versailles (1935–1940); Vichy's ambassador to Washington as of July 1940.

Herberts, Jean A colleague at Rist's research institute; anti-Nazi German refugee inducted into the French army.

Héring, Pierre Military governor of Paris (1939–1940); admired by de Gaulle for his teaching of a rapid military displacement strategy.

Héritier, Lucien Odd-job man at Rist's research institute.

Hermant, Max Director of the Insurance Committee, July 1940.

Herriot, Édouard President of the Chamber of Deputies under the Third Republic.

Herriot, Mme Arrested with her husband, Édouard, in December 1942.

Herzen, Alexander (1812–1870) Activist thinker and writer known as the father of Russian socialism. Grandfather of Germaine Rist.

Hess, Rudolf Deputy Führer from 1933 until May 1941, when he flew to Scotland, apparently thinking he could negotiate peace with the United Kingdom.

Hickerson, John D. Member of the Permanent Joint Board on Defense (U.S. and Canada), 1940–1946.

Hillaert, M. Belgian sugar producer from the Oise; partner in the Béguins' paper manufacturing firm.

Himmler, Heinrich Powerful member of Hitler's government who oversaw all security forces and coordinated Nazi Germany's mass exterminations.

Hoare, Sir Samuel British ambassador to Madrid.

Hohenstaufen German dynasty of kings (1138–1254) that produced three Holy Roman emperors.

Hölderlin, Friedrich (1770–1843) German lyric poet of the Romantic movement; author of *Hyperion*, an epistolary novel.

Homolle, Michel General secretary of the Suez Company; became its general manager after the war.

Hore Belisha, Baron Isaac War minister in Chamberlain's cabinet (1937–January 1940).

Hu Shih Republic of China's ambassador to the United States (1938–1942).

Hudelo, Louis (See Stavisky affair) Former police prefect who served as board chairman for a company set up by Alexandre Stavisky to cover his fraud. Tainted by the Stavisky scandal, Hudelo asked Laval for protection. The latter apparently tried to suppress the incident and close the case, which in spite of his precautions popped up again in 1934.

Hughes, Charles E. Chief Justice; read the oath of office at Roosevelt's 1941 inauguration ceremony.

Hugo, Victor (1802–1885) Major writer of the French Romantic movement. His involvement in France's political life as an advocate of republicanism and social justice led him to spend twenty years in exile.

Huizinga, Johan Author of *Incertitudes, essai de diagnostic du mal dont souffre notre temps*, 1939.

Hull, Cordell American secretary of state (1933–1944).

Huntziger, Charles French general who commanded French armies in the Ardennes (1939–1940) and negotiated the armistice with the Germans; one of the signatories of the anti-Jewish statute of 3 October 1940.

İnönü, Ismet President of Turkey (1938–1950).

Institute The French Institute, created in 1795, consisted of the five French academies of arts and sciences.

Iorga, Nicolae Romanian historian and writer who presided over a short-lived government (1931–1932). A prominent member of the National Renaissance Front, King Carol's fascist organization, Iorga was assassinated by the rival Iron Guard on 27 November 1940.

ISRES (Scientific Institute for Economic and Social Research) Founded in 1934 by Charles Rist; located at 4 rue Michelet in Paris.

Istel, André Banker. Technical adviser at the finance ministry in Paul Reynaud's cabinet. During World War II he served as financial adviser for the provisional government of the French Republic before representing the Republic at the great postwar monetary meetings.

Izard, Georges French writer and politician; joined the Resistance after being released from prison by the Germans for health reasons.

Jacob, Charles Geology professor and member of the French Academy. As a Vichy appointee, he headed the C.N.R.S. (National Scientific Research Center) from 1940 until the Liberation.

Jacquier, Paul Senator from Haute-Savoie (1935–1940).

Jahan, Henry Inspector of finances; manager at the Banque de Paris et des Pays-Bas.

Janson, Paul-Émile Belgian politician arrested in France and sent to Buchenwald, where he died.

Jaoul, Raymond Electromechanical engineer; manager of Matériel Téléphonique.

Jardel, Jean Pétain's secretary-general.

Jay, Nelson D. President of the Morgan Bank in Paris.

Jeanneney, Jean-Marcel Son of Jules Jeanneney; professor of political economy at the Law Faculty in Grenoble (where Senate president Jules Jeanneney settled after Pétain dissolved Parliament in 1942).

Jeanneney, Jean-Noël French historian, media expert, author, and statesman.

Jeanneney, Jules President of the French Senate when World War II erupted.

Jodl, Alfred Josef Ferdinand German general hanged as a war criminal after World War II.

Jonas On a list of Jews who left France between 25 May and 30 June 1940.

Jouhaux, Léon Influential French trade unionist imprisoned at Buchenwald.

Journal Officiel Official gazette that publishes legal information put out by the French government.

Jouvenel, Henry de (1876–1935) French statesman and journalist; editor of *Le Matin*; married to Colette, 1912–1924.

Juin, General Alphonse Pierre Commander of French forces in North Africa; notably effective in the Italian campaign of World War II.

Jullien, Armand Assistant manager at the Banque de Paris et des Pays-Bas.

Keitel, General Wilhelm Senior German military commander; hanged for war crimes in 1946.

Kemal, Mustafa (1881–1938) Founder and first president of the Turkish republic. In gratitude, the nation gave him the title Atatürk (Father of the Turks).

Keynes, John Maynard British economist. His economic views on regulating business cycles with fiscal policy ran counter to Rist's advocacy of reliance on the gold standard. As adviser of the British Treasury, Keynes authored the British plan for monetary stabilization after World War II.

King, Mackenzie Canadian prime minister (1926–1930 and 1935–1948).

Kittredge, Eleanor Wife of Tracy Kittredge. Mrs. Kittredge published an interview with Charles Rist during his 1940 trip to the United States: "A Philosopher amid the Currency Maze" (*New York Times*, 31 March 1940).

Kittredge, Tracy Barrett Representative of the Rockefeller Foundation in Paris.

Klein Chief administrator in the navy and one of Léonard Rist's fellow prisoners who paid a visit to Charles Rist.

Knickerbocker, Hubert Renfro ("Red") American journalist who reported on German politics during World War II.

Knox, Colonel Stuart Roosevelt ally; secretary of the navy during World War II.

Koenig, General Marie Pierre Fought with de Gaulle's Free French Forces; appointed governor of Paris by de Gaulle on 21 August 1944.

Köster, Roland (1883–1935) German ambassador to France (1932–1935).

Krug von Nidda, Roland Germany's consul general in Vichy.

Künwald, Gottfried Financier and former president of the Austrian central bank; assassinated in 1938.

Kutuzov, Prince Mikhail (1745–1813) Commander of the Russian forces who put an end to Napoleon's invasion of 1812 using a strategy of retreat and harassment.

Labbé, Robert Assistant secretary general for the national economy.

Laborde, Admiral Jean de Scuttled the French fleet in Toulon, November 1942; received a death sentence (commuted) after the war for not having allowed the fleet to defect to the Allies.

Laboulaye, André Former French ambassador to Washington.

Lachenal, Gustave Genevan fiscal expert.

Lacoste, Robert Active in the "Libération Nord," a Resistance movement in the occupied zone.

Lacroix, Marie de Daughter of Victor de Lacroix; married Noël Rist.

Lacroix, Victor de Diplomat; French ambassador to Prague until 1939; became father-in-law of Noël Rist.

Lafaye, Dr. Noël Rist's supervisor at the Pasteur Institute.

Lagache, Hélène Sister of Françoise Rist; died of undiagnosed diphtheria in 1942.

La Laurencie, Lieutenant General Leon-Benoit de Fornel de Sent to a concentration camp by Laval for favoring an Anglo-American victory (1942–1944).

Lambert Perhaps Marcel Lambert, a Banque de France board member and administrator for the Ateliers et Forges de la Loire, or else Alfred Lambert-Ribot, formerly on the Foundries Committee.

Lammers, Clemens German economist.

Lamson, André With the Ministry of Native Affairs in Morocco (1936–1943).

Lamure, de Rist lunched at his place while in Washington, D.C., 9 March 1940.

Langeron, Mme Wife of Roger Langeron.

Langeron, Roger Paris prefect of police since March 1934; arrested by the Gestapo on 24 January 1941.

Larminat, General Edgar de Important military leader of Free French Forces.

Laroche, Jules Former French ambassador to Poland.

La Rocque, Colonel Francois de Leader of the Croix-de-Feu (a far-right league of World War I veterans) and then of the Parti Social Français, a fascist party. Broke with Pétain and joined the Resistance.

La Rocque, Pierre de Brother of Colonel de La Rocque; adviser to the Comte de Paris, Henri Robert d'Orléans.

Lattre de Tassigny, Jean de French general who led the French First Army (1944–1945).

Laure, Émile French general who commanded the Eighth Army in the Lorraine region in 1940; freed from a German prison by Pétain's intervention; served in Pétain's cabinet.

Laurent, Jacques Industrialist; Banque de France trustee; ex officio member of the Foreign Exchange Committee.

Laurent-Atthalin, Baron André Council of State attorney; named president of the Banque des Pays de l'Europe Centrale in 1935; chairman of the Banque de Paris et des Pays-Bas as of October 1940.

Laval, Pierre Laval, a proponent of collaboration with Germany, was twice prime minister (11 July 1940–13 December 1940 and 18 April 1942–20 August 1944) under the Vichy regime. Executed for treason immediately after the war.

Laveleye, Émile de (1822–1892) Belgian economist; wrote *De l'avenir des peuples catholiques*.

Lavisse, Ernest (1842–1922) French historian.

Lazard, Max Son of a founder of the Lazard Bank, his social work focused on unemployment and other labor issues.

Leahy, Admiral William D. U.S. ambassador to Vichy (1941–1942).

Lebreton, André General secretary of the Ugine steelworks and Mario Rist's boss.

Lebrun, Albert President of France (1932–1940). Although Lebrun never officially resigned, he was replaced by Philippe Pétain by a vote of the Parliament on 10 July 1940.

Leclerc, General Philippe Much-decorated leader of Free French Forces.

Ledoux, Frédéric Businessman; trustee of the Société Pennaroya and of the Casa Velasquez in Madrid.

Lefebvre, Georges French historian specializing in the revolutionary period.

Leffingwell, Russell C. Director of the Morgan Bank in New York.

Léger, Alexis (Saint-John Perse) French poet and diplomat; general secretary of the French Foreign Office until 1940.

Legueu, François French writer and politician specializing in economic matters.

Leith-Ross, Sir Frederick Britain's chief economic adviser (1932–1945).

Lemaître, Henri Assistant director of Rist's research institute, ISRES.

Lenin, Vladimir Ilyich (1870–1924) Russian revolutionary; founder of the Soviet Union.

Lequerica, José-Felix de Named Spain's ambassador to Paris in 1939, Lequerica was instrumental in the persecution of Spanish refugees from the Civil War; Spanish minister of foreign affairs (1944–1945).

Le Rond, Henri Edouard French general who served on the front in World War I, participated in the Paris Peace Conference, and headed the Interallied Committee overseeing the Upper Silesia plebiscite mandated by the Versailles Treaty to determine the border between Germany and Poland.

Leroy, Maxime Sociologist and historian who taught at the École Libre des Sciences Politiques; wrote *La Pensée sociale de Charles Rist*.

Leroy-Beaulieu, Paul Finance inspector; foreign trade director at the finance ministry.

Le Roy Ladurie, Jacques Minister of agriculture in 1942 under Laval; joined the Resistance in 1943.

Lesseps, Ferdinand de Suez Canal Company administrator.

Lesseps, Mathieu de Grandson of Ferdinand de Lesseps.

Letter Rogatory Court's formal request for documents or other assistance.

Le Verrier, Madeleine Succeeded Louise Weiss in 1934 as head of the weekly L'Europe nouvelle.

Leverve, Gaston Secretary of the Union Internationale des Chemins de Fer; expert on railroads.

Levy (*La relève*) Laval's scheme by which one French prisoner of war would be sent home for every three French workers who went "voluntarily" to work in Germany. Two French laws created the S.T.O. (Compulsory Work Service): the Law of 4 September 1942 and the Law of 16 February 1943.

Lévy, General Mentioned (15 February 1942) as having married Mme Bloch's sister.

Leyendecker Architect in Versailles.

Leygues, Georges (1857–1933) French politician who held several posts during the Third Republic, including prime minister (1920–1921) and foreign minister.

Liberation Committee in Algiers A committee formed by generals Giraud and de Gaulle to coordinate their efforts to liberate France.

Libération Nord Important Resistance movement of occupied France.

Lichtenberger, André Writer and historian specializing in the study of socialism; editor in chief of *L'Opinion*.

Ligne, Prince de Belgian nobleman; president of the Red Cross in Brussels.

Lindbergh, Charles Celebrated pilot who was outspokenly antiwar until the bombing of Pearl Harbor.

Lippmann, Walter Award-winning U.S. newspaper columnist and political commentator. Of German-Jewish lineage, Lippmann had a degree from Harvard and spoke French and German.

Litvinov, Maxim Maximovich Russian revolutionary and diplomat. His Jewish origins led to his being replaced as commissar of foreign affairs by Molotov before the signing of the Nazi-Soviet Pact. Soviet ambassador to the United States (1941–1943).

Loisy, Alfred Firmin de Author of books on religion; excommunicated by the Catholic Church.

Lorch, A. Anti-Nazi German refugee; prisoner in a French camp for foreigners in Cheverny, September–October 1939. He had arrived in France in 1933, applied for French citizenship, and enlisted in the French army (C. Rist, *Papiers Charles Rist*, 80).

Lot, Ferdinand French historian and professor specializing in late Roman/early medieval culture.

Lothian, Lord (Philip Kerr) British ambassador to Washington.

Louis XIV (1638–1715) Flamboyant "Sun King" of France.

Louis XV (1710–1774) Great-grandson of Louis XIV. Presided over France's defeat in the Seven Years' War (1756–1763).

Louis-Napoleon Bonaparte (1808–1873) President of France's Second Republic (1848–1852); ruler of the Second French Empire (1852–1870).

Louis-Philippe (1773–1850) French king during the "July Monarchy" (1830 to 1848).

Lubin, Germaine Paris Opera diva admired by Hitler.

Luchaire, Jean Supporter of Vichy's National Revolution; founded the collaborationist paper *Les Nouveaux Temps* in 1940.

Ludendorff, General Erich (1865–1937) Primary German strategist in World War I.

Lvov, Prince Georgy (1861–1925) Appointed by Czar Nicolas II as head of Russia's provisional government in March 1917, Lvov was forced to resign four months later. He was soon arrested by the Bolsheviks but escaped and spent the rest of his life in Paris.

Mackenzie King, W. L. Long-serving Canadian prime minister (1935–1948).

MacMahon, Marshal Patrice de (1808–1893) Fought in several wars and became president of France's Third Republic (1873–1879).

Madgearu, Virgil Romanian minister of industry, then of finances at the time of Rist's missions to Romania in 1929 and 1932; assassinated by Codreanu's Iron Guard.

Magna Olga Monod-Herzen, familiarly known as Magna, was the mother of Jeanne and Germaine, Charles Rist's wife. Magna was a daughter of Alexander Herzen, the anti-tsarist Russian revolutionary, and the wife of Gabriel Monod.

Maindras Mentioned by François Legueu (14 March 1941) as a French general who gives him military advice.

Maisky, Ivan Soviet ambassador to London during World War II (1932–1943); active in normalizing relations with the Allies after the Nazi-Soviet Pact broke down; Moscow's deputy commissar of foreign affairs (1943–1945).

Maistre, Joseph de (1753–1821) Royalist, counter-Enlightenment philosopher, and diplomat.

Man, Henri de Belgian socialist who saw the Nazis in 1940 as deliverance for the working classes from a "decrepit" world.

Mandel, Georges Jewish statesman who opposed the armistice with Germany and hoped to lead a French government in exile in North Africa; arrested in August 1941 on Laval's orders, along with others who had sailed to North Africa on the *Massilia*; murdered by the French Milice in July 1944.

Mange, Michel Expert on rail transport.

Maniu, Iuliu Romanian prime minister for three terms (1928–1933); co-founded the National Peasants' Party.

Mannheimer, Fritz (1890–1939) Powerful German Jewish financier during the interwar years.

Manstein, General Erich von German field marshal in World War II.

Marchand, Camille Replaced Langeron as Paris's police prefect in 1941.

Marcilly, Henri Chassain de Former French ambassador to Bern, Switzerland.

Mariejol, Jean-Hippolyte (1855–1934) French historian who specialized in the sixteenth and seventeenth centuries.

Marin, Louis French professor and politician; minister of state in Reynaud's cabinet (1940); opposed the armistice but maintained links to the Vichy government for a time before joining the Gaullists.

Marion, Paul French journalist who joined the French Communist Party in 1922 and contributed to *L'Humanité*. Later he switched allegiances, serving as Vichy's minister of information (1941–1944), playing an important role with the Legion of French Volunteers against Bolshevism and supporting recruitment for the Waffen SS.

Marjolin, Robert Future general secretary for the OECE (Organization for European Economic Cooperation), Marjolin worked with Rist at ISRES from 1934 until the war. (See his article "Le directeur de l'Institut scientifique de recherches économiques et sociales" in *Revue d'Economie politique*.)

Marlio, Louis Aluminum and hydroelectricity mogul.

Marmont, Marshal Auguste de (1774–1852) Named marshal of France by Napoleon. In 1814, having retreated to Essonne, south of Paris, Marmont betrayed Napoleon by negotiating with the Allies to surrender.

Marquet, Adrien Formed the Neosocialists with Déat, then served as Vichy's minister of the interior (1940); strong advocate of collaborationist persecutions during the war.

Marx, Jean Head of the Services des oeuvres françaises à l'étranger (Bureau of Cultural Relations) at the foreign ministry. Because he was Jewish, he was obliged to leave this post in the summer of 1940.

Masse, Pierre French senator arrested in 1941; held variously at Drancy, Compiègne, and la Santé; finally deported to Auschwitz, where he died in 1942.

Massigli, René French diplomat specializing in German affairs; demoted in 1938 from his senior position in the foreign office to an ambassadorship in Turkey. In 1940, having been removed by the Vichy government from this post, he returned to France, made contact with Resistance leaders, and in 1943 became de Gaulle's commissioner for foreign affairs.

Matsuoka, Yōsuke Japanese foreign minister (1940–1941).

Matthews, Harrison Freeman First secretary at the American embassy in France.

Mattioli Head of the Banque Française et Italienne.

Maublanc, de One of two people associated with the Ugine steelworks plant seen by Mario Rist in the spring of 1941 regarding his desire to be employed there.

Maupassant, Guy de (1850–1893) French writer whose short story "Boule de Suif" (1880) depicts a group traveling together in a stagecoach during the

Franco-Prussian War, a microcosm of French society.

Maurin, General Louis French minister of war (November 1934–June 1935 and January–June 1936).

Maurras, Charles Influential leader of l'Action Française, advocating monarchism and a return to the ideas of pre-Revolutionary France.

Maury, Pierre French Protestant pastor at the Passy-Annonciation reformed parish in Paris. After the war he became president of the National Council of the French Reformed Church and a member of the Ecumenical Council of Churches.

Maxilly-sur-Léman Village near which the Rists' country house, Le Très-Clos, was located.

Mazarin, Cardinal Jules (1602–1661) Chief minister of France under Louis XIII and Louis XIV, from 1642 until his death.

Ménard, General Mentioned as having a post in France's war ministry, October 1939.

Mendès France, Pierre Left-wing French politician; arrested on Laval's orders in August 1941 along with others who had sailed to North Africa on the *Massilia*; escaped and joined de Gaulle's Free French in London; served as de Gaulle's finance commissioner in Algeria and, after the Liberation, as minister for national economy in France's provisional government.

Ménétrel, Bernard Pétain's personal physician and friend; known as Pétain's éminence grise.

Menthon, François de Law professor; French minister of justice after the Liberation.

Mény, Jules-Adolphe Engineer; trustee for the Compagnie Française des Pétroles (French Petroleum Company);

became president of the company in 1940 when he replaced Ernest Mercier.

Mercier, Ernest Electric power and oil magnate.

Merle d'Aubigné, Guy Brother of Robert Merle d'Aubigné; imprisoned with Rist's son Léonard in an internment camp.

Merle d'Aubigné, Robert Professor of medicine.

Merlier, Octave Administrator of the French Institute in Athens; suspended from his duties for having proclaimed his Gaullism too loudly, then imprisoned upon his return to France.

Merz, Charles Journalist with the *New York Times*.

Metaxas, General Ioannis Greek dictator (1936–1941).

Metternich, Prince Klemens von (1773–1859) Foreign minister of the Holy Roman Empire, then of the Austrian Empire (1809–1848).

Mettetal, Maître Well-regarded lawyer in the Vichy camp whom Charles Rist enlisted to protect Françoise, the Jewish wife of Rist's son Claude, as well as their three daughters, from persecution.

Metz, Victor de Director of the Compagnie Française des Pétroles.

Meyer, André Partner with the Lazard Frères Bank; awarded a Legion of Honor for his role in saving Citroën from bankruptcy; as Jews, he and his family were forced to flee in 1940.

Meyer, Arthur (1844–1924) Publisher of the influential newspaper *Le Gaulois*; conservative royalist and supporter of Boulangism.

Meyer, Eugene Editor and publisher of the *Washington Post*.

Meynial, Pierre Trustee of the Morgan Bank in Paris.

Michael I A figurehead, Michael became the last king of Romania as the result of a pro-German coup against his father, King Carol II, in September 1940.

Michaud, René President of the Seine's Court of Commerce.

Michelet, Jules (1798–1874) French historian with Huguenot roots and republican leanings; quoted extensively by Rist. Michelet's massive *Histoire de France*, inspired by the French Revolution to focus on the struggle of the French people for liberation, was published in 1867, notable for its author's romantic imagination and democratic idealism.

Michelson, Alexandre French economist of Russian origin; general secretary of the Institut International des Finances Publiques.

Mikhailovich, Drazha Anticommunist leader of Serbian Chetniks in conflict with Tito's Yugoslav Partisans during World War II.

Milice Paramilitary force created by the Vichy regime as an auxiliary to the Nazi occupiers.

Militärbefehlshaber Military governor.

Millerand, Alexandre Former president of the republic; senator from the Oise; neighbor and friend of the Rists in Versailles.

Millerand, Jacques Son of Alexandre Millerand; neighbor of the Rists.

Mireaux, Émile Co-director of *Le Temps*.

Mittelhauser, Eugène Commander in chief of the Levant Army (Syria and Lebanon) in 1940, General Mittelhauser threw his support to Pétain and Vichy France.

Molotov, Vyacheslav Foreign affairs minister for the Soviet Union (1939–1949).

Mönick, Emmanuel After being recalled by Vichy as general secretary of the French Protectorate of Morocco, Mönick joined the Resistance and was appointed governor of the Banque de France after the liberation.

Monnet, Jean International financier and proponent of European unity. In September 1939 Monnet was cabinet attaché to the Council presidency, charged with coordinating Allied purchasing missions, armaments, and transport.

Monod, Gabriel (1844–1912) French historian and educator who came from a long line of Protestant pastors; left-wing intellectual and passionate Dreyfusard who co-founded *La Revue historique* in 1876; father of Germaine Rist.

Monod, Germaine Red Cross nurse; sister of Gustave-Adolphe Monod; daughter of Marcel Monod.

Monod, Gustave-Adolphe Germaine Rist's cousin; former adviser to French legislator Jean Zay; sacked as inspector general of education by Vichy's minister of education in November 1940.

Monod, Isabelle ("Bellah") Germaine Rist's aunt.

Monod, Jacques Professor of literature; nephew of Gustave-Adolphe Monod.

Monod, Marcel Pastor of the Reformed Church of France in Paris, then in Versailles.

Monod, Noël Executive with Peugeot; distant cousin of Germaine Rist. His sister married Jean-Marcel Jeanneney, Jules Jeanneney's only son.

Monod, Olga (née Herzen) See Magna.

Monod, Philippe Minister plenipotentiary (see 9 June 1940); half-brother of Jacques Monod.

Monod, Wilfred (1867–1943) French theologian who founded the Order of Watchers, a community of Protestant hermits, in 1923; wrote *La Nuée de témoins*.

Monroe Doctrine The 1823 doctrine written by James Monroe differentiating between the Old and New World spheres of influence and warning that European colonization in the Americas would no longer be tolerated by the United States, but that the United States would not interfere in internal European affairs.

Montaigne, Michel de (1533–1592) Renaissance writer, famous for his *Essais* (1580).

Montesquieu, Charles-Louis de Secondat (1689–1755) Enlightenment philosopher whose theory of separation of powers became widely influential.

Montgomery, Field Marshal Bernard ("Monty") British general in command of the Eighth Army that defeated Rommel in North Africa; commanded Allied forces on D-Day, 6 June 1944.

Montoire-sur-le-Loir Site of a meeting between Hitler and Pétain on 24 October 1940 that marked the beginning of French collaboration. Laval had met here with Hitler two days earlier and suggested that the latter meet with Pétain.

Monzie, Anatole de Deputy from le Lot; public works minister; friend of Otto Abetz and Darquier de Pellepoix.

Morand, Paul Novelist-diplomat; head of the French mission for economic warfare in Great Britain.

Moreau, Émile Former governor of the Banque de France; president of the Paribas board.

Moreau-Néret, Olivier Former inspector of public finances; general secretary for economic matters at the Ministry of Finance in 1940; quit in 1941 to work for Crédit Lyonnais.

Moret, Clément Governor of the Banque de France (1930–1934).

Morgan, J. P., "Jack," Jr. Wealthy banker and philanthropist.

Morgan Bank J. P. Morgan & Co., a bank founded by J. Pierpont Morgan in the United States, forerunner of JPMorgan Chase and Morgan Stanley.

Morgenthau, Henry, Jr. American secretary of the Treasury (1934–1945).

Morin, Jean Worked with Charles Rist at ISRES.

Morrow, Dwight (1873–1931) American banker, legislator, and diplomat; great friend of Charles Rist. His daughter, the pioneering aviator Anne Morrow, married Charles Lindbergh in 1929.

Moysset, Henri Historian of nineteenth-century French socialism and professor at the Naval Academy, Hautes Etudes Navales; minister of information, then minister of state, under Pétain. Moysset and Rochat were Rist's usual contacts in the Vichy government.

Munich Pact An agreement signed by Germany, France, the United Kingdom, and Italy in September 1938 allowing Nazi Germany to annex Czechoslovakia's Sudetenland.

Murphy, Robert D. U.S. consul in France (1939–1941); American representative in Algeria at the time of the landing. He was then General Eisenhower's political adviser.

Museum of Man (*Groupe du musée de l'Homme*) First Resistance network set up in France in response to de Gaulle's 18 June 1940 radio appeal.

Mussolini, Benito Italy's prime minister (1922–1925), then head of government (1925–1943). His official title after 1936 was His Excellency Benito Mussolini, Head of Government, Duce of Fascism, and Founder of the Empire.

Nalèche, Étienne de Suez Company trustee; editor of the *Journal des débats*.

Napoleon Bonaparte (1769–1821) French military leader and emperor (1804–1815) whose military campaigns are frequently compared to those of Hitler in Rist's diary.

Navicert Certificate specifying the contents of a neutral ship's cargo, issued especially by a blockading power in time of war.

Nehru, Jawaharlal (Pandit) Leader of India's independence movement; first prime minister (1947–1964).

Neisser, Albert Anti-Nazi Austrian refugee; professor of Italian law; arrived in France in 1938; friend of one of Charles Rist's sons (C. Rist, *Papiers Charles Rist*, 80).

Nelson, Admiral Horatio (1758–1805) Heroic commander in England's navy during the Napoleonic Wars.

Neuflize, Baron Jacques de Director of the Protestant bank of the same name and trustee of the Ottoman Bank.

Newton, Isaac (1642–1727) Great English mathematician and physicist.

Nietzsche, Friedrich (1844–1900) Rist admired Nietzsche's ideas on life affirmation and abhorred the way the German philosopher's writings were appropriated by Nazi Germany.

Noël, Léon French ambassador in Warsaw (1935–1939). Refused to sign the armistice agreement of June 1940, at which he was a delegate; served briefly in the Vichy government, then resigned and in 1943 began organizing clandestine meetings for the Resistance.

Noguès, Charles General in charge of French forces in North Africa (1939–1943); arrested the French politicians who arrived on the *Massilia* in Casablanca, 24 June 1940; resisted the Allied invasion of November 1942; resigned as France's resident general in Morocco, 1943.

Norman, Montagu Governor of the Bank of England (1920–1944); member of the Anglo-German fellowship.

Nouveaux Temps, Les **(1940–1944)** Collaborationist daily founded by Jean Luchaire.

O'Brien, Dr. Daniel Medical doctor and Rockefeller Foundation representative in Europe. When the Paris office was closed after the German occupation, O'Brien relocated to London.

Officiel, L' Official bulletin of the French State under the Vichy regime.

Offrey Secretary to William C. Bullitt at the U.S. embassy in France.

Orléans, Duke of Anti-Jewish statements of the duke were cited by Toussenel in an 1845 book.

Ortega y Gasset, José Spanish essayist and philosopher; admired by Rist for his critique of the bourgeoisie in *La Rebelión de las masas* (1930).

Ostersetzer, Wilhelm Anti-Nazi Austrian engineer and friend of Claude Rist; sent to a French prison camp after war was declared (C. Rist, *Papiers Charles Rist*, 80). One of Rist's "protegés," he was liberated from his camp and given shelter at Claude Rist's house. (See note in 29 January 1940 diary entry.)

Osusky, Stefan Czechoslovakian representative in Paris during the Munich crisis.

Oudot, Émile Manager (1920–1937) then administrator of Paribas.

Page, Mrs. Arranged for Rist to meet Wendell Willkie on his visit to New York in 1940.

Pagès, Georges (1867–1939) French historian; author of *La Guerre de Trente Ans, 1618–1648*.

Painvin, Georges Aluminum manufacturer.

Pannier, Jacques Parisian pastor; wrote *L'Eglise réformée de Paris sous Louis XIII, 1621–1629*, a work on the Protestants of Paris.

Papi, Giuseppe Ugo Italian economist; secretary-general of the International Institute of Agriculture (1939–1946).

Paribas Banque de Paris et des Pays-Bas.

Paris, Comte de, Henri Robert d'Orléans Pretender to the French throne (1940–1999).

Parmentier, André In 1943, as Vichy's prefect of Rouen, Parmentier ordered the arrest of the region's Jews and was then named general director of the national police by Pierre Laval.

Parodi, Alexandre Council of State attorney; former managing director for labor; future chief representative of the provisional government of occupied France in 1944; friend of Jean Rist.

Parodi, Jacqueline Alexandre Parodi's sister.

Parodi, René Deputy prosecutor in Paris; active in the Libération Nord alongside Robert Lacoste, Albert Gazier, and Robert Pineau; taken at the same time as the leaders of Combat Zone North.

Paswolski, Leo Special aide to U.S. Secretary of State Cordell Hull.

Paulus, Field Marshal Friedrich von Commanded the German assault on Stalingrad in 1942.

Payot, René Swiss journalist and radio commentator.

Pécate Neighbor of the Rists in La Boufource; village blacksmith.

Péret, Raoul French politician who was appointed French finance minister in 1926 in Briand's eighth cabinet. His resignation, after efforts at financial reform failed, led to the collapse of Briand's government.

Pernot, Georges Senator from Le Doubs; appointed blockade minister on 13 September 1939. (See his *Journal de guerre*.)

Pernot, Maurice Journalist and writer; brother of Blockade Minister Georges Pernot.

Perrin, René Head of Ugine's steelworks and of the Compagnie Française de Raffinage (French Refining Company).

Perruche, Commandant With French military intelligence in 1939.

Perse, Saint-John See Léger, Alexis.

Pesson-Deprêt, Mme Militant member of the Abolitionist Federation and of the Union against the Trafficking of Human Beings.

Pesson-Didion, Maurice Trustee of the Morgan Bank in Paris, also of Matériel Téléphonique.

Pétain, Marshal Philippe Viewed as a hero of World War I, at the age of eighty-four Pétain became chief of state of the Vichy government (11 July 1940– 19 August 1944), which collaborated with the Nazis.

Peter II King of Yugoslavia as the result of a military coup on 27 March 1941.

Petrelli Italian banker.

Peyrecave, René de Aide to French industrialist Louis Renault.

Peyrouton, Marcel Served in various capacities in Pétain's cabinets, including minister of the interior (September 1940–February 1941).

Philip, André Protestant politician and economist who served with de Gaulle as an interior minister for the Free French and later as finance minister in 1946 and 1947.

Philip II (1527–1598) Son of Charles V, King Philip II oversaw a vast Spanish Empire and championed the Catholic counter-Reformation and Inquisition.

Philippe, Raymond Played an important role in the great monetary maneuvers of the 1920s, particularly regarding the stabilization of the franc.

Piatier, André Economist; secretary of the Institut International de Finances Publiques; colleague at Rist's research institute.

Picabia, Gabrielle Buffet Wife of Francis Picabia (French painter associated with the Dadaists and Surrealists).

Picard, Jean Assistant secretary-general of the Foundries Committee; general secretary of the Ministry of Armament's mission in London, pre-Vichy. (See 24 January 1940.)

Pichon, Adolphe With the Union des Industries Métallurgiques et Minières (Union of Metallurgic and Mining Industries); old friend of the Rists.

Picquart, General Georges (1854–1914) As chief of the Deuxième Bureau (military intelligence), Picquart discovered the document that ultimately led to Alfred Dreyfus's exoneration. Later promoted to general, Picquart served under Georges Clemenceau as minister of war (1906–1909).

Piétri, François Minister of posts, telegraphs, and telephones for a brief period; French ambassador to Spain (1940–1944) during the Nazi occupation.

Pillet-Will, Jean Son of Count Frédéric Pillet-Will, who had been on the boards of the Banque de Paris et des Pays-Bas and the Ottoman Bank.

Pilori, Le Anti-Semitic newspaper published in Paris during the war and funded by the Germans.

Pineau, Christian French Resistance leader arrested by the Gestapo in 1943. A survivor of Buchenwald, he served the French government in several ministerial roles after the war.

Pitt, William (1708–1778) "The Great Commoner" who refused to accept a title until 1766, Pitt led during the Seven Years' War as Britain's secretary of state.

Planque, Jacques Banker and Société Générale partner.

Pleven, René General director for Europe of the Automatic Telephone Company.

Poincaré, Raymond (1860–1934) French prime minister on five occasions from 1912 to 1929; president (1913–1920).

Poissonnier Stockbroker in Paris; neighbor of the Rists in Versailles.

Popular Front Left-wing coalition that governed France from 1936 to 1938 (Blum, Chautemps, and Daladier revolved in office as head of state).

Portes, Comtesse Hélène de Described by *Time* magazine (5 August 1940) as "short, homely, plain, dark, nervous, jealous and not very bright," Hélène, daughter of a Marseilles dockworker, married a count, set up a salon in Paris, separated from the count, and became the lover of Paul Reynaud. She was viewed as an "evil genius" who meddled in Reynaud's career and pressured him to resign as France's prime minister on 16 June 1940. The comtesse died on 28 June 1940 as the result of a car crash when she and Reynaud were traveling in the south of France.

Potut, Georges Former student of Rist's; journalist; former Radical deputy from la Nièvre; prefect for the Loire (1941–1943).

Poussin, Nicolas (1594–1665) Seventeenth-century French painter.

P.P.F. (Le Parti Populaire Français) Fascist, anti-Semitic party headed by Jacques Doriot.

Prételat, Gaston Member of France's Supreme War Council in 1940; commander of the armies in the East.

Prince, Albert "A junior judge in the *Paris Parquet* (Public Prosecutor's Office) ... Prince was scheduled to testify about how his superior, the former prosecutor Pressard, had kept Stavisky out of jail for so long" when he was found dead on a railroad track, run over by a train (David Clay Large, *Between Two Fires: Europe's Path in the 1930s*, 53).

Proudhon, Pierre-Joseph (1809–1865)
Calling himself an "anarchist," Proudhon asserted "Property is Theft!" and
advocated "order without power,"
advocating workers' associations and
cooperatives as a substitute for private
property. Rist's own early advocacy of
workers' associations and cooperatives
was clearly influenced by Proudhon.
(See Rist's "La Pensée économique de
Proudhon," *Revue d'histoire économique
et sociale*, no. 2 [1955]: 129–65).

Puaux, Gabriel French ambassador; high
commissioner in Syria and Lebanon.

Pubston Mentioned 15 March 1940 as
having been sent by U.S. Secretary of
the Treasury Morgenthau to discuss
agricultural purchases with Rist.

Pucheu, Pierre As Vichy's enthusiastic
minister of the interior (1941–1942), he
formed the anti-Jewish Police aux Questions Juives as well as anticommunist
and anti-Masonic organizations. Executed in Algeria, March 1944.

Pujo, Bertrand French air force general
and briefly Pétain's air minister (June–
July 1940); president of Air France.

Purvis, Arthur B Director-general of the
British Purchasing Commission during
the war.

Quai d'Orsay French Foreign Office.

Quesnay, Eric Third son of Pierre and
Mme Quesnay.

Quesnay, Mme The widow of Pierre
Quesnay; her brother Ramsay was Finland's minister of foreign affairs.

Quesnay, Pierre Former head of economic services at the Banque de France
during the time when Charles Rist was
deputy governor; Rist's colleague and
confidant.

Quesnay, Pierre (fils) Eldest son of
Pierre and Mme Quesnay.

Queuille, Henri Radical senator from
Corrèze; served in various posts in
France's Third Republic, including
minister of agriculture (1938–1940);
joined de Gaulle in London in 1943 and
became vice president of the government in exile in Algeria; prime minister
(1948–1949, 1950, and 1951).

Quinet, Edgar (1803–1875) Author of
L'Enseignement du Peuple (1849) and *La
République: Conditions de la régénération
de la France* (1872).

Quiñones de León Spanish diplo-
mat; former Spanish ambassador in
Paris; personal friend of Pétain and
Alfonso XIII.

Quisling, Abraham Vidkun Taking
advantage of the Nazi invasion of Norway in 1940, Quisling seized power and
became notorious for his government's
collaboration with Nazi Germany.

Raeder, Erich Led the German navy in
World War II until he resigned in 1943.

Raffard, Roger Member of Mario Rist's
regiment.

Raspail, François Vincent (1794–1878)
Scientist and political reformer; imprisoned after the 1848 Revolution, then
spent a decade in exile, returning to
France in 1862.

Ratier Son of one of the Rists' neighbors
in Versailles.

Reconnaissance Française, La Described by Rist as "an association of fair
ladies and Americans."

Reibel, Charles Senator from Seine-
et-Oise; undersecretary of state
(1920–1921).

Reichenau, Walter von Led the German
armies invading Poland, Belgium, and
France; enthusiastic supporter of Hitler
and Nazism.

**Reichstadt, Duke of (son of Napoleon I;
Napoleon II, 1811–1832)** His ashes

were brought from Vienna to Paris on 15 December 1940 as a "gift" from Adolf Hitler.

Reichswehr [Reich Defense] The name of Germany's army from 1919 to 1935.

Renan, Ernest (1823–1892) French historian who published works on early Christianity and on national identity.

Renard, Pierre Friend of Mario Rist who volunteered in Syria; brought back to France at the end of 1940 for having tried to go over to the Resistance.

Réquin, E. French general who commanded the Fourth Army (1939–1940).

Reuter, Paul Professor at the Law Faculty in Aix-en-Provence.

Reynaud, Paul Named French finance minister in 1938; prime minister (21 March–16 June 1940).

Ribbentrop, Joachim von Germany's foreign minister (1938–1945).

Ribbentrop Bureau Office set up by Hitler's minister of foreign affairs, Joachim von Ribbentrop, to read, digest, and translate foreign newspapers for Hitler.

Ricard, J. H. Agronomic engineer who served as minister of agriculture in the administrations of Millerand and Georges Leygues (1920–1921).

Richelieu, Cardinal Armand du Plessis de (1585–1642) Rose to prominence as King Louis XIII's principal minister, advocating centralization of power and opposition to Huguenots, the Habsburg Dynasty, and feudal lords.

Riefler, Winfield W. American economist.

Riom trial (19 February 1942–21 May 1943) An unsuccessful trial held by the Vichy regime to cast blame for France's defeat on the Third Republic and show that France, not Germany, was responsible for the war. Defendants: Léon Blum, Édouard Daladier, Paul Reynaud, Georges Mandel, Maurice Gamelin, Guy La Chambre, and Robert Jacomet.

Ripert, Georges As dean of the Paris Law Faculty and Vichy's minister of education (September–December 1940), he played an active role in the exclusion of Jews from the universities.

*Rist, André Son of Jean and Jeannette Rist.

*Rist, Antoinette Daughter of Claude and Françoise Rist.

Rist, Bernard Son of Édouard and Madeleine Rist.

*Rist, Claude Second son of Charles and Germaine Rist.

*Rist, Colas Son of Mario and Lolli Rist.

*Rist, Édouard Charles Rist's elder brother.

*Rist, Éléonore ("Lolli") Gaede Wife of Mario Rist; daughter of Wilhelm and Leni Gaede, who fled Nazi Germany with Lolli and her two sisters in 1933 and went to the United States.

*Rist, Eva Cornier Wife of Léonard Rist.

*Rist, Françoise Gorodiche Wife of Claude Rist.

*Rist, Germaine Monod Wife of Charles Rist; daughter of Gabriel Monod and Olga Monod-Herzen ("Magna").

*Rist, Isabelle Daughter of Claude and Françoise Rist.

*Rist, Jean Eldest son of Charles and Germaine Rist.

*Rist, Jean-Franklin Son of Mario and Lolli Rist.

*Rist, Jeannette Cestre Wife of Jean Rist.

*Rist, Léonard Third son of Charles and Germaine Rist.

*Rist, Madeleine Roy Second wife of Édouard Rist.

*Rist, Marcel Son of Jean and Jeannette Rist.

*Rist, Marie-Claire Daughter of Claude and Françoise Rist.

*Rist, Marie de Lacroix Wife of Noël Rist.

*Rist, Mario Fifth son of Charles and Germaine Rist.

*Rist, Noël Fourth son of Charles and Germaine Rist.

Rist, Olivier Son of Édouard and Madeleine Rist.

*Rist, Simone Daughter of Jean and Jeannette Rist.

Ritz, Monsieur An Alsatian interpreter at the Kommandantur in Versailles.

Rivaud, Albert Professor of philosophy; served briefly as minister of national education (16 June–12 July 1940).

Rives Germaine Rist's cousins in Nantes.

Rivière, Jacques (1886–1925) Editor of *La Nouvelle Revue française* (1919–1925). Author of a memoir of his time as a German prisoner of war during World War I.

Robineau, Georges (1860–1927) Governor of the Banque de France (1920–1926).

Rochat, Charles General secretary at Foreign Affairs. Moysset and Rochat were Rist's usual contacts in the Vichy government.

Rockefeller Foundation Funded Rist's research institute, ISRES, for many years.

Rohan-Chabot, Vicomte de (Jean H. de Rohan) Member of the Suez Canal Company board.

Rollin, Henri French navy officer and historian; author of *La Révolution russe, ses origines, ses résultats* (1931).

Romier, Lucien Journalist and personal friend of Pétain; appointed minister of state under Laval (April 1942–December 1943); editor of *Le Figaro* (1925–1927 and 1934–1942).

Romier, Mme Wife of Lucien Romier.

Rommel, Erwin German field marshal known as the Desert Fox.

Ronsard, Pierre de (1524–1585) Leader of the Pléiade group of French poets.

Röpke, Wilhelm Influential German economist.

Rothschild, Maurice de On a list of Jews who left France between 25 May and 30 June 1940.

Rousseau, Emmanuel Honorary member of Vichy's Council of State who served on the board of trustees for the Suez Canal Company.

Rousseau, Jean-Jacques (1712–1778) French Enlightenment philosopher whose writings helped to bring about the French Revolution.

Roussel Director of Le Matériel Téléphonique.

Roussy de Sales, Raoul de Bilingual French journalist and historian who lived in the United States and worked for closer understanding between the French and American democracies. His book *The Making of Tomorrow* appeared in 1942 shortly before he died.

Roussy, Gustave In 1937 a Swiss-French medical researcher. Under German pressure, the Vichy government removed Roussy from his position as rector of the University of Paris. He had defended his students, who demonstrated at the Tomb of the Unknown Soldier on Armistice Day, 11 November 1940.

Rucart, Marc Minister of justice under the Third Republic; member of the National Council of Resistance during World War II.

Rueff, Jacques Appointed as second deputy-governor of the Banque de France in 1939, then in 1940 as finance ministry inspector; exempted by Pétain from anti-Jewish laws.

Rueff, Maurice Banker.

Rundstedt, Gerd von German marshal sacked by Hitler; later served on the Court of Honor that expelled hundreds of officers after the 20 July attack on the Führer.

Ryti, Risto President of Finland (19 December 1940–1 August 1944).

Sainte-Beuve, Charles Augustin (1804–1869) Nineteenth-century literary critic. His "Monday Chats" appeared in *Le Constitutionnel*, a French newspaper.

Saint-Étienne Chief town of the Loire department, a coal mining city some eight miles north of Firminy; a necessary transfer point on the way to Firminy and Fraisses. The family of Charles Trocmé moved to Saint-Étienne in June 1942. (See 10 November 1942.)

Saint-Gobain A French manufacturing corporation founded in 1665.

Saint-Quentin, Count René de French ambassador to Washington.

Saradjoglou, Sükrü Turkish foreign affairs minister (1938–1942); Council president (1942–1946).

Sarraut, Maurice Journalist and important Radical leader under the Third Republic. Suspected of being a Freemason, he was murdered on 2 December 1943 by Laval's Milice.

Sauvy, Alfred French economist who specialized in demographics.

Savoie French spelling of Savoy.

Saxony, Duke of (Johann Georg I) (1585–1656) Elector of Saxony (1611–1656) during the Thirty Years' War.

Say, Jean-Baptiste Léon (1826–1896) French economist appointed as minister of finance in December 1872 by Adolph Thiers.

Scapini, Georges Deputy from Paris; named Vichy's ambassador to Germany; chief of the Diplomatic Service for Prisoners of War (1940–1944).

Schacht, Hjalmar Reich minister of economics (1934–1937); president of the Reichsbank (1923–1930 and 1933–1939).

Schaefer, Dr. Carl German commissioner appointed to the Banque de France; chief surveillance officer over French banks in the occupied zone (July 1940–July 1941).

Schairer German refugee in England and friend of Goerdeler.

*****Schaller, Constant** General Schaller was married to Charles Rist's sister Gabrielle.

Schaller, Florence Italian teacher; daughter of Gabrielle and Constant Schaller; niece of Charles Rist.

*****Schaller, Gabrielle** Sister of Charles Rist.

Schaller, Marc ("Marco") Son of Constant and Gabrielle; nephew of Charles Rist; killed at Neufchâteau in June 1940.

Scharnhorst, Gerhard von (1755–1813) Prussian general during the Napoleonic Wars. After the defeat at Jena in 1806, he led a reform commission that gradually modernized Prussia's army.

Schiller, Friedrich von (1759–1805) German writer, poet, philosopher, and historian. Author of *Geschichte des dreissigjährigen Kriegs* [The History of the Thirty Years' War].

Schneider, Georges Chief engineer with the office of Mines, obliged as a Jew to quit his job; he and his family were sheltered at the Rists' house in Haute-Savoie during the war.

Schuschnigg, Kurt von Austrian chancellor following Dollfuss's assassination (1934–1938).

Sciences Po Elite school in Paris founded in 1872 to prepare France's political and diplomatic corps.

Scott, Sir Walter (1771–1832) Scottish historical novelist.

Secours National This organization, originally created to aid military personnel and civilian victims of World War I, was revived in 1939. It became a powerful propaganda tool of the collaborationist government.

Ségur, Louis Philippe, Comte de (1753–1830) French statesman and writer who fought in the American Revolutionary War in 1781; served as a diplomat in the court of Catherine II of Russia; commented favorably on the results of the French Revolution upon his return to Paris in 1789.

Seignobos, Charles French historian; member of the League of the Rights of Man.

Serrigny, General Bernard Head of the Petroleum Federation; friend of Pétain.

Serruys, Daniel High commissioner at the Ministry of National Economy in Daladier's cabinet (September 1939–March 1940).

Sert i Badia, Josep Maria Spanish muralist and friend of Salvador Dali.

Seydoux, Roger Director of the École Libre des Sciences Politiques.

Shotwell, James T. Bryce Professor of International Relations at Columbia University.

Sieburg, Friedrich German journalist; author of *Gott in Frankreich*, 1929. The book was popular between the wars, and a French version – *Dieu est-il français?* [Is God French?] – was published in 1930 by Bernard Grasset.

Siegfried, André French political writer and sociologist.

Simon, Manfred German-born journalist; attaché at the French embassy in Switzerland who provided Charles Rist with information on Nazis and anti-Nazis.

Simović, Dušan T. Yugoslav general. Two days after Yugoslavia's signing of the Axis Tripartite Pact (25 March 1940), Simović led the antifascist military in a coup d'état. He then served as

Yugoslavia's prime minister until January 1942.

Simson, Theodore English engraver and old friend of the Rists.

Skilton U.S. assistant secretary of state with whom Rist discussed the nickel embargo during Rist's visit to Canada in April 1940.

Smith, Hugh Representative of the Hambro Bank in London.

Smuts, Joan-Christian Prime minister of the Union of South Africa.

S.N.C.F. (Société nationale des chemins de fer français) French National Railway Company.

Snyder, Carl American statistician and author of several books, including *Capitalism, the Creator* (1940).

Société Lyonnaise des Eaux et de l'Éclairage Lyonnaise Water and Light.

Société Pennaroya Mining company.

Solente, Henri Engineer; served on the boards of Union d'Escompte Bank and British Petroleum.

Somerville, James English admiral who "neutralized" the French fleet at Mers-el-Kébir on 3 July 1940.

Sommier, Edme Industrialist in the sugar-refining business.

Sorel, Albert (1842–1906) French historian, professor at the École Libre des Sciences Politiques in Paris.

Spitzer, Janine Secretary at ISRES, Rist's research institute. Rist tried to help when her Jewish father was arrested.

Spitzer, Robert Janine Spitzer's father, who collaborated on plays with Paul Géraldy.

Staël, Germaine de (1766–1817) Greatly influential Swiss writer whose *Considérations sur les principaux événements de la Révolution française* was published posthumously in 1818.

Stamp, Lord Charles Statistical economist; former British representative to the Dawes and Young committees on German reparations.

Stanley Journalist with the *Nickel*.

Starhemberg, Prince Ernst Rüdiger von Austrian politician who took part in Hitler's 1922 putsch in Munich, then organized the *Heimwehren* (a militarist organization) in 1927 before becoming minister, then vice-chancellor, in 1934–1936. However, he did not support the Anschluss and left for Argentina during the war.

Stauffenberg, "Count" (*Graf*) Claus von Leading member of the failed July 1944 plot to assassinate Hitler, for which he was executed shortly afterward.

Stauss, Emil-Georg von Deutsche Bank manager.

Stavisky affair (6 February 1934) A 1934 scandal brought about by embezzler Alexandre Stavisky, a Russian-born Jew, who issued worthless bonds valued at millions of francs. His death in January 1934 led to exposure of the close involvement of many ministers in his shenanigans and cover-ups and resulted in a political shakeup in February, under pressure from the right. The suspicion was that Stavisky had been deliberately killed to protect higher-ups. But French premier Chautemps was only replaced by someone from his own party, Daladier, who proceeded to fire the right-wing prefect of the Paris police. This led to the 6 February crisis during which right-wing groups including the Croix-de-Feu and Action Française rioted, provoking a police repression that resulted in fourteen deaths. The Third Republic survived until 1940, but Daladier was forced to resign. The Stavisky affair, which left France divided, was symptomatic of a general European shift away from democratic values.

Stein, Baron Heinrich vom (1757–1831) After Napoleon defeated the Prussian army at Jena in 1806, Baron vom Stein was granted wide ministerial powers by King Frederick William III. His reforms, which helped to bring about German unification, included the abolition of serfdom, taxation of nobles, and establishment of municipalities.

Stendhal Pen name of Marie-Henri Beyle (1783–1842). Influential realist author of several novels as well as a *Life of Napoleon*. Rist alludes to three of his books in the diary.

Stere Similar to the cord; a metric unit used for measuring firewood.

Stewart, Walter W. American economist.

Stimson, Henry Lewis American secretary of war (1940–1945).

Ştirbey, Prince Barbu Romanian prime minister in 1927. His influence derived primarily from his intimate relationship with Queen Marie.

STO Service du Travail Obligatoire: Compulsory work service, starting in June 1942, which sent hundreds of thousands of young Frenchmen to work in Germany.

Strode, George K. After the Rockefeller Foundation's International Health Division (I.H.D.) office in Paris was closed as a result of the German occupation, Dr. Strode helped to set up a hygiene institute in Marseille.

Stucki, Walter Swiss ambassador to Paris.

Stülpnagel, Karl-Heinrich von Commander of the German occupation forces in France.

Sturmführer Nazi paramilitary rank.

Sueur, Jean Cousin of the Rists.

Sully, First Duke of (Maximilien de Bethune) (1560–1641) Faithful Huguenot minister of King Henry IV of France. Among other services, he reformed France's system of collecting revenues.

Sûrete Générale France's domestic intelligence service in charge of counterintelligence and internal security; merged with regular police administration after World War II.

Synarchy According to a conspiracy theory that gained popularity during the war, a right-wing coalition including La Cagoule and the Banque Worms had plotted to bring about France's defeat in order to avoid a communist takeover (or to profit the presumed bankers and industrialist conspirators). A fascist Europe would then be run by the Synarchy of bankers and industrialists. (See Worms, Maison.)

Syveton, Gabriel (1864–1904) Co-founded the Ligue de la patrie française (League of the French Fatherland) in 1898 to counter the League of the Rights of Man and bring together influential members of the anti-Dreyfus faction.

Taittinger, Pierre Founder of Champagne Taittinger; formed the right-wing, anticommunist Jeunesses patriotes (Young Patriots) in 1924; became chairman of the municipal council of Paris in 1943; during the Liberation, pleaded with both the Germans and the F.F.I. to leave Paris an "open city"; arrested after the Liberation.

Talleyrand, Charles Maurice de (1754–1838) French Enlightenment figure in political power for most of his life; Napoleon's minister of foreign affairs (1797–1807 and 1814–1815).

Tarde, Guillaume de State councilor and vice president of the Compagnie Nationale des Chemins de Fer (National Railroad Company).

Tardieu, André Three-time prime minister of France (1929–1932). Pierre Laval was his minister of labor and social security provisions in 1930 and 1932.

Tarle, Yevgeny Russian army officer; professor of history at the Leningrad Historical Research Institute; author of books on European and Russian history.

Tcherichowsky Sent to the United States on behalf of France's public works ministry in March 1940.

Teleki, Count Pál Head of the Hungarian government from February 1939 until his suicide in April 1941.

Temps, Le (25 April 1861–30 November 1942) Major newspaper of the French Republic; viewed as having collaborated during the war, its place was taken in 1944 by *Le Monde*.

Tereschenko, Mikhail Ivanovitch Revolutionary Ukrainian economist and financier; Russian foreign minister for a brief period in 1917.

Terray Louis de Vogüé's son-in-law; assistant to Jacques Barnaud.

Tessan, François de Radical-Socialist French politician who served in various posts, including undersecretary of state for Foreign Affairs in the 1930s; died 22 April 1944 at Buchenwald.

Théry, Edmond (1854–1925) Author of *La Transformation économique de la Russie* (1914).

Thiers, Adolphe (1797–1877) French statesman whose government succeeded in crushing the revolutionary Paris Commune of 1871; served provisionally as president of France until constitutional laws created the Third Republic in 1875.

Thomasson, Paul de Inspector of finances; manager with the Banque d'Indochine; trustee of the Ottoman

Bank, as well as of the Banque de Syrie et du Liban.

Thuillier, Joseph Manager with the Société Lyonnaise des Eaux et de l'Eclairage.

Thyssen, Fritz Initially a Nazi supporter, this German industrialist became disillusioned and left Germany at the beginning of the war. It seems it was he who suggested that the Allies make an expedition to Norway in order to cut off the Swedish "iron route."

Tilho, General Jean Explorer; officer of the colonial army.

Timoshenko, Semyon Soviet military commander who launched the Second Battle of Kharkov in May 1942.

Tirard, Paul Senior member of the Council of State; former French High Commissioner for the Rhineland (1918–1930).

Tirpitz Son of Admiral Alfred von Tirpitz; founder of the German Imperial Fleet; state secretary of the Imperial German Navy (1889–1916).

Tocqueville, Alexis de (1805–1859) French writer and politician famous for his sociological and political analyses. His *Recollections*, a private journal about the Revolution of 1848, was published posthumously in 1893.

Tojo, General Hideki Japan's prime minister (1941–1942); responsible for the bombing of Pearl Harbor.

Toussenel, Alphonse (1803–1885) Nineteenth-century anti-Semitic utopian socialist.

Towers, Graham Canada's first Bank of Canada governor.

Tréfouël, Jacques Director of the Pasteur Institute.

Très-Clos, Le The Rist family's summer home in Haute-Savoie is located in the district of Maxilly-sur-Léman, some 5 miles southeast of Evian, on a mountain slope overlooking Lake Geneva. The house was built in 1932 using Charles Rist's own design. On 26 June 1940 Charles Rist writes: "We learned that Haute-Savoie is not occupied. Le Très-Clos remains one of the only safe places." Le Très-Clos became a shelter for the Schneiders, Jewish friends of the Rists, for the duration of the war, even though after November 1942 this area too came under German occupation. "La Cabane," on the lake shore, some 6 miles northeast of Le Très-Clos, is a one-room wooden cabin where the families of Charles Rist's sons, particularly those of Mario and Claude Rist, would stay.

Trocmé, André Pastor Trocmé, the celebrated protector of Jews in Le Chambon-sur-Lignon, was the first cousin of Henri Trocmé, husband of Charles Rist's sister Ève.

Trocmé, Charles Son of Charles Rist's sister Ève and good friend of Jean Rist. The families of Charles Trocmé and Jean Rist became part of a network for the protection of Jews following Charles Trocmé's move to Saint-Étienne in 1942.

Trocmé, Daniel Son of Charles Rist's sister Ève; arrested in June 1943 by the Gestapo when they came for the young refugees he was sheltering; died in a German concentration camp (Majdanek) in 1944.

*Trocmé, Ève Sister of Charles Rist; wife of Henri Trocmé.

Trocmé, François Rist's nephew; son of Ève and Henri Trocmé; engineer with the Société des Produits Azotés (Nitrogenous Products Company).

*Trocmé, Henri Husband of Charles Rist's sister Ève; vice principal of the École des Roches; killed on a road in Normandy by an American military truck in December 1944.

Trocmé-Aubin, Élizabeth Rist's niece; daughter of Ève and Henri Trocmé.

Truptil, Roger-Jean Banker; mission attaché for London's finance ministry. Rist wrote a preface to his book *Le Système bancaire anglais et la place de Londres* (1934).

Tsouderos, Emmanouil Appointed governor of Greece's Central Bank in 1931; became prime minister of the Greek government in exile during World War II.

Tuck, Pinckney Chargé d'affaires at the American embassy in Vichy from April 1942 until the Germans invaded the unoccupied zone in the south of France later that year.

Turenne, Vicomte de (1611–1675) Seventeenth-century French general.

Tyler, William R. An American born in France, Tyler was with Guaranty Trust Bank in the United States.

Unruh, Fritz von German Expressionist antiwar and anti-Nazi playwright obliged to flee his country in 1932, residing in the United States and France thereafter.

Vaihinger, Hans (1852–1933) German philosopher and Kant scholar.

Valéry, Paul French Symbolist poet, intellectual, and academic. Valéry, like many Frenchmen, was not pleased by the British takeover of Syria, which had been a French mandate.

Vallat, Xavier Appointed in March 1941 as Vichy's commissioner-general for Jewish Questions; replaced in May 1942 by Darquier de Pellepoix.

Vallin, Charles Initially a right-wing Vichy sympathizer, Vallin joined de Gaulle in London in 1942.

Valrun Encountered by Rist at Roussy de Sales's in New York on 17 March 1940.

Vergniaud President of Aciéries Jacob Holtzer, where Jean Rist worked as an engineer.

Vésinet, Le Town where Claude Rist's family lived. They rented a house in Le Vésinet because Claude Rist could drive to his lab in Le Pecq from there. The house has been described by one of the daughters as having a garden in a leafy suburb – "quiet, with English undertones, and a lot of Resistance activity."

Veslot, Doctor Medical doctor; acquaintance of the Rists.

Victor, Prince (1862–1926) Bonapartist pretender to the French throne. His brother Prince Louis fought with the Russian army.

Vignasse, La Located at Mandelieu-La Napoule on the French Riviera, this property belonging to Françoise Gorodiche Rist's parents became a refuge for the Gorodiche family until Germany took over the free zone in November 1942.

Vildé, Boris French ethnographer of Russian origin; leader of the Resistance group Museum of Man, which produced an anti-Nazi newspaper.

Villard Deputy governor of the Banque de France.

Villey-Desmeserets, Achille Seine prefect (1934–1940).

Viner, Jacob Canadian economist.

Vitry, Raoul de École des Mines engineer; administrator of Péchiney, an aluminum conglomerate; served as a member of the blockade ministry's advisory committee.

Vogüé, Bertrand de Administrator with Veuve Clicquot in Reims.

Vogüé, Marquis Louis de Chairman of the board, Suez Company (1927–1948).

Wagemann, Ernst Friedrich German economist; friend of Rist; director of the Institut für Konjunkturforschung (research institute) in Berlin; collaborated with ISRES between the wars.

Waldeck-Rousseau, Pierre (1846–1904) Influential statesman of the Third Republic; prime minister (1899–1902).

Wallace, Henry U.S. secretary of agriculture (1933–1940); vice president (1941–1945).

Wallenberg, Marcus Head of a dynasty of Swedish businessmen.

Wallenstein, Albrecht von (1583–1634) Bohemian commander of the Habsburg armies during the Thirty Years' War.

Wallon, Henri Specialist in child psychology; Marxist; named secretary of national education in 1944.

Ward, Dudley London economist; manager of the British Overseas Bank; served as British representative to the Dawes Commission on German reparations.

Watteau, General Appointed by Marshal Pétain to serve as a judge at the Riom trial.

Welles, Sumner U.S. undersecretary of state (1937–1943).

Wendel, François de French industrialist and politician. The de Wendel family was an old dynasty, owners of the Lorraine steelworks. In World War II the de Wendels' factories in Lorraine were confiscated.

Wendel, Humbert de Brother of François de Wendel.

Wenger, Léon Director of the Comptoir Européen de Crédit; responsible for purchases of Romanian oil, which remained in German hands until the end of the war.

Weygand, Maxime Commander in chief of French forces in the eastern Mediterranean and then of the entire French army from May 1940 until the armistice

with Germany; Pétain's minister of national defense.

White, Dr. Harry D. Director of the division of Monetary Research of the U.S. Treasury; author of the American plan for monetary stabilization after World War II.

Wibratte, Louis Vice president and future president of Paribas; also during this period, head of the board for Chemins de Fer Marocains (Moroccan Railway).

Widmann, Marcel Friend of Noël Rist; forestry inspector in Thonon, Haute-Savoie.

Wilhelm II German emperor who abdicated at the end of World War I.

Willard, Marcel Rist describes Willard (22 August 1944) as a communist who had reportedly been named to the Ministry of Justice.

William III (1650–1702) Protestant ruler of the British Isles following the Glorious Revolution.

Willkie, Wendell Republican who ran against Roosevelt in the 1940 presidential election.

Wilson, General Henry Maitland Supreme Allied Commander in the Mediterranean as of January 1944.

Wilson, H. S. Young Englishman who wrote a moving testimonial to Rist's sister Ève.

Wilson, Horace Adviser to Neville Chamberlain who advocated appeasement vis-à-vis Hitler.

Winant, John Gilbert Roosevelt appointee as ambassador to Britain (1941–1946).

Winter family The Winters' house was next door to the Rists'; Germaine Rist kept an eye on things there in the absence of the Jewish owners.

Worms, Maison (House of) Worms et Cie was created in Paris in 1841 by

Hypolite Worms, a shipping agent. The company began by dealing in coal, importing English coal to France. Gradually the Maison Worms became a shipping empire with operations throughout northern Africa. Worms et Cie supplied merchant and other ships during World War I. The company evolved into the Banque Worms, which provided much of France's investment capital in the 1930s. Worms et Cie continued to maintain close ties with England and to carry on its import operations during World War II, angering the Vichy French authorities. At the same time, Banque Worms became the focus of conspiracy theories positing a pro-German Synarchy. Worms et Cie was investigated on collaborationist charges after the war, but the charges were dropped.

Wulf, Comte de The name used by a young air force cadet who swindled Rist's sister Gabrielle by pretending to know her missing son, Marco.

Ybarnégaray, Jean French minister of state (10 May–16 June 1940) under Paul Reynaud; served under Pétain until 6 September 1940; arrested in 1943 for Resistance activities.

Young, Norman Egerton Financial adviser at the British embassy in Paris (1939–1940) and commissioner of the British government with the Suez Canal Company (1939–1945).

Zaleski, Count August Poland's minister of foreign affairs.

Zambeaux, Charles Assistant district attorney in Versailles; friend of Mario Rist.

Zay, Jean French minister of national education and fine arts (1936–1939); arrested for desertion after having sailed on the *Massilia* in June 1940. Zay, who was Jewish, was imprisoned and ultimately assassinated on 20 June 1944 by Darnand's Milice.

Zola, Émile (1840–1902) French writer. His 1898 letter in support of Dreyfus ("J'accuse") marked a turning point in the Dreyfus affair.

Zuber, Alfred Distant cousin of Germaine Rist; paper mill industrialist in Thann.

Works Cited

Amouroux, Henri. *La Vie des français sous l'occupation*. Paris: Librairie Arthème Fayard, 1961.

Auboin, Roger. "Les Missions en Roumanie, 1929–1932." *Revue d'Économie Politique* (1955): 927–43.

———. *Les Vraies Questions monétaires*. Paris: Hachette, 1973.

Bamberger, Marc. *Les Chômeurs*. Foreword by Charles Rist. Paris: Librairie du Recueil Sirey, 1941.

Bardoux, Jacques. *La Délivrance de Paris, séances secrètes et négotiations clandestines, octobre 1943–octobre 1944*. Paris: Fayard, 1958.

Barrès, Maurice. *Mes Cahiers*. Vol. 8. Paris: Plon, 1929.

Blumenson, Martin. *Le Réseau du musée de l'Homme*. Paris: Editions du Seuil, 1979.

Boegner, Phillipe. *Ici, on a aimé les Juifs*. Paris: Lattès, 1982.

Bois, Élie-Joseph. *Truth on the Tragedy of France*. Translation of *Le Malheur de la France* by N. Scarlyn Wilson. London: Hodder and Stoughton, 1941.

Boret, Victor. "L'Illusion de l'or" [The Gold Illusion]. *Les Nouveaux Temps*, 11 April 1941.

Bourde, Paul. *Essai sur la Révolution et la religion*. Paris: Hartmann, 1939.

Broglie, Duke of. *Souvenirs, 1785–1870*. 4 vols. Paris: Calmann Lévy, 1886.

Caillaux, Joseph. *Mémoires*. Vol. 1: *Ma jeunesse orgueilleuse*. Paris: Plon, 1942.

Cambon, Paul. *Correspondance, 1870–1924*. Paris: Grasset, 1940–1946.

Caulaincourt, Armand-Augustin-Louis, Marquis de. *Mémoires du Général de Caulaincourt, Duc de Vicence*. Tome Troisième: *L'Agonie de Fontainebleau*. Paris: Plon, 1933.

Champion, Edmé. *Philosophie de l'Histoire de France*. Paris: Charpentier, 1882.

———. *Vue générale de l'histoire de France*. Paris: Colin, 1907. [reissue of *Philosophie de l'Histoire de France*]

Chardonne, Jacques. *Voir la figure – Réflexions sur ce temps*. Paris: Grasset, 1941.

Charles Rist et les siens. Paris: Banque de France, 17 November 2006.

Charles-Roux, François. *Cinq mois tragiques aux Affaires étrangères, 21 mai–1er novembre 1940*. Paris: Plon, 1949.

Charléty, Sébastien. *La Restauration (1815–1820)*. In Ernest Lavisse, l'*Histoire de France depuis les origines jusqu'à la Révolution*. 18 vols. Paris: Hachette, 1901–1911.

Courtin, René, and Teitgen et Menthon. *Rapport sur la politique économique d'après-guerre*. Published secretly in

November 1943 by the General Studies Committee of the Resistance.

Deloraine, Maurice. *Des ondes et des hommes – Jeunesse des télécommunications et de l'ITT.* Paris: Flammarion, 1974.

Desjardins, Paul, and H. F. Stewart. *French Patriotism in the Nineteenth Century, traced in contemporary texts.* Cambridge: Cambridge University Press, 1923.

Du Moulin de la Barthète. *Le Temps des illusions – Souvenirs (juillet 1940–avril 1942).* Genève: Les Éditions du cheval ailé, 1946.

Fabre-Luce, Alfred. *Journal de la France, 1939–1940.* Paris: J.E.P., 1940.

Ford, Franklin L. *Political Murder: From Tyrannicide to Terrorism.* Cambridge, MA: Harvard University Press, 1985.

Gosse, Lucienne. *Chronique d'une vie française, René Gosse, 1883–1943.* Paris: Plon, 1963.

Granet, Marie, and Henri Michel. *Combat, histoire d'un mouvement de résistance.* Paris: Presses Universitaires de France, 1957.

Halévy, Elie. *L'ère des tyrannies, études sur le socialisme et la guerre.* Paris: Gallimard, 1938. Translated as *The Era of Tyrannies: Essays on Socialism and War* by R. K. Webb (New York: Doubleday, 1965).

Henry-Haye, Gaston. *La Grande Eclipse franco-américaine.* Paris: Plon, 1972.

Huizinga, Johan. *Incertitudes, essai de diagnostic du mal dont souffre notre temps.* Paris: Librairie de Médicis, 1939. A translation by J. Roebroek of *In de schaduwen van morgen,* 1935.

Jeanneney, Jean-Noël. *François de Wendel en République.* Paris: le Seuil, 1976.

Jeanneney, Jules. *Journal politique,* September 1939–July 1942. Jean-Noël Jeanneney, ed. Armand Colin 1972.

Kittredge, Eleanor. "A Philosopher amid the Currency Maze." Interview with Charles Rist. *New York Times,* 31 March 1940, 8, 23.

Klein, Benoît. *Pétain: J'accepte de répondre: les interrogatoires avant le procès.* Waterloo, Belgium: André Versaille, 2011.

Langeron, Roger. *Paris, juin 1940.* Paris: Flammarion, 1946.

Large, David Clay. *Between Two Fires: Europe's Path in the 1930s.* New York: Norton, 1991.

Laroche, Jules. *La Pologne de Pilsudski – Souvenirs d'une ambassade, 1926–1935.* Paris: Flammarion, 1953.

Laveleye, Émile de. *De l'avenir des peuples catholiques.* Paris: G. Baillière et Cie, 1876.

Leahy, William D. *I Was There.* New York: Whittlesey House, McGraw-Hill, 1950.

———. Telegram dated 27 August 1941. Department of State Archives, 701.5III/817.

———. Telegrams dated 26 and 27 September 1941. Department of State Archives, 701.5III/839 and 846.

———. Telegram dated 27 September 1941. Department of State Archives, 701.5III/840.

———. Telegrams dated 20 and 27 October 1941. State Department Archives, 701.5III/848 and 851.

Lefebvre, Georges. *Napoléon.* Paris: F. Alcan, 1935.

Leroy, Maxime. *La Pensée sociale de Charles Rist.* Paris: Librairie du Recueil Sirey, 1955.

Loisy, Alfred Firmin. *La Crise morale du temps présent et l'éducation humaine.* Paris: Nourry, 1937.

———. *Mémoires pour servir à l'histoire religieuse de notre temps.* 3 vols. Paris: Nourry, 1930, 1931.

———. *La Religion.* Paris: Nourry, 1917.

Man, Henri de. *Après coup.* Paris: Editions de la Toison d'or, 1941.

Marjolin, Robert. "Le directeur de l'Institut scientifique de recherches économiques et sociales." *Revue d'Économie politique* (November–December 1955): 913–22.

———. "Evolution des Transports." *Revue d'Économie politique*, 1956.

———. *Prix, monnaie et production. Essai sur les mouvements économiques de longue duré.* Paris: Presses Universitaires de France, 1941.

Marrus, Michael R., and Robert O. Paxton. *Vichy France and the Jews.* New York: Schocken Books, 1983.

"Memorandum of Conversation, by the Under Secretary of State (Welles)." *Foreign Relations* (641.116/2603). Vol. 3, p. 96, 9 February 1940.

Michelet, Jules. "Catherine de Médicis," *Histoire de France* (1833–1841), Tome X [History of France, Vol. 10].

Monod, Wilfred. *La Nuée de témoins.* Paris: Fischbacher, 1929.

Montaigne. "Of Vanity." *Essays.* Vol. 17, ch. 9. Translated by Charles Cotton. Edited by William C. Hazilitt. New York: A. L. Burt, 1894.

Moreau, Emile. *Souvenirs d'un gouverneur de la Banque de France, Histoire de la stabilisation du franc (1926–28).* Paris: Marie-Thérèse Génin, 1954.

Nicolas (Trocmé), Françoise. *Les Ascendants Rist.* A genealogy beginning with Charles Rist's father, Adrien Rist. Typescript provided to the translator by the author.

———. Video interviews with the translator. November 12 and December 3, 2010. Paris.

Nicoullaud, M. Charles. *Récits d'une Tante; Mémoires de la Comtesse de Boigne, née d'Osmond.* Vol. 1, p. 291. Paris: Plon, 1907–1908.

Nietzsche, Friedrich. *The Will to Power.* Translated by Kaufmann-Hollingdale. New York: Vintage, 1968.

Ortega y Gasset, José. *Révolte des masses.* Translated by Louis Parrot. Paris: Delamain et Boutelleau, 1937.

Pagès, Georges. *La Guerre de Trente Ans, 1618–1648.* Paris: Payot, 1939.

Pannier, Jacques. *L'Eglise réformée de Paris sous Louis XIII, 1621–1629.* Paris: Champion, 1931–1932.

Paxton, Robert O. *Vichy France: Old Guard and New Order, 1940–1944.* New York: Knopf, 1972.

Pernot, Georges. *Journal de guerre.* Paris: Les Belles Lettres, 1971.

Pigeat, Passerose Rueff, and Henri Pigeat (former head of France Press). Telephone interview, 20 March 2011.

Pinard, Isabelle Rist. Email of 6 March 2011.

———. Video interviews, Saint-Jean-du-Gard, France. November 9, 2010.

Proudhon, Pierre-Joseph. *La Révolution sociale demontrée par le coup d'état du 2 décembre 1851.* 1936. Paris: Garnier 1852.

Quinet, Edgar. *L'Enseignement du peuple.* Paris: Chamerot, 1850.

———. *La République: Conditions de la Régéneration de la France.* Vols. 28 and 48. Paris: E. Dentu, 1872.

Renan, Ernest. *Questions Contemporaines.* Paris: Michel Lévy Frères, 1868.

Revue d'économie politique. Issue dedicated to Charles Rist. November–December 1955.

Rist, André. "Jean Rist (1900–1944), Le Fils, Ingénieur et Résistant." In *Charles Rist et les Siens,* 17–28.

———. Emails to the translator. 4 May 2010, 13 September 2010, and 16 November 2011.

———. Video interviews with the translator. 17 November 2010.

Rist, Antoinette. Video interviews with (February, November 2011) and email letters to the translator (2010–2012).

Rist, Charles. *Jean Rist, 1900–1944.* Biographical brochure, n.d. Family archives.

———. (with Charles Gide). *Histoire des doctrines économiques.* Paris: Sirey, 1909.

———. "Notice biographique." *Revue d'économie politique.* (November–December 1955): 977–1045.

———. *Papiers Charles Rist.* Papers archived at the Banque de France. Paris: Secrétariat du Conseil Général, September 2006.

———. "La Pensée économique de Proudhon." *Revue d'histoire économique et sociale,* no. 2 (1955): 129–65. The essay was written as an introduction for a reprint by Marcel Rivière of Proudhon's *Manuel de spéculation en Bourse.*

Rist, Colas. "The Anti-Jewish Laws of Vichy." Personal document provided to the translator. See appendix 2 of the present text.

———. "Charles Rist, Moraliste." In *Charles Rist et les Siens,* 5–16.

———. Email of 4 March 2011.

Rist, Jean. *Pages de journal avril–juin 1918, janvier 1941–décembre 1942.* Family archives. Typescript.

———. *Projet de Laboratoire de Sidérurgie.* Paris: IRSID, Imprimerie Tancrede, 1948.

Rivière, Jacques. *L'Allemand: Souvenirs et réflexions d'un prisonnier de guerre.* Paris: Éditions de la Nouvelle Revue Française, 1918.

Rollin, Henri. *La révolution russe; ses origines – ses résultats.* Paris: Delagrave, 1931.

Röpke, Wilhelm. *Die Gesellschaftskrisis der Gegenwart.* Rentsch: Erlenbach-Zürich, 1942.

Roskill, S. *Hankey, Man of Secrets.* London: Collins, 1974.

Rueff, Jacques. *De l'aube au crépuscule.* Paris: Plon, 1977.

Sainte-Beuve, Charles-Augustin. *Cahiers.* Texte établi par Jules Troubat. Paris: Alphonse Lemerre, 1876.

———. *Causeries du lundi.* Vol. 6. Paris: Garnier, 1852.

———. *Causeries du lundi.* Vol. 15. Paris: Garnier, 1862.

———. "De la connaissance de l'homme au XVIIIe siècle." *Nouveaux Lundis.* Vol. 3. Paris: Michel Lévy Frères, 1870.

———. *Nouveaux Lundis.* Vol. 12. Paris: Calmann Lévy, 1884.

Sauvy, Alfred. *Histoire économique de la France entre les deux guerres.* Paris: Fayard, 1965.

Schiller, Friedrich von. *Geschichte des dreissigjährigen Kriegs.* Leipzig: Goschen, 1802.

Scott, Sir Walter. *Peveril du Pic.* Translated by Jean-Baptiste Defauconpret. Paris: Furne, Charles Gosselin, et Perrotin, 1835.

———. *Peveril of the Peak.* London: Routledge & Sons, 1879.

Serrigny, Bernard. *Trente ans avec Pétain.* Paris: Plon, 1959.

Sieburg, Friedrich. *Dieu est-il français?* Translated by Maurice Betz. Paris: Bernard Grasset, 1930.

———. *Gott in Frankreich.* Frankfurt: Societäts-Verlag, 1929.

Siegfried, André. *Suez, Panama et les grandes routes du trafic mondial.* Paris: Colin, 1941.

Sorel, Albert. *L'Europe et la Révolution française.* Vol. 5. Paris: Plon, 1907.

Stokesbury, James L. *A Short History of World War II.* New York: William Morrow, 1980.

Tarle, Eugène. *La Campagne de Russie, 1812.* Paris: Nouvelle Revue Française, 1941.

Théry, Edmond. *La Transformation économique de la Russie*. Paris: Économiste européen, 1914.

Tocqueville, Alexis de. *Souvenirs*. Paris: Calmann Lévy, 1893.

Tournoux, Raymond. *Pétain et la France*. Paris: Plon, 1980.

Toussenel, Alphonse. *Les Juifs rois de l'époque: histoire de la féodalité financière*. Paris: Gabriel de Gonet, 1847.

Truptil, Roger-Jean. *Le Système bancaire anglais et la place de Londres*. Paris: Librairie du Recueil Sirey, 1934.

Vaihinger, Hans. *Nietzsche als Philosoph*. Langensalza: Hermann Beyer & Söhne, 1930.

Weygand, General Maxime. *Rappelé au service*. Paris: Flammarion, 1950.

Index

CHARLES RIST (1874–1955) was a prominent French economist whose account of life in France during the German occupation was informed by his wide reading; his personal and professional experience; his acquaintance with people in all walks of life; his knowledge of several languages; and his ability to follow news, particularly radio broadcasts, from abroad. Rist moved in the highest circles of government, banking, and business, with intimate connections to the Resistance movement (via his son Jean) and to Jews (including his daughter-in-law and three granddaughters). At the same time, he counted among his acquaintances U.S. President Franklin D. Roosevelt and diplomats from numerous countries. Owing to his position, family background, and fluency in several languages, Rist was ideally placed to make an excellent witness.

MICHELE MCKAY AYNESWORTH is an award-winning translator and Editor in Chief of *Source*, the quarterly online publication of American Translators Association's Literary Division. She received grants from the National Endowment for the Arts and from the Kittredge Foundation to research and translate Charles Rist's diary. Her many literary translations from Spanish include Roberto Arlt's *Mad Toy*, short stories by Fernando Sorrentino, and poetry by Guillermo Saavedra and Edgar Brau. She has also translated extensively from French and Spanish for *The Posen Library of Jewish Culture and Civilization*.